D1170734

WHY THIS WORLD

WHY THIS WORLD

A BIOGRAPHY OF CLARICE LISPECTOR

Benjamin Moser

2009

OXFORD
UNIVERSITY PRESS

Oxford University Press, Inc., publishes works that further
Oxford University's objective of excellence
in research, scholarship, and education.

Oxford New York
Auckland Cape Town Dar es Salaam Hong Kong Karachi
Kuala Lumpur Madrid Melbourne Mexico City Nairobi
New Delhi Shanghai Taipei Toronto

With offices in
Argentina Austria Brazil Chile Czech Republic France Greece
Guatemala Hungary Italy Japan Poland Portugal Singapore
South Korea Switzerland Thailand Turkey Ukraine Vietnam

Published by Oxford University Press, Inc.
198 Madison Avenue, New York, NY 10016

www.oup.com

The dingbat used in the interior is taken from the first edition
of Clarice Lispector's first novel, *Perto do coração selvagem*,
published by A Noite Editora,
Rio de Janeiro, December 1943.

Library of Congress Cataloging-in-Publication Data
Moser, Benjamin.
Why this world : a biography of Clarice Lispector / Benjamin Moser.
p. cm.
Includes bibliographical references and index.
ISBN 978-0-19-538556-4
1. Lispector, Clarice. 2. Authors, Brazilian—20th century—Biography.
I. Title.
PQ9697.L585Z777 2009
869.3'42—dc22
[B]
2008055639

2 3 4 5 6 7 8 9

Printed in the United States of America
on acid-free paper

To Arthur Japin and Lex Jansen

CONTENTS

Western Ukraine
circa 1920
N
POLAND
VOLHYNIA
Kiev
UKRAINE
Lvov
GALICIA
Haysyn
PODOLIA
Teplyk
Chechelnik
Savran
Pervomays'k
BESSARABIA
KHERSON
R. Dniester
Kishinev
Odessa
0 50 100 miles
0 100 200 km
ROMANIA
Bucharest
Black Sea
R. Danube

N
R. Amazonas
Belém do Pará
R. Tocantins
B R A Z I L
PARAHYBA
Parahyba
PERNAMBUCO
Recife
Maceió
ALAGOAS
BAHIA
R. S. Francisco
Salvador
MINAS GERAIS
Belo Horizonte
ATLANTIC
OCEAN
RIO DE JANEIRO
Rio de Janeiro
São Paulo
R. Paraná
R. Paraguay
RIO GRANDE DO SUL
Porto Alegre
R. Paraná
Brazil in 1922
0 100 200 300 400 500 miles
0 500 1000 km

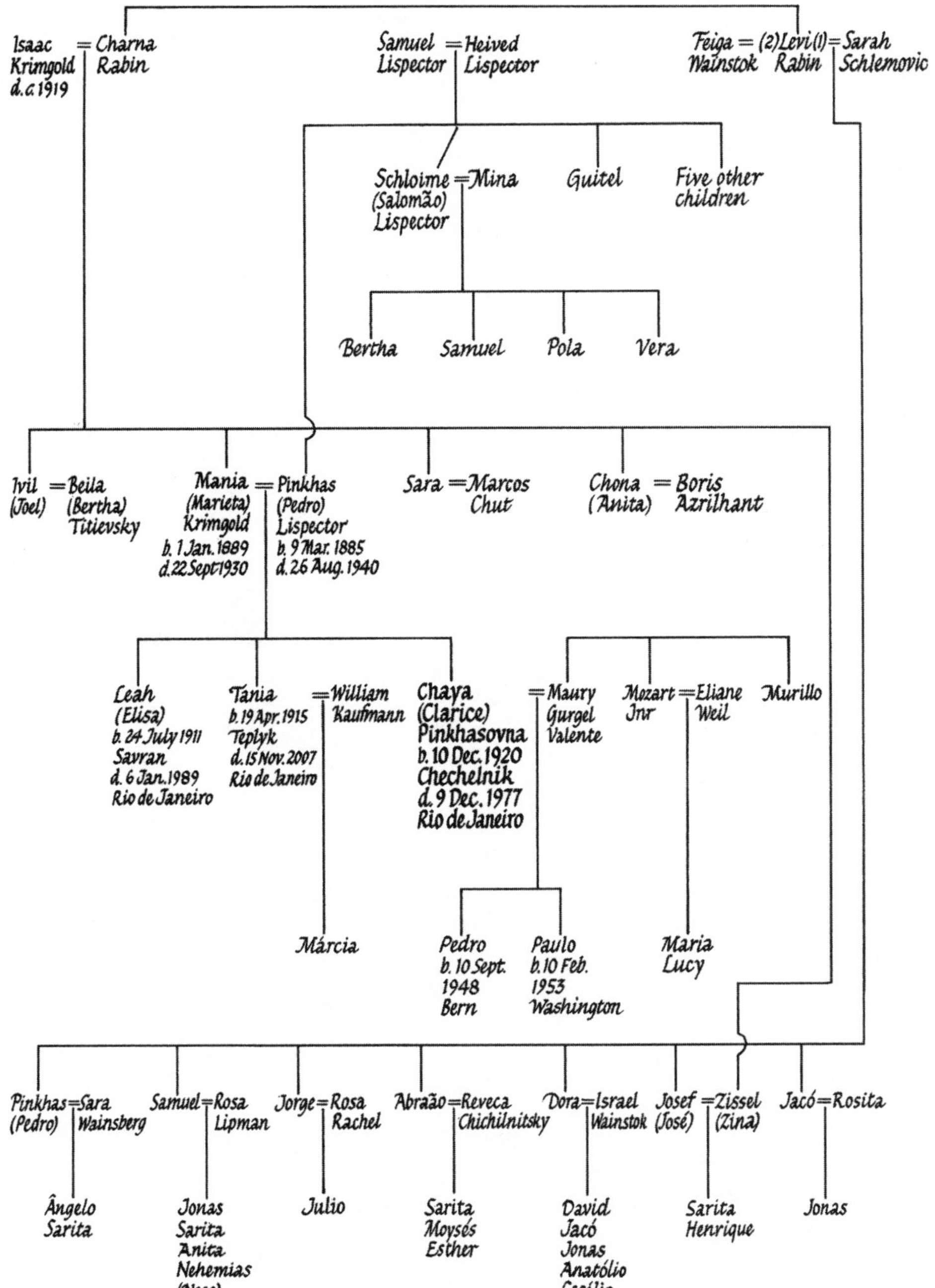

Isaac Krimgold d. c. 1919
= Charna Rabin
Samuel Lispector
= Heived Lispector
Feiga Wainstok
= (2) Levi Rabin (1) =
Sarah Schlemovic
Schloime (Salomão) Lispector
= Mina
Guitel
Five other children
Bertha
Samuel
Pola
Vera
Ivil (Joel)
= Beila (Bertha) Titievsky
Mania (Marieta) Krimgold b. 1 Jan. 1889 d. 22 Sept 1930
= Pinkhas (Pedro) Lispector b. 9 Mar. 1885 d. 26 Aug. 1940
Sara
= Marcos Chut
Chona (Anita)
= Boris Azrilhant
Leah (Elisa) b. 24 July 1911 Savran d. 6 Jan. 1989 Rio de Janeiro
Tania b. 19 Apr. 1915 Teplyk d. 15 Nov. 2007 Rio de Janeiro
= William Kaufmann
Chaya (Clarice) Pinkhasovna b. 10 Dec. 1920 Chechelnik d. 9 Dec. 1977 Rio de Janeiro
= Maury Gurgel Valente
Mozart Jnr
= Eliane Weil
Murillo
Márcia
Pedro b. 10 Sept. 1948 Bern
Paulo b. 10 Feb. 1953 Washington
Maria Lucy
Pinkhas (Pedro)
= Sara Wainsberg
Samuel
= Rosa Lipman
Jorge
= Rosa Rachel
Abrãao
= Reveca Chichilnitsky
Dora
= Israel Wainstok
Josef (José)
= Zissel (Zina)
Jacó
= Rosita
Ângelo Sarita
Jonas Sarita Anita Nehemias (Neco)
Julio
Sarita Moysés Esther
David Jacó Jonas Anatólio Cecília
Sarita Henrique
Jonas

WHY THIS WORLD

Cleanse thy clothes, and if possible, let all thy garments be white, for all this is helpful in leading the heart towards the fear of God and the love of God. If it be night, kindle many lights, until all be bright. Then take ink, pen and a table to thy hand and remember that thou art about to serve God in joy of the gladness of heart. Now begin to combine a few or many letters, to permute and to combine them until thy heart be warm. Then be mindful of their movements and of what thou canst bring forth by moving them. And when thou feelest that thy heart is already warm and when thou seest that by combinations of letters thou canst grasp new things which by human tradition or by thyself thou wouldst not be able to know and when thou art thus prepared to receive the influx of divine power which flows into thee, then turn all thy true thought to imagine the Name and His exalted angels in thy heart as if they were human beings sitting or standing about thee.

—ABRAHAM ABULAFIA
(1240–after 1290)

INTRODUCTION: THE SPHINX

In 1946, the young Brazilian writer Clarice Lispector was returning from Rio de Janeiro to Italy, where her husband was vice consul in Naples. She had traveled home as a diplomatic courier, carrying dispatches to the Brazilian Ministry of Foreign Relations, but with the usual routes between Europe and South America disrupted by the war, her journey to rejoin her husband followed an unconventional itinerary. From Rio she flew to Natal, on the northeastern tip of Brazil, then onward to the British base at Ascension Island in the South Atlantic, to the American air station in Liberia, to the French bases in Rabat and Casablanca, and then via Cairo and Athens to Rome.

Before each leg of the trip, she had a few hours, or days, to look around. In Cairo, the Brazilian consul and his wife invited her to a cabaret, where they were amazed to see the exotic belly dance performed to the familiar strains of a hit of Rio's 1937 Carnival, Carmen Miranda's "I Want Mommy."

Egypt itself failed to impress her, she wrote a friend back in Rio de Janeiro. "I saw the pyramids, the Sphinx—a Mohammedan read my palm in the 'desert sands' and said I had a pure heart.... Speaking of sphinxes, pyramids, piasters, it's all in horribly bad taste. It's almost immodest to live in Cairo. The problem is trying to feel anything that hasn't been accounted for by a guide."[1]

Clarice Lispector never returned to Egypt. But many years later she recalled her brief sightseeing tour, when, in the "desert sands," she stared down no one less than the Sphinx herself.

"I did not decipher her," wrote the proud, beautiful Clarice. "But neither did she decipher me."[2]

By the time she died in 1977, Clarice Lispector was one of the mythical figures of Brazil, the Sphinx of Rio de Janeiro, a woman who fascinated her countrymen virtually from adolescence. "The sight of her was a shock," the poet Ferreira Gullar remembered of their first meeting. "Her green almond eyes, her high cheekbones, she looked like a she-wolf, a fascinating wolf.... I thought that if I saw her again I would fall hopelessly in love with her."[3] "There were men who couldn't forget me for ten years," she admitted. "There was an American poet who threatened to commit suicide because I wasn't interested."[4] The translator Gregory Rabassa recalled being "flabbergasted to meet that rare person who looked like Marlene Dietrich and wrote like Virginia Woolf."[5]

In Brazil today, her arresting face adorns postage stamps. Her name lends class to luxury condominiums. Her works, often dismissed during her lifetime as hermetic or incomprehensible, are sold in vending machines in subway stations. The Internet is alight with hundreds of thousands of her fans, and a month rarely goes by without the appearance of a book examining one side or another of her life and work. Her first name is enough to identify her to educated Brazilians, who, a Spanish publisher noticed, "all knew her, had been to her house, and have some anecdote to tell about her, as the Argentines do with Borges. Or at the very least they went to her funeral."[6]

The French writer Hélène Cixous declared that Clarice Lispector was what Kafka would have been had he been a woman, or "if Rilke had been a Jewish Brazilian born in the Ukraine. If Rimbaud had been a mother, if he had reached the age of fifty. If Heidegger could have ceased being German."[7] The attempts to describe this indescribable woman often go on in this vein, grasping at superlatives, though those who knew her, either in person or from her books, also insist that the most striking aspect of her personality, her aura of mystery, evades description. "Clarice," the poet Carlos Drummond de Andrade wrote when she died, "came from one mystery / and departed for another."[8]

Her indecipherable air fascinated and disquieted all who encountered her. After her death, a friend wrote that "Clarice was a foreigner on earth, going through the world as if she'd arrived in the dead of night in an unknown city amidst a general transport strike."[9]

"Maybe her closest friends and the friends of those friends know something about her life," an interviewer wrote in 1961. "Where she came from, where she was born, how old she is, how she lives. But she never talks about that, 'since it's very personal.'"[10] She gave very little away. A decade later another frustrated journalist summed up Clarice's responses to an interview: "I don't know, I'm not familiar with it, I've never heard of it, I'm not aware, That's not my area, It's hard to explain, I don't know, I don't consider, I've never heard, I'm not familiar with, There isn't, I don't think."[11] The year before her death a reporter who had come all the way from Argentina tried to draw her out. "They say you're evasive, difficult, that you don't talk. It doesn't seem that way to me." Clarice answered, "Obviously they were right." After extracting monosyllabic replies, the reporter filled the silence with a story about another writer.

> But she said nothing. I don't even know if she looked at me. She stood up and said:
>
> "I might go to Buenos Aires this winter. Don't forget to take the book I gave you. There you'll find material for your article."
>
> [She was] very tall, with auburn hair and skin, [and] I remember her wearing a long brown silk dress. But I could be wrong. As we were leaving I paused in front of an oil portrait of her face.
>
> "De Chirico," she said before I could ask. And then, at the elevator: "Sorry, I don't like to talk."[12]

In this void of information, a whole mythology sprang up. Reading accounts of her at different points in her life, one can hardly believe they concern the same person. The points of disagreement were not trivial. "Clarice Lispector" was once thought to be a pseudonym, and her original name was not known until after her death. Where exactly she was born and how old she was were also unclear. Her nationality was questioned and the identity of her native language was obscure. One authority will testify that she was right-wing and another will hint that she was a Communist. One will insist that she was a pious Catholic, though she was actually a Jew. Rumor will sometimes have it that she was a lesbian, though at one point rumor also had it that she was, in fact, a man.

What makes this tangle of contradictions so odd is that Clarice Lispector is not a hazy figure known from shreds of antique papyrus. She has been dead hardly thirty years. Many people survive who knew her well. She was prominent virtually from adolescence, her life was extensively documented in the press, and she left behind an extensive correspondence. Still, few great modern artists are quite as fundamentally unfamiliar. How can a person who lived in a large Western city in the middle of the twentieth century, who gave interviews, lived in high-rise apartments, and traveled by air, remain so enigmatic?

She herself once wrote, "I am so mysterious that I don't even understand myself."[13]

"My mystery," she insisted elsewhere, "is that I have no mystery."[14] Clarice Lispector could be chatty and forthcoming as frequently as she was silent and incomprehensible. To general bemusement, she insisted that she was a simple housewife, and those who arrived expecting to encounter a Sphinx just as often found a Jewish mother offering them cake and Coca-Cola. "I need money," she told one journalist. "The position of a myth is not very comfortable."[15] Late in life, explaining why she gave up on interviews, she said, "They wouldn't understand a Clarice Lispector who paints her toenails red."[16]

More than anything, she wanted to be respected as a human being. She was mortified when the famous singer Maria Bethânia threw herself at her feet, exclaiming, "My goddess!"[17] "My God," exclaimed one of Clarice's protagonists, "but it was easier to be a saint than a person!"[18] In a melancholy piece called "Profile of a Chosen Being," she describes her rebellion against her image: "The being attempted an underground work of destroying the photograph: he did or said things so opposite to the photograph that it bristled in the drawer. His hope was to make himself more vivid than the photograph. But what happened? It happened that everything the being did only retouched the portrait, embellished it."[19]

The legend was stronger than she was. Toward the end of her life she was asked about an unkind comment that appeared in a newspaper. "I got pretty annoyed," she admitted, "but then I got over it. If I ran into [its author] the only thing I would say is: listen, when you write about me, it's Clarice with a c, not with two s's, all right?"[20]

Still, she never entirely gave up hope of being seen as a real person, and her protests against her own mythology surface in unexpected places. In a newspaper piece that she wrote about—of all things—the new capital of Brasília, an odd exclamation appears: "The sacred monster has died: in her place was born a little girl who lost her mother."[21]

"Facts and particulars annoy me," she wrote, presumably including those surrounding her own curriculum vitae. She went to lengths, in her life and her writing, to rub them out. Yet on the other hand few people have exposed themselves so completely. Through all the many facets of her work—in novels, stories, correspondence, and journalism, in the splendid prose that made her "the princess of the Portuguese language"—a single personality is relentlessly dissected and fascinatingly revealed in perhaps the greatest spiritual autobiography of the twentieth century.

"Alongside my desire to defend my privacy, I have the intense desire to confess in public and not to a priest."[22] Her brand of confession was concerned with the inner truths she painstakingly unearthed throughout a life of unceasing meditation. This is the reason Clarice Lispector has been compared less often to other writers than to mystics and saints. "The novels of Clarice Lispector often make us think of the autobiography of St. Teresa," *Le Monde* wrote.[23] Like the reader of St. Teresa or St. John of the Cross, the reader of Clarice Lispector sees a soul turned inside out.

She emerged from the world of the Eastern European Jews, a world of holy men and miracles that had already experienced its first intimations of doom. She brought that dying society's burning religious vocation into a new world, a world in which God was dead. Like Kafka, she despaired; but unlike Kafka she eventually, and excruciatingly, struck out in search of the God that had abandoned her. She recounted her quest in terms that, like Kafka's, necessarily hearkened back to the world she had left, describing the soul of a Jewish mystic who knows that God is dead and, in the kind of paradox that recurs throughout her work, is determined to find Him anyway.

The soul exposed in her work is the soul of a single woman, but within it one finds the full range of human experience. This is why Clarice Lispector has been described as just about everything: a woman and a man, a native and a foreigner, a Jew and a Christian, a child and an adult, an animal and a person, a lesbian and a housewife, a witch and a saint. Because she described so much of her intimate experience she could credibly be everything for everyone, venerated by those who found in her expressive genius a mirror of their own souls. As she said, "I am all of yourselves."[24]

❦

"There is much I cannot tell you. I am not going to be autobiographical. I want to be 'bio.' "[25] But even a universal artist emerges from a specific context, and the context that produced Clarice Lispector was unimaginable for most Brazilians, and certainly for her middle-class readers. It is no wonder that she never spoke of it. Born thousands of miles from Brazil amid a horrifying civil war, her mother condemned to death by an act of unspeakable violence, Clarice's background was unimaginably poor and violent.

By adolescence, she seemed to have triumphed over her origins, and for the rest of her life she avoided even the vaguest reference to them. Perhaps she feared that nobody would understand. And so she held her tongue, a “monument,” a “sacred monster,” bound to a legend she knew would outlive her and which she reluctantly, ironically embraced. Twenty-eight years after her first meeting with the Sphinx, she wrote that she was considering paying another visit.

“I’ll see who devours whom.”[26]

1

FUN VONEN IS A YID?

"Clarice was called alienated, cerebral, 'intimist' and tedious by hard-line Communist critics. She only reacted when offended by the stupid accusation that she was a foreigner."[1] "She always got very annoyed when people suggested she wasn't entirely Brazilian," her closest friend wrote. "True, she was born in Russia, but she had come here when she was only two months old. She wanted to be Brazilian in every way."[2] "I am Brazilian," she declared, "and that is that."[3]

> I was born in the Ukraine, my parents' country. I was born in a village called Chechelnik, so small and insignificant that it isn't even on the map. When my mother was pregnant with me, my parents were heading toward the United States or Brazil, they still hadn't decided. They stopped in Chechelnik so I could be born and then continued on their journey. I arrived in Brazil when I was *only two months old.*[4]

Though she had arrived in earliest infancy, Clarice Lispector always struck many Brazilians as foreign, not because of her European birth or the many years she spent abroad, but because of the way she spoke. She lisped, and her rasping, throaty r's gave her an odd accent. "I am not French," she explained, which is how she sounded. "This *r* of mine is a speech defect: I simply have a tongue-tie. Now that my Brazilianness has been cleared up..."[5]

She claimed that her friend Pedro Bloch, a pioneer Brazilian speech therapist, had offered to carry out an operation that would fix the problem. But Dr. Bloch said her pronunciation was natural enough for a child who had imitated her foreign parents' speech: the throaty r's, if not the lisp, were, in fact, common among the children of Jewish immigrants in Brazil.[6] It was through training, not surgery, that Dr. Bloch managed to correct the problem. But only temporarily.

Despite her constant disavowals, she stubbornly refused to shed this immediately noticeable sign of her foreignness. She would struggle throughout her life between a need to belong and a dogged insistence on maintaining her apartness.

A few months after his successful treatment, Dr. Bloch ran into Clarice. He noted that she had started using her old r's again. Her explanation was simple. "She told him she didn't like losing her characteristics."[7]

There was no characteristic Clarice Lispector might have wanted to lose more than her place of birth. For this reason, despite the tongue that tied her to it, despite the sometimes horrifying honesty of her writing, she has a reputation for being something of a liar. White lies, such as the few years she was given to shaving off her age, are seen as a beautiful woman's coquettishness. Yet almost every lie she told has to do with the circumstances of her birth.

In her published writings Clarice was more concerned about the metaphysical meaning of birth than the actual topographical circumstances of her own. Still, those circumstances haunted her. In interviews, she insisted that she knew nothing about the place she came from. In the 1960s, she gave an interview to the writer Renard Perez, the longest she ever granted; the kind and gentle Perez surely put her at ease. Before publishing the piece, he gave it to her for approval. Her single objection was to the first sentence: "When, shortly after the Revolution, the Lispectors decided to emigrate from Russia to America . . ." "It wasn't shortly afterwards!" she protested. "It was many, many years afterwards!" Perez obliged, and the published piece began, "When the Lispectors decided to emigrate from Russia to America (this, many years after the Revolution) . . ."[8]

And she lied about how old she was when she came to Brazil. In the passage cited earlier, she italicizes her insistence that she was *only two months old* when her family disembarked. As she well knew, however, she was over a year old. It is a small difference—too young, either way, to remember any other homeland—but her insistence on shaving it down to the smallest credible integer is odd. Why bother?

Clarice Lispector wanted nothing more than to rewrite the story of her birth. In private notes composed when she was in her thirties and living abroad, she wrote, "I am going back to the place where I come from. The ideal would be to go to the little town in Russia, and to be born in other circumstances."

The thought occurred to her as she was falling asleep. She then dreamed that she had been banned from Russia in a public trial. A man says "only feminine women were allowed in Russia—and I was not feminine." Two gestures had inadvertently betrayed her, the judge explains: "1st I had lighted my own cigarette, but a woman should wait with her cigarette in her hand until a man lights it. 2nd I had pushed my own chair to the table though I should have waited for a man to do it for me."[9]

And so she was forbidden to return. In her second novel, perhaps thinking of the finality of her departure, she wrote, "The place she was born—she was vaguely surprised it still existed, as if it too were something she had lost."[10]

In a novel based on her family's emigration, Elisa Lispector, Clarice's oldest sister, repeatedly poses a question: *Fun vonen is a yid?* Literally, it means "Where is a Jew from?" and is the polite way a Yiddish-speaker inquires about another's origin. Throughout her life Clarice struggled to answer. "The question of origin," one critic wrote, "is so obsessive that one can say that Clarice Lispector's entire body of work is built around it."[11]

In photographs, she hardly looks like she could be from anywhere but Brazil. Perfectly at home on Copacabana Beach, she wore the dramatic makeup and the loud jewelry of the *grande* Rio *dame* of her day. There was no hungry ghetto waif in the woman hitting the slopes in Switzerland or wafting down the Grand Canal in a gondola. In one photograph, she stands next to Carolina Maria de Jesus, a black woman whose harrowing memoir of Brazilian poverty, *Child of the Dark*, was one of the literary revelations of 1960. Beside the famously beautiful Clarice, whose tailored suit and wraparound sunglasses make her look like a movie star, Carolina looks tense and out of place, as if someone dragged Clarice's maid into the picture. No one would guess that Clarice's background was even more miserable than Carolina's.

Yet in real life Clarice often gave the impression of foreignness. Memoirs frequently mention her strangeness. There was that odd voice, and that odd name, so unusual in Brazil that when her first book appeared a critic referred to "this unpleasant name, likely a pseudonym."[12] There was the strange way she dressed; after separating from her husband, she had little money to update her wardrobe, and she wore the old clothes, purchased abroad, that for years afterward made her look "foreign, out of season."[13]

Her oddness disturbed people. "They accuse her of being alienated," one critic wrote in 1969, "of dealing with motifs and themes that have nothing to do with her homeland, in a language that recalls the English writers. There are no chandeliers in Brazil, and nobody knows where that besieged city is."[14]

(*The Chandelier*, the title of her second novel; *The Besieged City*, of her third.)

"I must seem stubborn, with the eye of a foreigner who doesn't speak the language of the country," she wrote.[15] Yet her attachment to the country that had saved her family, where she spent her life, and whose language was the medium of her art, was natural and genuine.

More remarkable is how often *others* insist on her attachment to Brazil. One never sees writers on Machado de Assis, for example, asserting that he was truly Brazilian. In writing on Clarice Lispector, such assertions are almost inevitable. The editors of the popular paperback series "Our Classics" chose, as one of only two extracts from Clarice's five-hundred-plus-page book of newspaper columns, a few short paragraphs she wrote in response to a question about her nationality. "I belong to Brazil," was her answer.[16]

A full third of the flap copy of one biography is dedicated to insisting that she was Brazilian: "This mark of her origin [i.e., her foreign birth], however, is the contrary of what she tried to live, and what this biography asserts, based upon a vast correspondence and dozens of interviews: Brazil was more than her adoptive country, it was her true home."[17] On the popular social-networking Web site Orkut, the Clarice Lispector group, with more than 210,000 members, announces that it is a "community dedicated to the greatest and most intense BRAZILIAN writer ever. I said: BRAZILIAN."

But from the very beginning readers understood that she was an outsider. "Clarice Lispector," writes Carlos Mendes de Sousa, "is the first, most radical affirmation of a *non-place* in Brazilian literature."[18] She is both Brazil's greatest modern writer and, in a profound sense, not a Brazilian writer at all. The poet Lêdo Ivo captured the paradox: "There will probably never be a tangible and acceptable explanation for the language and style of Clarice Lispector. The foreignness of her prose is one of the most overwhelming facts of our literary history, and, even, of the history of our language. This borderland prose, of immigrants and emigrants, has nothing to do with any of our illustrious predecessors.... You could say that she, a naturalized Brazilian, naturalized a language."[19]

"My homeland left no trace on me, except through the blood heritage. I never set foot in Russia," Clarice Lispector said.[20] In public she referred to her family's origins no more than a handful of times. When she did, it was either vaguely—"I asked my father how long there had been Lispectors in the Ukraine, and he said: generations and generations"[21]—or falsely. Her published references to her ethnicity are so sparse that many imagined she was ashamed of it.[22]

Fun vonen is a yid? It is not surprising that she longed to rewrite the story of her origin, in the winter of 1920 in the *goubernia* of Podolia, which until shortly before had been part of the Russian Empire and which is today in the southwestern part of the Republic of Ukraine. "I am sure that in the cradle my first wish was to belong," she wrote. "*For reasons that do not matter here*, I must have somehow felt that I didn't belong to anything or anyone."[23]

The emphasis is added: she never explained those reasons. But the least one can say about the time and place of her birth is that they were badly chosen. Even in the panoply of murder and epidemic and war that passes for Ukrainian history, from the Mongol sack of Kiev in 1240 through the nuclear explosion in Chernobyl in 1986, 1920 stands out as a particularly horrifying year.

Worse was still to come: twelve years later, Stalin began his systematic starvation of the country's peasants, killing more people than died during the First World War on all sides put together.[24] Nine years after that, Hitler's invasion killed 5.3 million people, one inhabitant in six.[25] "Ukraine is not yet dead," the national anthem marvels.

In this bleak panorama not every catastrophe can be duly commemorated. But though mostly forgotten today, what befell the Jews of the Ukraine around the time of Clarice Lispector's birth was a disaster on a scale never before imagined. Perhaps 250,000 were killed: excepting the Holocaust, the worst anti-Semitic episode in history.

In 1919 a writer declared that during the First World War, "what the Jews of Eastern Europe were threatened with was not the temporary suffering and decimation inevitable in war, but the total extermination by ingenious and rapid torture of a whole race."[26] When that sentence was published, the writer believed that horror to be in the past. The real drama was about to begin.

2

THAT IRRATIONAL SOMETHING

One little corner of the tsar's enormous empire, Chechelnik, in the western Ukrainian province of Podolia, was typical of the grubby places where, until the turn of the twentieth century, most of the world's Jews lived. Before World War I it had around eight thousand inhabitants, a third of whom were Jewish. An emigrant from Chechelnik to New York, Nathan Hofferman, emphasized that "the majority of Jews were poor. And not the standard of 'poor' which is accepted here in the States, but literally poor. Which meant not having a slice of bread to feed the children, that were plentiful."

> Some lived in hovels of two or three rooms with earthen floors, half naked, cold in the winter and hot in the summer.... Child mortality was high, but the birth rate was also high, since according to Jewish law birth control is taboo. There was no sanitation, all the infant and child sicknesses were of epidemic proportions, and medical help was very scarce.... When I said no sanitation, I did not exaggerate. Most homes did not even have an outhouse. People relieved themselves in the back of the house, in small ravines on the edge of the town. The only cleaners were the pigs that roamed in the streets and the rains that washed it down to the stream.

Grain was the economic mainstay. As Jews were not allowed to own land or farm, many of the smaller traders were Jews, who also bought and sold livestock. "At the top of the town was a large open plaza where the peasants and horse traders bought and sold horses," Hofferman remembered. "At the foot of the town there was another plaza where they traded cattle. The procedure was the same as with the horses except, that here was cow shit and at the other horseshit."[1]

Chechelnik today does not seem so terrible. Its ramshackle village architecture, colorfully painted in green and purple, is interrupted by a few crumbling concrete Soviet interventions. Other buildings remember vanished populations: the Catholics who worshipped in the Polish church are long gone, and the synagogue where Mania and Pinkhas Lispector would have brought their newborn daughter to be blessed is in a sad state, empty, open to the elements behind its still impressive stone façade.[2]

It is the kind of town where a can-do mayor owns the grocery store, the gas station, and the hotel; where poultry wanders down the main street, Lenin Boulevard; and where people fondly recall the Brazilian ambassador, wearing shorts and sandals, arriving a few years back to scout out a place for a monument to Clarice Lispector. (For its inauguration he was more formally attired.) Chechelnik does not have a lot of monuments, and it does not see a lot of ambassadors.

Atop a high ridge, the town offers commanding views over the green hills of the surrounding countryside, views not designed to delight tourists but to offer fair warning of impending invasion. The place was always endangered, a vulnerable frontier post sitting on the border of what, in the fifteenth and sixteenth centuries, were the Turkish and Polish empires.

The Lispector family would not be the town's first refugees. Chechelnik was founded by refugees, and is even named for them. The story goes that the root of the word Chechelnik, *kaçan lik*, is the Turkic word for "refugee." Its first settlers arrived under the leadership of a Tatar renegade, Chagan, who married an Orthodox girl, was baptized, and settled on the right bank of the Savranka River.[3] Following Chagan's lead, more refugees arrived at the beginning of the sixteenth century, runaway serfs whose lives under their Polish owners were bad enough to risk settling in a territory subject to the terror of unremitting Tatar invasion. An elaborate system of tunnels underneath the buildings provided shelter. There were three main interconnected passageways, some as deep as five meters under the ground and up to two meters tall. Most houses, and almost all Jewish houses, had camouflaged entrances to the catacombs in their basement. In peacetime they were used for storage; during invasions the whole town disappeared underground, the whole population, animals included. The system's engineers had taken care to provide access to an underground river, where the animals could drink.[4]

By the seventeenth century, under Polish rule, Chechelnik was officially elevated from a village to a township; and around 1780 the Jews erected the handsome synagogue whose precarious ruins still stand. It was a time of religious strife, often intra-Christian. The town's rulers, the princely Lubomirski family, tried to "Polonize" the locals, building a Catholic church and seizing the lands of Orthodox foundations.

The princes also introduced the town's claim to its extremely modest fame, a large stud farm that produced valuable horses. For Clarice Lispector's birthplace, this is an almost uncannily appropriate industry. "Trying to put into sentences my most hidden and subtle sensation," she wrote, "I would say: given the choice I would have been born a horse."[5]

"After entering the town, we see a Roman Catholic church with a green roof and a high bell tower," the Polish traveler Kraszewski wrote after a visit in 1843. "Only vases decorate the tops of the walls that surround the ruins of Prince Lubomirski's palace. . . . The town and market are empty, houses are poor, low, lopsided, and made of clay. Local Jews speak more Russian than Polish and look very different from Jews in Poland."[6]

By the beginning of the twentieth century, a century after Chechelnik had passed into Russian hands, there were few Russians in the area. The peasants were Orthodox and spoke Ukrainian. The gentry was Polish and Catholic; these were the people who worshipped at the impressive Catholic church Kraszewski noticed, which was much fancier than its Orthodox cousin across town. Despite the poverty the Russian government enforced, the Jews survived, often barely, in commerce, frequently as cattle traders. All the stores in Chechelnik belonged to Jews, except the drugstore, which belonged to a Pole, and the liquor store, which was part of the government vodka monopoly.

Can a place impress its traits on one who abandoned it in infancy? It would seem not. Yet the fact remains that a great mystic was born in a area famed for its great mystics. Perhaps the most remarkable fact about the area Clarice Lispector came from was not its poverty or oppression but its electric relationship to the divine. Isolated and poor, the Jews of Podolia were frequently swept up by millenarian waves.

The Hasidic movement, with its emphasis on a direct, personal experience of God, made its first appearance, and burned most intensely, in benighted Podolia. The movement's founder, the Ba'al Shem Tov, died not far from Chechelnik, in Medzhybyzh, and the tomb of the apostle of Hasidism, Nachman of Bratzlav, is even closer by, in Uman. In the eighteenth century, the greatest scholar of Jewish mysticism has written, "within a geographically small area and also within a surprisingly short period, the ghetto gave birth to a whole galaxy of saint-mystics, each of them a startling individuality."[7]

The Western Ukraine not only produced many of the great Jewish mystics. Its Christian population, too, periodically burned with religious frenzy. The area's official churches included the Russian Orthodox, Roman Catholic, Lutheran, Ukrainian Autocephalous, and Ukrainian Greek Catholic. It was a place where the Virgin Mary appeared to villagers with something like regularity and where statues of Christ were known spontaneously to bleed. It was a place where, around the time of Clarice's birth, preachers led a whole constellation of charismatic sects, with names like the Flagellants, the Painters, the Israelites, the Foot-washers, the Tanzbrüder, the Studenbrüder, and the Milk-Drinkers of Saint Uncle Kornei and Aunt Melanie.

"How difficult it is to write the history of the [Ukrainian] borderlands," one scholar has noted, "without, temporarily, believing in divine apparitions. Ghosts, miracles, occurrences that today cannot be explained, made up a major part of everyday life."[8]

"Her eyes," a friend of Clarice Lispector's wrote, "had the dull dazzle of the mystic."[9] "I am a mystic," she told an interviewer. "I have no religion, because I don't like liturgy, ritual. A critic for *Le Monde*, in Paris, once said that I recalled Saint Teresa of Avila and St. John of the Cross—authors, incidentally, I never read. Alceu Amoroso Lima... I once called, asking to see him. He said: I know, you want to talk about God."[10]

Such was the fascination of Clarice Lispector's mysterious figure, and so little known about her origins, that in her own lifetime a whole body of legend sprang up around her. In this she resembled the Jewish saints of her homeland, the Hasidic *zaddikim*, "bearers of that irrational something," mythic figures in their own day, about whom an "overwhelming wealth of tales" indissolubly mix "triviality and profundity, traditional or borrowed ideas and true originality."[11]

Yet though she did not provide them herself, though she tried to rewrite the story of those origins, records do survive describing the family's life in the Ukraine. The most important were left by Elisa Lispector, her oldest sister: an unpublished typescript called "Old Pictures" and a novel, *In Exile*, published in 1948, telling in thinly veiled terms the story of the family's emigration.[12]

Elisa, born Leah on July 24, 1911, was old enough to have a clear memory of the country the family was forced to abandon. She hardly knew her paternal grandparents, though she was haunted by the figure of her grandfather, Shmuel

Lispector, the very type of the studious, pious Eastern European Jew. Obedient to the commandment prohibiting the reproduction of the human figure, Shmuel Lispector never allowed himself to be photographed.

He lived in the tiny shtetl of Teplyk, not far from Chechelnik. Quiet and affable, he realized early on that he was "not destined for the things of this world."[13] When given the choice of studying the Holy Scriptures or working in the little shop full of "products with many different odors, and the noisy and irascible customers," he naturally chose the former. A cousin of Elisa and Clarice's remembered his fame as a saint and a wise man, whose knowledge of the holy books attracted scholars from the whole region. His concentration on his studies was absolute.[14] This was possible because, according to custom, he had married a rich woman, Heived, or Eve. Learned men were sought-after husbands for the daughters of richer, but presumably less refined, families. "The rich parents supported the pair, enjoyed their offsprings and basked in the glory and respect of the son-in-law, who continued his studies," wrote Nathan Hofferman. These marriages between poor men of scholarly background and richer girls from merchant families were neither unequal nor uncommon.

The marriage, as was also the custom, was arranged, and produced five children, the youngest of whom, Pinkhas, Clarice's father, was born in Teplyk on March 3, 1885.[15] Elisa never met her grandfather, who died in his forties, but neither did she see much of her grandmother, who lived to be ninety-three. "Grandmother Heived visited us only once in Haysyn, where we lived. I don't remember her well. I don't think she stayed long. She was careful about getting in other people's way, afraid of inconveniencing them. So the image that I have of her is of a docile, shy creature, of few words—a silence and a standoffish manner that her daughters-in-law easily interpreted as touchiness mixed with domineering."[16]

When it came time for Pinkhas to marry, Shmuel hired a matchmaker. The prospect turned up was Mania Krimgold, who was born on New Year's Day 1889.[17] Like his father, Pinkhas also married a woman whose father could support his studies. Pinkhas was not destined to become a scholar, but the match was wise in another way: Mania's jewels would salvage her family from the coming war.

❧

By traditional reckoning, Mania's father, Isaac Krimgold, was not a good Jew, and so what might have been a straightforward marriage became a complicated amorous history. As a young man, he had met Mania's mother, Charna Rabin, at a wedding party.

Elisa remembered him as "tall and strong as an oak, dignified, straight-backed." Well-off, he had a grocery store in a town near Pervomays'k, at some distance from Teplyk, and, for his dealings in timber, rented land from a Russian nobleman.[18] He had somewhat loose manners and close contact with gentiles. "In the big warehouse where he stored wood, he even occasionally drank a bit of vodka, and it was not unusual for him to fraternize with the lumberjacks."[19]

Unlike the strictly pious Lispectors, Isaac Krimgold was not religious. He headed to town to attend the synagogue only on the most important holidays. Charna's father found this laxity unacceptable and denied his permission. Both Charna and Isaac married others. Isaac's wife gave him three children, "and, when she died, he confessed that he did not mourn. She was hot-tempered, he said." Charna, too, had one child before being widowed in her turn. Years later, she and Isaac met again and were finally married. Elisa remembered her "pious and modest" grandmother warmly, "her clothing and her jewelry almost sumptuous." They had three daughters, including Mania, or Marian, the oldest. For little Elisa, her grandparents' house, where she spent her summer holidays, was a thing of beauty: the veranda with its stained-glass windows where they took tea every afternoon, the river she played in with the neighbor children.

But Charna died prematurely, and Isaac married a third time. That wife, too, he had to bury.

Mania grew up in that large house, surrounded by trees. Like her father, she was independent and informal, "having always lived in the countryside, and not in one of the narrow alleys of the Jewish neighborhoods."[20] Yet her country background did not imply a lack of culture and elegance; to the contrary, like her famous daughter Clarice, she gave an impression of refinement. "She knew how to speak, she knew how to walk. She only wore clothes from designers in Kiev and Odessa. She always had an understanding word for one person, a coin for another."[21]

This was the woman the matchmaker found for Pinkhas Lispector. The bride and groom were allowed to see each other before the wedding, "in the presence of chaperones, of course."[22] After their marriage, which took place in about 1910, they moved. They would never again stay long in one place. By July 24, 1911, they were in the town of Savran, when their first child, Elisa, *née* Leah, was born.

The young family knew periods of peace and prosperity. Elisa remembered the brilliance of their Friday evenings, her mother magnificent in her pearls, lighting the Sabbath candles; the table, in the splendidly clean house, decked with the delicacies of the Eastern European Jews; the Saturday mornings spent in prayer in the synagogue; the afternoons of reading and visiting family and friends; and then, when the first stars appeared in the sky, her father's prayer over a glass of wine, "praising God for having distinguished between the sacred and the profane, between light and darkness, between the Sabbath and the days of work."[23]

> But my mother was at her most brilliant on the nights that other couples came to visit. Nobody was as fascinating a conversationalist, moving so gracefully through a world she enchanted. Because on the nights when my parents hosted their friends, who were young like they were, the house, with its windows open to the night in the summer, and cozy in the winter, was a true celebration.[24]

Their marriage was arranged, but "love was the feeling that united them, I'm sure of it now, remembering them together," Elisa wrote. "A halo surrounded them. There was a great understanding of mutual admiration. It was not unusual for me to catch them speaking more with their eyes than with words." Elisa contrasts the radiant Mania with the slightly reserved Pinkhas: "Thin face. Sad expression. My father always wore a sad expression, but of an imposing seriousness."

> An aspect of his character was not to be lavish with praise, and not because he did not recognize someone's qualities, but because he lacked that streak of servility that can be seen in certain people and which flattery only worsens. Quite to the contrary: the more he recognized someone's noble qualities, the greater his restraint in dealing with him. An expression he used with some frequency was *a fainer mensch* (a distinguished person), but if the person had won his complete admiration, he simply called him a *mensch* (a person). So when he said so-and-so is a *mensch*, he was paying him his highest honor.[25]

Pinkhas had inherited his father's seriousness, as well as his dedication to study. Elisa remembers him as ambitious: "He felt the world moving ahead all around him and did not want to be left behind."

Yet the world was determined to leave Pinkhas Lispector behind. His plight was that of generations of talented Russian Jews. His strictly traditional father, who allowed him to dress in a modern style, must have recognized that Pinkhas's generation would not be as closely bound to old orthodoxies. But the ambitious Russian Jew broke loose from these traditions only to find he had no future in his own country. " 'Jew' was the slur they used to block his way to the university," Elisa wrote, recording that as a young man Pinkhas "was fascinated by mathematics and physics, but was always blocked by an immovable barrier: the stigma of being Jewish."[26]

Instead of becoming a scientist or mathematician, Pinkhas had to be content with selling odds and ends in a rundown hamlet. "Father never learned a manual skill either, since all the men of his pedigree were dedicated to the study of Torah, and that, he knew from experience, meant nothing in terms of earning a living. And he wanted to earn, he wanted to live. He wanted to see the world. When he married, he even moved to another town. His eyes were open to the future, along with a boundless desire for knowledge."[27]

The life of a shopkeeper, selling shoes, cloth, hats, and accessories, "acquired in Kiev and Odessa, which is why he had a very select clientele," may have been a bitter comedown.[28] But during Elisa's earliest years he and his family prospered, though, as Clarice remembered, "his real talent was for spiritual matters."[29]

Like so many Russian Jews, Pinkhas turned inward. When the weather was so bad that no customers appeared, he went into the back of the shop, turned on a kerosene lamp, and started to read "everything he could bring back from the big bookstores he visited on his frequent journeys. But, besides Bialik and Dostoevsky, he also read, or rather studied, the Gemara (Talmud). The pious religious feelings of his father, whom he always saw hunched over the Holy Books, had become, in him, a way of thinking that was both spiritual and humanistic."[30]

Despite the humiliations that awaited the Jews in Russia, Pinkhas, according to Elisa, had never thought about emigrating, and nobody in his family had ever done so.[31] That was not Mania's case. Around 1909, her first cousins, the five sons of her maternal uncle Levy Rabin, went to Argentina,[32] headed, like thousands of others, for Baron Maurice de Hirsch's agricultural colonies.

The greatest Jewish philanthropist of his day, Hirsch, a Bavarian banker and industrialist, poured his vast fortune into causes all over the world, making princely gifts to educational and medical institutions throughout Europe, the United States, Canada, and Palestine. When the Russian government rebuffed his offer of two million pounds to create a system of secular Jewish schools in the Pale of Settlement, he turned his attention to helping the Russian Jews emigrate. Through his foundation, the Jewish Colonization Association, Hirsch bought up land in the United States, Canada, Brazil, and especially the enormous, fertile, empty Argentine Republic. In that country alone he eventually acquired over *seventeen million* acres.[33]

Like the Zionists, whose dream of a Jewish state he did not share, Hirsch believed that agricultural labor was the key to regenerating the Jewish people. But though the Jewish Colonization Association (JCA) provided much of the colonies' infrastructure, Hirsch's scheme was no more socialist than was

Hirsch himself. The immigrants were expected to buy the land they worked, and the colonies were meant to become self-governing municipalities. As conditions worsened in Russia after the 1905 Revolution, Jews flooded into Argentina. Between 1906 and 1912, around thirteen thousand arrived annually. Among these were Mania Lispector's five cousins, who found work with "La Jewish."

From the beginning, however, Hirsch's project in Argentina was troubled. Forbidden to work in agriculture in their homeland, the Russian Jews were essentially an urban, commercial people. Despite the training and assistance the JCA offered, they could not readily adapt to farming the pampas. Within two years of the colonies' founding in 1891, almost a third of the original colonists had departed for the United States. And though conditions eventually improved, the remainder steadily gravitated toward the cities.

Among those who left the countryside were the Rabin brothers. Of the five, only Abraham, who settled in Buenos Aires, remained long in Argentina.[34] The other four went to Brazil. For some reason, one of them, Joseph, now Brazilianized as José, ended up in Maceió, in the northeastern state of Alagoas. Maceió was an unlikely destination, located in the poorest and most backward region of the country. The bigger, more prosperous city of Recife, not too far away, was a more promising target, and it was there that the other three brothers settled, sporting the Brazilian names Pedro, Samuel, and Jorge. There they took up the traditional entry profession of immigrant Jew: peddling.[35]

By the beginning of 1914, therefore, five of the seven Rabin children were safely in South America. Sarah Rabin, their mother, was dead. Only Dora and Jacob, with their father, Levy, remained in the Ukraine. Dora soon met a young man from Chechelnik, Israel Wainstok, to whom she became engaged. They had planned to leave Russia immediately, but their plans were put off and they settled down in Chechelnik. There Israel's widowed mother, Feiga, married the widower Levy Rabin, Dora's father and Charna Krimgold's brother.[36]

The last of the family to depart before the war was Mania's sister Zicela Krimgold, who was engaged to her first cousin José Rabin, the brother who had settled in Maceió. It is not clear whether this union had already been planned before José and his brothers departed for Argentina five years before. In any case, José and Zicela, now answering to the more Brazilian-sounding name Zina, were married in Recife on April 24, 1914.

They escaped Europe just in time. For some reason, Dora and Israel Wainstok, along with their now married parents, Levy and Feiga Rabin, stayed behind. Perhaps they had spent their savings sending relatives on ahead of them and planned to join them later. Whatever the reason, it was a nearly fatal miscalculation.

❧

When the world war broke out in August, the normal paths of emigration—overland from Russia, through central Europe, and via Hamburg or the Holland ports to the Americas—were closed to the eastern Jews. Hundreds of thousands were being slaughtered on the front. Along it, as in the West, there was little movement after the armies dug into their trenches. And as in the West, millions of people were slaughtered for the gain of a few kilometers.

Pinkhas and Mania were lucky in one respect. Compared to many Russian Jews, they made it through the war with relative ease. In distant Savran, far from the front, many of the horrors of the First World War would pass them by. But amid the chaos that was swallowing up the country, Pinkhas's business did not prosper. By April 19, 1915, when their second daughter, Tania, was born, they had already left Savran and returned to Pinkhas's hometown, Teplyk.

But in contrast to France and Belgium, the Eastern Front was the scene of pogroms that surpassed anything that had come before them, and these would reach the Lispectors in due course. In the Polish and Ukrainian regions—whose loyalty the Russian Crown had good reason to suspect—attacks on Jews began almost as soon as the war did. They started with rumors: that Jews were smuggling gold to the Germans in the bodies of slaughtered geese; that they had put the plans for an antitsarist mutiny into a bottle and thrown it into the sea, where it could float to Danzig; that they were flashing coded lights from windows to assist the Austrian advance; that they were disrupting the telephones and fiddling with the telegraphs.[37] The Russian Jewish writer S. An-Ski records a rumor he heard from a hotel maid in Russian Warsaw:

> "The telephones," she said vaguely. "They tell the Germans everything. On Sunday, when the flying machines came over, the Jews sent them all sorts of signals—they told them that the biggest generals were in the church. So they started bombing it. Luckily, they missed."
>
> The elderly maid went on, delivering a recitation that she apparently replayed for every guest she met. The bombs had killed or wounded a dozen people, she said, all of them Poles, and all because the "Jews have an ointment, which they smear on their bodies so the bombs won't hurt them."[38]

Before long these absurdities devolved into slaughter. A wave of pogroms swept across the Pale. Though 650,000 Jews eventually served in the Russian army and 100,000 died in the war,[39] their loyalties were suspect, especially in the lands that switched hands over the course of the war.

In Galicia, to the northwest of Podolia, as many as 450,000 Jews (more than half the Jewish population) were uprooted by the war. In one forty-eight-hour period in May 1915, the entire population of forty thousand Jews was evicted from Kaunas, in Lithuania.[40] All told, around 600,000 Jews were deported. Up to 200,000 Jewish civilians were murdered.[41]

As the war drew to its bloody and protracted end, law and order vanished from the collapsing Russian Empire. The removal of the bungling tsar in the revolution of March 1917 at first seemed to herald a new dawn for Russia. Overnight the country went from a repressive police state to "the freest country in the world." But the two liberal governments that succeeded the tsar did not end the war. Instead, eager to show that the revolutionary democracy was as patriotically committed to the defense of the fatherland as any dictatorship, the provisional government threw the tattered army into a great offensive in June 1917, whose calamitous failure bled the government of the almost universal popular support that had greeted its establishment only a few months earlier. And it opened the way for the demagogue Vladimir Lenin to take control of the capital in November, in large part because he promised to end the war.

This he did, though not as quickly as he promised. In the Polish town of Brest-Litovsk, his deputy Trotsky spun the peace talks out for several months, hoping that the delay would spark a revolution in Germany and Austria. It did not. Instead, at the end of February 1918, the Germans, frustrated with the intransigence of the Bolsheviks, recommenced hostilities. Lenin had no army to resist the German advance. Within a couple of weeks the Germans had advanced across enormous swaths of Russian territory. With the Germans nearing the capital, Petrograd, Lenin suddenly capitulated on March 3, 1918, signing a treaty whose terms were even worse than those he could have achieved at the end of 1917.

The treaty eventually ensured the independence of Finland, Estonia, Latvia, Lithuania, and Poland. In the Ukraine, the picture was complicated. Most Russians did not then, and do not now, easily accept the idea that the Ukrainians were a separate people, or that their language, related to but quite distinct from Russian, was anything more than a peasant dialect. The Ukrainians themselves were cautious. Like many nationalist movements in the former Russian Empire, the Ukrainians, at the beginning of 1917, initially wanted nothing more than autonomy: the freedom to use their own language, especially in the schools and in the government.[42]

After Lenin's coup in November, the Ukrainian government distanced itself further from the government in Petrograd. But they stopped short of full independence. This reassured the Jews, whose two principal goals, Jewish autonomy and the continued unity of Russia, were respected.[43] But the honeymoon was about to end, with the government under pressure from the Bolsheviks in the north and the Jews alarmed by the wave of pogroms breaking out in Podolia, Volhynia, and Kiev.[44] The government responded by allowing the formation of Jewish military units for self-defense.[45] The self-defense units never got off the ground, and the Jews in the western Ukraine were left defenseless.

On January 25, 1918, the Ukrainian Rada declared the independence of the Ukrainian People's Republic.[46] Soon after the declaration Kiev was occupied by Bolshevik forces. But not for long: by April the Rada had been overthrown in a German-sponsored coup, establishing the so-called hetmanate under General Pavlo Skoropads'kyi, who took the traditional Ukrainian title of hetman, and creating a German military protectorate in exchange for supplies of food and raw materials.[47] The German grain confiscations stirred peasant resistance, and the Germans were quick to blame the Jews.[48]

Meanwhile, the divided country faced a Bolshevik invasion. The presence of Jews, especially Trotsky (born Lev Bronstein), at the highest levels of the Bolshevik organization meant that, though a large majority and all Jewish political parties opposed the Bolsheviks, the idea that the Jews were behind the Bolsheviks quickly took root. "The Trotskys make the revolutions," people grimly quipped, "the Bronsteins pay the price."

Throughout 1918 there were sporadic pogroms, sparked, to some extent, by the anarchy unleashed by the general German surrender on November 11, 1918, which ended the Ukrainian protectorate and created a power vacuum. Deprived of its critical German support, the hetman's puppet government proved too weak to restore order. Throughout November and December the Ukrainian National Movement, known as the Directorate, fought a civil war to depose the hetman. Headed by the former journalist Simon Petlura, the Directorate eventually vanquished the hetman.

But as Petlura was conquering the Ukraine, the Bolsheviks were invading from the north and east. In many cases, Petlura had only nominal control over his troops, who splintered into detachments under local warlords. These "generals" were often no more than thugs and criminals who used the chaos of the civil war to plunder the defenseless population. For the Jews, this was the worst possible scenario.

In Elisa Lispector's unpublished memoirs, she remembered with special affection the making of liquors in the autumn:

> The wines, the cider, the fine liquors, especially *vishniak*, ruby-colored cherry liquor. This wasn't child's play. It was the occupation of grownups with real skill. That is why that expertise demanded respect. That is also the reason we felt such horror one day, when—returning from a hiding place after a terrific pogrom, and finding the house turned inside out, the cabinets and the secret drawers for the good silver and embroidered linens ransacked, the furniture broken and hacked to pieces—we saw red rivers running all over the floor, the wines and liquors, with their indescribable taste, transformed into rivers of blood.[49]

Soon news came of another disaster. Law and order had vanished and highwaymen invaded defenseless towns, taking hostages and then demanding outrageous "levies" to free them. When they appeared in Isaac Krimgold's town, in one of the first pogroms that followed the October Revolution, they took a group of young people hostage, promising to free them in exchange for money. Isaac and some neighbors offered to change places with the hostages, and with great difficulty the sum demanded was collected. The bandits murdered the hostages anyway.[50]

Of herself, Elisa writes, "She shouldn't have mentioned Grandfather. Mother also knew what 'they' had done to him." In Isaac's lovely house, where Elisa fondly remembered bathing in the stream and playing in the surrounding woods, "they broke the colored glass on the porch, tore down the wall around his garden, and cut down all the trees. Now anyone could go into Grandfather's house. The house no longer belonged to him."[51]

The final clipped sentences in her lightly fictionalized novel may reproduce a childhood memory of Elisa's. Perhaps it was in those terms that her parents explained to the little girl that her grandfather had been murdered.

3

THE AVERAGE POGROM

At the end of December 1918 the great wave of pogroms began. It was a series of attacks "unparalleled in history, [covering] the fields and towns of the Ukraine with rivers of Jewish blood," an epidemic "exceeding all other periods in its refined cruelty, in the merciless thoroughness of the acts of violence, and in the naked bloodthirstiness of the barbarous criminals."[1]

According to a contemporary report, the "average pogrom" went something like this:

> The gang breaks into the township, spreads all over the streets, separate groups break into the Jewish houses, killing without distinction of age and sex everybody they meet, with the exception of women, who are bestially violated before they are murdered, and men are forced to give up all there is in the house before being killed.
>
> Everything that can be removed is taken away, the rest is destroyed, the walls, doors, and windows are broken in search of money. On one group departing another comes, then a third, until absolutely nothing is left that could possibly be taken away. All clothing and linen is taken, not only from those who escape death, but also from the corpses of the dead. A new administration is established in the place, and a deputation of the Jews miraculously preserved go to them or to the Christians who are supposed to be friendly to Jews, and request protection. As a rule the new authorities consent to grant the protection on the condition that a certain contribution is paid by the Jews. With great difficulty a contribution is paid and then a new claim arrives from the authorities for contributions in

> kind, and it is the duty of the Jews to obtain a certain number of boots and a certain quantity of meat for the soldiers. In the meantime small groups continue terrorizing the Jews, exact money, murder and violate. Then the town is occupied by the Soviet troops, who often continue the robbery of their predecessors. But soon all the gangs return, as the front fluctuates and the place continually changes hands. Thus, for instance, Boguslav was taken five times during one week. Every change of Government or administration brings new pogroms, and the end of it is that the terrorized population, ruined and exhausted, naked and barefooted, without a single coin in their pocket, fly heedless of the climatic conditions and risking the dangers of the journey, to the nearest town in the vain hope of getting protection there.

There were at least a thousand such pogroms, committed by every side in the war. The Russian Red Cross estimated that by 1920 at least forty thousand Jews had been killed but acknowledged that the true total would never be known. Their statistics, after all, did not include "those who died during their wanderings from one town to another in search of an asylum, those who were thrown out of trains and shot, those who were drowned in the rivers, and those who were murdered in forests and other lonely and sequestered places. In the above totals we have not included those who died from wounds, from infection, and from starvation and exposure."[2]

Like millions of others, Mania, Pinkhas, Elisa, and Tania Lispector were trapped in this horror. At some point after April 19, 1915, when Tania was born in Pinkhas's native Teplyk, the family moved to Haysyn, only a few miles away.[3] Then as now, there were more opportunities in Haysyn, which was something of a regional center.

Pinkhas desperately tried to scrape by working as a traveling salesman or petty trader, and when the White Army arrived he was absent, unable to rejoin his family in the war zone. Among the Jews, rumors circulated that the Whites would be better than the Reds, that they would bring peace, but there was no reliable news.

On a night Elisa recalls in her novel, there were shots; fires broke out. Something awful was happening, but no one knew what. This had become a common enough occurrence. "Every morning," Elisa wrote, "a surprise. We never knew in whose hands the night's battle had left the town."[4] Mania, in charge of a group of terrified refugees, was unsure what to do. She decided to leave the house and find out.

At this point in Elisa's narrative there is a strange lacuna. "So it was up to her," Elisa writes of her mother, "to save her daughters, and the women and children who had taken refuge in her house." She goes out.

> She was in the street, her hair blowing in the wind, the snow almost to her waist. When she saw two militiamen coming in her direction, she fell at their feet, begging for help. *She cried, imploringly kissing their muddy boots. After that the images blurred fantastically in the dim moonlight.* As in a dream, in the dense fog, she saw men running and firing at each other, and then, for what seemed like an eternity, the world was deserted. So with sluggish, elastic steps, she walked home....
>
> Without knowing what to do, Marim [Mania] let herself slide into a chair, and there she remained quietly and meekly.[5]

In her unpublished memoir Elisa writes simply, "The trauma resulting from one of those fateful pogroms caused my mother to fall ill."[6] In the passage above from her novel *In Exile*, she hints at the trauma indirectly. Until Mania falls at the feet of the soldiers there is no suggestion of sickness. Afterward, though, Mania faced a slow and horrible demise, dying young from some untreatable disease.

It is no surprise that Mania's daughters did not fill in the gaps. At the very end of her life, Clarice confided to her closest friend that her mother was raped by a gang of Russian soldiers.[7] From them, she contracted syphilis, which in the ghastly conditions of the civil war went untreated. Perhaps if she had reached a hospital sooner she would have stood a better chance. But it would be another twenty years before penicillin, the most effective treatment, entered common use. By then, after a decade of horrible suffering, Mania, the elegant, intelligent, free-spirited girl from the Podolia countryside, would be lying in a Brazilian graveyard.

"There is something I would like to say but I can't. And it will be very difficult for someone to write my biography," Clarice Lispector wrote in an unpublished manuscript.[8] Is this "something" a reference to the rape of her mother, one of the central facts of her life?

Every account of the pogroms records the prevalence of rape. Along with robbery of Jewish property, it was one of the indispensable characteristics of the pogroms. This is not unusual; rape is an essential element of ethnic cleansing, designed as much to humiliate a people as to kill and expel them. The Ukraine of the civil war era was no different.

In the sense that Mania's two oldest daughters were not killed or raped, that her third daughter survived a birth to a syphilitic mother, that her husband survived, and that she herself lived long enough to see her family safely established abroad, she was luckier than many. In the panoply of horrors that was the civil war–era Ukraine, Mania can even be said to have got off lightly.

Thousands of girls were gang-raped; after one pogrom, "many of the victims were later found with knife and saber wounds to their small vaginas."[9] The Russian Red Cross recorded the aftermath of an "ordinary, simple pogrom" in Ladyshenka, one town east of Pinkhas and Tania's native Teplyk. "On July 9th a peasant brought to the Jewish hospital in Uman the last two Jews from Ladyshenka (before the war Ladyshenka counted a Jewish population of 1,600). These were two young Jewish girls, frightfully beaten and bruised, one with her nose cut off and the other with her arms broken. They are both in Kiev now and both suffer from venereal disease."[10]

It is hard to know exactly when Mania Lispector was attacked; there are several conflicting possibilities. Elisa sets her elusive scene in the winter, with heavy snow all around; the major attacks on Haysyn occurred in the summer. The neighborhood of Haysyn, where the family lived, was one of the heaviest hit areas in all of the Ukraine. Pogroms were more common there than in any other part of Podolia, which after Kiev was the most brutalized province in the Ukraine.

In the small district of Haysyn, there were no fewer than twenty-nine pogroms up to September 19, 1919. Many more followed. In 1919 the Red Cross noted, "The pogroms in Trostianetz [just south of Haysyn] on May 10th and in Gaisin [Haysyn] on May 12th may be classed among the most cruel ever perpetrated." In Haysyn on May 12 to 13 at least 350 people were killed.[11] From July 15 to 20 Haysyn was hit again.[12] Was it during one of these attacks that Mania Lispector was raped? In 1968, in her only direct allusion to these events, Clarice gives a hint of the timing:

> I was prepared for birth in such a beautiful way. My mother was already sick, and a common superstition had it that pregnancy would cure a woman of her illness. So I was deliberately created: with love and hope. Except that I didn't cure my mother. And to this day that guilt weighs on me: they made me for a specific mission, and I let them down. As if they were counting on me in the trenches of a war and I had deserted. I know that my parents forgave me for being born in vain and for having betrayed

their great hope. But I can't forgive myself. I simply wanted a miracle: for my birth to cure my mother.[13]

This would mean that Mania had taken ill some time before March 1920, when Clarice was conceived. How reliable is this account, though? The Lispectors came from a backwoods town and had no advanced secular education to explain the cause of syphilis. Still, it was an old and greatly feared disease, and it is surprising that Mania and Pinkhas would have risked sex, not to speak of pregnancy, knowing that she was infected.

But a danger widely understood in more sophisticated places might have appeared mysterious in Podolia. The region hardly groaned under excessive medical attention. It boasted no more than one doctor for every twenty thousand people. That, by comparison, is half the number in Afghanistan today, one-sixth the number in Cambodia, and one twenty-fifth the number in Brazil. And that was in peacetime.[14]

In the desperate circumstances of the civil war, when even that paltry medical care was nonexistent, Pinkhas and Mania probably did rely on local superstition, which would have been the normal course for the poor people of the obscure regions of the Ukraine. In such areas, people believed that

unclean or divine forces caused illness, which fell into the same category as misfortune, economic ruin, and crop failures.... Hasidic *tsadikim* [saints], midwives, clairvoyants, and sorcerers all bore the power to heal. They cured with a blessing, an incantation, an amulet, a potent herbal drink, or a night-long vigil at the synagogue. Places and objects, as well as individuals, possessed miraculous qualities. Water from a particular well, earth from a special place, herbs from a special spot, the excrement from a hen grouse, all worked in healing the sick.[15]

In rural Podolia, such beliefs were specific to certain localities.[16] To this day in Chechelnik, though not as close as Uman, only a few miles away, the local population believe that genital "bubbles," or chancres, will disappear during pregnancy. Primary syphilis appears as a hard, painless chancre, on an average of twenty-one days after initial infection. Then, in many cases, the primary lesion disappears. The symptoms return later in a much more painful and visible secondary stage. So if Clarice was conceived as a response to her mother's primary syphilis, Pinkhas and Mania, seeing the chancre disappear, would surely have hoped that the old popular wisdom was true. But their hopes would have been dashed when the infection returned in a more laming form. The disease's second stage would probably have begun when Mania's pregnancy was already advanced, which means that Clarice was very lucky to be born without congenital syphilis: 40 percent of births to syphilitic mothers are stillborn. As many as 70 percent of the survivors are infected, and 12 percent of these will die prematurely. In the middle of a war zone, without adequate nutrition, the percentages would be even higher. To the extent that one can speak of luck in a situation such as this one, Clarice was extremely lucky.

The progress of the disease varies. But if Clarice was conceived in about March 1920, this suggests that Mania was probably attacked in or after the summer of 1919, when the wave of pogroms struck the family's native region with such force. They were almost certainly fleeing by that time, though Clarice's declaration on the subject is a masterpiece of elision. The family's flight sounds like a holiday outing. But she makes clear that she was born en route: "When my mother was pregnant with me, my parents were heading toward the United States or Brazil, they still hadn't decided which. They stopped in Chechelnik so I could be born and then continued on their journey."[17]

In her novel, *In Exile*, Elisa recalls a pogrom, probably one of the attacks in Haysyn in the summer of 1919, that left the family's home uninhabitable: "The doors had been yanked out of their jambs; the broken windows stared silently out at the street, like blinded eyes."[18] The family fled to another house, where they hid in the kitchen, seeing the city in flames and hearing machine-gun fire throughout the night. There, a teenage boy, wounded and bleeding from his head, staggered in and expired in plain sight of Elisa and her mother. But there is a moment of hope: Pinkhas, hungry and terrified, finally manages to rejoin his family.

There is widespread hunger. Soup kitchens open, and cooperatives, but it is too little and too late. A scene from Elisa's book bears an eerie echo of something Clarice would later write:

> Ethel [Tania] stirred drowsily and asked for some bread.
>
> "There isn't any, sweetheart. It's night. I'll buy some tomorrow."
>
> "But I want some. Daddy brought some, I saw it. I saw white bread."
>
> Then she turned over and went back to sleep, sucking her thumb in an instinctive effort to fool her hunger.[19]

Years later, Clarice wrote a short piece that at first glance seems to reflect a middle-class Brazilian's concern for her less fortunate fellow citizens. But it is probably a fragment of autobiography:

> I can't. I can't keep thinking about a scene that flashed through my mind, a real scene. A child has hunger pangs at night and says to his mother: I'm hungry, mommy. She says sweetly: sleep. He says: but I'm hungry. She insists: sleep. He says: I can't, I'm hungry. She repeats, exasperated: sleep. He insists. She cries out, hurting: go to sleep, you brat! The two remain motionless, silent, in the darkness. Is he asleep? she thinks, wide awake. And he is too terrified to complain. In the black night the two lie awake. Until, out of pain and fatigue, both nod off, in a nest of resignation. And I cannot stand resignation. Ah: with what hunger and pleasure do I gulp down revolt.[20]

When Haysyn is taken by the Red Army, the new governors promptly forbid commerce, removing any way for Pinkhas to earn a living. Mania and Pinkhas decide to take their chances and escape. As in tsarist (and Soviet) times, they need an internal passport to leave the city, and once they are outside they are accosted by a slimy Jewish character, "Barukh," who promises to escort them across the border for a payment of 500,000 rubles. Barukh prides himself on his lack of sentimentalism and his hardheaded realism, which allows him to move with the times. He makes pointed comments that indicate a lowly class origin ("Me, I'm no rabbi's son").[21] Like many unscrupulous Jews, he makes a living exploiting the desperate refugees.

"What interested them," wrote Israel Wainstok, who was fleeing at the same time, "wasn't saving refugees but making sure they got all the money they could get out of these people."[22] With no other choice—the Jews so hated in Russia were also generally forbidden to depart legally—Pinkhas hands over all the money he has left.

On their first attempt to cross the border, Barukh sends a message advising them against it; the crossings are too heavily guarded. All they can do is return to the nearest city. They have nothing left and no means of earning more. Both Elisa and Tania recall that Mania saved them with a hidden purse of jewels. These were the jewels she, the well-to-do daughter of a prosperous trader, had brought to her marriage; these were the jewels that would save the lives of her family. But they were the same jewels that, if discovered, could have meant the death of that same family. Mania's gamble—that the bandits who infested the roads, preying on the helpless refugee population, would not find her out—was a desperate gesture. It was also the gesture of a courageous and formidable woman.

"What does this mean?" Pinkhas demands in understandable terror when Mania calmly reveals the hidden purse. "How dare you? If 'they' had found it, what would have happened to us?"[23] But the success of her bet allows the family to survive in a new town, Chechelnik, due south of Haysyn on the most direct road to Kishinev. They had relatives there, Mania's cousin Dora; Dora's husband, Israel Wainstok; and Dora's widowed father, married to Israel's mother, Faiga.[24]

In Elisa's book, the family stays in the unnamed town through several seasons. This may explain Clarice's claim that she was born during the family's emigration, between their first and second attempts to escape. In this village, probably Chechelnik, they celebrated Passover on April 3, 1920. That year, in the "ghost town," the family must have recalled with a shiver the deliverance from Egyptian bondage. They themselves were not yet free.

Throughout the summer and autumn they waited for Barukh, their Moses, to resurface.[25] They were kept from starvation by the fortuitous appearance of a sick, elderly man, who approached Pinkhas in the street and offered to teach him a trade, soap making, in exchange for helping him reach the next town, in the direction of his own native village. Pinkhas quickly learned how to make soap, which gave the family a fragile source of income.

But Chechelnik, founded as a refuge from Tatars and landlords, offered cold comfort. A couple of weeks after Passover, a detachment from the Ukrainian Galician army appeared. They were soon chased away by local Poles. In June, the Red Army arrived, and its soldiers were greeted as liberators. As elsewhere, however, the Soviet soldiers quickly wore out their welcome. The peasantry rebelled against taxes levied in food, which had the effect of inducing mass starvation.

The south of Podolia seethed with counterrevolution; by summer no fewer than five Red Army divisions had arrived to quell the disturbance, and Olgopol County, where Chechelnik is located, was the most unstable area in all of Podolia. The Cheka, predecessor to the KGB, attributed most of the problems to the complex geography of the area (it is hilly and forested and thus ideal for guerrilla warfare) and to the "national-petit-bourgeois mentality" of the local residents. But even they mentioned the "tactless behavior" of the Soviet troops.[26]

There is no mention of attacks on the Jews, but the Jews doubtless suffered more than their share throughout the year Mania was pregnant with Clarice. In 1920 in the little town of Chechelnik alone, five hundred peasant households were ransacked. Businesses were destroyed, fields went unplanted, epidemics raged. Starvation was the rule. Six years earlier, 8,867 people had lived in Chechelnik. By January 1921 the population had been more than halved.

In these circumstances, in temperatures that reached 20 degrees below zero, Chaya Pinkhasovna Lispector was born to a syphilitic mother on December 10, 1920.

4

THE MISSING NAME

The fragile child became a famous artist in a country her parents could then have hardly imagined. But it would be under another name. The name she received in Chechelnik, Chaya, which in Hebrew means "life"—and which also has the appropriate connotation "animal"—would disappear, reappearing only in Hebrew on her tombstone and not widely known in Brazil until decades after her death.

Her writing is full of secret names. "One can say that in the work of Clarice Lispector there is a hidden name, or that her whole body of work is constructed upon her own name, disseminated and hidden," one of her most perceptive critics has written.[1] The name Clarice is hidden inside the name Lucrécia, the heroine of her third novel, *The Besieged City*. The protagonist of *An Apprenticeship* has the un-Brazilian name Lori, which is made of the first and last letters of the name Lispector.[2] These may be coincidences, though they probably are not. Clarice's work abounds with explicit instances of these sorts of word games: "I want to say things wrong. Like: Sued. That means God [Deus]."[3] Or "But Brasília doesn't pour. It is backwards. Like this: ruop (pour)."[4]

The question of names and naming, the process by which things are called into being, dominates Clarice Lispector's work. These questions, which she ultimately invests with great mystical import, may have had their origins in her own childhood, when she was suddenly assigned another name. In the posthumously published *A Breath of Life (Pulsations)*, Clarice puts the following words into the mouth of her character Angela Pralini: "I quickly ran down the list of my possessions and was startled to realize that there is only one thing that has not yet been taken from us: our own names. Angela Pralini, a name as gratuitous as yours and which became the title of my quavering identity. Where can that identity take me? What am I to do with myself?"[5] Like so many of Clarice's fictional creations, Angela is an avatar of her author. But Clarice's name *had* been taken from her; Chaya had become Clarice, and Clarice never, as far as is known, referred to her secret name, except obliquely: "I lost myself so many years ago that I hesitate to try to find myself again. I am afraid to begin. Existing so often gives me palpitations. I am so afraid to be myself. I am so dangerous. They gave me a name and alienated me from myself."[6]

The fear of losing her identity pursued her throughout her life, as in a letter she sent a friend three years before her death: "I was awakened by a terrible nightmare: I dreamed that I was leaving Brazil (as in fact I am, in August) and when I came back I learned that lots of people were writing things and signing my name to them. I complained, I said it wasn't me, but nobody believed me, and they mocked me. I couldn't take it any more and woke up. I was so nervous and electric and exhausted that I broke a glass."[7]

She created a myth about her name, which already appears in her first novel, published when she was twenty-three. She embroidered the legend throughout her life, claiming, improbably, that Lispector was a Latin name. By breaking it into parts—*lis*, lily, as in *fleur de lis*, and *pector*, chest or breast—she produced a nonsensical combination, "breast-lily." On her deathbed, in a small scribbled fragment, she imbued this fantastical name with poetic resonance:

> I am an object loved by God. And that makes flowers blossom upon my breast. He created me in the same way I created the sentence I just wrote: "I am an object loved by God" and he enjoyed creating me as much as I enjoyed creating the phrase. And the more spirit the human object has, the greater is God's satisfaction.
>
> White lilies pressing against the nudity of my breast. The lilies I offer to whatever hurts inside you.[8]

But the ultimate reality is beyond names and language. The mystical experience, which she would dramatize most memorably in her novel *The Passion According to G.H.*, is the process of removing language to discover an ultimate, and necessarily nameless, truth. Before her old life is shattered by a blinding mystical vision, the protagonist, G. H., summarizes her biography: "The rest was the way I had gradually become the person who has my name. And I ended up being my name. All you have to do is look on the leather of my luggage and see the initials G. H.—and there I am."[9]

In Chechelnik her name was about all the infant Chaya had. As Mania's illness advanced, household tasks increasingly devolved upon Elisa, the oldest daughter. The nine-year-old had already lived through more than her share of horrors, and the physical burden of running the household added to her psychological trauma.

The effects on her, she remembers in the most poignant scene in her book, were visible. And they caused her father to adopt a different attitude toward his oldest daughter: "He silently caressed her head, sometimes only barely pausing to glance at her thin face; her long, scrawny limbs; her expressionless mouth; her wild eyes. She was ugly, hideous, and it hurt him to see it. What hurt him most was her premature seriousness, the mark of her heavy responsibilities."[10]

This was not a family that needed more problems. But, sure enough, Pinkhas soon came down with the typhus fever that was then raging. Typhus, a disease of filth, is exactly the disease one would expect to find in a devastated country like the Ukraine. It is transmitted by rats and lice and thrives amid misery, in places where public hygiene has completely broken down. "The lice that carry typhus fever are common in large aggregations of persons who do not bathe or change clothes with any regularity and are forced by circumstances to live in close quarters. These are also the situations that infantry, refugees and prisoners are likely to find themselves."[11] Between twenty and thirty million people were infected in the typhus epidemic of 1918–1922. At least three million died.

Throughout the winter, as her father lay motionless in bed, Elisa writes, her mother, "forgetting her own illness," left every day to exchange some bit of their meager property for food for her family. In the Ukraine, in 1921, this was a grueling task, even for a healthy person. The country, known as the great breadbasket or granary of Europe, which before the war had produced an annual *surplus* of 300 million tons of grain, was starving.

No less than Vidkun Quisling, whose eager participation in the Nazi occupation of Norway made his name synonymous with treason, visited the Ukraine with a League of Nations commission. He described the scene:

> The land is burnt black and stripped of trees and plants. One sees the straw of the roofs used as food for men and cattle, the miserable and often poisonous surrogates used for human first; hears the people tell how they have already eaten all the dogs, cats and crows they could get hold of, even dead cattle, leather of the harnesses, wood of the furniture. You hear of and get proof of necrophagy and cannibalism, speak with persons who have eaten

their children or sisters and brothers, see the people lying like skeletons only in the houses, dying or awaiting death without any relief in view. You see the hospitals, which in reality are only places where the starving people are brought together to get a certain care, but where there are no beds, no linen, no medicine, and often no physician, the people lying narrowly together on the floor in the utmost misery. You taste the food which is given in those hospitals: a soup, salt water. You see the heaps of dead bodies, often with open eyes, nobody having cared to shut them.[12]

From 1921 to 1922 a million people in the Ukraine died of starvation. In 1922 Quisling estimated that, of the three million Jews in the country, "the number of Jewish sufferers from starvation and disease does not fall far short of 2,000,000."[13]

Trapped in a war zone with millions of starving people, her husband immobilized by disease, her three young children hungry and helpless, her own health shattered, and without money or property to fall back on, Mania struggled to feed her family. Finally, when there was nothing left to sell, Mania, already partly paralyzed and in the middle of the Ukrainian winter, removed her own shoes, sold them, and wrapped her feet with rags. Elisa remembered her perfect composure.[14]

Yet in the hellish context of the Ukraine, the family was, once again, luckier than many. Thanks to Mania's determination and the bits of jewelry she still had, they were not among the million people who died of starvation, and Pinkhas was not one of the three million who died in the typhus epidemic. After he recovered, the family tried once more to escape. With a group of other emigrants they left the city, reaching the forest at night. In Elisa's book there is no sign of Barukh, who presumably absconded with their money. Pinkhas carried their baggage on his back, Clarice tied to his chest, supporting the crippled Mania on his arm. After an exhausting journey throughout the night, they reached an abandoned village, where they slept the rest of the following day. Finally, at night, they arrived at the moonlit Dniester, where canoes waited to ferry them across to Romania. Elisa recalls, "To her surprise, the village faced the night with its doors and windows open, fearlessly! Here no one was afraid of the dark, or of the fugitives the night always hid. And there was light in the houses. Great kerosene lamps cleanly lit the simple, pleasant homes, and upon the tables there was bread, real bread, tea, and plates of meat. Then they slept in beds, real beds... beds for normal people."[15] This is Soroca, a town with a large Gypsy population just over the Dniester, in what is now the Republic of Moldova. The Lispectors would never return to their homeland.

The closest Clarice ever got to her birthplace was Warsaw, where her husband was the Brazilian ambassador in the 1960s. She was by then a famous writer, and the Soviet government, anxious as ever to burnish its "cultural" credentials, offered her the opportunity to visit the land of her birth. She refused. "I literally never set foot there: I was carried. But I remember one evening, in Poland, at the home of one of the secretaries of the embassy, I went out onto the terrace alone: a great black forest movingly pointed me the way to the Ukraine. I felt the call. Russia had me too. But I belong to Brazil."[16]

5

STATUE OF LIBERTY

They left the Ukraine in the winter of 1921.[1] From Soroca they traveled south to Kishinev, in Romania, now Chişinău, the capital of Moldova. Compared to the Ukraine, the new land was prosperous, but it was also overflowing with some of the millions of refugees who had fled the world war and the Russian civil war. Europe was overwhelmed with these desperate people, and not only Europe: there were fifty Russian exiles in Abyssinia, a hundred thousand in China.[2]

Their numbers and desperate plight inspired contempt in many members of the established Jewish community. "Some Romanian Jews," Israel Wainstok wrote in his Yiddish memoir, "looked down at the thousands of thousands of refugees like damaged goods, washed downstream by a flood." Kishinev was " 'like the garden of the Lord in the land of Egypt,' " he wrote. "The Jews who lived there did good business and earned a lot of money. They showed themselves indifferent to the terrible situation of the Jewish refugees from Russia, who were exiled there and in other Romanian cities, drifting from synagogues to streets, awaiting some help from their friends and relatives in America."[3]

Pinkhas Lispector was unable to find work. The family traveled south into what is now Romania, stopping in Galatz (now Galaţi), an industrial center in the Danube delta, and eventually reaching Bucharest. "Bucharest was particularly inhospitable," Elisa wrote. "Its sinuous streets all intertwined. By God it seemed more like a nightmare than reality." They found provisional lodgings in a miserable hotel, "black from the smoke that escaped from the iron brazier that wasn't enough to cook on or to heat the room, the room black from the almost total lack of light, even by day (because it was a room at the back), and from the sadness and worries that weighed upon us all."[4]

According to *In Exile*, the family then moved to a refugee hostel. The five people were given two narrow beds in a long corridor with hundreds of other people, many of whom were sick. One day, when Pinkhas returned after another day vainly searching for employment, he found that his own daughters had fallen victim to an outbreak of measles and been removed to a hospital in a distant part of the city. Some responsible party also evacuated his wife, whose illness had progressed so far that "she found it increasingly impossible to drag herself every day to the free kitchen, where they served a dirty, greasy soup."[5]

As at so many desperate points on this seemingly impossible journey, a kind of luck was with them. On the street Pinkhas ran into a *landsman*, a neighbor from his hometown, whom Elisa calls Herschel. Herschel had a bit of money and offered a loan to Pinkhas, with which the family managed to leave the hostel. Their circumstances improved, but they were not exactly well-to-do. Elisa, who herself no longer had any shoes, had to lug a pot to the communal soup kitchen, as she had to do in Haysyn after the Revolution. It was humiliating and painful, but there was hope: Pinkhas, with Herschel's loan, started selling shoes in the marketplace. Her mother remained in the charity hospital. They were allowed to visit her only once a week, bringing bread, grapes, and apples, and then leaving her behind until the next week, when the "disdainful, severe" public charity again allowed them back.

"And then there were the uncertainties," Elisa writes. "Uncertainties about how long we would have to be there (it ended up being months) and about where we would go. Until almost the day we left, we didn't have any hope, we couldn't see any promised land. The letters Mother and Father wrote to America and Brazil took a long time to reach their destinations, and the answers took even longer. And what worried us the most was the friendly and reticent tone in which those answers were given."[6]

❧

Mania's half-siblings, children of Isaac Krimgold and his first wife, were in the United States, by far the most popular destination for Jewish emigrants. But on May 19, 1921, the U.S. Congress passed the Emergency Quota Act, slashing by 75 percent the numbers of Eastern Europeans allowed entry. Brazil was still open, and probably the most attractive option anyway, given the greater number of relatives the family had there. But both countries required an invitation from someone who could guarantee they would not become wards of the state.

At last the invitation, with its "friendly and reticent tone," arrived from Brazil. The family was issued a Russian passport on January 27, 1922, valid for travel to Brazil.[7] It is hard to imagine a more joyless family portrait than the one staring out from this document. Elisa thought that Pinkhas was "the most pathetic figure. Yet full of dignity. . . . He was not a man who would turn up anywhere without a collar and a tie! . . . The face is grave, with a dark complexion and large mustache, and he is dressed like Charlie Chaplin: a dark coat and vest, quite threadbare and much too big for his emaciated body, an old crumpled shirt, and, knotted around his high collar, yes, knotted, is a poor substitute for a tie." Elisa and Tania look thin and exhausted, "frightened by a world made of foreign countries, populated by strange people."[8] The youngest daughter is a tiny blur. The most striking face is Mania's; she looks much older than her thirty-two years. She stares straight out, her jaw clenched. It is the same defiant gaze, "too intense for anyone to stand for long," that would make her famous daughter instantly recognizable.

Soon after the Russian consulate in Bucharest issued them a passport for Brazil, the Lispectors traveled via Budapest and Prague to Hamburg, where they boarded a Brazilian ship, the *Cuyabá*. With twenty-five other immigrants, they traveled in third class.[9] One can only imagine what an ordeal the voyage must have been for Mania. The Atlantic crossing was a trial even for the healthy, and the experience of steerage is a staple of immigrant literature.

Filth, and a stench enhanced by faulty ventilation, created on most of these ships an atmosphere an American report described as "almost unendurable. . . . In many instances, persons, after recovering from seasickness, continue to lie in their berths in a sort of stupor, due to breathing air whose oxygen has been mostly replaced by foul gases." An American investigator, disguised as a Bohemian peasant, described the tiny quarters where the immigrants were piled atop one another, the open troughs that served as toilets, the smell of the vomit emitting from the seasick passengers. "Everything," she concluded, "was dirty, sticky and disagreeable to the touch. Every impression was offensive."[10] In her own book Elisa mentions the heat and the suffocating, poisonous air in the hold. One evening, when she was lying in bed unable to sleep, an enormous rat ran across her pillow, brushing against her face, "its little eyes sparkling in its gray, repellent fur."[11]

Unlike the hardships they faced in Europe, this one at least would be only temporary, and Mania and Pinkhas Lispector were surely comforted by the knowledge that their journey was about to end. Their children would grow up in a free country, one relatively unburdened by anti-Semitism. This was not because Brazil was historically well-disposed toward Jews. It was a Portuguese colony and hosted the Inquisition in colonial times, when professing Jews were barred. But it had nothing like the endemic anti-Semitism of Eastern Europe. This was in part because when the Lispectors arrived the "Jewish Question" was almost entirely academic.

Aside from a few small Sephardic communities in the Amazonian cities, few Jews lived there. In 1920, probably no more than fifteen thousand Jews lived in the entire enormous country. The previous thirty years had seen more than 2.6 million other immigrants arrive, mostly from southern Europe, along with an important contingent of Japanese. But only a handful of the new immigrants were Jews.[12] Like the Lispectors' relatives, many had originally arrived with the Jewish Colonization Association, either through Argentina, like the Rabin brothers, or through the far south of Brazil, where the Association had two agricultural colonies. But from the beginning the Jewish immigrants were drawn to the cities.

They mainly gravitated to the large southern cities of Rio de Janeiro and São Paulo. The northeastern city where the Lispectors disembarked, Maceió, south of Recife in the small state of Alagoas, contained no more than a handful of Jewish families. These included Mania's sister Zicela and her husband, Joseph Rabin. When they greeted their relatives at the port of Maceió, the gulf between them must have been yawning. The Rabins and the Lispectors had not seen each other in almost a decade. Brazilianized as Zina and José, the Rabins had had time to grow comfortable in their new home. They had a successful business, spoke Portuguese, and had two Brazilian-born children, Sara and Henrique. Most of all, they had not experienced the hellish years the Lispectors had spent trapped in the Ukraine.

Though the dock was graced with its own replica of the Statue of Liberty, Maceió could not be easily confused with Manhattan. Three years after the Lispectors' arrival, in 1925, the capital of Alagoas boasted no more than seven cafés, six hotels, and three cinemas.[13] Not a lot happened there, and not a lot ever had. Between 1695, when Zumbi, the leader of the free black republic of Palmares, in the interior of Alagoas, was killed, and 1990, when corrupt local wastrel Fernando Collor de Mello was elected president of Brazil, it was a stranger to the headlines, a sleepy backwater in the poorest part of the country. The rivers were full of piranhas, and it is unlikely that Pinkhas and Mania Lispector were much heartened by the attractions Maceió offers the visitor today. The tropical climate must have seemed stifling to people used to the temperate Ukraine, and they were not likely to be spending much time on its wide beaches. Still, after all the family had experienced, Maceió, with its colonial plazas lined by tamarind and coconut trees, with its blue sea dotted with the distinct triangular sails of the *jangadas*, would certainly have seemed attractive.

In Maceió the family took Brazilian names. Pinkhas became Pedro, Mania became Marieta, Leah became Elisa, and Chaya became Clarice. Only Tania, whose name was common in the new country, kept hers. Clarice, not yet a year and a half old, would have no memory of Chaya, no memory of the horrors of the Ukraine.

Though in the bright tropical light the family might not have immediately noticed, in some ways Alagoas would not have been entirely exotic to them. It had much in common with the family's homeland. Like Podolia, it was rural and preindustrial, and as in Podolia there was an extreme gap between the impoverished majority and the great landed magnates. Alagoas was Brazil's most densely populated state, with eight hundred thousand inhabitants in 1912. But Maceió had only around forty thousand people, and it was by far the largest city.[14] The almost entirely rural population was concentrated on the plantations that produced the region's principal products, sugar and cotton. For practical purposes, these estates were small independent principalities, ruled by an intermarried oligarchy fiercely protective of its prerogatives.

This social structure was perhaps inevitable. Whereas the maldistribution of the rich Ukrainian lands was the result of perverse political leadership, Alagoas's social problems were preordained by its geography and the commodities that geography could support. Neither, to say the least, encouraged the development of an egalitarian society. Sugar required enormous investments of money and labor. Brazil is vast on paper, but its fertile lands, especially in the northeast, peter off quickly as one moves west from the coast. There was never enough land to spawn an independent class of middling freeholders, and the area's frequent, severe droughts, which could last years, weeded out all but the strongest planters. Early in the country's history, landholding was concentrated in a few hands. And once the price of sugar fell from its historic highs in the seventeenth century, Alagoas, and places like it, were bound to stagnate.

Economic matters were made worse by the failure of Brazil to create cities. What cities existed were spread far apart and, with a few exceptions, such as Rio de Janeiro, were rarely cities in the true sense of the word. (Even Rio, even at the beginning of the twentieth century, was mainly a port and a seat of government rather than a city with a dynamic, self-sustaining economy, such as São Paulo became.) Maceió and places like it were simple outgrowths of the countryside.

They shipped rural commodities abroad and imported advanced products for the plantations. They were, secondarily, social, religious, and educational centers for the elite, who mainly resided on their estates. They were country people, and the money they spent in town was country money. Practically all urban economic activities were related to the plantation.

This was true even in the metropolis of the Brazilian Northeast, Recife. In a commemorative volume published in 1925 the advertisements are almost exclusively dedicated to rural products.[15] Besides the handful of ads for hotels, dentists, and tobacconists, the merchants of Recife trumpeted their expertise in cotton and castor seeds, the export of leather and hides, the grinding of coffee and flour. Even the industrial products are advertised for their usefulness in the countryside: motors for their convenience in sugar mills, machines for combing cotton.

Yet the traditional rural order was eroding. The abolition of slavery in 1888 caused a revolution in Brazilian rural society. The effects were not immediately apparent, but by 1900 the Brazilian south, helped by a quickly expanding supply of free labor, was rapidly industrializing. The most visible result was the explosive growth of the modern city of São Paulo. Other important cities also emerged at this time, such as Belo Horizonte, Porto Alegre, and Curitiba. The northeastern states were left behind economically, but their cities were expanding, especially as former slaves abandoned the increasingly forlorn countryside.

It was a great opportunity for immigrants. Millions poured into Brazil to take advantage of the growing economy. The Portuguese gravitated to Rio de Janeiro, the Japanese and Italians to São Paulo. Even places like Maceió were expanding, but they were not attracting the proto-middle-class immigrants arriving in the south. Instead they were filling with rural workers accustomed to slavery, people who generally lacked the basic education and skills required to go into business for themselves. Arriving in preindustrial towns that offered little in the way of work and generally unused to the cash economy, these people needed basic, cheap goods and services: the pots and pans and scraps of cloth indispensable to even the poorest household. Maceió had little in the way of a native middle class. A clever immigrant, even with a tiny bit of capital, might fill the niche.

Pinkhas, now Pedro, Lispector, had high hopes. "Father wanted to try a new life," Elisa wrote. "He wanted to live in freedom." In the passport photo she saw "his eyes fixed on the camera with something between bitterness and defiance. Since wasn't he the first of the many generations of his family who had the courage to emigrate?"[16]

In Maceió the example of José Rabin's successful business may have inspired him. Rabin began as a *klientelchik*, a peddler. It was a profession the Jews had long exercised in Europe. In Brazil, the first peddlers were Levantine Christians who had arrived slightly earlier than the Jews, and who, in emerging Brazilian cities, performed a vital service. The urban population had grown much faster than the petty retail and banking services the new inhabitants required. These were often the most basic clothing and household products, but there were few outlets that provided them. In these cash-poor regions, the Jews offered even the cheapest goods on credit. This gave the humblest immigrant something to sell and allowed even the humblest consumer to acquire needed merchandise.

The Jewish peddlers not only reached customers traditional retailers ignored, but they traveled to areas where traditional retailers would never have dreamed of turning a profit. They brought goods to the smallest towns of the American West; they had outposts in the pampa and the veld and the outback, places much more far-flung than Maceió, which, even if it didn't amount to much, was at least an established city, a state capital. In fact, the cities of the Brazilian Northeast, most of which had previously been nothing more than ports for the plantations, were ripe for peddling. Urban populations were increasing with the decline of the rural economy. The cities were filling with just the kinds of people that an entrepreneur at the very bottom of the ladder could sell to.

For most Jews, peddling was simply a first step into the economies of their new homes. Though the work was arduous, they were spurred on by dreams of betterment for themselves and their children. The immigrant peddler, carrying his goods on his back, dreamed of a fixed shop. "It was not a very pleasant or respectable way to make a living," wrote Israel Wainstok of his early career in Recife. "Still, however, many good people had worked their way up from peddling to become big businessmen and industrialists. So I too took to peddling, not that I had a choice!"[17]

Toward the end of her life, Clarice described her father's profession as that of a "commercial representative." "That wasn't exactly it," a friend said. "She said that as an affectionate way of dealing with the family's poverty in Recife.... It was a commercial activity, but quite a different one.... He wandered through the streets of the poorest neighborhoods of Recife with a handcart, announcing, shouting with his foreign accent and his tired voice: *Bey clooooooaz, bey clooooooaz*.... He would buy up old, used clothes, and resell them to bigger dealers in the city.... To this day I can still hear Clarice's voice imitating her father with immense tenderness, *Bey clooooooaz*; I've never forgotten it."[18]

Most peddlers ended up in small-time commerce; some failed entirely. Even fewer founded great fortunes. In the United States, names like Guggenheim, Annenberg, and Levi Strauss owe their luster to Jewish peddlers. By the time the Lispectors arrived, José Rabin, who himself began as a peddler, had managed to place himself at the head of a small network of other peddlers, presumably more recent arrivals. These borrowed a small bit of money from him and set themselves up in business, peddling different goods in different areas of the city and returning a percentage of their intake to him. He was not a rich man, but he was on his way up.

José Rabin was also, it appears from Elisa's book, cruel. After all the Lispectors had gone through, the chilly welcome that awaited them in Maceió was the last thing they had reckoned on, though they had perhaps had a hint of it in the "friendly and reticent tone" of the letters that reached them in Romania. Having survived racial persecution, civil war, rape, disease, and exile, they now faced the tyranny of petty relatives. Elisa's book, written almost thirty years after these events, still smarts with anger over the humiliation José and Zina dealt her parents.

Some of the friction could be attributed to the vastly different experiences the two families had had of the previous decade. "How little they knew each other!" Elisa marvels. "Where were the bonds of understanding, the slightest wisp of affinity?" But if we are to believe Elisa, her parents were also the victims of a deliberate campaign of mortification. José frequently bullied Pedro by shaking his head whenever a difficulty arose and saying, more in sorrow than in anger, "Ah, so you mean after all the trouble we took, after all our expenses in bringing you over..."[19] He constantly sought refined new ways to remind Pedro of his great debt in bringing them to Brazil.

It is hard to imagine the difficulties of Pedro Lispector's position. Indeed, his entire life was an unrelenting, heartbreaking struggle. His crippled wife was in and out of the charity hospital. He had three small girls to raise. He constantly received letters from frantic relatives in Russia pleading with him, the lucky one, to save them. After his epic struggle to carry his family to safety halfway around the world, he found only an arrogant and miserly brother-in-law.

Pedro made a bit of money teaching Hebrew to ungrateful children, and he sold pieces of linen on commission from José, who, to emphasize his mistrust, "meticulously counted them and then passed them to his wife, who painstakingly recounted them." To keep his wife and children from the hunger that was a constant menace, he trudged day after day through the feverish streets of Maceió, earning a pittance. It was never enough. Elisa movingly recalls his sadness and desperation, the hours he spent silently smoking on the balcony, seeking a way out.

At length he remembered the skill the old man had taught him back in Chechelnik. He could manufacture soap. In exchange for José's initial investment, he proposed, he would provide the labor. In the torrid heat of Maceió, he spent hour after hour, day after day, stirring a boiling cauldron, breathing "the nauseating atmosphere of the tallow, the caustic poison of the tar."[20] He thought this enterprise would put him on a more equal footing with his brother-in-law. But it was to no avail. "On the days you're not making soap, what are you doing, watching other people work?" José taunted him.[21] Pedro was in no position to resist, and his self-esteem slowly eroded. There was still not enough to eat at home. Even in his rare free time he had to depend on his wife's relatives for entertainment. Clarice later claimed that he immediately learned Portuguese. But Elisa wrote that in Maceió he had not yet had time to learn the new language. For his connection to the outside world he relied on the Yiddish newspaper *Der Tog* (The Day), which he borrowed from his brother-in-law. But eventually José stopped lending it.

Elisa records her own increasing loneliness and her flights into the fantasy world she created to escape the grim reality of her life. She had learned some Portuguese, but not enough. At school she was mocked for her accent.

> "Say *cadeado* [padlock], say it." The bullying children surrounded her.
>
> "*Ca-de-a-do*," she repeated, emphasizing every syllable, afraid to make a mistake. The other girls laughed, jumping around her, one pulling her skirt, another, her ragged hair.[22]

As the humiliations piled up, Pedro, whose ambitions had already been thwarted by the tsarist government, civil war, and emigration, began to pass those ambitions to his daughters. One night, as he sat listening to the sound of a piano coming out of a neighbor's window, he said to Elisa, "I can have you taught music. Of course I can." Piano lessons may have seemed extravagant for a man who could hardly afford to feed his family, but they were a small price to pay for a bit of dignity, for the feeling that his children would have a better life. Elisa wrote that he was determined for the world to see what kind of daughters he had.[23]

His sacrifices were not in vain. One of those daughters would place the poor peddler's name among the great names of Brazil. But Pedro Lispector would not live to see it.

6

GRIENE GRINGOS

According to Elisa, the final blow to their lives in Maceió came when Marieta returned from one of her prolonged stays in the hospital. She had undergone a lengthy and fruitless treatment, and Zina, who in Elisa's account was complicit in her husband's cruelty, began whispering conspiratorial words into her sister's ill and desperate ears. She encouraged Marieta to blame Pedro for the family's difficulties, and when he came home from another arduous day of work, Marieta vomited cruel and violent words at her husband, words that drove him to tears. Even years later, Elisa remembered the incident with horror.

The next day, according to Elisa, Pedro informed José that he was leaving the city. He took the boat to Recife, the capital of Pernambuco. Four months later, he had saved enough to send for his wife and daughters. Tania Lispector Kaufmann remembered the circumstances of the departure in another way: "Elisa might not have felt very good about the cousins. She was around 12 or 13. She might have had bad memories, as children sometimes do. There are always little tensions. But they weren't the reason we went to Recife. Maceió, in those days, was little more than a village, so it was only natural to head to a bigger city like Recife, which was the capital of the Northeast. We all depended on Recife, which had more things to buy, and more competent doctors."[1]

They had spent three years in Maceió, of which Clarice would have no memory; she was five years old when they moved to Recife, which she would always think of as her hometown. "Pernambuco leaves such an impression that all I can say is that none, but none, of my travels throughout the world contributed anything to my writings. But Recife never fades."[2] "I grew up in Recife," she wrote elsewhere, "and I think that living in the North or the Northeast of Brazil is to experience most intensely, to see most closely, the true life of Brazil. . . . My superstitions were learned in Pernambuco, my favorite foods are from Pernambuco."[3]

In the seventeenth century Pernambuco had been conquered by the Dutch, who transformed the sleepy backwater of Recife into South America's richest and most diverse city. It was populated by Africans and Indians, Dutch and Portuguese, Germans, Italians, Spaniards, Englishmen, and Poles. Because "a greater degree of religious freedom was allowed in Netherlands Brazil than anywhere else in the Western world," including in Holland, Jews flocked there, so many that in Recife they may have outnumbered white Gentiles.[4] The first synagogue in the New World, Kahal zur Israel, was founded on the Rua dos Judeus, Jews Street, in 1637. One priest muttered that Recife and its twin city, Olinda, were "*como a Sodoma, & Gomorra.*"[5]

There had been Jews in the Brazilian Northeast before the Dutch conquest, mainly forcibly converted Portuguese Jews and their descendents, who sought safety away from the more tightly policed metropolis. But though there was no Court of the Holy Office in Brazil, it was not entirely safe from the Inquisition, and periodic persecutions claimed many prominent Brazilians. Among the victims were Bento Teixeira, author of the first literary work written in Brazil, the *Prosopopéia* ("A bad poem, a poor imitation of Camões, and its main intention was to praise the governor of the *capitania* of Pernambuco," wrote Clarice's friend Erico Verissimo), and the family of Branca Dias, a prominent resident of Olinda who was the first person to provide education to women in Brazil.[6] But under the Dutch, who took control of northeastern Brazil in 1630, the community blossomed. Many "crypto-Jews" who had been forced to disguise their backgrounds reemerged, and many Jews, mainly Portuguese who had taken refuge in Amsterdam, appeared in Recife.

Arrival in the new land also brought novel problems. In about 1636 the community dispatched a letter to a rabbi in Salonica, Haim Shabetai, asking whether they could adjust their prayers to the conditions of the southern hemisphere, where the seasons were reversed: "And should we pray for rain between the months of Tishrei and Nissan, as other Jews do throughout the world, or should we adapt our prayers to the seasons of the year in Brazil?"[7] The local Portuguese and their allies, having contracted enormous debts to the Dutch,[8] mounted a fierce campaign to retake Pernambuco, and several times almost succeeded, besieging hungry Recife. At one especially desperate moment two ships, the *Falcon* and the *Elizabeth*, magically appeared, inspiring the famous rabbi Isaac Aboab da Fonseca, who was a member of the Amsterdam tribunal that later excommunicated Spinoza, to compose a long song of praise, "Zekher assiti lenifla'ot El" ("I wish to recall the miracles of God"). This was the first Hebrew poem written in the New World.

But God proved stingy with his miracles. He did not again intervene to rescue Netherlands Brazil. The Portuguese succeeded in taking Recife in 1654, putting an end to a brief golden age. With the reconquest, the Jews were expelled and the Inquisition reinstated. Twenty-three Recife Jews made their way to another Dutch colony, New Amsterdam, where on the island of Manhattan they laid the foundations for the greatest diaspora Jewish community the world has ever seen. The temple the exiled members of Kahal zur Israel founded there, Congregation Shearith Israel, exists to this day in a lavish building on Central Park West.

For American Jewry, 1654 was a beginning. For Brazil it marked an end. Some of the Jews who remained converted to Christianity and maintained their religious beliefs in secret, some for generations. Eventually, however, they melted into Luso-Brazilian society, and by 1925, when the Lispector family arrived in Recife, there was no living connection to the Jews of Netherlands Brazil. The Jews of Recife, like all the Jews of Brazil, were recent arrivals.

In Pernambuco today, the brief period of Dutch rule awakens an interest that borders on the fetishistic. Every taxi driver, it seems, can recite the achievements of the Dutch governor Johan Maurits van Nassau-Siegen, and citizens openly long to have been colonized not by the bumbling Portuguese but by the tolerant and competent Dutch. This fascination is such a part of Pernambuco's mentality, such a cornerstone of the state's identity, that it seems it has always been thus.

In fact, however, it is relatively recent. During the three centuries that followed the fall of Dutch Recife, the conquest of Pernambuco was presented as a triumph of a Catholic, Portuguese, and unitary state, an event so important that it was generally understood to mark the birth of the Brazilian nation. The large numbers of Jews in Dutch Recife also meant that the tone of these criticisms was often anti-Semitic. As late as 1979 the famous sociologist Gilberto Freyre could approvingly cite an earlier historian who saw the war against the Dutch as a struggle between "the cross and the shop-counter."[9]

Historians have always been attracted to the colorful Dutch interim. "No period of national history possesses such abundant literature as the troubled Dutch domination of eastern Brazil," wrote Alfredo de Carvalho in 1898. But the pro-Dutch view began to be popularized only in the middle of the twentieth century. Books such as José Antônio Gonsalves de Mello's *Tempo dos Flamengos* (The Flemish Time), published in 1947, emphasized aspects of Dutch rule that were appealing to a modern, democratic Brazil: the colony's religious tolerance, along with its substantial artistic and scientific achievements. Two years later another writer compared the two colonial powers: "[With the institution of the Inquisition] the Portuguese expelled the classes that had freed themselves from feudalism... while the Dutch shook off old systems and embraced private initiative."[10]

The result of this revisionism, and the Dutchophilia it sparked, is that to be Jewish in Pernambuco today is to be directly connected to the most glorious moment in local history. The recent rediscovery, excavation, and reconstruction of the synagogue of Kahal zur Israel was a great boon to the Jewish community, which has rather unexpectedly found itself a central feature of *pernambucanidade*, Pernambuco's identity.

This situation could not be more different from the way it was shortly before the First World War, when the first Jews arrived in Recife. The immigrants, who were almost exclusively poor people from Eastern Europe, knew only vaguely that there had been an earlier community. They knew nothing about this past, and the locals, even the most sophisticated, knew nothing about the Jews.[11]

Take this exchange from 1922, the year the Lispector family arrived in Brazil. The correspondents are two prominent Pernambucans, Gilberto Freyre and Manuel de Oliveira Lima. Freyre was probably Brazil's most famous scholar; Oliveira Lima was one of Brazil's greatest historians, a man of immense learning who left a personal library of forty thousand volumes to the Catholic University in Washington. In 1922 both were living in the United States. On January 18, 1922, Freyre writes, "Mr. Goldberg has returned to Boston. We're so alike, in our tastes, our affinities, our interests! He's going to introduce me to David Prinski, the great Jewish intellectual, whose house is the meeting place of all sorts of literary people. By the way: how do you say 'Yiddish' in Portuguese?" Oliveira Lima answered, "I don't know how to say 'Yiddish' in Portuguese, or even what it is. I'd like to know, because I never stop learning." Freyre replied, "By the way: 'Yiddish' is the name of the Jews, their *modern* language and literature. You say 'so-and-so is Yiddish,' 'Yiddish literature,' etc. I thought there was a word for that in Portuguese."[12] (There is: *ídiche*.)

If this was the level of Jewish cultural literacy of internationally educated intellectuals, one can imagine the situation among the common people in this backward part of Brazil. "The less sophisticated people, especially outside the big cities," wrote Samuel Malamud, a prominent lawyer and friend of the Lispectors, "confused the Jew with Judas, and they imagined him as something out of the ordinary, like the devil, with horns and a tail. The Jews they had daily contact with—either the peddlers who sold clothes, bed- and tableware, jewelry, and furniture, or even the businesspeople who were already established in different sectors—were called Russians, Poles, or simply 'gringos,' a word meaning any foreigner. For the Jews, 'gringo' was the same as *griener* (green), in Yiddish, meaning the ones who had just arrived in the country."[13] To most Brazilians the Jews were no different from other immigrant foreigners—Portuguese, Lebanese, Italians, Spaniards. As a separate category, Jews were unknown, and anti-Semitism hardly existed, even as a concept.

The joke that a Jew trapped alone on a desert island would build two synagogues, the one he attended and the one he wouldn't be caught dead in, also applied to the young *kehilah* of Boa Vista, Recife's Jewish neighborhood. Mania Lispector's relatives had been among the first Jews in the city. In November 1911 there were only eight Jewish men in Recife, including her cousin Pinkhas Rabin.[14] Pinkhas had the honor of importing the city's first Torah scroll in 1913, but the honor seems to have gone to his head. According to Avrum Ishie's Yiddish memoir of 1956, Rabin's stinginess with his holy book annoyed much of the community. Repulsed by his attitude, other men ordered their own Torah from Palestine. When it arrived in 1914, there were already four *minyanim*, or forty adult men, in the city. Two years later, the nascent community acquired a building to house a school and other Jewish institutions. "But we really were Jews," Avrum Ishie recalled. A second group didn't like the building, so they found their own and established a competing school. Later the Zionist Club and the Socialist Club, located next door to each other in tiny houses on the Rua da Glória, would struggle to win the little community's hearts and minds.

Despite these predictable squabbles, the community, evicted from the steppes of the Ukraine, Bessarabia, and White Russia and plunked down halfway across the world, was remarkably cohesive. They might not always have liked each other, but at the end of the day they simply had more in common with their fellow Jewish immigrants than with their exotic neighbors. The immigrants were, first of all, poor, at least when they arrived. One of the attractions of Recife was its location at the northeastern tip of South America; as the closest major Brazilian port to Europe, it was cheaper to get there than to the more famous destinations further south. Many stayed in Recife because they could not afford the glitzier options of Rio de Janeiro, São Paulo, and Buenos Aires.[15]

Recife's convenient location was not the only reason they chose the Northeast. Because the Jewish immigrants worked in similar professions, they needed each other's support. With increasing immigration, the large centers—Rio, São Paulo, Montevideo, Buenos Aires—were increasingly spoken for. Markets for the kinds of goods the Jews specialized in were nearly saturated.[16] But there was still opportunity, and less competition, in the second-tier cities. In Recife, as in the much smaller Maceió, these peddlers often began selling merchandise, such as bits of cloth, on consignment, carrying it through the poor surroundings of Recife, the rough-and-tumble backlands of Pernambuco, and even into neighboring states.

A decade after the first Jews arrived, the community had settled into the neighborhood of Boa Vista. The area was named after a palace built by the most celebrated of the Dutch governors, and though his princely splendor was far in the past, Boa Vista was still in the busy commercial heart of the city. Many of the original pioneers had by now managed to leave peddling and settle into a less arduous life of shopkeeping. In Brazil, they worked in jobs similar to those that had always employed Jews in Europe. In the old country, the Jews, such as Mania Lispector's murdered father, were timber merchants; in the new country, which abounded with tropical forests, many Jews set themselves up as traders in wood. Others sold wood products, especially furniture, and other household items such as linens and dishes. And as in Europe there were many Jewish tailors and jewelers. Just as their distant relatives in the seventeenth century had had to adapt their prayers to the southern seasons, the immigrants had to adapt their offerings to the new climate; unlike in chilly Podolia, in sweltering Recife umbrellas were as often used to protect from the sun as from the rain.

Recife may have been an important city in the Brazilian Northeast, but its economy was hardly more diversified or developed than Maceió's. There was little manufacturing in the city. It was left to the Jews of Boa Vista to introduce items such as ready-made towels, sheets, and tablecloths (before this innovation, people had always made their own from rough bolts of cloth) as well as to amplify the primitive system of credit. Just as the Jewish peddlers allowed the poorest consumers to buy cloth and pots and pans on generous terms, the shopkeepers of Boa Vista later introduced credit and installment plans for bigger items, such as refrigerators, a practice long since fully naturalized in Brazil.

The center of this community was the Praça Maciel Pinheiro, known in Yiddish as the *pletzele*, or little square, and it was here, at number 367, that Clarice Lispector would spend her childhood. "The house was so old that the floorboards bounced when we walked," Tania Lispector remembered. "It had colonial windows, a balcony, colonial roof tiles, it really was very old.... We lived on the second floor. We eventually moved because we were afraid that the house would fall over."[17] (It is, however, still there.) The square was named for a local hero of the Paraguayan War and was ornamented with a large and splendid fountain made in Lisbon and decorated with the likenesses of Indians. But "there weren't many friendships with the Pernambucans," Tania recalled, meaning the

Gentiles;[18] indeed the *pletzele* and the surrounding streets were almost as Jewish as the *shtetlach* its inhabitants had recently abandoned.

Just on the small square itself were Jacob and Lea Lederman's *sodevosser* (soda water) parlor; the furniture stores of Maurício Gandelsman, Adolfo Cornistean, Benjamim Berenstein, Moisés Rastolder, Isaac Schwarts, Israel Fainbaum, Leopoldo Edelman, and the Iampolsky brothers; a ready-made clothes store belonging to Júlio and Ana Guendler and Moisés Rochman; the variety store of the memoirist Avrum Ishie Vainer; and Natan and Freida Pincovsky's fabric shop.[19] The Rua Imperatriz, which led from the *pletzele* down to the Capibaribe River, was also heavily Jewish. There was the Casas Feld, an upscale clothing shop presided over by Luiz Feldmus and his wife, a glamorous figure known in Recife as Madame Clara. There were Jewish bakeries and Jewish dry-goods stores, a Jewish school, and Jacob Berenstein's Livraria Imperatriz, long the best bookshop in Recife and a gathering place of the city's intelligentsia.

There were also the institutions, the schools, the synagogues. A few feet from the Lispectors' door, on the corner of the Rua do Aragão, was the Cooperativa Banco Popular Israelita de Pernambuco, a volunteer "bank" that operated with donations from the community, open from seven to ten on Wednesday evenings. The Cooperativa, which charged no interest on what now would be called microloans, was an essential ingredient in the community's upward mobility, helping new arrivals set up as peddlers, and peddlers set up as shopkeepers.

Months before her death Clarice Lispector made her final trip to Recife to give a speech at the university. She insisted on staying in the Hotel São Domingos, on the corner of the Praça Maciel Pinheiro, on the site of the old Jewish bank. She spent hours gazing out the window at the little square where she grew up. "That little garden in the square, where taxi drivers flirted with maids, seemed like a forest to me, a world—my world, where I hid things I could never again recover."[20] After all those years only the color of the house had changed. "I remember looking out from the balcony on the Praça Maciel Pinheiro, in Recife, and being afraid of falling: I thought everything was so tall.... It was painted pink. Does a color end? It vanishes into the air, my God."[21]

An interviewer asked, "We know that you spent your childhood here in Recife, but does Recife still exist within Clarice Lispector?" She answered, "It is all alive inside me."[22]

❧

Her father's poverty and her mother's illness conspired against it, but in interviews and occasional writing Clarice always remembered a happy childhood. "Look, I didn't know we were poor, see?" she said in a later interview. "Not too long ago I asked Elisa, my oldest sister, if we ever went hungry and she said almost. In Recife, in a square, there was a man who sold a kind of orangeade that the oranges had managed to avoid. That and a piece of bread was our lunch."[23]

Clarice was lucky to be the youngest child. Unlike her parents and her sisters, she had no memory of the family's trials in Europe. Where her sisters had been tortured and starved, she was cosseted and spoiled. Her sister Tania remembered that Clarice was strikingly beautiful even as a baby, and that the family and their neighbors doted on her.[24] Mischievous and energetic, Clarice was a gifted mimic by the age of four, Tania said. "She went to the kindergarten (one of the first of its kind and very different from the way they are today), a pretty strict place, and Clarice, who was already critical and analytical at that age, came home and imitated the teacher's every move, to hilarious effect. We asked her to do it again and she did, imitating the way the teacher ordered the group around, interrupting every activity to say 'Clap your hands, now relax.' "[25] Seventy years later, Tania could still recall her amazement when they went to the doctor or the dentist and Clarice could immediately imitate all the postures of everyone in the waiting room.

Where Elisa and Tania were somewhat timid, Clarice was a natural leader. "Clarice had lots of friends at school. But she was selective, and she was the one who chose her friends," Tania remembered. "I was kind of bossy," Clarice admitted. She was also "very imaginative. She was the one who made up the games," Tania said. "One of them, for example, with a little cousin her age, Clarice in the lead, went like this: 'Let's play "Two Ladies." ' And they would spend hours playing, irreverently imitating the words and attitudes of housewives." "Before I could read and write I already made up stories," Clarice recalled. "I even invented, with a somewhat passive friend of mine, a never-ending story.... I started, everything got very difficult, they both died.... Then she came in and said they weren't actually as dead as all that. And then it all started over again."[26]

Bertha Lispector Cohen, her cousin, recalled that Clarice had names for all the tiles in the shower and for all her pens and pencils. "When I started to read and write, I also started to write little stories," she said.[27] After seeing a play she returned home inspired to write her own, *Poor Little Rich Girl*, three acts in two pages, which she hid and then lost. She wrote to the children's page of the *Diário de Pernambuco*, which on Thursdays published stories sent in by young readers. "I kept sending and sending my stories, but they never published them, and I knew why. Because the others went like this: 'Once upon a time, and so on and so forth.' And mine were sensations."[28] "They were stories without fairies, without pirates. So nobody wanted to publish them."[29]

"She didn't study much," Tania said,[30] but she always got good grades. "In everything except behavior," Clarice added.[31] At her first school, the João

Barbalho School, a few streets from the Praça Maciel Pinheiro, she became the inseparable companion of Leopoldo Nachbin, a little boy her age who himself had a colorful family history. His father, Jacob Nachbin, had immigrated to Brazil at some point after the First World War. An orphan and an autodidact, he nonetheless became a celebrity in the Yiddish press of the country, traveling to Argentina and Uruguay and later back to Europe, where he was supposed to recruit more immigrants for Brazil. Despite his utter lack of education, he nonetheless became the first Jewish historian to examine the history of the Jewish communities in Brazil, and was a noted poet besides. Eventually he abandoned his Brazilian family and went to the United States.[32]

Leopoldo, the son he left behind in Recife, grew up to be Brazil's greatest mathematician. At the João Barbalho School in Recife, however, Leopoldo Nachbin and Clarice Lispector were just "the two impossibles of the class." The teacher separated them, but in vain: "Leopoldo and I just shouted across the room whatever we had to say to each other." Leopoldo became, besides her father, Clarice's first masculine protector, "and he did such a good job that for the rest of my life I have accepted and wanted masculine protection."[33]

With a friend she stole roses from the gardens of the better-off residents of Recife: "It was a street without trams, where cars rarely passed. In the midst of my silence and the silence of the rose, there was my desire to possess it as something all my own." She and a friend ran into the garden, plucked a rose, and made their escape. "It was so good that I simply began stealing roses. The process was always the same: the girl on the lookout, I running in, breaking the stem, and fleeing with the rose in my hand. Always, my heart beating; always a glory that nobody could take from me."[34]

The fullest portrait of this bright, impish child can be found in her own first novel, *Near to the Wild Heart*, published when she was twenty-three. Like so many of Clarice's fictional manufactures, the main character, Joana, bears a striking resemblance to her creator: the same family circumstances, the same headstrong personality, the same resistance to convention. ("To what extent are you Joana?" an interviewer once asked. She replied: "*Madame Bovary c'est moi.*")[35] And the same nearness to the wild heart, the same animal-like existence. "Not having been born an animal is one of my secret nostalgias," Clarice once wrote.[36] "Maybe it's because I'm a Sagittarian, half beast."[37] People who met her frequently compared her to an animal, often a feline: elegant, unknowable, potentially violent. "She was perfectly dressed, long and beautiful, like one of those Egyptian cats," one friend remembered.[38] "Her Slavic face impressed me, strong and beautiful, with something of a feline animal," the poet Ferreira Gullar remembered. "For me she had the aura of a myth, so impressed had I been by her strange books, woven from a magical language, without an equivalent in Brazilian literature."[39] "Other people think I seem like a tiger, like a panther," Clarice told an interviewer. He replied, "Because of your eyes—but that's not it. It's because you have a cat's inner composure, that feline way of always being on the lookout."[40] Joana, Clarice wrote, "seemed like a wild cat, her eyes blazing above her fiery cheeks."[41]

As a girl, Clarice was "surrounded by cats": "I had a cat who sometimes had a litter. And I wouldn't let them get rid of any of the kittens. The result was that the house was happy for me, but hellish for the grownups."[42] She spent hours with the chickens and hens in the yard: "I understand a hen, perfectly. I mean, the intimate life of a hen, I know how it is."[43] When, as an adult, friends recommended a movie starring a French actress who, they said, bore a striking resemblance to Clarice, she had eyes only for the woman's horse. "I identified more strongly with the black horse than with Barbara Laage," she wrote.[44]

"The people here look at me as if I had come straight from the Zoological Gardens," she wrote a friend from the city of Belo Horizonte. "I entirely agree."[45] The cat-like eyes and their intense gaze, "which no one could stand for long," were unsettling, and became increasingly so as she aged.[46] "Who was she? the viper," Joana says to herself, using the word her hateful aunt uses to describe her: "She is a strange animal, Alberto," says the aunt, "without friends and without God—may he forgive me!" And Joana's own husband, shocked by her behavior, explodes, "Wicked... Evil... Viper! Viper! Viper!"[47]

She confessed to stealing roses, but there is no evidence that the young Clarice, like Joana, engaged in shoplifting, and certainly no hint that she, like Joana, was given to flinging heavy objects at the heads of elderly men. Nonetheless, as most of Clarice Lispector's later work will prove, this alliance with the animal kingdom is far more disturbing than any juvenile delinquency. Joana's family is right to be shocked by her, for Joana is simply the most notable early instance of the embrace of an animal nature that, in Clarice Lispector, approaches a philosophical ideal. This is her complete refusal of any anthropocentric morality.

Morality, Fernando Pessoa wrote, is "the effort to elevate human life, to give it a human value."[48] It is this attempt to cut life down to human size—any sense that life is human or that the universe is organized to comfort humans—that Clarice will most famously reject in *The Passion According to G. H.*, the monumental novel of 1964 in which the protagonist realizes her identity to a cockroach. Clarice's amorality, as she herself will come to realize, is so horrifying and absolute that taking it to its logical end means madness: in that book she appalls herself much as Joana shocks her relatives.

Given the savage circumstances of Clarice's early life, she could hardly have reached any other conclusion than that life is not human and has no "human value." There was no more reason for her existence than there was for the cockroach's. Blind luck was the only reason she had survived the Ukrainian horrors when so many millions of others had perished. The conclusion that the nature of the world is random and senseless was the only logical one, but to understand the random animal nature of the world was necessarily to reject the conventional morality that meant assigning human meanings to the inhuman world. A person with her history could never be satisfied by a lame fiction of a universe subject to human control.

Life, instead, was neutral and universal, without human value, beyond human knowledge and therefore—like the great holy name of God, which for the Jews is simultaneously unknowable *and* the ultimate mystical goal—beyond human language, impossible to name or describe. All humans can do is place themselves in contact with that universal life. This is the importance of Joana's animality, for this will become the mystical goal of Clarice Lispector's writing.

In childhood, of course, Clarice did not enunciate this concept as clearly as she would in her maturity. But the feline beauty, the intellectual and spiritual rebelliousness already fascinated and disturbed. Of Joana, Clarice wrote, "She had a crystalline, hard quality that simultaneously attracted and repulsed."[49] And of herself, she said, "As I well know, for they have told me so themselves, certain people think I am dangerous."[50]

Joana is not only animal-like; she is also, like Clarice, an eccentric linguistic prodigy. "As a little girl she could play with a word for a whole afternoon," Clarice wrote of her.[51] In one of the last manuscript fragments, found after her death, Clarice scrawled, "A question from when I was a little girl that I can answer only now: are rocks made, or are they born? Answer: rocks are."[52]

Like Clarice, Joana is close to her father, a widower, whom she seeks out to show off her newest inventions.

> "Daddy, I made up a poem."
>
> "What's it called?"
>
> "Me and the sun." Without waiting long she recited: "The hens who are in the yard already ate two earthworms but I didn't see it."

"Yes? What do you and the sun have to do with the poem?"

She looked at him for a second. He hadn't understood....

"The sun is shining on the earthworms, Daddy, and I made the poem and I didn't see the earthworms."[53]

This is the same child who, in her submissions to the *Diário de Pernambuco*'s children's page, found it impossible to write the "Once upon a time" stories the editors expected. In *Near to the Wild Heart* she gives an example of the child's tendency to use words to evoke sensations, the word "Lalande," which she invents and then defines: "It's like angel tears. Do you know what angel tears are? A kind of little narcissus, which the slightest breeze pushes from one side to the other. Lalande is also the sea in the morning, when no one has yet gazed upon the beach, when the sun is still to rise. Every time I say: Lalande, you should feel the fresh and salty breeze from the sea, you should walk along the still-dark beach, slowly, naked. Soon you will feel Lalande..."[54]

In a late book of stories, *Where Were You at Night,* Clarice proves that she never lost the habit of inventing names, spending pages playing with the name of an alarm clock, Sveglia. "A quarrel is Sveglia. I've just had one with the owner of the clock. I said: since you won't let me see Sveglia, at least describe to me his works. Then she became furious—and that is Sveglia—and said that she had tons of problems—to have problems is not Sveglia. Then I tried to calm her down, and everything was O.K."[55]

These nonsensical riffs, especially when sustained over many pages, have an unsettling, hypnotic effect. At first incomprehensible, like a pointillist painting seen from too close, they gather speed and power as they move forward. Joana, telling such stories at school, "surpassed herself, taking the girls along with her will and her word, filled with an ardent and cutting wit, like light licks. Until, finally enveloped, they inhaled her brilliant and suffocating air."[56]

7

THE MAGICAL STORIES

These childish games, however charming, were not simple pastimes. Their purpose was deadly serious. For over Clarice Lispector's happy childhood hung the terrible and unremitting sight of her paralyzed mother, Mania Krimgold Lispector, cast into a bewilderingly foreign country, unable to move or speak, trapped in a rocking chair, slowly and painfully dying. This was the dominant impression of Clarice's childhood, and perhaps of her life. Like the lost or hidden name, the dying mother, and her child's longing for her, would recur in almost everything Clarice wrote.

"She was like a statue in the house," Clarice's cousin Anita Rabin remembered.[1] Elisa wrote, "Every afternoon, she sat on the balcony of the old house on the Rua da Imperatriz, dressed in stiff linen, her smooth black hair combed back, her useless arms crossed on her chest. After looking down to see what was happening on the street, pausing to look at one or other passer-by, she dropped her head to the side, her eyes staring off, like slightly deadened blue beads."[2]

"I was so happy that I hid from myself the pain of seeing my mother like that," Clarice said. "I felt so guilty, because I thought my birth had caused it. But they said she was already paralyzed."[3] Even her happiest moments were overshadowed by the woman sitting paralyzed on the balcony. In a telling anecdote, Clarice recalled the Carnival of 1929. It was to be her first, since "amidst the worries about my sick mother, nobody in the house paid much attention to a child's Carnival." In other years the most she got was permission to stay downstairs in the doorway until eleven, with a bag of confetti and a little ampoule of perfume to squirt on the revelers.

This Carnival was to be different, though, "as if the streets of Recife finally explained why they had been made." A friend's mother had decided to dress up her daughter in pink crepe paper and offered to make Clarice, eight years old, a costume as well; she would be dressed up as a rose. "When I was all dressed up in crepe paper, with my hair in rollers and still without my lipstick and rouge—my mother's health abruptly took a turn for the worst, there was a sudden tumult in the house, and I had to run off to the pharmacy to buy her medicine. I ran dressed as a *rose*... running, running, baffled, astonished, through the streamers, confetti, and cries of Carnival. The happiness of those other people frightened me. When, hours later, things had calmed down at home, my sister did my hair and makeup. But something had died inside me."[4]

The mutilated woman was completely dependent on her husband and her daughters, especially the eldest, Elisa, whose book speaks movingly of the emotional and material strain of her mother's illness, both on her father, whose "rebelliousness had given way to a profound sadness,"[5] and on herself. Most of her childhood had already been robbed by the terror of the Ukraine; now, in the new country, she was forced to spend what was left of it in constant attendance on her helpless mother.

She longed to leave the house—"sad, and uninviting for outsiders"—but when she did, to go to the Jewish club, for example, located on the same Praça Maciel Pinheiro, she was so unused to social interaction that she felt even more out of place and hurried home.[6] Over the distressing protests of her mother, she had to leave for school. "My daughter, I don't want to live, I can't go on," the mother tells the Elisa of *In Exile* in a particularly pathetic scene. "Mother," the girl answers, trying to encourage her, "you won't get better this way. Take pity on yourself, and on us. Stop crying. I have to go to school." "No, don't go today, just today," her mother pleads.[7]

However awful the situation, Elisa, Tania, and Pedro were at least in a position to help. Pedro could work to earn money to pay for her medicines; Tania and Elisa could feed her, undress her, put her to bed. But Clarice was too small to be able to offer any real assistance. The only help she could offer was magical. She implored God to help her mother, and, according to Bertha Lispector Cohen, she put together little plays to entertain her, sometimes succeeding in making the doomed "statue" laugh. Anita Rabin remembered that, when Clarice was inventing stories, using props such as pencils or tiles, she contrived magical endings in which a miraculous intervention cured her mother's illness. "We were always worried about it," Anita said. "I was struck by that dream, that something could cure her."[8]

A little girl's stories were not enough to save a woman with a devastating terminal illness. And Mania no longer wanted to be saved. "Don't cry when I die," Elisa remembered her mother saying. "It will be such a great relief for me."[9] Mania knew the end was nearing. "Resigned and God-fearing, Mother asked Father to buy her a new *sidur* (prayer book), and she prayed for an entire week, at the end of which she died."[10]

Mania Krimgold Lispector was forty-two years old when, on September 21, 1930, her long suffering finally ended. She was buried in the Israelite Cemetery of Barro, a distant suburb of Recife. Her mother Charna's silver candlesticks, which she had miraculously rescued from their homeland, were given, as she had asked, to the small local synagogue. The family avoided reference to her, Elisa wrote, having "tacitly agreed to avoid the subject, omitting her name, because she was present in all their thoughts and actions."[11]

Clarice's trick had failed. Her dreams of divine intervention were disappointed. But the habit she learned in early childhood, of playing with words and telling stories to assure a miraculous outcome, stuck. Half a century later, when Clarice Lispector, herself consumed by a terminal disease, left her house for the last time, she would resort to the same tactic. "Let's pretend that we're not going to the hospital, that I'm not sick, and that we're going to Paris," her friend Olga Borelli recalled her saying in a taxi on the way to the hospital. "I remember her words perfectly," Olga went on.

> So we started making plans and talking about everything we would do in Paris. The taxi driver, poor thing, already tired from working all night long, timidly asked: "Can I go on the trip too?" And Clarice said: "Of course you can, and you can even bring your girlfriend." He said: "My girlfriend is an old lady, seventy years old, and I don't have any money." Clarice answered: "She's coming too. Let's pretend you won the lottery." When we got to the hospital, Clarice asked how much it was. Only twenty cruzeiros, and she gave him two hundred.[12]

Needless to say, the trip to Paris never happened. Clarice Lispector died six weeks later.

A friend once asked what Clarice thought of a painting in an Italian museum. "Ah," he answered, when she couldn't remember it, "it's true, you're one of those people who only remembers things that happened before they were ten years old."[13]

Her early childhood, its lost happiness and its immitigable tragedies, were never far from her mind. A late essay on the new capital of Brasília includes an unexpected lament: "Ah, poor me. So without a mother. It is a duty to have a mother. It is a thing of nature."[14] An interviewer discovered what was really on her mind:

—Do you have peace [*paz*—a homophone of *pais*, parents], Clarice?
—Neither father [*pai*] nor mother.
—I said "peace."
—How odd, I thought you said "father." I was thinking about my mother a few seconds before. I thought—mama—and then I didn't hear anything else. Peace? Who does?[15]

Though in the real world stories and myths proved unequal to a deadly virus, she clung to them. "She was devastated by her mother's death," said Anita Levy. "They told her [at school] that you couldn't leave scissors open on the table. At home she had seen a pair of scissors open on the table. So she said that was the reason. That was why her mother died. Because someone left out an open pair of scissors."[16]

For a child, miraculous stories might have been a reasonable means of sparking divine intervention, and an open pair of scissors as good an explanation as any for an incomprehensible disaster. But the woman sitting in a taxi half a century later, dreaming of Paris on her way to the hospital, was not a child. Stories had proven powerless to save her mother, and she could not have reasonably believed in their efficacy. For an adult, silent acceptance might have seemed more fitting.

Yet that woman had dedicated her life to writing. She scribbled notes into her last hours. Why, having seen the impotence of this activity so forcefully demonstrated, did she continue to bother? Part of it, surely, was a reflex, a resort, in a desperate situation, to an old tactic. Part of it was to comfort the other people in the taxi, distraught by their friend's illness. In 1977, however, the illusion was not for herself. The disappointment she experienced as a nine-year-old girl taught her how worthless such poetic efforts were. Writing was the last thing that could tack a happy ending onto the end of a stubborn reality.

But the habit stuck. Throughout her life she would search for justifications for her activities. She clung to a hope that there was something she could do to save the world. She always, sometimes bitterly, lamented her powerlessness—

> In Recife, where I lived until I was twelve, there was often a crowd on the streets, listening to someone speak ardently about the social tragedy. And I remember how I trembled and how I promised myself that this would one day be my task: to defend the rights of others.
>
> Yet what did I end up being, and so early? I ended up as a person who searches for what she deeply feels and uses the word to express it.
>
> It's little, it's very little.[17]

—but she never sought to deny or disguise it. The problem was not hers alone: many artists were distressed by their powerlessness in the face of the horrors of the twentieth century. The atomic bombs exploded; the gas chambers hissed; a raped mother stared blankly from her rocking chair.

One could choose to embrace irrelevance, making art for art's sake. Or one could address one's palpable inconsequence with engagement: using fiction or drama or architecture to redress social injustices. This approach was especially attractive in Brazil, where so many wrongs demanded righting. But the problems persisted, despite (or, as in many parts of Latin America, because of) political activism. Artists who sought a greater meaning for their work were frustrated. "If you write a novel alone you sit and you weave a little narrative," V. S. Naipaul has said. "And it's O.K., but it's of no account. If you're a romantic writer, you write novels about men and women falling in love, etc., give a little narrative here and there. But again, it's of no account."[18]

Despite her fanciful jaunt to Paris on the way to the hospital, Clarice Lispector entertained no illusions about the greater meaning of her work. She was an animal and destined to die as one, and she never forgot the lessons she learned before she was ten years old. "It changes nothing," she emphasized in one of her last interviews. "It changes nothing. I write without the hope that anything I write can change anything at all. It changes nothing."[19]

What, then, was the point? She would always try to discover it. But the basic instinct never changed. Among her last notes is this: "I write as if to save somebody's life. Probably my own life."[20]

"Every story of a person is the story of his failure," Clarice wrote, perhaps thinking of her own.[21] "I was guilty from birth, she who was born with the mortal sin."[22] As long as her mother was alive, she could still hold out hope that her birth had not been in vain. With Mania's death that possibility vanished, and a note of sadness appeared in the happy child's personality. "I often found her crying silently, alone," Tania remembered.[23]

Her sadness and disbelief soon turned into a kind of revolt, a word that frequently recurs in her writings: the same word, perhaps not coincidentally, that Elisa attaches to their father in his youth. In the year her mother died Clarice composed a two-part piano piece: "The first was soft, the second somewhat military, somewhat violent, a revolt, I suppose." This, in lieu of studying with the immense Dona Pupu, "who could not have been fatter" and who presided over the piano lessons Pedro Lispector had, with considerable difficulty, arranged for his daughters. Tania and Elisa enjoyed the lessons; Elisa was a talented musician and went on to study at the Recife Conservatory. Clarice, however, spent her time in class wondering how a woman as fat as Dona Pupu had ever managed to get married; she was far more interested in her own inventions than in the assigned works.[24]

Tania, moved by Clarice's quiet suffering, helped her with this and other difficulties. When Clarice didn't want to practice piano, Tania helped her by playing the black keys while Clarice played the white, "until, to Clarice's great relief, the piano lessons were called off." After seeing her crying, Tania wrote, "I, as the older sister, out of love and pity, to a certain extent adopted her," filling in for their lost mother. "This maternal-filial bond united us forever. We were more than sisters."[25]

In a fragment written in English during the years Clarice lived in the United States, she recalls her childhood and the origins of her bond with Tania. " 'Till you were about 10 [Tania said to Clarice] I was not very aware of you, suddenly I became aware how interesting you were.' I suppose she really meant: I became aware how much you needed me. I don't know what to do when the person comes to me; I'm the one to go to the person. To be selected is disturbing. I have to ask, I have to select."[26]

Through the unlikely vehicle of a piece of chewing gum, Tania introduced her younger sister to the "painful and dramatic" concept of eternity. Tania bought her the gum, novel in Recife, and said, "Be careful not to lose it, because it never ends. It lasts a lifetime." The perplexed Clarice took it, "almost unable to believe in the miracle," and Tania ordered her to "chew it forever." Clarice was terrified, not wanting to confess that she was unequal to eternity, that the idea tormented her, but she didn't dare. Finally, when they were going into school, she managed to drop the gum into the sand, feigning distress and embarrassed to be lying to her sister. "But I was relieved. Without the weight of eternity upon me."[27]

At school Clarice didn't study much, though she got good grades. In the third grade, before her mother died, she went to a new school, the Colégio Hebreo-Idisch-Brasileiro, on the Rua da Glória, a block or so away from the Praça Maciel Pinheiro. As the name indicates, the school taught Hebrew and Yiddish in addition to the usual disciplines. But despite her obvious talents, she did not go straight into the fourth grade, her cousin Samuel Lispector recalled. "She was really small and couldn't even carry the bigger books, like an atlas, which was enormous. Then my uncle decided: 'The book is too big for you. You're not going to fourth grade.' So she repeated a year."[28]

Perhaps her size was not the only reason she was held back. In the public school she would not have had Hebrew classes, which the other students would already have started. She seems, however, to have had a talent for the language. There are no references to Hebrew in her work, but the child with the gift for words apparently made up the gap quickly, for she was chosen to give one of the three year-end discourses the students presented to the faculty and parents, in Hebrew, Yiddish, and Portuguese. The small Clarice gave the Hebrew discourse, which means she was at the top of the class.[29]

Recife's Hebrew teacher, Moysés Lazar, was a man of such progressive ideas that, Anita Rabin remembered, "We were horrified by some of the things he said [in religion class], and he wasn't one of those people who said, No, you just have to believe it."[30] Clarice badgered him with her questions: "How did it happen?" she demanded, when he told how God gave the Torah to Moses. "God put the Torah in his hand?" Lazar told the girl, "Look, nobody saw it."[31]

These questions never left Clarice. In a manuscript from the end of her life, she wrote, "But there are questions that nobody can answer for me: who made the world? Was the world made? But where? in what place? And if it was 'God'—who made 'God'?"[32]

Another friend remembers a heated discussion. "She was tall, thin. She was talking to her Hebrew teacher, Lazar, who was an eminence. He didn't just teach the abc's. I was walking by. And Clarice was persistently asking what the difference was between a man and a woman. She kept hammering away, demanding an explanation! She wouldn't let go of it. Because she already had a different kind of mind."[33] Lazar may have been the model for a recurrent figure in Clarice's writing: the old teacher, alternatively exasperated and fascinated by a precocious girl. "I knew about the existence of this teacher," Tania Kaufmann told an interviewer, "but I never knew that Clarice felt that way about him when she was a little girl. She was always a surprise for me."[34]

The teacher appears in *Near to the Wild Heart*, and he appears in "The Disasters of Sofia," the story of a wild, brilliant nine-year-old girl who torments a teacher she both loves and despises. The girl, whose mother has recently died, tries ceaselessly to provoke him, but she can never get the better of him, until the day he assigns the class a writing composition. He gives the outline of the plot, which the students are to re-create, using their own words: "A very poor man dreamt that he discovered a treasure and became very rich; upon awaking, he gathered his belongings and went off in search of the treasure; tired, he returned to his poor, poor house; and since he had nothing to eat, he began planting his own poor yard; he planted so much, he harvested so much, he started to sell so much that he ended up very rich."[35]

"Since all I knew was how to 'use my own words,' writing was easy," the girl remembers. She is the first to leave, insolently handing her notebook to the teacher and escaping to the recess area. She returns to the classroom, where the teacher has read her story and where she feels she has stumbled into a great danger. "To my sudden torture, without taking his eyes off me, he slowly began to take off his glasses. And he looked at me with naked eyes that had many eyelashes. I had never seen his eyes that, with their numberless cilia, looked like two sweet cockroaches," she wrote. The professor has been changed by her story of "the hidden treasure," "the treasure that is hidden where it is least expected."[36]

Her fear of the teacher strips away his human layers—his glasses are an example—and to her horror she sees what they both are, "anonymous as a belly opened for an intestinal operation," what she called the "wild heart" of life. "I saw inside the eye. Which was as incomprehensible as an eye. An eye open with its mobile gelatin. With its organic tears." Finally, breaking the silence, the teacher tells Sofia, "Your composition about the treasure is very pretty. You...—for a moment he added nothing. He looked at me smoothly, indiscreetly, as intimate as if he were my heart. —You're a very funny girl, he finally said."[37]

8

NATIONAL MELODRAMA

On July 26, 1930, weeks before Mania Lispector's death, the humble neighborhood of Boa Vista unwittingly stepped into the national limelight when the governor of Paraíba, which borders Pernambuco to the north, was gunned down in the Confeitaria Glória, on the Rua Nova. Clarice's cousin Samuel Lispector watched the tumult from the balcony of their house with Elisa and Tania.[1] Running to the scene of the crime, another cousin, David Wainstok, arrived in time to see João Pessoa laid out on a bench in the neighboring pharmacy, "his shirt drenched in blood."[2]

The macabre event had revolutionary consequences, but the ensuing national melodrama had decidedly domestic origins. João Pessoa Cavalcanti de Albuquerque, its first victim, bore a name enclosing three northeastern dynasties. His uncle, Epitácio Pessoa, was president of Brazil from 1919 to 1922; the Cavalcantis and the Albuquerques, with their innumerable ramifications, were among the first families of Pernambuco. João Pessoa ran on an anti-oligarchic platform.

After his elevation to the governorship of Paraíba, João Pessoa became a candidate for the national vice presidency in the elections of March 1930. He and the presidential candidate, Getúlio Vargas, lost amid widespread voting fraud. In their protests against the results, they took care to stress that they would remain "within the existing order" and in accordance with Brazil's "political habits and customs."[3]

Since Brazil gained independence—peacefully—in 1822, the country had known only one revolution, the bloodless revolt in 1889 that replaced the elderly and benign Emperor Dom Pedro II with a republic. Their relatively orderly politics was a source of pride for Brazilians, who watched, scoffing and appalled, as Spanish America was bled by endless coups and feuds; the reference to their "political habits and customs" may be a veiled attack on Brazil's chaotic neighbors.

But the peaceful changes of power at the national level masked a level of violence, corruption, and fraud that suggested the national politicians were only barely able to keep a lid on. The northeast, with its masses of illiterate rural workers living in conditions of near-slavery, was in the hands of a few powerful families, like those from which João Pessoa descended. Votes could be easily bought or manipulated. In the more modern south, there was a long-standing rivalry between the largest and most powerful state, São Paulo, and the states of Minas Gerais and Rio Grande do Sul. Since the foundation of the Republic in 1889, the presidency had usually passed from a São Paulo candidate to a candidate supported by Minas Gerais and Rio Grande do Sul.

In 1930, this tenuous arrangement was threatened when the outgoing president, a São Paulo man, attempted to install another *paulista* as his successor. For Getúlio Vargas, the opposition leader from Rio Grande do Sul, and his vice presidential candidate, João Pessoa, who represented the northeastern landed interests, this was a step too far, though Vargas was not in principle opposed to fraud; in Rio Grande do Sul, he garnered 298,000 votes against the opposition's 982. But it was their turn. Still, armed revolt, so rare in Brazil, did not seem a real option, and it looked like the losing parties would have to swallow their defeat.

Until, that is, João Pessoa was gunned down in the Confeitaria Glória. Given the country's tense political state, people immediately assumed the motives were political. In fact, the unwitting culprit was a poetess named Anaíde Beiriz, a Paraíban flapper whose vanguardism had so scandalized Paraíba's society that children were reportedly forbidden to speak her name. A catalogue of Anaíde's sins gives a good idea of how archaic northeastern society was: she wore makeup, had short hair, and smoked. She said that she did not want to marry or have children. And she went out into the street without a chaperone.

Anaíde was also the lover of João Dantas, a bitter political enemy of João Pessoa. Dantas, a Paraíba lawyer, was allied to a rural clan who opposed Pessoa's attempt to regularize taxation of the state's cotton production. Pessoa's police raided Dantas's law office, where they found letters from Anaíde; these, Pessoa's newspapers insinuated, narrated all sorts of dirty acts. Though neither Anaíde nor Dantas was married, this was too heavy for Paraíba. Anaíde's family disowned her, forcing her to decamp to Recife. It was in that city that João Dantas, thirsting for revenge, walked into the Confeitaria Glória, said, "I am João Dantas, whom you so humiliated and mistreated," and fired two bullets into his rival's chest.

This drama ended badly for all involved: Dantas was killed in prison, following which a desolate Anaíde committed suicide. But in a less tense political situation it probably would have been forgotten as the small-town soap opera that it was. Instead, the murder of João Pessoa unleashed passions that Getúlio Vargas's partisans carefully stoked. The name of the capital of Paraíba was changed to João Pessoa, and the gubernatorial corpse was paraded through the entire length of Brazil, from Paraíba to Rio de Janeiro, provoking mass hysteria at each of its many stops.

Finally, at the funeral in the capital, a multitude arrived to hear inflamed discourses: "We are not going to bury him," one fiery orator proclaimed. "We are going to leave him standing, standing strong the way he always lived, standing tall, unlike his murderers, standing tall: his heart above his stomach and his head above his heart."[4]

Four days after Mania Lispector's death, Getúlio Vargas began an armed revolution in Rio Grande do Sul. Twenty-eight days later, in a gesture of defiant machismo, Vargas's gauchos tied their horses to the obelisk at the end of Rio de Janeiro's grandest boulevard, the Avenida Rio Branco, taking symbolic possession of the capital.

For the next quarter-century, under different names and with one important hiatus, Vargas's provisional government ruled Brazil. When the melancholy strongman, who had ridden into office on a wave of national melodrama, finally departed, he did so in a fashion befitting his entrance. In 1954, in the presidential palace, clad in his pajamas, he shot himself through the heart.

It was a sensational end to the most sensational career in twentieth-century Brazilian politics. The country Getúlio left behind was very different from the one that hailed him in Rio at the end of 1930. He summed up all the contradictions of Brazil. He was short and balding and preceded by an enormous pot belly, and women found him hard to resist. To his supporters' claim that he was the "father of the poor," his opponents sneered that he was also the "mother of the rich."[5] He ruled Brazil as a Fascist dictator, yet he, alone among Latin American leaders, sent troops to fight Fascism.

His ability to be all things to all people was the key to his extraordinary staying power. Since the fall of the emperor forty-one years before, Brazil had proven extremely difficult to govern. If there had been no widespread civil war, there was certainly reason to fear one, as the bickering of various regional and class-based parties threatened, every four years, to split the nation once and for all. The southern states were booming as the northeast withered; the new urban middle classes, with their democratic aspirations, were pitted against the old and still powerful rural oligarchy.

The civil war kept threatening to arrive. It had almost come in 1925, with the famous Prestes Column, a middle-class military movement under the leadership of an army engineer, Luís Carlos Prestes, known as the "Knight of Hope." For two years and five months Prestes led fifteen hundred men throughout almost every corner of Brazil, twenty-five thousand kilometers in all, always just a step ahead of the army. Preaching equality, they died at an alarming rate from cholera, exhaustion, and army attacks before finally fleeing the country. Prestes proved an unwitting ally of Getúlio Vargas, who would become his archenemy; the Prestes Column contributed more than any other movement to the conviction that the Old Republic was bankrupt, waiting to be swept away.

When Vargas's Revolution of 1930 did sweep it away, the country's political unrest did not end. A little more than a year later, civil war almost arrived again, after July 9, 1932. The state of São Paulo, the country's wealthiest and most dynamic, rose against Getúlio Vargas's strongly centralizing constitution, which would have removed much of the state's autonomy. São Paulo went on a war footing: ladies offered up their gold jewelry, and men dug trenches around the city. For two months the federal army besieged São Paulo, until the worn-out rebels finally succumbed.

Though Getúlio then appeased the state, suspending some of the more rebarbative provisions of the new constitution and instructing the Bank of Brazil to assume the São Paulo banks' war debt, the revolt gave him exactly what he needed: a mandate to proceed with the centralization of the Brazilian state. The rebellion was the last gasp of the old political system, based on personalities and regional and class divisions. The new political parties were radical and ideological, on the right and left, as they were in Europe. And, as in Europe, Brazilian politics soon gravitated toward two poles: the Communists on the left and the Integralists, the home-grown Nazis, on the right. Both threatened Getúlio Vargas, and the existence of both threatened the Jews.

Like the São Paulo secessionists, the Communists signed their own death warrants with a premature revolt. At the end of 1935 Communist soldiers rebelled—it began in Recife and Natal—murdering senior officers in their beds.[6] But they overestimated their support in the armed forces, and the rebellion quickly evaporated. Luís Carlos Prestes, the leader of the Communists, eluded capture until March 1936. In a horrifying episode that has become the symbol of Vargas's cruelty, Prestes's pregnant wife, Olga Benário Prestes, born Jewish in Munich, was deported to Germany. There, at Bernburg, aged thirty-three, she was gassed.

According to Gustavo Barroso, Communism equaled capitalism equaled Judaism.[7] The formula would not suggest it, but Gustavo Barroso was taken very seriously as an intellectual, and was even elected, three times, as president of the Brazilian Academy, the country's most prestigious academic and intellectual society. His large body of anti-Semitic writings betray a veritable obsession. He was Brazil's first translator, in 1936, of the *Protocols of the Elders of Zion*, whose publishers, Agência Minerva of São Paulo, emphasized that by making this book available, they did "*not* want to offend or injure, and much less promote a racist campaign, but *only* to increase knowledge of a question—the Jewish Question—of the highest relevance to humanity."[8] Barroso was a leading light of Integralism, Brazil's derivative Nazi movement; Argentina's pro-Nazi *Deutsche La Plata Zeitung* described Barroso as the "Führer of Integralism."[9]

His rival for the title was the wannabe tropical Hitler, Plínio Salgado, who, like Barroso, was a mediocre novelist with big ideas. Like many of the Integralists, Salgado was strongly influenced by the Catholic writers who emerged in the 1920s, with their suggestions of mystic nationalism. Clarice Lispector would later become close to some of these figures, such as Augusto Frederico Schmidt and Octávio de Faria. Barroso, Salgado's rival, attacked him for his associations with Jews, notably Horácio Lafer, a São Paulo politician related to the Segall-Klabin clan, Brazil's richest and most prominent Jewish family. And in October 1934 Salgado met the prominent rabbi Isaías Raffalovich, who was cordially assured that the Integralists "would leave the Jewish question out of the program."[10] This he did not do.

Still, though there is doubt as to the Integralists' genocidal intentions, there were no doubts about their inspiration. Salgado grew a Hitler moustache, clad his followers in green shirts, and ornamented them with Nazi-style armbands. In place of the swastika came the Greek letter sigma, which stood for "the sum of all values." And in place of "Heil Hitler" they greeted one another with the word "Anauê," which was supposedly Tupi, the indigenous language of Brazil, for "You are my brother" but turned out to be made up.

As in Europe, such kitsch would have been simply embarrassing if it had not had devastating consequences. The Integralists, like the Nazis, took to beating up their political opponents, especially Communists, in the streets, and earned a fearsome reputation. Getúlio Vargas, with his gift for being all things to all people, relied on the Integralists during the early years of his reign. He could hardly ignore them: the party had four hundred thousand *paid-up* members, an unheard-of number for a Brazilian political party, and many thousands more were sympathizers. Their blend of nationalism and Catholicism, their call for an authoritarian, hierarchical system, for a return to "values," for a "spiritual revival," had broad appeal to people scarred by the global economic downturn and disgusted by the everyday sleaze of politics. And their attacks on Communists, their call to put the national interest above petty local feuds, were certainly useful to Getúlio Vargas.

Not all Integralists were anti-Semites, Clarice's cousin Bertha Lispector Cohen remembers. The ideology had been imported from Europe, but it did not necessarily win many converts as enthusiastic as Gustavo Barroso. Bertha even had friends who belonged to the party. "They thought that ideology was going to change the world, was going to change Brazil," she said. "Of course," she adds with a dismissive wave of the hand, "it didn't change a thing."[11]

But a lot of Integralists were in fact anti-Semites. Bertha's brother Samuel Lispector remembers the climate of fear that spread among the Jews of Boa Vista: "We were scared. We knew what *could* happen. We had seen it in Europe. There was fear, quite a lot of fear." At school, where Samuel remembers students and even some teachers wearing the green shirt and the sigma armband, Jewish students were frequently harassed. "'You're a Jew, you shouldn't be here,' they said." He paused. "You never forget that."[12]

Another cousin, David Wainstok, went to a new school at the end of 1933, when the Integralist movement was in full swing, and was also distressed to see students and teachers sporting the green shirts. "We, the Jews at the school, were provoked by 'shock brigades' who attacked us as we left the classroom. We had no alternative but to confront them, sometimes attacking, sometimes fighting. On several occasions we arrived home with battle scars."[13]

"The Rua da Imperatriz was all Jewish," one immigrant remembered. This was the street where, since shortly before Mania's death, Clarice, Tania, Elisa, and Pedro Lispector had been living, a busy commercial street that connects the Praça Maciel Pinheiro, the *pletzele*, to the Capibaribe River. He remembered green-shirted Integralists shouting slogans in the street, fired up by Plínio Salgado's articles attacking the Jews. "They made trouble, threw rocks; and the boys, their sons, who are now big shots in the state and whose names I can't mention, would say: 'You're a Jew, and when we're in charge, we'll kick all of you out.'" There was also the equation of Jews with Communists, which grew throughout the 1930s. "Back then, the police were very uneducated, and they would come into the library and confiscate all the books they thought smacked of Communism. A friend of mine, for example, owned *The Red Rover*, an adventure story, and it was seized."[14]

Fortunately, on his rare visits to Recife, which after all was not an Integralist stronghold, the leader failed to burnish his party's mystique. "His grotesque, puny figure, with his little Hitler moustache and his strained and wheezing voice, stuffed in a uniform that contrasted with his appearance, made him look a bit comical," David Wainstok recalled. "Once Plínio came to Recife to give a speech at the famous Law School. His followers had prepared a pompous march in the Fascist style. The 'national chief' didn't manage to get through his harangue. At a certain point, a law student retorted in a ringing voice, perturbing the speaker and his acolytes. Just then the lights went out and the papers on the orator's desk blew away. Simultaneously, vials of sulfuric acid fell from the galleries, the stink impregnating the room. A general stampede ensued, as the crowd ran for the exits."[15]

Another occasion, a martial parade, this time *sans* "national chief," resulted in a similar rout. "They were uniformed, brandishing their flags, their symbols, and, to a ruffle of the drums, marching in all their glory through the Rua Nova"—where João Pessoa was killed, just across the river from the Lispectors' home—"in the busy center of town. Suddenly, from a few buildings, green-painted hens, with the sigma on their wings, began a squawking descent upon the marchers. A great confusion erupted, and the marchers scattered, astonished by the unexpected event. The grotesque spectacle offered considerable hilarity to the onlookers."[16]

9

ONLY FOR MADMEN

Brazil's troubled politics, even when acted out just beneath their windows, did not distract the Lispectors from their own family dramas. The girls were growing older. Elisa, nineteen when her mother died, was now of marriageable age and had a suitor who, like her, was a Jewish immigrant. Yet unlike the cerebral Elisa—who completed the advanced *curso comercial*, below university level but nonetheless higher than most girls attained, and who was by now a talented conservatory-trained pianist—the prospective bridegroom was "an uneducated shopkeeper."[1]

But it was not just that, according to Tania. Elisa had taken care of a household for as long as she could remember, ever since her mother fell sick. Now she was finally independent. She had a job, her sisters were old enough to take care of themselves, and she was simply not ready to start over as a wife and mother. Still, she got engaged, accepting a ring from the young man. She soon began to have her doubts, ultimately dispatching her youngest sister, Clarice, to the man's house with the ring and an apology. "What could I do?" her father asked Dora Wainstok, his wife's cousin. "Z'hot gepisht met tranen [She had wet herself with tears]!"[2] (Devastated, the suitor eventually moved to Israel.)

It was a typical reaction for Pedro Lispector. He was an exceptionally tolerant and good-hearted man, Tania remembered. "He had the finest character of any man I ever knew," she said.[3] "He had a great deal of Biblical education.... He read the newspaper from New York, *The Day*, in Yiddish. He had very advanced ideas. He was an advanced man. He never laid a finger on a daughter of his. He was exceptional. If the circumstances had been different, he could have had a better life."[4]

At age ninety-one, Tania still remembered her wonderment at her father's reaction when, as a teenager, she came out in favor of "free love" and proclaimed that she wasn't going to get married. From a girl in the small, conservative Jewish community of Recife of the 1930s, this was a provocation, and Tania braced herself for the reaction. "Other fathers would have beat a child who said something like that. I'm sure he *was* shocked, but he asked instead why I thought that way. We talked about it. And then, as I'm sure he knew I would, I forgot about the whole thing."[5]

Clarice herself was beginning to blossom. In 1932 she entered the Ginásio Pernambucano, the most prestigious secondary school in the state, housed in an elegant building on the Capibaribe River, not far from Boa Vista. Only the best students were admitted, and of the forty-three that passed the examination that year, three were Lispectors: Tania, Clarice, and their cousin Bertha.[6] The school was not only prestigious, it was also free, which the Jewish school was not, surely a consideration for Pedro Lispector, who was always teetering on the brink of poverty. Clarice was already flirtatious, Bertha remembered, unafraid of boys, and the beauty that would make her legendary was already apparent. In her first year at the new school she and a colleague were voted the prettiest girls in the class.[7]

She had her first boyfriend, whose Sephardic origin raised a few eyebrows at home. "Father thought he should be Ashkenazic," Tania said. "He ended up accepting him, as he always did. But by that time they had already split up, because he told Clarice he wanted eight or nine children. He became a doctor, got married—and ended up having no children at all."[8]

All three daughters recalled that Pedro Lispector was a great mathematician.[9] It is hard to know precisely what this means, but Clarice must have inherited from him some of his interest in numbers. Her childhood friend Leopoldo Nachbin, who had an education that Pedro Lispector did not and who was recognized internationally as a great mathematician, happily concurred when Clarice said that "mathematics and physics are not only the product of reasoning: they are as much an art as Bach."[10]

As a child her interest in numbers was conventional. She had a pedagogical bent and taught math and Portuguese to neighborhood children. "Mathematics fascinated me, and I was only a little girl when I put an ad in the paper as a tutor. A lady called me, said she had two sons, gave me the address and I went. She looked at me and said: 'Oh, sweetie, you're too young.' So I said: 'Listen, if your kids don't improve their grades, then you don't have to pay me anything.' She was intrigued and hired me. And they did improve."[11] Clarice's little cousin Anatólio (Tutú) Wainstok, whom she also taught to read, proved a disappointing pupil. "Tutú," she pleaded, "how are you going to learn if you don't do your homework?" "Clarice," he answered, "I'm doing you a favor by letting you teach me. You wanted to do it so badly!"[12] His shamefaced teacher was unable to respond.

As an adult, however, her interest in mathematics reflected her broader concern with abstraction and its connection to the divine. Mystical numbers, like hidden names, assumed an important role in her work. Part of this interest was whimsical, as Olga Borelli, who accompanied her in the last years of her life, attested: "When she had me type for her, she would say: 'Count seven, seven spaces between paragraphs, seven. Then, try not to go over thirteen pages.' So superstitious! When it was a story, she said: 'Don't put as many spaces in, so it won't go over thirteen pages.' She really liked the numbers 9, 7, and 5. It's a rather strange thing she had, but she would ask the publisher not to let something run more than x number pages.... It's almost cabbalistic, isn't it? She had a lot of that."[13]

The number seven, she wrote, was "my secret and cabbalistic number"; it recurs throughout her work. In her late short story "Where Were You at Night" she describes a "failed woman writer" who takes her journal, bound in red leather, and writes "July 7, 1974. [i.e., 7/7/74]. I, I, I, I, I, I, I!"—seven times.[14] There are the seven notes out of which can be composed "all the music that exists and existed and ever shall exist";[15] and there is a recurrence of "theosophical additions," numbers that can be added to reveal a magical sum. The year 1978, for example, has an ultimate total of seven: 1 + 9 + 7 + 8 = 25, and 2 + 5 = 7. "I tell you that 1978 is the true cabbalistic year, since the final sum of its units is seven. So I have polished the instants of time, made the stars shine anew, washed the moon with milk and the sun with liquid gold. At the beginning of every year I begin to live."[16] She would die a couple of weeks short of the true cabbalistic year.

But there was more to her interest in numerology than superstitious games. "My passion for the essence of numbers, wherein I foretell the core of their own rigid and fatal destiny," was, like her meditations on the neutral pronoun "it," a desire for the pure truth, neutral, unclassifiable and beyond language, that was the ultimate mystical reality.[17] In her late works, bare numbers themselves are conflated with God, now without the mathematics that binds them, one to another, to lend them a syntactical meaning. On their own, numbers, like the paintings she created at the end of her life, were pure abstractions, and as such connected to the random mystery of life itself. In her late abstract masterpiece

Água viva she rejects "the meaning that her father's mathematics provide and elects instead the sheer it" of the unadorned number: "I still have the power of reason—I studied mathematics which is the madness of reason—but now I want the plasma—I want to feed directly from the placenta."[18]

As always, her mother's silent presence is implied.

The budding mathematician was in many ways precocious "in picking up on a mood, for example, in learning the intimate atmosphere of a person." But perhaps because she didn't have a mother who could teach her these things, she was also remarkably tardy in learning about "what the Americans call the facts of life." At thirteen, she wrote, "as if I only then [was] mature enough to receive a shocking reality," she confided her secret to a close friend: "I didn't know [the facts of life] and just pretended to know. She could hardly believe it, since I had pretended so well. . . . I was paralyzed looking at her, a mixture of perplexity, terror, indignation, and mortally wounded innocence. Mentally I stuttered: but why? but why? The shock was so great—and for a few months traumatic—that there and then, on the corner of the street, I swore out loud that I would never marry."[19]

This shock soon passed; what did not, the great event of Clarice's adolescence, was her discovery of literature. In childhood the creative drive was always there, from naming her pencils and the tiles in her shower, to composing the three-page play *Poor Little Rich Girl*, to telling her miraculous stories about her mother. But a little girl's fantasies are one thing, and literature is another; just as numbers require rules to give them human meaning, words, too, demand a form to turn them into literature. "When I learned how to read and write, I devoured books! I thought books were like trees, like animals: something that was born! I didn't know there was an author! Eventually I figured out that there was an author. So I said: That's what I want, too."[20]

The year after her mother's death the family moved farther down the Rua Imperatriz. Next door, where the street met the Capibaribe River, a Bessarabian immigrant, Jacob Bernstein, had opened a bookstore that would become a Recife institution, the Livraria Imperatriz, which exists to this day. The shop, long the city's best, was a meeting place for the local intelligentsia, some of whom became outstanding figures in Pernambuco and Brazil. The sociologist Gilberto Freyre was one; his famous study *The Masters and the Slaves* was first sold in Bernstein's store (though Bernstein, correctly, found it slightly anti-Semitic). Through his bookstore, Jacob Bernstein became one of the first Recife Jews to enter the local bourgeoisie.[21]

Bernstein's daughter Reveca was the same age as Clarice. According to Reveca's sister Suzana, Clarice for a time had the run of the bookstore and the Bernsteins' large private library. There she read classic Brazilian authors such as Machado de Assis and the children's writer Monteiro Lobato, books her father could not afford. Suzana remembered that the two were close friends.

Clarice, however, recalled Reveca less tenderly. "She was all revenge," Clarice wrote. "What a talent she had for cruelty." One day Reveca announced casually that she owned Monteiro Lobato's *As Reinações de Narizinho*, "a thick book, my God, a book to live with, eating it, sleeping it." As Reveca well knew, Clarice could never afford such a book, so she told her to come by the next day, when she would let her borrow it. Elated, Clarice returned as told, "literally running" through the mildewed streets of Recife. When she arrived, Reveca put into motion her "quiet and diabolical plan." With fake regret, she told Clarice that she didn't have the book yet, and asked her to come back the next day. The next day she invented another excuse and told her to come back the next day. "How long? I went to her house every day, without missing a single one. Sometimes she said: well, the book was here yesterday afternoon, but you only came in the morning, so I loaned it to another girl."

At length Mrs. Bernstein grew suspicious and demanded to know why the "blonde girl standing in the doorway, exhausted, in the wind of the streets of Recife," kept showing up at her house. When she found out, she was horrified by the discovery of the kind of daughter she had. "But that book never left this house, and you didn't even want to read it!" she said, appalled, to her daughter, ordering her then and there to loan it to Clarice. Mrs. Bernstein added that Clarice could keep the book as long as she wanted.

"Arriving back home, I didn't start to read it. I pretended I didn't have it, in order to have, later, the shock of discovering it. I opened it hours later, read a few marvelous lines, closed it again, walked around the house, put it off even more by going to eat a piece of bread with butter, pretended I didn't know where I had left it, found it, opened it for a few instants. I created the most false difficulties for that covert thing that was joy. Joy would always be covert for me."[22]

In 1933, Clarice Lispector decided to become a writer.

> When, consciously, thirteen years old, I consciously claimed the desire to write—I wrote as a child, but I had not claimed a destiny—, when I claimed the desire to write, I suddenly found myself in a void. And in that void there was nobody who could help me. I had to lift up myself from a nothingness,

> I myself had to understand myself, I myself had to invent, in a manner of speaking, my own truth. I started, and it wasn't even from the beginning. The papers piled up—the meanings contradicted one another, the despair of not being able was one more obstacle for really not being able to. The never-ending story which I then began to write (under much influence from *Steppenwolf*, by Hermann Hesse), what a pity that I didn't keep it: I tore it up, despising an entire attempt at apprenticeship, at self-knowledge. And doing everything in such secrecy. I didn't tell anyone; I lived that pain alone. One thing I had already guessed: I would have to try to write always, not waiting for a better moment because that would simply never come. Writing was always difficult for me, even though I had begun with what is known as vocation. Vocation is different from talent. One can have vocation and not talent; one can be called and not know how to go.[23]

These first efforts, she said, were "chaotic... entirely outside of reality," and fed by a reading that she remembered as being like that of a "starving person, avid; I read randomly, sometimes up to two books a day."[24] She read the Brazilian classics, such as Machado de Assis, and anything else she could find on the shelves of the library, where she chose her books by their titles. Two books, she always remembered, left the deepest impression. The first was *Crime and Punishment*, a dramatization of human failing and mystic salvation that would have appealed to a person who felt abandoned by God: Dostoevsky had also been a favorite of her father's. The second, perhaps more interestingly, was Hermann Hesse's *Steppenwolf*, an experimental novel published in Germany in 1927. It is easy to see why the book was so attractive to Clarice, whom it left with a "real fever." So many of its concepts reverberate in her experience that it almost seems to have been written specifically to influence Clarice Lispector. Hesse's books have always found a particular resonance with teenagers, for whom the longing for love and the question of what sort of life one ought to lead are at their most acute. *Narcissus and Goldmund* (1930), an allegory of two friends, one a scholarly monk, one a passionate sensualist, outlines two paths that love can take; *Siddhartha* (1922), his fictionalized life of the Buddha, popularized Eastern spiritual concepts in a world that, after the First World War, had been disillusioned by all its institutions, including religious.

Steppenwolf is a book about the glory of art and the price the artist pays for it. Like many of Clarice's own future books, *Steppenwolf* is a philosophical meditation hung on a fantastic, loosely constructed story, that of the "wolf of the steppes," Harry Haller, a scholar and artist whose nickname comes from his half-human, half-animal nature. Haller is "an animal who wandered into a world that to him was strange and incomprehensible, who could no longer find his home, passion, or sustenance."[25] His "Steppenwolf Treatise," prefaced with the warning that it is "Only for Madmen," lays out a life project for the future artist. The path of art, and the independence it requires, is a terrible one, he seems to be warning the adolescent Clarice. But Haller also notes, "Those who have no wolf inside them are not, for that reason, happy."[26]

"There are quite a lot of people just like Harry," Hesse wrote. "Many artists belong to this species. These people all have two souls, two beings inside them, in whom the divine and the diabolic, the mother's blood and the father's, the capacity for happiness and for suffering, are as tightly and inimically bound as the wolf and the man were inside Harry." Such people are "near to the wild heart," but they also know "that man is perhaps not simply a half-witted beast, but also a child of God, destined for immortality."[27]

Like other productions—novelistic, poetic, and cinematic—of Weimar Germany, Hesse's novel more closely resembles a dreamscape than it does a traditional novel. It tells a story, but the story is simply a framework for the exploration of sensory and philosophical possibilities. The real appeal of *Steppenwolf* to a budding adolescent writer such as Clarice Lispector was the freedom it offered to pursue her vocation, to describe the inner life.

"The interior journey fascinated me," she wrote of her "germination" by Hesse. The possibility he demonstrated, of writing about that journey, was a revelation for the girl whose stories had never been straightforward and who was always much less interested in the novelistic apparatus of plot and character than in the process through which writing could arrive at an inner truth. In *Água viva*, published three years before her death, she sought to write a book that was like music or sculpture; in the posthumous fragment *A Breath of Life*, "pure movement," she conceded only three sentences to traditional storytelling: "Quickly, because facts and particulars annoy me. So let's see: born in Rio de Janeiro, 34 years old, five foot six and of good family though the daughter of poor parents. Married a businessman, etc."[28]

It was not, she later remembered, that she did not want to write the kind of "once upon a time" stories the editors of the children's section in the *Diário de Pernambuco* expected. It was that she couldn't. As an adult, remembering this rebuff, she decided to try again. "I had changed so much since then," she figured, "that I might be ready for a real 'once upon a time.' So I asked: why don't I begin? Right now? It would be easy, I felt. So I started. Yet as soon as I wrote the first sentence, I immediately saw it was still impossible. I had written: 'Once upon a time there was a bird, my God.'"[29]

10

FLYING DOWN TO RIO

When Clarice Lispector was fifteen, a year after she discovered the possibility of writing, her father made his final move. Now the destination was Rio de Janeiro. Then as now, the city enjoyed a spectacular natural setting, with giant granite-and-quartz mountains plunging into the sea, primeval forests beginning just behind modern apartment buildings, and miles of great crescent-shaped beaches.

Unlike now, when the city is associated with violence and drugs, Rio was then at the height of its international reputation. Whereas previously ships traveling to Buenos Aires advertised that they made no stops in Brazil—the foreign mind, when it thought of it at all, imagined a place of monkeys, yellow fever, and cholera—Rio had transformed itself into one of the globe's ritziest destinations. Cruise ships streamed into the Bay of Guanabara, offloading their well-heeled passengers into the new hotels modeled on the white-wedding-cake originals of the French Riviera: the Hotel Glória, near downtown, opened in 1922; the legendary Copacabana Palace opened a year later, on a beach that was then still out of town.

The visitors spent their evenings in ritzy venues such as the Casino da Urca, underneath the Sugar Loaf, where rising stars like Carmen Miranda sang and danced into the early hours. Smart tourists would time their visits to coincide with the five days of the February Carnival, an entirely new event despite its ancient origins. Like any other city in the Catholic world, Rio had always had a Lenten carnival. But under the careful tending of Getúlio Vargas's government, with its unerring flair for public relations, the old festival was reorganized, expanded, and promoted heavily abroad.

It was a Hollywood production, and Hollywood took note. Dolores Del Rio put in an appearance for the 1933 film musical *Flying Down to Rio*, which launched the careers of Fred Astaire and Ginger Rogers and featured dancing on the wings of airplanes. In those years Orson Welles flew down to Rio and Carmen Miranda flew up to Hollywood from a city she, more than anyone else, made synonymous with dancing and beaches and pretty girls. São Paulo, with its rising industrial power, rivaled Rio for economic dominance, but inside Brazil there was only one undisputed capital, and outside, in the eyes of the world, Brazil was Rio, and Rio was Carnival.

Ginger and Fred were not the only people arriving in Rio. Pedro Lispector was part of a rush of less glitzy newcomers, the migrants that flowed into the capital in an unbroken stream. They came from all over the world, but the two main currents came from the northeast, the poorest and most backward part of Brazil, and from Portugal, one of the poorest and most backward countries in Europe.

By 1909, Rio de Janeiro's population of around one million included two hundred thousand citizens born in Portugal, and that number did not include the Brazilian-born children of Portuguese parents, who, if included, would have at least doubled that number.[1] Between 1901 and 1950, almost a million Portuguese citizens arrived in Brazil,[2] an enormous percentage of a population that barely numbered six million in 1920 and that represents almost twice the current population of Lisbon. Many, if not most, of these immigrants chose Rio de Janeiro, where they joined the lower middle class: shopkeepers, artisans, and small businesspeople. They dominated certain professions: bakers were almost always Portuguese; Carmen Miranda's father was a barber.

The Portuguese often had some bankable skills. In contrast, the uneducated and unskilled northeasterners, many of whom had been slaves or were the children of slaves, arrived in a city that had no use for them. They congregated in the slums, the *favelas*, that sprang up at the turn of the century. As the northeast continued its unstoppable decline into the twentieth century, more and more new arrivals joined those early unfortunates. But Rio was not generating new industry, and the newcomers could not be absorbed into an economy that was still mainly geared toward the export of agricultural products. The northeasterners often found that they had traded misery in one place for misery in another.

Pedro Lispector had more in common with the Portuguese immigrants than with those who were by now his fellow northeasterners. After years of work, his business in Recife was still not thriving, and he hoped that the capital would offer a wider field for his ambitions. He also hoped that Rio de Janeiro, with its large Jewish community, might offer suitable husbands for his daughters. Elisa was now twenty-four, Tania was twenty, and Clarice was fifteen. In Recife, with its two hundred Jewish families, they had presumably examined the offerings and found them wanting. In Rio they would have a wider choice.

Clarice never described the departure from Recife, where she had spent her entire childhood. She remembered the English boat that brought them to Rio in third class: "It was terribly exciting. I didn't know English and chose from the menu whatever my child's finger pointed out. I remember that I once picked cooked white beans, and nothing else. Disappointed, I had to eat it, poor me. A random bad choice. It happens."[3]

Though she rarely returned, she spoke of Pernambuco often ("Recife never fades"),[4] and alongside her throaty r's she kept the place's distinctive accent, a combination that made her an odd apparition in Rio. In a short elegiac essay, she imagined once again peering out the window of the house where she spent her childhood: "That is the river. That is the clock. It is Recife.... I see it more clearly now: that is the house, my house, the bridge, the river, the prison, the square blocks of buildings, the stairway, where I no longer stand."[5]

Only two of his daughters accompanied Pedro to Rio. Elisa stayed behind working in Recife, rejoining the family a few weeks later. Shortly after she arrived, she took the civil service examination for the Labor Ministry, an open competition, and earned the highest score in the whole country.

But at that time there were no openings in the Ministry. However, for the first time in their lives, the Lispectors had connections. These came in the shape of the extravagantly named Agamemnon Sérgio de Godoy Magalhães, a Recife politician who had been sitting next to his friend João Pessoa when he was gunned down in the Confeitaria Glória. On the back of the ensuing revolution, Magalhães had managed to become minister of labor. Before reaching this exalted position, he had been a geography teacher at the Ginásio Pernambucano, where his students included Clarice and Tania Lispector.

Tania decided to help her family, and she proved a well-chosen ambassadress. With her full figure and black hair, the twenty-two-year-old Tania was "sensuous," a neighbor remembered, "voluptuous, like a gypsy."[6] In her nicest dress, she went to the ministry in downtown Rio. "I explained that Elisa had come in first, and that she needed to work, that we needed to help our father because our mother had died," Tania remembered. "And he remembered me and Clarice from Recife, and promised to help us."[7] With a nod from the minister, Elisa was hired by the Ministry, where she would spend the rest of her working life.

This promising start was difficult for Pedro to follow. He had come to Rio to improve the family's fortunes, but he was barely more successful there than he had been in Recife. In the new city he sought work in commerce, as a sales representative, but had trouble finding a good job. For a time it seemed that another kind of happiness was in the cards, when, for the first time since Mania's death, he met a woman. There was talk of marriage, but the woman apparently thought he had money and left him when she discovered he didn't: another humiliation in a life that had already offered plenty.

Elisa's income took off some of the financial pressure, and at the beginning of 1938 Tania, too, found a public service job. In January of that year, Pedro's hope of finding his daughters Jewish husbands bore its first and only fruit, when Tania married William Kaufmann, a furniture salesman and decorator from Bessarabia (today's Moldova), across the Dniester from the Lispector family's own homeland. Clarice was impressed by her sister's choice, who, she thought, looked like a movie star.[8] Tania moved from Tijuca, where Pedro had settled the family, to Catete, on the other side of downtown, where she and William found an apartment on a street bordering the gardens of the Presidential Palace.

Inside that palace, Getúlio Vargas was now Brazil's absolute ruler. The development would not have enhanced Pedro Lispector's optimism. On September 29, 1937, a few months before Tania's wedding, the army chief of staff called a press conference to reveal a "document of great importance." The secret service, the general disclosed, had got their hands on a plan for implementing a Communist regime in the country, with the help of "Moscow gold." A cry immediately went up from the usual quarters—the great landowners, the Integralists, and the military, along with the frightened middle class—demanding defense of the "Nation and its traditions."[9]

Just who was behind this devious scheme was made clear by its name: the Cohen Plan. By the time it became obvious that the Cohen Plan, as the name also suggested, was a crude Integralist forgery, it had already achieved its objective. On November 10, Vargas answered the carefully orchestrated outcry to prevent the nation from falling into Muscovite hands. In the name of "national security," he suspended all political rights, individual and collective; called off presidential elections; disempowered the courts and the independent judiciary; and surrounded both houses of Congress with military police.

The name of the new regime, the Estado Novo, New State, was borrowed from Portugal. There, in 1933, under the same name, António de Oliveira Salazar—who encouraged people to call him "God's Chosen"—had established a regime that would become one of the twentieth century's most enduring tyrannies. There were other inspirations for Vargas's coup, especially Mussolini's Italy, and the constitution sanctifying his seizure of power became known as the *polaca* because it was said to be modeled on that of Poland.

The word *polaca* had a different connotation, however. In Rio de Janeiro, "Polish girl" meant whore, and many of the prostitutes in Rio—as in São Paulo, Montevideo, and Buenos Aires—were in fact from Poland and were Jewish.[10] Many were the orphans of the Great War, women who had not, like the Lispector girls, managed to escape safely abroad. Such girls, or those whose families had been reduced to destitution, were completely uneducated and easy enough to lure away to South America on the promise of marriage or a new life abroad. "The Man from Buenos Aires," in Scholem Aleichem's story of that name, was a pimp, a member of a fearsome Jewish mafia known as the Zwi Migdal, first based in Buenos Aires and which, when things heated up there, moved to Rio. For a time, it controlled the white slave trade in South America.

The Jewish presence in this business had not, of course, gone unremarked, and the existence of Jewish prostitutes and pimps was a prominent item on the Integralists' list of complaints against the Jews. In fact, on June 7, 1937, before the Cohen Plan and the Estado Novo, a secret circular was in force to bar all Jews, including tourists and businesspeople, from entering Brazil. This was not only the work of Integralists. It reflected the broad anti-Semitism in the upper echelons of the Brazilian Foreign Ministry, as well as in the government.[11]

This anti-Semitism was generally not, as for example in Argentina, translated into attacks on the Jews who already lived in Brazil. As Getúlio Vargas would go on to prove, the official Brazilian attitude was much more slippery. Even people who in their public life were quite determined to enforce anti-Semitic policies could be helpful to individual Jews—in part because it probably didn't always occur to them, in a country with a tiny Jewish population, to wonder whether the people they were dealing with were Jews. An example was none other than Agamemnon Magalhães, minister of labor, who was willing to lend a hand to Tania and Elisa Lispector even as he was agitating within the cabinet to keep Brazil closed to the increasingly desperate refugees from Nazi Germany.[12]

Brazil was, in any case, far from unique in denying refuge to these people. Other large countries—the United States, Canada, Britain, Argentina, South Africa, Australia—as well as a host of smaller countries, from Ecuador to Liberia, shut their doors to the European Jews. Brazil grudgingly allowed in a few—between

1933 and 1942 almost twenty-five thousand Jews legally entered Brazil—though the Vargas regime considered Jewish immigration undesirable.[13]

In a country under heavy censorship, this undesirability was not advertised. It didn't need to be. "We knew there were secret protocols to prohibit the entry of Jews into Brazil," said one Recife Jew. "But they didn't say there was—we felt it. It was the time of the concentration camps.... Sometimes they would say it was because the Jews were intellectuals and not farmers. There were already way too many intellectuals in Brazil. Then they said they wouldn't bring progress to the country. So they never said Jews can't get in. We talked about it in the community. In my house we talked about it."[14]

The Jews paid a high price for Vargas's grasp for absolute power. There was the price paid by Jewish Communists such as Olga Benário Prestes, the pregnant twenty-eight-year-old wife of the Brazilian Communist leader, deported to Germany and gassed. In the same year, 1936, Clarice's cousin David Wainstok, a medical student in Recife, would also pay a price when, on suspicion of Communist sympathies, he was arrested and brutally tortured in Recife. "Brought up in a home where Zionism was the highest ideal, by parents who dreamt the dream of all the Jewish generations, the young Jewish student went a step beyond his parents, attempting to hasten the Jewish prophesies of 'the end of days' and 'the earth shall be filled with wisdom,'" his father, Israel Wainstok, wrote in his Yiddish memoirs, making an explicit connection between his son's Zionist upbringing and his thirst for social justice. After his arrest, "a black night descended on our family life. It stretched on and on, so many nights, weeks, and months."[15] David's sister Cecília recalled a climate of terror. Their mother, Dora Rabin Wainstok, had buried all of David's questionable books behind the house and covered them with cement, perhaps sparing the family greater complications; terrified Cecilia, a little girl, was followed to school by plainclothes police. After a year in the very prison that Clarice remembered seeing from her window, across the bridge from her house, he was finally released.

At the Ginásio Pernambucano, the school Tania and Clarice had attended in Recife, a certain Father Cabral began denouncing the Jewish girls for "seducing Christian boys,"[16] and before long Jewish girls were expelled, as the school resolved to concentrate exclusively on educating boys. There are differing accounts of whether this was a direct reaction to Father Cabral's agitation. But the Jews felt it was aimed at them; because the school was located in their neighborhood, and because it was free to those students who could pass its rigorous entrance examinations, it was attractive to a poor community that put a premium on education. The Jewish girls were forced to depart only a year after the Lispectors left Recife.

The equation of Judaism with Communism was potentially as dangerous to the Brazilian Jews as it had been to the Jews of Russia and Germany, though this equation had not, of course, been derived from an objective observance of actual Jews among the ranks of the Communists. As Gustavo Barroso's formula had it, Communism equaled capitalism equaled Judaism. The Estado Novo took strong steps to repress all three. The Communists had been dealt with after 1935, and, as in Mussolini's Italy and Perón's Argentina, Brazil's nascent industries were brought under a corporatist umbrella that did little to stimulate further economic growth.

At a time of world Jewish crisis, for people who had already survived the terrible massacres that followed the First World War and the Russian Revolution, any hint of repression would have been demoralizing, at the very least. Even Pedro Lispector, low as he was on the totem pole of Brazilian society, was a target of the Estado Novo's new security measures. "He was a Zionist," said Tania, "and he raised money for the Jewish National Fund. We had the little box in our house, where we put a coin on every occasion, whenever we could, for the Jews in Palestine."[17]

This activism in no way distinguished Pedro Lispector from any other Jews, in Brazil or anywhere else; Pedro Lispector's and Israel Wainstok's homes were not the only households in which "Zionism was the highest ideal." Shortly after his arrival in Rio, in March 1935, Pedro had served on the executive committee of the Zionist Federation when it was preparing its third national conference,[18] unaware that this ideology, which would not have seemed to present much of a threat to Brazilian national security, would soon be banned as indicative of allegiance to a foreign government. (Of course, in 1937, when the ban took effect, there was no such thing as a Zionist government.) The *pushke*, the four-inch-tall metal box that Tania remembered, was declared "illegal and dangerous."[19] Even the word "Zionism" was banned; one lecturer was forced to refer to "a certain idea, well known to all, which Herzl helped to establish."[20]

Luckily for the Brazilian Jews, the Integralists overplayed their hand, squandering the advantage they had gained when Vargas, adopting much of their rhetoric, cracked down on the Communist Party in 1935 and then, in 1937, instituted the Estado Novo. They resented Vargas's ban on political parties, which included theirs. Plínio Salgado, their leader, who had always seen Vargas as a useful idiot, decided that it was time to install an Integralist dictator—himself—in his stead.

On the night of May 11, 1938, while Salgado waited in elegance above the fray in São Paulo, an Integralist battalion attacked Guanabara Palace in Rio de Janeiro, while Vargas and his family were asleep inside. Luckily, his gun-toting twenty-two-year-old daughter Alzira, a future friend of Clarice Lispector's, managed to telephone around, rallying the troops, who, after long uncertain hours for the Palace's residents, brought down the uprising toward noon of the next day. The plotters suffered far less than their Communist rivals. Salgado was dispatched to cool his heels in Portugal, where Gustavo Barroso soon joined him, and most of the military officers who participated in the coup were given token punishments or none at all.

Getúlio Vargas saw no point in retribution. The Integralists, the party of the right, had fumbled in exactly the same way that the Communists, the party of the left, had botched their chances three years before. It was a golden opportunity for the dictator to disencumber himself of any significant opposition without sullying his own hands. Though the Integralists, and many of their ideas, would return to haunt Brazil, their threat to the country's Jews was now past.

The thirst for justice, the "dream of all the Jewish generations" that led the Communist idealist Olga Benário Prestes to the gas chamber and David Wainstok to the dungeons of Recife, took Clarice Lispector down another path.

After arriving in Rio de Janeiro in 1935, she spent a short time at a dinky neighborhood school in Tijuca before entering, on March 2, 1937, the preparatory course for the National Law Faculty of the University of Brazil. It was a most unusual decision for a woman—there were no more than a handful of female lawyers in the country—just as it was for a student of her background. The legal profession was everywhere in Brazil a preserve of the elite, and no school in the country was more prestigious than the law school in the capital. The girl from the Podolia *shtetl* was about to enter the top echelons of Brazilian society.

Careerism, however, was not what propelled Clarice into law school. The yearning for justice was bred in her bones. She had seen her mother's horrible death, and her brilliant father, unable to study, was reduced to peddling scraps of cloth. She had grown up poor in Recife, but she was also aware that her family, despite their struggles, were better off than many. "When I was a little girl," she later wrote, "my family jokingly called me the 'protector of animals.' Because all someone had to do was accuse someone and I would leap to their defense. And I felt the social drama with such intensity that I lived with my heart perplexed by the great injustices which the so-called underprivileged classes suffered. In Recife I visited our maid's house on Sundays, in the slums. And what I saw there made me promise that I wouldn't let it go on."[21]

Her advocacy of the defenseless was so fervent that people started saying she would be a lawyer. "That stuck in my mind," she wrote, "and since I didn't have any other ideas about what to study, I went to study law."[22] Her father, however, warned against it. He told one of her sisters that he was afraid she would end up thinking too much and fly off the handle. "Obviously," she commented in a letter a few years later, "it wasn't law school that made me like that. But now I understand so well what he meant."[23]

Clarice had, however, a concrete goal. "My idea—an adolescent absurdity!—was to study law in order to reform the prisons," she said.[24] This was not a notion plucked out of nowhere, for in those years a movement existed in Brazil to reform the country's prisons. Its most famous fruit was the House of Detention in São Paulo, a model institution open to visitors from across the world.

The anthropologist Claude Lévi-Strauss, who made his name in Brazil, came, and so did the Austrian Jewish writer Stefan Zweig, who visited in 1936, discovering that "exemplary cleanliness and hygiene transformed the prison into a factory of work. The prisoners made the bread, prepared the medicines, served in the clinic and the hospital, planted vegetables, washed the clothes, made pictures and drawings, and took classes."[25]

The authorities packed more and more prisoners into the building, and it soon became Latin America's largest, famed not for prisoners sketching and planting vegetables but for a rate of violence so appalling that its nickname, Carandirú, became a byword for horror. In 1992, the prisoners revolted, a massacre that left as many as 250 people dead, after which the model prison was finally shuttered.

❦

The "tall, thoughtful, rebellious" blonde girl with the strange accent and outstanding scholastic record made a strong impression.[26] At the school where she took extracurricular English classes, one teacher devised a special exercise to discover more about her, assigning an English essay on the question "What do you do during the day?" When Clarice returned a banal recitation of her daily activities, the disappointed teacher said, "I thought you were a painter, or that you played the piano." A few years later, Clarice ran into the woman again and mentioned that she had published her first novel. "But you were a writer?" the teacher exclaimed. That, she admitted, was what she hoped to learn in assigning the composition.[27]

But Clarice Lispector was never obvious. She was tentatively taking her first steps as a writer, in secret, "creating her mask," as she put it, "with great pain. Because to know that from that point on you are going to play a role is a scary surprise. It is the horrible liberty of not being. It is the hour of decision."[28] The decision had already been made, though as far as the outside world knew, her energies were directed toward the law school. She took the entrance examination in February 1939, scoring first in her preparatory class and fourth of the three hundred candidates nationally,[29] and prepared to enter the University of Brazil.

"I was a confused and perplexed adolescent who had a mute and intense question: 'what is the world like? and why this world?' Later I learned many things. But the adolescent's question remained, mute and nagging."[30] From almost before she entered university, she knew that she would not find answers in the law. Her mask had already been chosen when she read *Steppenwolf* and resolved to become a writer; a brief stint working in a lawyer's office confirmed that she had no vocation for paperwork.

In those days, however, not all students entered law school in order to become lawyers; relatively few, in fact, actually ended up practicing law. It was a training ground for influential journalists, politicians, diplomats, and businessmen, almost anyone aspiring to a nonscientific profession. This was partly because until the year Clarice was born, 1920, giant Brazil did not have a single university. It had schools of medicine, law, engineering, and so on, but no single institution offering a full range of disciplines. (By contrast, in Spanish America, Lima, Mexico City, and Santo Domingo had universities by the middle of the sixteenth century.) The National Law Faculty—housed in the former Imperial Senate, across from a large park, the Campo de Santana, where large bucktoothed rodents called agoutis wandered across the grass—was the most prominent institution of higher learning in Brazil.

As such, it was open to foreign influence, including "scientific racism." Many of the Foreign Ministry officials who barred Jewish refugees from Brazil had issued from the school, their outlooks formed by writers such as Arthur de Gobineau, who arrived in Rio on a diplomatic mission in 1870 and loathed almost every aspect of the country, with the single exception of its blond Habsburg emperor, Dom Pedro II. Gobineau's claims that only heavy doses of European blood could fortify Brazil's lamentably dark population found approving audiences inside the school. Related claims by other authors, including the proto-Nazi Houston Stewart Chamberlain, met with sympathy there, too, along with the notion of a strong centralized state that was so important to both the Integralists and Getúlio Vargas. "The intellectual roots of Integralism were not popular," one scholar writes. "Rather, they sprang from Brazil's prestigious law faculties, where Integralists, like many of the diplomats in charge of making and implementing immigration policy, frequently linked communism and 'international Jewish finance' in their manifestoes."[31]

At the school, one of racial fortification's leading advocates, Francisco José Oliveira Vianna, was himself a mulatto.[32] The ideology's absurdity, however, did not mean it was without consequence, inside or outside the country. But on the other side, a growing chorus condemned the dictatorship's affinities with the Axis—and even, increasingly, the dictatorship itself.

Politics were not the reason Clarice Lispector was never much interested in law school. Her grades, which in secondary school had always been outstanding, were respectable rather than stellar, and on December 17, 1943, she didn't even bother to attend the graduation ceremony.

She moved on almost before she started. During her first year of university, she had discovered an outlet for her true vocation, and on May 25, 1940, she published her first known story, "Triumph," in *Pan*. This was a magazine of a type then popular in Brazil, a general-interest periodical that translated and reprinted all kinds of news, essays, stories, and reportage from foreign publications, alongside contributions from Brazilian writers. Since its first issue, at the end of 1935, its political orientation had changed along with the country's. In that edition, *Pan* was unabashedly pro-Fascist. Benito Mussolini was the "man of the issue," "the most vigorous universal personality of this century," and amid the carnage of the Ethiopian War the back cover featured a cartoon showing "the heroic crusader, so civilized by Fascism, attacking African barbarity, to liberate, disinterestedly, the beautiful black slave."[33]

By the time Clarice published her story, that orientation was far in the past, as indeed it was in most of the Brazilian press, heavily censored since the beginning of the Estado Novo. Clarice's own concerns were closer to home. Appropriately enough for a first story, "Triumph" tells of a beginning writer and his frustrations, seen from his lover's perspective: "He said he needed special conditions in order to produce, to continue his novel, undermined from the very beginning by an absolute inability to concentrate. He went off to try to find the 'atmosphere.'" He has sacrificed his girlfriend on the altar of literature, though she remembers hearing him say, "the wide beloved shoulders trembling in a laugh, that it was nothing more than a joke, an experience to insert on the page of a book."[34]

The short tale includes the unexpected verbal flourishes ("the wide beloved shoulders trembling in a laugh") that would become trademarks of Clarice

Lispector's. And they already include a doubt about the role of literature in life. Clarice mocks the maudlin drama the writer makes of his petty troubles. At the same time, she sympathizes with his torment, as when Luísa, the girlfriend, finds a note the writer has left behind: "'I can't write. I can't write. With these words I am scratching a wound. My mediocrity is so...' Luísa interrupts her reading. What she had always felt, just vaguely: mediocrity." In those lines, the young writer's fear of her own mediocrity comes through, a fear of failure that belies the triumph of the title. That comes when the naked Luísa enters the bath, feels the sensation of the water running over her body in the hot morning sun, and suddenly realizes that he will come back to her. She—the animal, the body, the woman—was stronger than his doubts. Life triumphs over literature.

It is a skilled performance by a nineteen-year-old girl, as Pedro Lispector would have sensed, proud of his youngest daughter's appearance in a prominent national magazine. Even if he, like most parents, placed an exaggerated value on the productions of his children, he could not have known that he was witnessing the beginning of one of the most extraordinary careers in twentieth-century literature. Perhaps this pride was a small compensation for the fear and depression he felt at the progress of Adolf Hitler across his home continent, a progress that, in mid-1940, seemed unstoppable. When Russia was invaded, he sought news of his relatives through the Red Cross. There was none.

Despite a life of setbacks, "years of heartbreaks, of fruitless, inglorious struggles," he had not given up. He loved reading and music. "He often came home radiant: 'I bought tickets for us to go hear Yehudi Menuhin.' Or it was Brailowski, or Arthur Rubinstein. It was always thanks to him that we got to go to the theater and hear good music," Elisa wrote. "He was a dedicated activist: working for the Jewish National Fund, the Keren Hayesod, contributing to help the refugees from the war."[35]

These were little compensations in a life that was one unremitting battle. "He never knew what it was to spend a single day without worries, without having to work, without having to save," Elisa wrote. "Simply without having to think about the day a note was due. Because the truth is that Daddy never had any talent for business, and if people thought we had any claims to wealth, it was only because of the firmness of his character. Whatever happened, Daddy always paid his bills the day they were due. And the day before if possible, which for him was a victory."[36]

Like Clarice, Elisa, too, was starting to publish her work. She showed a story to her father, who, after reading it, sat thinking.

> "Let me suggest a topic. Write about a man who got lost, a man who lost his way."
>
> For a while he sat there silently, and then went into his room. He added nothing. And I sat there imagining what would have made him feel shipwrecked, at what point he had gotten lost in his doubts, oscillating between two worlds, lost among different cultures?
>
> Because then Father was in his fifties, and he had built nothing: All his deepest aspirations had remained incomplete.[37]

In secret, Elisa started gathering notes for a book based on her father's suggestion.

In August, Pedro had a mild health complaint that led him to a doctor. He learned that his gall bladder would have to be removed, a common surgery scheduled for August 23, 1940. In the Brazil of 1940 any surgery was risky, but his daughters did not think there was any reason to be alarmed. But he returned from the clinic in considerable pain, dying three days later. After a life that had included poverty and exile, the martyrdom of his beloved wife, and the unceasing struggle to raise and establish his daughters in a completely foreign country, he was dead at the age of fifty-five.

"I am going to use a very strong word," his daughter Tania said. A person of great refinement and discretion, Tania did not use strong words, so it was all the more surprising to hear her claim that her father was murdered. "It was a routine operation," she said, her pain and bewilderment audible sixty-six years later. "And then, after he died, we went to the clinic and tried to talk to the doctors. They wouldn't see us, they wouldn't give us any answers."[38]

It was a final defeat in a life that had known little else, a last humiliation for the brilliant Jewish boy from the Ukrainian backwoods, who dreamed of studying mathematics and religion and was forced instead into a distant exile, his wife condemned to a slow extinction, his own ceaseless struggle for a better life never gratified. If he had lived a short time longer, he would have seen the sudden, unexpected fame of his beautiful youngest daughter and the emergence of the Jewish state he had dreamed of. Instead, his death was not reckoned important enough to merit an explanation from the doctors who caused it.

A few years later, Clarice wrote a friend, "Once he said: if I were to write, I would write a book about a man who saw that he had lost. I cannot think about that without unbearable physical pain."[39]

Once again, Tania stepped into the parental role. She insisted that the newly orphaned Elisa and Clarice move in with her and William, though their apartment, across the street from the gardens of the Catete Palace, was so small that Elisa had to sleep in the living room and Clarice was forced into the tiny maid's room. There she spent much of her time studying and writing, and in addition to her law studies she soon began working as a journalist.

In those days, few Brazilian women, with the exception of the occasional society lady, worked for newspapers. Those few were of high caliber, however, including the poet Cecília Meireles, who had worked for the *Diário de Notícias* in the 1930s, and the novelist Rachel de Queiroz, who in the next decade worked for *Cruzeiro*.[40] A woman in the newsroom was an unusual phenomenon and required a bit of adaptation; her colleagues, embarrassed to use dirty language in front of a woman, had to resort to tapping on the tables instead.[41]

Clarice's induction into this world came thanks to one of only three people outside Italy who truly understood Fascism: this, according to no less an authority than Benito Mussolini.[42] The all-powerful Lourival Fontes was Getúlio Vargas's éminence grise, in charge of the Department of Press and Propaganda, the organ that, through "seduction, bribery, and coercion," controlled the Brazilian press. He helped certain Jewish refugees, including Stefan Zweig, the Hungarian philologist Paulo Rónai, and the French publisher Max Fischer, even as he shut down Jewish newspapers.

From the Tiradentes Palace, a neoclassical pile in downtown Rio that, until 1937, had housed the now extinct Congress, Lourival Fontes reigned over the Brazilian press. His office ornamented by a gigantic portrait of Vargas—his job was to prove that Getúlio "neither peed nor shat"[43]—the smooth-talking Fontes managed to make overt censorship almost redundant; with the suppression of the Communists and the Integralists, most of the press agreed with the government anyway, and when they didn't it was easy enough to rearrange their access to newsprint or public funding. "Living from literary or journalistic talent was almost impossible, except if you worked for Lourival Fontes."[44]

The Department of Press and Propaganda was the only authorized voice in the country. The dictatorship had taken over Rádio Nacional (Brazil's most powerful), the evening paper *A Noite*, the news service Agência Nacional, and a host of magazines, including *Vamos Lêr!* (Let's Read!), "a publication for its time, a publication for the man of the dynamic and tremulous era of zeppelins, of fantastic speed 'records,' of 'skyscrapers,' and of television."[45] It was probably at *Vamos Lêr!* that Clarice Lispector caught the eye of Lourival Fontes. Just as Tania had done when she convinced Agamemnon Magalhães to employ Elisa, Clarice strode into the office of Fontes's secretary, Raymundo Magalhães Júnior.

"I went with enormous shyness, but I was bold at the same time," she recalled. "I went to the magazines and said: 'I have a story, do you want to publish it?'

I remember one time it was Raymundo Magalhães, Jr., who looked at it, read a bit of it, looked at me, and said: 'Who did you copy this from?' I said nobody, it's mine. He said: 'Did you translate it?' I said no. He said: 'Then I'll publish it.' "[46]

This was probably "Jimmy and I," which appeared in *Vamos Lêr!* on October 10, 1940. Clarice Lispector is occasionally thought of as a feminist writer, but she wrote few stories as overt. "What could I do, after all?" the protagonist asks. "Ever since I was a little girl, I had seen and felt the predominance of men's ideas over women's. Before she got married, according to Aunt Emília, Mother was a firecracker, a tempestuous redhead, with her own ideas about the freedom and equality of women. But along came Daddy, very serious and tall, who also had his own ideas, about...the freedom and equality of women," Clarice wrote, with an unaccustomed political stridence and verbal clumsiness. Other themes reappear: when the narrator dumps her lover, Jimmy, she thinks, "Well, figure it out! We're just animals....I didn't think this was an argument, but it made me feel a bit better. I was a little sad when I went to bed. But I woke up happy, a pure animal."[47]

Perhaps it was the publication of this story that emboldened Clarice to approach Magalhães's boss. Lourival Fontes may have been a Fascist propagandist, but he was also a cultured man with a weakness for beautiful literary women: In the same year he hired Clarice Lispector, he married the poetess Adalgisa Nery. Still, it required some nerve to knock on his door. "In those days," Tania said, "you didn't do *anything* without connections. Nobody showed up and asked for a job. It was all through your cousin or your brother-in-law. But Clarice did. He liked her and he hired her."[48]

Fontes put her to work at the Agência Nacional, the national wire service, which distributed laudatory news to papers and radio stations all over Brazil. She was first meant to work as a translator, but there were already enough translators, so she was assigned to work as an editor and a reporter, the only woman so employed. Perhaps the only person actually employed at all: her enthusiasm contrasted with the lazy atmosphere of the newsroom. Their job was not, after all, to discover news, but to dress up items from other papers, making it sound official before redistributing it to other outlets.[49]

It was a young group, and her friend Francisco de Assis Barbosa, then twenty-eight, recalled the impression she made: "A marvelous being. Beautiful, attractive, but completely unpretentious. She always wore white. A blouse and a skirt. A leather belt. Nothing else. Low shoes, maybe sandals. Light brown hair. Ah, yes, long shoulder-length hair. She spoke softly. A slight accent, revealing her Jewish origins. She laughed a lot. She enjoyed life. She was happy with life. She was ready to live."[50]

11

GOD STIRS THE WATERS

Among the bored young staff of the Agência Nacional was Lúcio Cardoso, a twenty-six-year-old from a small town who was already hailed as one of the most talented writers of his generation. His father, Joaquim Lúcio Cardoso, had studied engineering but left university without a degree, due to the death of his own father. He then headed into the backlands of the interior state of Minas Gerais, where he enjoyed a period of great prosperity, at one time accumulating eight thousand head of cattle, only to fall into debt and be forced to hand over his fortune to a textile factory owner. After the death of his wife, he created, like Pedro Lispector in Maceió, a soap factory. But his volatile personality brought him trouble with the local merchants, who boycotted his products. His business ventures failed, Joaquim and his second wife, Dona Nhanhá, raised their six children in relative poverty.[1]

Their town of Curvelo was typical of the backwoods of Minas Gerais, a state said to imprint a special character on its inhabitants, and one whose personality occupies a prominent place in Brazilian mythology. The *mineiros*, the stereotype goes, are tight-fisted, wary, and religious; there is a joke that Minas tables have drawers built into them, the better, at the first approach of a visitor, to hide the silverware. It is a place where mannered elocutions play an important role in the local language. Nobody in Minas is crazy, the preferred euphemism is "systematic." There is a taboo against overt descriptions of medical procedures: "They opened him, and closed him back up" is the most that can be conceded of a surgery. A *mineiro*, above all, does not draw attention to himself. One native, returning home from São Paulo, recalls his puzzlement at being the object of amazed stares. He finally realized that he was wearing a red shirt.[2]

That was in the capital, Belo Horizonte, one of Brazil's largest and most modern cities, in the 1960s. Four decades earlier, in the no-name village of Curvelo, it was presumably even easier to provoke a scandal. And nobody did it quite as well as Joaquin and Nhanhá Cardoso's youngest son, Lúcio, who refused to go to school, was obsessed with movie stars, and played with dolls. This last point especially galled his father, who fought with his wife about it. "It's your fault," he would charge, "you brought him up clinging to your skirts, and the result is this queer. Where did you ever hear of a boy playing with dolls? Why doesn't he like playing with the other boys? He's a nervous kid who's never going to amount to anything."[3]

It was impossible to keep him in school, but he was curious about everything, and his older sister, Maria Helena, who became the best chronicler of his life, oriented his reading. He read many of the same authors that Clarice read as a girl, a mix that ranged from Dostoevsky to the romantic novels serialized in the newspapers, which Lúcio and Maria Helena followed avidly.[4] The family moved to Rio de Janeiro, and he was sent to boarding school, where he was predictably miserable, eventually ending up working at an insurance company, A Equitativa, run by his uncle. "I was always a terrible worker," he said. "All I did was write poetry."[5]

But he was finally free and in the capital. He was twenty-two when, in 1934, with the help of the Catholic poet and industrialist Augusto Frederico Schmidt, he published his first novel, *Maleita*. By the time he published his third novel, *The Light in the Basement*, two years later, he had attracted the attention of Brazil's ultimate cultural arbiter, Mário de Andrade, who dispatched a typically colorful letter from São Paulo. "Artistically it is terrible," Andrade thundered. "Socially it is detestable. But I understood its point... to return the spiritual dimension to the materialistic literature that is now being made in Brazil. God has returned to stir the face of the waters. Finally."[6]

Since 1826, when the first history of Brazilian literature was published, most Brazilian writers had followed the advice of the pioneer historian who insisted that the country "must remain independent, and seek its only guide in observation... free in its poetry as in its government."[7] That the historian was French and the book published in Paris gave this advice to ignore Europe even more authority. "Whoever examines the Brazilian literature of the present day immediately recognizes its primary trait, a certain instinct of nationality," Brazil's classic novelist, Machado de Assis, wrote in 1873. "Poetry, novels, all... dress themselves in the colors of the country."[8]

The result was that Brazilian literature was mostly a literature about Brazil, and only to a much lesser degree a literature written by Brazilians. It was local, regional, and patriotic, composed by self-conscious Brazilians dedicated to creating, or opposing, a certain image of Brazil. They celebrated the country's particularities—its natural beauty, its history, its popular culture, the heritage of the Indian and the African—and they denounced the country's social problems, its poverty, its injustice, its failure to live up to its apparently limitless potential. Most often they did both.

In this aspect, Brazil's literature resembles Russia's. Both colossal countries are part of the Western world and, in an important way, outside it. They have used literature to bridge the seemingly unbridgeable gaps imposed by their history and geography. Their regions are spread across enormous distances; the life of their modern cities is often unimaginable in their backward countryside; their upper classes cannot imagine, except through literature, the lives of their mammoth underclasses. And their elites, despite their preoccupation with national "authenticity," were long under the sway of France, which gave much of their literature, even at its most nationalistic, a colonial, derivative flavor.

In the twentieth century, the trend largely continued, even despite the revolution known as "22," the Modern Art Week held in São Paulo in 1922. Though not published until 1928, the paradigmatic "22" novel was Mário de Andrade's *Macunaíma*, an ironic recycling of many of the old national clichés: Macunaíma himself is an Indian who comes to the big city of São Paulo, and Mário de Andrade's concern for emancipating the national, Brazilian language from its colonial Portuguese baggage is also typical. Though the novel's subtitle, *The Hero with No Character*, is also satirically intended, it nevertheless places the book within the ideological tradition of Brazilian literature, in which people are not shown as fully human but are instead meant to advance or attack one ideological position or another. Mário de Andrade elsewhere defined his goal as "to make the Brazilian one hundred percent Brazilian, to nationalize a nation that is as yet so lacking in national characteristics."[9] It is a surprising statement from a man who knew better than anyone how many national characteristics Brazil had; he was a pioneer collector of Brazilian art and devoted years to cataloguing the country's musical traditions.

The urge to "nationalize a nation" found sympathetic listeners in both Communism and Fascism, which encouraged artists to look at the national "reality." Writers influenced by Communists tended to use their fiction to denounce class oppression and assert the claims of Brazil's oppressed workers in the city and, especially, in the country. Fascist-influenced writers also discovered, again especially in the country, the *völkische* values of the country's common people. These contrasted, of course, with the "commercialism" of the foreign cities.

The northeast, where Clarice Lispector grew up and where Brazil's social contrasts were at their sharpest, was a favorite stage. The years following 1922 saw a blossoming of northeastern-themed novels, "using a Brazilian language within a Brazilian reality," Clarice Lispector wrote, in one of her rare forays into literary criticism. "This was all the result of 1922.... We are hungry for knowledge about ourselves, because we need ourselves more than we need others."[10]

Yet the quest for this knowledge usually delivered dry books. By using fiction as a vehicle to discover some general truth about some aspect of Brazil, writers sacrificed detail for the sweep, the panorama, the *grande ligne*. It was an inevitable result of the task. As in Germany, where urban intellectuals traipsed through hill and dale in search of some imagined place more "real" than Munich or Hamburg; as in Argentina and Uruguay, where the national gaucho poetry turned out to be written not by gauchos but, in Borges's words, by "educated people, gentlemen from Buenos Aires or Montevideo," the attempt to "liberate" Brazil was conducted by educated urban people who decided what they wanted to find before they went out to discover it. It was a Brazil seen from outside in, and the predictable result of the focus on reality was a country just as imaginary as the romantic productions that preceded it.

Above all, this literature was materialistic rather than spiritual, which is why, despite his reservations about the book's artistic and social qualities, Mário de Andrade welcomed Lúcio Cardoso's *The Light in the Basement.*

God had, indeed, returned to stir the waters. But Lúcio Cardoso was not the first godly writer to appear in the years following 1922. Another was Augusto Frederico Schmidt, Lúcio Cardoso's first publisher, who in 1928, at twenty-two, published his own collection of poetry entitled *Song of the Brazilian Augusto Frederico Schmidt.* On the first page the poet put to rest the assertion of nationality in his title:

I no longer want love
I no longer want to sing to my homeland.
I am lost in this world.
I no longer want Brazil,
I no longer want geography
Nor the picturesque.

At the time, Schmidt was running a Catholic magazine called *The Order*, which attracted writers who would come to be associated, like Schmidt himself, with the "introspective school." This was a loose grouping of writers whose concerns were less social and national than internal and spiritual. They included Vinicius de Moraes, later famed as a bohemian poet who married nine times and became an early champion of bossa nova; the beloved poetess Cecília Meireles; the aristocratic novelist Octávio de Faria, whose enormous thirteen-volume cycle *Bourgeois Tragedy* is one of the famous unread works of Brazilian literature; and the half-blind Cornélio Penna, whose novel *Border* appeared in 1936, the same year as *The Light in the Basement.* "Everything happens on the border between dream and reality, between past and present, between the natural and the prenatural, between clarity and madness," wrote a preeminent critic, Tristão de Athayde, of the book.[11] The description could also serve for the works of Lúcio Cardoso, who was first published by Schmidt—or, for that matter, of Hermann Hesse.[12] The Catholic faith of many of these writers led some to associate, usually temporarily, with Integralism and to defend certain reactionary propositions, such as militating in favor of silent films.

But Catholicism played a different role in the works of the homosexuals among them, including Mário de Andrade, Octávio de Faria, Cornélio Penna, and Lúcio Cardoso. For these people, the Church was a logical home. Not only because, in Brazil as everywhere else, it was chockablock with gay men, but because of the redemption the Church promised those weighed down by the awareness of sin. These people did not see art as a way of addressing social issues, or of refining the national language, or of asserting the preeminence of one political party over another. Their mission was much more urgent: they sought to be saved through art. Writing was for them a spiritual exercise, not an intellectual one.

That is what Clarice Lispector, "guilty from birth, she who was born with the mortal sin,"[13] had in common with Lúcio Cardoso. "Beauty was a quality, not a form; a content, not an arrangement," one writer has said of the worldview of the poor Jews of Eastern Europe. When he wrote that the "Jews would have been deeply puzzled by the idea that the aesthetic and the moral are distinct realms,"[14] he might as well have been speaking of the works of Lúcio Cardoso and other gay Catholics, whose frenzied work was in large part an urgent mission to save souls they feared irrevocably damned.

This was also the goal of Clarice Lispector and many other Jewish writers, faced with the silence of a God who, despite their fervent prayers, withdrew from them over and over again. Both were rejects, and both thirsted for the redemption they despaired of finding. It is no wonder that Clarice Lispector fell passionately in love with Lúcio Cardoso.

She was not the only one. Many people fell in love with Lúcio, a friend remembered.[15] He was strikingly handsome, brilliantly witty, and endlessly creative. "It just poured out of him!" said another. He would sit in cafés, writing one page after another, tearing one sheet out of the typewriter and immediately beginning another.[16] He completed his novel *Inácio* in a mere four days.[17] "What a verbal talent he had, my God, Lúcio Cardoso," another friend recalled. "And what an ability to work, even though he stayed out all night drinking. He got up early and wrote, wrote, wrote. What he published isn't half of what he wrote."[18]

He was a natural writer, a natural talker, and a natural seducer. On his first meeting with Luiz Carlos Lacerda, a teenager who later became a well-known film director, he scribbled off a poem for him and then took him back to his apartment. Lacerda, young and naïve, assumed they would live happily ever after. A few days later, he was devastated when he walked by Lúcio's apartment in Ipanema, saw the light on, rang up, and got no answer. After waiting a while, he saw another boy emerge and understood that he was just another notch on the bedpost.[19]

Lúcio never had a lasting relationship. As anguished and tormented as the characters in his books, he apparently never wanted one either, though he was constantly falling in love with different men. When he died, Clarice wrote, "In so many things, we were so fantastic that, if it hadn't been for the impossibility, we might have gotten married."[20] Clarice's friend Rosa Cass disagrees, seeing a different impossibility. "It wasn't just that he was gay," she emphasizes. "They were too much alike. He needed his solitude, he was a 'star,' unearthly. The two of them would have been an impossible couple."[21]

That did not prevent Clarice from trying. "He'll never marry you, he's homosexual," their colleague Francisco de Assis Barbosa told her. "But I'll save him," Clarice retorted. "He'll like me."[22] The relationship, needless to say, never got off the ground. This was probably just as well, because anecdotes suggest that Lúcio would have made a difficult spouse.

"'Lúcio went crazy, Helena,'" a coworker told his sister when she arrived at his office in downtown Rio. "'He sold me a suit because he needed money and now he's entertaining himself by throwing bills and coins out of the window, half of what I just paid him.'...I went to the window, laughing myself. Below, the Rua Álvaro Alvim was full of people, and more were streaming in every minute, attracted by the noise of the crowd chasing after the money that was ceaselessly falling from that miraculous window."[23]

The prankishness also had a dark side. Once he told people that he had hired someone to kill him, the better to comprehend the feeling of being persecuted.[24] He did not need to resort to such theatrics. The tenants' union in his building tried to kick him out, in a letter that made reference to Oscar Wilde.[25] He himself repeatedly tried to correct his homosexuality, sometimes going so far as to punish himself like a medieval penitent. "This perpetual tendency to self-destruction," he wrote. "Yes, it has long been inside me, and I know it as a sick man comes to understand his own illness."[26] He began to drink.

Her encounter with Lúcio Cardoso caused Clarice a fever as intense as her discovery of Hermann Hesse had provoked a few years earlier. Under his influence, and with the new world opened to her by the university and by her employment as a journalist, she began to write and publish prolifically.

Her longest and most ambitious piece of early writing is an enigmatic novella from October 1941, by which time reality had sunk in and she had abandoned her former hope of "rescuing" Lúcio.[27] "Obsession" introduces a dark character, Daniel, who will reappear at length in her second novel, *The Chandelier*, and who is almost certainly Lúcio Cardoso, the guide through occult realms.

Clarice tells the story as conventionally as her protagonist, Cristina, lives. One sees the young writer grasping at fictional devices, still unsure of her narrative footing. Unlike most of her writing, "Obsession" also has a clear traditional plot. "I must tell a bit about myself before I met Daniel," she writes with uncharacteristic explicitness. "I was always calm and never showed any sign of possessing the elements that Daniel developed in me."[28]

Cristina had wanted only to "marry, have children, and, finally, be happy." She weds the dull Jaime and lives in a world where "the people around me move peacefully, their foreheads smooth and free of worries, in a circle where habit had long since opened clear paths, in which facts were reasonably explained by visible causes, and the most extraordinary were attributed, not out of mysticism but out of convention, to God."[29]

Perhaps her disappointed love for Lúcio led Clarice to the skepticism about marriage that returns again and again in her work. In any case, Clarice mocks Cristina's smug, safe world, which is rocked by a nearly fatal bout with typhoid fever, the same disease that nearly killed Pedro Lispector in Bessarabia. After she recovers, the family sends her to the better air of Belo Horizonte, the capital of Minas Gerais, Lúcio Cardoso's native province, and places her in a boardinghouse. Free of the cozy certainties of her home, she finds herself "suddenly thrown into a liberty I had not requested and did not know how to use."[30]

At this point in the story, Cristina, like her author, fumbles back to narrative convention. "But I have to start from the beginning, place a little order in this narrative of mine," she stammers, her disorder provoked by a mysterious figure who is also staying in the boardinghouse. She overhears him saying unconventional, disturbing things. "Daniel was the danger," she realizes. "What interests me more than anything else," Daniel says, "is feeling, accumulating desires, filling myself with myself. Accomplishment opens me, empties me, satisfies me." She recognizes in him "the destiny of the wanderers of the earth, of those who no longer measure their actions as Good and Bad."[31]

This amorality will mark many of Clarice's characters. Her recognition of the random nature of the universe, her knowledge that hers was not a world in which "facts were reasonably explained by visible causes," had always been present to her. What, for example, were the "reasonable explanations" for the tragedy of her mother? But for Cristina it is a revelation: Daniel "awakens" her, not least to her animal nature ("my addled eyes, attesting to my animal ingenuity") but also to her human possibilities. " 'To reach one's potential,' he said, 'that is the highest and most noble human goal' "—and the state of artistic creation was the greatest available joy.[32]

Cristina, predictably enough, falls madly in love with Daniel, whom she considers a genius, and who awakens in her a fierce latent desire. He warns her, though, that this desire can lead to madness, a "privileged" madness. "Cristina, do you know you're alive?" he badgers her. "Cristina, is it good to be unconscious? Cristina, you don't want anything at all, do you?" He longed to "breathe into my body a bit of venom, of the good and terrible venom."[33]

Cristina's mother becomes ill, and she returns to Jaime. There is no word from Daniel. She grows to fear the madness he has breathed into her and remembers him saying, "You have to know how to feel, but you also have to know how to stop feeling, because if the experience is sublime it can also become dangerous." Madness looms as she attempts to settle back into the bourgeois routine she had left. " 'It's hot, isn't it, Cristina?'—Jaime said. 'I've been trying this stitch for two weeks and I can't do it,' said Mother. Jaime interrupted, stretching. 'Imagine, crocheting in weather like this.' "[34]

Tormented by guilt—"But my god (lowercase, as he had taught me), I am not guilty, I am not guilty"—she nonetheless longs to reencounter the profundity of real life that she had experienced with Daniel, that "feeling that inside my body and spirit there vibrated a deeper and more intense life."[35] She leaves a cruel note for Jaime and returns to Daniel. One day she comes home to find Daniel sullen, and hungry. She discovers that the man who has exercised such fascination over her cannot even prepare his own meals. Her love ferments into contempt, and she returns to her milquetoast husband.

The forty pages of "Obsession" introduce many of the themes Clarice Lispector's subsequent writing would expand. There is an epiphany that shakes up a humdrum life, awakening the protagonist to the possibility of mystical knowledge. There is the condescending view of that conventional, "human" life ("Marry, have children, and, finally, be happy"), coexisting alongside a scared awareness that a full embrace of the irrational, "animal" life involves, and even invites, a descent into madness. "Two souls, alas! inhabit my breast," the Steppenwolf quotes the lament of Faust, the two souls the artist, breathing in the "good and terrible venom," strives to unite, always afraid of casting off the melancholy burden of sanity.

Another theme appears at the end of the story. When Cristina returns to Jaime, she discovers that her absence has killed her mother.

As she was writing her first stories, Clarice also met many of the "introspective" group, who, along with Lúcio Cardoso, gathered at the Bar Recreio in downtown Rio. She had plenty to do as a journalist and a student, and was anyway little given to literary chitchat, but she nonetheless encountered the slightly older writers—Octávio de Faria, Vinicius de Moraes, and Cornélio Penna—interested, like her, in metaphysics, and through the Agência Nacional she met Augusto Frederico Schmidt, whom she was to interview about industrial fibers. The admiration she expressed for his poetry caused them to veer off-topic, and a long friendship began.[36]

The Agência Nacional was a government organ, and the young reporter was dispatched to interview her share of generals and admirals and visiting dignitaries. Yet a skeptical and irreverent personality shines through even those articles most carefully pitched to flatter Getúlio Vargas's regime. A case is the ironically titled "School of Happiness," a puff piece about Mrs. Darcy Vargas's new school for five thousand girls, an island of industry and learning based on Father Edward Flanagan's Boys Town in Nebraska. "They can hardly suspect, Darcy Vargas's girls, that they are beginning life surrounded by that rarest of sentiments: that of pure goodness, which asks nothing for itself, wanting only to give," wrote Clarice with a straight face. "The young women will learn that they have the solemn duty to be happy."[37]

Writing only a few months after her father's untimely death, during a hopeless love affair with a man who could not love her as she desired, Clarice Lispector was understandably skeptical about the ability of an institution to teach happiness—and indeed about the very possibility of happiness. Despite her recent successes and the relish with which she pursued her writing and journalism, she was skeptical about other ideas, too.

In *A Época*, the law students' magazine, she published a short essay titled "Observations on the Right to Punish" in August 1941. Her interest in crime and punishment, related of course to the notions of guilt and sin that had always preoccupied her, had brought her to law school in the first place. "There is no right to punish. There is only the power to punish," she wrote. "A man is punished for his crime because the State is stronger than he; the great crime of War is not punished, because beyond the individual there is mankind, and beyond mankind there is nothing else at all."[38]

This is an extravagant declaration. On a practical, political level, it is an assertion, in a dictatorship, of the fundamental illegitimacy of any state. More fascinatingly, it is an assertion of atheism from one who would become famous as a mystic. By the time she wrote that sentence, Clarice Lispector had already shown the interest in the inner life that had drawn her to Lúcio Cardoso, Augusto Frederico Schmidt, and other Catholic writers. She had been raised by a man whose main talent, she said, was for "spiritual things." As her early writing suggests, and the whole of her life would prove, her interests were spiritual rather than material. Whatever material or ideological strains her early writing betrays—the rather strident feminism, for example—would soon disappear.

Because the story of her life, as a writer and a mystic, is in great part a story of her movement *toward* God, this initial rejection must be seen as a starting point. It was, in fact, nothing more than what she had already felt when her mother died: "I see myself small, weak, and helpless in the enormous house of my childhood, where nobody could help me and where I felt abandoned by God."[39] It is also the point that separates her from her Catholic colleagues. Her rejection of God is quite different from the loss of faith that Christian writers record. Their wavering faith can be ascribed to personal circumstances, interior circumstances; Lúcio Cardoso's homosexuality, for example, was an internal characteristic that placed him apart from the teachings of the Church. The impulses that force a Jewish mystic into himself come from outside: the persecution, exile, and segregation that have haunted so many Jewish generations. "The spiritual experience of the mystics was almost inextricably intertwined with the historical experience of the Jewish people," Gershom Scholem has noted. Certainly, as a general rule, mystical revolutions follow upheaval: "Mysticism as a historical phenomenon is a product of crises."[40]

Seeing her parents' suffering, exile, and ungratified toils, it was easy enough for Clarice Lispector to reject God, or, at the very most, to feel rejected by the God who had withdrawn from her family and her people. "I am Jewish, you know," she said in a rare declaration. "But I don't believe this nonsense about the Jews being God's chosen people. That's ridiculous. The Germans ought to be because they did what they did. How did being chosen ever help the Jews?"[41]

It is her only known reference to the Holocaust, and it is typically indirect ("they did what they did"). References to the trauma her family experienced in the Ukraine are equally infrequent and elliptical. Yet the harrowing historical circumstances of her early life are the fundamental point that allies her to the Jewish mystics who preceded her. Like her, they would transform their real traumas into complex allegories that only rarely alluded to the historical circumstances that produced them.

In Jewish history, in its cycles of catastrophes followed by mystical revivals, God must repeatedly retreat in order for the Jews to blaze different paths to him.[42] The retreat is terrible. Many will not survive it, including those it does not physically destroy. This is the case of Elisa Lispector, her childhood robbed and her adult life one of pain and solitude.

But a few religious and artistic geniuses transfigure the horror of their people's history into their own individual creation. And when they do, because of the tragic consistency of the Jewish historical experience, they will find themselves re-creating the entire ethical and spiritual structure of Judaism. God had to withdraw from Clarice Lispector to allow her to begin her own work of creation.

In August 1941, a year after her father's death, when she declared that "beyond mankind there is nothing else at all," God had, once again, turned his face from his chosen people. Hitler was advancing unimpeded across Europe. The girl who had survived one genocide now looked helplessly on as another unfolded.

"In the great cataclysm now stirring the Jewish people more deeply than in the entire history of Exile... the story [of Jewish mysticism] is not ended, it has not yet become history, and the secret life it holds can break out tomorrow in you or in me," Gershom Scholem wrote in May 1941. "Under what aspects this invisible stream of Jewish mysticism will again come to the surface we cannot tell."[43]

Two months later Clarice Lispector confessed to Lúcio Cardoso her "great desire": "To prove to myself and others that I am more than just a woman. I know you don't believe it. But I didn't believe it either, judging by what I've done up to now. And I'm nothing more than potential—I feel a fresh spring within me but cannot locate its source."[44]

When, after her father's death, Clarice Lispector drifted away from institutional Judaism, she was no more than reflecting the slow but inevitable dissolution of the religion practiced in places such as Chechelnik. That Eastern European world, where the majority of the world's Jews had lived at the beginning of the twentieth century, was disintegrating, and in the next couple of years would be irremediably destroyed.

Even without the Holocaust, the traditional society would not have survived. It had already been bled by mass emigration; in Brazil, as in all the countries where the emigrants settled, the economic and social barriers to advancement were nothing like they had been in the Russian Empire. By the second generation, the immigrant Jews entered the middle class everywhere. In those countries, as in the European homeland itself, modern people no longer found the old beliefs adequate. The greatest mass movement in recent Jewish history was Zionism, which, though it heralded the return of the children of Israel to their ancestral home, was a secular nationalist movement surprisingly unconnected to the ancient tradition of Jewish millenarianism.

The loss of the old universe did not go unmourned, nor was it unanimously greeted as an emancipation. It is perhaps in Kafka where one feels with the greatest intensity the Jewish despair at the loss of God. Clarice Lispector's renunciation of God, in this context, was no more than a reflection of a lóss that the Jewish world as a whole had experienced. And it was all the more cruelly ironic that they were singled out for persecution just as they had lost their old faith. "They could no longer find any meaning in their suffering, or any guilt," Stefan Zweig wrote. "Those exiled in the middle ages, their ancestors, at least knew why they were suffering: for their faith, for their law. They still had an unbreakable trust in their God.... They lived and suffered in the proud delusion that they were a people chosen by the Creator of the world and of mankind for a special destiny and mission."[45]

But in 1941 that God was dead. The Torah and Talmud were no longer consoling trees of life, and the immense edifice of the cabala, the intricacies of its metaphysics refined and elaborated by centuries of mystical geniuses, lay in ruins. Only the facts of exile and persecution, and the thirst for redemption they engendered, were unchanged. It may have seemed a dead end, the same dead end Kafka confronted. But the combination could present a challenge to a person with an extraordinary spiritual vocation and the linguistic power to express it. After all, the longing for redemption born of hard persecution had shaped the Jewish mind-set for centuries. When Clarice Lispector began to enunciate her own speculations about the divine, she would echo the writings of earlier generations who sought the eternal amid crisis and exile.

12

STRAIGHT FROM THE ZOO

In Clarice Lispector's writings, there are echoes of another great Jewish thinker, another product of exile, who faced the death of God and sought to re-create a moral universe in His absence. Thanks to the recent discovery in Clarice Lispector's library of a French anthology of Spinoza, the connection is not merely speculative, a possible result of a coincidence of historical circumstances. The book comes complete with her annotations and the handwritten date February 14, 1941.[1] Even without this important information, the novel she began in March 1942, *Near to the Wild Heart*, makes it obvious that she had read Spinoza attentively.

"They could ask him to write articles about Spinoza, as long as he didn't have to be a lawyer, watching and dealing with those affrontingly human people, walking by, shamelessly exposing themselves," one long passage begins. (The "he" is the law student Otávio, the future husband of the protagonist, Joana.) He makes annotations:

> The pure scientist stops believing in what he likes, but cannot keep himself from liking what he believes. The need to like: the sign of mankind. —Do not forget: "the intellectual love of God" is the true knowledge and excludes any mysticism or adoration. —Many answers are found in affirmations of Spinoza's. In the idea for example that there can be no thought without extension (aspect of God) and vice-versa, is not the mortality of the soul confirmed? Of course: mortality as a distinct and reasoning soul, clear impossibility of the pure form of St. Thomas's angels. Mortality in relation to the human. Immortality through the transformation in

> nature.—Inside the world there is no room for other creations. There is only the opportunity for reintegration and continuation. Everything that could exist, already does. Nothing else can be created, only revealed.[2]

This passage is noteworthy in many ways. It is not very well digested, first of all: parts are lifted almost verbatim from the notes in the back of her copy of Spinoza ("Inside the world there is no room for other creations. There is only the opportunity for reintegration and continuation. Everything that could exist, already does," for example.) Though it has somehow escaped the attention of her many commentators, it is by far the longest citation to be found in her extensive body of work, which otherwise includes only a handful of quotations, these rarely more than a sentence or two. The rather dry recitation is unusual, a staccato presentation interesting because it also, in a few lines, offers a list of many of the philosophical preoccupations that Clarice, throughout her life, would so vividly animate and illustrate.

The list goes on: "If it is true that the more man evolves, the more he tries to synthesize, abstract, and establish principles and laws for his life, how could God—in any sense of the word, even in that of the conscious God of the religions—how could God lack absolute laws for his own perfection?"[3]

Clarice will often mock this "conscious God of the religions," but only because she so desperately longed for the same perfection and assurance that Spinoza, too, had rejected as impossible.

> A God possessed of free will is lesser than a God with a single law. In the same way that a concept is all the more true when it need not transform itself when faced with every individual case. God's perfection is proven more by the impossibility of miracles than by their possibility. For the humanized God of the religions, to perform miracles is to commit an injustice—at the same time thousands of other people require the same miracle—or to recognize a mistake and correct it—which, more than an act of goodness or a "proof of character," means having made a mistake in the first place.—Neither comprehension nor will belong to the nature of God, Spinoza says. That makes me happier, and leaves me freer. Because the idea of a conscious God is horribly unsatisfying.[4]

Perhaps Clarice was thinking of her mother as she wrote these lines, remembering her own failure to generate a miracle: the idea that a "conscious God" had saved someone else instead might have been unbearable. An unconscious God would have been a bit more satisfactory, at least on an intellectual level:

God had not, for example, *actively* killed her mother. She concludes with one of Spinoza's most famous sentences, one for which *Near to the Wild Heart*, with its emphasis on the wild energy pulsing through the universe, might have stood as an extended poetic metaphor: "He would garnish the top of the study with a literal translation from Spinoza: 'Bodies are distinguished from one another in respect of motion and rest, quickness and slowness, and not in respect of substance.' "[5]

Clarice's philosophical involvement with Spinoza was not a matter of copying down phrases and then forgetting them. His thoughts would be incorporated into her own, and though she would never quote from him at such length, Spinozistic phrases recur throughout her work. *The Chandelier*, her second novel, also contains a near-quote from Spinoza: "In order to be born, things must have life, since birth is a movement—if we say that the movement is only necessary for the thing giving birth, a thing cannot give birth to something outside its own nature and therefore always gives birth to something of its own species and so it is with movements as well."[6] In her third novel, *The Besieged City*, we find the line "Error was impossible—everything that existed was perfect—things only begin to exist once they are perfect."[7] She repeated this two decades later, in *An Apprenticeship or the Book of Pleasures*: "Everything that existed was of a great perfection."[8]

These concepts may seem abstruse, but Clarice returned to her paperback Spinoza many times in the following years. Was it simply for these ideas, or was it for a moral and philosophical model? As portrayed by Arnold Zweig, who wrote the book's long introduction and whose more famous brother Stefan had killed himself near Rio only a month before Clarice began writing *Near to the Wild Heart*, Spinoza was a secular saint. His exhortations to remain true to one's own nature would have resounded with Clarice; his "grandiose pantheism had exercised a particular influence upon poets and poetic natures, and on those of Faustian temperaments."[9]

Her parents were dead, and in Rio de Janeiro there was no body concerned, as in Spinoza's Amsterdam, with enforcing orthodoxy. She did not have to break with any traditional strictures, as Spinoza had. Yet they shared certain important biographical similarities. Spinoza's parents were Jewish exiles from Portugal who had arrived in Amsterdam ten years before he was born. He lost his mother when he was six and would spend his whole life mourning her. (Arnold Zweig attributed Spinoza's famous formula "Deus sive natura"—God: that is to say, nature—to this early loss. The idea "magically and mystically elevates to a principle of the world this alliance and this marriage, whose destruction had been the dark star of his childhood.")[10] They both lost their fathers when they were twenty, and both left organized Judaism after their father's death. They were both thwarted in their first love, Clarice for Lúcio and Spinoza for his teacher's daughter. And both impressed others as being "aristocratic" and, tellingly, "foreign."

Perhaps these similarities drew Clarice close to the great philosopher, in whom she found a confirmation of her own rejection of "the humanized God of the religions," that conscious God who actively meddles in human affairs. It must have come as a relief to her, whose life had made her well aware of the absurdity of relying on miracles, or any other interventions. "The idea of a conscious God is horribly unsatisfying," she wrote.[11]

What was real was the divine eminence that manifested itself in the amoral animal nature, the "wild heart" that animated the universe. For Spinoza as for Clarice Lispector, fidelity to this divine inner nature was the noblest goal of all.

"I meant to cry on the journey, because I always get nostalgic for myself. But luckily I'm a good healthy animal and slept very well, thanks. 'God' calls me to him, when required," Clarice wrote Lúcio Cardoso in July 1941. She was in Belo Horizonte, where Lúcio had spent part of his childhood, and her impressions of the place were not flattering. "The women here are almost all dark and short, with straight hair and listless expressions. Anyway, you almost only see men on the streets. Apparently the women betake themselves to their homes to do their duty, giving the world a dozen kids a year. The people here look at me as if I had come straight from the Zoological Gardens. I agree entirely."[12]

In 1941, her reporting job brought her there and to several other destinations, including to the old hill station of Petrópolis in the mountains above Rio de Janeiro, where Stefan Zweig had arrived in September and would kill himself in February. The city was the resort of the nineteenth-century emperor Dom Pedro II. He escaped the awful heat of the seaside capital in a large pink palace that Getúlio Vargas was busily restoring as the Imperial Museum, sprucing up the temples of previous dynasties having been a hobby of dictators since at least Egyptian times. Clarice was one of the museum's first visitors—the public wouldn't be admitted until 1943—and on May 1, 1941, covering the Labor Day celebrations for the Agência Nacional, she got to meet Getúlio Vargas himself.

Throughout the year, she published her writing, not only in the provincial organs that ran the Agência Nacional's stories but also in the capital's literary magazines, where her stories, and at least one poem, appeared.[13] "There was a paper, *Dom Casmurro,*" she remembered. "I took some...some things over there. Just like that, without knowing anyone....They loved it, they thought I was gorgeous! They said I had the prettiest voice in the world! And they published it. And they didn't pay. Of course! Of course!"[14]

The pages of *Dom Casmurro* give an idea of the interests of Rio de Janeiro's lettered classes at that time. The paper was serious but playful—the women's pages carried articles about how to whiten one's teeth—and reflects the very serious position literature still enjoyed in Brazilian society. There are articles on the origins of Nietzsche, the death of Christ, the animal in painting, Peruvian popular poetry, "Our Mother, Greece," and "Let's talk about Freud." There are articles of local interest, about the sermons of Padre Antônio Vieira, the novels of Eça de Queiroz, the baroque churches of Minas Gerais, and "The Academy and the Brazilian Language."

It is a wide range, but despite its catholicity of interest, there is no mention of politics, and the only cause the paper espoused, amid a world war, was a campaign, week after week, to raise money to provide the poet Castro Alves with a properly glorious tomb. In an atmosphere of censorship and Brazilian neutrality, the paper expressed its political orientation obliquely, with a heavy emphasis on French culture ("Vigée Le Brun," "Recalling Pierre Loti"), including articles published in French. This was the culture Brazilians had traditionally admired and, as such, would have raised few eyebrows among the censors. With Getúlio Vargas still flirting with both sides, that was the best the editors of *Dom Casmurro* could do.

By July 1941, when she wrote Lúcio Cardoso from Belo Horizonte, Clarice had abandoned her attempt to "save" him from his homosexuality. "PS," she wrote at the end, hinting at a more compromising earlier communication, "you don't have to 'tear up' *this* letter." The twin disasters of disappointment in love and losing her father, combined with the pressures of school and her demanding job, had taken a toll. For the first time in her life she was hospitalized for depression, prescribed "sleep therapy," in which drugs induced her to sleep for most of a week.[15] The practice was thought to help the body recover from stresses both physical and psychological. By the end of the year, she picked up enough to begin a new romance with a law school colleague, Maury Gurgel Valente.

Maury's past was as colorful, if not as terrible, as hers. His mother, Maria José Ferreira de Souza, known as Zuza, was the daughter of a rubber baron from the Amazonian state of Pará. Like many others, and indeed like the entire

Amazonian economy, he was ruined when Brazil lost its monopoly on rubber, unable to compete with slave labor in the Belgian Congo and the plantations the British began with seeds smuggled out of Brazil. After the dramatic theft of the seeds, and the even more dramatic attempts of botanists at Kew Gardens in London to discover how they could be transplanted, Britain's tropical colonies, especially Malaya, began growing rubber in great quantities. By World War I, the economy of northern Brazil was a shambles, leaving such famous monuments as the sumptuous opera house, the Teatro Amazonas, in the ephemeral boomtown of Manaus.

Once the seeds started sprouting in Malaya, Zuza had to earn a living. The daughter of a rich businessman, she had lived in France for five years and in England for another five, and the skills she learned there could be parlayed into a decent living as a language teacher back in Brazil. These early travels seem to have instilled a diplomatic vocation in the family: her brother, Glauco Ferreira de Souza, died as Brazilian ambassador to La Paz, and all three of her sons—Mozart Jr., born in 1917; Maury, born in 1921; and Murillo, born in 1925—became ambassadors.

Zuza's husband, Mozart Gurgel Valente, was a dentist from a family of provincial gentry in Aracati, in the northeastern state of Ceará. Their sons were born in Rio de Janeiro, but the boys grew up in a place remote and exotic even by Amazonian standards: the territory (now state) of Acre, on the Bolivian border. Dr. Mozart went there to try to rescue one of Zuza's father's last remaining rubber plantations, spending years laboring in vain. Eventually, they returned to Zuza's hometown of Belém do Pará, an important city at the mouth of the Amazon.

Maury started law school in 1938, and by the end of 1941 he and Clarice were a couple. She departed for a couple of weeks' sojourn at a secluded resort in the state of Rio de Janeiro in January 1942, and they wrote each other almost every day. His letters to her reveal a combination of timidity and admiration in a sensitive young man fascinated by literature even as he prepared for a life in the bureaucracy. "I end letters like this," he wrote her, " 'I have the honor to repeat to Your Excellency the protests of my highest esteem and most distinct consideration.' What a crock," he lamented. "Only one thing would do me good right now. To fall asleep with my head on your lap, while you whispered sweet tasty nothings to help me forget the rottenness of the world."[16]

His love for his fellow law student is tempered by the insecurity her superior intelligence provokes. He is unsure about his writing: "Warning to readers: Mortal danger—This letter is full of bad literature," he writes in one letter.[17] A few days later he adds, "I request 'Teach' to underline all the childish expressions in my letters, so I can correct them."[18]

She, in return, writes tenderly: "How are you, sweetheart? How are your hands?"[19] And again: "Curious little rat, your hands in mine are always a nice dose of humanity, don't you think?"[20] At the same time, she inevitably engages in philosophical speculations of the kind that intimidate her adoring young boyfriend: "Why not give oneself over to the world, even without understanding it? It is absurd to seek an individual solution. That is spread out among the centuries, all mankind, all nature. And even your greatest idol in literature or science did nothing more than blindly add another element to the problem. Another thing: what would you, *you individually*, do if not for the evil in the world? Its absence would be the ideal for all mankind, as a whole. For a single person, it wouldn't be enough."[21]

He tries to bring her back down to earth, back down to his humble level. "I have to confess," he writes her after reading her last letter, "that as I read it, I got smaller and smaller. . . . That letter wasn't for me, it was a pamphlet directed to all HUMANITY. . . . I'm much simper than that. My wretched little worrying has nothing to do with the great problems. Oh! Goddess Clarice! . . . Don't terrorize me with your anti-aircraft guns—I fly too close to the ground—all you have to do is reach out your hand to grab me."[22]

"I laughed a lot when I read your letter," she responded. "I could have expected an answer like that. But the truth is: I wasn't trying to make myself huge or intelligent." She alluded to a particularly negative description of herself: "When I told you I was egocentric, I wasn't just saying so. I really am. And lots of other, even worse, things. . . . I was never very open or sweet. I'm not sure if certain circumstances in my life made me that way, clumsy when it comes to confessions. And proud (why, my God? . . . I'm laughing, don't be scared—it's nothing tragic)."[23]

She recalled the source of her annoyance to Tania: "There was a fight between us because he interpreted a letter I sent him as literary. You know that's the thing that can offend me the most. I want a regular life and that's why I try to separate it from literature." Her letter seemed spontaneous and natural to her, and when Maury acted overwhelmed, she even went so far as to write breaking off their relationship.[24]

But after the disappointment with Lúcio, who was older, sexually unattainable, and an established writer, she must have welcomed the frantic attentions of Maury, younger, less intellectual, and madly in love with her. Yet she also seems to have kept him at a certain distance. "You don't have any other objections to me, besides the ones that just arrived all typed up?" the besotted boy asked anxiously a few days later. "I don't think you do, because if you did you would tell me, right?... Can I still call you my girlfriend?"[25]

She must have given him the green light, because the romance continued. Another obstacle did not depend on either of them. In August 1940, Maury passed the foreign service examination and entered the diplomatic corps, his official inauguration pending his graduation from university. At the time, Brazilian diplomats were not allowed to marry foreigners, and Clarice Lispector was still a foreigner. She could not request Brazilian nationality until her twenty-first birthday, December 10, 1941.

Soon thereafter, with the help of her old family friend Samuel Malamud, a native of Podolia who was now a lawyer, she started preparing the paperwork. Because of the war and her desire to marry, there was some urgency to her request, as her surviving letters to Getúlio Vargas demonstrate. She wrote the president, and then waited almost half a year before addressing him again. This step was necessary because Vargas—in a fashion reminiscent of Nicholas II, who, as his enormous empire crumbled, busily devoted his personal attention to each and every individual who petitioned to change his name—wondered in writing why it had taken the applicant so long to apply for naturalization. "As soon as I reached my majority and, with it, acquired the right to apply [for Brazilian nationality] I hastened to do so immediately, and it took me only three months to finalize a process that almost always requires a year of effort," she wrote the "Chief of the Nation," of whose "proverbial magnanimity" she professed herself a "sincere admirer."[26]

In her first letter to him she described herself as

> a twenty-one-year-old Russian who has been in Brazil for twenty one years minus a few months. Who does not know a single word of Russian but who thinks, speaks, writes, and acts in Portuguese, making of this language her profession, and basing upon it all her plans for the near and distant future. Who has neither father nor mother—the former, like the sisters of the undersigned, a naturalized Brazilian—and who for that reason feels in no way connected to the country she came from, not even through the stories she has heard about it. Who, if she was forced to return to Russia, would feel irredeemably foreign there, without a friend, without a profession, without a hope.[27]

She does not linger on "the stories she has heard about it," which presumably would not have fortified her desire to return; and when Malamud suggested she would not be granted naturalization, his client burst into tears, before he assured her he was joking.[28] In her letter to the president, she regretted that her youth had prevented her from having lent any great services to the nation, but she pointed out that through her work in the official press she had aided "in the distribution and propaganda of Your Excellency's government."[29]

Her petition was supported by the man who was now her boss, André Carrazzoni, director of the newspaper *A Noite*. "Clarice Lispector is a smart girl, an excellent reporter, and, in contrast to almost all women, actually knows how to write," he assured a friend in the Ministry of Justice.[30]

These appeals had their desired effect, and on January 12, 1943, Clarice Lispector was naturalized. Eleven days later, she married Maury Gurgel Valente.

In a notebook recording conversations with her young son Pedro, Clarice remembered him asking, "The first time you saw my father (he corrected himself and said) the first time you saw Maury, was he a stranger to you?" Clarice answered, "He was." Pedro persisted: "But you wanted to marry that stranger?" She said she did. Her son retorted, "Did you marry the person you wanted?"[31]

She left the question unanswered, at least in the version she recorded, which begs the question of how she felt about the marriage. There was her love for Lúcio Cardoso, which would last the rest of their lives, but she knew a sexual relationship with him was not in the cards. Her letters from early 1941 make it clear that she felt very affectionately toward Maury, and he was certainly in love with her.

But not everyone thought the marriage was a good idea. "Elisa was dead-set against it, because he was a goy," said Tania, who used legalistic arguments to bring her older sister around. "I said that Father was the only one who could forbid it, and he was no longer with us. Besides, Clarice was now an adult and could decide for herself." Her father, Tania thought, would have opposed the match, at least at first. But if he had been convinced that marrying Maury was what Clarice really wanted, he would have come around. Still, other family members were also uncomfortable about the match. Bertha Lispector Cohen asked how her cousin felt about marrying a Catholic. "I don't see a solution for the Jewish question," Clarice replied, ambiguously as usual. Bertha's brother Samuel said the resistance to her marrying a non-Jew came more from fear than from ethnic or religious pride.[32] The Jews did not trust the goyim, and in 1943, they had good reason.

At the time, it was extremely rare, indeed almost unheard of, for a Jewish girl in Brazil to marry outside the faith. Far more than lengthy citations from Spinoza, the marriage was a declaration of her independence from the community that raised her. Perhaps the sisters feared the family's disapproval, which is why few family members were present at the civil ceremony. Maury's parents came, but the Wainstok family, then living in Niterói, across the bay from Rio de Janeiro, learned about the wedding only when Elisa and Tania made a trip across to tell them. The witnesses were not relatives but the bride and groom's bosses: André Carrazzoni, the director of *A Noite*, who had helped Clarice with her naturalization, and Dora Alencar de Vasconcellos, one of the earliest women to enter the foreign service, whom Clarice would reencounter in the United States many years later.

But the main skepticism about the marriage was Clarice's own. The doubts that nagged her had little or nothing to do with questions about Maury or about marrying outside of her own community. They were about marriage itself. It is, in fact, remarkable how many of her early stories, many written before she met Maury, express this skepticism. In "Obsession" there is the dismissive description of the unimaginative Cristina's future plans ("Marry, have children, and, finally, be happy"), in "Jimmy and I" the fear of how marriage limited women ("Mother [had] her own ideas about the freedom and equality of women. But along came Daddy, very serious and tall, who also had his own ideas, about... the freedom and equality of women").[33] In "The Escape," a story from 1940, a housewife flees her home: "She had been married for twelve years and three hours of freedom had almost entirely restored her to herself."[34] But it is impossible to pry oneself free of the marriage trap. Like Cristina in "Obsession," who after her thrilling experiences with Daniel finally returns to her dullard husband, Jaime, the woman in "The Escape," without the money to support an independent life, returns home, defeated, as well.

In "Gertrude Asks for Advice," a teenage girl seeks a doctor's help with her screaming existential doubts: "I came to ask what to do with myself," as she puts it. More than anything else—already with a sense, her author's as well, that she had a genial vocation and destiny—she wants the world to "finally see that she was someone, someone extraordinary, someone misunderstood!" Faced with this explosion of vitality, the doctor simply says, "You'll get over it. You don't need to work or do anything extraordinary. If you want—he was going to use his old ruse and he smiled—if you want, you should find a boyfriend."[35]

13

HURRICANE CLARICE

Much of *Near to the Wild Heart*, the novel Clarice wrote from March to November 1942, the year preceding her marriage, is a meditation on its impossibility. "The Marriage," the opening chapter of the second part of the book, starts with Joana, the wild heroine, daydreaming. She knows her fantasy, about standing atop a staircase, is nonsense—"Absurd. So it was a lie"—but she wants to keep on dreaming nonetheless, and when she is interrupted by her husband she struggles to recapture it. "She stopped moving for a moment and only her eyes were batting quickly, searching for the sensation. Oh yes," Joana dreams, before the dream vanishes and she is back to her life with Otávio, a mediocre intellectual who is writing a book on common law.[1]

"What an animal," she thinks, looking at Otávio—the word, as always in Clarice, ambiguous—and the force of her thought jolts him. "He interrupted his reading and looked at her terrified, as if she had thrown something at him." Joana, however, is satisfied that she has stirred him to feel something, and she realizes that she hates him. "It was his fault, she thought coldly, waiting for another wave of anger. It was his fault, it was his fault. His presence, and more than his presence: the knowledge that he existed left her without freedom," Joana thinks. Her rage crests and then passes, but "she thinks: even so, in spite of death, I will leave him someday."[2]

Joana, elemental, passionate, and cruel ("like the devil," "the snake"), exerts a fascination over Otávio that he himself mistrusts. The first time he sees her, she is stroking the belly of a pregnant dog. "She had a hard and crystalline quality that simultaneously attracted and repulsed him.... Those lines of Joana's, fragile, a sketch, were uncomfortable. Full of feeling, with open eyes, incandescent.

She wasn't overly pretty or refined. Even her sensuality must have been different from his, excessively luminous," he thinks. He leaves his childhood love, Lídia, for Joana, who is haunted by a "fear of not loving, worse than the fear of not being loved."[3]

Joana's marriage to Otávio founders, and he returns to Lídia, who gets pregnant. Joana invites Lídia over for what the pregnant woman expects will be an animated discussion, only to find that Joana offers no resistance.

"Would you like to be married—really married—to him?" Joana asked.

Lídia looked at her quickly, trying to know if there were any sarcasm in the question:

"I would."

"Why?" Joana was surprised. "Don't you see you don't gain anything by that? You already have everything you'd have in a marriage." —Lídia blushed, but I have no malice, ugly and clean woman. "I bet you've spent your whole life wanting to get married."

Lídia made a movement of revolt: she was being touched right on her wound, coldly.

"Yes. Every woman . . ."—she concurred.

"Not me. I didn't plan to marry. The funny thing is that I'm still sure I didn't get married. . . . I thought more or less: that marriage is the end, after I got married nothing else could happen to me. Imagine: always having someone next to you, never to be alone—My God!—not to be alone with yourself, never, never. And to be a married woman, I mean, a person with a defined destiny. From that point on all you can do is wait for death. I thought: you don't even have the freedom to be unhappy because you'd be dragging someone else down with you. There's always someone watching, looking you over, watching your every move. And even the fatigue of life has a certain beauty when borne alone and desperately—I thought. But together, eating every day the same saltless bread, watching one's own defeat in the defeat of the other. . . . Not to mention the weight of the habits reflected in the habits of the other, the weight of the shared bed, the shared table, the shared life, preparing and threatening the shared death. I always said: never."

"Why did you get married?" Lídia asked.

"I don't know. I just know that 'I don't know' isn't just my ignorance in relationship to this particular case, but regards the basis of things.—I'm avoiding the question, soon she'll look at me in that way I'm already familiar with.—I must have gotten married because I wanted to get married.

> Because Otávio wanted to marry me. That's it, that's it: I've got it: instead of asking to live with me without getting married, he suggested something else. It's all the same, anyway. And I was giddy, Otávio's good looking, right? I didn't remember anything else.—Pause.—How do you want him: with your body?"[4]

Joana tells Lídia, "Stay with Otávio. Have your baby, be happy, and leave me alone."[5] In a dreamlike sequence that recalls Andrey Bely or Kafka—or, even more strikingly, the scenes from *Steppenwolf* that find Harry Haller wandering the streets, walking into shady doors and striking up hazy conversations with vague and formless people—a featureless man follows Joana through the streets. She goes with him to his house, where he lives with another woman. She returns a few times, and they presumably have a sexual relationship, though Joana never bothers to ask him his name.

At length Joana makes her unhurried way back to Otávio, and when she arrives she scandalizes him, as usual. This time it isn't so much her wildness, which attracted him away from the placid Lídia in the first place. It is her complete indifference to the rules of conventional behavior, her failure to hold him to a standard she does not so much flout as utterly fails to realize exists. She knew, he learns, and didn't much care about his affair with Lídia.

> What . . . , a shaking, gasping rage thrashed around inside him, so she knew about Lídia, about the baby . . . she knew and she didn't say a word. . . . She betrayed me. . . . —The asphyxiating weight pressed into him ever deeper.—She calmly allowed my infamy . . . she kept on sleeping beside me, putting up with me . . . for how long? Why? but great God why?! . . .
>
> "Wicked."
>
> Joana jumped, rapidly lifted her head.
>
> "Evil."
>
> His voice could barely be contained in his swollen throat, the veins in his neck and forehead throbbed thick, gnarled, in triumph.
>
> "It was your aunt who called you a snake. Snake, indeed. Snake! Snake! Snake!"[6]

What shocks Otávio, and so many other characters in the book—the aunt, for example—is the girl's amorality, her nearness to the "wild heart." Joana is an animal, "natural" rather than human. Over the course of the book Clarice compares her to a snake, a dog, a wildcat, a horse, and a bird. Joana's failure to acknowledge or understand the codes of human behavior jolts people. She is never actively malicious; she simply inhabits another world, beyond good and evil, like a pet uncomprehendingly shitting on the carpet.

"Evil is not living, and that's it. Dying is already something else," Joana says. "Dying is different from good and evil."[7] Joana's young creator, of course, had reason to reject the conventional morality that had proven so futile in her own experience. The lives of her parents put the lie to any notions of a benevolent order, any illusion of a compassionate personal god who would reward the good and punish the bad.

Yet from her infancy she had been intimately acquainted with the reality of evil. Aware of what happened to her raped mother, her murdered grandfather, and her ruined father, amid the greatest disaster in the history of her people's long history, how could she proclaim that evil was nothing more than "not living"? It is easy to understand why Clarice, and Joana, would be indifferent or rebellious. But this pure rejection of morality, which includes a rejection of the notion of evil itself, begs other questions.

Here we see the unmistakable imprint of Spinoza, who equates Nature with God and both with an absence of good and evil. "All things which are in Nature, are either things or actions. Now good and evil are neither things nor actions. Therefore good and evil do not exist in Nature," he wrote.[8] As a child of Nature, Joana is neither good nor evil, and does not even seem aware of these categories. Like Joana, Nature has "positive" attributes, freedom, for instance, alongside the "negative": Joana is violent, thieving, aggressive.

A Spinozistic conception of Nature implies that the same rules that apply to man apply equally to God, who is no longer a moral being, bound by notions of good and evil, meddling in human affairs, rewarding and punishing, but a philosophical category equivalent to Nature. This is no longer "the humanized God of the religions," which Spinoza also calls "superstition" and "inadequate ideas," and which would have triumphed but for "mathematics which is concerned not with ends, but only with the essences and properties of figures, [showing] men another standard of truth."[9]

In *Near to the Wild Heart*, Otávio longs for an absurdly humanized god: "To kneel down before God and ask. For what? Absolution. Such a big word, so full of meaning. He wasn't guilty—or was he? of what?—he knew he was, yet he continued with the thought—he wasn't guilty, but how he would love to be absolved. Upon his forehead the large fat fingers of God, blessing him like a good father, a father made of earth and world, containing everything,

everything, without failing to possess so much as a particle that could later tell him: yes, but I didn't pardon you!"[10]

In a long prayer-like rumination that is the novel's climactic passage, there is no longer any question of begging favors from the god of the large fat fingers. Instead Joana pushes her Spinozistic conception further. Just as there is no meaningful separation between man and animal, between Joana and the cat or the snake, neither man nor animal is separate from God, the single, infinite, and eternal "one substance" that is synonymous with Nature: one substance in constant transition, linked in an infinite chain of cause and effect.

The idea is the foundation of Spinoza's thought, and in the ecstatic passage that closes Clarice Lispector's book it recurs clearly as the narration shifts, almost imperceptibly, from Joana's third person into the author's first.

> What rose within her was not courage, she was substance alone, less than human, how could she be a hero and want to conquer things? She wasn't a woman, she existed and what she had inside her were movements lifting her always in transition. Perhaps she had once modified with her wild strength the air around her and no one would ever notice, perhaps she had invented new matter with her breath and didn't know it, only felt something that her little woman's head could never understand. Throngs of warm thoughts burst out and scattered through her frightened body and what mattered about them was that they concealed a vital impulse, what mattered about them is that in the exact instant of their birth there was the blind and real substance creating itself, lifting itself, straining like an air bubble from beneath the water's surface, almost breaking through... She noticed that she had not yet fallen asleep, she thought she would still have to burst into flames. That it would end at once the long gestation of childhood and from her painful immaturity her own being would explode, finally finally free! No, no, there is no God, I want to be alone. And a day will come, yes, a day will come in me the capacity as red and affirmative as it is clear and smooth, one day whatever I do is blindly safely unconsciously, walking over myself, on my truth, as completely immersed in whatever I do that I shall not be able to speak, and especially a day will come in which all my movement will be creation, birth, I will break all of the nos that exist inside me, I shall prove to myself that there is nothing to fear, that whatever I am will always be wherever there is a woman who shares my origins, I will erect inside me what I am one day, with one gesture my waves will rise up powerful, pure water drowning doubt, conscience, I shall be strong as the soul of an animal and when I speak they will be words not thought out

> and slow, not lightly felt, not full of human will, not the past corroding the future,! whatever I say shall resound fatal and entire! there will be no space inside me for me to know that time, men, dimensions, exist, there will be no space inside me to so much as notice that I will be creating instant by instant, no instant by instant: always molten, because then I shall live, only then shall I live more fully than in childhood, I shall be as brutal and misshapen as a stone, I shall be light and vague as something felt and not understand, I shall surpass myself in waves, ah, God, and may everything come and fall upon me, even the incomprehension of myself in certain blank moments because all I need to do is fulfill myself and then nothing can block my path to death-without-fear, from any struggle or rest I shall rise up strong and beautiful as a young horse.[11]

If, like Joana, the author of *Near to the Wild Heart* feared that "after I got married nothing else could happen to me," she was mistaken. The book, published in mid-December 1943, caused a furor.

When Clarice began writing it, in March 1942, she was still in law school and still working as a journalist. In February, she had transferred to the newspaper *A Noite*, once one of the glories of Brazilian journalism. Its newsroom shared a floor with *Vamos Lêr!* The job was less a new one than it was an extension of her previous posting, because like the Agência Nacional (and, for that matter, *Vamos Lêr!*), *A Noite* was now a middling government organ, aiding, as Clarice put it in her petition for naturalization, "in the distribution and propaganda of Your Excellency's government."[12]

Some of her colleagues made the move with her. Francisco de Assis Barbosa was one, and she turned to him for help with the novel she had begun writing. "Groping in the darkness," she pieced the book together by jotting down her ideas in a notebook whenever they occurred to her.[13] To concentrate, she quit the tiny maid's room in the apartment she shared with her sisters and brother-in-law and spent a month in a nearby boardinghouse, where she worked intensely. At length the book took shape, but she feared it was more a pile of notes than a full-fledged novel.[14] Lúcio Cardoso assured her that the fragments were a book in themselves. Barbosa read the originals chapter by chapter, but Clarice rejected his occasional suggestions with characteristic vividness: "When I reread what I've written," she told him, "I feel like I'm swallowing my own vomit."[15]

Lúcio suggested a title, borrowed from James Joyce's *Portrait of the Artist as a Young Man*: "He was alone. He was unheeded, happy, and near to the wild heart of life." This became the book's epigraph, which, together with the occasional use of the stream-of-consciousness method, led certain critics to describe the book as Joycean. The comparison annoyed Clarice. "I discovered the quote, the title of the book, and Joyce himself once the book was already finished. I wrote it in eight or nine months, while I was studying, working, and getting engaged—but the book has no direct influence from my studies, my engagement, Joyce, or my work."[16]

Barbosa, who together with Lúcio was one of the book's first readers, recalled his amazement. "As I devoured the chapters the author was typing, it slowly dawned on me that this was an extraordinary literary revelation," he said. "The excitement of Clarice, hurricane Clarice."[17] He steered it to the book-publishing wing of their employer, *A Noite*, where it appeared with a bright pink cover, typical for books by women, in December 1943. It was not a lucrative arrangement for the new author. "I didn't have to pay anything [to have it published], but I didn't make any money either. If there was any profit, they kept it," Clarice said.[18] A thousand copies were printed; in lieu of payment she got to keep a hundred. As soon as the book was ready, she began sending it out to critics.

"Everyone wanted to know who that girl was," the journalist Joel Silveira remembered. "Nobody had any idea. Suddenly everyone was talking about it."[19] The reviews still bear witness to the excitement "hurricane Clarice" unleashed among the Brazilian intelligentsia. For almost a year after publication, articles about the book appeared continuously in every major city in Brazil. Sixteen years later, a journalist wrote, "We have no memory of a more sensational debut, which lifted to such prominence a name that, until shortly before, had been completely unknown."[20]

Clarice Lispector, critics wrote, was "the rarest literary personality in our world of letters"; "something exceptional;" possessed of a "bewildering verbal richness." "The whole book is a miracle of balance, perfectly engineered," combining the "intellectual lucidity of the characters of Dostoevsky with the purity of a child."[21] In October 1944, the book won the prestigious Graça Aranha Prize for the best debut novel of 1943. The prize was a confirmation of what the *Folha Carioca* had discovered earlier that year when it asked its readers to elect the best novel of 1943. *Near to the Wild Heart* won with 457 votes. Considering that only nine hundred copies had actually been put on sale, it was a spectacular number. But it was appropriate to a book *A Manhã* declared to be "the greatest debut novel a woman had written in all of Brazilian literature."[22] Another critic went further: "*Near to the Wild Heart* is the greatest novel a woman has ever written in the Portuguese language."[23]

The author of the last statement, the young poet Lêdo Ivo, sought her out after reading the book. "I met Clarice Lispector at the exact moment she published *Near to the Wild Heart*," he remembered. "The meeting took place in a restaurant in Cinelândia. We had lunch and our conversation strayed from literary matters. . . . The least I can say is that she was stunning. It was autumn, the leaves in the square were falling, and the grayness of the day helped underscore the beauty and luminosity of Clarice Lispector. Alongside the foreign climate was that strange voice, the guttural diction which rings in my ears to this day. I was not yet twenty years old—and, under the impact of her book, felt that I was standing before Virginia Woolf or Rosamund Lehmann."[24]

The book's "strange voice," the "foreign climate" of its unusual language, made the deepest impression on its early readers. It did have certain points of resemblance with earlier Brazilian writing. "Clarice Lispector's work appears in our literary world as the most serious attempt at the introspective novel," wrote the dean of São Paulo critics, Sérgio Milliet. "For the first time, a Brazilian author goes beyond simple approximation in this almost virgin field of our literature; for the first time, an author penetrates the depths of the psychological complexity of the modern soul." But the affinity with other "introspective" writers, even those as close to her as Lúcio Cardoso, was superficial, as another prominent critic realized when writing that Clarice Lispector had "shifted the center of gravity around which the Brazilian novel had been revolving for about twenty years."[25]

It is remarkable how rarely critics compared the work to that of any other Brazilian writer. Instead, they mentioned Joyce, Virginia Woolf, Katherine Mansfield, Dostoevsky, Proust, Gide, and Charles Morgan. This was not simply because the entire question of Brazil, that "certain instinct of nationality" Machado de Assis considered to be the heart of Brazilian literature, is absent from *Near to the Wild Heart*. It was that its language did not sound Brazilian. Lêdo Ivo, remembering Clarice's "strange voice" and "guttural diction," writes, "Clarice Lispector was a foreigner. . . . The foreignness of her prose is one of the most overwhelming facts of our literary history, and even of the history of our language."[26]

Later this language would be naturalized as that of a great Brazilian writer. But for the time being it sounded exotic. "In Brazil we see a certain stylistic conformity," wrote Antonio Candido, criticizing those writers who, whatever their other merits, think "that the generous impulse that inspires them is more important than the roughness of their material."[27] And Sérgio Milliet noted that the wonder of the book was the author's achievement of "the precious and precise harmony between expression and substance."[28]

This is the core of the fascination of *Near to the Wild Heart*, and of Clarice Lispector. It was not a matter of style versus substance, nor a simple question of emphasis, that separated her from those writers for whom "the generous impulse that inspires them is more important than the roughness of their material." It was a fundamentally different conception of art. In that first book, she summed up the impulse Candido and Milliet sensed when she wrote, "Vision consists of capturing the symbol of the thing in the thing itself." The remark was important enough for her to repeat it a hundred pages later—"the symbol of the thing in the thing itself"—and was the heart of her entire artistic project.[29]

But as the phrase suggests, that project was less artistic than spiritual. The possibility of uniting a thing and its symbol, of reconnecting language to reality, and vice versa, is not an intellectual or artistic endeavor. It is instead intimately connected to the sacred realms of sexuality and creation. A word that does not describe a preexisting thing but actually *is* that thing, or a word that *creates* the thing it describes: the search for that mystic word, the "word that has its own light," is the search of a lifetime. That search was an urgent preoccupation of centuries of Jewish mystics. Just as God, in Clarice's writing, is utterly devoid of any moral meaning, so does language signify nothing beyond what it expresses: "the symbol of the thing in the thing itself."

The unprecedented ovation that greeted Clarice Lispector's debut was also the beginning of the legend of Clarice Lispector, a tissue of rumors, mysteries, conjectures, and lies that in the public mind became inseparable from the woman herself. In 1961, a magazine reporter wrote, "There is a great curiosity surrounding the person of Clarice. She seldom appears in literary circles, avoids television programs and autograph sessions, and only a few rare people have been lucky enough to talk to her. 'Clarice Lispector doesn't exist,' some say. 'It's the pseudonym of someone who lives in Europe.' 'She's a beautiful woman,' claim others. 'I don't know her,' says a third. 'But I think she's a man. I've heard he's a diplomat.'"[30]

The beginning of this legend can be dated to Sérgio Milliet's influential essay of January 1944, when he noted the oddness of the author's "strange and even unpleasant name, likely a pseudonym."[31] When she read the article, Clarice wrote Milliet to thank him for his warm review, and to clear up the matter of her name. "I was prepared, I don't know why especially, for an acid beginning and a solitary end. Your words disarmed me. I suddenly even felt uneasy at being so well received. I who didn't expect to be received at all. Besides, the repulsion of others—I thought—would make me harder, more bound to the path of the work I had chosen. PS. The name is really my own."[32]

The legend of Clarice Lispector could henceforth be freely embroidered, in part because she was not around to give it the lie. Less than a month after *Near to the Wild Heart* was published, she left Rio de Janeiro. She would not return for any length of time for almost two decades. The letter she sent Milliet came from Belém do Pará, at the mouth of the Amazon. It was an unusual destination for a diplomat, but Maury was posted there because sleepy Belém, like much of northern Brazil, had suddenly become an essential theater in the war that was consuming the world.

14

TRAMPOLINE TO VICTORY

In 1942, while Clarice Lispector had been applying for Brazilian citizenship, dating Maury, and writing her first novel, Brazilian foreign policy was undergoing a revolution. In some respects, Brazil might have been a logical partner of the Axis. It had a dictatorship inspired by and sympathetic to continental Fascism. It hosted enormous concentrations of German, Italian, and Japanese immigrants. Its leader, Getúlio Vargas, had given every indication that he wished to maintain friendly relations with the Axis, going so far as to send warm birthday greetings to Adolf Hitler. As late as August 1940 he gave a speech aboard the navy ship *Minas Gerais* that contained the ominous line "New forces are rising in the West."[1]

As ever, of course, the "father of the poor" and the "mother of the rich" was playing both sides. A man who had survived so long atop Brazil's byzantine politics was not, at the end of the day, fool enough to bet on the Axis, especially once he noted the immense benefits a closer alliance with the United States would bring. Vargas saw that the country could use U.S. help to solidify its industrial base and to consolidate its political preeminence in South America; with Argentina more or less openly siding with Hitler, an Allied victory would place Brazil in a position of unquestioned dominance. He could use the war to refurbish his military, upgrade his domestic infrastructure, and extend his diplomatic influence.

Brazil had always needed the United States, but now the United States needed Brazil. The Americans would pay handsomely for Brazilian cooperation; Brazil's vast natural resources were critical to the war effort. But its trump card was its location, the "Brazilian bulge" of its northeastern flank, the easternmost part of the Americas. The bulge was a vital link in the chain of communications that ran from Miami through the Caribbean and the Guianas to French West Africa. It was the only secure route across the Atlantic, known in the corny parlance of the day as the "trampoline to victory." Without Brazilian cooperation, it would have been useless.

The air routes were so essential that, while Vargas flirted with the Axis, there was even talk in Washington of forcibly occupying northeastern Brazil, which one American report described as one of the four most strategically valuable places in the world, along with the Suez Canal, Gibraltar, and the Bosporous.[2] That chatter was rendered moot by mid-1941. When both Brazil and the United States were still officially neutral, Vargas allowed Pan-American Airways to begin constructing a giant air base at Natal, just north of Recife, which became the largest air base outside U.S. territory. "Without Natal serving as the 'trampoline to victory,'" one historian has noted, "the Allied supply problems of 1942 and 1943 might have been insurmountable."[3]

In January 1942, just after Pearl Harbor, the American nations gathered for a critical conference in Rio de Janeiro. The scene of the meeting was Tiradentes Palace, where until recently Lourival Fontes, one of the three non-Italians who "really understood" Fascism, had lorded over the Brazilian press. The conference concluded with a diplomatic triumph for Sumner Welles, leader of the U.S. delegation, when every nation in the hemisphere, with the exception of Argentina and Chile, broke off relations with the Axis. The announcement was greeted with jubilation in the streets of Rio de Janeiro.

It was not a Brazilian declaration of war, however, though the Axis treated it as such. This was a mistake, for there were many elements in the army, especially Integralist alumni, who were sympathetic to the Fascists. These included such influential individuals as the minister of war, Pedro Aurélio de Gois Monteiro, and the virulently anti-Semitic chief of the Rio police, Filinto Müller, who was answerable only to Vargas himself. There were also large numbers of Axis nationals in the country, as well as politicians and journalists with Fascist leanings.

All were silenced once Hitler and Mussolini began torpedoing Brazilian ships, killing hundreds. The *Baependi* went down with 250 soldiers and seven officers, along with two artillery batteries and other equipment. Another ship, packed with pilgrims en route to a Eucharistic Congress in São Paulo, was also sunk.[4] In response to the predictably widespread popular revulsion, the government issued a decree on March 11, 1942, enabling the government to make good the damage by seizing the property of Axis nationals.

Pogrom-like scenes, aimed especially at the most visible Axis citizens, the Japanese, soon followed. Where Italians and Germans could often pass as Brazilians, the Japanese could not; and as in the United States, where were interned though no such collective punishment was or Italian Americans, the Japanese were singled out, even Italy and Germany, had not attacked Brazil. And there were lots of Jap Brazilian colony, hundreds of thousands strong, was the largest Japanese community outside Japan. Their businesses were impounded and they were hounded out of coastal areas, where they were suspected of holding secret communication with Axis submarines.[5]

The accusations recall in uncanny detail those leveled against the Jews during World War I: flashing mirrors, mysterious radio signals, unaccounted-for bumps in the night. The Axis languages were banned, an especially devastating handicap for the Japanese. Relatively recent arrivals who often spoke no Portuguese, they found themselves isolated in an environment in which all foreigners were suspect.

Clarice Lispector's old neighborhood in Recife witnessed an odd inversion of the situation in Germany a few years before. As they watched the rise of Vargas and his erstwhile Integralist allies, and as they saw the disaster unfolding in Europe, the Brazilian Jews feared for their safety. Suddenly, however, being Jewish was an advantage; large signs reading FIRMA JUDAICA sprouted in the shop windows along the Rua Nova, where João Pessoa had been shot.

"Who was Axis, who wasn't," one Jewish woman said, recalling those times. "Everyone was a foreigner. They needed to know who was Jewish, who was German, who wasn't a Nazi." A friendly Japanese man who owned a nearby ice-cream parlor had his establishment sacked. "They destroyed everything, even though they liked him, his delicious ice cream. It was a beautiful ice cream parlor, it even had an orchestra."[6]

"The Jews were terrified because they remembered the pogroms in Europe," a witness recalled. "They put themselves in those people's places. It was a kind of empathy. They weren't happy about it, because they knew their families were in Europe."[7] Jewish enterprises that left any doubt about their allegiance were not safe. Messrs. Stillman and Dimenstein, proprietors of a Recife garment manufactory called Fábrica de capas Argentina, learned this in the nick of time. When local toughs approached, they quickly scotched the suspicious suggestion of Argentina in the name of their business.

After a single German submarine torpedoed six Brazilian ships between August 15 and August 19, the pressure to enter the war became irresistible. Getúlio Vargas declared war on August 22, 1942, soon going further than any other Latin American nation (read: Argentina) and volunteering troops, the twenty-five-thousand-man strong Força Expedicionária Brasileira, or FEB, which was to be placed fully under U.S. command.

There was some doubt that Brazil could pull off such a major operation. The nation had not been involved in an international conflict since the Paraguayan War ended seventy-two years before. A wit quipped, "A cobra will smoke before Brazilian troops enter the war." When the FEB disembarked in Italy in 1944, their symbol was a snake with a pipe in its mouth.

Clarice and Maury Gurgel Valente arrived in Belém do Pará on January 20, 1944. The mildewed, languid city at the mouth of the great river is a sensual place, the capital of the state of Pará, as big as Western Europe. Every afternoon, with clock-like regularity, and never for more than an hour, a torrential downpour drenches the city, washing the air of the putrid smells of rotting fish that drift from its enormous riverside market. Belém is isolated from the rest of Brazil geographically and culturally, its population marked more strongly by the Indian than the African.

"One cannot imagine the city of Belém in the rest of Brazil," the great journalist Euclides da Cunha wrote at the beginning of the century.[8] At the time, Belém was in the midst of its fabulous rubber boom, which left it with an imposing collection of fin de siècle buildings, and which had also, for a time, made Maury's grandfather rich, an important rubber grower and proprietor of his own bank. Maury's mother grew up in the city, and he and his brothers had spent part of their own childhood there.

It was a happy time for Clarice and Maury. In the name of the Foreign Ministry, Maury was charged with meeting and greeting the many foreign dignitaries who were passing through on their way to Europe, Africa, and Asia. By January 1944, the "trampoline to victory" was not as essential as it had been before the Allies retook North Africa, but it was still important enough to host a visitor of the caliber of Eleanor Roosevelt, who put in an appearance on March 14. Clarice was on hand to welcome her. "I wore my black dress," she reported to her sisters. "She is extremely nice, very simple, dresses modestly, and much prettier in person than in pictures or films. The next day, she gave a collective interview to the press. I went, sending the report over the phone to *A Noite*, even though I'm not officially employed, because I didn't want to lose the opportunity."[9]

And she got drunk for the first time, at the house of the U.S. consul. "Wow! How nauseating," she wrote Tania. "A hangover just like in the movies. It's good that I drank so I could get rid of anything tempting there might have been in the idea, so praised and sung by the poets.... It was the first time and the last, no doubt about it."[10]

Despite such flashes of excitement, she had little to do for the first time in her life. She was no longer in school and did not have a job. "I'm a bit lost here," she wrote Lúcio Cardoso a couple of weeks after she arrived. "I do almost nothing. I started to look for work and start to torture myself until I decide not to go out: and then the freedom goes nowhere and then I go out again and then I get even more revolted. I've read everything that's fallen into my hands. *Madame Bovary* fell straight into my hands and I reread it. I took advantage of the death scene to cry all the sorrows I've ever had along with those I haven't.—I never had exactly what's known as 'a group' but I've always had a few friends."[11]

The unaccustomed freedom was par for the course for many foreign service wives, whose ranks Clarice now joined. The Foreign Ministry, known as Itamaraty for the neoclassical Itamaraty Palace that housed it, was, and remains, the snootiest club in Brazil. In a country where connections mattered far more than talent, Itamaraty's reputation for strict meritocracy attracted many of Brazil's best minds. And its diplomats' talent in ensuring the nation's security without resort to war gave them a nearly mythical aura of competence in a country that generally had little confidence in its governors.

Needless to say, the foreign service tended to be populated by people with a background more like Maury's than Clarice's. The diplomatic wives were for the most part pretty, well-bred, upper-class women, whose function, in a world of embassies and servants, was largely decorative.[12] Few women had Clarice's advanced education, and even fewer her humble origins. There were no Jews in the foreign service—when Clarice married Maury, there was only one other Jewish spouse in Itamaraty[13]—and dark-skinned Brazilians, the large majority of the country's population, were equally absent. The Foreign Service was meritocratic, but the criteria for admission, an excellent education including knowledge of French and English, ensured that it would be heavily staffed by the old elite families who, as anywhere else, tended to be conservative, religious, and nationalistic.

Indeed, as Hitler marched across Europe, Itamaraty played a leading role in keeping Jews out of Brazil. The racist ideology many diplomats had absorbed at the National Law School in Rio de Janeiro made the Foreign Ministry a bastion of anti-Semitism; during the war Brazilian diplomats charged with shaping immigration policy frequently, and fiercely, argued against admitting Jews. In the memos sent back to Rio they commonly made, for example, the connection, which on the surface ought to have been absurd, between Communism and "international Jewish finance."[14]

There were some exceptions. The most highly placed was Luiz Martins de Souza Dantas, ambassador to France until 1942, when he was removed from his post for issuing large numbers of fraudulent visas to desperate Jews, at least several hundred of whom managed to make their way to Brazil.[15] Paulo Carneiro, later Brazil's ambassador to UNESCO, worked for the Brazilian commercial office in Paris during the war, when he took passports home and doctored them on his kitchen table.[16]

The most famous of these heroes was João Guimarães Rosa, whose *Sagarana*, published two years after *Near to the Wild Heart*, announced the arrival of the other great master of twentieth-century Brazilian prose. With Aracy Moebius de Carvalho, his German Brazilian wife, taking the lead, the couple issued illegal visas from the consulate in Hamburg; Aracy even used her diplomatic passport to escort Jews to the ships waiting to take them to safety. After the Brazilian declaration of war, the couple spent four months interned in Baden-Baden, until they were finally exchanged for German diplomats in Brazil.[17]

Clarice was now a foreign service wife, but for the time being, though far from home, she was not yet abroad in the diplomatic cocoon. Despite her occasional boredom, she loved Belém, where she spent much of her time reading the books—Sartre, Rilke, Proust, Rosamund Lehmann, and Virginia Woolf in addition to Flaubert—that she bought at the Our Lady, Queen of Sorrows Bookstore.[18] Many of her choices seem to have been influenced by reviewers' comparisons of *Near to the Wild Heart* to the works of other writers. As the reviews flowed in from all corners of Brazil, dispatched by Tania from Rio, some critics received personal responses from the author, including the author of the most prominent negative review, the young critic Álvaro Lins.

Lins's objections to the book now make for amusing reading. "It is true that every work of literature should be the expression, the revelation of a personality. There is, however, in masculine temperaments, a greater tendency to hide the author behind his creations, to disconnect from the finished and completed work. That means that a writer can put all of his personality into a work, but diluting himself inside it so that the spectator sees only the object and not the man." Lins suggests that "feminine temperaments" are incapable of this kind of distance, except for the odd case of "androgynous intelligence." Interestingly, however, he uses the term "magic realism" to describe the book: "Realism defined not only as the observation of the exterior aspects of human phenomena, but as an intuition for the knowledge of the intimate and mysterious reality of these same phenomena." This may be the first use of the term to describe the work of a Latin American writer.[19]

"Reviews in general are no good for me," Clarice wrote Tania. "The one by Álvaro Lins... made me despondent, and that was good in a way. I wrote him that I didn't know Joyce or Virginia Woolf or Proust when I wrote the book, because the man all but called me their 'sales representative.'"[20] Years later, still irritated by the comparison, she wrote, "I don't like when they say that I have an affinity with Virginia Woolf (I only read her, by the way, after writing my first book): it's that I don't want to forgive her for committing suicide. The terrible duty is to go to the end."[21] She also dismissed any comparison to Sartre: "It so happens that I only learned of the existence of Sartre when I was writing my second book. My nausea is different from Sartre's, because when I was a child I couldn't stand milk, and almost vomited it back up when I was forced to drink it. They dripped lemon juice into my mouth. I mean, I know what nausea is, in my entire body, in my entire soul. It's not Sartrean."[22]

After his review appeared on March 12, she wrote Lúcio Cardoso. "I liked it so much. I was scared by what you said—that it's possible that this book will be my most important. I feel like tearing it up in order to get my freedom back: it's horrible to already be complete." A tone of fragility and insecurity creeps through in this letter. She addresses him as unreachable, superior, almost in the same way Maury addressed *her* before they were married. "I'm having that impulse toward sincerity and confession that I so often have with you," she told Lúcio. "But I don't know, maybe because you've never felt the same impulse toward me, I suddenly end up finding the words I want to say but not wanting to say them."[23] In a similar vein, she wrote a few months later, "Today I had my picture taken which must look horrible because I looked horrible. But if it comes out all right I'll send one to you. Do you want it? Poor thing you don't want a picture or a letter. I invented that you think of me as a friend just because I am your friend: what a little tragedy."[24] He answered, with calm authority, "There is no little tragedy: I really am your friend and would be terribly sorry if you didn't believe it."[25]

Their collaboration, so important to the making of *Near to the Wild Heart*, continued in *The Chandelier*, the book she had begun in March 1943, a few weeks after her marriage, when she was still living in Rio. *Near to the Wild Heart* would not be published until December, but Clarice was already going off in a different direction. In Belém, she ate *açaí*, a favorite treat of the Amazonian regions, in order to concentrate on it.[26] But the results were disappointing, she wrote Tania in February: "I'm horribly frayed: everything I've written is rubbish; flavorless, self-imitating, or in an easy tone that neither interests nor satisfies me."[27]

Still, she was happy to be back at work. As she told an interviewer (probably her first), "I write because I find in it a pleasure that I don't know how to translate. I'm not pretentious. I write for myself, to hear my soul talking and singing, sometimes crying." In the same interview she agreed that her writing was, in a sense, autobiographical, referring to the book she was reading at the time: "After all Flaubert was right when he said: '*Madame Bovary c'est moi.*' One is always at the forefront."[28]

By May, she was ready to show parts of her new work to Lúcio. "Now I'd like to write a calm and clean book, without any strong words, but something real—real like something dreamed, like something thought—something real and very delicate."[29] But the book would not be finished in Belém. On July 5, 1944, a month after D-Day and the liberation of Rome, the announcement came that Maury Gurgel Valente was being removed to the consulate in Naples.

15

PRINCIPESSA DI NAPOLI

After a few days in Rio de Janeiro,[1] Clarice and Maury began their trip to Europe on July 19. Their tortured itinerary proved just how difficult it was to get across the Atlantic in those days. Their first stop was the "trampoline to victory," the great U.S. base at Parnamirim, Natal, where they spent five days awaiting transport. The base was luxurious: its cinema showed films still not available in Rio, its mess hall served delicious food, and its apartments sported enormous electric refrigerators.[2] Maury went first, traveling with the other diplomats, who were to reopen the consulate before bringing over their dependents. Their journey was grueling: from Rio to Natal to Ascension Island to Accra to Robertsfield (Liberia) to Dakar to Tindouf to Marrakech to Casablanca to Oran to Algiers, where Maury and his colleagues finally got to rest.

Clarice, meanwhile, was stuck in Natal. She moved from the U.S. base to the "horrid little Grand Hotel here," she wrote Lúcio. "Maury left yesterday and I'm waiting for transport maybe over the weekend." She spent a total of twelve days in Natal, "a little city without character, even that of age," missing her sisters, Maury, and her friends from Rio and Belém.[3]

For the first time since she arrived in Maceió as an immigrant infant, she was going to leave Brazil. The circumstances would have been hard to imagine when she arrived twenty-two years before in steerage class, a poor, hungry child from a family of ragged refugees. There was no sign of her family's epic struggle in the beautiful young woman, an admired writer and respected journalist, who sat waiting for her plane at the Grand Hotel, a distinguished Catholic name in her diplomatic passport.

It was a triumph of sorts, but it was not unambiguous. In the years since her family disembarked in the shadow of the faux Statue of Liberty on the docks of Maceió, she had put down deep roots in the only country she knew. "Clarice should never have left Brazil," said Eliane Weil, who met her a few weeks later in Algiers. "She wasn't like those other women. Only a very few had any education. They were trained to help their husbands, to look after the children and the servants. Clarice was educated, she had a profession, she had a life in Brazil."[4]

The experience of living abroad would be as difficult as it was rewarding, but first she had to get there. On July 30, she embarked from Natal. "I traveled with a bunch of missionaries and looking at a little holy woman asleep in front of me, I myself felt weak and horribly spiritual, free of hunger, ready to convince the blacks of Africa that there is no need of anything, except civilization," she wrote Lúcio.[5]

The next day, she arrived at the U.S. Army Air Corps facility at Fisherman's Lake, Liberia, where she spent a day and a night. Despite being surrounded by Liberian villagers who were intrigued by her smooth blond hair, she was not struck by the place's exoticism. "I had to keep telling myself: this is Africa—in order to feel anything. I've never seen anyone who was less of a tourist." On August 1, she reached Bolama in Portuguese Guinea, where she had lunch and saw the nature of the colonial regime. She would still be writing about the experience as late as 1974. "[Seeing Guineans being whipped,] I asked: but do you have to treat them as if they weren't human beings? He answered: they won't work any other way. I thought about it: mysterious Africa."[6] She left mysterious Africa through Dakar, flying all night to Lisbon.[7]

Thanks to her parents' sacrifices, Clarice Lispector could arrive, well-fed and well-dressed, married to a diplomat with a salary paid in dollars, back in her native continent. It is unlikely that she had any knowledge of the extent of the horrors being visited upon her people. Since the 1930s it had been widely known that the European Jews were being persecuted, but the exact nature of that persecution was not yet imagined. Brazil had spent years under the censorship of the Estado Novo. The Yiddish papers, which would have taken the greatest interest in the subject, were still closed; the Portuguese-language papers either weren't interested or were barred from reporting on it. "We didn't know," said Tania Lispector Kaufmann. "We were busy working, and people didn't really talk about it."[8] For the most part, the Brazilian Jews were in the dark. "When the war ended, many journalists and writers . . . came to Latin America," another Brazilian remembered. "Because here we didn't know anything. The papers didn't write about it because it was a dictatorship. So they invited journalists and writers who had been in Europe."[9]

Neutral Lisbon, where Clarice arrived on August 2, 1944, was better off than most of the continent, but it was still ratty and poor. "Lisbon must be terrible to live and work in," she wrote Lúcio a few weeks later. "As Maria Archer said, dignity is the downfall of the Portuguese."[10] Archer, a novelist who grew up in Portuguese Africa, was one of the many cultural figures impressed by the young Brazilian. Clarice wrote Tania and Elisa that Ribeiro Couto, a Brazilian writer and diplomat, "gave a dinner for, among others, João Gaspar Simões, a great Portuguese critic." (He is today mainly remembered as the first biographer of Fernando Pessoa.) "We talked quite a lot. He liked me and wanted the book (you can't imagine what a success I was that night. They were all imitating me, they were all 'charmed')."[11]

She made an enduring friend in the Portuguese poet Natércia Freire. "The four hours we spent together were very little for me and for all we had to say to one another. But one day we will meet again, I will listen a lot and talk a lot."[12] They never did meet again, but those four hours made a deep enough impression on Natércia that they were corresponding as late as 1972. ("My God, we have lived so much!" Clarice wrote.)[13]

The trip was not all fun, she wrote Lúcio. "I don't know if it's because of the special situation of waiting and anxiety, but I felt an unease I haven't felt in a long time. But for some reason you do feel like you're at home—maybe that's the reason, who knows?"[14] And she wrote Tania, "I'm not enjoying travelling. I'd like to be there with you or with Maury. The whole world is lightly annoying, it seems. What matters in life is being close to the people you love. That is the most important truth in the world."[15]

After a week and a half in Lisbon, "Mme Clarisse Gurgel Valente, courrier diplomatique,"[16] departed for Morocco bearing correspondence for Dr. Vasco Tristão Leitão da Cunha, the representative of Brazil to the Provisional Government of the French Republic, located at Algiers. Clarice passed through Casablanca, which was "cute, but really different from the film *Casablanca*," she wrote her sisters. "The poorer women aren't veiled. It's funny to see them covered, veiled, sometimes wearing short dresses and shoes and socks à la Carmen Miranda," the inevitable ambassadress of Brazilian fashion.[17] From Casablanca, Clarice continued to Algiers.

"Things are the same everywhere—the sigh of a well-traveled little lady," she wrote Lúcio. "Cinemas across the world are called Odeon, Capital, Empire, Rex, Olympia; the women wear Carmen Miranda shoes, even when their faces are veiled. The truth is still the same: we ourselves are the main thing and we're the only ones without Carmen Miranda shoes."[18] From Algiers, she wrote Tania and Elisa, "The truth is I don't know how to write letters about trips; the truth is I don't even know how to travel. It's funny how, passing through all these places, I see very little. I think nature all looks pretty much alike, and things are all pretty much alike. I knew more about a veiled Arab woman when I was in Rio. Anyway, I hope I'll never expect myself to take a stand. That would tire me. . . . This whole month I haven't done anything, read anything, anything at all—I am entirely Clarice Gurgel Valente. And I'm in a good mood."[19]

In Algiers, she stayed at the Brazilian legation, in her brother-in-law Mozart Gurgel Valente's room; he was relegated to the sofa. It was her first extended experience of diplomatic society, and she was not impressed, she wrote Elisa and Tania back in Rio.

> Lots of these people are extremely snobbish, hard and merciless, though not actively bad-natured. I think it's funny to hear them talk about nobilities and aristocracies and to see myself sitting there in the middle of them all, with the kindest and most delicate look I can muster. I've never heard so much serious and irremediable nonsense as over the month of this trip. People full of certainties and judgments, whose empty lives are filled up with social pleasures and daintiness. Of course you have to know the real person beneath all that. But though I've always been a protector of animals the task is difficult.[20]

The picture was not all bleak, though, and over her twelve eventful days in Algiers she made lasting friends. One was a young Jewish Frenchwoman named Eliane Weil, who had escaped the Nazis in Paris and made her way to Algeria on the last ship from Marseilles. There, where she worked in psychological operations for the Americans, she met Mozart, four years Maury's senior, who had been in Algiers since April 1943. They fell in love, but, as Clarice and Maury had discovered, Brazilian diplomats were not allowed to marry foreigners.

Luckily, a quirk of genealogy was on their side: Eliane's mother, Lucy Israel, had chanced to be born in Rio in 1899. The family were among the first Jews to settle in Brazil, but they returned to Europe when Lucy was seven. In Paris, Lucy married an Alsatian Jew, Léon Weil, in 1920, making their daughter Eliane legally a "Brazilian, born in Paris," just as Lucy had been a "Frenchwoman, born in Rio de Janeiro." Her papers had to be processed, and then, reborn as a Brazilian national, she married Mozart in Rome in December 1944, becoming the third Jewish spouse in Itamaraty.

Another surprise awaited Mozart and Maury when, a few weeks earlier, Elza Cansanção Medeiros showed up at the legation in Algiers. Their father was the Medeiros family's dentist back in Copacabana; the families were neighbors who had known each other for years, and the last place they expected to run into nineteen-year-old Elza was at the legation in Algiers. "What are you doing here?" the astonished brothers demanded. "How did your father let you come?" He hadn't, Elza replied. Her father cut her off when she became the first female volunteer for the FEB.[21]

Dr. Medeiros was not the only one to regard the Brazilian nurses with skepticism. Santinha Dutra, the "little saint," renowned for her reactionary Catholicism and married to the minister of war, saw the volunteer nurses as "prostitutes going off to war to make their careers." She convinced her husband, Eurico Gaspar Dutra, to put the nurses in a position as neither soldiers nor officers. That, Elza remembered, meant they couldn't eat: there were messes for soldiers and messes for officers, but none for the nurses. Luckily, the president of the Red Cross in Recife, who owned a biscuit factory, had given her a couple of boxes of his manufacture, which is all they had to eat on the trip from Brazil to Algeria.

Safely arrived, Elza was greeted by another astonished family friend, Dr. Vasco Leitão da Cunha, who helped the young women find lodgings in the servants' wing of a nearby hotel. Dr. Vasco, the representative of Brazil to the French Provisional Government, was about to take up his position as consul general in the newly reopened embassy in Rome. Clarice liked the talented and charming Dr. Vasco a great deal, as did everyone else who knew him; over the course of his career in Itamaraty, he held the essential ambassadorships in Washington and Moscow and rose to become minister of foreign relations. He and Mozart accompanied Clarice to Italy by ship, "to Taranto, without letting go for a minute of the obligatory life jacket, escorted by two destroyers." "In Taranto we took the private plane of the commander-in-chief of Allied forces in the Mediterranean, until we arrived in this city."[22]

They arrived on August 24, the day before the liberation of Paris. Like so many other people throughout the world, Elisa Lispector, back in Rio, spent a night sleepless with joy and excitement.[23]

Long before the Second World War, the Naples consulate had played a vital role in Brazilian history. With the abolition of slavery in 1888, Brazil began to look abroad for sources of free labor to work its booming coffee plantations.

Impoverished Italy, with its large surplus of agricultural workers, was an ideal solution. Italians, unlike Jews or Japanese, also met the requirements of Brazilian racial theorists: they were white, Latin Catholics who could be painlessly absorbed. Hundreds of thousands arrived, especially in the south, so many that they account for the ancestors of a full 15 percent of the current Brazilian population.[24] Like the Italians who arrived in the United States and Argentina, most of those bound for Brazil sailed from Naples, their papers stamped at the Brazilian consulate.

Now the consulate that Maury Gurgel Valente was helping to reopen was the base for another critical operation, assisting the twenty-five thousand soldiers of the Brazilian Expeditionary Force. In 1944, Naples could hardly be described as a station on the "Elizabeth Arden career," the chain of ritzy postings diplomats coveted. Maury learned in Algiers that among the comforts he would have to do without were pillows and lunch.[25]

The city had been liberated less than a year before, on October 1, 1943. Its population had been reduced to misery. "Nothing, absolutely nothing that can be tackled by the human digestive system is wasted in Naples," wrote the well-known English travel writer Norman Lewis. "The butchers' shops that have opened here and there sell nothing we would consider acceptable as meat, but their displays of scraps of offal are set out with art, and handled with reverence: chickens' heads—from which the beak has been neatly trimmed—cost five lire; a little grey pile of chickens' intestines in a brightly polished saucer, five lire; a gizzard, three lire; calves' trotters two lire apiece; a large piece of windpipe, seven lire."[26]

In addition, much of the city had been booby-trapped by the departing Germans. The explosion of buildings was a regular occurrence, and the unguarded city had been stripped: "Nothing has been too large or too small—from telegraph poles to phials of penicillin—to escape the Neapolitan kleptomania. A week or two ago an orchestra playing at the San Carlo to an audience largely clothed in Allied hospital blankets, returned from a five-minute interval to find all its instruments missing."[27]

The sky was electric with omens. Vesuvius had erupted on March 19, and the population was charged with a religious fever whose manifestations would not have seemed unusual to one from northeastern Brazil:

> Churches are suddenly full of images that talk, bleed, sweat, nod their heads and exude health-giving liquors to be mopped up by handkerchiefs, or even collected in bottles, and anxious, ecstatic crowds gather waiting for these marvels to happen. Every day the newspapers report new miracles.

In the church of Santo Agnello, a speaking crucifix carries on a regular conversation with the image of Santa Maria d'Intercessione—a fact confirmed by reporters on the spot. The image of Santa Maria del Carmine, first recorded as having bowed its head to avoid a cannon-shot during the siege of Naples by Alfonso of Aragon, now does this as a matter of daily routine.[28]

Bread, meat, oil, and pasta were all very expensive, even a year after the liberation, wrote Rubem Braga, the correspondent of the *Diário Carioca*.[29] "The people of Naples live badly, dress badly, eat little—and their freedom is full of restrictions," Braga wrote. "The black market works everywhere: sometimes you have the tragic, comic impression that everyone is trying to find something to buy for 20 lire to resell for 40 lire to someone else who will resell it for 70 lire to someone else, who will resell it yet again—and so forth, until, at some point in the chain, a citizen will decide to use the article with money discovered God knows where." But Braga added, "You don't see hunger, the absolute hunger that is said to reign in Greece and other places. Food is expensive and rare but it exists."[30]

In this garden spot, Clarice and Maury began their overseas careers. In her correspondence, Clarice did not dwell on, or even much mention, the troubles. "It is beautiful here," she wrote Lúcio. "It's a dirty, disorganized city, as if the main thing was the sea, the people, the things. People seem to live provisionally. And everything here has a washed-out color, but not as if seen through a veil: those are the colors themselves."[31]

She described the situation a bit to Elisa, to whom she generally wrote more descriptive letters than to Tania or Lúcio. "The population clearly live from smuggling, the black market, prostitution, attacks, and robbery. The middle class suffers."[32] A few weeks later, she elaborated: "It's true that they blame the war for lots of things that always existed here. Prostitution, for example, was always a big profession here. They've told us now that boys on the street offer their sisters, the husband who says he has a very pretty girl and it turns out to be his wife, etc.; but everyone says it's always been that way."[33]

She was reading a great deal, mainly in Italian. In that language, she renewed her acquaintance with Katherine Mansfield. Mansfield's *Bliss* had made a decisive impact on her a few years before; it was the first book she purchased with her salary as a journalist. "This book is me!" she recalled exclaiming when she first opened it. Now, in Naples, reading Mansfield's letters, she wrote Lúcio, "There can be no greater life than hers, and I simply don't know what to do. What an absolutely extraordinary thing she is."[34]

Clarice's admiration for and identification with Mansfield is interesting. There is the admiration a writer would naturally feel for a great predecessor. But the statement "There is no greater life than hers" begs the question of what Clarice meant in reference to a life that included lovers of both sexes, venereal disease, depression, tuberculosis, and death at age thirty-four. Perhaps it was Mansfield's selfless dedication to her art. But another possibility is Mansfield's defiance of convention, her ceaseless, doomed fight for freedom. For the young author of *Near to the Wild Heart* as for her rebellious creation Joana, freedom, personal and artistic, was the highest good. The message of Katherine Mansfield's life would have especially appealed to Clarice as she was being swallowed up by the diplomatic corps, careful, closed, and highly mannered, even in wartime.

"In general I have been a 'social success,'" she wrote Lúcio. "It's just that afterwards Maury and I end up pale, exhausted, looking at one another, detesting the populations and full of hate and purity.... Everyone is intelligent, good-looking, polite, gives alms and reads books; but why don't they go to any hell they can find? I myself would be happy to, if I knew that the place of 'suffering humanity' was in heaven. My God, after all I'm not a missionary."[35]

Despite this bravura, she was not adverse to "suffering humanity," or even to missionary work. Soon after her arrival, she invested her energies in helping to care for the "smoking cobras," the troops of the FEB who had disembarked in Naples to the bewilderment of the Italians. On November 15, the anniversary of the foundation of the Brazilian Republic, Vasco Leitão da Cunha gave a speech outlining the reasons for Brazil's entry into the war, referring to the Italian submarines that had attacked Brazilian shipping. This needed emphasis, for most Italians had no idea what the Brazilians were doing there. "Hundreds of Italians that I have spoken to—people of all social classes and educational levels, including political journalists—had absolutely no idea of the cowardly actions of Italian submarines, killing the men, women, and children of a neutral country," Rubem Braga wrote.

> The Fascist censorship hid the fact. According to Fascist propaganda, the United States forced Brazil to enter the war. The great protest marches of the Brazilian people after the torpedoing of our ships by German and Italian submarines were not, as it's easy enough to imagine, reported here. Once Brazil entered the war, Mussolini's propaganda machine started to take more interest in our country. At the same time that our entry into the

> conflict was ridiculed in the most vile manner—attacking not only our government's position but the Brazilian people themselves—they invented stories about thousands of Italian immigrants suffering horrors in prisons and concentration camps in Brazil.[36]

It was the usual Fascist propaganda, but the Brazilians were not fighting the Italians, who had surrendered in 1943. They were up against the Germans. It was bad enough that they were underequipped and undertrained and that their general condition reflected the lamentable conditions of public health in Brazil.[37] Worst of all, they were racially "mongrelized," a point that pro-Nazi Brazilians had hammered on when stressing the folly of Brazil's entering the war. Rubem Braga emphasized their toughness: "They're as good fighters as anyone else—and they don't believe in the legend of 'supermen' that—though it shames me to say it—has been promoted by our own 'sociologists,' some of whom, as I myself know, [are] of 'inferior' racial composition themselves."[38]

On this point, the Nazis showed more delicacy. In the leaflets they spread to the Brazilian soldiers, the Germans used the same arguments employed by the domestic fifth column, the single difference being the Germans' bad Portuguese. "The main argument is the question of why the Brazilians are fighting in Italy—though their author never explains why the Germans are fighting in the same country." The flyers also promise good food for prisoners and deserters, "without distinction of race or nation, and not only good food but consideration, since there 'everyone is respectfully treated.' Not a word of racism. The strongest phrase, which deserved a special font, was this deep philosophical truth: 'In war, the main thing is to get home alive.' What a nice thought in the mouths of the German soldiers—the supposed authors of the message. Here is Mr. Hitler, pacifistic and anti-racist—in Portuguese."[39]

Hitler's "pacifist and anti-racist" armies inflicted heavy casualties on the Brazilian troops, who streamed back to the hospitals that Elza Cansanção Medeiros and her fellow nurses were staffing. The camp hospitals, just behind the front, were the first station. For those wounded soldiers who could travel and who were expected to recover within a few days, there was an evacuation hospital about twenty kilometers behind the front. The worst cases headed to the main U.S. hospital in Naples.[40]

Symbolically enough, the hospital was located at the Mostra d'Oltremare, the Overseas Exhibition, an ultramodern fairground complex Mussolini had inaugurated in May 1940.[41] It celebrated exactly the same "heroic crusader, so civilized by Fascism, attacking African barbarity, to liberate, disinterestedly, the beautiful black slave" that *Pan*, where Clarice published her first story, had honored a decade before.[42] Only four years after the complex's pompous inauguration, the pavilions commemorating the Italian colonies Eritrea, Ethiopia, Albania, and Libya were already housing the latest victims of those "heroic crusaders," the Allied soldiers wounded in the Italian campaign.

There, Elza Cansanção Medeiros, a nineteen-year-old from a well-to-do Rio family, whose English came from an Oxford-educated governess, recalled her despair at finding the hospital run by "TEXANS!" "What they speak is almost a dialect, with their mouths half-closed. It was a horror! In a few days I was crying desperately, since I had to translate the doctors' words for the patients, and vice-versa."[43]

The nurses needed all the help they could get and were happy to have the reinforcement of Mrs. Clarice Gurgel Valente, who, despite her dismissive remarks about "suffering humanity," proved an indefatigable humanitarian. Because there were no social workers with the Brazilian army, Clarice "requested authorization from the military authorities, both Brazilian and American, to visit the hospital every day and chat a bit with the sick men," Elza remembered. "It was hard to obtain the authorization, since she was a civilian, who, though a member of our diplomatic corps, had no military position. After a long struggle, she received her authorization. She started coming to the hospital every day, a real Samaritan. That gracious figure passed from bed to bed, always with a happy smile on her lips, conversing with the soldiers, reading them letters from home, giving them advice, writing for those who couldn't or didn't know how, organizing games for the wounded men, and distributing the poor things we could offer our sick men."[44]

The great mystic, Elza remembered, had a particular gift for clipping toenails.[45] Rubem Braga gives an idea of the letters Clarice might have read, or even written. Wounded and stranded overseas, the soldiers' thoughts were never far from home. "One of them—the censor tells me, without violating his professional oath—wrote an enormous sentimental drivel, saying he missed her to death, living without her was a tragedy, I don't know how I can take it, this separation is a piercing agony, I weep when I think of you, and at the end of it added PS—Tell me who won the game against Bangu.... Another, writing to his wife, spoke about how he longed for her, about the Fatherland, and then said: 'Woman, don't forget to weed the yard, it was really ugly the last time I was there.' "[46]

"I visit all the sick men every day," Clarice told Lúcio in March. "I give them what they need, I talk to them, I fight to get them things from the administration, in other words I'm amazing. I go every morning and it annoys me when I can't, since the men are waiting for me, and since I miss them myself."[47]

She didn't limit herself to bedside visits. Elza recalled "arriving from an infirmary where some of [the] wounded officers were, and happening upon a conversation between Miss Clarice and the patients, who were about to be evacuated to the United States, where they would have to stay for many months, learning to use mechanical limbs." One of these officers said:

> "Ah, Miss Clarice, how I would love to eat a bit of Brazilian food before heading to the United States, I miss Brazil so much, the food there, and now it'll be so long before I can have some good Brazilian beans, or rice with sweet sauce!"
>
> Miss Clarice stood silently, thinking, thinking, and having reached a decision replied:
>
> "Well then, if your doctor agrees, come to the consulate tomorrow, and I'll see what I can do, with our rations, to make a Brazilian meal."

"Reading this now," Elza comments, "it seems very unremarkable, but only someone who has been in a country devastated by the War can realize what a sacrifice this invitation represented, because even the diplomatic corps had great difficulty finding food. Even more so because it was five extra people, who wanted the kinds of food not normally covered by the rations. . . . Our good fairy spared no sacrifice, and the following day the mutilated officers received a warm reception at the consulate, with good Brazilian food, lovingly prepared by Miss Clarice."[48]

The girl who had left Europe as a hunted refugee had returned to help the victims of another war, a "good fairy" for Elza, the "Principessa di Napoli" for Rubem Braga and Joel Silveira, another reporter, who in February 1945 traveled two thousand kilometers through the war zone to visit her.[49] Photographs show her at the height of her beauty, which stood out all the more dramatically in her devastated surroundings. The greatest compliment she ever received, she wrote, came when she and Maury were walking down a Naples street. "And a man said loudly to another, so that I would hear it: 'That is the kind of woman we are counting on to rebuild Italy.' "[50]

16

THE SOCIETY OF SHADOWS

In October 1944, back in Rio, Clarice Lispector was awarded the Graça Aranha Prize for best novel of the year, bringing *Near to the Wild Heart* a fresh round of publicity. In the enormous apartment on the Via Giambattista Pergolesi, which she and Maury shared with the consulate, the consul, Mozart Gurgel Valente's fiancée, Eliane Weil, and the second secretary of the embassy, Clarice was putting the finishing touches on *The Chandelier*, the novel she had begun in Rio the previous March. As she had done when she was trying to finish *Near to the Wild Heart* in Tania and William Kaufmann's crowded apartment, she locked herself away to work.[1]

"My housewifely duties are null, happily," she wrote Elisa in November. "I don't make any decisions and only get involved occasionally; because otherwise it would all become my responsibility and even things that were meant to be bad would be explained as my mistakes. I have better things to do than take care of a kind of boardinghouse: for example, sitting and staring at the wall."[2]

That was not all she was doing, of course. By November, the new book was ready, she wrote Lúcio. "The only thing that's missing is everything I can't say. I also have the idea that it was already finished when I left Brazil; and that I didn't think it was complete, like a mother who looks at her enormous daughter and says: you can tell she's still not ready to get married." She asked him to "find [her] a husband at the Editora José Olympio," then the most prestigious publisher in Rio.[3] She surely thought that after the thundering success of *Near to the Wild Heart* she would have her pick of publishers.

She was wrong. Despite the accolades for *Near to the Wild Heart*, her next book would not be published by José Olympio. Rubem Braga helped place it with the Editora Agir, a Catholic publisher. Clarice thought it a strange choice, writing to Elisa, "I admit I don't understand why the Editora Agir, run essentially by Catholics, is accepting a book that isn't Catholic and that isn't written by a Catholic. I think it's very odd."[4] And when Elisa sent her more information about the house, Clarice responded, "I can see that I could become a nun if I wanted to: my poor book is so surrounded by an orgy of Catholic books."[5]

To Lúcio she reported, "Tania had serious doubts about *The Chandelier*. Including about the title."[6] He, too, had expressed his reservations, writing earlier, "I like the title *The Chandelier* but not much. I think it's a bit Mansfieldian and too poor for a person as rich as you."[7] Clarice responded, "[The title] stays even though [Tania's] right. Nothing in it is very good. My problem is that I only have defects, so if I take out the defects there's almost nothing left but a magazine for teenage girls."[8]

One reason *The Chandelier* had problems finding a publisher is surely that it stands out, in a strange and difficult body of work, as perhaps her strangest and most difficult book. It is her least translated major work, and though Clarice Lispector is perhaps the most studied Brazilian writer of her century, there is remarkably little critical writing on *The Chandelier*. Yet the book's difficulty is, in a way, what makes it linger in the mind. Clarice often said that her books profited by rereading, and that is certainly true of *The Chandelier*.

Unlike her first novel, written in fragments and constantly jumping from scene to scene, *The Chandelier* is a coherent whole. Though its long segments purportedly describe events, they consist almost entirely of long interior monologues, interrupted only by the odd and jarring fragment of dialogue or action. The book moves in slow waves that crest in moments of revelation. The pages between these epiphanies are precisely the moments when the book is most intolerable to the reader, who is forced to follow the interior movement of another person in such microscopic detail. Used to epiphanies, expecting continual stimulus and surprise, the reader approaching the book for the first time is quickly baffled.

Yet the book's glacial intensity has a special fascination. In it Clarice comes as close as she ever would to mirroring in her prose the actual experience of writing, which is made of lulls and tedium and boredom only occasionally punctuated by climaxes and joy. What is true of literature is also, more emphatically, true of life itself—"Literature is life, living," as she said—tedium relieved by intense experience. The book is too concentrated to be read with divided attention, and the focus it demands is exhausting. Reading the book, one recalls Clarice's friend Olga Borelli's description of her at the end of her life: "Her eyes seemed to peer into all the mysteries of life: profound, serene, they locked onto people like the eyes of one's own conscience, too intense for anyone to stand for long."[9] Only when read slowly, pensively, and undistracted, three or five pages at a time, does *The Chandelier* reveal its penetrating genius.

The Chandelier lends itself even less than most of Clarice's works to a description of its plot or characters. The names are general and vague: the protagonist, Virginia, grows up in a rural place called Quiet Farm near the town of Upper Marsh, from which she eventually moves to "the city." The characters have almost no external characteristics. Nobody has a last name, and only a few have a profession, a family, or a home. The drama of Virginia's life, which is the story of the book, is almost entirely internal, though it is often shocked from the outside; these shocks are the bits of dialogue, the extraneous people and events, that infringe upon her wraithlike existence. As in so many of Clarice's books, the real tension comes from the individual's attempt to safeguard her inner world from assaults from without.

Virginia's attempts to make contact with that external world end, without exception, in failure; on the last page of the book she is hit by a car. The symbolism, not subtle, recurs in Clarice Lispector's work. In *Near to the Wild Heart* it appears at the end: "Joana had already dressed the doll, had already undressed her, she had imagined her going to a party where she would shine among all the other girls. A blue car crossed the girl's body, killed her. Then along came the fairy and the girl came back to life."[10] The reverberations of the stories Clarice told to resurrect her mother are clear enough. The theme traversed her entire life. In her final novel, *The Hour of the Star*, the protagonist is run over by an oncoming Mercedes.

The knowledge of the crude and inevitable end does not, however, result in a fatalistic worldview. Instead, it illuminates the individual's struggle even more brightly. Virginia does not resist the attacks of other people, but neither is she attached to them. The people around her are ghosts. The punctuation of the following passage, in which a potential friend tries to bring Virginia into the everyday world, gives a banal conversation an ethereal, chant-like rhythm: "Virginia come one day to my house... I'm not just saying that, she repeated... Come... I live alone... We'll have a nice chat just between us girls, we'll talk about bras, menstrual cramps... whatever you want... all right?"[11] The invitation is ridiculous, but in these passages Clarice is not belittling the woman issuing it. Virginia is incapable of participating in normal life, incapable of seeking fulfillment in friendship. Nothing can remedy her isolation: not her move from the countryside to the city, not family, not sex, not friendship.

This is partly because the external world, for Virginia, does not exist. Nothing can be expected from it. Incidentally, this is another reason why comparisons of Clarice Lispector to Sartre are so misplaced: the world of politics, of "new men" and revolution and ideology, is utterly foreign to her. For one of her background, having seen where revolution and ideology lead, it probably could not be otherwise. Virginia's freedom comes only from within. This perfection is not permanent or definitive. It can be only briefly but dazzlingly glimpsed. The longing for these states of grace is the source of the energy of Clarice Lispector's characters, who devote themselves to meditation, prayer, and creation with an intensity that would be impossible absent the certainty of doom. In a long metaphor for Clarice Lispector's own creation, the young Virginia shapes figurines out of mud:

> But what she loved more than anything was making clay figurines, which no one had taught her.... When she wanted to with great strength she went down the road to the river. On one of its banks, which was slippery but scaleable, she found the best clay that one could desire: white, supple, sticky, cold.... She got a clear and tender material from which she could shape a world. How, how to explain the miracle.... She grew scared, thoughtful. She said nothing, she didn't move but inside without any words she repeated: I am nothing, I have no pride, anything can happen to me if - - - they want they can stop me from mixing the clay - - - they can crush me, ruin me entirely, I know that I am nothing. - - - it was less than a vision, it was a sensation in the body, a frightened thought about what allowed her to accomplish so much with the clay and the water and before which she had to humble herself with seriousness.

Her silent knowledge that she could be crushed, that she is nothing, and her obstinate determination to continue creating surround her creation with a spiritual halo, and her own role in it becomes divine.

> But sometimes she remembered the wet clay and ran fearful out to the terrace—she plunged her fingers into that mixture, cold, mute, constant as waiting, kneading, kneading, slowly extracting forms. She made children, horses, a mother with a child, a mother alone, a girl making things out of clay, a boy at rest, a happy girl, a girl seeing if it would rain, a flower, a comet with a tail sprinkled with washed and sparkling sand, a wilted flower beneath the sun, the cemetery of Upper Marsh, a girl looking....

> Much more, much more. Little forms that meant nothing but which were in reality mysterious and calm. Sometimes tall like a tall tree, but they weren't trees, they weren't anything.... Sometimes like a little running river, but they weren't a river, they weren't anything.... Sometimes a little object with an almost starry form but tired like a person. A work that would never end: that was the most beautiful and careful thing she had ever known: since if she could make anything that existed and anything that did not![12]

The strange syntax and the unexpected adjectives that made Clarice Lispector's language sound so foreign when it first appeared remain striking today, especially when given another layer of foreignness by translation. Coupled with its impossible poetic images—how can one sculpt a "girl seeing if it would rain"?—the passage produces in the reader the same vertiginous experience that one can imagine Virginia felt while creating her world of mud and sand. Like Clarice—"I write for myself, to hear my soul talking and singing, sometimes crying"—the ecstasy of contemplation and creation is the highest freedom Virginia finds.

❦

As a girl, and then as a young woman, Virginia, like Joana, is transgressive and sometimes violent. Yet Joana seems less defiant than indifferent to, or even ignorant of, the expectations of the outside world, of the usual ways children deal with adults, women deal with men, or humans deal with animals. In this sense, Joana is already free. Virginia, in contrast, must seek her freedom. She is not naturally inclined to resistance. As a child she is happy to submit to the will of her wicked, sentimental brother Daniel, and she meekly consents to being belittled in her adult relationships. Even her violence is not entirely her own. Her instructor is Daniel, who resembles the figure of the same name, perhaps inspired by Lúcio Cardoso, in Clarice's early story "Obsession."

When they are children, Daniel guides Virginia into the occult mysteries of the Society of Shadows, whose mottos are "Solitude" and "Truth." His bullying and cruelty meet no resistance from Virginia, who finds "sweetness" in submitting to him. The Society of Shadows—that is, Daniel—orders her to spend long periods in prayer or meditation, sometimes in the basement, sometimes in the forest surrounding their large, partly ruined country house. And the Society commands Virginia to tell her father that their sister is secretly seeing a young man. It later appears that this act has ruined her sister's chance at love.[13]

Virginia's sin is thrilling: "She had committed a corrupt and vile act. Never however had she felt she had acted so freely and with such freshness of desire."

She fantasizes about kicking a helpless dog off a bridge, and then giving herself sexually to a passing man.[14] These acts, needless to say, meet no censure from the author. Virginia, like Joana, exists outside the conventional world of beauty and ugliness, virtue and sin. But where Joana's acts are spontaneous and natural, Virginia, under the sway of Daniel and the Society of Shadows, requires instruction, for these acts are contrary to her nature.

Whatever their origins or results, all Virginia's interactions with the outer world require great effort, and she struggles to achieve the independence that comes naturally to Joana. Grown up, at a dinner party in the city, she seeks liberation in a meager little rebellion: "How to free oneself? not to free oneself from something but just free oneself because she wouldn't be able to say from what. She not-thought for an instant, her head bent. She took a napkin, a round piece of bread...with an extraordinary effort, breaking in herself a stupefied resistance, deflecting destiny, she threw them out the window—and in that way kept her power."[15]

In the long, dreamlike sequence that follows, Virginia seeks to escape "other people's laughter and brilliance" by drinking, not for the alcohol but for the meditations the drink provokes in her about the nature of sensation, and the language that does not describe but creates it. In doing so, she rediscovers the freedom she had as a child sculpting figures in the clay:

> She drank the liquor with pleasure and melancholy—trying once again to think about her childhood and simply not knowing how to get near it, since she had so forgotten it and since it seemed so vague and common—wanting to fasten the anise in the way one looks at an immobile object, but almost not possessing its taste because it flowed, disappeared—and she only grasped the memory like a firefly that does nothing but disappear—she liked the notion that occurred to her: like a firefly that does nothing but disappear...and she noted that it was the first time in her life that she had thought about fireflies even though she had lived near them for so long....She reflected confusedly on the pleasure of thinking of something for the first time. That was it, the anise purple like a memory. She surreptitiously kept a mouthful on her tongue without swallowing it in order to possess the anise present with its perfume: then it inexplicably withheld its smell and taste when it was stopped, the alcohol numbing and warming her mouth. Defeated, she swallowed the now-old liquor, it descended her throat and in a surprise she noted that it had been "anise" for a second while it ran down her throat or after? or before? Not "during," not "while" but shorter: it was anise for a second as a touch of the point of a needle

on the skin, except that the point of the needle gave an acute sensation and the fleeting taste of the anise was wide, calm, still as a field, that was it, a field of anise, like looking at a field of anise. It seemed she had never tasted anise but had already tasted it, never in the present but in the past: after it happened she sat thinking about this and the thought...was the taste of anise. She moved in a vague victory. She was coming to understand more and more about the anise, so much that she could almost no longer relate it to the liquid in the crystal bottle—the anise did not exist in that balanced mass but when that mass divided into particles and spread out as a taste inside of people.... Beneath an attitude of calm and hard clarity she addressed no one and abandoned herself attentive as to a dream she would forget. Behind secure movements she attempted with danger and delicateness to touch the same light and elusive, to find the nucleus made of a single instant, before the quality came to rest on things, before what really came unbalanced in tomorrow—and there was a feeling ahead and another falling away, the tenuous triumph and the defeat, perhaps nothing more than breathing. Life making itself, the evolution of the being without the destiny—the progression from the morning not aiming for the night but attaining it.[16]

❧

The passage above illustrates the impossibility of describing *The Chandelier* in the conventional terms of plot and character. It is the same frustration that awaits a reader expecting plot and character, for if on one level the book is the story of a woman's life, *The Chandelier*'s real drama resides in Clarice Lispector's attempt to deploy, and build upon, the poetic inner language she had discovered in *Near to the Wild Heart*.

Certain sequences of *The Chandelier* resemble Joana's poetical riffs. But where those were limited to shorter passages, in *The Chandelier* they can stretch, as above, over many pages. "She wanted to tell or hear a long story made only out of words," Virginia says,[17] and in this sentiment Clarice Lispector seems to answer modernist writers such as Gertrude Stein, or even the Dadaists. Unlike the latter, though, who were given to composing poems by drawing words at random from a paper bag, Clarice Lispector, by shuffling words around, is not trying to discard meaning. She is trying to find it. "There is so much talk," she wrote years later, "or rather, used to be, about my 'words,' about my 'sentences.' As if they were verbal. Yet none of them, but absolutely none, of the words in the book was—a game."[18]

As Sérgio Milliet recognized when he wrote of "the precious and precise harmony between expression and substance," the union of *forme* and *fond* was the great achievement of her first book.[19] *The Chandelier* pushes her quest even further. One can see the point of attaining that "precious and precise harmony" in the passage describing Virginia's attempts to capture the flavor of the anise liquor. In itself, the flavor of anise is not important. The taste of a drink on the tongue is such an infinitesimal part of human experience that it hardly seems worth expending so much effort to capture it. "Her impression then was that she could only reach things through words," she writes in *The Chandelier*.[20] But if human language, weighed down by reflexive syntax and clichéd meanings, is unequal even to that trivial experience, what use can it be for describing anything greater?

When Clarice writes "The thought . . . was the taste of anise," that Virginia's thinking about the taste *creates* the taste, she identifies the point at which a thing is named as the point where that thing comes to exist. The name of the thing *is* the thing, and by discovering the name one creates it. The hidden name is "the symbol of the thing in the thing itself" that already appeared in *Near to the Wild Heart*: the purest language possible, what could be called the concrete spiritual goal of these linguistic exercises. The point where the name of a thing becomes identical to the thing itself, the "word that has its own light," is the ultimate reality.

The discovery of the holy name, synonymous with God, was the highest goal of the Jewish mystics, and the methods Virginia uses to describe the anise liquor resemble their methods. "The Society of Shadows must perfect its members," Daniel tells Virginia, "and orders you to turn everything on its head." The repetition of nonsensical words, the combination of letters, the parsing of verses, the search for a logic other than the strictly literal were common tools, and they could produce paradoxical or even absurd results. By dislocating her language (the liquor is purple, it is a field, it is a needle on the skin), by splitting and rearranging its words, Clarice is attempting to coax shades of significance from them, finding the word that might create the flavor of the liquor on Virginia's tongue.

The search for hidden meanings within language is a very serious activity, like Virginia's sculpting of mud figurines, tied to creation itself. "Absolutely none of the words in the book was—a game," Clarice insisted, for if something as fleeting and unimportant as the flavor of anise liquor can be captured, then some greater truth might be, too.

For Clarice Lispector, as for Virginia, the search for the hidden word is internal and solitary—"Truth" and "Solitude" are the mottos of the Society of

Shadows—and it promises no final result, no permanent rapture, no definitive salvation. In this book, Clarice is still grasping for this language, which she does not yet completely dominate, but the ecstasy of the search is the highest state Virginia attains. "There were days like that, when she understood so well, and saw so much, that she ended in a gentle and dizzy intoxication, as if her perceptions without thought were whisking her off on a brilliant and sweet current to where, to where . . ."[21]

17

VOLUME IN THE BRAIN

The completion of *The Chandelier* came at a time of intense activity in the Naples consulate. On December 18, Mozart Gurgel Valente and Eliane Weil, now a naturalized Brazilian, married there, with Maury and Dr. Vasco serving as witnesses. And business was booming at the hospital, where the casualties from the Brazilian Expeditionary Force were pouring in. In four bloody and protracted assaults beginning on November 24, the Brazilians invested a German position at Monte Castello, near Bologna, finally conquering it on February 21, 1945.

These victories pushed the war ever farther from Naples. A degree of travel was now possible, and Rome, where Mozart was employed at the embassy to the Vatican, was an obvious destination. Clarice and Maury went for New Year's 1945, at the invitation of Vasco Leitão da Cunha,[1] and in May. The impoverished city was happy to welcome them, Eliane remembered. In wartime conditions, Maury and Mozart were no longer simple civil servants, and in ruined Italy their wives were in demand by ritzy houses such as Gucci, Fendi, and Leonardo, who were seeking out those few women with dollars in their pockets to rebuild their clientele. The prices, Eliane was delighted to recall, were expensive but doable.[2]

A similar principle operated in the Roman art world, where the collapse of the Italian economy had affected painters as much as the rest of the population. As it happened, Landulpho Borges da Fonseca, a colleague of Mozart's, was an aficionado of contemporary painting and sought out the city's artists. Perhaps the most famous of these was Giorgio de Chirico, a fifty-six-year-old who had settled in Rome in 1944 and who had taken a leading role in the Surrealist movement earlier in his career.

"I was in Rome," Clarice wrote, "and a friend of mine said that De Chirico would surely like to paint me. And he asked him. And said he'd have to see me first. And he saw me and said: I will paint your... your portrait."[3] She went to his studio in the Piazza di Spagna, steps from the house where Keats died, to pose for the small portrait. "His pictures are in almost all the museums," she told Elisa and Tania. "You've definitely seen reproductions of them. Mine is little, excellent, beautiful, with expression and everything. He charges a lot, naturally, but he charged me less. And while he was painting a buyer appeared. Of course he didn't sell it.... Mine is just of my head, neck, and a bit of my shoulders. Everything smaller. I posed in that blue velvet dress from the Mayflower, remember Tania?"[4]

The picture shows Clarice's head tilted slightly to the right, her eyes, distrustful or defiant, looking out to the left. Her red lips, right in the center of the picture, are the most notable flash of color in the otherwise dark picture, which captures astonishingly well the intense interior focus, the "brilliant and suffocating air" that comes across so forcefully in her books.

Though it became one of the most celebrated images of Clarice Lispector, the model, never easily impressed by famous names, had her doubts: not only about her own appearance, which she later described as "a bit affected," but about the artist himself. De Chirico, she told an interviewer a few years later, was a "painter in decline who has lost his artistic feeling."[5]

Nonetheless, the portrait is a small witness to a great moment. As Clarice was posing on May 8, 1945, she and the painter heard the newspaper boy shouting from the square below "È finita la guerra!" Upon hearing the news, she wrote her sisters, "I gave a shout, the painter stopped, we talked about people's strange lack of happiness, and then he kept on painting."[6]

❦

With the end of the war, dramatic events ceased to occupy Clarice. Her book was finished, the Brazilian soldiers went home, and the Naples consulate, lately a witness to momentous events, settled into its routine as a sleepy office in an impoverished backwater. Clarice traveled a bit and read a great deal, including Proust, Kafka, and Lúcio Cardoso's translation of Emily Brontë's poetry. "How well she understands me, Lúcio, I feel like putting it that way. It's been so long since I read poetry, I felt I had ascended to the sky, to the open air. I even felt like crying but luckily I didn't because when I cry it soothes me, and I don't want to be soothed, neither for her sake, nor for mine."[7]

She met another great poet, Giuseppe Ungaretti, with whom she had much in common. If Clarice was called "hermetic," Ungaretti was the proud founder of the so-called hermetic school. Clarice was a Jewish Brazilian born in the Ukraine; Ungaretti was a Jewish Italian born in Egypt. Unlike Clarice, Ungaretti had been a Fascist—Jewish Fascists were not uncommon in Italy, at least in the early years—though in 1936, disillusioned with politics, he went to Brazil, where he taught at the University of São Paulo. Before returning to Italy in 1942, he explored much of the country and came to know many of its leading writers. It was Clarice Lispector, however, who increased his "respect for the Portuguese language, thanks to her poetic intensity, her invention."[8] Meeting her in Italy, he and his daughter translated part of *Near to the Wild Heart*, which they published in a literary magazine.[9]

But her closest friend was her dog, Dilermando, whom she found in a Naples street. "One look at him was all I needed to fall in love with his face," she recounted in her children's book *The Woman Who Killed the Fish.*

> Despite being Italian, he had a Brazilian face and the face of someone named Dilermando. I paid his owner some money and took Dilermando home. I immediately gave him food. He looked so happy to have me as his owner that he spent the whole day looking at me and wagging his tail. Apparently his other owner beat him.... Dilermando liked me so much that he almost went crazy when he smelled with his snout my woman-mother scent and the scent of the perfume I always wear.... He hated taking baths and thought we were bad when we forced him to make the sacrifice. Since it was a lot of work to make him bathe every day, and since he fled the bathroom all soaped up, I ended up bathing him only twice a week. The result, of course, is that he had a very strong dog scent which I immediately smelled with my snout, because people too have snouts.[10]

Her love for Dilermando, "the purest person in Naples," inspired the only expression of resentment toward Maury in her known correspondence. "The dog got sick, I took him to the veterinarian and the fool told me he was incurable," she wrote Tania. "And there I was crying, I spent the day nervous and sad about the idea that they'd have to kill him, I who love him so much. Maury, as always, reacted normally and wouldn't regret it too much. But we're thinking about having him x-rayed and then he'll be cured, they promised me."[11]

"When I was typing, he sat, half stretched out, at my side, in the exact posture of the Sphinx, snoozing. If I stopped typing because I had come across an obstacle and was getting discouraged, he immediately opened his eyes, raised his head high, looked at me, one of his ears cocked, waiting.... No human being ever gave me the feeling of being so completely loved as I was loved without restrictions by that dog."[12]

Despite these friendships, Clarice had to find a role for herself as the dust of the war began to settle and the novelty of being abroad wore off. It was not easy, and references to loneliness and depression begin appearing in her letters with ever greater frequency. Even before the war's end, she had expressed frustration with being cut off from her friends and family: "While you live in Brazil," she wrote Lúcio in November 1944, "I am drinking tea with milk at a girls' school."[13]

In May she wrote her sisters, "I feel a real thirst to be there with you. The water I have found in this world outside is very dirty, even when it's champagne."[14] In August she told Natércia Freire, "I'm dying of longing for home and for Brazil. This life of 'married to a diplomat' is the first destiny I have. This isn't traveling: traveling is leaving and going home whenever you want to, traveling is being able to move. But traveling this way is awful: it's serving out sentences in different places. The impressions you have after a year in a place end up killing your first impressions. At the end of it all you end up 'educated.' But that's not my style. I never minded being ignorant."[15]

In a similar vein, about a trip to Florence she was planning, she told Elisa that her life was providing her "a quick and suburban little culture that's useful later on in 'drawing rooms,'" and reported, "The ambassadors respect me.... People think I'm 'interesting.'...I agree with everything, too, I never disagree with anything that's said, I'm very tactful and I win over the necessary people. As you can see, I'm a good diplomatic wife. Since people vaguely know that I am 'a writer,' my God, they would surely allow me to eat with my feet or wipe my mouth with my hair."[16]

Between books, working erratically, she struggled with artistic doubts: "All I have is the nostalgia that comes from a mistaken life, from an excessively sensitive temperament, from perhaps a forced or mistaken vocation," she wrote Tania in September.[17] She said to Lúcio, "I haven't really liked Italy, just as I couldn't really like any place; since something stands between me and any thing, as if I were one of those people whose eyes are covered with a white film. I horribly regret to have to say that that veil is precisely my desire to work and to see too much."[18]

Seeing too much, "an excessively sensitive temperament": this was how her sister-in-law Eliane remembered her at this time. "She felt everything others felt," Eliane said. "She felt what they were feeling even before they did."[19] This extremely refined sensibility was her great strength as a writer: "You pick up a thousand waves that I can't catch," Rubem Braga told her. "I feel like a cheap radio, only getting the station around the corner, where you get radar, television, shortwave."[20] But it was also very painful, as Clarice wrote later: "I can no longer carry the pain of the world. What am I to do, if I feel totally what others are and feel?"[21]

A perceptive reviewer of *The Chandelier* captured Clarice's dilemma: "Possessed of an enormous talent and a rare personality, she will have to suffer, fatally, the disadvantages of both, since she so amply enjoys their benefits."[22] From Florence, which she visited at the end of 1945, she wrote Elisa and Tania, "I try to do what I *ought* to do, and be the way one *ought* to be, and to adapt to the world around me—I manage to do it, but at the price of my intimate balance, I feel it. . . . I go through phases of being irritable, depressed. My memory doesn't exist: I forget things from one room to the next."[23]

Many years later, Clarice underlined the following sentences in a newspaper article entitled "Volume in the Brain":

> The research showed that the same physical events are perceived by some people as if they were louder, shinier, quicker, more odorous or colorful than they are for others. . . . In some people, the volume is turned up to the maximum, amplifying the intensity of all sensory experiences. These people are called "amplifiers." . . . A level that provokes slight discomfort in "dampeners" can mean intense suffering for "amplifiers." . . . At the other extreme, the "amplifier" is an introvert who avoids the busy existence of the "dampener." He is the kind who complains about the volume of the radio, the seasoning of the food, the brightness of the wallpaper. If it's up to him, he prefers to be alone, quiet, in solitary environments.

At the top of the page she scrawled, "Everything touches me—I see too much, I hear too much, everything demands too much of me."[24]

The words "diplomatic corps" are often read as synonymous with stuffiness and exclusivity, describing an institution constitutionally incompatible with an artist whose heroes—Spinoza, Katherine Mansfield, Lúcio Cardoso—were the embodiment of rebellion. This is how Clarice would later remember her years as a foreign service wife: "I remembered a time in which I arrived at the refinement (!?) of having the waiter at home pass fingerbowls to all the guests in the following way: every fingerbowl had a rose petal floating in the liquid."[25]

Even before she married Maury, Clarice had already started rebelling against the diplomatic world. "Ever since I've been going out with Itamarati," she confessed to Tania and William, "I've especially liked using really vulgar slang."[26] Within Itamaraty, however, she had a great deal of freedom. Her duties as the wife of a vice consul, low on the totem pole, were not onerous. She had an ample and guaranteed income, which, vitally, allowed her the space and time to write. She had good friends, including Maury, Eliane and Mozart Gurgel Valente, and Vasco Leitão da Cunha, not to mention Dilermando the dog. Life in the foreign service was not perfect, but in many ways it was less demanding than working as a journalist in Rio.

There is no doubt that she hated being away from Brazil and that she feared exile: "I am sure that in my cradle my first wish was to belong," she said, and belonging to Brazil was very important to her. "I lived mentally in Brazil, I lived 'on borrowed time.' Simply because I like living in Brazil, Brazil is the only place in the world where I don't ask myself, terrified: what am I doing here after all, why am I here, my God. Because it's here I have to be, where I have my roots."[27] Certainly she missed her sisters and her friends. But a simpler explanation for her unhappiness at this time was that the excitement of her new life—marriage, success, travel, as well as the usefulness she had felt at the hospital—had ebbed. There was now room for a resurgence of the depression that had already tormented her before she married. "My problems are those of a person with a sick soul," she wrote Tania, "and cannot be understood by people who are, thank God, healthy."[28]

There was hope on the horizon, however. In December, Maury was promoted from vice consul to consul. She wrote Tania and Elisa, "I feel very well, . . . I'm having fun in Rome and . . . just by looking at me you can tell I'm much more rested."[29] One reason for her newfound repose was the knowledge that a trip to Brazil was only six weeks away.

The country Clarice returned to in January 1946 was very different from the one she had left eighteen months before. The end of the war brought the end of Getúlio Vargas's fifteen-year reign. Many Brazilians were embarrassed to be fighting Fascism in Italy in the name of a quasi-Fascist dictatorship at home; for Elza Cansanção Medeiros, Rubem Braga, and many of the Brazilian troops, the fight to free Europe was, at the same time, a fight to free Brazil.[30] For the time being, Getúlio Vargas's long run was up. He was deposed on October 29, 1945.

The new president was the bland Eurico Gaspar Dutra, Vargas's former minister of war. A close collaborator of Vargas, he was a conservative choice. This he proved when, under the sway of the reactionary Catholic wife who had compared the war nurses to gold-digging whores, he outlawed gambling in a country addicted to games of chance. Dutra's election did not signify a break with the old regime, nor was it intended to. Still, the end of the war and the return of democracy brought Brazil much needed air, and Brazil brought much needed air to Clarice Lispector.

It was a brief visit, less than two months. She saw the publication of *The Chandelier*, and she met many people whom she would count among her closest friends. First among them was Bluma Chafir Wainer, a Jewish woman from Bahia whom Clarice met through Rubem Braga. Unlike Clarice, Bluma did not photograph well, and with her big nose and large teeth she could hardly be called beautiful. Yet those who knew her unanimously recall her great charm and appeal. "She was even more beautiful than Clarice," said the journalist Joel Silveira, "because Clarice was often withdrawn, dejected. Bluma was witty, vibrant, fun."[31]

Bluma attracted important and powerful men. Her husband, Samuel Wainer, was one of the most influential journalists in Brazil. His anti-Vargas, pro-Communist monthly *Diretrizes*, founded at great personal risk in 1938, had at first operated with significant support from the Jewish middle class in Rio, the shopkeepers, dentists, and lawyers who bought ads to help him when the magazine was starting out. Later, in a chapter baroque even by the standards of Brazilian political journalism, Samuel Wainer became Getúlio Vargas's closest ally in the media. Bluma, a committed leftist of great moral integrity, would be appalled by her husband's closeness to Getúlio: "The ends do not justify the means" was a favorite saying of hers.[32] Though she never joined the Communist Party, the police kept an eye on her. Like Clarice, she was a free thinker who scorned convention. She frequented bars, not to drink but to participate in political and intellectual debates, "in the European manner,"[33] a phrase that seems to mean "without her husband," upon whom she did not depend socially or intellectually.

Or, as it turned out, sexually. Unlike Clarice, who tended to leave her transgressions in the pages of her books, Bluma acted on them. Married to Samuel Wainer since 1933, in 1938 she fell in love with Rubem Braga, a young, married colleague of Samuel's. Bluma got pregnant, left her husband, and advised Braga that she was ready to live by his side. Panicked, Rubem fled to southern Brazil; Bluma, in Rio, had no choice but to abort.

Such was her charm, however, that Samuel took her back, ensuring that there would be no scandal, and Rubem Braga, decades later, confided that she was the love of his life.[34] In 1946 Bluma and Clarice became instant friends, and the beautiful, sophisticated, intelligent pair did not escape the notice of the artistic and journalistic circles of Rio de Janeiro. They were from humble immigrant backgrounds working in the press at a time when few women did. More strikingly, they *looked* nothing like the Jews of legend. "Before, even the philo-Semites tended to mythologize the Jews. They saw them as something wise, mysterious, something out of the Old Testament. Bluma and Clarice were young, beautiful, sensual, cultivated," said the journalist Alberto Dines. "They changed the idea of Jewish women in this country."[35]

When *Near to the Wild Heart* was published, Clarice, at the behest of Lúcio Cardoso, sent several copies to literary acquaintances in Minas Gerais. One made its way to Fernando Sabino, a young man very much on the make. In 1941, at age seventeen, Sabino published his first book. He sent it to Mário de Andrade, the pope of Brazilian literature, in São Paulo; Andrade, with some exaggeration, saw a resemblance to the work of Machado de Assis. Soon thereafter, Fernando—good-looking, a champion swimmer, but from an unspectacular middle-class background—managed to marry Helena Valladares, daughter of the powerful governor of Minas Gerais. As a wedding gift, Getúlio Vargas himself granted Fernando Sabino a generous lifetime pension, lifting him at a stroke from the penury in which most Brazilian writers lived.[36]

"I didn't know who she was," Sabino wrote of receiving Clarice's book, which he enthusiastically reviewed. "I also didn't know who had suggested it—perhaps Lúcio Cardoso. The book stunned me.... When she returned to Brazil, Rubem [Braga] introduced us. She stunned me."[37] Their meetings in Rio, where he had moved in 1944, made a deep impression on them both; he became, after her sisters and Bluma Wainer, Clarice's most frequent correspondent. "We spent hours talking in our meetings at a café downtown. Or even in my house, where she met, besides Helena, my friends from Minas, Otto Lara Resende, Paulo Mendes Campos (later Hélio Pellegrino)."[38]

This group, which included Rubem Braga, would be of the first significance in Clarice's life. Paulo Mendes Campos, an old friend of Fernando's, had come to Rio to meet the visiting Chilean poet Pablo Neruda. He never left. Though very short, he was refined, charming, and attractive; his lovers eventually included Clarice Lispector. Like her, and like Fernando Sabino, Paulo showed great early promise. "In a literary career, the glory comes at the beginning," he later reflected. "The rest of one's life is an intensive school of anonymity and oblivion."[39] Indeed, though he was a lyrical poet of rare quality, he never enjoyed real fame. But when Clarice met him, he was, in the words of another friend, "Byron, aged twenty three."[40]

❦

The thrill of these new friendships could not have made the return to Europe in mid-March any easier. "My joyous little departure face melted into tears in the plane," she wrote her new friends. "The happy Americans kept watching while I didn't know where to put all those tears and didn't even have enough tissues."[41] She returned via the "desert sands" of Egypt, where she went head-to-head with the Sphinx, and arrived back in Italy to find that Maury had almost finished the packing for their next post: the Swiss capital, Bern. Another, more painful departure awaited.

A report, which later turned out to be untrue, that Swiss hotels didn't accept dogs forced her to leave Dilermando behind. She found a nice girl to take care of him, but was heartbroken. "I can't stand to see a dog in the street, I don't like to look at them," she wrote her sisters. "You don't know what a revelation it was for me to have a dog, to see and feel the material a dog is made of. It's the sweetest thing I ever saw, and a dog has such patience with his own impotent nature and with the incomprehensible nature of others.... With their limited means, with a sweet dumbness, they find a way to understand us. And more than anything Dilermando was something of my own that I didn't have to share with anybody else."[42]

To excise the guilt of having abandoned Dilermando, she wrote a story, "The Crime," published in a Rio newspaper on August 25, 1945.[43] Expanded and rebaptized "The Crime of the Mathematics Professor," this is the earliest of the thirteen famous stories that became *Family Ties*. A man climbs a hill high above a city, carrying a dead dog in a sack.

> While I made you in my image, you made me in yours, he thought. I gave you the name of José so that you would have a name that at the same time could serve as your soul. And you, what name did you give me? You loved me so much more than I loved you, he reflected. We understood one another too well, you with the human name I gave you, I with the name you gave me and that you only pronounced with your eyes, the man thought tenderly. I remember when you were small, cute, and weak, wagging your tail, looking at me, and my surprising in you another way of having my soul. Every day you were a dog that could be abandoned.

When the inevitable abandonment comes, nobody even blames the mathematics teacher for his apparently victimless crime. "With an excuse that everyone approved of: because how could you make such a long journey with baggage and family and a dog on top of all that, said Marta." The abandonment of Dilermando seems to have reminded Clarice of her original sin, her failure to help her mother; the abandonment of the dog is a substitute for some greater, nameless crime: "There are so many ways to be guilty and to be lost forever; I chose to wound a dog. Because I knew it wasn't much and I couldn't be punished for it. Only now do I understand that it really is exempt from punishment, and forever. Nobody damns me for this crime. Neither the church. Not even you would condemn me," the teacher says, addressing the dead dog.

In its original version, the story is only a sketch of the more terrifying "Crime of the Mathematics Professor" she published in 1960. Yet even the preliminary story shows that, as in *Near to the Wild Heart*, Clarice was at her most powerful when, rather than trying to create complicated allegories, she sought the universal meaning within her particular experiences.

18

THE COUNTRY OF A THOUSAND YEARS OF PEACE

Even more than Venice, Clarice's new home, Switzerland, was the ultimate land of artistic death. Here Thomas Mann and Nabokov came to expire; here Nietzsche and Nijinsky went mad. The toy cities, the cuckoo clocks, the chocolates, and the neutrality could not have offered a greater contrast with the chaos, youth, and energy of Rio de Janeiro. Switzerland was somewhat less than Clarice could bear: "This Switzerland," she wrote Tania, "is a cemetery of sensations."[1]

Luckily, some of her new friends had followed her to Europe: Samuel and Bluma Wainer were now based in Paris. The founder of *Diretrizes* was now making a name for himself as a foreign correspondent, first as the only Brazilian to cover the Nuremberg trials, where he managed to interview Hitler's successor, Karl Doenitz, and now as a correspondent for another paper.[2] Samuel and Bluma came to Bern only a few weeks after Clarice and Maury arrived, and Samuel, at least, was not impressed.

"Wainer says that every day in Bern is Sunday," she wrote her sisters. "He said he couldn't stand it if we weren't here. He found it extremely boring and characterless."[3] "The way to do it is to look at Bern through the window and shut your mouth forcefully," she wrote Fernando Sabino and his friends. "Bern is pretty and calm, expensive and with ugly people; with the lack of meat, with the fish, cheese, milk, neutral people, I end up screaming. . . . The city lacks a demon."[4] To Elisa and Tania she added, "Bern is terribly silent: the people too are silent and laugh little. I'm the only one laughing."[5]

She managed to admire some aspects of the country. "The Swiss people got nothing for free. Everything in this country bears the mark of noble effort, of patient conquest. And what they achieved was not nothing—becoming a symbol of peace," she later wrote. But she tempered this admiration by adding, "This doesn't keep so many people, in silence, from throwing themselves off the Kirchenfeld Bridge."[6]

Her unspoken sympathy with these quiet suicides comes through in the atmosphere of despair that pervades her letters. The despair includes the Jewish terror of exile and a hint of what happened to her parents. "It's a shame that I don't have the patience to enjoy a life as tranquil as that of Bern," she wrote her sisters. "It's a farm.... And the silence of Bern—it seems that all the houses are empty, not to mention the calm in the streets.... Could it be that we just can no longer stand peace? In Bern nobody seems to need one another, that much is clear. They all work hard. It's strange to think that there isn't *really* a place one can live. It's all somebody else's country, where other people are happy."[7]

She was laughing a bit, though, and her letters can be enthusiastic and excited as often as they are depressed. One thing stayed the same: the terrible longing she felt for her sisters and her country. She virtually badgered Elisa and Tania to write more, and when letters did arrive, as on the day after her twenty-sixth birthday, she could hardly contain herself. "I was so moved, I cried out of happiness, gratitude, love, longing, joy. I decided to go straight to the cinema because I need to return to normal and then I can write you back, if I can respond in words to the love I've received."[8]

"It's bad to be away from the land where you grew up," she told Lúcio Cardoso. "It's horrible to hear foreign languages all around you, everything seems rootless; the real reasons for things are never revealed to foreigners, and the inhabitants of a place see us as gratuitous. If it was good for me, as medicine is good for the health, to see other places and other people, any benefit has long since worn off; I never thought I would be so inadaptable, I never thought I needed the things I had so much. Though now I'm ashamed not to live well in any place where the bells of the cathedral ring, where there's a river, where people work and do their shopping; but that's the way it is."[9]

"You have to be very happy to live in a small city, because it enlarges happiness just like it enlarges unhappiness," she told an interviewer in the 1960s, once she was back in Brazil. "So I'm going to stay here in Rio. See, in big cities everybody knows that in every apartment there's a kind of solidarity, because an unhappy person lives in every apartment."[10]

One reason for her unhappiness in Bern was the indifference that greeted *The Chandelier*. "The silence around your book is really too much," Fernando

Sabino wrote in May 1946.[11] He had written about it, as had a few other critics of note. Sérgio Milliet, who had heralded her first book, published a positive review; Oswald de Andrade, one of the country's most important writers, called it "terrifying;" another São Paulo reviewer called it "even more significant than her first" and claimed that it "places her in the first rank of our writers."[12] But the contrast with the excitement that greeted *Near to the Wild Heart* was dramatic. "I was prepared, I don't know why especially, for an acid beginning and a solitary end," she had written Milliet after her first book came out. Now she was surprised that even those critics who had praised her first book were ignoring the second. Shouldn't they at least "note the second one, destroying it or accepting it?" she asked Tania.[13]

For the most part *The Chandelier*, which is indeed extremely difficult, seems to have baffled Clarice's admirers and left most critics speechless.[14] The positive signs came from predictable corners. "*The Chandelier*—I still believe—is an authentic masterpiece," Lúcio Cardoso wrote her. "What a great book, what a personality, what a writer!"[15] The only real attack came from another usual suspect, Álvaro Lins, who had been almost alone in rejecting *Near to the Wild Heart*. "Everything he says is true," Clarice wrote Lúcio, "whether it's caused by some enmity for me or whether it's just something he dashed off without much thought.... Anyway, he acts like the man who beats his wife every day because she must have done *something*."[16] A month later, she was still thinking about Lins, telling Fernando Sabino, "Everything he says is true. You can't make art just because you have an unhappy and nutty temperament. A profound discouragement."[17]

This state of mind made progress on her new book, *The Besieged City*, fitful and uncertain, its creation surrounded by the kinds of doubts she did not record when writing her first two. "I'm struggling with the book, which is horrible. How did I find the courage to publish the other two? I don't know how to forgive the thoughtlessness of writing. But I've already based myself entirely on writing and if that desire goes, there won't be anything left. So that's the way it has to be," she wrote Tania. "But I've reached the conclusion that writing is what I want more than anything else in the world, even more than love."[18]

"Two souls, alas! inhabit my breast": Faust's cry, the leitmotif of Hesse's *Steppenwolf*, might also serve as a motto of *Near to the Wild Heart*. The struggle that book dramatizes—between the charismatic, beastly Joana and the placid bourgeoise Lídia, reflects the struggle between two fundamentally inimical halves of their creator. If, as Clarice said in reference to Joana, *Madame Bovary c'est moi,* Clarice was also Lídia, a conventional woman, a wife and a mother, a person who wished to live in peace with the world.

"I would like to spend at least one day watching Lídia walk from the kitchen to the living room, then have lunch beside her in a quiet room—a few flies, the silverware clinking," Joana says. "Then, in the afternoon, seated and watching her sew, helping her out here and there, the scissors, the thread, waiting for a shower and a snack, it would be nice, it would be spacious and fresh. Could a bit of that be what I've always been missing? Why is she so powerful? The fact that I never spent my afternoons sewing doesn't make me less than her, I suppose? Or does it?"[19]

Clarice and Joana have no contempt for Lídia. In interviews with those who knew Clarice Lispector, the word *careta* (prim, correct, square) occurs as often as words describing her eccentricity and genius. She was vain of her appearance, thought that her contributions as a mother far outranked her value as an artist, and published, alongside her vivifying mystical novels, tips on fixing mayonnaise and applying eye makeup. "Intuitively I never stopped believing that Clarice, Joana, and Lídia coexist inside you," Maury wrote her. "Joana and Lídia were, and are, the same person in Clarice."[20]

In Switzerland, the wobbly poise between Joana and Lídia inside Clarice threatened to slip. "I don't agree when you say that you make art because 'you have an unhappy and nutty temperament,'" Fernando Sabino wrote her. "I have a great, an enormous hope in you and I've already said that you have moved ahead of all of us, through the window, in advance of us all. I just hope intensely that you don't advance so far that you fall through the other side. You always have to find balance."[21]

But in Bern there was no place for Joana, consigned to a round of tea parties in polite company. Clarice, whose writings so rarely reflect anger or bitterness, never sounded more sardonic or mocking than in her descriptions of the people she encountered in Switzerland. "We went to see the Minister and his family. They're all great," she told Tania. "Except they're another species absolutely. His wife is a nice lady, from a nice family, simple, kind. But I have to keep my mouth shut the whole time because everything I say sounds 'original' and frightens her. I want to explain what I mean by 'original.' That lady is terrified of anything original. We went to see an exhibition of models of Vienna (not too interesting) and she said: this model is original but it's pretty. Speaking of an English lady who does a lot of sports: she's original, I don't like her.... What they really are is: best-sellers. Their opinions are best-sellers, their ideas are best-sellers."[22] She literally had to keep Joana packed away: "I'm trying to put off loaning them my book, in order not to 'hurt' them. Because I would be classified as 'modern art.'. . . From lying so much to try to have the same opinion as everyone else, because there's no point in arguing, I've been paralyzed."[23] The connotation cannot be accidental.

In Naples, she had ample opportunity to be useful, especially when caring for the wounded Brazilian soldiers. In Switzerland, the sense of uselessness oppressed her, and the possible reference to the mother she failed to rescue echoes the helplessness she felt toward the victims of a more recent tragedy. She confessed to Tania that she was "intimately bothered" by her inability to face up to "the situation of the War, the situation of people, those tragedies," adding, "[Although I feel] the necessity to do something, I feel that I don't have the means. You would say that I do, through my work. I've been thinking a lot about that but I don't see how, I mean, in a real way."[24] She tried to get a job at the Red Cross, but the local branch accepted only Swiss.[25]

With Joana banished from the country of a thousand years of peace, Clarice was increasingly unable to work at all. "I don't work any more, Fernando. I spend my days trying to trick my anxiety and to avoid horrifying myself. There are days when I lie down at three in the afternoon and get up at six to go to the sofa and close my eyes until seven which is dinner time," she wrote at the end of July.[26] "But I didn't want to rest!" Joana had shouted. "The blood ran through her more indolently, its rhythm domesticated, like an animal who shortened its paces in order to fit the cage."[27]

The caged animal, the Steppenwolf: "These people all have two souls, two beings inside them, in whom the divine and the diabolic, the mother's blood and the father's, the capacity for happiness and for suffering, are as tightly and inimically bound as the wolf and the man were inside Harry," Hesse wrote. Could the wolf and the man, Joana and Lídia, live side by side? Among Clarice's last notes is this: "Writing can drive a person mad. You must lead a serene life, well appointed, middle class. If you don't the madness comes. It is dangerous. You must shut your mouth and say nothing about what you know and what you know is so much, and is so glorious. I know, for example, God."[28]

She went to the movies every afternoon: "It hardly mattered what was on."[29] She saw some sights; she visited art exhibitions; and it was in Bern that she began her lifelong habit of visiting card readers and astrologers. She went to Paris a few times to visit Bluma Wainer and other friends; she and Maury took a happy trip to Spain and Portugal. In August 1947, she was on hand when Eva Perón's lavish

European "Rainbow Tour" disembarked in Bern. (Rumor had it that her unexpected detour to Switzerland had something to do with the country's banks.) When the Argentine first lady appeared at the train station, a volley of ripened tomatoes sailed from the crowd and splattered the Swiss foreign minister.[30] To Clarice, Evita seemed "slightly disgusted to see that not everybody likes her."[31] But the tomato incident gave Bluma hope for Switzerland: "In that tidy little Bern, with its polite people! It's good, this way not everything is lost. Our waiting for something to happen is not in vain."[32]

Her life was not without its distractions, but her pleasures were always transitory, and every time she thought she was recovering she ended up breaking down again. Nothing helped. "Every day I go up and down," she wrote Tania. "Even worse: sometimes I spend entire weeks without going up even a little bit. I've so lost my courage and energy that I no longer even complain about it. I can spend hours in an armchair, without so much as a book in my hand, without so much as the radio on—just sitting, waiting for the hours to pass by and for others just like them to appear."[33]

She sought distractions, private exercises, to rescue herself and Joana. In the footsteps of her father, she studied calculus: "Abstraction interests me more and more."[34] At Fernando's suggestion, she read a French translation of the *Imitation of Christ*, "which has purified me at times."[35] Bluma came to Switzerland, but Bluma's marriage was finally disintegrating and she herself was often depressed. "Everything here is quiet and clean," Bluma wrote in July from her hotel in Montparnasse. "Any coincidence with the cemetery is pure resemblance."[36]

By the end of the year, Clarice was seeing a therapist, Ulysses Girsoler, who provided her a lengthy Rorschach.[37] It is unclear whether he was a psychoanalyst and how he met Clarice. "He was a student, I think of painting," Clarice's friend Olga Borelli said. "And this Ulysses had such a violent passion for her that he had to move to another city, he left" (for Basel, and then Geneva). "Because Clarice was extremely beautiful, people fell in love with her. He left, and she always remembered him. He was blond, with light eyes, named Ulysses. So in homage, she used the name Ulysses in *An Apprenticeship*."[38]

Little is known about this Ulysses. He was not Swiss, and the few references to him in Clarice's correspondence suggest others that have not been published or made available. The longest is in a letter to Tania from October 1947 that probably refers to Ulysses:

> That boy, who is in Geneva, is completely neurasthenic. It seems he even gets up in the middle of the night to cry.... <u>Don't tell</u> <u>anyone</u>, <u>of course</u>. It seems he's even been going to a health clinic. Part of it has to do with

his being sick, and that depressed him. But I think that a lot of it comes from the uprooting of this life abroad. Not everyone is strong enough to stand not having their own surroundings, or friends. More and more, I admire Papa and others who, like him, managed to have a "new life"; you need a lot of courage to have a new life. In this career you're completely outside reality, you don't belong to anything—and the diplomatic environment is made up of shadows and shadows. It's even considered bad taste to have any personal tastes or to speak of oneself or even to speak of others. Nobody has a relationship with a diplomat—with a diplomat, you have lunch.[39]

Girsoler was the first in a long line of psychotherapists (if that is what he was) who either fell in love with Clarice or became too attached to her to be able to function with proper analytic distance. His prophetic Rorschach describes with uncanny precision the same drama Clarice had set out in *Near to the Wild Heart*: the struggle between impetuous Joana and placid Lídia.

"It is not necessary, after all, to say that the intelligence of Cl. V. is far above average. She knows it herself, though she has her doubts for the moment. She has a breadth of intellectual capacities that is almost too great to be completely employed," the diagnosis opens. "In Cl. V. the affectivity that actively touches the course of her associations [i.e., as the Rorschach drawings were shown] is of a disquieting power.... A great fantasy and a strong intuition are united.... The creative urge breaks through vehemently." Yet he warns against the danger:

[She has a] tendency to delve into a genial, undisciplined chaos. Affectivity occupies a much larger space than average and possesses a clearly egocentric character.— This affectivity directly requires a great intellectual effort from most of those affected by it.— The impulsive affectivity (which requires no accommodation) can in Cl. V., to the shock of those affected by it, become entirely explosive, and at such moments she can be whisked away without any control. During such outbursts she can perform entirely thoughtless actions and behave in a foolhardy fashion. For the time being this impulsive side is strongly repressed. We see that all her sentimental life is stretched between one extreme (impulsivity) all the way across the whole range to the other extreme (subtlety, sensibility, ability to feel all the possible emotions that other humans feel). —It will be very difficult for such a character to find balance.—a conscious domestication of these elementary impulses by intellectual participation. —The result is a more or less melancholy character. That is the reason for the possibility of a tendency

> to flee the world despite the great vitality. —There is a perseverance of a great number of thoughts, and especially when those thoughts are affectively related to conflicts. Cl. V. begins to think around the conflicts and a great amount of her originality and her creative strength is absorbed by this way of thinking in circles. The result of this manner of thinking [is] original symbols and partially thoughts that contain designs in a mystical form. —This depressive state often slides into a melancholy expression, but never for long since the reaction soon manifests itself once again on the side of vitality.

She is able to perform regular tasks, but "a great skepticism appears against the world, a doubt about people that reaches an outspoken opposition," including, "with the same energy, against herself."[40]

In her novel *An Apprenticeship or the Book of Pleasures*, Ulisses would be a rather pedantic teacher and philosopher; and her last, beloved dog would be called Ulisses, too. In a letter the real "Ulisses" sent to "Clarissa. Clarissima," he tells her, "It is an even harder thing to support [i.e., stand] real freedom."[41]

"My drama: is that I am free," she later wrote;[42] this was, in fact, much of the drama she experienced in Switzerland. From an artistic perspective, she had what so many writers dream of: unlimited hours in which to work unperturbed. But her days were amorphous and she stared out the window. "The solitude I always needed is at the same time entirely unbearable," she wrote Fernando.[43] She told Tania, "I would like to have a mathematical device to measure precisely every millimeter I move ahead, and every millimeter I fall behind."[44]

The months wore on; at the beginning of January 1947, she wrote Tania a long letter. For her substitute mother, who thought of herself as "more than a sister," it must have been even more painful to read than it was for Clarice to write.[45] It is hard to believe that its author is the same beautiful and alluring young woman who, less than a year earlier, had departed Rio de Janeiro, where she was fêted by many of her country's leading artists, and who took time out of her journey back to Europe to go eyeball-to-eyeball with the Sphinx. In her place appears a woman so despondent and helpless that her letter reads almost like a suicide note.

> Don't think that a person has the strength to lead any kind of life and stay the same.... I don't know how to explain my soul to you. But what I mean

is that we are very precious, and that there's only so much you can give up of yourself for the sake of other people and circumstances. . . . All I planned to do was tell you about my new character, or lack of character. . . . Darling, almost four years have greatly transformed me. From the moment I resigned myself, I lost all my vivacity and all my interest in things. Have you seen the way a castrated bull turns into an ox? That is what happened to me . . . despite the hard comparison. . . . To adapt to something I can't adapt to, to get over my dislikes and my dreams, I had to cut off my fetters—I cut off inside me the way I could hurt others and myself. And at the same time I cut off my strength. I hope you never see me resigned like this, because it's almost repugnant. . . . One day, a friend filled herself with courage, as she said, and asked me: "You were really different, weren't you?" She said she thought I had been passionate and lively, and that when she met me here she thought: either this excessive calm is a pose or she's changed so much that she's almost unrecognizable. Someone else told me that I move with the lassitude of a fifty-year-old woman . . . which can happen with someone who has made a pact with everyone, and who forgot that the vital center of a person has to be respected. Listen: respect even the bad parts of yourself—respect above all the bad parts of yourself—for the love of God, don't try to make yourself perfect—don't copy an ideal, copy yourself—that is the only way to live.

19

THE PUBLIC STATUE

> In Switzerland, in Bern, I lived on the Gerechtigkeitsgasse, that is, Justice Street. In front of my house, in the street, was the colored statue, holding the scales. Around, crushed kings begging perhaps for a pardon. In the winter, the little lake in the middle of which the statue stood, in the winter the freezing water, sometimes brittle with a thin layer of ice. In the spring red geraniums. . . . And the still-medieval street: I lived in the old part of the city. What saved me from the monotony of Bern was living in the Middle Ages, it was waiting for the snow to pass and for the red geraniums to be reflected once again in the water, it was having a son born there, it was writing one of my least liked books, *The Besieged City*, which, however, people come to like when they read it a second time; my gratitude to that book is enormous: the effort of writing it kept me busy, saved me from the appalling silence of Bern, and when I finished the last chapter I went to the hospital to give birth to the boy.[1]

For Virginia, in *The Chandelier*, the only reality was internal; the outside world was fuzzy and incomprehensible and finally did her in. Lucrécia Neves, heroine of *The Besieged City*, is the opposite. Her own intimate life is "barely useable," and so, "unintelligent," she looks outward, to the new city growing up around her. "Which was so important for a person in a certain way stupid; Lucrécia who did not possess the futilities of the imagination, but only the narrow existence of whatever she saw."[2] As a book about the external world, it is a singular instance in Clarice Lispector's work. Perhaps the book represented a final attempt for Clarice to get outside herself, to flee the "shipwreck of introspection,"[3] to escape the melancholy that threatened to do her in. "Breath deep the spring air," Bluma Wainer wrote Clarice after a visit to Bern in March 1947. "Think as little as possible and analyze even less."[4]

The name Lucrécia hides Clarice's own name, and unlike so many of Clarice's characters, who are extensions or enunciations of herself, Lucrécia is a true alter ego, a person who thinks as little as possible and analyzes even less. Unlike the vitally, painfully alive Clarice, Lucrécia achieves the ultimate in muteness and unreflection. In a chapter titled "The Public Statue," Clarice writes, "In the position she was in, Lucrécia Neves could even be transported to a public square. All she was missing were the sun and the rain. So that, covered with lime, she could finally be unnoticed by the inhabitants and finally seen daily without being noticed. Because that was the way a statue belonged to a city." It is hard not to think of the image of Justice outside her window in the Gerechtigkeitsgasse. Later, the metaphor reappears: "Slowly, as the man spoke, Lucrécia Neves grew larger, enigmatic, a statue at whose feet, during civic holidays, flowers were deposited."[5]

Lucrécia exists to satisfy her small, easily identifiable needs. Her story has an alluring simplicity: she grows up, gets married, is widowed, and marries again. It is impossible to escape the conclusion that Lucrécia is someone Clarice would have liked to be, or at least someone whose easier life part of her envied: happily superficial, content with tea parties and "best-seller" people. So many of Clarice's books end with car wrecks, submissions, and defeat; it is not by chance that *The Besieged City* has a happy ending.

Much of what brought Clarice misery and exile meant fulfillment and peace for Lucrécia. After spurning her dreamy adolescent boyfriend Perseu, whose name associates him with Pegasus, the flying horse of Greek antiquity, Lucrécia marries Mateus, a rich man from another city. Mateus offers Lucrécia much of what Maury could give Clarice. An outsider to her community, cultivated and worldly, Mateus promised financial security and the hope of seeing the world. "Every man seems to promise a woman a bigger city," Clarice writes. "Ah, Mateus is from another world, mama! he's from another city, he's cultured, he knows what's going on, he reads the paper, he knows other people," the ditzy Lucrécia tells her mother when she wants to get married. This is a perfect match. Lucrécia "wanted to be rich, possess things, and move up in the world."[6] But just as Clarice complained that "Bern is a tomb, even for the Swiss. And a Brazilian is nothing in Europe," Lucrécia finds, once she leaves her native São Geraldo, that she is out of place: "Once she left the town, her kind of beauty had disappeared, and her importance was diminished."[7] In her new place, she is "the most inexperienced member of the city,"[8] though she soon discovers a kind of satisfaction there.

Indeed, the catty remarks sprinkled through the book, so untypical of Clarice's writing, seem to reflect her unhappiness, not Lucrécia's. When she writes of Mateus, for example, that he had the "look of a lawyer or an engineer—such was his air of mystery,"[9] she probably was thinking of the lawyers and diplomats, the "best-sellers," that surrounded her in her exile. Lucrécia, by contrast, is usually in a good mood.

In the new place, the empty woman devotes herself to social climbing: "Lucrécia hoped to go two or three more times to the theater, looking forward to reaching a number that was difficult to count, like seven or nine, when she could add: 'I used to go to the theater all the time.'" She learns the customs of the new city, and she fits in perfectly. At first, at the theater, she is struck by the beauty of the performance, but this, too, passes, and the "best-seller" expression becomes second nature: "Because later she learned to say: I liked it a lot, the theater was nice, I had such a good time. . . . This is the most beautiful square I've ever seen, she would say, and then she could securely walk across the most beautiful square she had ever seen." A favorite saying is that something "works in theory, but not in practice."[10]

Lucrécia Neves, taking in the sights in the big city, shopping and visiting the theater, sounds rather like Clarice Lispector in Paris, where she spent a month at the beginning of 1947. "I don't know if I'm crazy about Paris," she wrote her sisters. "It's hard to say. With life the way it is, it seems that I'm 'a different person' in Paris. It's a dizziness that isn't pleasant at all. I've seen too many people, talked too much, told lies, been very nice. The person who's enjoying herself is a woman I don't know, a woman I detest, a woman who isn't your sister. She's just anybody."

She is Lucrécia, in other words. But Clarice, unfortunately for her peace of mind, could not turn herself into just anybody. "I was truly fatigued in Paris by all those intelligent people. You can't go to a theater without having to say if you liked it or not, and why you liked it and why you didn't. I learned to say 'I don't know,' which I was proud of, as a defense and a bad habit, because I end up really not wanting to think, besides just not wanting to *say* what I think."[11]

During Lucrécia's lifetime, the small settlement of São Geraldo becomes a full-fledged city. When she is a child, São Geraldo, rather like Chechelnik, is a little place, populated by wild horses. The history of the town's growth is the story of the expulsion of these horses; as it takes on ever more civilized airs, finally acquiring a viaduct and an embankment, the horses progressively emigrate, "delivering the metropolis to the Glory of its mechanism."[12]

As the city grows and the horses are expelled, the town's language evolves. São Geraldo's first citizens had no need of words. Lucrécia's ancient neighbor Efigênia, who by dint of long residence has become a kind of municipal totem, is almost as silent as the horses. "The spiritual life they vaguely attributed to Efigênia finally seemed to be summed up by the fact that she neither agreed nor disagreed, that she didn't participate even with herself, so austere she had become. To be as silent and hard as people who had never had to think. Whereas in São Geraldo people were starting to talk a lot."[13]

The symbol of São Geraldo's linguistic adolescence is Perseu, Lucrécia's first boyfriend, who experiences the same linguistic ecstasy that marked Joana and Virginia. Like the young Clarice Lispector, Perseu takes delight in a language that is still as sonorous and nonsensical as music.

> "Marine beings, when not affixed to the sea floor, adapt to a fluctuating or pelagic life," Perseu studied on the afternoon of May 15, 192....
>
> Heroic and empty, the citizen kept standing beside the open window. But in fact he could never transmit to anyone the extent to which he was harmonious, and even if he spoke, no word could convey the graciousness of his appearance: his extreme harmony was simply evident.
>
> "Pelagic animals reproduce with profusion," he said with hollow luminosity. Blind and glorious—that was all that could be known of him....
>
> "They feed on basic microvegetation, infusorials, etc."
>
> "Etc.!" he repeated brilliant, unconquerable....
>
> "This discoidal animal is formed according to the symmetry based on the number 4."
>
> That's what it said! And the sun beat down on the dusty page: a cockroach was even climbing up the house across the street....Then the boy said something as lustrous as a scarab:
>
> "Pelagic beings reproduce with extraordinary profusion," he finally exclaimed from memory.[14]

In choosing the outsider Mateus over the native Perseu, Lucrécia also elects a sophisticated language, one still foreign to the little town of her birth. But São Geraldo is catching up, and slick linguistic accretions are as much a part of its progress as the viaduct and the embankment. "The more São Geraldo grew, the more difficult it became for [Lucrécia] to speak clearly, so dissimulated had she become." Nothing, now, is wild; everything, even Mateus's last moments, are smothered by Lucrécia's syrupy words. "Even his death, she had tried to destroy.

She tried to console him, the only way to reduce the event to something recognizable: at least you're not dying away from home.... Foolish, as if dying didn't always take place away from home."[15]

Clarice's discontent with her own forcible domestication comes across rather loudly in her descriptions of the city's increasing pretensions. It is obvious enough that she hated for the horses to abandon São Geraldo. But *The Besieged City* is not a denunciation of bourgeois affectations. It is part of her lifelong quest for an authentic language.

Perhaps the initial impulse came from the hours she spent staring out of her window in Switzerland, contemplating the inflexible figure of Justice. The language of *The Besieged City* is the language of vision, and metaphors of seeing are sprinkled insistently throughout the book. At certain moments, vision even replaces spoken language, as when people "look" or "see" words rather than speaking or thinking them: "This city is mine, the woman looked."[16]

The gazes of its inhabitants, not bricks and asphalt, build the new city of São Geraldo. "The city was taking the form her gaze revealed." "Oh, but things were never seen: it was people who saw them." "She opened her eyelashes, staring blindly. After a time the things in the room recovered their own positions, recuperating the way they could be seen by her." "In truth it was a very crude function—she indicated the intimate name of things, she, the horses, and a few others; and later things would be seen by this name. Reality required the girl in order to take a form."[17]

At the end of Lucrécia's life, "looking was still her maximum reflection." Even as a child, she had "seen things as a horse does";[18] that is, Lucrécia is content not to see beyond the surface of things, and this is the positive value of her "superficiality." Clarice, whose relentless introspection had brought her to despair, could not follow Bluma Wainer's suggestion to be a bit more superficial herself, to "think as little as possible and analyze even less." "My misfortune is asking questions," she later wrote, "since I was little I was nothing but a question."[19]

Lucrécia must learn how "to look with a delicate effort at nothing more than the surface—and quickly not to look again."[20] The effort demands a certain determination; she is not, like Perseu or Efigênia, organically a part of the truth.[21] "She leaned over without any individuality, trying merely to look at things directly."[22] Merely—but this way of looking leads, paradoxically but inevitably, to Clarice's own metaphysical concerns. As it turns out, *not* being profound is simply another way of being profound.

Lucrécia's shallowness unites her not only with her immediate creator but with the divine act of creation itself. She creates the city; she creates every thing she looks at. "Some thing could not exist except under intense attention; looking with a severity and a hardness that made her seek not the cause of things, but the thing itself."[23] In other words, her insistent attention to surfaces is yet another way to approach "the thing itself" that Clarice had earlier sought in her previous books.

But what things can be fully seen by looking merely at their surfaces? The shape of a circle, for example, is indistinguishable from the circle itself, containing the entirety of itself in its symbol. This, not simply the untamed "wild heart," is the significance of the horses of São Geraldo. For Clarice, in this book as in so many others, the horse is a perfect creature, and becoming like a horse is a mystical goal, uniting soul and body, matter and spirit. A horse acts only according to its nature, free of the artifices of thought and analysis, and this is the freedom Clarice seems to long for: the freedom to do as she liked, yes, but more important the freedom from "the shipwreck of introspection." For a person tormented by her past and incapable of living in her present, the horse was also a solution.

And so, finally, was Lucrécia. "Everything she saw was *some thing*. In her and in a horse the impression was the expression."[24] *The impression was the expression*: Lucrécia, and the horses, are "the symbol of the thing in the thing itself." In a letter, Clarice further explains the phrase: "without the arms of intelligence, and aspiring to the kind of spiritual integrity of a horse, not 'sharing' what he sees, not having a mental or 'vocabular vision' of things, not feeling the need to complete an impression with an expression—a horse, in which there is the miracle of the impression being total—so real—that in him an impression is already an expression."[25]

What a horse feels, its "impressions," cannot be corrupted by the verbal, linguistic "expressions" that can only dilute or distort those original, authentic feelings. Lucrécia sees only surfaces and herself *is* nothing but surface, another means for Clarice to approach the same goal: the "word that has its own light," in which meaning and expression are finally united.

20

THE THIRD EXPERIENCE

"The word 'word' is ex-possible!"

"Ex-possible?"

"Yes! I'd rather say ex-possible than impossible! The word 'word' is ex-possible because it means word."[1]

One can only imagine with what thrill of motherly pride Clarice Lispector set down this dialogue with her son, Pedro. Named in memory of his grandfather and born in Bern on September 10, 1948, Pedro seemed to have absorbed the philosophical concerns that occupied his mother when he was in the womb. She was just completing *The Besieged City*: "When I finished the last chapter I went to the hospital to give birth to the boy."[2]

Pedro's birth initiated the third of her "three experiences": "I was born to love others, I was born to write, and I was born to raise my children." Not, however, in that order. Clarice often insisted that motherhood was much more important to her than literature: "There is no doubt that I am more important as a mother than as a writer."[3] Motherhood also offered her the possibility of piecing together an existence shattered when she lost her own mother: "If I wasn't a mother, I would be alone in the world."[4]

Motherhood was the one thing that both the wild Joana and the tame Lídia desired, and Clarice wanted it, too: "As for my children, their birth was not haphazard. I wanted to be a mother."[5] It was not easy, though, and the way Pedro came into the world was a taste of what was to come. The birth was induced with injections, but after almost fifteen hours of labor the baby had not come out, and the doctors decided to perform an emergency caesarian.[6]

Feverish and in pain, Clarice had to spend a couple of weeks in the hospital. "As for Maury, I have rarely seen his equal in my life. He is so good to me, thinks of everything, is enormously patient with me and surrounds me with more care and love than I deserve. I hope I never hurt him. Not only because he's been this way. In everything, he's one of the purest people I know. I couldn't have a better father for my son."[7]

Her first reports to her in-laws are full of a new mother's enthusiasm: "Little Pedro is very funny, constantly putting on weight and making faces. I'm sending an example, a terrible picture that is just a sample. In this photograph he is one week 'old.' This is the face he likes the most: opening his nostrils wide and transforming his mouth into a beak."[8] There were some doubts about the nanny: "She's maniacal about silence (imagine wanting more silence than in Bern!); she wants us to whisper and walk on tiptoes—which would teach the child bad habits: he'll be frightened in any other country."[9] Later, to Tania, she described the nurse as "a plague with a diploma."[10]

But the gravity of the new enterprise was not lost on her. "Every woman, when she learns she is pregnant, lifts her hand to her throat: she knows that she will give birth to a being who will inevitably follow the path of Christ, falling many times along the way under the weight of the cross. There is no escape."[11] Pedro would fall beneath the weight of his cross, causing her a pain as great as the loss of her mother. But for now, not even this foreknowledge would have contaminated her and Maury's happiness. Perhaps this is what she was thinking when, on December 24, 1971, she wrote a Christmas column called "Today a Child Is Born." The cross was looming in the future, but "for now, the joy belonged only to a little Jewish family."[12]

❦

In 1948, there was joy in other Jewish families. On November 29, 1947, under the gavel of its Brazilian president, Oswaldo Aranha, the United Nations General Assembly voted to partition Palestine. (The gesture earned Aranha fame as a friend of the Jews, notwithstanding his statement that the creation of Israel meant that Copacabana could now be returned to the Brazilians.)[13] By early May, when Clarice was finishing *The Besieged City,* Bluma's husband, the globetrotting reporter Samuel Wainer, was standing in front of the Café Brasil in Tel Aviv, a gathering place for the clandestine Jewish government, trying to contact the Irgun. Representatives of the Jewish terrorist organization duly appeared to describe, in detail, their famous attack on the King David Hotel.[14] On May 13, on his way out of the country, Wainer was almost blown up by a mine on the road to the airport. The next day the State of Israel was proclaimed.

And there was joy in Rio de Janeiro. Elisa Lispector's fictionalized memoir, *In Exile*, opens with Lizza's early-morning arrival at a train station. She hears a languid newspaper seller say "Read the *Diário*!" (Samuel Wainer's paper). "Latest news: Jewish state proclaimed! Read all about it! The *Diário*!"

> Lizza awoke from her stillness with a jolt in her heart. She bought a paper, feverishly opened it, and while her eyes ran across the news, a growing weariness spread through her entire being, as if a dark spring was flowing inside her and penetrating every corner of her soul. Now she would say she was peaceful—too peaceful for someone who had spent the last days in the sanatorium in unrelenting anxiety, following, through the newspapers and the radio, the events in Lake Success, relative to the problem of Palestine.
>
> "Jewish State!" she heard someone say, irritated, beneath the window of her wagon. "These Jews . . . "
>
> His steps moved off and the rest of the sentence broke off into the distance.
>
> Lizza heard him without resentment. She had heard similar comments so many times that they could no longer bother her. And now she was calmer than ever. A sweet hope in the destinies of the world was born inside her. Humanity was redeeming itself. Finally, it was paying its debt to the Jews. It was worth the suffering and the struggle. So many tears, so much blood. They did not die in vain.
>
> ". . . they did not die in vain . . . ," the wheels began to sing on the tracks, while the train began moving once again.[15]

The story that follows is the story of the Lispector family's flight from their homeland.[16] The creation of the Jewish state, and the happiness it gives the heroine, lends the dreadful suffering of its characters, especially Lizza, a kind of meaning, a hope that her family's and her people's sacrifices had been to some positive end, that their loved ones, and particularly her mother, "did not die in vain."

In both its explicit historical references and its insistent political bent, *In Exile* is unlike anything Clarice would write. Elisa, who was nine years older, not only remembered the whole hideous story of the family's flight from Europe. She could, in a sense, never forget it. An active Zionist, secretary of the Jewish Institute of Historical Research in Rio, she traveled to Israel in later years. More academically inclined than her younger sister, she earned degrees in sociology and art history, besides her piano studies at the Recife Conservatory, and she attentively followed literary and intellectual debates.[17]

As the phrase "someone who had spent the last days in the sanatorium in unrelenting anxiety" reveals, however, what she and Clarice did have in common were their terrible struggles with depression. After Elisa entered the federal bureaucracy, she was overtaken by sorrow and passed through a "tremendous crisis" upon her father's death.[18] This despair led her to write. Her first novel, *Across the Border*, was written in such secrecy that not even Tania knew she was working on it. Published in 1945, shortly after *Near to the Wild Heart*, it in fact considerably antedates Clarice's debut, completed by January 1942.[19]

The novel betrays its origins as the author's attempt to write her way out of her despondency. "In an outburst of pain, he began to write quickly, nervously, in shaky uneven handwriting, as if trying to free himself from a great oppression," the book opens.[20] *Across the Border* is the story of an immigrant writer, Sérgio, *né* Sergei, who has something in common both with Pedro Lispector and with his daughters. "When I say war psychosis, I mean from the tormented period we're going through," a colleague tells Sérgio. "I know you don't write about wars. I've read your writing. But there's a harmful influence in all of that. I don't know, maybe it's exile, the migrations through strange countries, your extreme solitude."[21]

A friend of Elisa's wrote that the book "was inspired by the figure of her father, to whom it is dedicated. It is his daughter's homage to the unfulfilled artist."[22] The figure of Sérgio announces Elisa's future theme: "extreme solitude." "Solitude became his only means of escaping the oppressive feeling that he was constantly failing, since he did not know how to live as others did."[23]

The book recalls Pedro Lispector's confession to Clarice and the words that inspired Elisa to begin writing it: "If I were to write, I would write a book about a man who saw that he had lost." The incapacity for living in the everyday world was shared by Clarice, who could never adapt to public life, as well as by Elisa, who dealt with her perpetual anxiety by shutting herself off from the world. Elisa was close to her friends and family, who remember her warmly. She had lovers, including the noted novelist Orígenes Lessa,[24] but she never married. Solitude was her great theme.

The legacy of the pogroms was an unrelenting depression, an inability to connect, that her friend Renard Perez noted. "I felt her inaptitude, her lack of preparedness for everyday life. A great insecurity, which became a wariness toward other people."[25] Like Sérgio, and like Clarice ("She was happy inside her neurosis. War neurosis.")[26], Elisa had her own crippling war neurosis. In her last novel, which, like *In Exile,* is strongly autobiographical, Elisa wrote, "But it is not good to survive. Believe me. One never entirely survives, and the part of us that remains grows weak not knowing what to do with one's time, which stands still, and with one's arid existence, which stagnates. Surviving means not knowing what to do with oneself."[27]

Elisa wrote for many of the same reasons that Clarice created Lucrécia. "If I could at least stop thinking, if only I could forget," Sérgio says. Like her sister, Elisa sought a solution in writing, but dwelling on misfortune was dangerous. "Writing, reliving, it may root out the evil, I tell myself, but the truth is that the more I touch the wound the more it bleeds." The antidote proved poisonous. "Will I never be able to put down this burden? always writing, writing. The idea never leaves me, and now I wonder why, what's the point? If I could stop, perhaps I could find peace."[28]

In May 1948, as war erupted in the Middle East, a pregnant Clarice, in placid Switzerland, finally completed *The Besieged City*. Her Italian maid, Rosa, shocked by the amount of time Clarice had spent revising it, concluded that it was better to be a cook than a writer, because "if you put too much salt in the food, there's nothing you can do about it."[29]

The book was swiftly rejected by the Editora Agir, the Catholic publishing house that had published *The Chandelier*. In early July, Clarice wrote Tania:

> I don't know if you know that Agir doesn't want to or can't publish my book—the fact is their reply was negative. So I don't have a publisher. I might send the book to Brazil with someone I know. You can let Lúcio Cardoso read it. He might find a publisher for me. If he doesn't, it doesn't matter. What I want is to get that book out of here. It's impossible to improve it. And besides, I urgently need to be free of it. When you give it to Lúcio, don't ask him to find a publisher. I'll write him myself about that. I don't even have the courage to ask you to read it. It is so tiresome, really. And you might suffer by having to tell me that you don't like it and feel bad about seeing me literarily lost.... Anyway, do whatever you want, whatever is easiest for you. I hope some day that I'll get out of this vicious circle into which my "soul has fallen."[30]

As always, Tania knew how to cheer up her younger sister, who thanked her exuberantly for her encouraging comments on the book: "I don't know how to tell you how I thank God, if God exists, for having you as a sister. You are the prize of my life. You are the sun of the Earth, and you give it beauty. Your existence gives meaning to life and makes it worth living."[31] Yet the news was discouraging; Agir's rejection was soon followed by a rejection from Jackson Editores.

She was elated to be a mother, but not even the birth of Pedro could shake Clarice out of her depression. In December, they moved house, leaving behind the Gerechtigkeitsgasse with its sculpture of Justice. She took a sculpture course, where she tried vainly to sculpt the head of a monkey in clay, and even learned how to knit.[32] She and Maury refused to learn how to play cards, though it might have enhanced their social lives: "But we don't want to on principle: playing cards would be an easy way to get out of the tedium and would work as a kind of morphine. Maybe I'll learn some day, but I'll hesitate a long time before I get there."[33]

She was, however, already taking other drugs. She recommended Bellergal to Tania, which is commonly prescribed for restlessness, fatigue, insomnia, and headache, but which also contains barbiturates and is contraindicated for pregnant women.[34] Pedro was already giving signs that he was not entirely normal. The first shock came when Clarice and Maury, who had to travel out of town, left him behind with his nanny. He was still very young and could not yet speak Portuguese. They were only gone for a few days, and when they returned, they found him speaking fluently the nanny's language. Clarice told Elisa that she was terrified by this abnormal precocity.[35]

The only thing that could really lift her spirits was the prospect of returning to Brazil. "I was so happy that Marcia [Tania's daughter] asked when I was coming back. Tell her that we might be there by the beginning of the year," she wrote Tania. "Tell her that all these years have dripped by and that I practically counted every drip—but that at the same time they've gone by incredibly fast because only a single thought connected them: this whole time was like the development of one single idea: return. Tell her that for that reason she shouldn't expect to see me come back laughing and jumping for joy: you never saw someone come out of prison laughing: it's a much deeper happiness."[36]

They would not return in 1948. Only on March 17, 1949, did the news come that Maury was being removed to Rio de Janeiro. "I'm writing from beneath the hair dryer," Clarice wrote her sisters a week later, "getting ready to go to Rome to have some clothes made. I can't tell you what I felt when I heard we would be leaving for Brazil. My great joy is inexpressible. My immediate reaction was my heart speeding up, my hands and feet going cold. Then I started sleeping badly and managed to lose even more weight. I'm so annoying that I'm already thinking that I'll have to leave Brazil again. I'm controlling myself so I don't get too happy. I'm so delighted. Maybe in Rio I'll be able to write again and revive myself."[37]

On June 3, 1949, the young family finally left Bern, sailing to Brazil from Genoa. "The food was awful, extremely greasy," on the Atlantic crossing, Clarice remembered. "I did what I could to feed without danger my eight-month-old boy."[38] The food improved once they arrived in Recife. A big lunch awaited, prepared by her aunt Mina Lispector. Like Tania, Mina had been a substitute mother for the girl, and Clarice remembered her with great tenderness. On her final visit to Recife, a few months before her death, Clarice named the person who had most marked her life: "Aunt Mina who gave me food. Who took care of me."[39]

Clarice had not seen the city of her childhood since 1935, when the family moved to Rio. It had not changed as much as she had. On her way to Aunt Mina's, she wanted to see the Avenida Conde de Boa Vista, the main artery through the Jewish neighborhood of Boa Vista. She remembered it as enormous and was disappointed when it turned out to be rather unimpressive. She had a similar notion of Recife's famous law school. "Children generally have a different idea of the dimension of things, you know how it is: I played on the stairs of the Law School and remembered it being enormous. On my way through Recife I saw it again, its actual size."[40]

She, Maury, and Pedro had only a few hours in Recife before they had to be back onboard, continuing on to Rio, where she hadn't been since March 1946. Her news of the city, and of Brazil, had come mainly from Bluma Wainer, who was increasingly depressed and had split from Samuel. Things had not been going well for years. Samuel, tirelessly building up one of the most extraordinary careers in the history of Brazilian journalism, was always darting off on exotic missions, leaving Bluma by herself in Paris or in Rio. "I spoke to Sam on the phone, and as I've already said and as always we didn't get past 'how are you? Everything ok? Etc.," she wrote Clarice in 1947.[41] By the next year, she told Clarice, "I'm turning to stone, nothing moves me or interests me any more." Samuel was gone again, flying from Palestine to Bogotá. "Miss Bluma will be alone once more. (I would like to find a word that means more than alone—you who understand the strength of words, find me one and send it)."[42]

The marriage was definitely over by the beginning of 1949, when Samuel met Getúlio Vargas in Rio Grande do Sul. In his home state, the erstwhile dictator, now a senator, was meticulously planning his return to the presidential palace. Samuel had come to see Getúlio as the leader of a genuinely national movement, with broad support from many sectors of society, as well as one committed to the democracy in place since 1945. He and Bluma had been leftists—Samuel, for example, was the first Brazilian to interview Tito—and Bluma still was. Her letters to Clarice record her enthusiasm over the Spanish Republican movement and her visit to Yugoslavia and are tinged with a mild anti-Americanism. In 1947, she reported, with understandable astonishment, that Brazil had agreed to import twenty-seven thousand tons of American bananas![43] For the woman whose motto was "The ends do *not* justify the means," Samuel's alliance with the dictator was the last straw.

Along with her reports on the unfolding political scene back home—"Brazil just keeps getting more and more Brazil," she sighed[44]—Bluma also urged her friend not to pine away for the place. "For the rest, the papers are full of news about wives who kill their husbands, husbands who kill their wives and respective lovers, and others, with less commotion, who simply kill themselves."[45]

21

HER EMPTY NECKLACES

For Clarice, arrival in Rio meant reunion with another old friend, Lúcio Cardoso. The boy who had dreamed of film stars in his small backwater now set up his own Chamber Theater to feature the works of classic authors, alongside his own work and that of his friends.[1] He had begun working in the theater in 1943, just when he met Clarice. It was a lifelong dream.

"Lúcio Cardoso—I remember well—attributed great importance to his work in the theater," said his friend the novelist Octávio de Faria. "It was inevitable, since he himself was essentially more a 'tragedian' than a novelist."[2] His theatrical work was artistically avant-garde and politically far ahead of his time, nowhere more than in racial questions. Though slavery had not been outlawed until 1888, within the living memory of many Brazilians, the country's elite held as a doctrine of faith that the country did not suffer racial divisions.[3] With Tomás Santa Rosa, who had illustrated the covers of *Near to the Wild Heart*, *The Chandelier*, and *The Besieged City*, Lúcio participated in the Black Experimental Theater of Abdias do Nascimento, an early Afro-Brazilian activist. Santa Rosa designed the sets and became codirector of Lúcio's *The Prodigal Son*, a biblical drama performed with an all-black cast.

Despite all the group's efforts, the play flopped. His sister recalled her "anguish seeing Pascola, the most renowned theater critic of the day, snoozing in the front row."[4] Undaunted, convinced that theater was a weak area in Brazilian culture, Lúcio determined to open the Chamber Theater in 1947. To get funding, he invited his writer friends to contribute articles. From Bern, Clarice Lispector sent a blurb: "The authors, set designers, and artists who work for the Chamber Theater guarantee the success of their undertaking—to return to the gesture its meaning and the word its irreplaceable tone; to allow silence, as in good music, to be heard as well, and not to relegate the sets to mere decoration nor to simple background—but to use all these elements in their specific theatrical purity, allowing them to form the invisible structure of a drama."[5] With her own theatrical flourish, she signed this sentence "Lili, queen of the desert."

To open this ambitious endeavor, Lúcio produced his own *The Silver String*. "I cannot recall a more carefully prepared, better worked-out, more impressive spectacle for our little group around Lúcio," Octávio de Faria recalled. "Ester Leão was the director and Lúcio Cardoso submitted (though, it is true, sometimes almost screaming) to all her demands. Sometimes I saw him on the verge of tears. It doesn't matter. The play opened, and the actress Alma Flora got almost all the applause."[6] As it happened, the poetically named Alma Flora had appeared at Recife's grandest venue, the Teatro Santa Isabel, when Clarice Lispector was a child. The spectacle had inspired her, age nine, to write her two-page, three-act play, *Poor Little Rich Girl*.[7]

Enthusiasm ran high, as always with Lúcio's undertakings. "I remember it like it was today," Faria continued.

> Lúcio Cardoso, wild about the new "diva" (he never got over his "passion" for Italian film divas), ordered up a huge "banquet," at Lapa 49, to commemorate Alma Flora's breakthrough. No end to the beer and the fresh crabs—except that there wasn't any money to pay for it...and there, in the middle of the table, a magnificent centerpiece of red roses (red, of course!...) dedicated to the diva being honored. It was a great party, one of the few happy, successful ones I can remember. It really was a breakthrough—not for Alma Flora, nor for Maria Sampaio (another actress, splendid, by the way), nor for Ester Leão, a notable director—but for Lúcio Cardoso, one of our greatest playwrights.

The inevitable hangover soon arrived. "Despite this great success, even *'d'éstime'* (in relation to the earlier plays), it was still a complete professional failure. It vanished without a trace."[8]

Still, Lúcio had managed, as always, to infect a group of Brazil's most talented artists with his extravagant dreams. Participating in his little theater were Marques Rebelo, whose chronicle of Rio de Janeiro in the 1940s is a classic of Brazilian literature; Nelson Rodrigues, later Brazil's most famous and controversial playwright; the landscape designer Burle Marx, celebrated for his gardens in the new capital, Brasília; and the great poet Cecília Meireles; not to mention Lúcio himself, the painter Santa Rosa, and, modestly and from afar, Clarice Lispector.

Lúcio's sister, Maria Helena Cardoso, captured the power of his irrepressible enthusiasm:

> I remember Nonô [her pet name for him] so joyful, his head full of fantasies, especially when thinking of traveling, and still young, with several books published and many still to be written, deciding to be a rancher some day. Infected by his enthusiasm, by the power of his faith and of his imagination, I seriously believed in all his whims, even the most impossible. For me, it was all feasible, nothing was impossible for him, whom I admired above all else: novels, poems, beautiful plantations conjured out of nothing. His slightest dreams were realities for me, such was the force of his imagination.[9]

Perhaps it was news of Lúcio's new theatrical venture that inspired Clarice, toward the end of her time in Switzerland, to write "The Choir of Angels," later published as "The Burnt Sinner and the Harmonious Angels." Or the piece may have been inspired by another friend, the Pernambuco poet João Cabral de Melo Neto, who had started a small press from his diplomatic posting in Spain and was eager to have something from Clarice. "I'm still waiting for the 'Choir of Angels,'" he wrote at the beginning of 1949. "You speak of it so fabulously that my hopes are rising."[10]

He never published it, and may indeed never have seen it, until the piece appeared in 1964 toward the back of *The Foreign Legion*, a volume of miscellany. It is Clarice's only incursion into drama. Though Tania's granddaughter Nicole Algranti produced it in 2006, "The Burnt Sinner" does not really seem destined for the stage, if only because of its length (thirteen pages). With a biblical rhythm and language that is also unique in her work, the play tells of a woman condemned to death.[11] Her sin is banal:

> *People*: So then she hid her lover from her husband, and her husband from her lover? That is the sin of sins.
>
> *Lover*: But I laugh not and for a moment neither do I suffer. I open the eyes I have kept closed out of vanity, and I ask you: who? who is this foreign woman, who is this solitary woman for whom a single heart was not enough?

The drama ends when the "foreign woman" is burned to death. Once she is gone the various characters have their say.

Priest: The beauty of a night without passion. What abundance, what consolation. "Great and incomprehensible are his works."

1st and 2nd Guards: As in war, good does not remain when evil is committed to the flames...

The newborn angels: ...we are born.

People: We do not understand and we do not understand.

Husband: I shall now return to the dead woman's house. Because there is my former spouse, awaiting me in her empty necklaces.

Priest: The silence of a night without sin... What clarity, what harmony.

Sleepy child: Mother, what has happened?

The newborn angels: Mama, what has happened?

Women of the people: My children, it was like this: etc. etc. and etc.

Member of the people: Forgive them, they believe in fatality and are therefore fatal themselves.

This odd short play reproduces with disquieting closeness the helplessness that comes through in Clarice's letters from exile in Switzerland, when her life was completely out of her hands, when people uttered high-sounding clichés all around her, and when she was completely subject to the will of others. In "The Burnt Sinner," the people have their say; the lover has his say; the husband has his say; the priest has his say; the guards have their say; and the angels have their say. The "foreign woman" herself, condemned to the flames, never says a word.

Finally back in Rio, Clarice began to find her voice. This time it was not just a quick visit. She would be in Brazil for over a year, while Maury was assigned to the ministry in Itamaraty Palace. After finding an apartment in Flamengo, close to Tania, her first order of business was to find a publisher for *The Besieged City*. She worked fast. She arrived in Brazil at the end of June and the book appeared by late August.[12] The publisher was, once again, A Noite, which had published *Near to the Wild Heart* five years before. It was the book publishing arm of the newspaper where she had worked earlier in her career, and it was a respectable enough choice, though the rejections from other, more prestigious houses—even Agir, which had produced *The Chandelier*—must have stung.

Worse, the book bombed. Only a handful of reviews appeared, and these were not positive. Even Sérgio Milliet, the São Paulo critic who had so vocally supported her earlier books, felt the despair so many readers have felt faced with what a close friend called "perhaps the least loved of Clarice Lispector's novels."[13] Milliet saw the book as rococo, "the writer tangled in her own web of precious images," the structure lost in the jungle of rhetorical flourishes. A shame, he continued, because the book "shows other ambitions, attempts psychological depth." He admires her linguistic invention but concludes, "The author succumbs beneath the weight of her own richness."[14]

Milliet has a point. Clarice said that it was her most difficult book to write,[15] and it is frustratingly difficult to read, hard to follow the curlicued inner movements of its heavily allegorical characters. "Its hermeticism has the texture of the hermeticism of dreams. May someone find the key," wrote the Portuguese critic João Gaspar Simões.[16] Clarice acknowledged the problem but hoped that closer acquaintance would reveal the book's merits, as it had for her law school friend San Tiago Dantas. "He opened the book, read it, and thought, 'Poor Clarice, she's really come down.' Two months later, he told me that when he was going to bed he wanted to read something and picked it up. Then he said: 'It's your best book yet.' "[17]

She acknowledged, though, that the book is incomplete: "*The Besieged City* was one of the most difficult books for me to write, because it demanded an exegesis I am incapable of performing. It's a dense, closed book. I was chasing after something and there was nobody to tell me what it was."[18] In retrospect, it is easy enough to see what she was chasing after. The refinement of her language had taken her so far. But in the broader sense *The Besieged City* has no point. Lucrécia's identification with the horses, and by extension Clarice's search for the union of expression and impression, was complete, as far as it could be.

But that search is, by definition, spiritual. And in *The Besieged City* Clarice is not yet ready to acknowledge frankly that the point of these extravagant linguistic exercises is to lead her to a God who had abandoned her and whom she had in turn rejected. In this book, it is as if she is still clinging to her statement of August 1941, that "beyond mankind there is nothing else at all." Though she had spent years refining her tools, her increasingly fantastic mastery of her language, she was as yet loath to use them. Hence the book's "dense, closed" air. Hence also, more than simple frustration at the restraints of diplomatic society, the foreign woman's silence.

On September 8, 1949, a few days after *The Besieged City* appeared, Maury received news of his next posting: Torquay, a Devon resort where the third round of the General Agreement on Tariffs and Trade was set to begin. Unlike his posting in Bern, which had lasted several years, the mission to Torquay was only a matter of six months, which for Clarice would mean more of a long holiday and less of an interminable prison sentence. And they would not have to leave immediately; they would remain in Rio for another year, until the end of September 1950.

While she was home, Clarice sketched out some stories and dabbled in journalism, but most of her time was taken up with her family and her new baby. She renewed her acquaintance with old friends, including Paulo Mendes Campos, who came to the apartment to interview her for the *Diário Carioca*. When he arrived, he found Pedro, "fat and happy," being transported from the bath to his bed. Clarice told Mendes Campos that maternity had taught her that "her voice was raspier, her gestures more brusque" than she had previously believed, and because her journalism, and presumably motherhood, was keeping her busy, she hadn't started thinking about another novel.[19]

That would have to wait until her arrival on the English Riviera, when the young family settled into one of the picturesque town's many hotels. The owners of these hotels had a reputation for snobbishness and intransigence later immortalized in the Monty Python spinoff *Fawlty Towers*. Like the hotels, not everything in the little beach town was as charming as it seemed. Agatha Christie was born there in 1890 and set many of her murder mysteries in the area, including her famous *Ten Little Indians*, also known as *And Then There Were None*. (Clarice Lispector would later translate Hercule Poirot's final case into Portuguese. She once said, "My ideal would be to write something that at least in the title recalled Agatha Christie.")[20]

With diplomats from thirty-eight countries streaming into town for the conference, Torquay's hospitality industry was presumably on its best behavior. Clarice's letters, at any rate, make no mention of any problems. She rather enjoyed England. "This here is a typical small town, with a whiff of Bern. If we weren't going to be here for such a short time, it would be unendurable. Everyone is more or less ugly, wearing horrible hats, and with horrible clothes in the shop windows... but though Torquay is boring I like England. The lack of sun, certain beaches with dark rocks, the lack of beauty—it all moves me much more than the beauty of Switzerland. Speaking of which, I hate it more and more. I hope never to return."[21]

She and Maury found time to visit Kents Cavern, a cave system near Torquay that has been inhabited by man for around forty thousand years (and that put in an appearance in Agatha Christie's *The Man in the Brown Suit*). The outing gave Clarice a certain perspective. "It was very nice. Though it causes a certain affliction. I left there determined not to worry about little things, since there were so very many years behind me. But when I got back to the hotel I realized that it was no use—prehistory has nothing to do with me, Pedro's food is more important."[22]

Pedro, who was already two, kept Clarice busy. He was learning English, which, Clarice wrote, he spoke like a backwoods Brazilian: "gude morningue," "looki di funni mani." It was quite an ordeal to find him a proper nanny; she went through three in two months and by the end of October was still "waiting for 'the woman of my life,'" she told Tania.[23] "He eats marvelously, is starving all the time, talking about food: 'good meat,' 'nice fish,' etc. He talks so much that if he wasn't my own I would get tired. The conversation doesn't vary much—it's about food, cars, busses, and then back to food."[24]

At least she couldn't be bored; unlike in Switzerland, she had little time to stare out the window. Her time in Rio and the relatively short trip to England had restored her spirits, even to the point that she could offer advice to Tania, normally the best adjusted of the three sisters. "Don't try to take certain problems so seriously," Clarice wrote with an unaccustomed lightheartedness. "Sometimes, when I look at things in the past that I thought were so important and that now are not important at all, I get annoyed with myself. Take care of yourself morally as well, my dear. Be happy, no matter what!"[25]

Toward the end of November she took a pleasant trip to London, where she visited the theaters and took in a show starring the American actor Tyrone Power. She liked London. "It wasn't the way I thought it would be. It's less 'obvious.'... It's not like Paris which is immediately and clearly Paris. You have to figure it out slowly, get acquainted with it slowly."[26] The memory of England remained with her, and in the 1960s she wrote a short piece about it: "I thought it was very natural to be in England, but now, when I think that I was there, my heart is filled with gratitude."[27]

Part of the happy tone of her letters from England may have come from the knowledge that she was pregnant again. It is not clear how far her pregnancy advanced, but around the beginning of 1951, on another trip to London, she suddenly fainted. "I almost died," she said years later. "I was taken unconscious to a hospital and when I opened my eyes there sitting next to me was João Cabral de Melo Neto. I'll never forget it."[28]

She lost the baby. In her great novel *The Passion According to G. H.* she would write, "Abandoning everything hurts like separating from a child not yet born."[29]

Clarice, Maury, and Pedro sailed for Brazil on March 24, 1951. More sad news awaited them upon their return. Bluma Wainer, who besides Clarice's sisters was her closest friend, had been suddenly attacked by a brain tumor. Samuel did not abandon Bluma now, though they had been separated for three years. Bluma may have found Samuel morally elastic in his political dealings, but she could not have accused him of a lack of loyalty. He had welcomed her back after the disastrous relationship with Rubem Braga, and now he paid for Bluma to go to the United States for treatment. But there was nothing for it. She returned to Rio, where Clarice helped nurse her, and died only a couple of months later. She was not quite thirty-six years old.[30]

In 1955, Rubem Braga dedicated a short essay to Bluma Wainer. All that remained of the love of his life was a plaster bust at the entrance to his apartment, commissioned from the eminent sculptor Bruno Giorgi.[31] "How many times did I see those eyes laughing in the daylight or softly shining in the dark, looking into mine. Now they look over me or past me, white, having returned with her to her goddess-like form. Now no one can hurt her; and all of us, in this city, who once knew her—and, more than any of them, he who most obstinately and anxiously loved her; he who today sees her like this, imprisoned in the motionless plaster, but free of all the pain and all the tumultuous passion of life—all of us died a bit when she departed."[32]

Perhaps it was just as well that Bluma departed when she did, sparing her the horror of watching Samuel Wainer become the éminence grise of the new Getúlio Vargas administration. The erstwhile publisher of *Diretrizes*, dedicated to combating the dictatorial Estado Novo, was now the media's most prominent pro-Getúlio voice. On the one hand, this was not saying much. Brazil's newspapers were unanimously opposed to Getúlio Vargas's return to power, but this was not because of their own strong democratic credentials; Brazilian newspapers had always been the bastion of a reactionary oligarchy, owned by a few very wealthy families who passed them down from one generation to the next.

Wainer saw, correctly, that the election of Vargas was a genuinely popular phenomenon. After his deposition in 1945, Getúlio had remained in the Senate, plotting to return to the presidential palace he had occupied for fifteen years, and biding his time while the politicians who replaced him discredited themselves. On October 3, 1950, when Clarice and Maury were settling into their Torquay hotel, Vargas was reelected with 48.7 percent of the vote, almost an absolute majority, unheard of in Brazil's fragmented political system.[33] As of January 31, 1951, Getúlio Vargas, democratically elected, was once again president of Brazil. "As I take office the people will climb the steps of Catete Palace with me," he declared melodramatically during the campaign. "And they will remain with me in power."[34]

A genuinely popular press was what Samuel and Bluma had hoped to create with *Diretrizes*, though Bluma, at least, would never have dreamed that a popular press meant one that supported Getúlio Vargas. In a secret meeting with the new president, Samuel agreed to start a newspaper to reflect the popular mood, helped along by a considerable loan—also, of course, secret—from the Banco do Brasil. On June 1, 1951, a ringing letter of endorsement from the president on its front page, *Última Hora* made its debut. As Samuel later described it, the paper was "ecumenical by vocation." In his memoir, he approvingly quotes a colleague who called him "the only journalist who can put out a paper that is capitalist in the first section and communist in the second,"[35] a perfect match for the "father of the poor" and the "mother of the rich." With *Última Hora*'s launch, Samuel Wainer had become one of the most powerful men in Brazil.

During her year in Rio de Janeiro, Clarice Lispector participated in the birth of another publication. *Comício* would not make the splash of *Última Hora*, and it would have been completely forgotten but for the outstanding quality of its contributors, who included most of the rising generation of Brazilian writers, including Paulo Mendes Campos, Fernando Sabino, and Clarice Lispector. Its founders were Rubem Braga and Joel Silveira, who had been a war correspondent with Braga in Italy, and its aims were lofty: to discuss "the dramatic and picturesque march of the affairs of this nation and, a bit, of others," though the editors made clear that their goal was not "to save the country once a week."[36]

Like the rest of the press, *Comício* was anti-Vargas, at least in theory. Typically enough for the time and place, however, most of its advertisers were delivered by Danton Coelho, Vargas's minister of labor, who "suggested" that his friends support it.[37] Its political orientation, or lack of one, however, mattered little to Teresa Quadros, the chatty, confident person in charge of the women's page. This is none other than Clarice Lispector, who took the job on the condition that she could work under a pseudonym, presumably to avoid staining her serious literary reputation.

In the pages of *Comício*, one finds Clarice dishing out advice on, for example, adapting one's perfume to different occasions: for a dinner, the Brazilian Sphinx suggests, choose something light, to avoid overpowering the smell of the food and ruining the other guests' appetites. "No matter how French your perfume is, it's often the grilled meat that matters." Deploy your jewelry with a bit of class: "Don't mix real jewels with fake ones. And try not to overdo it. Don't wear your diamonds with three rows of pearls, gold earrings and three gold bracelets on each arm, besides a gigantic aquamarine ring. You're not a jeweler's window, and you're not the Virgin of Pilar."[38]

In a voice exuding lofty control, Teresa Quadros also offered suggestions for getting women to calm down. "Act as if your problems don't exist," she wrote in the inaugural issue. "There are few problems that can't wait a week. Maybe you'll even be surprised to see they solve themselves." And in the next issue, Teresa wrote, "Worrying can become a habit, like biting your nails. Maybe the day will come when someone asks you: what are you worried about? And your honest answer should be: nothing, I'm just worried."[39]

Yet there was more to Clarice's page in *Comício*. "I didn't think the column was for strictly futile feminine topics, in the sense that feminine is generally understood by men and even by women themselves: as if women belonged to a closed community, separate, and in some sense segregated," she later wrote.[40] The page included much serious writing, including an introduction to a section called "The Peddler's Box." This is a veiled homage to her father and to the other Jewish peddlers who brought their wares to the wilds of Brazil.

> Amidst such a paradise [urban consumer society], it's hard for women to imagine the existence of places where the peddler and his box are awaited like the Messiah. But anyone who has crisscrossed the backwoods of Brazil knows that such places exist and that the peddler is also a pioneer, a tamer of the jungle, who brings, inside his box, the beginnings of civilization and the rudiments of hygiene, to places they could only otherwise reach with great difficulty. The anonymous figure of the peddler has never been adequately remembered by the men who wrote about our lives, by those who care about Brazilian things. Never has the peddler received the slightest homage. And he deserved it. Because along with his trinkets he also brought a bit of happiness.[41]

Clarice also published a short piece that must have been avant-garde for the day, certainly by the standards of the ladies' pages of Brazilian magazines: "Shakespeare's Sister," a reworking of Virginia Woolf's story about the hypothetical Judith Shakespeare, born with the same talents and the same inclinations as her brother but denied the opportunity to exercise them. She ended up killing herself. "Who," Clarice quoted Woolf's famous phrase, "shall measure the heat and violence of the poet's heart when caught and tangled in a woman's body?"[42]

22

MARBLE MAUSOLEUM

That violence and its repression is the theme of one of Clarice's great stories, "Love," written during this prolonged stay in Rio. Unlike Judith Shakespeare, Ana, its protagonist, is not a poet but a middle-class housewife, one who "had pacified life so well, taken such care for it not to explode."[1] She keeps an eye on her husband and children and regularly dusts the furniture, rather like Lídia in *Near to the Wild Heart*. And then, as in so many of Clarice's stories, Ana's unremarkable existence is shattered by an unremarkable event: returning from the grocery store, sitting in a tram, she sees a blind man chewing gum.

> Ana still had time to think for a second that her brothers were coming to dinner—her heart was beating violently, unhurriedly. Bent over, she looked deeply at the blind man, in the way one looks at something that cannot see back. He was chewing gum in the darkness. Without suffering, with open eyes. The chewing movement made him look like he was smiling and then suddenly not smiling, smiling and then not smiling—as if he had insulted her, Ana looked at him. And whoever saw her would have had the impression of a woman full of hate. But she kept looking at him, leaning over further and further—the tram suddenly jerked into motion throwing her back without warning, the heavy knit sack sliding off her lap, crashing onto the ground—Ana cried out, the conductor ordered a stop before realizing what was going on—the tram ground to a halt, the passengers looked scared.
>
> Unable to move to pick up her things, Ana straightened up, pale. An expression on her face, long since unused, welled up in her with difficulty,

> still uncertain, incomprehensible. The paperboy laughed and handed her the bundle. But the eggs had broken inside the newspapers that contained them. Viscous yellow yolks dripped through the fibers of the knit bag. The blind man interrupted his chewing and advanced his unsure hands, trying uselessly to grab whatever had happened. The package of eggs was tossed out of the sack and, amidst the smiles of the passengers and the signal from the conductor, the tram started up again.
>
> A few instants later nobody was looking at her. The tram shuddered along the tracks and the blind man chewing gum had been left behind forever. But the harm was done.[2]

Plunged into a kind of dreamy delirium ("Why? had she forgotten that there are blind people?"), Ana misses her stop and finds herself inside the primordial world of Rio's great Botanical Garden: "And suddenly, uneasily, she felt she had fallen into a trap. In the Garden a secret labor was being done that she was starting to perceive. On the trees the fruits were black, sweet as honey. On the ground there were dry seeds full of circumvolutions, like little rotting brains. The bench was stained with purple juices. The waters rustled with intense softness. The luxurious legs of a spider were fastened to the tree trunk. The crudity of the world was restful. And death was not what we thought."[3]

The Botanical Garden, with its rotting brains, is "so beautiful that she was scared of hell," and Ana's sudden awareness of the "wild heart," of the rotting, oozing, sprouting garden, brings her to the brink of insanity ("Madness is the neighbor of the most cruel sensitivity," Clarice wrote).[4] But unlike Joana, who had no ties and was free to come and go, Ana cannot linger in the garden, any more than Clarice could stay in the ancient caverns of Torquay: "Pedro's food is more important." Ana, too, has a child who needs to be fed, a dinner party to give.

She has lost track of time and must be freed by the night watchman. But her release from one form of madness deposits her in another. She runs home to find the "large, square living room," where "the clean doorknobs were shining, the glass in the windows was shining, the lamp was shining—what new land was this?" She shocks her son with her violent, fiery gaze, but she takes a deep breath and gives her dinner party, "a bit pale and laughing softly with the others." At the end of the night, her husband takes her back into her former world. "It's time to go to bed, he said, it's late. In a gesture that wasn't his, but which seemed natural, he clasped the woman's hand, taking her with him without looking back, removing her from the danger of life."[5]

After finishing this story in Rio, Clarice, too, subdued and calm as Ana, would be led away by her husband, on yet another long voyage, to yet another long silence.[6] The submission—of Joana to Lídia, of Clarice Lispector to Clarice Gurgel Valente—was painful, a violence against herself, but Clarice knew she could not linger indefinitely in the wild garden. "Ah!" Ana exclaims. "It was easier to be a saint than a person!"[7]

❦

"Love" was published in 1952 in a thin volume, really no more than a pamphlet, fifty-two pages long, called *Some Stories*. The book resulted from Fernando Sabino's friendship with José Simeão Leal, director of the Documentation Service of the Ministry of Education and Culture.[8] Sabino put in a word with Simeão Leal, who published a series called "Cadernos de Cultura," short books, including poetry, stories, and essays, by authors both domestic and international. The goal was to distribute these widely and cheaply, but only the second target was met; in Clarice's case at least, the book attracted no notice whatsoever.[9]

Besides "Love," the book included "Mystery in São Cristóvão," the story of three children, disguised in costumes, who sneak into a garden and steal hyacinths. The story recalled Clarice's own experiences as a girl in Recife, when she and her friend stole roses, and along with other short fiction, the story had earlier been auditioned in the pages of *Comício*. The book also included a longer work called "Family Ties," which would lend its name to the collection published in 1960. Like "Beginnings of a Fortune" and "Mystery in São Cristóvão," it had been written earlier, in Bern. The earliest piece was "The Dinner," written in 1943, at the time of *Near to the Wild Heart*, and published in a newspaper in 1946.[10]

"A Hen," like "Love," was a more recent production, composed during her visit to Rio. Many of these stories dramatize the Steppenwolf dilemma—"Two souls, alas! inhabit my breast"—that Clarice had already illustrated in the opposition of Joana to Lídia in *Near to the Wild Heart*. "Love" shows Ana faced with the same impasse, in a concise and more crystallized form. How to choose the wild heart—the wolf, the cat, the horse, the viper, the rotting brains of the Botanical Garden—when a person requires a human form in order to survive? How can a person be true to the animal side of her nature without going mad?

Clarice had written much about animal-like people, but "A Hen" was her first story about a human-like animal. "She was a Sunday hen. Still alive because it was only nine in the morning," it begins.[11] Indifferently selected to provide Sunday lunch, the hen unexpectedly revolts, flapping her way frantically across the rooftops and through the neighbors' back gardens, chased by a boy in whom her flight has awakened a dormant hunting instinct. "Alone in the world, without father or mother, she ran, panting, mute, concentrated. Sometimes, during her flight, she fluttered gasping on the edge of a roof and while the boy leapt over other rooftops she had a moment to regain her composure." At last the boy catches her and drags her by one wing back to the kitchen, where, "with a certain violence," he dumps her on the floor. Just when it seems that her game is up, however, and to her own and the family's astonishment, she lays an egg—"Her heart, so small on a plate, raised and lowered her feathers, filling with tepid warmth that thing that would never be more than an egg"—a bravura display of vitality that wins her a reprieve. The performance makes her "queen of the house," though this is unbeknownst to her. She settles into a routine. "But when all were quiet in the house and seemed to have forgotten her, she filled herself up with a small courage, remnants of the great escape—and circulated around the floor, her body advancing behind her head, leisurely as in a field, though her little head betrayed her: moving around rapid and vibrating, the old fright of her species already mechanized."[12]

The story, which is less than three pages long, is full of oblique references to Clarice's own life: the feeling of imprisonment and the longing for flight; the existence "without father or mother"; the virtuoso performance followed by a long period of silence. The reference to the "old fright of her species" suggests the ancestral Jewish fear of persecution, and the phrase "remnants of the great escape," coupled with the spectacle of a helpless, flightless, pregnant female running for her life, may refer to her mother's desperate escape from Europe.

But just as Mania Lispector's fate caught up with her, the hen has exhausted her energy in one fabulous feat. The "queen of the house" cannot avoid her destiny. She prospers for a time, "until one day they killed her, ate her, and the years went by."[13]

Like the hen's, Clarice's release into domestic tranquility was only temporary. As the hen was destined to be cooked for dinner, and as Ana inevitably had to return to her "large, square living room," Clarice was bound for large, square Washington, where Maury was posted as a second secretary in the Brazilian embassy. As always, she hated to leave Brazil. After her long years away, her months in Rio had brought her a modicum of professional success—writing for *Comício*, publishing her stories—and now she was heading back into a dreary exile. Like the hen protecting her egg, Clarice, too, was pregnant again.

She, Maury, and Pedro traveled to New York on an opulent English boat in first class. "But I didn't take advantage of it: I was too sad. I took a sixteen-year-old babysitter along to help. Except she didn't have the least intention of helping: she was fascinated by the trip and by diplomatic life. And Avani, weighed down with English books and her mind completely dazzled by her good luck, didn't so much as glance at my son."[14] For the festivities celebrating the crossing of the Equator, during which passengers were thrown fully dressed into the pool, the dejected Clarice stayed in her room.

They arrived in Washington on September 24, 1952. "Luckily you've been here," she wrote to Fernando Sabino and his wife, "so I don't have to make this vague and inorganic city concrete for you. It's beautiful, according to various laws of beauty that are not my own. There's no mess here, and I don't understand a city without a bit of confusion. But anyway, it's not my city."[15] It was, however, more congenial than Bern, with a much bigger city and a much bigger embassy, among whose employees Clarice could find a wider circle of Brazilians.

Several old friends were already there. There was Lauro Escorel, who had reviewed *Near to the Wild Heart* years before, and his pregnant wife, Sara, who, along with Clarice and Eliane, was one of three Jewish wives in Itamaraty. Sara went shopping for furniture with Clarice shortly after they arrived, but after a couple of days Clarice banned her from future trips. "But Clarice, what did I do?" Sara asked. "You make up your mind too quickly," Clarice snapped. There was also a friend from Clarice's student days, João Augusto de Araújo Castro, whom she had warmly recommended to Fernando Sabino, and Eliane and Mozart Gurgel Valente were close by in New York.

The ambassador was the wealthy banker Walther Moreira Salles, who owed his prestigious position to none other than Samuel Wainer. In exchange for a loan to purchase a rotary printing press for *Última Hora*, Samuel put in a good word with the president. Such was Wainer's influence, and such was *Última Hora*'s importance to the Vargas regime, that Getúlio passed over a powerful São Paulo industrialist and his own brother-in-law to please Wainer.[16] (Samuel never expected the loan to be called in, but when the political winds started blowing in a different direction, it would be.)

Soon after they arrived, Maury and Clarice bought the house at 4421 Ridge Street, a block from the country club in the leafy, correct suburb of Chevy Chase. It was the first house they had ever owned, and it proved an ideal place for a young family, close to town and good schools. The house, two stories, with a nice yard and a garden, was very comfortable, and it was there that she awaited the birth of her second child. The knowledge that she would have to have a caesarian, Lauro Escorel remembered, scared her to the point of panic.[17] This was probably because she remembered her awful experience in Bern when Pedro was born. But on February 10, 1953, a couple of weeks after Dwight Eisenhower's inauguration, Paulo Gurgel Valente was born at the George Washington University Hospital. "This birth had none of the horrible complications of the other one," she wrote Elisa.[18] The family was now complete.

Shortly after Paulo was born, another family arrived in Washington: Erico and Mafalda Verissimo and their teenage children, Clarissa and Luis Fernando. In May 1953, Erico Verissimo took up the post of director of cultural affairs in the "marble mausoleum" of the Pan-American Union, part of the Organization of American States. At age forty-seven, Verissimo was that rarest phenomenon: the Brazilian novelist who could live from his writing. (In the twentieth century, only Fernando Sabino and Jorge Amado could say the same.) Like Getúlio Vargas, he hailed from a small town in Brazil's southernmost state, Rio Grande do Sul, growing up in a rich family that was ruined by his late teens. A high school dropout, he tried his hand at several activities, including running a pharmacy in a small town (the pharmacy failed), before finding a job at the Livraria do Globo, the legendary bookstore and publishing house in the state capital, Porto Alegre.

There, at last, was a place for his talents. He started reading, writing, and translating; he was responsible for the translation of Katherine Mansfield's *Bliss* that had made such an impact on the young Clarice. In 1935, his novel *Crossroads and Destinies* won the Graça Aranha Prize, the same distinction *Near to the Wild Heart* claimed nine years later. More important from a marketing perspective, the book was widely denounced for Communism and indecency, raising Verissimo's national profile. But his real breakthrough came in 1939, when *Consider the Lilies of the Field* sold a "fabulous," and in Brazil unheard-of, sixty-two thousand copies.[19]

His increasing fame brought him an invitation from the State Department to visit the United States in 1941, followed in 1943 by an invitation to teach Brazilian literature at the University of California at Berkeley, where he stayed until 1945 and produced, in English, his short compendium *Brazilian Literature*. The book's beginning gives a good impression of the style that won him such a broad readership:

> In a small town of Brazil I saw many years ago a play staged and performed by amateurs, one of the scenes of which I will never forget. (The time was A.D. 1200, and the place somewhere in Europe.) The hero stepped over the proscenium and, beating his pasteboard cuirass with his clenched fists, cried out: "We are the brave and noble knights of the Middle Ages!"

> Later on, a friend of mine told me about another melodramatic play in which the central character, a fair and gallant lad, bidding farewell to his lovely bride, recited: "Oh, my beloved one, now I am going to take part in that tremendous campaign known in history by the name of the Thirty Years' War!"[20]

Early in his career, Brazil's cultural hogen-mogens—jealous, of course, of his success—attacked his warm, accessible style, until they were silenced by the appearance in 1949 of the first installment of *Time and the Wind.* Verissimo had started making notes on it in 1939, thinking of a single volume of roughly eight hundred pages, telling the story of a family and a city. The book ended up consuming fifteen years of work and running to 2,200 pages, in which the author, in dramatic narrative form, recounted the entire history of his native province of Rio Grande do Sul. Despite its enormous length, it is, to this day, one of the most beloved and widely read of Brazilian novels; it has frequently been adapted for film and television and its characters are household names.

Despite his success, however, Verissimo seems to have been nagged by doubts about his claims to literary quality. In an interview he gave Clarice Lispector in 1969, he said, "I plan, but I never stick rigorously to the plan I have sketched. Novels (you know this better than I do) are *arts* of the unconscious. On the other hand, I'm almost saying I consider myself more of an artisan than an artist. And that's why you can understand why the critics don't consider me profound."[21]

Clarice could not let the comment stand. Four years later, in her collection *Where Were You at Night*, she appended the following "Note to Erico Verissimo" to a story she had earlier published in *Comício*: "I don't agree when you said: 'Excuse me, but I'm not profound.' You are **profoundly** human—and what more can you want from a person? You have greatness of spirit. A kiss to you, Erico."[22]

Erico Verissimo's humanity made him a good choice for the prestigious post at the Pan-American Union, a position that brought him into contact with all kinds of supplicants. Luckily he was a very tactful man.

> There appeared a retired singer (contralto), who claimed to be the author of a Hymn of the Americas. She requested my good offices to get the piece adopted as the official anthem of the OAS. She showed me the music, crooned it for me in an affected but hesitant whisper. I moved my head in

> time with the hymn. I remember one irresistibly grotesque line: *solution by arbitration.* When the lady let out the final note, I declared that the anthem was truly gorgeous, "but you understand, for it to be adopted, we would have to convene a special meeting of the Council, get the unanimous approval of the representatives of the 21 countries in the Organization... Unviable." Sorry, very sorry.[23]

The position also included a great deal of travel throughout the Americas, when he had to leave Mafalda and his children at home. "My wife, who is horrified of air travel, is automatically widowed the moment I step onto a plane," Erico wrote.[24] Perhaps this fear and isolation helped bring Mafalda and Clarice together. With Erico so often abroad and Maury working long hours at the embassy, with their children occupied at school or with their own activities, the two women, away from their country and with time on their hands, grew very close, spending almost every afternoon together. Mafalda Verissimo became Clarice's closest friend since Bluma Wainer.

"I wasn't an intellectual," Mafalda told an interviewer, "but I knew how to listen. That was what she needed. She confided in me, naturally." That is the way her daughter, Clarissa Jaffe, recalls their friendship. "Clarice found in my mother someone she could relax with and let down her guard. My mother was a very uncomplicated woman, the exact opposite of Clarice."[25] "They could not have had more different personalities," Luis Fernando agrees, "[but] became childhood friends."[26] Mafalda saw in Clarice "an exceptionally intelligent woman and full of problems. I never saw a woman suffer as much."

In the long, empty afternoons, the two sat at the lunch counters in drugstores, "talking, drinking coffee, that horrible American coffee, and eating toast." The topics of their conversations were Clarice's personal history: Clarice constantly "spoke of Brazil, remembering the past, her family, her Jewish origins."[27] Perhaps under the weight of these memories, Clarice leaned ever harder on the sedatives she had been taking at least since 1948. "We sat around drinking coffee and taking Bellergal, isn't that crazy?" Mafalda said. "Bellergal was the tranquilizer of the day. It was a tiny little pill and we always had one with us."

Mafalda had started taking Bellergal because of her fear of flying, though she never developed a dependency. Such, unfortunately, was not the case with Clarice. Mafalda was struck by an incident at a cinema. Clarice wanted to see *Citizen Kane*, though she, like Maury, Erico, and Mafalda, had already seen it. They went again only because Clarice insisted. The film had barely started when they looked over to find her sound asleep. "She didn't see any of the movie," Mafalda said. "She must have taken more than one Bellergal."[28]

A passage from *The Apple in the Dark*, the novel Clarice wrote in Washington, recalls this habit: "Ah, she said with simplicity, it's like this: let's say someone is screaming and then someone else puts a pillow in their mouth so they don't have to hear the scream. Because when I take a pill, I don't hear my scream, I know I'm screaming but I don't hear it, that's how it is, she said adjusting her skirt."[29]

But Clarice's work was catching on. Even the collapse of *Comício* after less than six months ("Our *Comício*, you saw, died as soon as Tereza Quadros departed," Rubem Braga wrote in May 1953), did not mean that her commissions dried up.[30] While some *Comício* alumni went to work for Samuel Wainer, others, including Clarice, signed up with *Manchete*, a new magazine begun in April 1952, when Clarice was still in Rio.[31] Its founder was Adolpho Bloch, who, like Clarice, was born in the Ukraine and likewise fled during the pogroms. His family settled in Rio de Janeiro—they were neighbors of Lúcio Cardoso's—a few months before the Lispectors got to Maceió.[32] Starting with a tiny hand-operated printing press, Bloch built a media empire of which the flagship was *Manchete*, Brazil's equivalent of *Paris-Match* or *Life*. The editor in chief was an old friend of Clarice's, Otto Lara Resende. Otto, one of his father's twenty children, belonged to that celebrated group from Minas Gerais (along with Fernando Sabino, Paulo Mendes Campos, and the psychoanalyst Hélio Pellegrino) known as the "four *mineiros*." Like them, he had known Clarice since 1944, when Lúcio Cardoso had introduced *Near to the Wild Heart* to his literary friends in Minas.

Fernando, acting once again as Clarice's impresario, proposed on her behalf a kind of "note from the USA" for the new magazine.[33] The idea, readily accepted, ran into an obstacle when Clarice insisted on remaining anonymous. She suggested resuscitating Teresa Quadros, but the *Manchete* staff had other ideas; she and Fernando exchanged letters on the subject for most of 1953, Fernando sensitively parrying Clarice's exasperating resolve.

"She [Teresa] is much better than I am, sincerely: the magazine stands to gain more from her—she's eager, feminine, lively, doesn't have low blood pressure—a good journalist in other words," she insisted. To which Fernando replied, "I feel awkward telling them that you don't want to sign it: for two reasons: first, because despite the great respect and distinct consideration they have for the lovely Teresa Quadros, I know they want your name. That was how we discussed it; I don't know if you realize that you *have* a name." "It so happens," Clarice replied, rather petulantly meeting him halfway, "that I would only like to sign it

C. L." Fernando answered, "What people are interested in is Clarice Lispector, at least a Clarice Lispector reporting the news—even signing C. L."[34]

Clarice would, in fact, end up writing for *Manchete*, in 1968. Meanwhile, for the first time, a book of hers was being published abroad, an event that brought its own headaches. *Near to the Wild Heart* had been sold to Plon, in Paris, to the editor Pierre de Lescure. Along with "Vercors," the pseudonym of Jean Bruller, author of the celebrated novella *Le silence de la mer*, Lescure had founded the famous Resistance publishing house Les Éditions de Minuit.

In the spring of 1954, the translation arrived in Washington, riddled with faults, the work of a translator whose knowledge of Portuguese was clearly defective and who had not hesitated to hack out entire chapters of the book. Moreover, it seemed to be the final pass, and Clarice was given very little time to correct it.

Erico Verissimo told her to fire off a letter to Lescure,[35] which she did. "I hasten to inform you," she wrote in her most formal French, "that I cannot consent to the publication of the book in its current state." The translation was "scandalously bad... often even ridiculous." Finally, she wrote, "I prefer that the book not be published in France at all to having it appear so ridden with errors."[36] The poor translation was apparently the result of a miscommunication, because six weeks later she was assuring Lescure that she did not receive his earlier letters on the subject. Still, she was not ready to let the matter rest. "I admit, if you like, that the sentences do not reflect the usual manner of speaking, but I assure you that it is the same in Portuguese," she writes. "The punctuation I employed in the book is not accidental and does not result from an ignorance of the rules of grammar. You will agree that the elementary principles of punctuation are taught in every school. I am fully aware of the reasons that led me to choose this punctuation and I insist that it be respected."[37]

This is a point her translators would do well to recall: no matter how odd Clarice's prose sounds in translation, it sounds just as unusual in the original. "The foreignness of her prose is one of the most overwhelming facts of our literary history, and even of the history of our language," her friend the poet Lêdo Ivo wrote. The Canadian scholar Claire Varin has regretted her translators' tendency to "pluck the spines from the cactus."[38]

Notwithstanding her problems with the translation, Clarice assured Lescure that she regretted the phrase "scandalously bad." Worse, she wrote in June, she regretted that her communications had "damaged his health." The hero who had stood up to the German Occupation withered when confronted by Clarice Lispector. "As for myself," she added, "I am used, by temperament, to anxiety. But I take constant care not to disturb the tranquility of others."[39]

23

THE INTIMATE BALANCE

On July 15, 1954, the family flew to Rio for a two-month holiday, arriving just in time to witness one of the greatest uproars in modern Brazilian history. As was becoming usual, Samuel Wainer played a central role. Getúlio Vargas's only ally in the print media was an irresistible target for the president's enemies, who were led by a crusading—some said deranged—journalist named Carlos Lacerda. Carlos was an old friend of Samuel's from their leftist days, so close, in fact, that when Lacerda was expelled from the Communist Party (over a misunderstanding, he claimed), the first person he sought to console him was Bluma Wainer. The expulsion, however, enraged him, and he placed his considerable polemical talents at the service of anti-Communism.

A man of many enemies, Lacerda did not stop with attacking Communists; he detested the new incarnation of Getúlio Vargas as a democratically elected populist above all else and could not pardon his old friend Wainer's alliance with the president. His attacks on Wainer and *Última Hora* became steadily more aggressive until finally he got his biggest scoop. On July 12, 1953, his headline screamed: "WAINER NOT BORN IN BRAZIL." Wainer's nationality was of the greatest importance, because a foreigner could not legally own a Brazilian newspaper. Eliminating him and *Última Hora* would almost guarantee the fall of Getúlio Vargas.

The smoking gun was a yellowing document discovered in the archives of a Rio high school, in which Samuel's older brother, Artur, claimed that his brother was born not in São Paulo but in Bessarabia. Samuel hurriedly explained that "immigrant families, traumatized by the horrors of the war they had witnessed, were afraid that their children could be drafted into the army of the country where they were trying to rebuild their lives."[1] A comical drama ensued, with Wainer dredging up residents of Bom Retiro, São Paulo's Jewish neighborhood, to testify that they remembered attending his circumcision and Lacerda's allies dispatching their far-flung correspondents to exotic Bessarabia to try to uncover "Edenitz," the shtetl from which Samuel supposedly hailed. (The photographer they sent, Jean Manzon, was the only photographer who had captured the mad Nijinsky dancing.)

How exactly they were supposed to carry out this research in a Soviet Union where Stalin was barely cold in his grave was not thought out. Lacerda's detectives never found Edenitz. In fact, the town, now Edeniţ, did and does exist, today in northern Moldova, a few miles from Soroca, where the Lispector family crossed the Dniester. Though Wainer was briefly jailed over the scandal, he denied until the end that he was not a native Brazilian. (After his death, it turned out that he was, in fact, born in Bessarabia.)

Despite Samuel's exoneration, the scandal further established Carlos Lacerda as the government's most powerful enemy, and the points he scored against *Última Hora* weakened the already embattled Vargas. The coup de grâce came on the morning of August 5, 1954, three weeks into Clarice's visit to Rio, when Carlos Lacerda, arriving at his Copacabana apartment building, was shot. The assassin only hit Lacerda in the foot—for months afterward he paraded around in a theatrically large cast—but managed to kill an air force major walking alongside Lacerda.

From his hospital bed, Lacerda immediately declared that Samuel Wainer had nothing to do with the assassination attempt. Indeed, he was not interested in Wainer; his real target was the president himself.[2] Sure enough, the shot was traced back to one of Getúlio Vargas's palace guards, a corrupt, illiterate thug named Gregório Fortunato, acting without Getúlio's authorization or knowledge: Getúlio would not have ruled giant Brazil for most of a quarter-century if he had been that stupid. But the shot, as the president instantly realized, meant the end of his administration.

Rio boiled with indignation and intrigue. Under siege from every side, the wily old "father of the poor" still had one card up his sleeve. On August 23, 1954, Samuel Wainer's *Última Hora* published a dramatic headline: "GETÚLIO TO PEOPLE: I WILL ONLY LEAVE THE PALACE DEAD." He was not kidding. The next evening, after penning an inflammatory farewell letter, a pajama-clad Getúlio Vargas walked into his bedroom, took out a pistol, and fired a single shot into his heart.

Samuel's was the only newspaper not attacked by enraged mobs. That first day, it sold some eight hundred thousand copies,[3] as the offices of Standard Oil and the American embassy were attacked and Carlos Lacerda, still wearing a cast on his foot, fled the country. Vargas's thunderous suicide note, "Serenely I take the first step on the road to eternity as I leave life to enter history,"[4] rang day and night across the nation's airwaves.

"THE PRESIDENT KEPT HIS PROMISE," *Última Hora* blared.

A week after the attack on Carlos Lacerda, Clarice wrote Mafalda Verissimo, "I still haven't absorbed Rio, I'm slow and difficult. I'd need a few more months to understand the atmosphere again. But it sure is good. It's wild, it's astonishing, and it's every man for himself."[5] For a few days she escaped the capital's political chaos in the resort of Teresópolis; her apartment in Rio was only a few short blocks from Catete Palace, the center of the turmoil.[6] In this electric environment, Clarice managed to see old friends like Fernando Sabino and Lúcio Cardoso, and she cemented her relationship with José Simeão Leal, who, impressed by *Some Stories*, commissioned a full collection of stories, to include the previously published works. For the first time, Clarice was being paid for a book in advance. Like her Parisian debut, this blessing would soon prove ambiguous.

Just as she was starting to absorb wild and astonishing Rio, Clarice was yanked back to the suburban tranquility of Eisenhower's Washington, where she arrived on September 15. She had done it often enough before, but it never got easier. "For me, leaving Brazil is a serious matter," she wrote Fernando upon her return, "and no matter how 'graceful' I want to be, when it comes time to depart I really do cry. And I don't like for people to see me like that, even though they're polite tears, the tears of a second-rate artist, who doesn't have the director's permission to fix her hair."[7]

Once she got back, Clarice kept busy. She was learning to drive, again. "The teacher asked me flat out if I really had already learned to drive before. I answered that unfortunately I had. To which he said nothing. . . . Maury, next to me, feigns a courage worthy of note, so as not to dishearten me. He says that my only problem, just a little detail, is that I don't pay much attention to traffic."[8] She must have mastered the skill eventually. One of her son Paulo's first memories of her was in the car, on the way to school: "I must have been three or four, so it was in 1956 or 1957; the school atop a hill, the street snowed under, my mother driving, the car driving around and around until we got up there. . . . She may have given the impression of being 'dreaming awake,' of being connected to some reality other than the present one."[9]

She studied English as she studied driving: indifferently. She drank milkshakes and popped pills with Mafalda Verissimo, but in Washington she was increasingly realizing that the diplomatic life was impossible for her. "I wasn't much at ease in that milieu," said the woman who once boasted that she came straight from the Zoological Gardens. "All that formality... But I played my role.... I was more conciliatory than I am now. Whatever I thought was my duty, I did."[10] For years the notion of duty had sustained her: "I hated it, but I did what I had to.... I gave dinner parties, I did everything you're supposed to do, but with a disgust."[11] This was the time when she had "the waiter at home pass fingerbowls to all the guests in the following way: every fingerbowl had a rose petal floating in the liquid."

"Not only the hostess but every guest seemed satisfied that everything was going well. As if there was always the danger that that reality of silent waiters, flowers, and elegance was a bit above them—not because of their social background, just: above them.... The woman next to her said: 'The landscape there is superb!' And the hostess, in a tone of anguish, dreaminess, and sweetness answered hastily: 'Yes... it really is... isn't it?' "[12] This fictionalized fragment reads like a setup for so many of Clarice's stories: chaos shimmering through a veil of order, threatening at any moment to burst through the vigilantly maintained surface.

It did not, though, in Clarice's diplomatic role, even though her courtesy was often tested, including by anti-Semitism. Eliane Gurgel Valente recalled an embassy function in New York when a diplomat brought up the subject of Jews. "I can *smell* them," he said. Staring him straight in the eye, Clarice replied, "You must have a terrible cold, then, since you can't smell me and my sister-in-law."[13] In another recollection, Clarice, characteristically elliptical, does not name the disease, but it is easy enough to figure out what she is talking about:

> I remember an ambassadress in Washington who ordered around the wives of the diplomats serving there. She gave rude commands. She said for example to the wife of a secretary in the embassy: don't come to the reception dressed like a bum. To me—I don't know why—she never said anything, not a single rude word: she respected me. Sometimes she was distressed, and asked if she could come visit me. I said yes. She would come. I remember one time—sitting on the sofa of my own house—she confided to me in secret that she didn't like a certain kind of person. I was surprised because I was exactly that kind of person. She didn't know. She didn't know me or at least a part of me.

> Out of pure charity—in order not to embarrass her—I didn't tell her what I was. If I had she would be in an awful situation and have to apologize. I listened with my mouth shut. Later she was widowed and came to Rio. She called me. She had a present for me and asked me to visit her. I didn't. My goodness (?) has its limits: I cannot protect those who offend me.[14]

Despite her discomfort, Clarice was popular among her embassy colleagues, and the anti-Semitic ambassadress was not the only person who liked and respected her. She had Erico and Mafalda Verissimo, and when they returned to Brazil in 1956 she acquired an unlikely new friend. The new ambassador, Ernani do Amaral Peixoto, was married to none other than Getúlio Vargas's daughter Alzira. This was the same formidable woman who, at twenty-two, had protected Guanabara Palace, gun in hand, against the Integralist onslaught. Her martial readiness was only one reason she garnered wide respect. (Samuel Wainer, among others, was a great friend.) Often reckoned the brains behind her father's throne, she was a canny politician who for years was the most powerful woman in Brazil, the daughter of the president and the wife of Amaral Peixoto, whose posts previous to arrival in Washington included the governorship of Rio de Janeiro.[15]

Alzira took an instant liking to Clarice Lispector, whom she had met on an earlier visit to Washington.[16] Despite her redoubtable reputation, the ambassadress was devastated by her father's suicide. In Washington, perhaps as a way of working through her grief, she wrote a memoir, *Getúlio Vargas, My Father*, with Clarice's help. "You were very generous, I see now, in your statements about my literary 'genius,'" she wrote Clarice later. "You spared my *ego* as much as possible."[17] Clarice was not simply flattering her: the book is admirable. And Clarice could identify with Alzira's pain at the loss of her father.

Alzira's fifteen-year-old niece Edith Vargas, on a visit to Washington, noticed that her aunt was still melancholy at the loss and saw that Clarice, who "looked like a queen, there was a greatness within her," also seemed enveloped by sadness.[18] Much as Alzira had served as a privileged conduit to her father, Clarice, known as Alzira's "right arm," was the discreet and sympathetic emissary of the diplomats' wives to the ambassadress. Silvia de Seixas Corrêa (whose nephew married Eliane and Mozart's daughter Marilu), noted the same sadness, the same friendliness, the same beauty. Clarice never mentioned literature, her own or others.

Another diplomatic spouse, Lalá Ferreira, remembered an urgent call from Clarice, asking her to come to her house immediately. The reason, she learned upon arrival, was that Clarice had bought a record that she was afraid to listen to by herself. "They placed the LP in the record player and sat down to listen. After a moment, sighs, screams, heavy breathing, panting, squeaking doors, strange, phantasmagoric noises, followed one upon the other. Evening fell and the two sat terrified in the dusky light of the living room." It turned out to be a recording for use in theatrical productions of horror stories.

Lalá recalled another strange incident. At Christmastime, their American neighbors having festively decorated their lawns with the usual twinkling lights and sleigh bells and Santa Clauses, the Valente family was not to be outdone. "Lalá, tipped off by friends, went to see Clarice's decoration: irregular forms, cut out of sheets of plastic, in dark colors—gray, black, brown—hanging from the branches of the pine tree. There were no lights. The dark green of the pine and the white of the snow did not accentuate the Christmas 'decorations.' Lalá asked Clarice why she had selected those 'ornaments.' The answer: 'For me, that's what Christmas is.' "[19]

Through Alzira Vargas, Clarice met another lifelong friend, the young artist Maria Bonomi. Bonomi's mother, Georgina, was the illegitimate daughter of the Italian-born magnate Giuseppe Martinelli, famous for building the first skyscraper in São Paulo, the thirty-story Martinelli Building. Today it is hard to imagine that the immense metropolis of São Paulo ever took a dim view of the skyscraper, but the pioneering construction so wracked the nerves of the citizenry that to prove the building was safe Martinelli was obliged to move his own family into its gigantic penthouse, which soon became one of São Paulo's most glamorous addresses.

His granddaughter Maria Bonomi, born in Italy, came to Brazil as a young girl, after the war made it inadvisable to linger in Europe. Like Clarice, she was precocious, her talent encouraged by her family's intimacy with many of Brazil's leading artists. Her interests were early directed to graphic art, and in 1957, at twenty-two, she went to New York to study. Two years later, she participated in an exhibition at the Pan-American Union. To her surprise, she was selected to attend a White House dinner honoring foreign students. Driven to desperation by the occasion's sartorial requirements, she looked to the Brazilian embassy. Alzira Vargas took one look at her and said, "I know who can lend her some clothes. Clarice Gurgel Valente."[20]

Maria arrived in Chevy Chase and found Clarice "with a baby on her lap" and a selection of clothes all laid out: gown, gloves, shoes. "Dressed as Clarice," she went to the banquet. When she returned the clothes, they started talking. Maria told Clarice about her work, and though Clarice said that she "liked to write" she never mentioned that she was a published writer. When Maria returned to New York, she met one of the rare women in the Brazilian foreign service, the same Dora Alencar de Vasconcellos who had been a witness to Maury and Clarice's marriage. Clarice's name came up and Dora loudly regretted seeing Clarice, with all her genius, wasting away amid the tedium of diplomatic life.[21]

The best portrait of Clarice from her time in Washington, however, comes from João Cabral de Melo Neto, who visited her at the beginning of her stay there. He and other diplomats were at dinner at her house when the talk came around to death. Clarice had to go into the kitchen to check on something, and when she returned she was eager to get back to the subject. João Cabral remembered the incident in "A Story about Clarice Lispector," composed shortly after she died.

> One day, Clarice Lispector
> was swapping with friends
> ten thousand anecdotes about death,
> how serious it is, how carnivalesque.
>
> While they were talking, some others
> came back from the game.
> They sifted through every detail
> and analyzed every play.
>
> When the soccer talk died down,
> there came a yawning silence
> and Clarice's voice could be heard:
> As we were saying, about death . . .[22]

Life in Washington was more eventful than in a small embassy in a small Swiss city where, without friends or children, the feral, sparkling adolescent withered into a sad, solitary adult. In Washington, Clarice had plenty of people around her, made plenty of new friends, and received plenty of visitors: Tania, San Tiago Dantas, Rubem Braga, João Cabral de Melo Neto, Augusto Frederico Schmidt. She traveled a lot, returning to Brazil in 1956, visiting California and Mexico in 1957, and accompanying Alzira to Rotterdam in early 1959, where they baptized a new ship, the *Getúlio Vargas*, and stopped briefly in Greenland on the way back to Washington.

Yet amid these distractions, Clarice was always concerned with preserving the "intimate balance" without which she feared she would slip into madness. Now there was a new threat looming: from her boys. With two young sons to attend to, she could no longer lock herself away in her room to write. "I didn't want my children to feel that I was a mother-writer, a busy woman, without time for them. I tried to avoid letting that happen. I would sit on the sofa, with the typewriter on my lap, and write. When they were little, they could interrupt me whenever they wanted to. And *how* they interrupted."[23]

Despite her determination to keep herself available, her work did sometimes annoy them. Pedro once told her, in an authoritarian tone, "I don't want you to write! You're a mother!"[24] And Paulo, fed up with her writing for grown-ups, "ordered" her to write him a story about their bunny, Joãozinho, published a decade later as *The Mystery of the Thinking Rabbit*. The mystery is how Joãozinho, who is not very bright, manages to escape regularly from his apparently secure pen; it was based on a true story. Clarice offers no solution for the mystery, and when the book was published the letters streamed in. "The children's letters had the most varied solutions. I remember some of them: they accused the 'grownups' of killing the little rabbits, and then 'used the excuse that they had vanished.' Others said that the rabbits were so strong that they bent the bars of their cages and ran off. Still others thought that a big and powerful rabbit came at night to free them from their captivity."[25]

Pedro, the elder, was remarkable from the beginning, and Clarice kept a careful record of his development. In many of her notes, Pedro is doing nothing more than being a cute little kid. "At night, he called me to his bed," she noted for example. "—Mother, I'm sad. —Why? —Because it's night and I love you." On his sixth birthday, September 10, 1954, shortly before the family left Rio for Washington, he seemed bored by the approaching party, until Clarice finally dressed him in his new birthday clothes. "I'm so happy that me exists," he told her. He went through the usual phases: "1954—Period in which dinosaurs were his most important subject and the central object of his thoughts, including, apparently, of his nightmares."[26]

Yet from relatively early on, Pedro was not a normal child. His unusual intelligence impressed people from the very beginning. As an infant in Switzerland, his linguistic gifts had astonished and even frightened his parents. In Washington a couple of years later, Tania remembered Pedro seated on the sofa, reading the encyclopedia with Erico Verissimo. A diplomatic colleague recalled being stunned by a comment Pedro made à propos of a political discussion in

Washington: looking up from his playthings, the five-year-old said, "So you mean that a leftist party that takes power automatically shifts to the right?"[27]

In the notebook in which his mother recorded Pedro's wit and wisdom, Clarice made a curious notation that she may have looked back on, once the extent of the problem became clear, with a shudder. "Mommy," he told her, "I have special ears. I can hear music in my brain, and I can also hear voices that aren't there."[28] It is not clear just when Clarice and Maury began to worry about Pedro, but by the time he was nine years old, Clarice mentioned to her sisters that she was putting him into a guidance center, "where, besides schooling, he'll get help with his emotions."[29] (Already, in a letter of 1953, when he was five, she mentioned sending him to a psychologist.)[30]

Around the same time, she took Pedro to a psychiatrist who determined that Pedro would either turn out to be a genius or would go insane. It was a blunt way of saying what Ulysses Girsoler had told Pedro's mother a decade earlier, in Bern: "We see that all her sentimental life is stretched between one extreme (impulsivity) all the way to the other extreme (subtlety, sensibility, ability to feel all the possible emotions that other humans feel). —It will be very difficult for such a character to find balance."

Pedro inherited much of Clarice's character. He even bore her a remarkable physical resemblance: as a young man, he, too, was remarkably beautiful, "tall, strong, like a *muzhik,* one of Tolstoy's peasants," one friend remembered. As a boy, he was even more precociously intelligent than his brilliant mother had been. Clarice's powerful superego kept her emotions in check, if often only at great cost, and the controlled tension between impulsiveness and reason was a source of her creative power. But she always feared the danger. Those of her characters, Virginia, for instance, who try to keep their "intimate balance," always lost in the end.

24

REDEMPTION THROUGH SIN

"God knows what he is doing: I think it's right that the state of grace not be given to us frequently. If it were, we might pass over definitively to the *other side* of life, which is also real, but nobody would ever understand us. We would lose the common language," Clarice wrote.[1] Imagining that passage to the other side occupied her years in Washington, where she completed her longest, most complexly allegorical novel, *The Apple in the Dark*. Begun in Torquay and written in her suburban living room in Chevy Chase, the book describes, in poetic detail, a descent into madness.

The madness in *The Apple in the Dark* is a positive tool for knowledge, not a means for self-destruction. Yet self-destruction is its prerequisite. The old world of the protagonist, Martin, a statistician, a man of reason, is destroyed by a crime: he has killed his wife. But it turns out that the crime never took place; the medics got there on time.

The details of this crime hardly matter, to the character or the author. Over the course of the long book, Clarice devotes no more than a few dismissive lines to its particulars. Martin's sins are as neutral and amoral as Joana's and Virginia's: "Had he by chance felt horror after his crime? The man carefully felt around in his memory. Horror? and yet that was what language would expect of him."[2]

Clarice Lispector's obsession with crime stemmed from the guilt tied up with her existence: "guilty from birth, she who was born with the mortal sin."[3] Martin, too, is persecuted because he exists. His crime is simply a pretext, "useless: as long as he himself survived, others would call for him."[4] And they do: at the end of the book Martin is arrested. "Being" is not illegal, so he is arrested for a crime that can be given a name.

Clarice's view of crime is closely related to her amoral, "animal" view of the world, a view found in Spinoza: "Men commonly suppose that all things in nature act, as they do, with some goal in mind, and even maintain as a certainty that God himself directs everything toward a certain goal.... They believe that everything has been created with them in mind and say that the nature of a thing is good or bad, healthful or rotten and corrupted, depending on how they are themselves affected by it."[5]

The "moral" view of man and God, with man at the center of the universe and history a logical, meaningful process, was always ridiculous to Clarice. At the end of the book, a professor arrives to judge Martin. With all his bloated self-regard, the professor is a caricature of the critic, a personification of the whole edifice of false morality that Martin has rejected.

> "He's strict with his students, very strict," she repeated monotonously and without seeming to pay much attention to what she was saying. "One day a student was talking in class, and then at the end of the class, in front of them all, the professor called the student up and made such a moving speech, calling him son and asking him to lift his feelings to God, and the repentant boy couldn't stop sobbing. Nobody laughs at the professor, he doesn't allow it. The students laugh at the other teachers, but not at him."
>
> "Yes," said Martin, as a doctor would to a patient.
>
> "The student cried so much," said the exhausted woman, "that they had to give him a drink of water. He became a veritable slave of the professor. The professor is very well educated. The boy became a veritable slave, he's very well educated."
>
> For the first time Victoria seemed not to mind Martin's silence. And standing there, as if she had nothing else to do and no plans to leave, her features puckered up from fatigue, she kept on reciting:
>
> "To this day the professor uses the boy as an example. The boy looks like an angel, he grew paler, he looks like a saint. The professor was so pleased with what he accomplished, it was such a great moral victory, that he even put on some weight," she said exhausted.[6]

For Clarice Lispector, who did not possess the professor's moral clarity, crime could never be denounced out of hand. Spinoza wrote that "one and the same thing can be at the same time good, bad, and indifferent. For instance, music is good to the melancholy, bad to those who mourn, and neither good nor bad to the deaf."[7] Joana's transgressions were an essential part of her being; Virginia found freedom in her meager peccadilloes.

These crimes ("She took a napkin, a round piece of bread... with an extraordinary effort, breaking in herself a stupefied resistance, deflecting destiny, she threw them out the window—and in that way kept her power") bore a whiff of the teenager's rebellion.[8] In *The Apple in the Dark*, crime acquires a higher significance.

Martin's crime ushers him into a greater reality. Redemption through sin, enlightenment through crime: it is the kind of paradox in which Clarice Lispector delighted. With it, Clarice goes further than before, and further, too, than Kafka. Like him, she found locked doors, blocked passageways, and generalized punishment. But she also saw a different possibility: a state of grace.

The Apple in the Dark opens like a detective story. In a distant backwater, Martin is the only guest in a nearly abandoned hotel. The owner, a German, has a Ford parked out front; when the car disappears, Martin fears that the German has turned him in and flees on foot through a night "as dark as the night is while we sleep."[9] He awakens in an abandoned desert.

It is a rebirth, from darkness into light, from night into day, from the world of language to a world of silence: "One could not even imagine that that place had a name." Deprived of his senses—there is nothing to smell, nothing to hear, nothing to taste—all Martin can do is see, a "contented idiot."[10]

At last a thought occurs to him: "Today must be Sunday!" The first day, a name and a statistic for the world without meaning. But "without counting the days that had passed he had no reason to think it was Sunday. Martin then stopped, a bit weighed down by the need to be understood, from which he had not yet freed himself."[11]

A black bird appears, seeking refuge inside the palm of Martin's hand. He speaks to the bird, or tries to, but he cannot speak and the bird cannot, of course, understand. " 'I lost the language of others,' he then repeated very slowly as if the words were more obscure than they actually were. Then the man sat on a stone, erect, solemn, empty, officially holding the bird in his hand. Because something was happening to him. And it was something with a meaning. Though there was no synonym for this thing that was happening. A man was sitting down. And there was no synonym for anything, and so the man was seated."

Having lost the language of others, the term Clarice used for madness, Martin is haunted by the fear of the insanity that shadows the one who "passes over to the *other side* of life." "That man had always had a tendency to fall into profundity, which could one day lead him to an abyss." The best thing is to stop thinking entirely. "He was so repulsed by the fact of almost having thought that he pulled apart his teeth and made a painful face of hunger and helplessness: he turned worried to every side of the desolate land seeking amongst the stones a way of recovering the powerful previous stupidity that for him had become a source of pride and domination.... With enormous courage, that man had finally stopped being intelligent."[12]

Clarice disliked being called intelligent for the same reason many religiously inclined people distrust the word: God is by definition beyond human understanding, so attempts to reach the divine through "intelligence" are futile. The progress of the mystic takes him from rational thought to irrational meditation.

Yet one cannot linger in the irrational world. If the "state of grace" is the highest temptation, it is also a mortal danger. Losing language and human understanding—"intelligence"— is madness. The difference between the mystic and the madman is that the mystic can return, emerging from the state of grace and finding a human language to describe it.

❦

From wordlessly being—"But there was not a single synonym for a man seated with a bird in his hand"[13]—Martin must exit the irrational divine and become a full human, and to be human is to have a language.

The first words come, a cliché: " 'Like jewels, he thought, since he had always had a general tendency to compare things to jewels." Inspired, he launches into a long soliloquy. At its climax, his hand involuntarily contorts and crushes the little bird. It is a second crime. "He was impressed with himself. He had become a dangerous man."[14]

It is a painterly scene, forty pages of stillness, like a landscape of Magritte's or De Chirico's: the solitary man, the burning sun, the shimmering rocks, the dead bird, in the immense desert. The only action takes place inside Martin, who at its conclusion starts to walk away from the desert, arriving at length at a "poor and pretentious" farmhouse. He introduces himself as an engineer, which "lightly scandalizes" the plantation's boss, a tough woman named Victoria, who looks at him as if he were an animal, "as if she were professionally examining a horse."

> "Where are you from?"
>
> "Rio."
>
> "With that accent?"
>
> He didn't reply. With their eyes both agreed that it was a lie.[15]

Perhaps Martin was a foreigner all along. But his crime has placed him beyond classification. Imperious Victoria, "a woman as powerful as if she had one day found a key. Whose door, it is true, had been lost years before," sets him to work. All he can do is labor, and see: "The man expected nothing: he saw what he saw. As if his eyes were not made to conclude but only to look."[16]

His looking perturbs Victoria, who grows concerned by the appearance of the farm, "as if until the arrival of the man she had not noticed the slovenliness of the fields." Ermelinda, Victoria's childish, hypochondriac cousin, starts noticing things as well: "With the acuity of wonder, she noticed on her own hand a vein that she hadn't noticed in years, and saw that she had short thin fingers, and saw a skirt covering her knees."[17]

Martin's existence is perfect and simple: "When he was sleeping, he was sleeping. When he was working, he was working. Victoria commanded him, he commanded his own body." This ends when Victoria orders him to clean out the cows' stable. It is a sickening assignment. "Inside was an atmosphere of intestines and a difficult sleep full of flies. And only God feels no disgust." But conquering his disgust is the only way Martin can "free himself at last from the kingdom of rats and plants—and finally reach the mysterious breathing of larger animals."

Once he has, he must rediscover sex. For this experience he does not choose Ermelinda, who is in love with him, or Victoria, but a mulatto woman—significantly, she is nameless—"a young animal, he calculated her age by patting her." To her he is "strong as a bull." He takes her like an animal: "He would have to grab her or leave her. He grabbed her unhurriedly just as one day he had grabbed the little bird."[18]

After the act, "he also began to understand women again. He didn't understand them in a personal way, as if he were the owner of his own name. But he seemed to understand why women are born when a person is a man." As Martin enters the wet worlds of stables and sex, a drought is approaching. The days are beautiful and full of sun. "The countryside looks like a jewel, he then said blushing violently."[19]

After evolving from rock to plant to rat to cow to horse, Martin is a now a man. This, for Clarice, means finding a language, and Martin must rediscover symbols: "This necessity a person has to climb a mountain—and look. This was the first symbol he had touched since he had left home: 'climb a mountain.'" With this symbol, Martin draws nearer to Clarice's old ideal: "There Martin turned into the symbol of himself."[20]

But words barely fit a person so recently an animal. "Oh he was very helpless. He had lost the stage in which he had the dimensions of an animal, and in which understanding was silent as a hand picks up a thing." Seriously, ceremoniously, he takes up a pencil, but "the man seemed to have disappointedly lost the meaning of what he had wanted to write down.... Once again he rolled around the pencil, doubting and doubting again, with an unexpected respect for the written word.... So disloyal was the power of the simplest word upon the vastest of thoughts."

> And deflated, wearing glasses, everything that had seemed to him ready to be said had evaporated, now that he wanted to say it. The thing that had filled his days with reality was reduced to nothing when faced with an ultimatum to say it. One could see that that man was not an achiever, and like so many others, he only felt intentions, of which Hell is full. But for writing he was naked as if he had not been allowed to bring anything with him. Not even his own experience. And that man wearing glasses suddenly felt sincerely abashed in front of the white page as if his task were not to write down something that already existed but to create something that would then come to exist.... What was he waiting for with his hand ready? since he had had an experience, he had a pencil and a piece of paper, he had the intention and the desire—nobody ever had more than that. Yet it was the most helpless act he had ever performed.[21]

After a struggle that lasts many pages, "modest, serious, myopic, he simply wrote down: 'Things to do.'" Underneath he scrawls, "That." "'So I really did a great deal: I alluded!' And Martin was as happy as an artist: in itself the word 'that' contained everything he hadn't managed to say."[22]

Through writing, Martin builds a world, "asking, asking, asking—until little by little the world began to be created in response." "Yes. The reconstruction of the world. The man had just completely lost his shame. He wasn't even embarrassed to use words from his adolescence: he had to use them because the last time he had his own language was when he was an adolescent; adolescence meant risking everything—and now he was risking everything."[23] There are echoes here of Clarice's attempts as a child to save the world with magical stories. As she well knew, however, she did not save her mother. She did not remedy the social tragedy of Recife; she did not reform the penitentiaries; she did not rescue a war-ravaged nation. "I did not rebuild Italy. I tried to rebuild my home, rebuild my children, and myself. I failed."[24]

But her failure was only in the external world. Like Martin, she redirected this heroic impulse inward. "Reconstructing the world" was now a personal goal, as indistinguishable from her artistic mission as it had been when she was telling stories to save her mother. She could no longer expect to see her mother arise from her rocking chair. The child's desperation has been transformed into a mystical aim, a fantastic undertaking of breathtaking ambition: to reconstruct the world through words. "I write as if to save somebody's life," she wrote shortly before her death. "Probably my own life."[25]

As he embarks on this life-or-death enterprise, Martin hears from Victoria that their tomatoes are to be sold to a German. This, he presumes, is the same man from whose hotel he had fled. He knows that Victoria will turn him in. He wonders if there is time to escape. And he knows he will not try. Martin is still fantasizing about writing when the police arrive: "Above all... I swear that in my book I will have the courage to leave unexplained anything that cannot be explained."[26] The phrase could serve as a motto for *The Apple in the Dark*. The book is as challenging as *The Chandelier* or *The Besieged City*. But where those are sometimes impenetrable—"May someone find the key"—*The Apple in the Dark* combines their thematic intricacy with the powerful emotional currents of *Near to the Wild Heart*.

Now the richness of Clarice Lispector's thought, rather than being merely daunting, takes on an array of symbolic possibilities that are, along with her incredible linguistic invention, the glory of this novel. Even without the references to apples, crimes, and falls, it is obviously an allegory of creation, and an allegory of creation through the word: "And that man wearing glasses suddenly felt sincerely abashed in front of the white page as if his task were not to write down something that already existed but to create something that would then come to exist."[27]

Clarice had been pursuing these themes since the beginning. (The relationship between crime and creation is a further example.) Yet though *The Apple in the Dark* represents the unfolding of familiar ideas, it is nonetheless different from her earlier work. The difference lies in her willingness, for the first time, to say one word. "Oh God, Martin then said in calm despair. Oh God, he said."[28]

It is an excruciating moment. Clarice, with Martin, is going out to meet the God that had abandoned her in childhood. But what God is this? Clarice hints that the book is a Jewish parable. This is not indicated by the setting, an anonymous farm in the Brazilian interior, or from anything explicitly stated in the book. Clarice would never write, as did Elisa, "Latest news: Jewish state proclaimed! Read all about it!" Still, the clues are there, starting on the first page, where Martin's shadowy persecutor is identified as a German who owns a Ford. Feared but never actually seen, the only figure in the book who is not Brazilian finally brings about Martin's arrest.

There is no reason of plot or character for Clarice to assign this vague figure German nationality, especially in a book in which few characters have so much as a name: "the mulatto woman," "the professor." In a book by a Jewish writer of the 1950s, "German" was not a neutral description, especially when applied to a symbol of harassment and oppression. And "Ford," the only brand named in the whole book, recalls the notorious anti-Semite Henry Ford, whose venomous writings were widely distributed in Brazil.

Both names hint that the German's victim must be Jewish. The impression is strengthened by the goal of Martin's long confrontation with the blank page. He is searching for a specific, impossible word, "as if there were a word that if a man said it... That absent word that however sustained him. That however was him. That however was that thing that only died because the man died. That however was his own energy and the way he breathed."[29]

This unutterable word meant salvation. "And if this was the word—would that then be the way it happened? So he had had to live everything he had lived in order to experience something that could be said in a single word? if that word could be said, and he still hadn't said it. He had crossed the entire world, only because it was more difficult to take a single step? but if that step could never be taken!"[30]

The step that cannot be taken, the absent word that sustains him, is the hidden name, the "single word" that Clarice finally, elliptically, says. The name is a symbol of God and it *is* God, "the symbol of the thing in the thing itself." As Gershom Scholem has written, "This is the real and, if I may say so, the peculiarly Jewish object of mystical contemplation: The Name of God, which is something absolute, because it reflects the hidden meaning and totality of existence; the Name through which everything else acquires its meaning and which yet to the human mind has no concrete, particular meaning of its own."[31] Clarice's reluctant rediscovery of this God of the hidden name apparently signals a rejection of her declaration, in her early essay devoted to crime and punishment, that "beyond mankind there is nothing else at all."[32]

In light of her evolving thought, however, the phrase acquires a fascinating nuance. In Jewish tradition, nothing can be changed without coming into contact with the region of absolute being that the mystics call Nothing. Only when the soul has stripped itself of all limitation and, in mystical language, has descended into the depths of nothing, does it encounter the divine.[33] Martin is reborn when he descends into the empty desert, where human meaning ceases.

Reworked, disguised, but undeniably present, the Jewish motifs in Clarice Lispector's writings beg the question of the extent to which their inclusion was deliberate. She was not traditionally observant. Her presence in the synagogue ceased with her father's death, when she was twenty, and unlike the classical Jewish mystics she did not venerate, or even seem to notice, the religion's sacred texts.

Her personal experience was instead a microcosm of the broader Jewish historical experience. Persecution and exile—and the despair, and yearning for salvation, that went with them—gave her a psychological makeup similar to Jews of all ages. When these experiences were combined with an expressive genius, the results, naturally enough, bore certain similarities to the work of her predecessors.[34]

Despite her frequent descriptions of herself as nonintellectual, Clarice's relationship with Jewish mystical thought was probably more than a simple coincidence of biographical circumstances, however. Her sister Tania confirmed that at one point Clarice's reading included a great deal of cabbalistic literature. But this reading, for Clarice, was never the point, and she disowned it. "It is not only that I lack culture and erudition," she told an interviewer in the early 1960s, "it's that those subjects don't interest me. I used to regret it, but now I don't try to document myself; because I think that literature is not literature, it's life, living."[35]

The presentation of herself as "lacking culture and erudition" met with remarkable success. None less than Elizabeth Bishop, her neighbor in Rio, wrote Robert Lowell that "[Clarice is] the most non-literary writer I've ever known, and 'never cracks a book' as we used to say—She's never read anything, that I can discover—I think she's a 'self-taught' writer, like a primitive painter."[36]

In one sense, Bishop was spectacularly off the mark. Clarice's higher education, her work as a journalist, her experience in the foreign service, her knowledge of languages, and her practice in living on three continents made her, apart from her own artistic achievement, one of the most sophisticated women of her generation, and not only in Brazil. She was widely and deeply read, as the numerous allusions in her writing and correspondence prove. Autran Dourado, one of Brazil's leading novelists and intellectuals, recalls long Sundays spent with Clarice in complicated philosophical discussions ranging from Spinoza to Nietzsche.

In another sense, however, being a "primitive painter," "the most non-literary writer I've ever known," was a goal of Clarice's. She placed no value on learnedness or sophistication. From Naples she had written Natércia Freire of her impatience with the diplomatic life: "At the end of it all you end up 'educated.' But that's not my style. I never minded being ignorant."[37] She was interested in a different kind of knowledge, one that had nothing to do with advanced reading or philosophy. Suspecting that the answers to the "mute and intense question" that had troubled her as an adolescent—"what is the world like? and why this world?"—could not be discovered intellectually, she sought a higher kind of understanding. "You ought to know," a Spanish cabbalist muttered at the end of the thirteenth century, "that these philosophers whose wisdom you are praising, end where we begin."[38]

If *The Apple in the Dark* is a creation allegory, it differs in an important way from the traditional narratives. It is the story of the creation of a man, but it is also the story of how that man creates God. "Then in his colicky flesh he invented God. . . . A man in the dark was a creator. In the dark the great bargains are struck. When he said 'Oh God' Martin felt the first weight of relief in his chest."[39] This is Martin's essential, heroic, invention, and it comes through the word.

The story of Martin is the opposite of the biblical creation story. The man is himself created through sin, and the sinning man creates God; that invention, a further paradox, redeems the man. Clarice has at last said the word "God," but she will have Him only on her terms. "He knew that he would have to reduce himself when faced with the thing he had created until he could fit inside the world, and reduce himself until he became the son of the God that he had created because only that way would he receive any compassion. 'I am nothing,' and that way he fit inside the mystery."[40]

Even an invented God gives Martin a place in the world, along with that most human of sentiments, compassion. It is an element of the false morality from which Martin's crime freed him. But a man cannot live forever in a state of unforgiven sin, any more than he can linger too long in the state of grace. The moment Martin invents God is the moment he can finally come to terms with his crime: "I killed, I killed, he finally confessed."[41] Without God, even an artificial God, there can be no sin.

In these particulars, especially in the way Clarice reverses the creation story, Martin is related to that most famous figure of Jewish folklore, one Clarice surely knew from childhood: the Frankenstein-like Golem. The creation of the Golem, whose name comes from a Hebrew word meaning "unformed" or "amorphous," was the mystical reversion of the creation of Adam. The great folklorist Jacob Grimm, writing in 1808 in the *Journal for Hermits*, describes the Golem thus:

> The Polish Jews, after having spoken certain prayers and observed certain Feastdays, make the figure of a man out of clay or lime which, after they have pronounced the wonderworking *Shem hameforash* over it, comes to life. It is true this figure cannot speak, but it can understand what one says and commands it to do to a certain extent. They call it Golem and use it as a servant to do all sorts of house-work; he may never go out alone. On his forehead the word *Emet* (Truth; God) is written, but he increases from day to day and can easily become larger and stronger than his house-comrades, however small he may have been in the beginning. Being then afraid of him, they rub out the first letters so that nothing remains but *Met* (he is dead) whereupon he sinks together and becomes clay again.[42]

The similarities between Martin and the Golem are striking. Like the clay figurines Virginia creates in *The Chandelier*, golems are sculpted from mud, especially river mud: in the blazing desert Clarice stresses Martin's identity with the rocky earth. Like the Golem, Martin cannot originally speak and is used by Victoria as a house servant. He cannot leave the farm. As he masters human language he grows to a position of power over the original inhabitants of the house. Fearing him, Victoria has him taken away.

The *Shem hameforash,* the spoken form of God's unspeakable name, "that absent word that however sustained him," gives the Golem life. In the story of the Golem as in the story of Martin, man summons God into the world by using His name. With the discovery of the hidden name, man acquires the divine power over life and death.

25

THE WORST TEMPTATION

Clarice completed *The Apple in the Dark* in March 1956. "It was a fascinating book to write," she wrote Fernando Sabino in September. "I learned a lot doing it, I was shocked by the surprises it gave me—but it was also a great suffering."[1] But if she thought her suffering was through when she put the finishing touches on the last of the book's eleven drafts, she was mistaken. *The Apple in the Dark* met the fate of many works later acclaimed as masterpieces: it was nearly not published at all.

When she finished it, she sent copies to Erico Verissimo and to Fernando Sabino, once again acting as her literary agent. She wanted "a publisher who can publish it without delay, as quickly as possible—not a promise for whenever they have time." "Waiting isn't good for me," she added, "it trips me up, it makes me impatient."[2] At first, it seemed she would get her way. In June, to her delight, Fernando wrote her that Ênio Silveira from Civilização Brasileira would publish the book in October or November.[3]

Earlier that year, Silveira had scored a notable success with Fernando Sabino's own *A Time to Meet*, a kind of Brazilian *Catcher in the Rye* based on Fernando's teenage experiences in Minas Gerais. It became a best-seller, spawned dramatic adaptations, and was widely translated. Ênio himself, a leftist and later a prominent opponent of the military dictatorship, had studied at Columbia and even worked for a time at Alfred A. Knopf. What's more, he was completely "crushed by the impact of Clarice Lispector," "absolutely dazzled": "No book in Brazil and few abroad are at her level, it is something absolutely new, it makes a tremendous impact, etc."[4] Alas, by January 1957, when Fernando reported this news to Clarice, the dazzled and crushed Silveira was already backtracking. October and

November, the original publication dates, had come and gone. The reasons for the delay were obscure, Fernando wrote: "These days the publishing business is doing well in Brazil."[5]

This was true: the glamorous new president, Juscelino Kubitschek, had eliminated certain taxes, on paper, for example, that had a negative impact on the industry, and the publishing business exploded. In 1945 Brazil had produced an average of twenty million books a year; by 1962 this had more than tripled, to sixty-six million.[6] Still, Silveira was starting to fall back on time-honored excuses; he *was* still interested in it, Fernando assured Clarice, "even though it won't be so easy to sell," but he would do it by June 1957 at the latest, "for the prestige of the house."[7]

Clarice was growing nervous. Through Rubem Braga, who came to Washington in November, the book made its way to José Olympio, perhaps Rio's most prestigious publisher, who said that he would do it "immediately."[8] In the absence of a concrete commitment, Clarice's mood was souring, and she was losing her confidence in the book. She wrote Fernando that she was sure that José Olympio's enthusiasm could not withstand a reading of the book. Even if it did, she added, the book couldn't come out until 1958, which would not interest her. "When I write something, I stop liking it, little by little. . . . I feel like a girl putting together her trousseau and storing it in a chest. A bad marriage is better than no marriage; it's horrible to see a yellowing trousseau."[9]

At this point, she was even considering paying to publish it, and asked Fernando to help her get in touch with printers. She was especially discouraged because, as luck would have it, *The Apple in the Dark* was not the only book she was having trouble publishing. On her visit to Rio in 1954, Fernando's friend José Simeão Leal, who had published *Some Stories*, commissioned a full collection of stories. He even, for the first time in Clarice's career, paid her an advance. As she was writing *The Apple in the Dark*, she was also working on the collection that would become *Family Ties*.

The stories were completed in March 1955. They would eventually be recognized as a high point in Brazilian literature, as two of that literature's most famous writers saw immediately. Fernando Sabino wrote, "You've made eight stories like nobody has come even close to making in Brazil," adding that the book would be "exactly, sincerely, indisputably, and even humbly, the best book of stories ever published in Brazil."[10] Erico Verissimo told her, "I haven't written about your book of stories out of sheer embarrassment to tell you what I think of it. Here goes: the most important story collection published in this country since Machado de Assis," Brazil's classic novelist.[11]

Broader recognition, however, would have to wait. In June 1956, Simeão Leal told Clarice's agent that the book was in proofs.[12] In July, Clarice wrote Fernando, "My desire to get rid of things is almost a sickness; for example, I feel that I'll be constrained by Simeão Leal's book of stories forever."[13] Almost a year later, in March 1957, Rubem Braga was trying to wrest the stories free in order to publish them in the newspaper *O Estado de S. Paulo*.[14] Sabino tried to place them with Agir, publisher of *The Chandelier*.

Another humiliating year and a half went by, and Erico Verissimo found a publisher for both: Henrique Bertaso, of Globo, in the Verissimos' hometown of Porto Alegre. But, Erico added, Simeão Leal would "in no circumstances" return the originals of the stories, which were "already at the printer's." And just as Globo had agreed to publish *The Apple in the Dark*, the book appeared in the catalogue of Ênio Silveira's Civilização Brasileira.[15] Needless to say, it was not published at the appointed time. It is hard to understand why not. Civilização Brasileira was one of the most prolific publishers in Brazil; between 1961 and 1964, the house published a new title *every working day* of the year.[16] Why was it so hard to find a place for Clarice?

The exhausting seesaw of disappointed hopes and the depressing spectacle of being forced, in middle age and in midcareer, to beg for a publisher did not improve Clarice's mind-set. "Ever since you left I've lost the stimulus for everything, nothing is fun for me," she wrote Erico and Mafalda.[17] Her friends tried to cheer her up. "I know so well how you must be feeling," Fernando wrote her, "without news, without anything. But you can always count on me, I won't leave your book a single minute—I just regret that in Brazil the conditions of publishing it as it deserves don't exist."[18]

"You know perfectly well that you write the only prose of a Brazilian author that I would like to write myself," João Cabral de Melo Neto wrote, adding later, from Marseilles, where he was seeking treatment for depression, "What a thing, writing literature in Brazil. I think the best thing to do is nothing at all. In Brazil, all they understand is writing for newspapers. That's why we've got this superficial, improvised, fragmentary thing passing for a national literature."[19]

❦

"The strangest thing is happening to me," Clarice wrote to Fernando in 1956. "As time goes by, I feel that I live nowhere, and that no place 'wants me.'"[20] The sad truth was that Clarice was partly right. Outside the core of artists and intellectuals who had been fascinated by her since the appearance of *Near to the Wild Heart* over a decade before, Clarice was by now almost entirely forgotten.

Her subsequent novels had not burnished the celebrity she had earned with her first; moreover, she had been living abroad for many years. She was no longer a name, and, as the letters she was receiving from Fernando were making increasingly obvious, no publisher was eager to take on a difficult four-hundred-page cabbalistic allegory by an obscure writer, no matter what her reputation among certain intellectuals.

But that reputation, and the sincere dedication of her friends, was about to bear fruit. In November 1958, she received a letter from a young journalist named Nahum Sirotzky, a cousin of Samuel Wainer, who was launching a new magazine called *Senhor*, "Gentleman." Finally a place did want her, and on her terms. Sirotzky wrote, "We would like to read your stories which we never considered *intelligible*."[21]

Fernando Sabino and Paulo Mendes Campos had recommended one of the new stories, "The Smallest Woman in the World."[22] Alongside works by Ray Bradbury, W. H. Auden, Ernest Hemingway, and Carlos Lacerda—Samuel Wainer's archenemy—this story appeared in *Senhor*'s inaugural issue, March 1959.

"A Magazine for the Gentleman" was the brainchild of the brothers Simão and Sérgio Waissman. Their father was a publisher who specialized in selling encyclopedias and affordable classics on an installment plan. His sons wanted to produce a magazine to be the exciting public face of their own publishing company, Delta. *Senhor* turned out to be a sensation.

Earlier in his career, Sirotzky had been a correspondent in New York. His idea was to import the flavor of *The New Yorker*, *Esquire*, or the *Partisan Review* to Brazil. The old style was typified by *Dom Casmurro*, the most important literary publication of the previous generation, where Clarice had published some early work. Parodying the style he longed to replace, Sirotzky riffs, "This afternoon, a beautiful sunny day, my boss called me into his office and told me to interview so-and-so. I got onto the tram, the city was gorgeous, I ran up the stairs, knocked on the door, was let in and offered a cup of coffee."[23]

In the old-style magazines, Sirotzky said, "The delete key didn't exist." In his magazine, writers would be edited. This was a remarkable change, as Paulo Francis, *Senhor*'s fiction editor, recalled. He worked with Clarice, who, like other writers, appreciated his careful attention. "Clarice reacted completely normally, and sometimes rewrote passages that she agreed were unclear. In Brazil, in literature, that is taboo.... You don't touch the texts of the big names."[24] Except at *Senhor*, where they even rejected a piece by Erico Verissimo. (They paid him, but he, "extremely dignified," declined the money.)

Verissimo was not the only big name who had trouble getting into the pages of *Senhor*. Jânio Quadros, governor of the state of São Paulo and soon to be president of Brazil, fancied himself a litterateur and submitted several articles. Sirotzky rejected them, too. "I even rejected myself!" Sirotzky remembers. "I wasn't good enough for *Senhor*." The magazine's rigorous requirements for artistic excellence extended to questions of design: famous painters illustrated its covers, and even advertisements that did not meet its standards were rejected.

Clarice Lispector, however, was a favorite. She appeared in roughly one in every three issues. Her stories were prominently announced on the cover, and starting in 1961 she had a column in every issue. *Senhor*'s circulation peaked at twenty-five thousand, but "its influence in the Brazilian press needs no comment," Francis wrote; passed hand-to-hand, the magazine reached many more people than its circulation numbers indicated. For Clarice, the result was her first taste of genuine popularity.

One person it reached was Caetano Veloso, a teenager in a small town in the state of Bahia, soon to be one of Brazil's most famous musicians. The discovery was among the most important of his adolescence: "It was here that I was to discover sex, see *La Strada*, fall in love for the first (and for the second, even more startling) time, read Clarice Lispector, and—most important—hear João Gilberto," the inventor of the bossa nova.[25]

> It was the story "The Imitation of the Rose."...I was frightened. I was so happy to find a new, modern style—I was looking for or waiting for something that I could call *modern*, something I already called *modern*—but the aesthetic happiness (it even made me laugh) came with the experience of growing intimacy with the world of feelings that the words evoked, insinuated, let themselves acquire....So the person reading the story kept wanting, with that woman, to grasp the nuances of normality and, at the same time, to hand oneself over, with her, to the unspeakable luminosity of madness.[26]

"The Imitation of the Rose" captures the conundrum that had fascinated and tormented Clarice since childhood. It is a poetic encapsulation of the Steppenwolf dilemma, the conflict between Joana and Lídia: between, in Caetano Veloso's words, the "unspeakable luminosity of madness" and the "normality" of everyday life.

The title refers, of course, to another mystical work. "As for my reading," she wrote Fernando in 1953, "which is varied and probably mistaken, the best is the *Imitation of Christ*, but it is very difficult to imitate Him, and that's less obvious than it seems."[27] Less obvious because, as the housewife Laura remembers, waiting for her husband Armando to return home from work, "when they had given her the *Imitation of Christ* to read [in school], with a stupid ardor she had read it without understanding but, may God forgive her, she felt that whoever imitated Christ was lost—lost in light, but dangerously lost. Christ"—the humanized God—"was the worst temptation."[28]

As Laura sits waiting for Armando—"to the contrary of Carlota, who had made her home something that resembled herself, Laura had such pleasure in making her house something impersonal; somehow perfect because impersonal"—the reader understands that she is not a normal housewife. She has "finally returned from the perfection of the planet Mars," a spell in a mental hospital, and she is cured. Now she is back, to iron her husband's shirts and sleep peacefully at night. "How rich normal life was, she who had finally returned from extravagance. Even a vase of flowers. She looked at it."[29]

The sight of the perfect roses, however, unbalances her. "Oh! Nothing much, it just so happened that extreme beauty made people uncomfortable." She thinks about having the maid bring them over to her friend Carlota's house, where she and Armando are going to dinner. Despite the complications that could create, she has to get rid of them. "Could you go to Miss Carlota's house and leave these roses for her?" she asks the maid. "You say: 'Miss Carlota, these are from Miss Laura.' You say: 'Miss Carlota . . .' 'I know, I know,' said the patient maid."[30]

Like Clarice, who as a little girl in Recife stole roses, Laura fantasizes about keeping one. "She could at least take one rose for herself, nothing more than that: one rose for herself. And she would be the only one who would ever know, and after that never again, oh, she promised herself that she would never again let herself be tempted by perfection, never again!"[31]

The maid takes them, leaving Laura once again seated on the sofa, lost in reverie. By the time she hears her husband's key in the door, it is too late. Too late to greet him with a composure that will set his mind at ease. Too late for her to accept "humble joy and not the imitation of Christ." Too late.

"She was seated in her house dress. He knew that she had done everything possible not to become luminous and unreachable. With shyness and respect, he was looking at her. He had grown older, tired, curious. But there was not a word to say. From the open door he saw his wife who was seated straight-backed on the sofa, once again alert and calm as if in a train. Which had already departed."[32]

"Christ was the worst temptation," she writes. "Genius was the worst temptation," she adds a few pages later.[33] Clarice had always hovered between the imperatives of the mystic and the artist and the sincere desire to excel as a wife and mother.

But just as the train has already departed in "The Imitation of the Rose," it was obvious, if only in retrospect, that Clarice could not forever play the role of the diplomatic spouse. She, too, "had done everything possible not to become luminous and unreachable," but it was too violent an effort. So around the time her first stories started appearing in *Senhor*, she was making preparations to leave her husband and return, this time for good, to Rio de Janeiro.

With the advantage of hindsight, the skepticism about marriage that appears from the beginning of her career makes it less remarkable that her own marriage eventually ended than that it lasted as long as it did. Cristina, in "Obsession," mockingly speaks of wanting to "marry, have children, and, finally, be happy";[34] Joana thought that after marriage "all you can do is wait for death"; Virginia's relationships go nowhere; Lucrécia marries for money; and Martin kills his wife, or so he thinks. Solitude, the difficulty of human connection, is as much a theme of Clarice's as it is of her sister Elisa's.

And so the specific reasons behind Clarice's separation from Maury are, in some sense, superfluous. Things had not been going well for several years. Mafalda Verissimo, who left Washington in 1956, said, "The marriage was starting to go downhill. We did everything to try to get them to stay together, but it didn't work."[35]

There was, first of all, the pain of exile, which after fifteen years had become unbearable. Abroad, Clarice said, "[I] lived mentally in Brazil, I lived 'on borrowed time.' Simply because I like living in Brazil, Brazil is the only place in the world where I don't ask myself, terrified: what am I doing here after all, why am I here, my God."[36]

The frustrating difficulty of publishing her books could only have exacerbated her feeling that she was on the wrong track. At such a distance, even with Fernando's help, she could not personally look after her work, and the evidence, though gracefully disguised in his letters, that she was forgotten in her home country could not have made it easier for her to remain abroad.

Her distance from her sisters, too, was increasingly painful. "With the years of absence so many facts and thoughts have accumulated and not been transmitted that one involuntarily acquires an air of mystery," she wrote Tania. "If we were together, even if I didn't tell you, something always comes across through the face, through gestures, through being there."[37] Her sisters felt the distance, too. In *Body to Body*, the painful reckoning the lonely and insecure Elisa wrote after Clarice's death, a woman (Elisa) movingly writes to a man (Clarice) she has loved and lost:

In your letters, which I now recall so vividly, you loved me so much, you adored me, you enlarged me. You saw in me feelings I myself never suspected I had. And more: you induced me, almost implored me, to be happy, despite your absence.

Across that distance you exalted me.

In letters, our love was such a great love!

"... perhaps, even then, because of my sullen nature, I didn't know how to match with expansive love the love that overflowed in your letters, and for that too I repent."

Yet I loved you, and how!

And always you asked me to write more, you wanted to know about the smallest minutiae of my daily life.

"... it's one more reason that at first I didn't understand or accept that we gradually, mutually grew apart when you came back from your journey, and in reprisal I moved away."[38]

Clarice, in turn, had moved away from Maury. By all accounts he was, and remained, in love with her, and their relationship would remain strong for the rest of their lives. But she was tired of the diplomatic routine and increasingly desperate to return to Brazil. The couple tried to work out their problems, but Clarice finally decided to leave him. In an age when even international telephone contact was rare, expensive, and difficult, the decision to leave and take the boys back to Rio was difficult.

For six-year-old Paulo, he was not only leaving his father, he was also leaving his country, his language, his house, and his beloved nanny, Avani, who was like a second mother to him. Maury was now completely alone, without his sons and without a wife who, by all accounts, he always remained in love with. After her return, he sent an eloquent letter to Clarice begging for a second chance.

> I am going to write you asking for your forgiveness. Forgiveness with humility but without humiliation. I speak to you with the authority of someone who is suffering, who is profoundly alone, very unhappy, missing you and the boys in my body and soul. Many of the things that you are going to read will provoke you to anger and derision. I know it, but I can't help it. My friends have told me to try to reconcile through indirect means. That's not me, in the first place, and in the second place it wouldn't help, since you are too perceptive to accept "tactics," even though the intentions

are good. Maybe I should speak to Joana and not Clarice. Forgive me, Joana, for not having given you the support and the understanding that you had the right to expect from me. You told me that you weren't made for marriage before we got married. Instead of taking that as a slap in the face, I ought to have seen it as a request for support. I failed you in this and many other things. But intuitively I never stopped believing that inside you, Clarice, Joana and Lídia coexist. I rejected Joana because her world frightened me, instead of reaching out to her. I accepted, too much, the role of Otávio and ended up convincing myself that "we were unable to free ourselves for love." I was unable to undo Joana's fear of "connecting to a man without allowing him to imprison her." I didn't know how to free her from the "asphyxiating certainty that if a man took her in his arms, she wouldn't feel a very sweet sweetness in any of her boyfriends; it would be the opposite, like an acid lemon juice" and that "it would be dry wood close to the fire, bending, ready to burst" (I'm retranslating from the French). I was blind and didn't capture the deeper meaning of: "one becomes a monk because, in some way or another, he has inside himself enormous possibilities for pleasure, dangerous possibilities; which makes his fear all the greater." . . . [Joana had] a love so strong that she could only exhaust her passion through hatred. . . . I wasn't mature enough to understand that, in Joana or in Clarice, "hate can transform itself into love"; not being more than "a search for love." I didn't know how to free you from the "fear of not loving." Perhaps, like Otávio, I didn't like "the way a woman takes leave of herself" and needed her to be "cold and secure." I ended up saying, "like in childhood, almost victorious: 'it's not my fault.' " . . . I could never understand the intensity of a jealousy, always denied and profoundly repressed by Joana and Clarice, that would make them detest Otávio and Maury. . . . Lídia, to the contrary, and who is also a facet of Clarice, "isn't afraid of pleasure and accepts it without remorse." Forgive me, my darling, for not having known, though I vaguely felt the union of the two, for not having known how, in sixteen years of marriage, to reconcile them. For not knowing how to convince Joana that she and Lídia were, and are, the same person in *Clarice*. Joana didn't need to envy Lídia and you didn't need to envy the famous "sweet women" who came between us, in these sixteen years, toward whom you felt an unacknowledged and repressed jealousy that exploded in rage. . . . In these circumstances it isn't surprising that Joana saw marriage "as an end, like death." It's not surprising that Joana wanted to have a child with Otávio, to abandon her husband thereafter, giving him back to Lídia. Perfectly logical that Clarice, living out

> more or less Joana's destiny, would return Maury's "beauty" to the world, to the "sweet and thin women." I could go on quoting but I would have to copy out the whole of that great book, that profound document and testimony of the soul of an adolescent woman, of a great artist.... I can't accept it, though... that you are following, in a certain sense, in real life, Joana's destiny. In all sincerity, without even mentioning our boys who, as a result, will end up "losing their father," who is reduced to a mere bankroller of their lives and their studies. With all sincerity, the point of this letter is to tell you that, whether I am suffering or not, whether you come back to me or not, my part in these events is very, very big. For the love of God, don't interpret this letter as an accusation. I know that my immaturity, my distraction, my lack of support, were one side of the equation. I wasn't prepared, because of well-known circumstances from my childhood, to give you a strong hand, to help you resolve the conflict that you so eloquently reflected in your first book.[39]

As Maury understood, Joana was finally triumphant. Clarice was probably right when, as a young woman, she told him she was not made for marriage. Her constant struggle with depression and her despair at exile could not have made her easy to live with, and Maury, too, had grown depressed at his inability to help her. His own infidelities reflected desperation rather than a lack of affection. Even his second wife said that until he remarried, "sexually, physically, he always liked *her*. But she was not interested."[40]

He sent her a book about marital therapy, adding: "My intention in sending it to you is not to point an 'accusing finger' at you or anyone else. If there is any accusation it is against myself, who was stupid and blind. I am not trying to identify you with any of the extreme cases mentioned in the book. As the fado goes, my desire is to give you a kiss, like someone who knows that this smile, on *our* lips, will end.... I am more and more convinced that you are the woman of my life and that my search for you in others, in the many false Lídias of which the world is full, was the error of someone who gave up early on."[41]

26

BELONGING TO BRAZIL

But the train had already left. In July 1959, "luminous and unreachable," Clarice returned to Brazil, where, except for brief excursions, she would spend the rest of her life. When she had departed almost two decades before, barely out of adolescence, the country was in the grip of war and of the quasi-Fascist Estado Novo. She returned in middle age to find her country blossoming in a teenage exuberance, amid a cultural fluorescence that touched every area of national life.

For Europeans, the 1950s were the grim years of postwar reconstruction; for Americans, they reek of suburban conformity. For Brazilians, the decade following Vargas's suicide is remembered as a golden age, an unprecedented, and never repeated, era of national confidence. Hitherto depressed—"The stork," a historian wrote, "is the bird that symbolizes our country. Of advantageous stature, it has strong legs and robust wings, yet spends its days with one leg crossed over the other, sad, sad, with that sober, gloomy, unsightly sadness"[1]—Brazil was suddenly the happiest place around.

In those glorious years, "the Brazilian ceased to be a mutt among men and Brazil to be a mutt among nations."[2] Everything was "novo, nova." In 1959, João Gilberto launched the bossa nova and soon had Hollywood and the Riviera swaying along. The *cinema novo* arrived, determined to show Brazil's excluded in the urban slums and the rural backlands for the very first time. (Not to everyone's taste, this social emphasis earned the first cinema novo film, *Rio, 40 degrees* [1955], a ban from the censor. He reportedly alleged that "the average temperature in Rio never exceeded 39.6 degrees.")

And the "Novacap," the new capital, ultramodern Brasília, was rising in the remote highlands of the Brazilian interior. It may have cost 300 billion

Before the deluge, the family gathers for a wedding in the Ukraine, circa 1917. Clarice's older sisters, Elisa and Tania, are the little girls in the front row, left; behind them, their parents, Pinkhas and Mania. Seated front row center are Dora and Israel Wainstok, who would join the Lispectors in Recife.

Clarice's mother, Mania Krimgold, martyred in the Ukrainian pogroms. The specter of her dying mother would forever haunt Clarice.

Pinkhas Lispector, the "brilliant mathematician" whose ambitions, thwarted by persecution and exile, would be redeemed by the dazzling achievement of his youngest daughter.

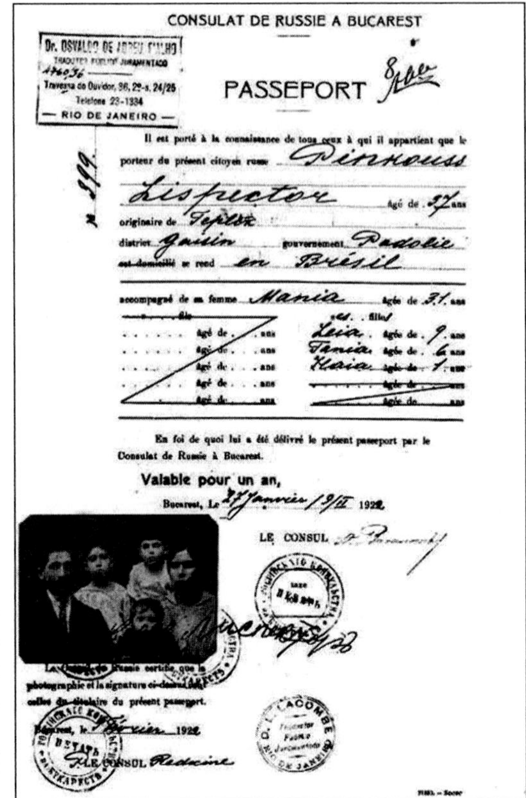

CONSULAT DE RUSSIE A BUCAREST

Traduteur Publico Juramentado
Travessa do Ouvidor, 36, 2º-s. 24/25
Telefone 23-1334
— RIO DE JANEIRO —

PASSEPORT

Il est porté à la connaissance de tous ceux à qui il appartient que le porteur du présent citoyen russe Pinkhouss Lispector âgé de 37 ans originaire de Teplik district Gaisin gouvernement Podolie se rend en Brésil

accompagné de sa femme Mania âgée de 31 ans

ses filles Leia âgée de 9 ans, Tania âgée de 6 ans, Haia âgée de 1 an

En foi de quoi lui a été délivré le présent passeport par le Consulat de Russie à Bucarest.

Valable pour un an,

Bucarest, Le 27 Janvier 1922

LE CONSUL

Le Consulat de Russie certifie que la photographie et la signature ci-dessus sont celles du titulaire du présent passeport.

Bucarest, le Février 1922

LE CONSUL

Tradutor Publico Juramentado
Rio de Janeiro

The document that saved the family, a Russian passport issued at Bucharest in 1922, valid for travel to Brazil. The baby, Clarice, would have no memory of the Ukrainian horrors.

The family in Brazil: Clarice clings to her paralyzed mother.

The sisters in Recife: Tania, Elisa, and Clarice.

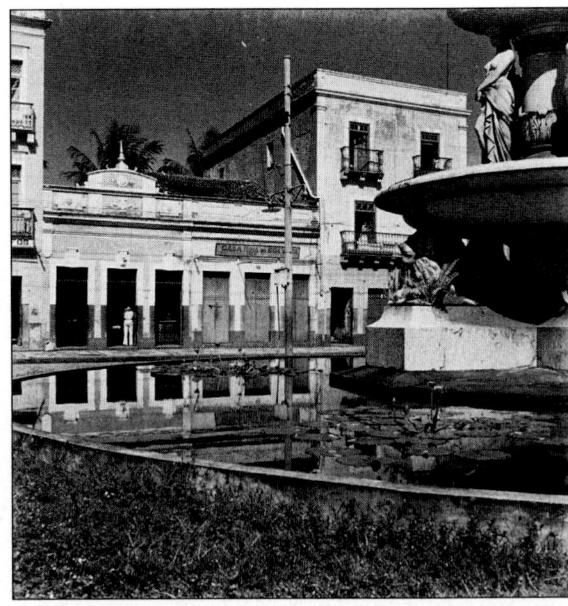

The Praça Maciel Pinheiro, Recife, known to the Jews as the *pletzele.* At right, the house the Lispectors lived in, so rickety that they were afraid it was going to fall over. It is still there today.

Clarice in Recife.

In Rio de Janeiro. The adolescent Clarice was already strikingly beautiful.

Clarice's first love, standing on Ipanema Beach. The gay writer Lúcio Cardoso was unavailable.

Shortly before his death, Clarice traveled to Minas Gerais with her beloved father for one of his rare holidays.

"More than just sisters": Clarice and Tania in Rio.

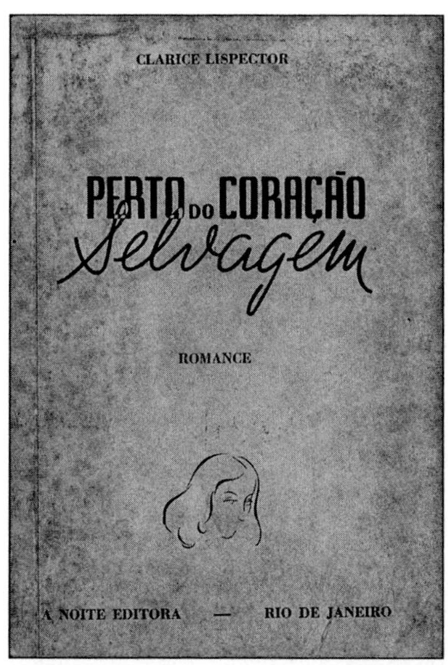

"Hurricane Clarice": *Near to the Wild Heart,* the work of an unknown twenty-three-year-old girl, astonished the intellectual and artistic world of Brazil when it appeared at the end of 1943.

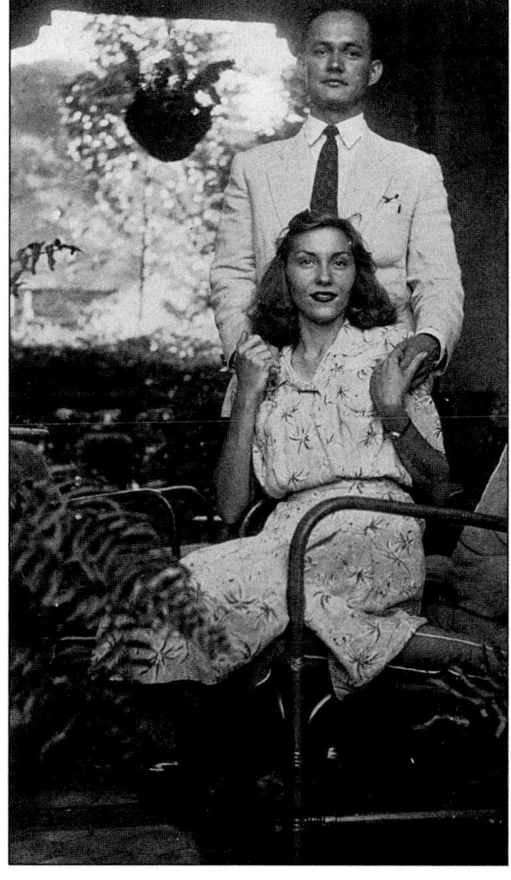

Clarice with the man she married shortly after the publication of her novel, the young diplomat Maury Gurgel Valente.

The homeless infant refugee returns to her native continent as an embassy wife: here, on the balcony of her apartment in ravaged Naples.

As Giorgio de Chirico was painting Clarice's portrait in his studio in the Piazza di Spagna, Rome, they heard a newsboy announce that the war was over.

Clarice with her diplomatic circle in Rome. Seated, left to right: Clarice's sister-in-law Eliane Gurgel Valente; Vasco Leitão da Cunha, consul in Rome; Clarice; Açucena Borges da Fonseca. Standing, left to right: Mário Soares Brandão; Clarice's husband, Maury; Landulpho Borges da Fonseca; and Maury's brother, and Eliane's husband, Mozart Gurgel Valente.

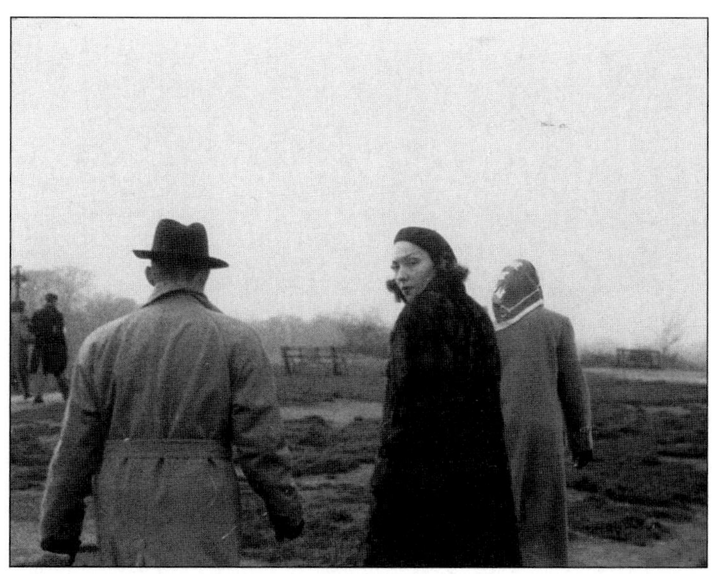

Clarice and Maury (left) on Mount Vesuvius, which had erupted shortly before their arrival in Italy.

Bluma Wainer and Clarice together in Bern, April 1946. Married to the powerful journalist Samuel Wainer, who was posted in Paris, the impressive Bluma would die young, not long after returning from Europe.

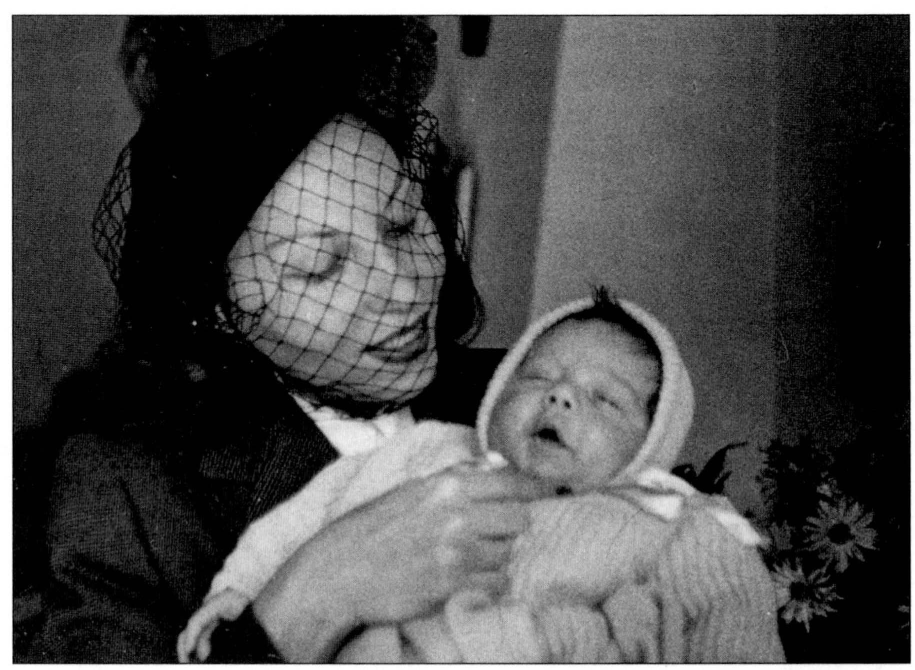

Clarice in Bern, with the newborn Pedro, named for her heroic late father.

Elisa Lispector, herself a respected novelist, chose solitude as her great theme.

In her diplomatic state, Clarice at a reception in Washington, heavily pregnant with Paulo.

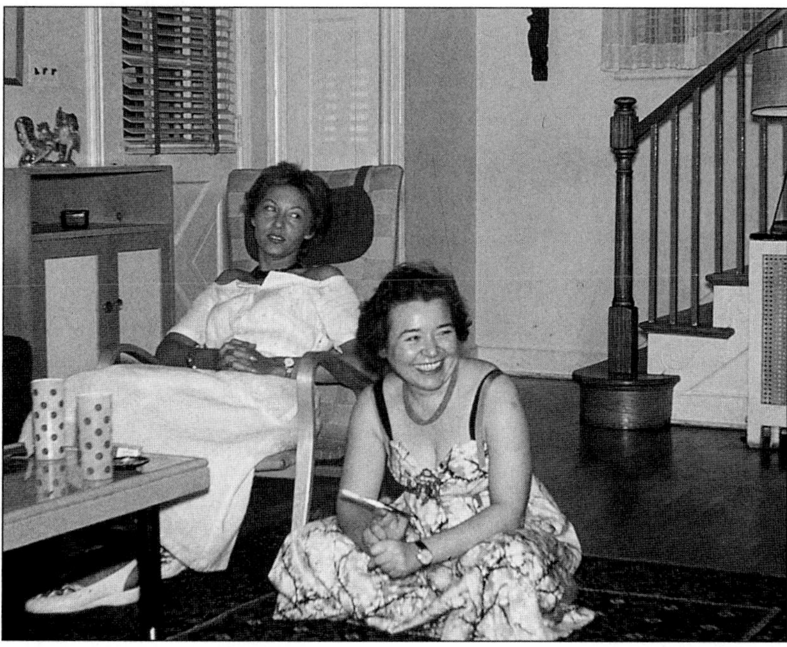

Clarice at home in Chevy Chase with Alzira Vargas. In her grief, the daughter of the suicidal dictator grew close to the writer.

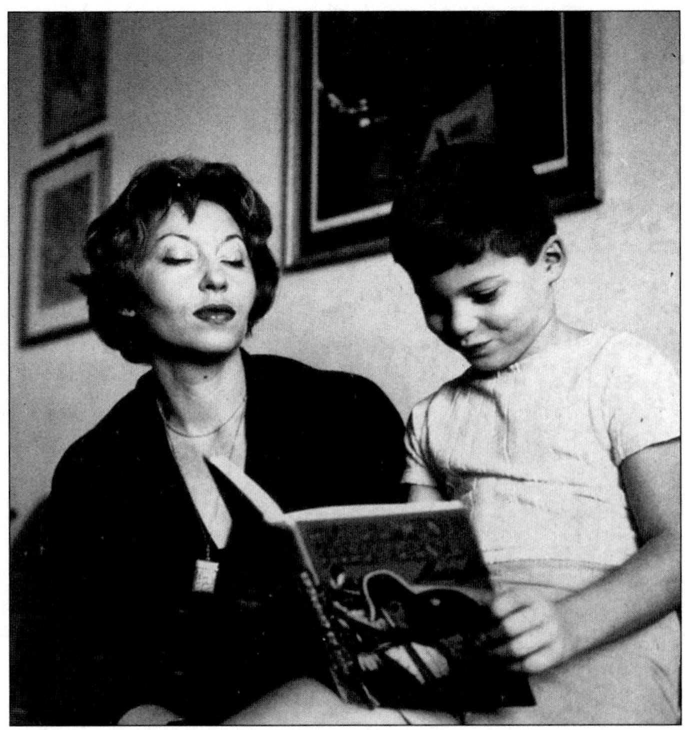

With Paulo: Clarice, newly popular since her return to her homeland, was becoming a figure of legend, universally known by her first name only.

Clarice, her two sons, and a friend on Leme Beach, with then glamorous Copacabana behind them. In 1959 Clarice finally returned to the country she had so longed for during her years abroad.

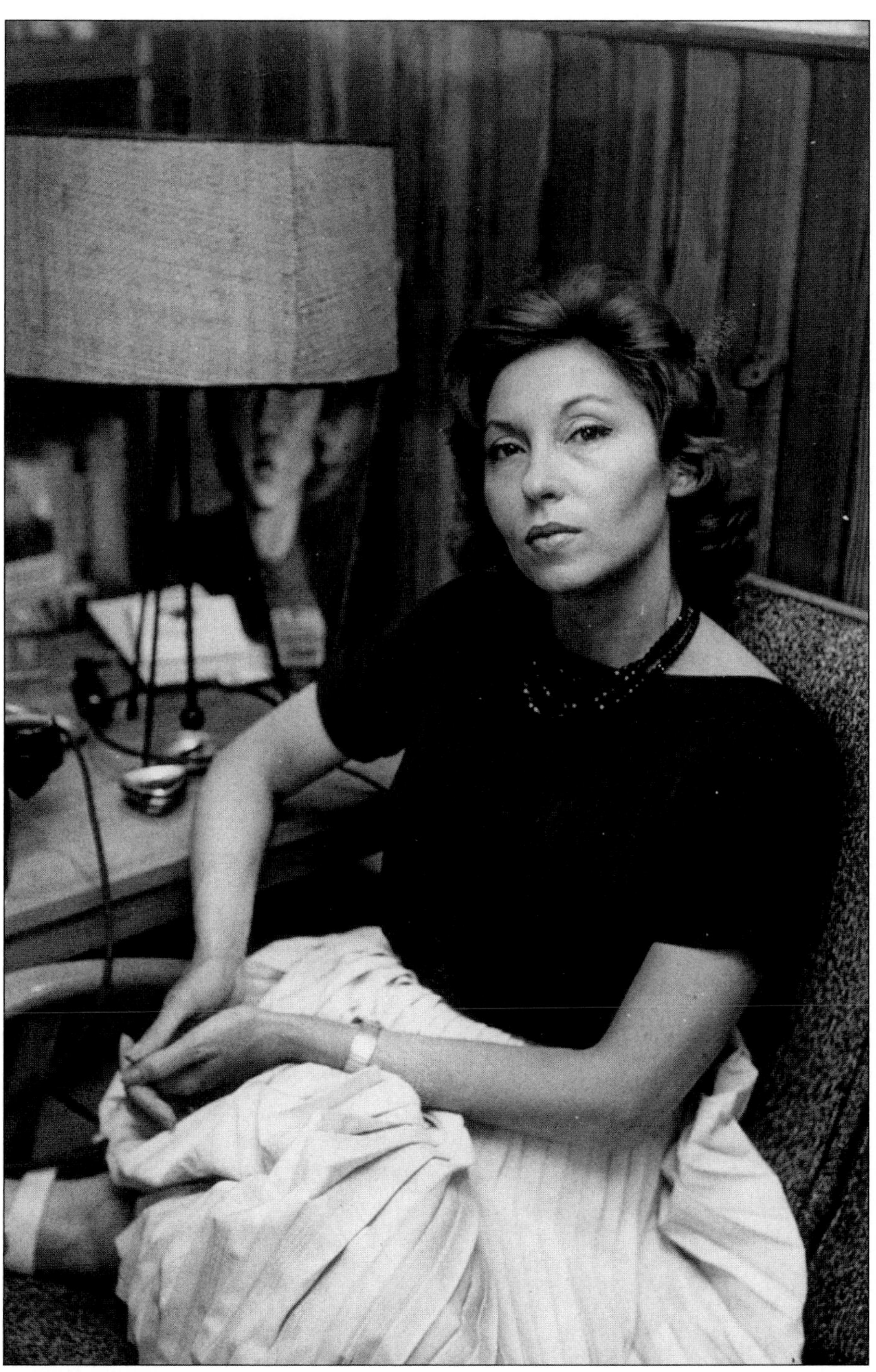

Clarice at home in Leme.

Clarice Lispector, surrounded by other leading intellectuals, marches against the dictatorship on June 22, 1968. From left to right: the painter Carlos Scliar; Clarice Lispector; Oscar Niemeyer, architect of Brasília; the actress Glauce Rocha; the cartoonist Ziraldo; and the musician Milton Nascimento.

With one of her oldest friends, Fernando Sabino.

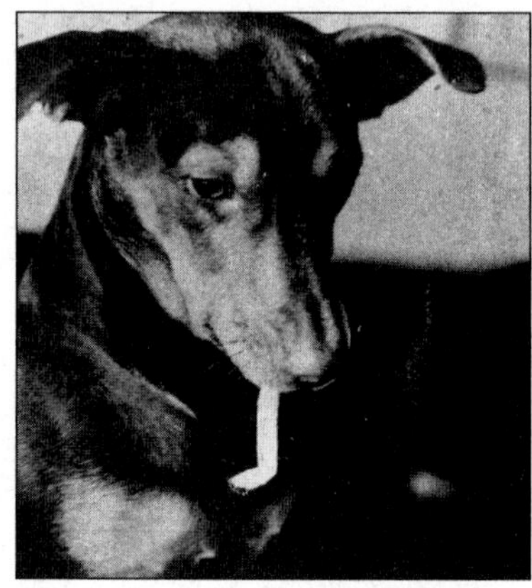

The mutt Ulisses, named for the mysterious painter or psychiatrist in Switzerland who had been in love with her. The smoking, drinking dog was himself a legend in Rio de Janeiro.

Clarice at home in the 1970s, surrounded by books and scattered manuscripts.

On her last visit to her hometown of Recife, Clarice signs books with her faithful friend Olga Borelli looking over her shoulder.

The writer toward the end of her life.

In her only televised interview, months before her death, Clarice enigmatically announced that she would be publishing a book with "thirteen names, thirteen titles." This was *The Hour of the Star*, composed of loose notes, written on checks, scraps of paper, and even boxes of cigarettes.

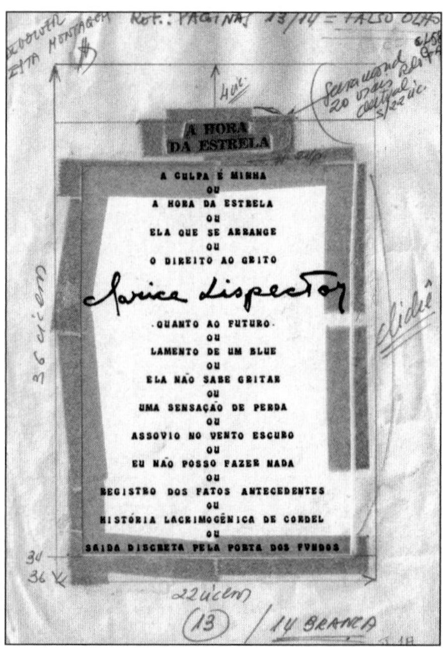

A HORA DA ESTRELA

A CULPA É MINHA
OU
A HORA DA ESTRELA
OU
ELA QUE SE ARRANGE
OU
O DIREITO AO GRITO

Clarice Lispector

.QUANTO AO FUTURO.
OU
LAMENTO DE UM BLUE
OU
ELA NÃO SABE GRITAR
OU
UMA SENSAÇÃO DE PERDA
OU
ASSOVIO NO VENTO ESCURO
OU
EU NÃO POSSO FAZER NADA
OU
REGISTRO DOS FATOS ANTECEDENTES
OU
HISTÓRIA LACRIMOGÊNICA DE CORDEL
OU
SAÍDA DISCRETA PELA PORTA DOS FUNDOS

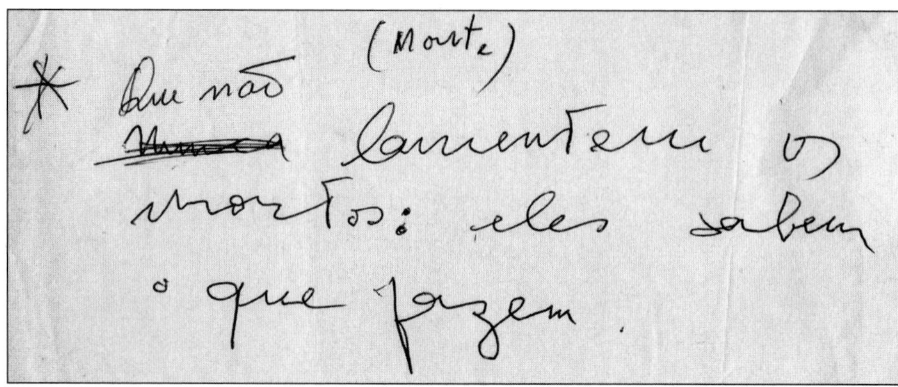

(Morte)
* Que não ~~Nunca~~ lamentem os mortos: eles sabem o que fazem.

In *The Hour of the Star* she announces her death; a few days after its publication she would be taken to the hospital. In this fragment, she writes: "Do not mourn the dead: they know what they are doing."

cruzeiros,[3] but it presented a bold new face to the world, and the world took notice, just as it had in 1958, when Brazil's soccer players—Garrincha, Didi, Vavá, and seventeen-year-old Pelé—won the World Cup. Brazil's luck had finally changed. In his small hometown in Bahia, Caetano Veloso was not the only Brazilian "looking for or waiting for something that I could call *modern*, something I already called *modern*."

Despite the renown she was starting to garner from her appearances in that most modern of Brazilian magazines, *Senhor*, Clarice's reentrance into Brazil was not easy. Paulo, her younger son, remembered, "With the separation from my father, she went through very anguished periods, of permanent 'material' (emotional?) need, of financial difficulties, of the weight, I imagine, of having to raise two children practically alone.... How much of this neediness was 'material'?"[4]

For the first time in her adult life, Clarice was under "material" pressure, though almost certainly less so than she felt. Maury sent five hundred dollars a month from Washington, a handsome sum, but from the beginning of her life without Maury, Clarice *felt* poor, perhaps out of fear of the poverty that haunted her childhood, and anxiety about money never left her. Financial worries became a constant complaint in her conversations and correspondence.

Yet Paulo was surely right to wonder "how much of this neediness was 'material.'" Clarice, after all, lived gracefully enough. After a month camping out at Tania's, she found an apartment in Leme, a small enclave at the end of Copacabana Beach, where she would spend the rest of her life.

Today one of the most densely packed areas on the planet—161,000 people crammed on the narrow strip between its legendary beach and the hills behind—Copacabana is a loud, hot victim of real estate speculation and Rio's half-century of decline. In 1959, however, when Clarice came back to Brazil, Copacabana was swanky. Chic shops and beach going by day, restaurants and casinos and discotheques by night, Copacabana was as much a symbol of the renascent, modern Brazil as Pelé and the bossa nova.

Not far from the massive white Copacabana Palace, whose opening in 1923 put Rio on the international tourist map, Leme emerged as a separate community, small, quiet, and exclusive. In contrast to chaotic Copacabana, Leme is no more than a couple of streets, lined with flame trees, between the beach and the mountains. Its far end is blocked by another mountain, so there is no through traffic. It boasts a small monastery, but in the 1950s and

1960s it was better known for high-end nightlife and for the calm waters of its beach.

Still, even in this pleasant spot and with a guaranteed alimony, Clarice did need to adjust to being a single mother. Her first priority was to publish the two books, *The Apple in the Dark* and *Family Ties*, that had been languishing in manuscript for almost five years. Her prospects were depressing. At the end of 1958, and despite all the years of promises to the contrary, Ênio Silveira of Civilização Brasileira had finally turned down *The Apple in the Dark*.

To Clarice's great surprise, the news triggered nationwide disgust. She got a hint of what was going on from Fernando Sabino, who wrote her in Washington in February 1959, "It was the straw that broke the camel's back, the resentment of writers in general with the way they are treated by publishers. It's a crisis and the thing ended up in the papers, triggering movements pro and con—they ended up, as always, getting the government involved, just to make it even more complicated."[5]

The outraged reaction reflected more than resentment at the shoddy treatment of one of the country's leading writers. "It wasn't just the rejection that unleashed the movement," a journalist wrote. "After all, any publisher can reject any book he chooses. It was the rejection of a manuscript that the publisher had himself requested, four years before."[6]

At first, still in Washington, Clarice heard none of the clatter, and when she did she was a bit embarrassed. "Really," she told a journalist after her return. "It's been said that there is a lot of curiosity about the book. I'm afraid that people will be disappointed. After all, I don't like to take credit for things that I haven't done. I'd like people to be interested in the book for what it is and not for what it's provoked."[7]

For an author whose books had languished for so long, however, any attention was useful, and the reaction to Silveira's dithering created a climate of interest around Clarice. "Result: from a writer whose work was almost exclusively known to a small group, Clarice Lispector became an author known across the whole country, in the face of that *wave*."[8] The surprising strength of the reaction shamed Silveira into a sort of action. By April 1959, he was writing to Clarice to promise that he would publish *The Apple in the Dark* before May 1960.[9]

Like so many of his previous dates, this one came and went without a whisper; Clarice had presumably heard the same line too many times before. At least both her books were now in her own hands, though. In March 1959, with the help of her sister-in-law Eliane, Clarice had managed to pry the stories of *Family Ties* free of José Simeão Leal.

"In 1959," wrote Paulo Francis, Clarice's editor at *Senhor*, "Clarice couldn't find a publisher in Brazil. She was well-known, yes, among intellectuals and writers. Publishers avoided her like the plague. The motives seemed obvious to me: she wasn't a disciple of 'socialist realism' or preoccupied with the little dramas of the little Brazilian bourgeoisie."[10]

Despite the outpouring of support, Clarice's bad luck continued. Agir, the Catholic publisher of *The Chandelier*, went so far as to send a draft contract for *Family Ties*, but that book never materialized either. "It is not for nothing that I understand those who are seeking their path," Clarice wrote a few years later. "How arduously I sought my own!"[11]

Her books in limbo, needing to find a way to make ends meet, Clarice embarked, almost as soon as she got back to Rio, on a new venture. At the invitation of the newspaper *Correio da Manhã*, the radical mystical author of *The Apple in the Dark* stepped aside to make way for a chatty, perky beauty columnist named Helen Palmer, who dispensed advice to her female readers with a wink and a smile. A descendent of Clarice's earlier alter ego, Teresa Quadros of *Comício*, Helen, unlike Teresa, had a secret mission: she was a paid agent of Pond's, purveyor of face creams.

According to the contract, Helen Palmer was not to name Pond's specifically. She would instead use more subtle devices to lure women to the beauty counter at their local pharmacy, a method the Pond's PR team spelled out in prepared pitches. Clarice sometimes used them verbatim. "If your skin is dried out, my friend—a look we all hate because it always adds a few years to our age—find a good special cream and use it daily, around the eyes and wherever wrinkles are appearing, massaging it lightly into your skin. Choose any cream with a base of anhydrous lanolin, for faster and deeper penetration, so it's more efficient than common lanolin. And nothing's better than lanolin for dry skin."[12] As it happened, Pond's included just this kind of "anhydrous lanolin."

But there was more to Helen Palmer than sales pitches. Like everything else in Brazil, Helen was modern, and she exhorted her readers to be modern, too. "You, my reader, don't limit your interests merely to the art of making yourself beautiful, being elegant, attracting masculine eyes. Futility is a weakness that has been overcome by the enlightened woman. And you," Helen nudged, "are an 'enlightened woman,' aren't you?" Clarice described this enlightened woman: "She studies, she reads, she's modern and interesting without ceasing to be a woman, a wife, a mother. She doesn't necessarily have to have a diploma or a title, but she knows something more than her knitting, her casseroles, and her gossip with the neighbors. Above all, she tries to be understanding and humane. She has a heart."[13] Modern was one thing, but Clarice and Helen had no patience for a woman who "smokes like a man, in public, crosses her legs with a shocking casualness, lets loose scandalous guffaws, drinks too much, uses tasteless slang, or demoralizes herself repeating vulgar words."[14] Clarice's new woman was, first and foremost, a lady.

If the descriptions now sound painfully dated, Helen Palmer's values were not foreign to Clarice Lispector, who had spent many years in diplomatic society. She was discreet to the point of being reclusive, and indeed something of a prude; friends recall that she was, for example, slightly ashamed to be separated from her husband. (Divorce would not be legal in Brazil until 1977.) Like Helen Palmer, Clarice was keen not to cause inconvenience. Her sister-in-law Eliane said that Clarice was overly sensitive to the feelings of others: "She felt what they were feeling even before they did."[15] Her friend Olga Borelli wrote that Clarice was "deeply feminine, insisting on good manners from herself as from others."[16] Vain of her feminine beauty, proud of the attraction she exercised over men, she nonetheless chafed at the limits placed on women in an extremely conservative society.

"I felt it too," Tania said, "I was very jealous of the men. You can't imagine what it was like to be a woman back then! We had to be housewives. When Clarice split from Maury and came back to Brazil, she didn't have a group. Her friends, Fernando, Rubem, Otto [Lara Resende], Hélio [Pellegrino], were married and went out drinking together. It was very hard to break through that."[17]

Clarice was not one to hang out in bars, but even if she had displayed an inclination toward the kind of social life her male friends enjoyed, she had very little time to carouse. Besides raising two children by herself, she was writing for *Senhor*, she was writing as Helen Palmer, and starting in April 1960 she was writing six columns a week under the name Ilka Soares. Unlike Helen Palmer and Teresa Quadros, Ilka Soares was a real person, and not just anyone: a gorgeous starlet, she was enough of a Rio it girl to have been selected in 1958 to accompany the gay Rock Hudson to the Carnival Ball in the Municipal Theater.[18]

Clarice's new job came thanks to Alberto Dines, a young Jewish journalist who lived in the same building, and on the same floor, as Tania and William Kaufmann. He approached Clarice with some misgiving, worried that a writer of her refinement would scorn such a mundane ghost-writing job, though he knew, through Otto Lara Resende, that Clarice was looking for work. Dines had recently assumed command of the *Diário da Noite*, the prestigious Rio paper where Clarice had worked before her marriage and which had published *Near to the Wild Heart* and *The Besieged City*. The once grand institution had tumbled from its formerly lofty heights. Dines was relaunching it as a tabloid, inspired by the *Daily Mirror* and *Daily Express*, and to get the renovated paper off the ground he needed star power.

Ilka herself lived one building away from Clarice, in Leme. Their contact was minimal: she met Clarice only once, in her apartment, where Clarice was "very reserved, smoked a lot." In giant Rio de Janeiro, Leme was a fairly intimate community, but even there Clarice was all but invisible. In all the years they lived next door to one another, Ilka never once ran into Clarice on the beach or in the cafés that were so important to the community's life.

Yet Clarice managed to create a new voice for Ilka's column, "Just for Women": confiding, approachable, and all about "you." "What you might not know is that even actresses find inspiration in the women they admire," "Ilka" wrote. "I've never moved away from the person that is you. I try to guess what kind of music you like to listen to, what kinds of feelings you'd like me to express, what kinds of looks you're thinking about for your new dress." To judge by the kinds of things Clarice thought "you" was interested in, "you" had not been rocked by feminism. "So now, talking about my favorite dishes, I'll be trying to guess what you like. Speaking of children, I'll be talking about how we care for our kids. We'll talk about fashion, with the same excitement that girlfriends talk about clothes. What I think you'd like to know about beauty is what you and I will talk about. And so many other things! Since one thing leads to another. Let's meet again soon. Till tomorrow."[19]

And Clarice dished out classy makeup tips: "The women of ancient Egypt were two thousand years ahead of the woman of today, as far as eyes were concerned. They, too, concentrated their seduction in their gaze, using a black substance called *kohl* to lengthen and darken their lashes. Back then they were already using green eye shadow, and we're not making that up, it's been proven. And wigs? Well, they used black wigs, for the 'sensual style of the Nile.'"[20]

The column was a success, Dines remembers, thanks to the dedication Clarice demonstrated in putting it together and in her access, through her international connections, to the foreign fashion magazines that provided photographs and illustrations.

Family Ties cemented her reputation. The publisher, at long last, was Francisco Alves, in São Paulo. When Clarice appeared in that city, reporters were keen to meet her. "Since her debut, a mystery has surrounded the admirable writer," wrote the *Diário de S. Paulo*, referring to her "hiding behind a pseudonym" and "spending most of her time abroad."[21] A week later, an impressive 150 people, including Alzira Vargas do Amaral Peixoto, attended a similar event in Rio. In photographs Clarice looks delighted, relieved that the book finally was there, gratified by the public's attention.

Perhaps the inquiring readers had gathered to see if Clarice actually existed. "There is a great curiosity surrounding the person of Clarice," one publication claimed at the time. "She seldom appears in literary circles, flees television programs and autograph sessions, and only a few rare people have been lucky enough to talk to her. 'Clarice Lispector doesn't exist,' some say. 'It's the pseudonym of someone who lives in Europe.' 'She's a beautiful woman,' claim others. 'I don't know her,' says a third. 'But I think she's a man. I've heard he's a diplomat.' "[22]

The presence of the author at least quieted the rumor that she was a man, though Clarice hardly rushed to fill in many details. "Maybe her closest friends and the friends of these friends know something about her life," wrote one frustrated interviewer. "Where she came from, where she was born, how old she is, how she lives. But she never talks about that, 'since it's very personal.' "[23]

What had changed, to generate this kind of interest? The question perplexed Clarice. One critic suggested "Clarice Lispector was fated to disappear momentarily, not only because she had left the country, but principally because her books had not had any great impact." Perhaps it was the taste for the "modern" that smoothed the path for her work, he speculated: "Because our artistic climate has changed so radically in the last four years, we are entirely ready to welcome her and acknowledge her as one of the best Brazilian writers of all time."[24]

A more obvious reason for its success is that *Family Ties* is simply easier to read than either *The Chandelier* or *The Besieged City*. Simeão Leal and Ênio Silveira, who had put off Clarice for so many years, could not have been delighted by a headline in the *Jornal do Comércio*: "Clarice Sells." "Her publishers describe sales of the story collection *Family Ties*, with which Clarice Lispector returned to the bookstores, as *spectacular*. CL, considered a writer for a small audience, is making her debut among the best-sellers."[25] *Family Ties* became the first of Clarice's books to earn a second edition, after the original two thousand copies sold out.

The stage was set, finally, for the appearance of *The Apple in the Dark*. Francisco Alves published it in July 1961, a year after *Family Ties*. The book, which had been plagued with problems from the beginning, was so full of errors that Clarice couldn't even look at it,[26] and she was embarrassed by its exorbitant price, 980 cruzeiros. (At the time, it was in fact the most expensive novel ever published in Brazil.)[27] In a copy she sent to Erico and Mafalda Verissimo, she stressed that she was dispatching an extremely valuable gift. "Luis Fernando," she added in a postscript to their son, "consider this book yours as well. Divide 980 by three and you will have your own precious part."[28]

Still, the book had been ready for five years, and, in Clarice's own words, "a bad marriage is better than no marriage." Twelve years had elapsed since her previous novel, *The Besieged City*, was published in 1949. Together with *Family Ties* and her appearances in *Senhor*, *The Apple in the Dark* marked the definitive return of a woman who not too long before had been painfully forgotten. Never again would it be thought that she was a man or that she was "hiding behind a pseudonym."

It was in the early 1960s that an obscure writer with a difficult reputation became a Brazilian institution, "Clarice," instantly recognizable from her first name alone. By 1963, a journalist could write, "Clarice Lispector has ceased to be a name and become a phenomenon in our literature. A phenomenon with all the characteristics of an emotional state: Clarice's admirers enter into [a] trance at the mere mention of her name.... And the great author of *Near to the Wild Heart* has been transformed into a sacred monster."[29]

After toiling for so long in obscurity, Clarice appreciated the praise for her work. But she hated being thought of as a "sacred monster." "I happen to write," she told a Jewish journalist, Rosa Cass, who later became a close friend. "And so it comes through literature. But if I were beautiful, or had money, for example, I wouldn't like for people to seek me out for that either. It's good to be accepted as a whole, starting even with one's defects, with little things, and reaching the bigger things later."[30]

It was not just social climbers who sought her out. She began receiving letters from people all over Brazil who opened their hearts to her, such as a paralyzed journalist in Minas Gerais whose career had been ended by an accident, and a teenage girl who sent her a humble poem and then asked, "Did I manage to say what I am?"[31] These letters are very moving to read, and the love they express for her must have been a comfort in difficult times.

On the whole, however, and though Brazilian literary celebrity was a modest outpost of fame, her humble eminence bothered her. "So many desire projection," she wrote. "Without knowing how this limits one's life. My little projection wounds my modesty. Even the things I'd like to say I cannot say anymore. Anonymity is as soft as a dream."[32] Anonymity had its price as well, of course, as she had learned during the five years during which her work was ignored, unpublishable. But professional success was not the same as celebrity, and she insisted that "I am not public domain. And I don't want to be looked at."[33]

Being looked at, she would soon learn, was not the only indignity that fame brought. When *The Apple in the Dark* won the Carmen Dolores Barbosa Prize for the best book published the preceding year, Clarice traveled to São Paulo to accept the award. She attended the ceremony on September 19, 1962, with her friend Maria Bonomi, the young artist who had worn Clarice's clothes to the White House. The ceremony was presided over by no one less than Jânio Quadros, former president of Brazil. Only a few months after his landslide election in January 1961 he quit abruptly, alleging, in a self-pitying letter to Congress, that "terrible forces" had compelled him to resign.

Even before this dramatic turn of events, Quadros was known to be an odd character. The handwritten decrees he fired off did little to change his eccentric reputation; he garnered special renown for outlawing the bikini on the Rio beaches.[34] He himself was hardly ready for Copacabana. His folksy image included a droopy moustache and even, the story goes, fake dandruff spread on the shoulders of his jackets. As if that were not enough, he was also missing an eye.

After proffering an endless speech at Mrs. Barbosa's gracious home, His Excellency invited Clarice into a private chamber, where he proceeded to grope her so passionately that in the course of fighting him off her dress was ripped. Clarice ran breathlessly out of the room and told Maria Bonomi that they had to leave immediately, throwing Maria's shawl over her shoulders to cover the slashed dress.

On the way back to Maria's house, a final indignity awaited the rattled laureate. Inside the prize envelope, the cash award: a grand total of twenty cruzeiros—for a book that cost 980.[35]

Jânio Quadros was not the only man interested in Clarice Lispector. "We all wanted to screw her!" exclaimed the irrepressible Nahum Sirotzky, her publisher at *Senhor*. "She was very, very sexy. But she was also inaccessible."[36] Putting it more delicately, Paulo Francis, *Senhor*'s fiction editor, recalled that there were many candidates for her hand. "But the price she would have had to pay for company, in terms of sensibility, would have been as high as the inevitable children."[37]

There was another problem. Three years after splitting with Maury and returning to Brazil, Clarice had still not entirely moved on, and Maury was, as ever, in love with her. Friends say the attraction was not one-sided. If Clarice didn't want to be married to him, neither was she entirely ready to give him up. Always very correct, she felt awkward about being separated from her husband of sixteen years, the father of her children.

After a decade steadily rising through the ranks in Washington, Maury had been promoted to ambassador. This long-awaited reward must have seemed a bit less electrifying when he received word of his new posting: dismal Communist Warsaw, whither he departed in March 1962. Alone in his new embassy, he longed for Clarice and his boys, and in mid-July, accepting his invitation, Clarice, Pedro, and Paulo departed for Poland.

It was the closest Clarice would ever come to her birthplace. The infant refugee from Chechelnik was now the tall, blonde ambassadress of Brazil, the only time in her life when she would bear that title. During this trip, a Soviet representative offered her a trip to her birthplace, which she refused, saying that she had never set foot there—she was an infant, carried by her parents—and never intended to.

Despite this categorical answer, she pondered the offer. "I remember one evening, in Poland, at the home of one of the secretaries of the embassy, I went out onto the terrace alone: a great black forest movingly pointed me the way to the Ukraine. I felt the call. Russia had me too. But I belong to Brazil."[38]

27

BETTER THAN BORGES

The reconciliation Maury hoped for did not take place. Friends warned Clarice against leading him on. When she returned to Rio de Janeiro, the diplomat Lauro Escorel, whom she had known since the days of *Near to the Wild Heart*, told her firmly that she either had to go back to him or let him go. If she was determined to break up with him, he said, she could not keep going on holidays with him and giving him false hopes. It was no good for him and it was no good for the children.[1]

Happily for him, Maury eventually put an end to her hesitation by meeting another woman on a visit to Rio. The new Mrs. Gurgel Valente was Isabel Leitão da Cunha, whose aristocratic background was as different from Clarice's as could be imagined. Her mother, Nininha, was a prominent socialite, and her father was none other than Vasco Leitão da Cunha, consul in Rome during Clarice's time in Naples. One of the outstanding Brazilian diplomats of his generation, by 1964 he had achieved Itamaraty's highest office, becoming minister of foreign affairs.

Maury had been aware of Isabel since she was a girl. Once, visiting her father at the consulate in Geneva, he had seen a picture of her on his desk, and he always spoke of how beautiful she was. Isabel was indeed beautiful, and having grown up in the foreign service she was far more suited to the diplomatic life than was Clarice. She was also twelve years younger than the first Mrs. Gurgel Valente, and this, by all accounts, Clarice found outrageous. After Isabel and Maury married in Montevideo—with divorce illegal in Brazil, Uruguay was Brazil's Las Vegas—Clarice majestically announced that their friends were not to "receive" the couple. Rubem Braga laughed: "You're just upset that she's so good looking—and so much younger.[2]

"That woman made my life hell" during the first years of her marriage, Isabel said, her impressions perhaps colored by the rivalry that will naturally subsist between a second wife and a first, particularly when the first was as famous and admired as Clarice. Whenever the boys were with their father, Clarice would badger Isabel constantly. "This is the mother of the Ambassador's children," she would grandly growl when Isabel picked up the phone. In classic Jewish mother style, she insisted on being informed of everything the boys ate when they were under Isabel's supervision, and she constantly pestered Maury to send more money.[3]

Once, when they were living in Warsaw, Maury and Isabel, who had not been to Brazil in a while, decided to come to Rio. Clarice was furious. She marched over to Itamaraty Palace and demanded an immediate audience with the minister. Diplomats required permission from the ministry to leave their posts, and the upshot of Clarice's visit to Dr. Vasco was that the permission was denied. "I was a married woman—my own father!" Isabel gasped, still annoyed forty years later.[4]

Maury's remarriage remained a delicate subject. When Clarice was writing a newspaper column in 1968 she replied to a reader's letter publicly. "F. N. M., you crafty fox... You muster this fake pity and tell me that you learned that my depression was a result of my ex-husband's marriage. Keep, dear lady, your pity for yourself, it is no use to me. And if you want to know the truth, which you certainly don't, here it is: when I separated from my husband, he waited for more than seven years for me to return."[5]

The reaction touched off by Maury's remarriage may have been extreme, but many friends report that in the early 1960s something in Clarice changed. All descriptions of her as a young woman record her almost excessive politeness. To those who knew her in the foreign service, this went far beyond the normal good manners required of diplomatic spouses: it was a profound empathy that drew all sorts of people to her, that made women confide in her and men fall in love with her.

"When she was in law school," Sara Escorel remembered, "she said: I am going be the best diplomatic wife ever. And she was. When she was married to Maury she was perfect." This perfection was not, of course, without its price. "I wasn't very comfortable in that setting.... All that formality... But I did my job.... I was more conciliatory than I am now," she said, looking back.[6]

The tension between the rebellious Joana and the placid Lídia, between the animal world and the artifice of human "civilization," was a favorite symbol, and in her letters Clarice mentioned her fear of losing her "intimate balance." In his perceptive letter, Maury expressed his fear that she was "following, in a certain sense, in real life, Joana's destiny." Already in Bern, her first analyst, Ulysses Girsoler, had warned of this unbearable tension in her personality: "It will be very difficult for such a character to find balance, [requiring] a conscious domestication of these elementary impulses by intellectual participation."

Clarice became demanding and, as her interactions with Maury and Isabel showed, even rude. Her friends noticed two major changes. First, she began calling people at all hours of the night, unable to sleep, tormented by unceasing anxiety. Second, her makeup became "scandalous"; the word is often repeated. Shortly before her divorce, she wrote Mafalda that her lipstick looked like she had "just finished eating a pork chop without a napkin."[7]

Many were surprised, considering how elegant Clarice had always been. She was disregarding Helen Palmer's own advice: "You naturally know that drawing attention to oneself is not done and always gives a bad impression of a woman. Whether with scandalous clothing, exotic hairstyles, ways of walking, manners, rude laughter, any way of calling attention to oneself deserves, in short, nothing more than a prize for vulgarity."[8]

Some attributed the change to her new psychoanalyst, Inês Besouchet. Though Clarice had been in psychiatric treatment on and off since before her marriage, and though his initial refusal to enter analysis was something she held against Maury, she was ashamed to be in therapy. In Brazil as elsewhere, there was in those years a stigma attached to psychotherapy; perhaps she feared a reputation for being crazy. But in Rio she found an analyst she could trust.

Like Clarice, Besouchet was Jewish. She had trained Clarice's friend Hélio Pellegrino, one of Fernando Sabino's Minas Gerais group. She was a leftist who had been exiled to Bolivia during one of Getúlio Vargas's governments. Wise and circumspect, keeping the distance from her patients that analysts are advised to maintain, Inês nonetheless became a close friend and was, with Tania, one of only two people to whom Clarice dedicated a book, *The Foreign Legion* (1964).[9]

Inês exhorted Clarice to free herself from the burden of always trying to meet other people's expectations. Perhaps if she lived in a less regimented environment, the reaction would not have been as violent. "Clarice's sincerity was so bruising that people sometimes confused it with eccentricity," said her friend Olga Borelli, who met her at the end of the decade. "She always—but always—did what she wanted, and when she wanted. Without asking anyone for permission. It was a strong feature of her character."[10]

"Clarice was an insoluble woman. She knew that," Paulo Francis wrote.[11] Yet, insoluble or not, Clarice *had*, her discomfort and depression notwithstanding, managed it for many years. Why was she so much less "conciliatory" now? The fact was that Clarice faced challenges that even the most stable personality would have found difficult to overcome.

She was glad to be back in Brazil. Professional success, after so many years of struggle, was gratifying. But her life was a struggle. She needed to earn a living, which *Senhor* and her journalism provided. But this work interfered with her "real" writing. She had not worked on a full-length book since 1956, when *The Apple in the Dark* was completed in Washington. Looking back on this period, she told an interviewer, "Sometimes my production is intense, and certain periods—hiatuses—when life becomes intolerable.... It's very difficult, this period between one work and the next, yet you have to empty out your head so that something else can be born—*if* it's born."[12]

But her greatest pain was the increasing illness of her son Pedro. The brilliant boy had become a troubled teenager. "When he entered adolescence he started closing down," Tania said. "Clarice did everything possible: she put him in analysis, in a bunch of treatments. Nothing helped."[13] As early as 1957, in Washington, Clarice had sought help, but eventually the eccentricities of an extraordinarily talented child hardened into full-blown schizophrenia.

Pedro lived in terrible anguish. Rosa Cass saw that the situation hurt his mother "*brutally*. She was afflicted, desperate." He was utterly unpredictable. At home, he would shout hysterically, so loud that the neighbors complained. They couldn't take him anywhere, not even to the movies, because he couldn't sit still. Another friend remembers a dinner during which Pedro constantly circled the table, his hands covering his face.

Treatment failed. The only thing that helped, according to Isabel Gurgel Valente, Maury's second wife, who took charge of him in the 1970s, was heavy medication. When his demons got to be overwhelming, he would start screaming "A shot! A shot!" While Pedro sat beside her, shrieking the entire way, Isabel would drive him to the hospital for his injection.

Having split with Maury, Clarice was deprived of a source of support, and as Pedro grew sicker her sense of loneliness became unrelenting. Always discreet, she shared the situation with few people; those friends who were aware of it discuss only their own impressions, rarely quoting her words. At the dinner party when Pedro circled the table, for example, Clarice pretended that she didn't notice him and continued on diplomatically with the conversation. But she did notice, and the guests knew she did, because though they sat there for hours, Clarice forgot to serve the food.

"When you have a child like that, you always think it's somehow your fault," Rosa said. "She just could not stand to see him like that. It hurt her too much." First she had failed to save her mother. Now she had to look on helplessly as her son went mad. It was another blow for a woman who had so much wanted to be a mother, perhaps partly in compensation for the tragedy of her own family. She was tremendously sensitive to any allusion to this failure. Her friend Otto Lara Resende recalled meeting her on the street in Leme, where he was walking with his young son André. "Who is that blonde lady?" André asked after they parted ways. "Something inside her is always throbbing. Does she have kids? I wouldn't want to be her child." A couple of years later, mentioning this to Clarice, but without the last sentence, Otto received a tough rebuke, delivered in an "overwhelming crescendo." "Tell your son that I can be a mother, yes. I can be his mother. I can be your mother, Otto. I can be the mother of humanity. I am the mother of humanity."[14]

She retreated even further into herself. "She had the face of someone who with the greatest dignity was always suffering.... She didn't invite effusive, affectionate, affective familiarity," said one of her editors at *Senhor*, recalling the magazine's great phase, when "every month, in our offices, two uncomfortable figures appeared, to hand over the best texts Brazilian literature produced at the time: Guimarães Rosa, with all his pretensions, and Clarice Lispector, with her anguishing silence."[15]

In about 1962 Clarice began her last love affair, with the poet and journalist Paulo Mendes Campos, known as Paulinho. She had known him since the time of *Near to the Wild Heart*, when she met Fernando Sabino and his friends from Minas Gerais. He was a kind of heterosexual version of Lúcio Cardoso. Both were from Minas and both were chronic miscreants, running away and getting expelled from various schools. Paulinho started courses in dentistry, veterinary science, and law; he entered, and then left, the Air Force Academy in Porto Alegre.[16]

Like Lúcio, he was Catholic; like Lúcio, he was good-looking and possessed an extraordinary and seductive talent for language. He was an outstanding poet, broadly and deeply read, eventually becoming director of rare books at the National Library. With Rubem Braga, he was one of Brazil's most famous practitioners of the brand of literary journalism known as the *crônica*.

Like Lúcio, he was bad with money; and like Lúcio, he was a bohemian and an alcoholic. "Drink consoles; man drinks; therefore, man must be consoled," he wrote, in one of his many discourses on the topic.[17] As he got older he became a bad drunk, aggressive and violent; his friends tended to avoid him. And if Lúcio's sexual orientation made him inaccessible to Clarice, Paulinho had a wife, an Englishwoman named Joan Abercrombie.

For a short time, Clarice and Paulinho lived a great passion, as everyone who knew them confirms. They were an odd match, Clarice tall, blonde, and bewitching, and Paulinho, no longer the Byron of his youth, short, dark, and, despite his charm, physically unattractive. A friend recalls seeing them enter a downtown restaurant and saying to her companion, "What is *Paulinho* doing with that *Valkyrie*?"[18] But as another friend, Ivan Lessa, says, "In terms of neurosis, they were born for one another."[19]

Glimpses of them together, however, were rare, even though, as Lessa says, Rio was "a village, in the best possible sense." This was especially true in literary circles, which Clarice avoided but in which Paulinho was a central figure. The affair surprised many of their common friends, though Clarice tried to be discreet about it. Lessa, who lived down the street from Clarice, often saw them walking furtively through the back streets of Leme. They also met in a *garconnière* Clarice and Paulinho shared with his friend, Sérgio Porto. To the doorman, Clarice announced herself as "Madame."

Yet if Clarice seemed to take almost nineteenth-century measures to conduct the affair discreetly, she was shockingly reckless with the one person who might be expected to object the most: Paulinho's wife, Joan Mendes Campos. Clarice's chronic insomnia and desperate loneliness led her to call Paulo at the oddest hours; in the middle of the night, knowing full well that his wife was in bed beside him, she poured out her heart, endlessly, to her lover.[20] This does not seem to be the act of indiscretion, or of a woman flaunting her affair to her rival. It suggests instead a terrible isolation, a need for emotional support that went far beyond sex; indeed Paulinho was far from the only person who received such calls in the middle of the night.

Joan tolerated the situation for a time. Eventually, however, enough was enough, and she threatened to take their children and return to England. Choosing his wife and family, Paulinho broke off the affair with Clarice. With it went their friendship. Clarice repeatedly asked the novelist Autran Dourado to try to patch things up, but he understood it was over and preferred not to get involved. The end of the relationship isolated Clarice still further from the literary milieu, from the adult world to which she had such fragile ties.

"She loved him until the day she died," her friend Rosa Cass remembered. And she seems to have taken a kind of revenge on the other woman when, more than a decade later, she wrote a short story about an Englishwoman, "Miss Algrave." In London, Miss Algrave knows she can seduce her boss. "She was sure he would accept. He was married to a pale and insignificant woman, Joan." On a more lyrical note, Clarice may have been thinking of Paulinho when she wrote, "Sometimes all the purity of body and soul is in illicit love, not blessed by a priest, but blessed by the love itself."[21]

Toward the middle of 1962, Clarice met the American poet Elizabeth Bishop. Bishop had been living in Brazil since 1951, when, on a cruise around South America, she disembarked at Santos for a two-week visit. She ended up staying for fifteen years. The reason was her relationship with the heiress Lota de Macedo Soares, with whom she lived in considerable splendor in their modernist mansion, Samambaia, in the mountains north of Rio. Lota was brilliant, one of the most important landscape architects in Brazilian history, having renovated a large section of Rio de Janeiro, but she was also tempestuous and depressive; she eventually committed suicide in Bishop's apartment in New York.

By the early 1960s, the relationship had taken a turn for the worse. Bishop was drinking heavily, and as her despair increased so did her view of Lota's country. Once a tropical paradise of waterfalls and Baroque churches, it was now a cesspool of ignorance and provincialism. Dismissive comments about Brazil and Brazilians began to fill her letters. She did, however, reserve one grudging exception:

> I have found one contemporary I like, however—living right down the street from us in Rio—I put off reading her because I thought I wouldn't like her, and now I find I not only like her stories very much but like her, too. She has a wonderful name—Clarice Lispector (Russian). Her 2 or 3 novels I don't think are so good but her short stories are almost like the stories I've always thought should be written about Brazil—Tchekovian, slightly sinister and fantastic—I am sending some to ENCOUNTER soon—She has a N.Y. publisher who wants them and maybe I'll do the whole book for her—I swore I'd never do any more translating—but I don't mind very short things and feel I should, really—She is rather large-boned fair and completely Oriental Russian-looking—"Khergis," I think is the race, something like that—like the girl in "The Magic Mountain," I imagine—

> but otherwise very Brazilian, and very shy. I know or care for so few of the "intellectuals" here that it is nice to find someone new—and Lota likes her, too, as much as I do, and even went to the length of reading a couple of the stories & agreeing with me they are good. (Lota won't read anything in Portuguese except the papers, and government reports now) Actually I think she is better than J. L. Borges—who is good, but not all that good![22]

Bishop was working on translations of Clarice's stories, but by the end of the year this romance, too, had soured. Her hopes for a productive literary collaboration were dashed when Clarice inexplicably vanished. In January 1963, she wrote to Robert Lowell:

> I have translated five of Clarice's stories—all the very short ones & one longer one. The New Yorker is interested—I think she needs money, so that would be good, the $ being what it is (almost twice as much already as when you were here)—then if they don't know them, Encounter, PR, etc. Alfred Knopf is also interested in seeing the whole book. But at the moment—just when I was ready to send off the batch, except for one, she has vanished on me—completely—and for about six weeks! Lota met her—she isn't cross or anything—and she seemed *delighted* with the translations, letters of interest, etc. I am mystified; L is fed up.... It is "temperament," maybe, or more likely just the usual "massive inertia" that one runs [into] at every turn—and that is driving Lota mad on her job. It makes one despair, really. Her novels are NOT good; the "essays" she does for *Senhor* are very bad—but in the stories she has awfully good things and they do sound pretty good in English and I was quite pleased with them. Oh dear.

Despite her annoyance, Bishop was not entirely ready—not yet, at least—to write off Clarice as yet another indolent Brazilian. "Clarice suffers from the same kind of dated-ness, provincialism, etc.—but she *really* has talent—and I have hopes,—(or had, until she disappeared)."[23]

Clarice's disappearance may have had something to do with yet another personal crisis. On December 7, 1962, a lifetime of heavy drinking and drug abuse finally caught up with her friend, mentor, and first love, Lúcio Cardoso.

Earlier that year, in May, he had had a warning. Arriving at his home in Ipanema, his sister Maria Helena "saw the muscles in his face ceaselessly trembling, while he, in the greatest affliction, tried to calm them with his hand." The crisis passed, but the doctor was clear. "Look, Lúcio, what you had was just a spasm, leaving your mouth a bit crooked and that drawling way of speaking. Thank God, because it could have been much worse. With time, if you keep doing your exercises in front of the mirror, everything will return to normal. But from now on don't overdo it, don't drink, don't wear yourself out partying, try to lead a calmer life, since if you go on like before something worse can happen." Despite his sister's desperate attempts to help him, he refused to heed the doctor's warning. "I'm not a child for you to be taking care of me," he told Maria Helena. "Don't touch those bottles! If I want to drink, neither you nor anybody else is going to stop me."[24]

Lúcio had never enjoyed the fame to which his volcanic creativity seemed to entitle him. His theatrical ventures had come to nothing, and his writing was met with incomprehension. In 1959, he published his masterpiece, *Chronicle of the Murdered House*, a long Faulknerian novel of his native Minas Gerais, an attack on "Minas, in its flesh and spirit,"[25] a meditation on good and evil and God complete with incest, homosexuality, and bestiality.

The novel predictably scandalized the more predictably scandalizable critics. His champion Octávio de Faria answered them, in words that hint at Lúcio's affinity with Clarice Lispector. "Are we going to abandon our attempts to reconstruct the world, this tremendous responsibility, on which our salvation may depend, in order to obey a half-dozen prejudices?"[26]

Even this notoriety did not bring him the wider audience he longed for. He struggled, increasingly worn down by alcohol, until December 7, 1962.

> I'll never forget that date: December 7, 1962 [his sister wrote]. It was a calm day, completely normal, until the afternoon. Between six-thirty and seven the phone rang.
>
> "Lelena, I'm at Lazzarini's house, helping out with a dinner for his friends."
>
> I recognized the voice of Nonô, whom I hadn't seen in more than two days. He sometimes vanished like that for a week, which worried me after his spasm.
>
> "Be careful, don't drink, don't take any pills."
>
> "Relax, I'm being a saint."[27]

Later that night, not having heard from him, she went to his apartment, directly behind hers. She found the door unlocked, which she thought was strange. She went in and discovered her brother gravely ill. Terrified, she called an ambulance; that night he fell into a coma. He emerged from the coma, but a massive stroke had paralyzed him forever. He would never again be able to speak normally, and his writing career was over.

Maria Helena cared for him for years, always hoping that their attempts at rehabilitation would pay off and allow him to resume his career. It was a painful struggle, days of hope punctuated by weeks and months of despair. In a moment of frustration, trying to get him to do his exercises, Maria Helena told him:

> "You're very stubborn, that's why so much has happened to you. Remember when you had your first sickness, just a spasm? I begged you, but you kept on drinking and popping pills. Did it work, your stubbornness?"
>
> He got even more irritated and to my surprise said:
>
> "It did. I died."[28]

"Clarice was finally heard from yesterday," Elizabeth Bishop wrote Robert Lowell around six weeks after Lúcio's stroke, "—apologies and tears, even, I think!—I couldn't even sound annoyed, of course—she has been sick, I think—and is having some sort of minor operation the end of this month—well—I think we'll be able to get off the batch of stories next week—Knopf is coming back in Feb. and it would be a good chance for her, too—I suppose the combination of Russian massive inertia and Brazilian does pile up. I do like her, too.—But I have been minding my loneliness here more lately, I'm afraid—HOWEVER—dear Clarice might have telephoned, in seven weeks—or had her maid telephone!"[29]

Bishop's attempts, however grudging, to promote Clarice in English would eventually pay off. In 1964, the *Kenyon Review* published "Three Stories by Clarice Lispector" in Bishop's translation.[30] And her efforts to interest Alfred Knopf resulted, in 1967, in the first book-length English translation of one of Clarice's works, *The Apple in the Dark*. Knopf reputedly said that he didn't understand a word of it. The translator was not Bishop, who found translating a work of that length "too boring & time-wasting,"[31] but Gregory Rabassa, the dean of translators of Latin American fiction.

He met Clarice a few months after Lúcio's stroke, when she was invited to the United States. "Clarice has been asked to another literary congress, at the University of Texas," Bishop wrote Lowell at the beginning of July, "and is being very coy & complicated—but I think is secretly very proud—and is going, of course. I'll help her with her speech. I suppose we are getting to be 'friends.'"[32] On August 26, the day Clarice left, Bishop, with her usual grudging, told Lowell that "she is off this morning to Texas for a Literary Conference—came & read me her lecture Saturday. But she's hopeless, really."

It was Clarice's first visit to the United States since she had left Washington in 1959, and it would be her last. During her few days in Austin, she made an amazing impression. Gregory Rabassa said that he was "astonished to meet that rare person who looked like Marlene Dietrich and wrote like Virginia Woolf."[33] A newspaper reporter wrote, "Mrs. Lispector is a stunning blonde with the charisma of a movie star, who lights up any room she enters."[34]

She was hardly treated like a movie star by the Brazilian consul, who "thought he had to invite [her] to dinner": "He took me, this representative of our country, to a third-rate restaurant, one of those with red-and-black-checked tablecloths. In the United States meat is expensive, fish is cheap. Before I could decide what I wanted, he said to the waiter: 'Fish for the lady.' I was surprised: it wasn't a fish restaurant. And he added, I swear: 'And for me a thick steak, very rare.' As he cut his steak, which I envied, he told me all about his misfortunes since his divorce. The fish, of course, was terrible. To help him economize and to get rid of him, I didn't order dessert."[35]

Though she began her talk by claiming that she was not a critic, and therefore not qualified to comment alongside the professors, Rabassa noted that "Clarice the novelist gave a much more cogent talk on literature than any of the many professional scholars and critics who shared the podium."[36] The speech reads like a mature version of the analytic journalistic voice from the beginning of her career.

The subject is avant-garde literature. In it, she addresses the issue of Brazil's insularity, the national self-obsession that characterized its literature. "We are hungry to know about ourselves, and urgently, because we still need ourselves more than we need others." All real art, she says, is avant-garde, since "all real life is experimentation," and any work that is not is simple imitation: "And there are some young writers who are a bit overintellectualized. It seems to me that they are not inspired by, shall we say, 'the thing itself,' but by other literature, 'the thing already literalized.' "[37]

She added a despairing appendix: "As for my own writing, I tell you—if anybody cares—that I am disillusioned. It's that writing didn't bring me what I wanted, which was peace. My literature is in no sense a catharsis that would do me good and is useless as a form of liberation. From here on out I may not write again, and only deepen the life within me. Or that deepening might lead me to write again. I can't say."[38]

28

THE COCKROACH

Back home in Brazil, Clarice's largely forgotten earlier work was getting a new lease on life. In 1963, Francisco Alves released an inexpensive paperback version of her once famous debut. "Published around twenty years ago, in a small printing, this *Near to the Wild Heart*, which many claim is Clarice Lispector's masterpiece, is completely unknown to today's readers," the introduction claimed.[1] In the same year, another publisher, José Álvaro, revived *The Chandelier. The Besieged City* followed in 1964.

This attention to her past production was flattering, but it was also a reminder of her difficulty looking toward the future. It had been so long since she had worked on a novel, seven years since she finished *The Apple in the Dark*. As her speech in Texas shows, she was profoundly anxious about being able to write. During such a "hiatus," she later said, "life becomes intolerable."[2]

No sooner did she give voice to this fear, however, than she produced, in a quick outburst at the end of 1963, one of the great novels of the twentieth century. "It's strange," she remembered of this time, "because I was in the worst of situations, sentimentally as well as in my family, everything complicated, and I wrote *The Passion*, which has nothing to do with that."[3]

In its ambition and eccentricity, in its sweeping redefinition of what a novel can be, *The Passion According to G. H.* recalls peculiar masterpieces such as *Moby-Dick* and *Tristram Shandy*. Yet it is not, at least not in the first place, literature. That, Clarice said in Texas, "is what other people call what we writers do."[4] She later wrote that "I am well aware of what the so-called true novel is. Yet when I read it, with its webs of facts and descriptions, I am simply bored. And when I write it is not the classical novel. But it *is* a novel."[5]

G. H., with its quick, sketchy plot, is instead the climax of a long personal quest. For the first time, Clarice writes in the first person. And for the first time she captures the full violence, the physical disgust, of her encounter with God.

Warning "possible readers" of the novel's shocking contents, Clarice opens with a brief and cryptic caveat in the preface. The book should be read only by "people who know that the approach, to anything at all, comes about gradually and agonizingly—and includes crossing through the opposite of the thing being approached." The reader who proceeds beyond this solemn admonition will see that Clarice is "gradually and agonizingly" approaching God. She, too, has passed through "the opposite of the thing being approached": one has only to recall her statement, made at age twenty-one, that "beyond mankind there is nothing else at all."

She does not disavow that apparently clear declaration of atheism, not even when she at last discovers God. Instead, and even more fundamentally than in *The Apple in the Dark*, she redefines its terms: "beyond mankind" and "nothing else at all." The result, which might be called mystical Spinozism or religious atheism, is her richest paradox yet.

The first section of *The Apple in the Dark* is called "How a Man Is Made." *The Passion According to G. H.* tells how a woman is unmade. G. H.'s crime, however, is far more repulsive and inhumane than Martin's supposed murder of his wife. Through it, she will not, like Martin, invent God. She will find God.

As she begins her monologue, G. H., a comfortable inhabitant of a Rio penthouse, tries to describe the life that had so unexpectedly ended the day before. The day started conventionally enough. Her maid having quit, G. H. resolved to tidy up the woman's room.

"Before I entered the room, what was I?" G. H. asks. "I was what others had always seen me be, and that was the way I knew myself." She had the occasional hint of something beyond that secondhand image: "Sometimes, looking at a snapshot taken on the beach or at a party, I noted with a light ironic apprehension something the smiling and darkened face revealed to me: a silence. A silence and a destiny that escaped me, I, hieroglyphic fragment of an empire dead or alive. When I looked at the portrait I saw the mystery. No. I am going to lose the rest of my fear of bad taste, I am going to begin my exercise in courage, being alive is not courage, knowing that one is alive is the courage—and I am going to say that in my photograph I saw The Mystery."[6]

These intuitions pass. G. H. is a presentable surface, not herself but a quote of herself, Clarice writes. "The rest was the way I had gradually become the person who has my name. And I ended up being my name. All you have to do is look on the leather of my luggage and see the initials G. H.—and there I am.... Around me I exude the tranquility that comes from reaching the point of being G. H. even on one's suitcases." In a short sentence that captures all the disjointed perfection of her style, Clarice emphasizes that G. H., even on her suitcases, no longer exists. "I finally got up from the breakfast table, that woman."[7]

In the maid's room, that woman expects chaos. Instead, to her shock, she finds a desert, "an entirely clean and vibrating room as in an insane asylum from which dangerous objects have been removed." "The room was the opposite of what I had created in my house, the opposite of the soft beauty that came from my talent for arrangement, my talent for living, the opposite of my serene irony, of my sweet and exempt irony: it was a violation of my quotation marks, of the quotation marks that made me a citation of myself. The room was the portrait of an empty stomach."[8]

Only one thing disturbs its perfect order: black carbon scratches on the dry white wall, outlines of a man, a woman, and a dog. Pondering the inscrutable drawing, she realizes that the black maid, whose name she has forgotten and whose face she has trouble calling to mind, had hated her.

The drawing, and the realization, unsettles her further, and she, in turn, conceives a hatred for that room. She resolves to make the desert flower: "And I would pour water and water that would run in rivers down the scraping on the wall." Overwhelmed by anger, she declares, "I wanted to kill something in there."[9]

Opening the door to the wardrobe—"and the darkness inside escaped like a puff"[10]—she sees a cockroach. Terrified, she slams the door, crushing the roach in its middle. A whitish substance begins to ooze from its body.

In *Near to the Wild Heart*, the cockroach represents Joana's amorality. In *The Besieged City*, Lucrécia identifies herself with the creature:

> "Daddy's complaining about the house," he said throwing with attention the stone far off. "It's full of flies... Last night I felt mosquitoes, moths, flying roaches, you don't even know what all's landing on top of you."
>
> "It's me," Lucrécia Neves said with great irony.[11]

Even in her journalism, Clarice displayed an unusual interest in the roach question. As Teresa Quadros, in 1952, she offered a gruesome recipe for annihilating them: "How can you kill roaches? Every night, in those disgusting little creatures' favorite haunts, leave the following recipe: sugar, flour, and plaster, mixed in equal parts. This delicacy will attract roaches, who eat it, radiant. After a while, the plaster will insidiously harden inside of them, causing certain death. The next morning, you will find dozens of little hard roaches, transformed into statues."[12] She used the same instructions as Ilka Soares in 1960. By 1962, writing in *Senhor*, she had fictionalized the recipe as "The Fifth Story," which she then republished in 1964 in her collection *The Foreign Legion*. "I complained about roaches," each of the story's five parts begins.

Roaches drove Clarice to murderous fantasies. In *G. H.* she explains:

> What I had always found repulsive in roaches is that they were obsolete yet still present. Knowing that they were already on the Earth, and the same as they are today, even before the first dinosaurs appeared, knowing that the first man already found them proliferated and crawling alive, knowing that they had witnessed the formation of the great deposits of oil and coal in the world, and there they were during the great advance and then during the great retreat of the glaciers—the peaceful resistance. I knew that roaches could resist for more than a month without food or water. And that they could even make a useable nutritive substance from wood. And that, even after being crushed, they slowly decompressed and kept on walking. Even when frozen, they kept on marching once thawed.[13]

In "The Disasters of Sofia," the child is shocked by the teacher's eyes. "With their numberless cilia, [they] looked like two sweet cockroaches." The teacher is shocked by Sofia's story of "the treasure hidden where it is least expected."[14] G. H. is about to discover the same.

As the door to the wardrobe crushes the roach, G. H. reaches an unprecedented crisis. She cannot resist or escape: "I was in the desert as I had never been before. It was a desert calling me as a monotonous and remote canticle calls. I was being seduced. And I was going toward that promising madness."[15]

The crux of G. H.'s crisis is the knowledge that the pus leaching through the roach's wound is the same matter as that at her own center. It is hard to imagine a substance further removed from "what I had created in my house, the opposite of the soft beauty that came from my talent for arrangement, my talent for living."[16]

This life inside the roach is anonymous, meaningless. This was not, of course, a new insight for Clarice. Comparing G. H. to a roach was consistent with her earlier comparisons of people to animals: Joana was a snake, Lucrécia a horse, Martin a cow, "he, too, pure, harmonious, and he too without meaning."

But for G. H., "faced with the living roach," the recognition that "the world is not human, and that we are not human" is a horror. She wants to scream, but she knows it is already too late. A scream would be an idiotic protest against being alive. "If I raised the alarm at being alive, voiceless and hard they would drag me away since they drag away those who depart the possible world, the exceptional being is dragged away, the screaming being."[17] Even worse: "I had nothing left to say. My agony was like that of wanting to speak before dying. I knew that I was saying farewell forever to some thing, something was going to die, and I wanted to say the word that at least summed up whatever it was that was dying."[18]

What is dying is, in Clarice's term, "civilization." She used the metaphor most extensively in *The Besieged City*. Lucrécia and her town, São Geraldo, begin as perfectly authentic, until civilization—viaducts, factories, statues—crowds out the wild horses. Already in *The Besieged City*, Clarice had conceived civilization as essentially linguistic. Language builds the town, literally: Lucrécia "indicated the intimate name of things.... Reality required the girl in order to take a form."[19] That civilization crumbles when its language is taken away. Alone in the maid's room, G. H. surveys the wreck, as it were, of São Geraldo. "An entire civilization had sprung up, with the guarantee that what one sees be mixed immediately with what one feels, an entire civilization whose foundation is salvation—so I was in its ruins."[20] G. H. must see without immediately translating the thing she sees into human language. At first, looking at the roach, she grotesquely personifies it, even using Clarice's favorite bad metaphor, the jewel: "Seen up close, the cockroach is an object of great luxury. A bride in black jewels."[21]

Lucrécia's way of seeing was "civilizing" and possessive: "This city is mine, the woman looked."[22] G. H. must unlearn that way of seeing: "And in this world that I was getting to know, there are several ways that mean seeing: a looking at the other without seeing it, a possessing the other, an eating the other, a simply being in a corner and the other being there as well: all this also means seeing. The roach was not seeing me directly, she was with me. The cockroach was not seeing me with its eyes but with its body."[23]

Her final attempt to "civilize" the cockroach is to wonder about its taste: "Would its eyes be salty? If I touched them—since I was gradually becoming ever dirtier—if I touched them with my mouth, would they taste salty?" "No, there was no salt in those eyes. I was sure that the eyes of the roach were tasteless. For salt I had always been ready, salt was the transcendence that I had used in order to be able to feel a taste, and to be able to flee what I called 'nothing.' For salt I had always been ready, for salt I had constructed my entire self."[24]

Bereft of salt, "transcendence," and "civilization" and, devastatingly, no longer able to discover human hope and beauty in the world, G. H. is left with the ooze coming out of the cockroach. It is the ultimate inhumanity. "Whatever comes out of the roach's belly is not transcendable—ah, I don't mean that it is the opposite of beauty, 'opposite of beauty' doesn't even make sense—whatever comes out of the roach's belly is: 'today,' blessed be the fruit of thy womb—I want the present without dressing it up with a future that redeems it, not even with a hope."[25] The passage is difficult to translate. The word *ventre* means, among other things, "womb," but in the first part of the sentence it suggests a belly or a stomach. Only when Clarice ironically quotes the "Ave Maria" does she clearly identify the roach with the Mother of God.

As she sheds her old world, she calls out desperately for her mother: "Mother: I killed a life, and there are no arms to receive me now and in the hour of our desert, amen. Mother, everything now has turned to hard gold. I interrupted an organized thing, mother, and that is worse than killing, that made me enter through a breach that showed me, worse than death, that showed me the thick and neutral life turning yellow. The roach is alive, her eye is fertilizing, I am afraid of my hoarseness, mother." In Portuguese the word for cockroach, *barata*, is feminine, regardless of the animal's biological gender. Here, however, Clarice is no longer using gender in a purely grammatical sense: "I had only thought of her as female, since things smashed at their waist are female." And not just any female: "Mother, all I did was want to kill, but just look at what I broke: I broke a casing! Killing is also forbidden because it breaks the hard casing, and one is left with the sticky life. From inside the hard casing is emerging a heart as thick and alive as pus, mother, blessed art thou among the roaches, now and in the hour of this thy my death, cockroach and jewel."[26] Hidden within G. H.'s confrontation with the dying cockroach is a memory of Clarice Lispector's own dying mother. The identity of her mother with the roach is one of the most shocking aspects of this whole unsettling book. Yet it is hard to escape the conclusion that this is what Clarice intended: "Mother, blessed art thou among the roaches."

One of the most eminent writers on Clarice Lispector, Claire Varin, has pointed out that "the disgusting roach appears explicitly as the only way to be born. A single narrow passage opens onto the room: 'through the roach.' "[27] The roach caught in the door of the wardrobe is described as a "prisoner at the waist,"[28] an allusion to the location of Clarice's mother's wound: "Things smashed at their waist are female." Like Mania Lispector, the cockroach is paralyzed, awaiting death: "Immobilized, it supported upon its dusty flank the burden of its own body."[29]

The cockroach is only half a body—"What I could see of her was only half of the body. The rest, which couldn't be seen, might be enormous, and divided among thousands of houses, behind things and wardrobes"—recalling a passage in one of Clarice's private notebooks, written in English, presumably in the United States, with Portuguese phrases sprinkled in: "I want somebody to hold my hand (That was how Papa, when I was hurting, helped me stand the pain)—I don't want to be a single body, I'm cut out from the rest of me—The rest of me is my mother! It's another body. To have a single body, surrounded by isolation it makes such a limited body. I feel anxiety, I'm afraid to be just one body. Little balls of mercury on the broken thermometer—My fear and anxiety is of being one body."[30]

The roach, the woman, and the mother share the organic life that is the most essential part of any creature. On the level of blood and guts, they are the one and the same.

❦

In 1964, the year *The Passion According to G. H.* was published, Clarice wrote, "If I had to give a title to my life it would be: in search of the thing itself."[31] Her goal is G. H.'s too. "Only then," when G. H. has stripped herself of human language and morality, "would I not be transcending and remain in the thing itself."

If Clarice knew what she was looking for, the "thing itself" remained elusive, except in abstract philosophical language. In *G. H.*, she broadens this language, offering new synonyms for the intangible "thing." It is neutral, inexpressive, tasteless, unsalted.[32] But no matter how many words she uses to describe it, it remains unfathomable. "I would horrify myself like a person who was blind and finally opened his eyes to see—but see what? a mute and incomprehensible triangle. Could that person consider himself no longer blind simply because he sees an incomprehensible triangle? I wonder: if I look at the darkness with a lens, will I see more than darkness?" At length, G. H. takes her "first steps into the nothing": "My first hesitant steps toward Life, and abandoning my life."[33]

In *The Apple in the Dark*, Clarice referred to the descent into the nothing. Still, the equivalence between "Life" and "the nothing" in *G. H.* is surprising, especially when Clarice stretches it even further, describing "a nothing that is the God."[34] The notion that God equals nothing is, however, a cabbalistic commonplace: "*Creation out of nothing* means to many mystics just *creation out of God*."[35] Read in this light, Clarice's statement that "above mankind there is nothing else at all" acquires an unexpected subtlety. Not above mankind but inside mankind is "the God," "nothing else at all." If God is nothing, God is also everything: "Life." This too is a Jewish definition: God is everything and nothing, the union of everything in the world and its opposite.[36] As G. H. says, "God is what exists, and all contradictions are inside the God, and for that reason do not contradict Him."[37]

The statement is logically agreeable. But after such a long and painful search, saying that God is "what exists" feels like a thundering letdown.

> Since prehistory I had started my march through the desert, and without a star to guide me, only perdition guiding me, only going astray guiding me—until, almost dead from the ecstasy of fatigue, illuminated by passion, I finally found the safe. And in the safe, sparkling with glory, the hidden secret. The most remote secret in the world, opaque, but blinding me with the irradiation of its simple existence, sparkling there with glory that hurt my eyes. Inside the safe the secret:
>
> A piece of thing.
>
> A piece of iron, a roach's antenna, a plaster chip.[38]

Finding the treasure of the world in "a piece of thing," or writing that "the divine for me *is* whatever is real,"[39] recalls the famous statement by Clarice's earlier mentor, Spinoza, that God is equivalent to Nature. And writing that "our condition is accepted as the only one possible, since it is the one that exists, and not any other," recalls Spinoza's proposition that "things could have been produced by God in no other way, and in no other order, than they have been produced."[40]

In repeating these definitions, Clarice is yet again rejecting what she already called, in *Near to the Wild Heart*, "the humanized God of the religions." It is a rejection that has an intellectual perfection to it. But for a woman longing to know God, the "thing itself" is so barren, so at "the opposite pole of the sentimental-human-Christian," that "in [her] old human terms, [it] means the worst, and, in human terms, the infernal."[41] The neutral God, "a piece of iron, a roach's antenna," can never satisfy a person longing for an emotional connection with the divine.

And so if Clarice must accept "our condition as the only one possible," she rages against it. The painstaking definitions, parsed over decades, have finally brought her to a God that can satisfy her rationally. But they are dry. The climax of her search, her most shocking and unforgettable symbol, is quite literally wet.

Abandoning hope and beauty and redemption but still desperate for union with the fundamental matter of the universe, G. H. takes the yellowish slime leaking from the belly of the cockroach and places it in her mouth.

❧

It is one thing to speculate about eating a roach as a possible outcome of an abstract philosophical search. "Why would I be disgusted by the matter coming out of the roach?" G. H. wonders. "Hadn't I drunk of the white milk that is the liquid maternal matter?" It is quite something else, of course, to actually eat a roach. "Give me your hand, don't abandon me, I swear I didn't want it either: I too lived well, I was a woman of whom you could say 'life and loves of G. H.' "[42]

Clarice was horrified by her own creation, she later remembered. "The thing escaped from my control when I, for example, realized that the woman was going to have to eat the insides of the roach. I trembled in fright."[43]

The woman eating a roach is so extreme a symbol, such a blunt illustration for Clarice's horror of encountering "the God," that it inevitably begs another question: Where, psychologically and artistically, can she possibly go from here? In *The Apple in the Dark* Clarice had already written that "Nobody could live based on having vomited or having seen someone vomit; they were not things to think about very much: they were facts of a life."[44] Thinking about these facts of life can lead in only one direction, as Clarice writes in *G. H.*: "Why not stay inside, without trying to cross over to the other shore?" She then answers her own question: "Staying inside the thing is madness."[45]

On the same page, she points out a possible solution: "It is like the sculpted eye of a statue which is empty and has no expression, since when art is good it is because it touched upon the inexpressive, the worst art is expressive, that art which transgresses the piece of iron and the piece of glass, and the smile, and the scream."[46]

29

AND REVOLUTION!

The ghastly magnificence of *The Passion According to G. H.* has placed it among the century's greatest novels. Shortly before her death, on her last visit to Recife, Clarice told a reporter that of all her books it was the one that "best corresponded to her demands as a writer."[1] It has inspired a gigantic bibliography, but at the time it came out it seems to have been all but ignored. Only one review was published in 1964, by Lúcio Cardoso's friend Walmir Ayala.[2]

This time, at least, Clarice did not have to search for a publisher. A strange turn of events had turned two of her closest friends, Fernando Sabino and Rubem Braga, into the proprietors of a publishing house. On March 28, 1960, they had traveled to Cuba as part of a delegation led by Clarice's future assailant, the one-eyed Jânio Quadros, who on October 3 would be elected president of Brazil. The group stayed in revolutionary Cuba for less than a week and returned to Brazil enthusiastic.

Unlike so many Latin American writers and intellectuals at the time, neither Braga nor Sabino were Communists. Sabino was Catholic and Braga a kind of Social Democrat. Their reports from Havana, therefore, are valuable indicators of the excitement that the Cuban Revolution sparked throughout the continent, even among people not automatically inclined to be swept away by the romance of Fidel Castro. Only thirty-three when he conquered the island, Castro, together with his cohort of "sincere," "honest" revolutionaries, appealed to dreamers, and not only dreamers, throughout Latin America.

Even the sober, wary Braga fell for it. He analyzed the Leader's handwriting and discovered in it no "despotic spirit." And if "good cashmere" was becoming hard to find in Havana, he wrote, that was only because "the government wants to use foreign currency to buy tractors, machines, factories, productive goods."[3]

Sabino, more romantic, showed a certain understanding for the regime's public executions and, perhaps even more embarrassingly, exulted that the Havana Country Club was now opened to the "humble people." How easy it would be to right the wrongs of a slave society, half a millennium old!

But these were articles in the local press, no different from, and indeed more skeptical than, many published during the Revolution's honeymoon. And they were nothing compared to the articles the world's most famous philosopher, Jean-Paul Sartre, had penned after his visit to Havana, from the beginning of February to mid-March 1960. The articles he published in *France-Soir* are what one would expect from a person who never met a bad leftist idea he didn't like, issuing apologies for everything from the more extreme elements in Algeria to the murder of Israeli athletes at the Munich Olympics.

At the invitation of Jorge Amado, Sartre and Simone de Beauvoir came to Brazil in August 1960, embarking on a triumphal tour of the country. For some reason, Sartre decided to cede his *France-Soir* articles to Sabino and Braga, who had been thinking about starting their own publishing house in order to avoid the exploitive royalties paid by existing houses. Sartre charged them nothing, and the Editôra do Autor had its first title: *Hurricane over Cuba*. But to produce it during Sartre's visit to Brazil, Sabino and Braga had to coordinate an amazing effort. With no experience in publishing, they gathered the rare originals of the articles, translated them, then edited, typeset, and printed the book—in little more than a week.[4]

The book betrays such ignorance of basic economic, historical, and political concepts that it is hard to imagine its author was seen as a global intellectual heavyweight, or indeed taken seriously at all. But it was the book of the moment by the man of the moment on the topic of the moment, and it launched the Editôra do Autor as prominently and lucratively as could be imagined.

By the time the publishing house appeared, Clarice already had a contract with Francisco Alves for *The Apple in the Dark* and *Family Ties*. But the Editôra do Autor was the most logical home for her next book, and it must have been a great relief to her to know that anything she wrote would be immediately welcomed by close friends and longtime admirers. By 1964, when Clarice published two books there, it had become known primarily for its finely produced editions of Brazilian writers, including Sabino and Braga, and for its pioneering anthologies of Brazil's modern poets.

In 1964, the Editôra do Autor had moved past Cuba, but Brazil, and Latin America, had certainly not. Fidel Castro elated the left, but after the fiasco of the

Bay of Pigs invasion in April 1961, Castro's embrace of Soviet Russia, and then the Cuban Missile Crisis of October 1962, he terrified the right.

These were not idle fears. During Jânio Quadros's visit to Cuba in 1960, after Castro listed Cuba's principal export products for the Brazilian delegation, his brother Raúl added, "And revolution!"[5] He was not kidding. In 1959, when the Cuban Revolution triumphed, Latin America had more democratic regimes than ever before in its history, with only five tiny exceptions: Nicaragua, Haiti, El Salvador, the Dominican Republic, and Paraguay. Upon taking power, the Cuban government immediately began sponsoring subversion across the continent. In 1959 it had bankrolled guerrillas in Panama, Haiti, and the Dominican Republic; by 1963 it started to support armed movements in Venezuela, Peru, Guatemala, and Argentina.[6]

No country was untouched, either by Cuba and its Soviet sponsors or by the brutal and panicked reaction. Fear of another Cuba galvanized the Latin American militaries into something like hysteria, and in this they were actively assisted by the United States, which feared a continent controlled by the Soviet Union. The reactions to the Cuban Revolution, by admirers and opponents, would form the bloodiest and most traumatic episode in Latin American history since the wars of independence a century and a half before.

In Brazil, too, the consequences would be terrible. They began on August 19, 1961, when Jânio Quadros awarded Che Guevara Brazil's highest honor, the Order of the Southern Cross. This was the kind of eccentricity for which Quadros, outlawer of the bikini, had become known. But it was a needless offense to the Kennedy administration, well disposed to the Brazilian government, and perfect ammunition for Quadros's domestic opponents.

Carlos Lacerda, the "destroyer of presidents" and Samuel Wainer's nemesis, had been an early supporter of Quadros, but now, as governor of the state of Guanabara, he turned against him. As Wainer learned, the famous polemicist was harshest on his erstwhile friends. Lacerda used the occasion to great effect, presenting the Key to the State to the anti-Castro leader Manuel Verona and accusing Quadros of wanting to lead Brazil to Communism.

This was very far from the case. The award to Guevara was thanks for respecting a Brazilian request not to execute twenty Catholic priests, who were instead exiled to Spain. But Quadros's foreign policy had already been raising eyebrows. Two of Clarice's oldest diplomatic friends were partially responsible for it. Araújo Castro had served in the New York consulate when Fernando Sabino lived there, and San Tiago Dantas, the brilliant Catholic lawyer, had fallen in love with Clarice on a visit to Paris in the 1940s. Both were respected establishment figures. Their plan for an "Independent Foreign Policy" was basically an attempt to increase Brazilian diplomatic influence in an international situation that, with the independence of former European colonies in Asia and Africa, was rapidly changing. The plan suggested that Brazil ought to maintain relations with all powers, which in practice meant China and the Soviet Union, with which Brazil had had no relations since 1947. This was controversial, but hardly a sign that Brazil was going Communist.

More alarming were signs that Quadros was simply unhinged. He planned, for example, to invade neighboring French Guiana, alleging that Brazil needed an outlet to the Caribbean, even though French Guiana is hundreds of miles from the Caribbean. The opposition, which had been dispirited by his overwhelming election victory, began to taunt him, and six days after he decorated Che Guevara he unexpectedly resigned the presidency. He had taken power only seven months before.

This resignation, too, was inspired by Cuba. In July 1959, Fidel Castro, caught in a power struggle with Cuba's president, Manuel Urrutia, borrowed a gambit from Perón and dramatically "resigned." The predictable outcry went a long way toward consolidating his absolute power; Urrutia ended his days as a Spanish teacher in Queens. Quadros apparently hoped that his sudden departure would unleash a similar reaction. But Brazilians were by and large relieved to see him go. (He briefly returned to politics in the 1980s. As mayor of São Paulo, he rekindled memories of his presidency by, among other things, banning homosexuals from the Municipal Theater's ballet school.)

Quadros's resignation unleashed a crisis. Under the Brazilian constitution, the president and vice president were elected separately and thus were not of the same party. Quadros's legal successor was João Goulart, known as Jango. Goulart was an unlikely revolutionary, and nothing in his curriculum suggested that he would push Brazil into the hands of the Communists. He was from a family of rich landowners in Rio Grande do Sul and was mainly known for his passionate appetite for the actresses and dancers that hung out in the exclusive clubs of Clarice's neighborhood, Leme.

Rather than seeing a friendly, mediocre playboy, however, the right wing looked at Jango and saw a much more powerful figure. Though he had been dead for seven years, Getúlio Vargas still dominated Brazilian politics. Jango and Getúlio were from the same town, São Borja, and Goulart had been Getúlio's minister of labor until 1954, when, seeing him as too sympathetic to labor unions, the military forced him out.

Those who imagined that Jango was a secret Communist were given an unexpected public relations lift when, upon Quadros's resignation, the vice president was found on a tour of Red China. Civil war briefly threatened when different army divisions declared themselves for or against Goulart, but after a ten-day crisis Jango was allowed to take power under a new "parliamentary" system designed to weaken the power of the executive.

Goulart thus struggled from the beginning, with Brazil terribly divided and without the talent necessary to reassure the right while also seeking to implement socially necessary reforms. At the center of his administration were two of Clarice's old friends, Samuel Wainer, who had known Goulart for years and whose *Última Hora* was the most powerful, and later only, pro-Goulart voice in the national press, and San Tiago Dantas.

Wainer thought little of Dantas—he saw him as power-hungry, "irremediably ambitious," and dangerously friendly to the Communists[7]—who became foreign minister and, after 1963, minister of finance. With Brazil's debt at a historic high and inflation spinning out of control, this was an unenviable position, especially with the Americans increasingly wary of Goulart's inability to stick to an economic plan. Moreover, San Tiago Dantas was dying of cancer, which did not help the government's chances of negotiating an economic settlement. The last time Clarice saw him was shortly before his death, at the marriage of one of his nieces. "He could hardly speak. He asked me what I was writing. I answered that I had just written a book and that the name was *The Passion According to G. H.* And he said that he liked the name very much. He would have liked the book, I know."[8]

He died on September 6, 1964, before *G. H.* came out. On March 31, Goulart was deposed in a military coup. Thousands were arrested or went into exile, most in less luxurious circumstances than Samuel Wainer. After taking refuge in the Chilean embassy, he made his way to Paris, where he spent four years being photographed in the company of Anita Ekberg, various Rothschilds, and the Shah's ex-wife, Princess Soraya.

The country he was forced to flee faced a grimmer future. The era of good feelings, of bossa nova and Brasília and girls from Ipanema, of energy and optimism and belief in the nation's future, was definitively over. Many, including Elizabeth Bishop, hailed the coup as a temporary expedient to save Brazil from Communism. It instead produced an unprecedented twenty-one years of military dictatorship.

30

THE EGG REALLY IS WHITE

The Passion According to G. H. was one of two books Clarice Lispector published in the watershed year 1964. In September, before the novel appeared, the Editôra do Autor published a collection of shorter writings, *The Foreign Legion*. If it is hard to imagine where Clarice—artistically, intellectually, spiritually—could go after the cockroach, *The Foreign Legion* offers several possibilities.

The book consists of stories and miscellany. There are older pieces, such as the beautiful and affecting "Journey to Petrópolis," first published in a newspaper in 1949, and "The Burnt Sinner and the Harmonious Angels," the play she wrote in Bern. There are also many pieces first published in *Senhor*, both long essays and short speculations: "If I get a present given thoughtfully by someone I don't like—how do I call what I feel? A person you no longer like and who no longer likes you—how do you call that sorrow and that spite?"[1] Or, revealingly, "Being born ruined my health."[2]

The title of the collection is borrowed from a story about a smart and curious little girl, Ofélia. The girl begins to visit the woman next door, who owns a tiny frightened chick, "the chick full of grace, [a] brief and yellow thing." Words cannot calm the baby bird's fright: "It was impossible to give him the reassuring word that would make him no longer be afraid, to console a thing that is afraid because it was born. How to promise him habit?"[3]

The story, which combines children and animals, announces a new strain in Clarice's writing. Indeed, some of the aphorisms, which may not have anything to do with either children or animals, come from a rubric in *Senhor* entitled, in English, "Children's Corner." She had been using the title since 1947, when she submitted some pieces to Samuel Wainer's *O Jornal*.[4] In *Senhor* she had a monthly column with the same title starting in October 1961, which displeased at least one of her editors: "My dislike of the name she'd chosen for her page wasn't enough for her to change it."[5]

It is, in fact, an odd title. It was in a foreign language, and the subject matter of her articles in *Senhor* was not children, except occasionally and incidentally. It is a revealing allusion to the writer's state of mind. "Children's Corner" is the title, also in English, of a series of piano pieces the French composer Claude Debussy dedicated to his daughter. Very difficult, they are not designed to be played by children but to express a nostalgia for childhood, and to evoke its mood.

As her use of the title indicates, the nostalgia for childhood grew particularly acute as Clarice aged. "I don't miss it, you understand?" Joana asks in *Near to the Wild Heart*. "I don't miss it, because I have my childhood more now than while it was happening."[6] Clarice increasingly did miss her own childhood, and she longed for the happy time before life had "tamed" her. In "Drawing a Boy," she writes, "One day we will domesticate him as a human, and will be able to draw him. Since that is what we did with ourselves and with God."[7]

The reference to the missing mother is not far behind. "He would trade all the possibilities of a world for: mother. Mother is: not to die."[8] In the title story, Clarice obviously identifies with both the bright impish Ofélia as well as with the helpless chick, who has lost his mother.

In one particularly moving anecdote, Clarice describes a coati, a long-tailed member of the raccoon family, whom she unexpectedly encounters, leashed like a dog, at a bus stop in Copacabana: "I imagine: if the man took him to play in the square, at some point the coati would grow uncomfortable: 'but, good God, why are the dogs looking at me like that?' I also imagine that, after a perfect day of being a dog, the coati would feel melancholic, looking at the stars: 'what's wrong with me, after all? what am I missing? I am as happy as any dog, so why this emptiness, this nostalgia? what is this anxiety, as if I only loved something I didn't know?' "[9] This is not G. H.'s monstrous mystical identification with the cockroach's entrails. It is softer and more sorrowful, the sympathy with the outsider that had always been natural to someone whose "first desire was the desire to belong."

The question of identifying with outsiders, which in Brazil traditionally meant the rural northeastern poor, had long been central to Brazilian culture, from the "northeastern novels" of the 1930s to the *cinema novo* of the 1950s. With the coup of 1964, the question of the social relevance of art was once again pushed to the forefront. The extent to which one was engaged, and with whom, became the main dividing line in Brazilian culture.

Clarice was not immune to the problems of her country, though she had difficulty conveying that solidarity in her work. In a short piece in *The Foreign Legion*, she explains that her social engagement was simply too obvious and natural:

> For example, my tolerance in relation to myself, as a person who writes, is to forgive myself for not knowing how to approach in a "literary" fashion (that is, transforming into the vehemence of art) the "social thing." As long as I have known myself the social fact has been more important to me than any other: in Recife the slums were the first truth for me. Long before I felt "art," I felt the profound beauty of the struggle. But I have a foolish way of approaching the social fact: what I wanted was to "do" something, as if writing was not doing. What I can't manage is to use writing for that, as much as my incapacity hurts and humiliates me. The problem of justice is in me a feeling so obvious and so basic that I can't surprise myself with it—and, without surprising myself, I can't write. And also because for me writing is searching. The feeling of justice was never a search for me, it never had to be discovered, and what astounds me is that it is not just as obvious for everyone.[10]

She did, however, have the ability to give voice to her rage at Brazil's injustices, as an essay published in *Senhor* and reprinted in *The Foreign Legion* illustrates. The piece is about Mineirinho, a murderer who had a girlfriend and was a devotee of St. George, and whom the police killed with "thirteen shots, when a single shot was enough." The extreme violence of his death revolted Clarice. "I became Mineirinho, massacred by the police. Whatever his crime had been, one bullet was enough, the rest was the desire to kill."[11]

> That is the law. But while something makes me hear the first and second shots with the relief of security, it puts me on alert at the third, unsettles me at the fourth, at the fifth and the sixth covers me with shame; the seventh and the eighth I hear with my heart beating in horror; at the ninth and tenth my mouth is quivering, at the eleventh I say God's name in fright, at the twelfth I call for my brother. The thirteenth shot kills me—because I am the other. Because I want to be the other.[12]

The three sentences of "The Greatest Experience" sum up this question as well as Clarice ever would: "I used to want to be others to learn about what wasn't me. Then I understood that I had already been others and it was easy. My greatest experience would be to be the other of others: and the other of others was me."[13]

The Foreign Legion also points in another direction: toward abstraction. With their strong emphasis on the interior worlds of her characters, Clarice's works had always had an important abstract element. "When art is good it is because it touched upon the inexpressive," she wrote in *G. H.* "The worst art is expressive, that art which transgresses the piece of iron and the piece of glass, and the smile, and the scream."[14]

The Foreign Legion is full of reflections on the meaning and process of writing, a subject Clarice had never addressed so extensively. In a short piece called "Novel," she wrote, "It would be more attractive if I made it more attractive. Using, for example, some of the things that frame a life or a thing or a novel or a character. It is perfectly acceptable to make something attractive, except for the danger that a painting is a painting because it is in a frame. For reading, of course, I prefer something attractive, it fatigues me less, it delimits me and surrounds me. In my writing, though, I must do without it. The experience was worthwhile, even if only for the person who wrote it."[15] This "attractiveness" was never the point of her writing, which was "the means of someone who has a word like bait: the word fishing whatever is not a word. When that non-word bites the bait, something was written."[16] Abstraction could be the most effective way of "baiting" meaning. "In painting as in music and literature, what is called abstract so often seems to me the figurative of a more delicate and more difficult reality, less visible to the naked eye."[17]

One of Clarice's greatest stories, "The Egg and the Hen," appears in *The Foreign Legion*. Since her childhood, growing up with chickens in the yard behind her house in Recife, Clarice had been interested in chickens and eggs. "I understand a hen, perfectly. I mean, the intimate life of a hen, I know how it is," she said. But the story has nothing to do with that. At the end of her life, when an interviewer asked her about the charge that she was "hermetic," she answered, "I understand myself. Well, there's one story I don't understand, 'The Egg and the Hen,' which is a mystery to me."[18]

"In the morning in the kitchen upon the table I see the egg," the story begins, conventionally enough. It soon becomes a meditation that recalls Gertrude Stein's cubist portraits in words.

> An egg is a thing that needs to be careful. That is why the hen is the disguise of the egg. So that the egg can move through time the hen exists. That is what mothers are for. —The egg lives on the run because it is always ahead of its time. —The egg for now will always be revolutionary. —It lives inside the hen so that they cannot call it white. The egg really is white. But it cannot be called white. Not because this harms it, but the people who call the egg white, those people die to the world. To call something white that is white can destroy humanity. Once a man was accused of being what he was, and was called That Man. They hadn't lied: He was. But to this day we have not got ourselves back, one after the next. The general law to keep us alive: one can say "a pretty face," but whoever says "the face" dies; because they have exhausted the topic.[19]

If this is not a traditional narrative, and is obscure in many places, if even Clarice claimed not to understand it, neither is it entirely opaque. It has a clear subject, and one familiar with her work will find in it many recognizable references. There is the mystery of motherhood and birth, the distance between language and meaning, and even, in the suggestion of revolution, an ironic nod to current politics.

In the same book, Clarice describes the new modernist capital of Brasília in terms similarly abstract.

> When I died, one day I opened my eyes and it was Brasília. I was alone in the world. There was a parked taxi. Without a driver. —Lúcio Costa and Oscar Niemeyer, two solitary men. —I look at Brasília as I look at Rome: Brasília began with a final simplification of ruins. The ivy has not yet grown. —Besides the wind is something else blowing. It can only be seen in the supernatural ripples of the lake. —Anywhere one is standing, a child can fall, and outside the world. Brasília is on the edge. —If I lived here, I would let my hair grow to the ground. —Brasília has a splendid past that no longer exists. . . . From my insomnia I look out the window of the hotel at three in the morning. Brasília is the landscape of insomnia. It never sleeps. —Here the organic being does not deteriorate.

> It petrifies. —I wanted to see spread throughout Brasília five hundred thousand needles of the blackest onyx. —Brasília is asexual. —The first instant of seeing is like a certain instant of drunkenness: feet that do not touch the ground.[20]

The ten pages of this meditation create in the reader precisely the drunken or prayerful feeling that Brasília created in Clarice. "Brasília: Five Days" is not a traditional essay, of course, but no other description of the city has ever come close to capturing its suffocating and enigmatic air. "As in anything else," she writes in *The Foreign Legion*, "in writing I also have a kind of worry about going too far. What would that be? For what? I restrain myself, as if holding the reins of a horse that could gallop off and take me God knows where."[21]

31

A COARSE CACTUS

In 1961, when *The Apple in the Dark* came out, Rosa Cass, a Jewish journalist who was a friend of Alberto Dines, interviewed Clarice for the *Jornal do Comércio*. "She hated interviews," Rosa remembered. "She answered *none* of my questions."[1] But the two women got on, and after the painfully improvised interview appeared, Rosa sent Clarice flowers to thank her.

Clarice never replied. Offended, Rosa did not contact her again until she came across *The Passion According to G. H.* Shocked and impressed, she forgot her previous annoyance and called Clarice. They discussed Beethoven. "How did he compose after he went deaf?" Clarice asked. "He could only hear the music inside him." Rosa answered. "And that was what I felt when reading your book: that solitude." Clarice said, "Imagine the solitude of the person who wrote it."[2]

The two women grew close, and Rosa had ample opportunity to see Clarice's solitude. Rosa worked as a journalist, but for Clarice's sake she took time off in the afternoons to attend matinees with her. Rosa, who after all had a job, had not seen a matinee since she was a girl, but she adjusted her work schedule to be able to spend more time with Clarice, who went to bed at nine; it was impossible to see her in the evenings. This kind of loyalty was common in Clarice's friends, at least for a time and from those who felt her vulnerability and wanted to help her, though she often exhausted even the most devoted.

She was not completely cut off, however. If *The Passion According to G. H.* had not been extensively reviewed when it first appeared, its impact, once readers began to absorb it, was profound and resulted in a certain popularization of Clarice. In 1965, the first of what would become dozens of theatrical adaptations of her work appeared in Rio; in 1966, the first book about her was published, *The World of Clarice Lispector*, by the philosopher Benedito Nunes.

She also found a new circle of friends around Pedro Bloch, cousin of Adolpho Bloch, the powerful owner of *Manchete*. Born, like Clarice, in the Ukraine, Dr. Bloch was a prominent playwright and physician, who specialized in disorders of the voice. He tried to cure Clarice of her throaty r's and her lisp, which, he said, might have resulted from her imitating her parents' speech in childhood. The interventions were successful, but then Clarice relapsed into her old accent: "She told him that she didn't like losing her characteristics."[3]

Bloch and his Uruguayan wife, Miriam, entertained prominent artists and intellectuals at their beach house in the resort of Cabo Frio. One who came was João Guimarães Rosa, the writer and diplomat who, from his post in Hamburg, had helped many Jews escape to Brazil. Three months before his stroke, Lúcio Cardoso had written that "Brazilian literature belongs to two princes, Guimarães Rosa and Clarice Lispector."[4] Now the two princes, one nearing the end of his life, grew close.

She had long admired him. When his masterpiece *Grande sertão: veredas* came out in 1956, she told Fernando Sabino, "I've never seen anything like it! It's the most beautiful thing in a long time. I don't know how far his inventive power can go, it surpasses any imaginable limit. I'm even giddy.... I'm even upset that I like it so much."[5] Clarice never wrote with such enthusiasm about a contemporary, and a few months before his death the older master gave her a great compliment. After citing by heart long passages from her books, he said "something I will never forget, so happy was I when I heard it: he said he read me, not for literature, but for life."[6]

In 1965, Clarice finally moved into the large three-bedroom apartment she had bought a couple of years earlier, in a building still under construction. It was close by the apartment she had been renting, also in Leme. After a lifetime on the move, Rua Gustavo Sampaio 88, one block from the beach, next door to the Leme Tennis Club, would be her final home. About a year after she moved in, she very nearly died there.

On September 12, 1966, Rosa Cass was at the Copacabana apartment of two sisters, Gilka and Gilda, practitioners of the Afro-Brazilian religion *umbanda*. Rosa was going through a difficult period in her life, and a friend had suggested that she visit Gilda, who could ritually "cleanse" her. During this cleansing, to Rosa's fright and astonishment, Gilda was suddenly possessed by a spirit that inspired the small woman to seize Rosa, lift her above her head, and spin her around. Once Rosa was safely back on the ground, the medium announced that a close girlfriend's life was in danger. At the time, Rosa's two closest friends were Clarice and the prominent novelist Nélida Piñon. Terrified, she wondered which of them was in danger, and she soon got her answer.

The next evening, Nélida was launching her first collection of stories, *Time of Fruit*, an occasion to which she had invited Clarice. A few hours before the event, Clarice called to say she would not be able to come. Nélida noted that her voice was weak, trailing off. Several hours later, at 3:35 in the morning, a neighbor spotted smoke coming out of the building across the street. She alerted her doorman, and they ran across to Clarice's building, where they found her apartment in flames.[7]

Clarice's two addictions, to cigarettes and sleeping pills, had finally caught up with her. She slept in a single bed under a curtained window, and she had always slept badly, going to sleep around nine and waking up in the early morning hours. That night, after taking her pills, she sat smoking in bed. She awoke to find the room in flames. In a panicked attempt to save her papers, she tried to put out the fire with her own hands. Her son Paulo brought her out of the blazing room and rang insistently on the doorbell of the next apartment. The frightened inhabitants, Saul and Heloísa Azevedo, awoke to find Clarice, burned all across her body, standing at their door. She did not say a single word. Saul and Paulo rushed to put out the fire while Heloísa led Clarice inside. Her partly melted nylon nightgown was stuck to her body, and when she walked across Heloísa's carpet, she left bloody footprints behind.

For three days, in the company of Tania, Elisa, and Rosa, Clarice hovered between life and death. Her right hand, her writing hand, was so badly damaged that there was talk of amputation. Tania pleaded with the doctors to wait another day, and the danger passed. During these three days, the surgeon prohibited visits. "But I want visits, I said, they distract me from the terrible pain. And everyone who did not obey the sign 'Silence,' I received them all, groaning in pain, as at a party I had become talkative and my voice was clear: my soul flowered like a coarse cactus.... It seemed that I vaguely felt that, while I suffered physically in such an unendurable way, that would be the proof of living to the maximum."[8]

The pain was monstrous. Besides the third-degree burns on her hand, her legs, too, had been terribly burned, though her face, luckily, had been spared. Almost forty years later, Rosa still shuddered when describing how the nurses had to clean the wounds, unanaesthetized, with a brush and soap. "When they took out the stitches from my operated hand, between the fingers, I screamed,"

Clarice wrote. "I screamed out of pain, and out of rage, since pain seems to be an offense to our physical wholeness. But I wasn't stupid. I took advantage of the pain and screamed for the past and the present. I even screamed for the future, my God."[9]

Clarice had to stay in the hospital for three full months, enduring surgery, skin grafts, and physiotherapy, which enabled her eventually to regain the use of her hand, at least for typing. For the rest of her life it would resemble a blackened claw. "The left hand was a miracle of elegance," her friend Olga Borelli wrote. "At work, agile and decided, it seemed to try to compensate for the deficiencies of the other, hard, with badly controlled gestures, with burnt fingers, bent back, deeply scarred."[10]

Her bedroom was completely gutted, with one exception: a missal a friend had given her, with the inscription "Pray for me." "The plaster fell from the walls and the ceiling, the furniture was reduced to powder, and the books as well. I won't even try to explain what happened: everything was burnt, but the missal remained intact, the cover only lightly singed."[11]

To Rosa, Clarice left the hospital even more beautiful than before, very thin, her features refined and given an even more intensely spiritual aspect by her suffering. But soon afterward, during her difficult convalescence, she began to gain weight and had to consult a dietician.[12] She would always remain a striking figure, but at age forty-six her famous beauty, which despite her many difficulties had never left her, was now in the past. According to her son Paulo, she suffered from "an unconfessed disillusionment with the loss of the beauty of her youth."[13]

"It seemed to me that she thought it was ugly to go out when one was no longer young," Clarice wrote. "The air so clean, the body dirty with fat and wrinkles. Especially the clarity of the sea, how it denudes. It wasn't for others that it was ugly for her to go out, everyone accepts that other people are old. But for herself."[14]

32

POSSIBLE DIALOGUES

As often before in Clarice's life, triumph soon followed disaster, and 1967 turned out, professionally at least, to be a good year. It saw the publication of the children's story *The Mystery of the Thinking Rabbit*, which she had written in Washington, in English, at Paulo's request. She had forgotten about it—"It wasn't much literature for me"[1]—until a publisher asked if she had anything for children. She pulled it out of the drawer, translated it, and published it.

The book won the Calunga Prize for the best children's book of the year, which made Clarice happy. "But I was even happier when it occurred to me that they call me a hermetic writer. How? When I write for children, I am understood, but when I write for adults I become *difficult*? Should I write for adults with the words and the feelings appropriate to a child? Can't I speak as an equal?"[2]

The next year saw her second incursion into children's literature, *The Woman Who Killed the Fish*, which opens with a confession: "The woman who killed the fish unfortunately is me. But I promise I didn't mean to. Me of all people! who doesn't have the heart to kill a living thing! I don't even always kill cockroaches."[3] In the book, she remembers all her pets, from Dilermando, whom she had to leave behind in Naples, to Jack, the dog she had in Washington. Like "The Crime of the Mathematics Professor," *The Woman Who Killed the Fish* was conceived because of a "feeling of guilt that [she] wanted to expiate."[4] In this case, the victims were two little red fish her son Pedro entrusted to her when he went away for a month. Busy working and absentminded, she simply forgot to feed them for a couple of days; when she finally remembered, they were dead. Once again, just as she had done following her mother's death, she told a story in order to assuage her guilt, reasserting the connection between crime and creation.

The chance "to speak as an equal," to adults, came when her old friend Alberto Dines, who had given her work at the *Diário da Noite* after her return to Brazil, got a phone call from another friend, Otto Lara Resende. As in 1960, Otto said, "Clarice is having trouble." And as in 1960, Dines, now editor in chief of the *Jornal do Brasil*, the country's most prestigious newspaper, was in a position to help. Dines was creating a new Saturday cultural supplement and was anxious to attract a more cultured readership for the section. He immediately offered Clarice a weekly column.

On August 19, 1967, she debuted as a *cronista*, or "chronicler." The *crônica* is a free-form literary column, and it was a Brazilian institution. The *cronistas* were popular and even revered. Whether this was because, as João Cabral de Melo Neto wrote, "in Brazil, all they understand is writing for newspapers," or simply because newspapers were still the primary medium in the country, the genre was genuinely popular. Its practitioners included many of Clarice's friends, including Paulo Mendes Campos, Rubem Braga, and Fernando Sabino.

Clarice feared that she was not up to the task and often confessed, over the six and a half years that she worked for the *Jornal do Brasil*, that she was a bit cowed by the genre.

> Besides being a neophyte in these matters, I'm also new to writing for money. I worked before in the press as a professional, without signing my name. Signing, however, automatically makes it more personal. And I feel a bit like I'm selling my soul. I told a friend about this and he said: but writing is selling one's soul a little bit. It's true. Even when it's not to make money, we expose ourselves a great deal. Though a doctor friend disagreed: she argued that in her profession she gives her whole soul too, yet she charges for it because she too has to live. So with great pleasure I sell you a certain part of my soul—the part of Saturday conversation.[5]

Part of her feeling of inadequacy may have come from being a rare female in an almost exclusively male domain. Only three or four women worked as literary columnists.[6] The men, particularly Rubem Braga, possessed a belle-lettristic grandiloquence, a self-conscious refinement of tone, utterly lacking in Clarice's work. Her columns were unabashedly personal and unabashedly feminine.

In them, Clarice did not abandon many of her old metaphysical themes, but she also chronicled her life as a mother and a housewife in directly personal terms. "I think that if I wrote about the problem of overproduction of coffee in Brazil I would end up making it personal," she said in one column.[7] She wrote about her children, her friends, her maids, her childhood, her travels, so much so that *Discovering the World*, the posthumously published collection of her columns, is the closest thing to an autobiography that Clarice left.

Her intimate "Saturday conversation" style annoyed some of the genre's grandees, who thought of the newspaper column as a minor art. Even Rubem Braga, a friend since Naples, apparently badmouthed her, earning a public riposte: "Someone told me that Rubem Braga said I was only good in my books, that my columns were no good," Clarice wrote. "Is that true, Rubem? Rubem, I do what I can. You can do more, but you shouldn't insist on others being able to do the same. I write my columns humbly, Rubem. I have no pretensions. But I get letters from readers and they like them. And I like to get them."[8]

The readers did like them. If *Senhor* introduced Clarice to the literati, the *Jornal do Brasil* brought her to the middle class, week after week, and her work as a columnist brought her a fame she had never known before. It even brought her an octopus. "I'm shy but I have the right to my impulses," exclaimed a woman who appeared at her door. "What you wrote in the paper today was exactly how I feel; and so I, who live across the street from you and saw your fire and know when the lights are on that you have insomnia, so I brought you an octopus."[9] To Clarice's astonishment, the woman proceeded to cook the octopus, a specialty of hers, then and there.

"I wrote nine books that made many people love me from afar," Clarice wrote about her newfound popularity. "But being a columnist has a mystery that I don't understand: it's that columnists, at least in Rio, are very loved. And writing this kind of Saturday column has brought me even more love. I feel so close to my readers."[10] She reflected the love she received back to her readers. One girl wrote to thank Clarice for helping her to love, and Clarice answered, thanking her: "Thank you also for the adolescent that I was and who wanted to be useful to people, to Brazil, to humanity, and wasn't even ashamed to use such imposing words for herself."[11]

A fascinating portrait of Clarice around this time emerges from the recollections of Maria Teresa Walcacer,[12] a twenty-year-old philosophy student who answered an advertisement for a "writer's secretary" around the time that Clarice started writing for the *Jornal do Brasil*. Upon arrival, Walcacer was shocked to find that the writer was none other than Clarice Lispector, who was seated beside the window interviewing the approximately forty candidates. Clarice told her that since the fire she could only type with difficulty, and that she needed someone who would respect every period and comma in her writing. She asked, finally, if

Maria Teresa had read any of her books. The young woman answered, "Almost all." Half an hour later she had the job.

> Why did I choose Maria Teresa, whose nickname is Teté? First because she was as capable as the others. Second, because she had already read some of my novels, she was familiar with my way of writing, and she would be sure to do as I said: when making a copy, she wouldn't add anything or take anything away. . . . Third, I chose Teté because she arrived in a miniskirt. A good representative of modern youth. She was the only one in a miniskirt. Fourth, I chose her because I like her voice. There are voices that leave me literally tired. My Teté has a pleasant voice.

Clarice promised the girl that it would be an ideal job for a student: "The secretary's only with me for a few hours, and has the rest of the time to study, go to class, see her boyfriend." Walcacer remembered it a bit differently: "I don't think she wanted a secretary, exactly, but someone to keep her company, or something like that. She asked me to do all kinds of things, to talk to her, to take her to a friend's house, to read stories to the boys, to take Pedro for a walk on the beach. She also asked me frequently to stay for lunch, or for dinner. She asked too much of me."

The house was in chaos. Maria Teresa, who had imagined a writer working in monastic seclusion, saw something very different. Paulo and Pedro interrupted constantly, the phone rang off the hook, the maid walked around, and Clarice's papers were spread all over the house. "If it had happened now, it certainly would have been a different story. But at the time, what inadequacy, what distance! I was so young, I had a boyfriend, I was in love, so it really wasn't a very attractive option to keep having dinner with that lady and her two rather problematic sons. . . . I also remember Pedro wandering around, with lost eyes. I have a somewhat gloomy memory of the daily life of that house."

In the same interview, Walcacer remembered her surprise at reading Clarice's description of her as perky and relaxed, when in fact she was going through a dark depression. "I was so insecure in front of that woman, that myth. In fact, I don't even think that I was wearing a miniskirt when we first met. That whole description seems a bit made up."

After four months, Maria Teresa fled.

In May 1968, fifteen years after Fernando Sabino had first broached the subject, Clarice began conducting interviews for *Manchete*, the Brazilian answer to *Paris-Match*. It was another prominent podium and raised her national profile. Many of the people she interviewed in "Possible Dialogues with Clarice Lispector" were old friends, such as Erico Verissimo and Alzira Vargas; her "first masculine protector," the mathematician Leopoldo Nachbin; and Hélio Pellegrino, the psychoanalyst who confessed that in another life he would like to be the "husband of Clarice Lispector, to whom I would dedicate myself with velvety and unsleeping dedication."[13]

Clarice told a reporter, "I exposed myself in those interviews and that was how I managed to gain the trust of the people I was interviewing until they exposed themselves. They are more conversations than the classical question-and-answer."[14] Some of the interviews are miracles of candor—on the interviewer's part. But her journalistic work took up so much of her time, and her natural timidity made it difficult. Hélio Pellegrino, noting her discomfort, said, "Clarice, let's just have a steak and a beer. Forget the questions. I'll write the interview."[15]

If *Manchete* brought her respect and a certain celebrity, it also brought humiliations. At the *Jornal do Brasil*, her great admirer Alberto Dines was keenly aware of her difficulties and published everything she sent, exactly as she sent it. "Once she sent in a column that was a single paragraph. And that is how it was published."[16] At *Manchete*, Lêdo Ivo, the poet who had known Clarice since 1944, once witnessed a terrible episode. In rejecting an article of Clarice's, Justino Martins, the magazine's director, suggested that, "in order to be more productive and competent, she ought to update her sexual agenda." The sensitive and discreet Clarice humbly answered, "I can't sleep with anyone, Justino. My whole body is burned."[17]

It was not easy for a woman who only a couple of years before had been beautiful and desirable to adapt to being outmoded. Lygia Marina de Moraes, who became Fernando Sabino's third wife in 1974, remembered her first meeting with Clarice. At a bar in Ipanema, Lygia and a friend struck up a conversation with the legendary Tom Jobim, one of the creators of bossa nova, who invited them to Clarice's house. The girls were stunned at the prospect of meeting, in a single day, Tom Jobim and Clarice Lispector.

"By then she was already CLARICE," remembered Lygia, intimidated to meet the icon. The icon, however, was not amused to see Tom arrive with two attractive young girls. In her "metallic voice," she told Jobim that Vinicius de Moraes, the famous poet and composer, had written a poem for her, and she asked Jobim to do the same. He offered to write some music for her instead, but then, a few minutes later, ended up scrawling a poem for Lygia. Clarice was terribly irritated and hurt.

She stopped trying to hide her wounds. Otto Lara Resende remembered having lunch with her and the writer Antônio Callado. "Suddenly she exploded at me: 'Why are you looking at me? Do you want to see my scars?' And she exhibited the legs that she and we were trying to escape."[18]

33

CULTURAL TERROR

At *Manchete*, though she had license to feature many of her prominent friends, Clarice also had to interview people whom she could not have found very appetizing. In early 1969, these included Yolanda Costa e Silva, wife of General Arthur Costa e Silva, whose reputation as the most disastrous president in Brazilian history has never been seriously challenged. The first lady was known for her devotion to plastic surgery and her habit of hanging around good-looking younger men.

Though Clarice wrote her son Paulo, "[Yolanda] doesn't have what it takes to be a first lady," Clarice could hardly grill her, and the interview is friendly.[1] Setting the tone, Clarice said, "I learned that you worry about the high rate of illiteracy in Brazil." She wondered how it felt to be a grandmother and inquired, perhaps a bit mischievously, about the first lady's "concept of elegance."[2] In a large picture of the two, Yolanda, clearly delighted to be in the magazine, radiates pleasure. A wary Clarice, hiding her burned hand behind a piece of paper, hardly cracks a smile.

Perhaps Yolanda would have been less delighted if she had recalled Clarice's participation in the March of the Hundred Thousand, one of the events that defined Brazil's tumultuous late 1960s. This was a gigantic protest held on June 26, 1968, in downtown Rio de Janeiro. Its target was Yolanda's husband, whose government had taken ever more sinister turns.

The first president following the 1964 military coup, Humberto de Alencar Castello Branco, was in many ways objectionable, not least in the way he arrived in office. He turned a blind eye to torture and illegally, temporarily, closed the Congress, whose president was Lúcio Cardoso's brother, Adauto Lúcio Cardoso.

His term also saw such absurdities as the arrest of Clarice's would-be publisher Ênio Silveira for the crime of hosting a *feijoada* for the deposed governor of Pernambuco.[3]

But at least Castello Branco was not a philistine—he enjoyed the theater—and was personally honorable. He protested the arrest of Silveira, accusing its authors of creating a "cultural terror." Rather than a full-fledged dictatorship, Castello Branco seemed to have imagined for Brazil a system along Mexican lines, in which the ruling party appointed new presidents on a regular schedule. The group—the party in the Mexican case, the military in Brazil—would keep power, but no single dictator could emerge.

When Castello Branco handed power to Costa e Silva in March 1967, all the contradictions inherent in this model came to the surface. Costa e Silva liked to be thought of as an intellectual, though he proudly, and no doubt correctly, claimed that the only books he read were books of crossword puzzles.[4] With his moustache, bemedaled uniform, and mirrored sunglasses, he looked more like a cartoonish Latin American dictator than any previous president of Brazil.

From the beginning of his administration, he sought ways to consolidate the dictatorial power implicit in the post-1964 political structure. Students, who were rioting and protesting everywhere from Paris to Prague, were a special target of the government. The measures taken to repress them appalled Clarice, who went so far as to send an open letter to the minister of education, published on February 25. "Being a student is a very serious matter," she wrote. "It is when ideas form, it is when one thinks the most about how to help Brazil. To the Minister or the President of the Republic: preventing young people from entering universities is a crime. Excuse the violence of the word. But it is the right word."[5]

An apparently innocuous issue set off the final confrontation. Poor students, who were dependent on a subsidized cafeteria known as the Calabouço, or "dungeon," asked for better service. Their protests led to a confrontation with the police on March 29, 1968. An apolitical student named Edson Luis de Lima Souto, seventeen years old, was shot and killed.

The murder shocked the nation, leading inevitably to more student protests and to violent police attacks. These included an attack on mourners attending a memorial mass for Edson Luis inside the gorgeous Candelária Church, where Rio's millionaires married and buried. Clarice Lispector appended a single sentence to her column of April 6: "I am sympathetic, in body and soul, to the tragedy of the students of Brazil."[6]

On June 21, Clarice joined a delegation of notables that called on the governor at Guanabara Palace, the same building Alzira Vargas had defended against the Integralist coup thirty years before. The leading names in Brazilian culture were there: the architect of Brasília, Oscar Niemeyer; the musicians Caetano Veloso, Gilberto Gil, Milton Nascimento, and Nara Leão; the actors Paulo Autran and Tônia Carrero. Hélio Pellegrino had been chosen as the spokesman for the group. He addressed the governor, Francisco Negrão de Lima, "firmly and respectfully, requesting him to stand up for the students.... The tense climate grew as Hélio Pellegrino recalled the latest police violence against the students, despite the governor's promises to the contrary. The governor tried to justify the reaction that a soldier might have if attacked by students.

At that point, the voice of Congressman Márcio Moreira Alves rang out, interrupting the governor and observing that to defend a soldier who had attacked students would be "to authorize the Police to keep gunning down the people." "Clarice Lispector almost fainted," recalled a journalist in attendance. "She had been tense the entire time, dying of fear that her friend Hélio would go too far. Every time the orator seemed to get carried away, Teresa Aragão, standing next to her, heard Clarice say in a prayerful whisper, 'For the love of God, Hélio, calm down.' With that ill-timed outburst, Teresa thought that our brilliant writer was going to have an attack."[7]

Five days later, the full range of Rio society united in protest against the regime's increasing brutality. The March of the Hundred Thousand was blessed by the same conservative cardinal-archbishop of Rio de Janeiro who four years earlier had consecrated the march celebrating the coup. It included 150 priests, sundry congressmen, enraged parents, and a whole contingent of artists.

At its head walked Clarice Lispector, arm in arm with Brazil's leading architects, musicians, writers, and intellectuals. The next day, beneath the headline "MARCH FOR FREEDOM TAKES OVER CITY," Chico Buarque and Clarice Lispector, separated by a battery of nuns, appeared in giant photographs on the front page of *Última Hora*.[8]

A woman who had never been involved in politics found herself a kind of patron saint of the student protests. Carlos Scliar, a painter who had first met Clarice in Naples, described her at these demonstrations as a "guardian... a protecting, generous, worried Jewish mother."[9]

❦

In her final interview, Clarice was asked if writing had any effect on the outside, political world. "It changes nothing," she insisted, again and again. "It changes nothing. I write without the hope that anything I write can change anything at all. It changes nothing."[10]

She had learned the lesson as a child, and she would be brutally reminded of it again in 1968. Soon after the March of the Hundred Thousand, the "cultural terror," of which the first military president had warned, arrived. Groups allied with the Costa e Silva government began by attacking theaters. In Rio, Chico Buarque's show *Roda-Viva* was violently dismantled; in São Paulo thugs forced famous actors to run naked from their dressing rooms and into the streets.[11]

Costa e Silva was looking for any pretext, however preposterous, to claim absolute power. He found it on September 2. Márcio Moreira Alves, the congressman whose fiery declarations in front of the governor of Guanabara had so agitated Clarice, returned to Brasília from São Paulo. There, in one of the theaters not yet shut down, he had seen Aristophanes's *Lysistrata*.

In a speech before Congress, Alves suggested that, in order to bring about the restoration of democracy, the wives and girlfriends of soldiers ought to follow the example of the Greek women who withheld sex from their husbands and thereby ended the Peloponnesian War. The speech garnered absolutely no notice and would have been instantly forgotten but for the government's determination to make an example of the congressman.[12]

With the honor of the armed forces at stake, Costa e Silva issued Institutional Act Number Five on December 13, 1968. The Act ordered the indefinite recess of the National Congress; declared a state of siege; allowed the president to govern by decree; suspended the rights of habeas corpus and free assembly; established "previous censorship" in the press, music, theater, and cinema; and banned from public life dozens of politicians, diplomats, and judges.

The AI-5, as it became known, was an assault on the rule of law never before contemplated, not even during Getúlio Vargas's Estado Novo, in the century and a half since Brazil gained its independence. Torture was institutionalized. Many of the nation's leading cultural and political figures were attacked. Clarice's friends Paulo Francis and Ferreira Gullar were immediately arrested,[13] as Chico Buarque would soon be; Caetano Veloso and Gilberto Gil were forced into exile. (In protest, the launch party for *The Woman Who Killed the Fish*, scheduled for the seventeenth, was canceled.)[14]

The day after the AI-5 was issued, Alberto Dines at the *Jornal do Brasil* concocted one of the front pages for which he would become famous. "Yesterday was the Day of the Blind," the paper noted, top right. Two censored articles on the front page were ostentatiously substituted by classified ads. The weather report, top left, read: "Black weather. Suffocating temperature. The air is unbreathable. The country is being swept by strong winds."[15]

On June 15, when there was still some hope that the protests and petitions might have some positive effect, Clarice wrote in her column, "As time goes by, especially in the last few years, I've lost the knack of being a person. I no longer know how one is supposed to be. And an entirely new kind of 'solitude of not belonging' started invading me like ivy on a wall."[16]

To escape her solitude, Clarice began reaching out to friends. Still unable to sleep, awake at all hours, she telephoned in the middle of the night, sometimes to confess terrible agonies, sometimes just to talk. In her heartbreaking and beautiful elegy for her sister, Elisa Lispector remembered these phone calls: "Today, to punish myself, I remember the impatience with which I answered the phone when you woke me up before dawn, just to chat—I didn't know that you were going to die, that is my only excuse, because, before you died, death did not really exist."[17]

The writer Affonso Romano de Sant'Anna and his wife, Marina Colasanti, Clarice's editor at the *Jornal do Brasil*, also got desperate calls from Clarice. "I still remember," Sant'Anna wrote, "that one day she called to say that she was completely lost. She no longer knew how to write.... Perplexed, unsure what to say, I made an excuse: 'Who am I, Clarice, to give you advice?'" Sant'Anna later learned that she asked the same question of Renaud, Rio's swankiest hairdresser, whose salon was in the Copacabana Palace.[18]

Clarice's further attempts at finding a life for herself were just as awkward as her ringing people up in the middle of the night. In Rio de Janeiro to this day, anecdotes of Clarice's social eccentricities abound. Once, Affonso and Marina were giving a dinner party and learned that Clarice wanted to be invited. Marina was thrilled, since she very rarely went out. At the appointed hour, Affonso went to pick up the famous writer and bring her to their house. She arrived, looking "imperial," walked into the living room and chatted awkwardly for a few minutes with the other guests. In the kitchen, she told Marina that she had a headache and had to leave immediately. Affonso drove her home.

It was not easier when she did stay. One host at a dinner party made borscht as a salute to her "Slavic origins." She took a spoonful and exclaimed that it was delicious. She didn't eat any more, though everyone pretended not to notice. She then proceeded to turn down drinks (she took sleeping pills), dessert (she was on a diet), coffee (she suffered from chronic insomnia). When she left at ten-thirty, the host wrote, "I felt I had survived once again."[19]

Even those who loved her best found her exhausting. She evoked a sense of protection in others, an urge to help her through her great suffering, though her friends make it clear she never asked for anything. "It was more a feeling she aroused in you," Rosa Cass said. And Clarice's neediness was draining. Tati de

Moraes, the first of Vinicius de Moraes's nine wives, once asked Rosa, "How long have you been friends with Clarice? Because nobody can stand it for long."[20]

If she was radically independent artistically and intellectually, emotionally she was as dependent as a child. In Clarice's private notebooks she recorded her difficulty in connecting with other people: "I wondered if I didn't avoid getting close to people out of fear of later coming to hate them. I get along badly with everyone. I have no tolerance. She told me . . . that I am someone to whom it is difficult to give affection. I answered: well, I'm not the type who inspires affection. She: you almost push away the hand people stretch out to help you. Sometimes, you need help, but you don't ask for it."[21] Clarice does not name the woman with whom she was having this conversation, but the tone of the conversation suggests a therapist, either Inês Besouchet or the woman she began seeing at the beginning of 1968, Anna Kattrin Kemper, known as Catarina. Kemper was a German friend of both Inês Besouchet and Hélio Pellegrino and had come to Rio de Janeiro after the war.

Clarice was ashamed of, or felt awkward about, her analysis and did not want it to become public knowledge. In June 1968, in a letter to Marly de Oliveira —a fellow diplomatic spouse who had become close to Clarice when, in the early 1960s, she published a long series of articles examining and attacking some critics' readings of Clarice's work, and who in 1968 also published a long poem in Clarice's honor, *The Gentle Panther*[22]—she asked her friend not to mention that she was seeing Kemper. At the same time, the letter also suggests that she never told Marly about the years she had spent with Inês Besouchet:

> I'm having a lot of difficulty with my novel: it's the first one I've talked to other people about, and it's the first whose ending I know in advance. There's still the shadow of *The Passion According to G. H.*: after that book I have the unpleasant impression that people expect something better from me. But I'm struggling against this nascent depression trying to find a better way to work and also leaning on Catarina (never tell anyone about my analysis: I wrote all my books before Catarina, except *The Mystery of the Thinking Rabbit*, which had been written since I was six anyway; so it's easy to explain me by saying that I write this way because of analysis. Eliane Zagury was one of the people who asked me if I am or have been in analysis, I denied it, and she said it was because my books have the profundity that is only attained in analysis).[23]

As Clarice was trying, however painfully and incompletely, to reach out to the world, her first love, the hero of her adolescence, Lúcio Cardoso, was dying, six years after his paralyzing stroke. After her accident, Clarice had met her friend in the hospital, where both of them were receiving therapy. "We fell into each others' arms."[24]

Nursed by his sister Maria Helena, Lúcio had become a talented painter, using only his left hand, though he never regained his ability to write. In the eloquent memoir Maria Helena published at Clarice's suggestion, she records his painful, fitful, exhausting progress, until, near the end, he finally managed to start writing again. Even his shortest notes gave them great hope.

"Can be 100 years—I have in the spirit young—life, happiness, everything!" he scrawled. "I, writer by fate." "I looked at him with great affection and admiration. God had tried him in the cruelest way yet he had more happiness and love in his heart than sadness and bitterness. The dark days passed quickly, followed by light, much light." After saying it for years in order to keep up his spirits, Maria Helena could finally exclaim, this time with conviction, "Darling, the day is not far off when you will be able to write novels again."[25]

The end soon followed, on September 22, 1968. When he was already in a coma, Clarice visited him. "I didn't go to the wake, nor to the funeral, nor to the mass because there was too much silence within me. In those days I was alone, I couldn't see people: I had seen death."[26]

34

"I HUMANIZED MYSELF"

Despite her physical handicaps, political disappointments, and personal bereavements, Clarice intensified her attempts to engage in the world, to rediscover "the knack of being a person," throughout 1968. Part of that process was *An Apprenticeship or The Book of Pleasures*, written in 1968 and published in the middle of the next year. She sometimes claimed to be unsatisfied with the result. "If the book is any good?" she wrote her son Paulo. "I think it's detestable and badly done, but the people who read it thought it was good."[1]

Though a best-seller when it was published, *An Apprenticeship* is now something of an orphan. Even some of her most sympathetic critics have gone so far as to accuse it of superficiality and flippancy, words that ought to give pause when used in connection with Clarice Lispector.[2] Perhaps some of this distaste is chronological: the book appeared between the summits of *The Passion According to G. H.* and the subsequent *Água viva*.

There is no question that *An Apprenticeship* requires a different kind of reading than Clarice's metaphysical works. She knew that *The Passion According to G. H.* would be a hard act to follow, as she noted in her letter to Marly de Oliveira. Indeed, artistically, that thunderous work would be difficult for any writer to surpass. But Clarice's project had never been primarily aesthetic. It was, as Martin said in *The Apple in the Dark*, "the reconstruction of the world."

So if *An Apprenticeship* lacks the titanic monumentality that readers of *The Apple in the Dark* and *The Passion According to G. H.* had come to associate with Clarice Lispector, its accessible language and its apparently banal love story mask a battle as fierce as any Clarice had ever waged. It records, quite literally, a struggle between life and death, between lucidity and madness, giving a rich and ambiguous answer to the question that *G. H.* begs.

Clarice's quest to identify with the inhuman world of "the God" reached a climax when G. H. placed the roach in her mouth. The moment was not only the climax of that great novel. It was the climax of a spiritual and artistic search that Clarice had been tracing for at least two decades, since *Near to the Wild Heart.* When the roach touches G. H.'s tongue, Clarice's original artistic project has finally been exhausted.

The book is so shocking and extreme that the reader almost fears for its author. Where could a person possibly go from there? The experience left only two possibilities. She could continue down that radical mystical path, which would mean madness, "in human terms, the infernal," "passing over definitively to the *other side* of life." In her newspaper column, Clarice wrote about the "great sacrifice of not being mad," a temptation she felt but nonetheless rejected. "I am not mad out of solidarity with the thousands of us who, in order to construct the possible, also sacrificed the truth which would be a madness."[3]

The other possibility was a return to the human world. After eating the roach, G. H., too, knows she has to reject the truth she found within it. At the end of the book, she announces plans to ring up her friends, put on a nice dress, and go out dancing. It is an explicit choice for the human over the divine, and it is the same choice Clarice made when composing *An Apprenticeship or The Book of Pleasures.* When it came out, an interviewer said, "I thought *The Book of Pleasures* was much easier to read than any of your other seven books. Do you think there's any basis for that?" Clarice answered, "There is. I humanized myself, the book reflects that."[4]

Coming from anybody else, this statement might seem enigmatic, or even incomprehensible. For Clarice Lispector, however, the desire to humanize herself represented a complete revolution, philosophically and spiritually. "A being's most pressing need was to become a human being," she wrote at the beginning of *An Apprenticeship or The Book of Pleasures.*[5]

This is such an explicit repudiation of so much of her previous work that it comes as a great surprise. It is the morality, "the effort to elevate human life, to give it a human value," that Clarice had so often, and so eloquently, rejected.[6] After so many years of searching for the impersonal, inhuman, divine life, the effort to "become a human being" could only be excruciating. In an important sense, it meant the negation of most of her oeuvre.

So it is not surprising that, upon the publication of *An Apprenticeship*, Clarice announced that she would not write again. "Why?" the interviewer asked. "What a question!" Clarice exclaimed. "Because it hurts so much."[7]

❧

"she was tired of the effort of the liberated animal," Clarice wrote at the beginning of *An Apprenticeship*, with the unorthodox capitalization and punctuation that characterizes it in parts.[8] It was one thing for an animal, or for Joana, to mate and then move on, but for a person to place freedom above all else was another matter. A person simply cannot survive without giving up a bit of freedom and accepting the necessary ties that bind her to others. For Clarice, that meant human love.

Love—her filial love for her parents; her maternal love for her ill son, Pedro; her erotic love for Lúcio and Maury and Paulinho—had so often brought her heartbreak, and she was wary of new ties. When her friend Sérgio Porto died within days of Lúcio Cardoso, she wrote, "No, I don't want to love anyone else because it hurts. I can't stand one more death of a person dear to me. My world is made of people who are mine—and I cannot lose them without losing myself."[9]

Maury understood her fear, if only once it was too late. In his letter attempting reconciliation, he wrote, "I wasn't mature enough to understand that, in Joana or in Clarice, 'hate can transform itself into love'; not being more than 'a search for love.' I didn't know how to free you from the 'fear of not loving.' "

An Apprenticeship is an attempt at another kind of freedom. Clarice had to escape the fear of not loving, as well as her fear that love was futile. "It's obvious that my love for the world never prevented wars and deaths," she wrote on March 9, 1968, perhaps thinking of her mother. "Love never kept me from crying tears of blood inside me. Nor did it prevent mortal separations."[10] But if she feared new wounds, she also knew that eating roaches in the maid's room would not help an actual person in an actual world overcome an immediate and desperate solitude.

For that, there was only human love, however imperfect and potentially disappointing. *An Apprenticeship* is accordingly a love story. It tells of a woman, Lori, gradually and meticulously shedding her isolation in order to learn how to love a man. Clarice explicitly links Lori's struggle to the political struggles of 1968. "Everyone was fighting for liberty—that was what she saw in the newspapers, and she rejoiced that finally they were no longer standing for injustice," she writes, before quoting a long song of freedom from Czechoslovakia.[11] There, as in Brazil, popular hopes of liberation would soon be crushed.

Lori's idea of freedom is not Joana's. In *Near to the Wild Heart*, which Clarice wrote shortly before embarking on her own failed marriage, as in stories such as "Obsession," in which she mocks Cristina's desire to "marry, have children, and, finally, be happy," Clarice is radically skeptical about the possibility of union between two people. So often in her work the isolation of the individual is absolute, the gap between people unbridgeable.

An Apprenticeship is Clarice's attempt to discover just how two people might be joined. Lori's is not an easy journey, and consequently the book is roughly written, lurching, sometimes giving the impression of an incomplete first draft. The formal perfection of *G. H.* has been swept away, though not its emotional charge: it contains some of the most moving and beautiful passages Clarice ever wrote.

It is the only one of Clarice's books that employs avant-garde devices in punctuation; it famously begins with a comma and ends with a colon. Words are not properly capitalized. One page reads "Luminescence..." and nothing else. The book advertises its own incompleteness, reflecting, on the page, the hesitations and doubts of the search it describes. As she had in *Near to the Wild Heart*, Clarice achieves, in *An Apprenticeship*, "the precious and precise harmony between expression and substance."

Like all of Clarice's works, *An Apprenticeship* has a strong autobiographical element, though unlike *G. H.* it is not written in the first person. But the "I" is hiding just below the surface. Clarice transformed long passages published in the *Jornal do Brasil* into this fiction, often doing little more than switching the "I" for "she." On May 18, 1968, for example, she wrote in the newspaper, "Tomorrow I will probably have some happiness, also without great ecstasies, and that isn't bad either. But I'm not really enjoying this pact with the mediocrity of living." In *An Apprenticeship*, this became "The next day she would probably have some happiness, also without great ecstasies, just a bit of happiness, and that wouldn't be bad either. That was how she tried to make peace with the mediocrity of living."[12]

The word "Clarice" hid within "Lucrécia," and the first and the last two letters of "Lispector" lurk inside the odd and improbable name of the protagonist, Lori, short for Loreley, who hints at a hidden name: "Pretend that she was lying in the transparent palm of the hand of God, not Lori but the secret name that for the time being she still could not enjoy."[13]

Lori is a childless schoolteacher who lives alone, but other than that she and Clarice have much in common. Like Clarice, Lori has spent long periods abroad, particularly in Paris and Bern. Her face is compared to the Sphinx: "Decipher me or I shall devour you." Her makeup is a bit too much. She suffers from paralyzing social anxiety: "It seemed to her that the tortures of a timid person had never been completely described—in the moving taxi she was dying a bit."[14] She takes pills to sleep; she consults fortunetellers; her mother is dead.

Her potential lover is Ulisses, a professor of philosophy. Though some critics supposed the name referred to Homer or Joyce, Clarice stated that Ulisses was "a philosophy teacher I met in Switzerland."[15] This is the reappearance of the mysterious Ulysses Girsoler, who was so in love with the young Clarice that he had to move to a different city. Could *An Apprenticeship* mask Clarice's regret at not having seized that chance at love? Did she wonder if it might have turned out more happily than her loves for Lúcio Cardoso, Maury Gurgel Valente, or Paulo Mendes Campos? In Switzerland she was, of course, married, but Ulysses was always on her mind, even decades after she left Bern. She gave his name to this character, and a few years later she named her dog Ulisses, too.

This figure has annoyed some readers. Even Fernando Sabino, who confessed himself "stunned" by the book—"I no longer deserve to be your reader. You have gone too far for me"—was puzzled by him. "Who is that man? What is he saying? Why is he so pedantic and professorial? What's his problem?"[16]

Ulisses has taken upon himself the task of educating Lori for love. He does have a rather finicky tone, like Girsoler's in the Rorschach he wrote up for Clarice. He speaks in parables and essays with an air of all-knowingness and superiority, which, together with Lori's often meek girlishness, have disconcerted Clarice's feminist readers: "This didactic sense of mine, which is a desire to transmit, I also have it with you, Lori, even though you are my worst student."[17]

Yet Clarice must have felt understood by Girsoler, whose description of her character is very accurate, even premonitory, notwithstanding its wooden language. Lori, too, feels that Ulisses, despite his "pedantic and professorial" tone, understands her. They meet on a street corner, where she is waiting for a taxi, and he desires her physically. But her notion of love is pure and absolute, different from his humanity. "Through her serious defects—which one day she might be able to mention without boasting—she had now arrived at being able to love. Even that glorification: she loved the Nothing. The awareness of her permanent human fall had led her to the love of Nothing."[18]

Over the course of the book, this pure philosophical love gradually makes way for a more human communion, emotional and, finally, carnal. Ulisses patiently trains Lori for their ultimate sexual encounter in a courtship that, like therapy sessions, takes the form of scheduled meetings, which Lori may or may not cancel. Like a therapist, Ulisses is neither offended nor surprised by her caprices, patiently trying to awaken her to the wonders of the world.

> "But in your travels it's impossible for you never to have been among orange trees, sun, and flowers with bees. Not only the dark cold but also the rest?"
>
> "No," she said solemnly. "Those things are not for me. I am a big city woman."
>
> "First of all, Campos is not what I would call a big city. And anyway those things, as symbols are for everyone. That is why you never learned to have them."
>
> "And that can be learned? Orange trees, sun, and bees on flowers?"
>
> "It can be learned when one no longer has as a strong guide one's own nature. Lori, Lori, listen: one can learn anything, even how to love! And the strangest thing of all, Lori, you can learn to have joy!"[19]

Lori's skepticism in the face of this is understandable. But though she sometimes cancels their meetings and plays little games with Ulisses, she never spurns or mocks his advice, so desperate is she to liberate herself from her loneliness and rejoin the human world. The "strong guide" of her own nature has failed her, leading her only to isolation. "Your advice. But there is a great, the biggest obstacle for me to move ahead: me myself. I have been the biggest difficulty along my path. It is with enormous effort that I manage to impose myself upon myself. . . . I am an insurmountable mountain along my own path. But sometimes with a word of yours or a word I read, suddenly everything becomes clear."[20]

It would be a mistake to see Lori's desire to submit to this man primarily in the terms of gender dynamics, though the book certainly begs the question. ("It was a freedom that he was offering her. Yet she would have rather he ordered her around, setting a date and a time.") This is not a coquettish pose. She needs help, and she feels that in Ulisses she has an ally: "Lori put up with the struggle because Ulisses, in his struggle with her, was not her adversary: he was struggling for her."[21]

Ever since her mother's death, Clarice's awareness of her own inadequacy and failure had been one of the strongest aspects of her character. "When I speak of *humility,*" she wrote in October 1969, "I don't mean humility in the Christian sense (as an ideal that can be reached or not); I mean the humility that comes from the full awareness of being truly unable."[22]

❦

In an ironic echo of *The Passion According to G. H.*, Ulisses says to Lori, "Your mouth, as I have told you, is passionate. It is through your mouth that you will come to eat the world." In *An Apprenticeship*, no less than in *G. H.*, the heroine makes contact with the world orally. This was a favorite theme of Clarice's. Lori teaches her pupils something that recalls Virginia's discoveries. "She wanted them to know... that the taste of a fruit is in the contact of the fruit with the palate and not in the fruit itself."[23]

The Portuguese verb *comer* means to eat, and in Brazil it is also common slang for fucking, a meaning Clarice suggests in these final chapters. Eating leads to sex, *comer* to *comer*. Lori's redemption begins when she bites an apple—unlike a roach this is a food a person is allowed—and culminates when she finally goes to bed with Ulisses.

The Fall Lori's apple triggers is nothing like the dry horror that greets G. H. in the maid's room, when, in supreme isolation, all human qualities melt away. Lori leaves the divine perfection of that state and falls into her humanity, a state of grace, "light, so light," that for Lori means profound pleasure in herself and the world.

"One who is capable of intense suffering can also be capable of intense joy," Ulisses had told her, and in this state she discovers an "exalted physical happiness with which nothing could be compared. The body was transformed into a gift. And she felt that it was a gift because she was feeling, from a direct source, the indubitable blessing of existing materially." G. H.'s state of grace made her less human; Lori's makes her more. "She had experienced something that seemed to redeem the human condition, though at the same time it accentuated the narrow limits of that condition. And exactly because after grace the human condition revealed itself in all its imploring poverty, one learned to love more, to hope more. One began to have a kind of trust in suffering and in its ways that were so often intolerable."[24]

❦

As Lori becomes more human, she is also tempted to humanize God. For the first time Clarice lets a character invest a God with human attributes, as when

Lori prays that "the God" will "relieve my soul, make me feel that Thy hand is holding mine."[25] The hand recalls the hand G. H. invented to accompany her as she told what happened in the maid's room. It also recalls the gesture Clarice mentioned in her unpublished notes: "I want somebody to hold my hand (That was how Papa, when I was hurting, helped me stand the pain)."

Has Clarice started to think of God as a comforting father figure? Surely not. But the desire to submit to a superior guiding presence animates *An Apprenticeship*. Ulisses is as much father or therapist as lover. Lori needs someone above her, some kind of mediation between herself and "a God so vast that he was the world with its galaxies."[26] Having abandoned the religion of her childhood, determined to seek strength and guidance from herself alone, she is worn out by her hard-won independence, "tired of the effort of the liberated animal."

In her utter abandonment, Lori even equates herself with the most famous of humanized gods: "Christ was Christ for others, but who? Who was Christ for Christ?" Loving God's "impersonal vastness and without even wanting him to exist" is not enough for a person requiring urgent and immediate assistance. But the consoling lie of a Christ-like god is impossible for Lori, who "violently rejected a God to whom one could appeal. But she also didn't want to appeal: she was lost and confused."[27]

It is remarkable how rarely in Clarice's work sex has any emotional content, any meaning beside the purely animal: Joana and Martin, among others, see it as a physical satisfaction, never a remedy for their emotional isolation. Through sex, Lori learns to be emotionally intimate with another human being, without renouncing her animal physicality. Lori's answer comes when she finally goes to bed with Ulisses, one of Clarice's rare happy endings.

The physical union of two people is a perfect solution to Lori's previously irremediable solitude. "After Ulisses had been hers, being human seemed now to be the best way of being a living animal." In the final two paragraphs of the book, which ends with a colon, Lori has abandoned the quest for a humanized god. Instead she finds a deified human.[28]

> My love, you don't believe in the God because we erred by humanizing Him. We humanized Him because we don't understand Him, so it didn't work. I am sure that He is not human. But even though He is not human, He still sometimes makes us divine. You think that—
>
> I think—the man interrupted and his voice was slow and muffled because he was suffering from life and love—this is what I think:

35

MONSTRE SACRÉ

Alas, finding solutions to real problems in the real world was even harder for Clarice than finding solutions in her books. Lori's answer to her isolation turned out to be as theoretical a response as *G. H.* had been. With her burned body and her difficulties connecting to people outside of her writing, Clarice still struggled to discover the "knack of being a person."

Her struggles with her ill son, Pedro, had grown more acute. He was almost twenty-one when *An Apprenticeship* appeared, a grown man, and as he grew older his schizophrenia had taken deeper root. During the first half of 1969, Paulo was an exchange student in Warsaw, Indiana, and her letters to him offer rare glimpses of Pedro's condition. He suddenly developed a fear of going to the movies. In June, she had to commit him to a clinic: "He went and he's still there but it seems he'll leave on the 30th of this month. He's much better. I visit him often. Today, Sunday, I took him to lunch.... Don't worry: it's a comfortable treatment center, with a bar where you can eat sandwiches and drink sodas."[1]

The effect of all this was not emboldening. "Pedro isn't well at all and that takes away my joy in life," she wrote Paulo. Her own health, fragile since the accident, suffered. "Today I had a real hysterical crisis and when he saw it Pedro said: I'm going to call Daddy. Your father doesn't have the slightest notion of what's going on here."[2]

Maury did, of course, know what was going on. He and Pedro had not lived under the same roof for a decade, but the boys often visited their father and Pedro's condition was evident even to casual observers. Still, Clarice generally avoided the painful subject.

Even a person in much better shape than Clarice would have had a hard time dealing with a son so far gone. "Today Pedro went to have lunch with your father, luckily. I was literally getting sick with Pedro over the last few days, since now he stands in front of me or follows me around saying literally without stopping: mother, mother, mother."[3]

Despite all this, Clarice had not given up on Pedro. As she wrote Paulo, "Hope is the last thing that dies."[4] A manuscript she wrote a year or so later suggests that her hope for Pedro was still alive: "The madness of the creators is different from the madness of the mentally ill. They—for some reason of which I am not aware erred along their paths. They are cases for the comprehensive and tough intelligent doctor—whereas creators find fulfillment in the act of madness itself. I know a 'he' who will soon be cured."[5]

Around the time that she was writing *An Apprenticeship*, Clarice found her own father figure, though their relationship lacked the sexual component that brought Lori into harmony with the world. For some reason, her analysis with the German Catarina Kemper had not lasted, and she became a patient of a Jewish psychiatrist named Jacob David Azulay. She would see Azulay five days a week, for an hour each day, "without ever being late or missing a single session," for a total of six years.[6]

During these meetings, Azulay remembered, Clarice played with her own writing, "citing passages, and constructing her books during our sessions." He jotted down some of her phrases, which do indeed sound like phrases in her books. "I am nothing," she said, for example. "I feel like those insects who shed their skin. Now I lost the skin. The name of that skin is Clarice Lispector."

She had, Azulay could not help but notice, "an enormous maternal and paternal deficit."

> She was a rough diamond, wild. She had no method. Clarice happened like a volcanic eruption. That little girl who came from down there... As if a volcano had exploded and she had come along with it! Part of her was so childish. She had a fear, a youngest daughter's respect for her sisters... I think that she didn't allow herself to go further in her writing, in erotic matters for example, because of a very large super-ego. I think her sisters, mainly, acted as a very apparent super-ego.

Clarice had always been very close to her sisters, especially to Tania, to whom she was closer in age. Elisa, however, may have been surprised to learn how much respect—and even, apparently, awe—Clarice had for her. By the end of the 1960s, Elisa was herself an established writer. In 1962, with Clarice's encouragement, she had entered a contest sponsored by the publisher José Olympio, and the novel she submitted, *The Stone Wall*, won first prize out of 119 entries. It was also later distinguished with a prize from the Brazilian Academy of Letters.[7] In 1965, *Thereza's Longest Day* was published.[8]

Elisa had a very respectable reputation, though she lacked her youngest sister's genius and, consequently, never enjoyed her fame. She was painfully aware of her inferiority, which only reinforced the self-image that comes across so brutally in all her writings: of a solitary woman, unimportant, unloved, utterly alone. "I have heard," she wrote in her fictionalized memoir of Clarice, "that when a person is not loved by anyone, not even by an animal, by a cat, for example, or a dog, that person becomes dry and tough. Well, I was slowly transformed into a woman of straw."[9]

Her solitude was, to some extent, self-imposed. Many people were fond of Elisa. One friend, the novelist Maria Alice Barroso, remembered that Elisa avoided discussing personal matters, preferring to talk about literature. She called Maria Alice frequently, but when it came to face-to-face visits she tended to become reclusive. "She *cultivated* that solitude," Barroso said. "You had to force her to accept invitations. She always talked about not feeling well. She was pessimistic." Still, Barroso knew that her friendship was important to Elisa and that her standoffishness came out of shyness and insecurity rather than unsociability.

Azulay's recollection of Clarice's "enormous maternal and paternal deficit" and her deep respect for, and even fear of, her older sisters is interesting in this light. Despite Clarice's almost religious veneration of Tania and Elisa, a reader of her book about Clarice cannot escape the impression that part of Elisa felt estranged from, inferior to, and unloved by her youngest sister. And Elisa noted the same behaviors in Clarice—the unreachability, the unsociability—that other people regretted in Elisa.

The horrors of their childhood had alienated them from the world of others, and the pogroms of Podolia cast a long shadow, even half a century on. First among them was a terrible difficulty in connecting to other people. "Surviving means not knowing what to do with oneself," Elisa had once written, recalling Clarice's poignant statement, in a letter from Switzerland to her sisters: "There isn't *really* a place one can live. It's all somebody else's country, where other people are happy."

Their letters from Clarice's years abroad suggest that it was Elisa, whom Clarice called by the Portuguese diminutive, Leinha, of her Hebrew name, Leah, who had moved away from Clarice. Clarice was no stranger to depression, of course, but in her letters to her sisters she was just as often exorbitantly loving and enthusiastic. Elisa's tremendous insecurity can be gauged from Clarice's responses to her. "But, darling, why are you so pessimistic?" she asked from Rome, already in 1945. "My little Elisa, it makes me suffer to see you like this, it makes me suffer to hear you say bad things about yourself, it humiliates me, it makes me suffer. Even saying that you don't like Leda's article, you make so many excuses for yourself. A dumb article, empty and pretentious. And about the lava [that Clarice had sent her from Vesuvius], 'I'm all the more sorry that I can't match such kindnesses.' But darling, you seem to suffer from the love one gives you."[10]

In February 1947, Clarice was complaining to Tania that "Elisa's letters to me are getting shorter and shorter and with less in them. And when she says anything, she usually adds, as in the most recent letter: 'but you'd say that none of that has anything to do with you.' As if it were possible for me not to have anything to do with your lives."[11]

Later that same year, still in Bern, Clarice offered Tania some advice about the exhaustion she was suffering, making explicit the connection between the sisters' problems and their early years. Tania seemed to have been wearing herself out with worries about her young daughter Marcia. "Listen, little darling, you might be trying to make up for the fact that we have the idea that we didn't do everything we could have for Mama. What I said is that you somehow seem to be wanting to <u>sacrifice yourself</u>—and that's the same thing that happens, in another area, with Elisa. Realize, darling, you now want to do a thousand things, to dedicate yourself terribly to the house and to Marcia, to <u>make up for</u>, not only the idea that you didn't do enough before, but to make up for the fact that when we were little, we didn't get, because of the way things were, all the attention we needed."[12]

When Clarice was living in the United States Tania came to visit, and in 1956 a visit from Elisa was so immanent that Clarice could write, "Elisa, dear, we're all eager for you to arrive, I'm even trying not to think about it so I don't get too excited. Paulo got jealous. When I said you were coming, he was very happy. But I added: she's my sister. He, after a pause, said: don't say that or I'll cry. I think he wants an aunt, but one that has nothing to do with me."[13] For some reason, the trip kept getting put off and ended up never happening at all.

Much less than Elisa, though, who lived alone and who never married or had children, Clarice's solitude was not due to a lack of company. As Maria Teresa Walcacer noticed during her four months' employment, Clarice was surrounded by people. There were her two sons, first of all. And like all middle-class Brazilians, Clarice had live-in servants. Despite her frequent complaints of poverty, she had quite a collection. She grew close to many of them and they featured prominently in her writings, from the absent black maid of *G. H.* to the women she described in her letters and journalistic anecdotes:

> The cook is Jandira. But this one is powerful. So powerful that she is clairvoyant. One of my sisters was visiting me. Jandira came into the living room, looked at her seriously and suddenly said: "The journey you are thinking about taking will come to pass, and you are going through a very happy period in your life." And she left the room. My sister looked at me in fright. A bit embarrassed, I made a gesture with my hands that signified that there was nothing I could do about it and explained: "It's that she's clairvoyant." My sister answered calmly: "Fine. Everyone gets the maid they deserve."[14]

Another presence in her home was Siléa Marchi, who, because of her nursing experience, had been hired to help Clarice after her accident and would remain with her until her death. Siléa was the all-purpose companion Clarice required and that Maria Teresa Walcacer could not be. Siléa slept in the house from Monday to Friday and was available to take Clarice to the doctor and to help with Pedro, as well as doing Clarice's shopping and anything else that needed doing.

At the end of 1970, the household acquired a new member, Olga Borelli, who would become the key figure in the last years of Clarice's life and whose tireless dedication and intellectual affinity facilitated the creation of Clarice's great final works. The writer, with her "enormous maternal and paternal deficit," found in Olga the last of her mother figures, and the childless Olga, who seems to have spent much of her life in search of a charitable mission, found in Clarice a project worthy of her colossal devotion.

Olga was one of the many people who, moved by her writings, sought out Clarice in those years. In one of her newspaper columns, Clarice mentioned her perplexity at the outpourings of affection she received. "I'm going to call Elsie [Lessa], who's been writing columns for longer than I have, to ask her what to do with the marvelous phone calls I get, with the roses pungent with such beauty that people send me, with the simple and profound letters that people send me."[15]

While she was reading *The Passion According to G. H.*, Olga caught a glimpse of the writer on television. She had the strange sensation that she had known her for years, and decided to seek her out. She rang to ask Clarice to participate in a fundraiser for the Fundação Romão Duarte, where Olga was a volunteer. As it so happened, this was the same orphanage Clarice had visited in 1941, at the very beginning of her journalistic career, when she wrote a long piece about the institution's two-hundredth anniversary.[16] Three decades later, she would return to autograph her two children's books for the residents of the orphanage.

The two women had a chance to talk. "Her bearing," Olga remembered of this first meeting, "had something of the humility of a peasant mixed with the hauteur of a queen." Two days later, Olga received a summons to Clarice's home, where the writer handed her a letter.

> 11-12-70. Olga, I'm typing this letter because my handwriting is awful.
>
> I have found a new friend. Which is too bad for you. I am an insecure, indecisive, directionless, rudderless person: the truth is I don't know what to do with myself. I am a very fearful person. I have very serious real problems that I will tell you about later. And other problems, with my personality. Do you want to be my friend despite all that?
>
> If you do, don't say I didn't warn you. I don't have qualities, only fragilities. But sometimes... sometimes I have hope. The passage from life to death frightens me: it's like passing from hate which has an objective and is limited, to love which is limitless. When I die (as a matter of speaking) I hope you will be near. You seemed to me to be a person of enormous sensitivity, but strong.
>
> You were my best birthday present. Because on Thursday the 10th it was my birthday and you gave me a little baby Jesus who looks like a happy child playing in his rough cradle. Even though, without knowing it, you gave me a birthday present, I still think my birthday present was you yourself appearing, at a difficult time, of great solitude.
>
> We need to talk. It so happens that I thought that nothing was any use any more. Then I saw an ad for a perfume by Coty, called Unexpected. The perfume is cheap. But it helped me remember that good unexpected things happen too. And whenever I'm discouraged, I put on Unexpected. It gives me luck. You, for example, were not expected. And I unexpectedly accepted an afternoon signing books.
>
> Yours, Clarice[17]

Olga, who, by a magical coincidence, would indeed be nearby when Clarice died, was the daughter of Italian immigrants and she had been a nun. She spent years throwing herself with tremendous energy and enthusiasm into various charitable efforts, working with Peace Corps volunteers, teaching sewing classes in slums, volunteering at the orphanage, giving workshops on communication, and starting various organizations that promoted theater and dance. But her greatest project, one might even say her legacy, was Clarice Lispector, to whom she dedicated herself completely.

Her possessiveness alienated many of Clarice's oldest friends, but even they recognized that Olga's unstinting commitment was a godsend for a progressively weakening Clarice. She acted as a kind of ambassadress between the writer and the outside world. "When I met Clarice," Olga remembered after her friend's death, "I saw the great solitude in which she lived, as a person and as a writer within Brazilian literature. It was as if I said to the world: Look at this marvelous person that you don't know about. Because at that time she was absolutely, absolutely dysfunctional socially. Nobody sought out Clarice, there was little discussion of her work."[18]

This was the kind of thing that annoyed Clarice's many friends and admirers, who did not need Olga to remind them of Clarice Lispector "as a person and as a writer." She was far from forgotten by the public and was surrounded by people who cared a great deal about her. But in a broader sense Borelli was, of course, correct. The same friends attest that Clarice had a harder and harder time functioning normally and badly needed help.

Around this time it became increasingly common to refer to Clarice Lispector as a *monstre sacré*, a person whose combination of genius and oddity placed her somehow outside normal human society. The epithet pained her terribly. "Suddenly I discover that I am becoming for them [her readers] a sacred monster," she told an interviewer.[19] To another, she expressed her "horror at the *monstre sacré*."[20] "One of the things that makes me unhappy is this story about the sacred monster: others fear me for no reason, and I end up fearing myself. The truth is that other people created a myth around me, which trips me up a great deal: it scares people off and I end up alone. But you know that I am very easy to get along with, even if my soul is complex."[21]

Yet there is no question that this was how many people saw her: weird, mysterious, and difficult, an unknowable mystical genius far above, and outside, the common run of humanity. The reputation isolated her just at the time that she most needed help. "Christ was Christ for others, but who? Who was Christ for Christ?" she had wondered in *An Apprenticeship*. The ex-nun arrived just as Clarice was desperate for a savior.

36

THE STORY OF INSTANTS THAT FLEE

Unlike Lori, Clarice would not have another sexual relationship. In the final years of her life, her close relationships would be either filial, such as those with Jacob David Azulay and Olga Borelli, or maternal. Like a true youngest child, Clarice took full advantage of Olga's incredible patience. "It's not easy to be friends with very self-centered people," Olga remembered.

> Clarice was that type and so she was demanding and consuming of the people she liked. She had great trouble sleeping and called me countless times in the middle of the night to say that she was upset and tense. I don't think I'll ever forget the time I went to Salvador to teach a class. One night, arriving back at the hotel, I got an urgent message to call her. On the phone her voice was strange. "Olga, I'm so distressed. An enormous anguish. I don't know what's going to happen to me. Come back as soon as you possibly can." I canceled everything and returned to find her the next day at lunchtime, laughing, in a good mood. Do you know what she said to me? That I took her too seriously and had acted hastily by coming back early. Of course I was very annoyed, but I learned a lot from the incident.[1]

The book of stories Clarice published in 1971, *Covert Joy*, reflects a growing preoccupation with childhood. Almost all of the book's twenty-five pieces had appeared elsewhere, mostly in *The Foreign Legion*, but three exceptions are instructive. The title story recalls the neighbor girl in Recife whose father owned a bookstore and who tortured the young Clarice with the promise of a book.

"Remains of Carnival" is the story of the little girl dressed as a rose whose carnival was ruined by a crisis in her mother's health; in "A Hundred Years of Pardon" Clarice remembers stealing roses from the gardens of Recife's well-to-do.

So much of her work had been autobiographical, but rarely in the sense of these memories of her childhood in Recife. She had almost never written about herself so literally, preferring to hide behind her characters or inside her allegories. When she did appear, it was in newspaper columns or in little stories like those that make up the second half of *The Foreign Legion*.

To a reader, it does not much matter whether these stories are "true." But Clarice was not really satisfied with this kind of autobiographical writing. The inclusion of so many personal anecdotes, so many extracts taken directly from her newspaper columns, may have been one reason she professed to be unsatisfied with *An Apprenticeship*. Writing, especially about herself, had always been a means of learning about the world beyond the self rather than a merely descriptive, or even memoiristic, end.

"I am not going to be autobiographical. I want to be 'bio,'" Clarice wrote in the book she was working on around the time she met Olga Borelli, *Água viva*. In a note she spelled out this goal: "I must, Olga, find another way of writing. Very close to the truth (which?), but not personal."[2] This was the problem she had been struggling with since she began *An Apprenticeship*, when she confessed to her friends, and even to her hairdresser, that she "no longer knew how to write."

In *Água viva*, she would discover a means of writing about herself in a way that transformed her individual experience into a universal poetry. In a body of work as emotionally powerful, formally innovative, and philosophically radical as Clarice Lispector's, *Água viva* stands out as a particularly magnificent triumph. The reviews reflect the same amazement Clarice had provoked thirty years before, when she published *Near to the Wild Heart*. "With this fiction," wrote a critic who had attacked *An Apprenticeship*, "Clarice Lispector awakens the literature currently being produced in Brazil from a depressing and degrading lethargy and elevates it to a level of universal perennity and perfection."[3] The book has inspired passions. The famous Brazilian singer Cazuza, for example, read it 111 times.[4]

In the form in which it was eventually published, *Água viva* is short, less than ninety pages of big print. Its brevity and apparent simplicity mask several years of struggle. A first version, entitled *Beyond Thought: Monologue with Life*, was already complete by July 12, 1971, when Clarice met Alexandrino Severino, a Portuguese professor at Vanderbilt University. She gave him a copy of the manuscript for translation into English, along with specific procedural instructions. He was not to budge so much as a single comma.[5]

She was still "drying out the book," she told Severino, before handing it over to her publisher. This was now Editora Sabiá, which Rubem Braga and Fernando Sabino had founded after quarreling with their partner at the Editôra do Autor, and where they had already published *An Apprenticeship* and *Covert Joy*. But a year later, in June 1972, the book had not appeared, and Severino wrote to ask if she still wanted him to proceed.

When she answered, the manuscript had another name. "As for the book—I interrupted it—because I thought it wasn't achieving what I wanted to achieve," she wrote. "I can't publish it as it is. Either I am not going to publish it or I am going to work on it. Maybe in a few months I will work on the *Loud Object*."[6]

The process of "drying out," Severino noticed when he finally saw the subsequent version, consisted mainly in removing its many explicit biographical references. But *Loud Object*, weighing in at 185 pages, was even longer than *Beyond Thought* (151). The manuscript seems to capture an everyday voice utterly unrefined by literary or fictional artifice.

Clarice reminisces about her pets—abandoned Dilermando from Naples makes an appearance—listing almost every animal she ever owned or wrote about. As if she can no longer think of anything else to write about, she goes into great detail about her favorite flowers. One of them remits her to her origins, a reference surprising because so rare: "The sunflower is the great child of the sun. So much that it is born with the instinct to turn its enormous corolla toward its creator. It doesn't matter if it's a father or mother. I don't know. Is the sunflower a masculine or feminine flower? I think masculine. But one thing is for sure: the sunflower is Ukrainian."[7]

If at times this manuscript is as brilliant and inspired as the mature work of a great artist, at other times it is as dull and uninspired as a housewife's neighborly chitchat. Clarice often claimed that she was a simple housewife, and in this formless, plotless conversation, an unfiltered "brainstorm"—she uses the English word—in which she types anything and everything that pops into her mind, that is often exactly how she sounds.

She complains, for example, about money, another constant topic: "I'm back. The day is still very nice. But things are very expensive—I say this because of the price the man asked to fix [the record player]. I have to work hard to get the things I want or need." She defends herself against her mythology: "I mean to say that my house is not metaphysical. They can hardly forgive bad food. All I do is open and close my purse to hand out money to buy things. . . . Besides eating we talk a lot about what's going on in Brazil and in the world. We talk about what clothes are appropriate to different occasions." And: "I sleep too and how! My readers think I'm always an insomniac. But that's not true. I sleep too."[8]

Loud Object's direct and confessional tone, the sense it offers of Clarice's unfiltered conversational voice—she frequently pauses to answer the phone, light a cigarette, or pour herself a drink of water—can distract the reader from the reality that it, too, is a fiction. In *Beyond Thought*, she bluntly addresses the reader: "Here's what's happening. I had been writing this book for years, spread out in newspaper columns, without noticing, ignorant of myself as I am, that I was writing <u>my</u> book. That is the explanation for readers who recognize this: because they have already read it in the paper. I like the truth."[9]

She apparently did not like the truth enough to refrain from retouching it in the second draft. The critic Lícia Manzo points out that *Loud Object* contains a new, and completely contradictory, explanation: "This book, for obvious reasons, was going to be called *Beyond Thought*. Many pages have already been published. But when I published them I didn't mention that they had been extracted from *Loud Object* or *Beyond Thought*."[10]

It does not particularly matter whether Clarice took her newspaper articles and stitched them into a manuscript or whether she plundered a manuscript for material for her journalism. Yet the two conflicting explanations emphasize that in *Loud Object* she is still wrestling, and somewhat guiltily, with fictionalization.

Perhaps the least satisfying part of *An Apprenticeship* was the way Clarice extracted large chunks from her newspaper columns and dropped them, often unmodified, into her novel. The process could work flawlessly, but sometimes the pieces felt undigested. In *Loud Object* she does the same thing. A column about her childhood friend Leopoldo Nachbin appears, for example, modified only by the replacement of his name with the words "a he." The deliberate anonymity belongs to her project of depersonalizing her personal experience, replacing proper names with less specific pronouns. But the effort is halfhearted. She still names their school and their city, Recife. She must have known that these reminiscences were out of place, since almost none reached the final book. In the drafts, doubts about how to use her personal experience lead to repeated meditations on the creative process itself.

Throughout *Loud Object*, she is aware that she is doing something completely different, but she does not yet know what or how: "What will my liberty lead to? What is this that I'm writing? As far as I know I never saw anybody write like this." Such remarks frequently recur in the manuscript. The knowledge of the novelty of her invention is sometimes thrilling, sometimes frightening, and in one case is followed by a surprising interjection: "Who invented the chair? Someone with love for himself. So he invented greater comfort for the body. Then the centuries went by and nobody noticed a chair because using it was a merely automatic question. One needs courage to do a 'brainstorm': we never know what might come and frighten us. The sacred monster died. In its place was born a little girl who lost her mother."[11]

Of all Clarice Lispector's works, *Água viva* gives the strongest impression of having been spontaneously committed to paper. Yet perhaps none was as painstakingly composed. Even the apparently artless exclamation about her mother reappears in at least two other books, including an essay she later published about Brasília. As she writes in *Loud Object*, "Art is not purity: it is purification. Art is not liberty: it is liberation."[12]

For the first time in her career, Clarice had help in the work of "purification." She had always done this by herself: she typed out a mind-bending eleven versions of the lengthy *Apple in the Dark* and spent three years revising *The Besieged City*. Her journalism had occasionally been edited, but nobody had ever touched her literary work. Olga Borelli was the first person, including Lúcio Cardoso and Fernando Sabino, to edit Clarice.

A sensitive, well-educated reader with a refined sense of language, Olga proved ideal for the task. Her posthumous memoir of her friend, *Clarice Lispector: Sketch for a Possible Portrait*, displays her writerly talents with concision and elegance.[13] It stands out in the vast body of reminisces by Clarice's friends as by far the best, though Olga, unlike so many of them, was not a professional writer.

She would have a hand in all of Clarice's late works, but the first challenge was helping transform the lumpy and chaotic *Loud Object* into the classic *Água viva*. "Structuring" a book was the hardest task in writing, Clarice complained. As she grew older, editing herself had become more and more exhausting and she needed a sympathetic reader.

"She just didn't have the nerve to structure those manuscripts, all those fragments," Olga remembered. "One day, seeing all that material, I said Clarice, why aren't you writing? The book is ready. She said, no, I don't feel like it, don't bother with it. So I said, No, I'll help you. So I started to structure the book. That was when I got to like structuring and worked up the courage, later, to try my hand at the others."[14]

Without this help, *Água viva* might never have been completed. Clarice had serious doubts about the work. "She was insecure and asked a few people for their opinion," Olga recalled. "With other books Clarice didn't show that insecurity. With *Água viva* she did. That was the only time I saw Clarice hesitate before handing in a book to the publisher. She herself said that."[15]

"I don't know why you liked my book *Loud Object*," Clarice wrote Marly de Oliveira. "Since once the first impulse had passed, I reread it and was horrified. It's so bad, so bad, that I'm not going to publish it, I already pulled it from the publishers."[16] Olga's delicate interventions may have saved the book, and with it the new kind of writing Clarice was pioneering.

Her editorial method, Olga said, was "breathing together, it's breathing together."

> Because there is a logic in life, in events, as there is in a book. They follow one another, they must. Since if I took a fragment and wanted to move it further ahead, there wouldn't be anywhere to put it. It was like a puzzle. I took all the fragments and collected them, kept them in an envelope. On the back of a check, a piece of paper, a napkin...I still have some of those things at home, and some of them still even smell of her lipstick. She would wipe her lips and then stick it in her purse.... Suddenly she noted something down. After collecting all those fragments, I started to note, to number them. So it's not difficult to structure Clarice, or it's infinitely difficult, unless you commune with her and already are in the habit of reading her.[17]

❦

As ultimately published in August 1973, the book was called *Água viva.* This is the only one of Clarice's titles that offers no ready translation. Literally "living water," the words can mean a spring or a fountain, a meaning often suggested inside the book, but to a Brazilian the words will first of all refer to a jellyfish. This was not the meaning Clarice intended—"I preferred *Água viva*, a thing that bubbles. At the source"[18]—but for a work without plot or story, the hint of invertebrate floating is especially apt. Perhaps this is what Olga Borelli had in mind when she compared this book to those that had come before it: "*The Passion According to G. H.* has a backbone, doesn't it?"[19]

Água viva does not, and this initially made Clarice nervous. "That book, I spent three years without daring to publish it, thinking it would be awful. Because it didn't have a story, it didn't have a plot."[20] The question of what exactly she was writing preoccupied Clarice, and with good reason. "This is not a book because this is not how one writes," she announces at the beginning.[21]

It does not, in fact, resemble anything written at the time, in Brazil or anywhere else. Its closest cousins are visual or musical, a resemblance Clarice emphasizes by turning the narrator, a writer in the earlier versions, into a painter; she herself was dabbling in painting at the time. The epigraph comes from the Belgian artist Michel Seuphor: "There must be a painting totally free of dependence on the figure—or object—which, like music, illustrates nothing, tells no story, and launches no myth. Such painting would simply evoke the incommunicable kingdoms of the spirit, where dream becomes thought, where line becomes existence." The title *Beyond Thought* referred to these "incommunicable kingdoms of the spirit," the unconscious realm she had meant to simulate, and provoke. "Could it be that what I am writing you is beyond thought? Reason is what it isn't. Whoever can stop reasoning—which is terribly difficult—let them come along with me."[22]

She is writing not for the mind but for the ears and nerves and eyes: "I see words. What I am saying is the pure present and this book is a straight line in space."[23]

> This text I am giving you is not to be seen from close by: it gains its previously invisible secret roundedness when seen from a plane in high flight.[24]

> This is not a story because I don't know any stories like this, but all I know how to do is go along saying and doing: it is the story of instants that flee like fugitive tracks seen from the window of a train.[25]

Clarice compares the book to scents ("What am I doing in writing you? trying to photograph perfume"), to tastes ("How to reproduce the taste in words? The taste is one and the words are many"), and touches, though her most insistent metaphor is of sound: "I know what I am doing here: I am improvising. But what's wrong with that? improvising as in jazz they improvise music, jazz in fury, I improvise in front of the crowd." This is abstract music, "a melody without words": "Dissonance is harmonious to me. Melody sometimes wears me out. And also the so-called 'leit-motif.' I want in music and in what I write to you and in what I paint, I want geometric streaks that cross in the air and form a disharmony that I understand. Pure 'it.'"[26]

The Chandelier, published almost three decades before, moved with agonizing slowness, a tension built up, page after glacial page, to climaxes that, because so unexpected, were as potent as the cresting of great waves. Though essential to its power, the long intervals could also make the book unendurable. Freed from the constraints of plot or storytelling, *Água viva* is all cresting. "What I write is all climax? My days are all climax: I live on the edge."[27]

"I think *Água viva* is the fragmentation of her thought made concrete in a book," said Olga Borelli. "There are several moments in *Água viva* where I feel that: days of light, days of darkness, days of discoveries, days of great happiness, of climax.... She loved to live in a climax, in the climax of things."[28]

Clarice's relentless revision of the fragments that make up *Água viva*, some of whose ancestors go as far back as *The Foreign Legion*, nine years before, her paring them down and fitting them together, finding the "climaxes" inside them, seeking "the *is* of a thing,"[29] make the book peculiarly hypnotic. The quest for the "is" and the "it" is not, as such, new to her work, but when shorn of the intermediate devices of story and character, her writing gains a riveting immediacy.

As Borelli understood, this "spineless" writing is not random, or even abstract. Instead, its consistency more properly belongs to the realm of thought or dreams, in which ideas and images connect with a logic that may not be immediately apparent but is nonetheless real. This was the writing Clarice described when she wrote in *The Foreign Legion* that "in painting as in music and literature, what is called abstract so often seems to me the figurative of a more delicate and more difficult reality, less visible to the naked eye."[30]

When *The Besieged City* appeared, a critic wrote, "Its hermeticism has the texture of the hermeticism of dreams. May someone find the key." In contrast to that earlier novel, however, the dreamlike *Água viva* is not hermetic in the least. It can be opened to any page, just as a painting can be viewed from any angle, and it pulses with a sensuality that gives it an unequaled and direct emotional appeal: "I see that I've never told you how I listen to music—I press my hand lightly to the record player and my hand vibrates spreading waves through my whole body: that is how I hear the electricity of the vibration, last substratum in the domain of reality, and the world trembles inside my hands."[31]

The "more delicate and more difficult reality" Clarice captures is not time lost but time present, "the instant-now." Her ability to arrest time, which itself has no beginning or end, is the most uncanny aspect of the book.

Now it is an instant.
Now it is another.[32]

The pulsating, fragmentary form conveys the actual experience of being alive, moving through time, better than any artificially constructed perspective could. The narrator, and with her the reader, is attentive to each passing instant and electrified by the sad beauty of her inescapable destination: death, approaching with each tick of the clock.

As time runs out, awareness of the passing instants takes on the solemnity of a religious ritual. Time belongs to the occult force that Clarice assigns the neutral English pronoun "it," the unpronounceable and unknowable name: "the God" or, elsewhere, "X." "The transcendence inside me is the 'it' alive and soft and has the thought that an oyster has. Does the oyster when torn from its root feel anxiety? It is troubled in its life without eyes. I used to squeeze drops of lemon onto the living oyster and watch with horror and fascination as it writhed all over. And I was eating the living it. The living it is the God."[33]

Alongside the "life without eyes" that a person shares with an oyster (and a cockroach) is a deeply human religious impulse. As the author nears her own denouement, she, "an unbeliever who profoundly wants to hand myself over," is overcome by a longing for the God who had abandoned her, and whom she in turn had abandoned.[34]

> Even for the unbelievers there is the instant of despair which is divine: the absence of the God is an act of religion. Right this instant I am asking the God to help me.... The God must come to me since I have not gone to Him. Let the God come: please.... I am troubled and harsh and hopeless. Though I have love inside me. But I don't know how to use love. Sometimes it scratches like barbs. If I received so much love inside me yet still remain troubled it is because I need the God to come. To come before it is too late.[35]

At the end of *An Apprenticeship*, Clarice had written, "Though He is not human, He still sometimes makes us divine." The dominant impression of *Água viva* is not of the divine "it" but of the woman with her hand on the record player, feeling the ultimate substrata of the universe and radiating her own "it" outward, the God that is inside her, the God that *is* her: "I am not joking because I am not a synonym," she writes. "I am the name itself."[36]

37

PURGED

By the time Clarice at last completed *Água viva*, Fernando Sabino and Rubem Braga were no longer in the publishing business. Their editorial ventures had taken too much time away from their own writing, and they sold Sabiá to the prestigious José Olympio. For some reason, perhaps because she was still insecure about the reception *Água viva* would meet, she did not follow her previous titles to José Olympio, choosing instead Artenova, run by the sometime poet and film producer Álvaro Pacheco, who also worked at the *Jornal do Brasil.* Clarice had come to know him when she called him to express her admiration for a book of his poetry. In early 1973, he published an anthology of her older material called *The Imitation of the Rose*, soon followed by *Água viva* in August.

In September, Clarice decided to go on a vacation. With the exception of visits to conferences, including her one brief trip to Texas, she had not taken a proper holiday since 1959. This was not because she had lost her wanderlust. Olga Borelli remembered that Clarice went through "periods of great dynamism: she would start exercising, riding a stationary bicycle, applying creams to her face, wearing a lot of perfume. She would drink orange, melon, or strawberry juice, cutting out sodas." And she would dream of travel.

> She would call travel agencies, making appointments, dreaming of itineraries and spending day after day fantasizing about the places she would visit: contemplating landscapes and listening to the buzz of the insects in the Italian summer afternoon; or ecstatically watching the snow fall, transmuting the glimmering yellow-gold of the European autumn into purplish tones. She would watch the smoke rising from the chimneys and

> hear the rain falling heavily on the rooftops and tumbling over the paving-stones. She would delicately walk through the flowering gardens of the Rosegarten, in Switzerland, on her way to the museum with works by Paul Klee....
>
> It was all so real that suddenly there was nothing left to be seen or experienced; an inevitable sluggishness came over her when she imagined her dreams transformed into reality. Exhausted, she would cancel the trip.[1]

This time, Clarice actually managed to get on the plane. She had not been to Europe for fourteen years, since she visited the Netherlands with Alzira Vargas in 1959. She and Olga embarked on a one-month trip across the continent, following a sentimental itinerary that showed her new friend the places she had lived as a young woman: London, Paris, Rome, Zurich, Lausanne, and Bern.

The day they arrived at Gatwick, September 11, 1973, was a watershed in Latin American history and would touch the lives of millions of people, including Clarice's own. As she was flying over the Atlantic a brutal military coup was beginning in Santiago de Chile. In one of the continent's most venerable democracies, the presidential palace was bombed and the leftist president, Salvador Allende, committed suicide in his office. Forty-five thousand people were arrested, and, with the active encouragement of the Nixon administration, a little-known thug named Augusto Pinochet was installed as military dictator.

Brazil, too, was still suffering under a tense military dictatorship. Artur Costa e Silva had been removed from office following a stroke in August 1969, eventually succeeded by Emílio Garrastazú Medici, a hard-line general who encouraged the further institutionalization of torture and censorship. Torture in Brazil became an international scandal, even earning an unprecedented papal condemnation in March 1970.[2]

Censorship reached absurd heights, perhaps most emblematically in September 1972, when Filinto Müller, a pro-government politician (formerly Getúlio Vargas's anti-Semitic police chief), found that his statement that there was no censorship in Brazil had been censored.[3] This state of affairs produced some memorable protest journalism, starting with Alberto Dines's front page of the *Jornal do Brasil* in 1968, announcing the imposition of the AI-5. To mock the censors, editors took to featuring, in place of repressed articles, classified advertisements, favorite recipes, or long extracts from the poetry of Camões.

When news of the coup in Chile arrived in Rio, the censors stationed at the *Jornal do Brasil* informed Dines that he could place the death of Allende on the front page on the condition that he not make it the headline. Meeting the request, he ordered a page prepared with no headlines or photographs at all, notifying Brazil of the coup in long columns of uninterrupted black print.[4]

This was not the kind of thing that endeared the paper, then still Brazil's most influential, to the military authorities. At the time of Allende's overthrow, the country was tensely anticipating its upcoming "elections." Under the regime, presidents were chosen by the Congress, which the military controlled. The owner of the *Jornal do Brasil*, Manuel Francisco do Nascimento Brito, was opposed to Ernesto Geisel, a general who was one of the contenders, and this opinion was known in high circles. In the backroom politicking that led to Geisel's appointment, Nascimento Brito bet on the wrong horse.

Geisel, from Rio Grande do Sul, was the son of a German immigrant, and German was the language of his childhood home. Geisel was not outspokenly anti-Semitic and had not been an Integralist, but there were a few elements in his biography that raised Jewish eyebrows, such as his youthful affiliation with the active Nazi sympathizer General Álcio Souto.[5] He is recorded as describing Professor Eugênio Gudin (who was not Jewish) as "that crook Gudin, who is a rogue, a shameless Jew."[6] Unlike many elements in the Brazilian military, who were awed by Israel's martial prowess, there is no hint that he was favorably disposed to the Jews.

The Yom Kippur War influenced Geisel's thinking, as it did that of so many others. It broke out a bit more than a month after *Água viva*'s publication, and three months before Geisel's "election." As director of Petrobras, the giant national oil company, Geisel already had strong Arab connections; Brazil was not (as it later would become) self-sufficient in energy.[7] The war and the new administration brought about a revolution in Brazilian foreign policy; the country whose ambassador had presided over the United Nations vote authorizing the creation of the State of Israel now threw its diplomatic support to the Arab nations.

The *Jornal do Brasil*, reflecting Brazil's traditional foreign policy orientation, had always been pro-Jewish and Zionist. Nascimento Brito, its rich and influential owner, was an admirer of Israel; he had even sent his son to a kibbutz on his first trip abroad. But business was business, and his indiscreet opposition to Geisel created the need for a gesture toward the new ruling clique. As Samuel Wainer, among others, had learned, the military regime could make life very difficult for an uncooperative media magnate.

The solution he hit upon was clear enough: fire the Jews. That this move might have appealed to Geisel is suggested by the rest of his comment about the "crook" Eugênio Gudin: "*O Globo* opens its columns for Gudin to write his drivel every day." *O Globo* was the *Jornal do Brasil*'s principal competitor in Rio, and a hint of Geisel's distaste for the "shameless Jew" in its pages might have reached the ears of, and suggested an opportunity for, Nascimento Brito.

In December, Clarice Lispector heard a rumor that she would be let go at the end of the year. Panicked, she called up Alberto Dines and Álvaro Pacheco, who stayed at her apartment most of the night, assuring her that she had nothing to worry about and that it was all a misunderstanding. The next morning Alberto Dines awoke to see an announcement of his dismissal on the front page of his own newspaper.[8]

The stated reason was "a lack of discipline," though Dines had run the paper for years and had never heard such a complaint. It was not done all at once; "his people" were let go one by one. "I was very careful not to bring on too many Jews, so that they couldn't accuse me of favoritism. And those I did hire were of the highest quality. Nobody could say that Clarice Lispector didn't deserve to be there," Dines recalled. "The paper ended up *Judenrein*. But they did it carefully enough that it wasn't immediately obvious. They never said it, but the result was clear enough. Typically Brazilian."[9] Not one of the non-Jews he had hired were dismissed.

On January 2, 1974, Clarice received an envelope with her still unpublished columns and a dry letter, "not even thanking [her] for [her] services over the last seven years."[10] Outraged, she hired a lawyer, but Dines said that despite the insult and the serious damage to her income the loss of her job represented, she was secretly proud of having been fired. Her prominence in the 1968 demonstrations notwithstanding, it was the first time in her life she had gotten into trouble for being "political," though of course nothing in her columns related directly to the country's tense politics. She had always wanted to "belong," and now, for the first time, she belonged to the growing opposition to a dictatorship she despised.

Her dismissal was also a tacit slap in the face of the cartoonist Henfil. In the satirical magazine *O Pasquim*, which, despite its relatively (and necessarily) anodyne content, became a symbol of resistance to the dictatorship, Henfil had been assigning prominent Brazilians whom he judged to be insufficiently "engaged" to what he called the "Cemetery of the Living Dead." At the beginning of 1972 he buried Clarice Lispector. The attack occasioned protests, including from the writer herself. In the next issue Henfil drew a fretting and hysterical Clarice, "a simple writer about flowers, birds, people, the beauty of life..."

She ended up in the cemetery, Henfil wrote, because she was a reincarnation of Pontius Pilate. He drew her inside a glass dome, washing her hands, surrounded by birds and flowers, while Christ was being crucified.[11] Clarice was offended by the ugly and unprovoked attack, which came complete with the original anti-Semitic slur, collaboration with Christ's crucifixion. In public, all she said was "If I ran into Henfil the only thing I would say is: listen, when you write about me, it's Clarice with a c, not with two s's, all right?"[12]

Now she, too, was an unambiguous victim of the dictatorship, and Alberto Dines thought that she also liked "belonging" to a Jewish identity she rarely discussed with Gentiles. This identity was not without its anxieties, financial and personal. During the Yom Kippur War, she called up a friend of Lebanese descent and asked point-blank if she would like her less if she knew Clarice was Jewish. The friend and her mother both assured Clarice that it made no difference to them and that she was always welcome to the Arab foods Clarice often enjoyed in their home.[13]

"Clarice didn't like labels," Dines says. "But around that time we were talking about the Jewish motifs in her work and she asked me if they were obvious. I said that she was like Kafka, whose literature is very Jewish though he never deals with Judaism as such. And she liked the comparison."[14]

38

BATUBA JANTIRAM LECOLI?

Another phase of Clarice's life, commenced around the same time she started writing for the *Jornal do Brasil*, ended in 1973, when her psychoanalyst, Jacob David Azulay, suggested that they call off her therapy. She had been seeing Dr. Azulay four or five times a week for the previous six years. "I was exhausted," Azulay told an interviewer. "Clarice drained me more than all my other patients put together. The results were minimal. I was very tired of her and she of me. The effort that I made with her and that she made with me was very great for the little we got in return."[1]

Clarice begged him not to abandon her, and so he suggested she try group analysis. This soon failed; all of Azulay's patients wanted to be in the same group as the famous writer, and she could not adapt to the group.[2] Azulay explained:

> She was a fantastic figure, an extremely generous woman, but even so it was not easy to be with her. She carried a load of anxiety that I have rarely seen in my life. It's very difficult to be around someone like that. Full-time self-centered, not because she wanted to be, out of vanity, but a real difficulty, in connecting. She couldn't turn herself off, and when her anxiety heated up, it reached overpowering levels, and she had no rest, she could not calm down. At those times living was a torment for her. She couldn't stand herself. And other people couldn't stand her. I myself, as her analyst, couldn't stand her.[3]

The doctor was stunned to learn just how many tranquilizers and antidepressants Clarice was taking. He himself did not prescribe them, aware of what had happened a few years before when she fell asleep with a cigarette in her hand. A different doctor, and probably several, gave her whatever she wanted. "When she told me she took that amount of stuff I simply did not believe her. I said, 'Clarice, that's unacceptable, bring it here and show me.' She brought it, it was true. So she swallowed that colossal amount of medicine and even then often couldn't sleep."[4]

The analysis having failed, and group analysis having only attracted tourists, Dr. Azulay offered Clarice, terrified of being abandoned, another alternative. She could see him once a week, not as a patient but as a friend, and he would try to do what he could for her. "I think that was when I was most useful to her. That was when I thought: I'm not going to be her analyst, I'm going to be an advisor, confidant, teacher. Clarice was very naïve, and people often took advantage of her. With her royalties, for example, it was always like that. And she didn't have a father, a mother, anyone to help her with it. I liked her a lot and decided to be that person."[5]

In 1973, Pedro, twenty-five years old, moved to Montevideo, where Maury was ambassador to the Latin American Free Trade Association. He had sought the posting in part because Montevideo was the closest foreign post to Rio, and there he could take the more active role he had always desired in the lives of his grown sons. This was especially essential for Pedro, the burden of whose illness Clarice could no longer carry alone. Isabel Gurgel Valente, Maury's beautiful, aristocratic second wife, whom Clarice had so tormented during the first years of her marriage, became an unexpected ally in the struggle to care for Pedro.

Isabel was interested in psychology—she later trained as a psychoanalyst—and cared so well for Pedro that Clarice's feelings toward her changed completely, from sullen resentment to gratitude. Clarice felt terribly guilty about her inability to cope with Pedro, but after all the long years of trying she was no longer strong enough to deal with his incurable schizophrenia. For a woman who had so eagerly wanted to be a mother and who was proud to say "There is no question that as a mother I am more important than as a writer," this felt like a particularly bitter failure.[6]

Perhaps it was this failure that led Clarice to seek out children she could mother more successfully, and to fall into a childlike role herself. For the past few years, Clarice had been increasingly retreating from the adult world, as Olga Borelli stepped into the maternal role and Jacob David Azulay into the paternal. As she neared the end of her life, her memories of her happiest time, her early childhood, crept into her consciousness with increasing insistence. In a draft of *Água viva*, she wrote:

> I am walking a tightrope now because I'm not writing well. It's because I'm hiding something. Here's what it is: I bought a doll for myself. To sleep with me. I'm only a little bit embarrassed. But when I was a girl I wanted a pretty doll so badly. I only had those little ones made of rags. Filled with dried flowers or straw. I had so much love to give. And now my love was so great that it became compulsive. She is pretty. I've already kissed her and hugged her. I sleep clutching her to me. I animate objects. She closes her eyes when she is horizontal. She just didn't inherit my hair which is soft enough to drive you crazy: hers is shiny and rough. Her name is Laura. And now I have a girl—since I only had sons. She's so sweet. Now I gave Laura to a poor girl because I wanted to see a girl happy.[7]

In the form of the doll, she was almost literally clinging to her childhood. Her desire to rediscover the rebelliousness that she had most memorably described in *Near to the Wild Heart* appears in another scene in *Loud Object*, which, like the passage above, did not make it to the final draft:

> I buy clothes ready-to-wear but I wanted to have a black knit dress made. I received it at home and expected a masterpiece. What it was was horrible. In a rage I ripped it to shreds with my two hands. The person watching said: but it still could have been adjusted! The little temperamental one. But I felt so good afterwards. So sated finally that I understood that I have to return to wildness every once in a while. I seek out the animal state. And every time I fall into it I am being me. And how good it is to do what you want without even thinking about it beforehand.[8]

The scene recalls the animal ferocity of Joana. But that wild young girl was painfully fading, even dying. In *Água viva*, she wrote:

> On Sunday inebriated with the sun and with Jupiter I was alone in the house. I suddenly doubled over as if in childbirth—and I saw that the girl in me was dying. I will never forget that bloody Sunday. To heal the wound took days.
>
> And here I am tough and silent and heroic. Without a girl inside me.[9]

To compensate for this loss, Clarice sought the company of children,[10] and her mothering impulse now extended to Dr. Azulay's precocious nine-year-old daughter, Andréa. Azulay had shown Clarice some of her writings, and Clarice was instantly smitten by an intelligence and innocence that must have reminded her of her own. She wrote Andréa a letter:

> To the beautiful princess Andréa de Azulay,
>
> You need to know that you already are a writer. But don't pay any attention to that, pretend you're not. What I wish for you is to be known and admired only by a delicate but large group of people spread across the world. I hope that you never attain cruel popularity because that is bad and invades the sacred intimacy of our hearts. Write about eggs because that works. It also works to write about stars. And about the warmth that animals give us. Surround yourself with divine and human protection, always have a father and mother—write whatever you like without worrying about anyone else. Do you understand?
>
> A kiss on your princess hands.
>
> Clarice[11]

Like so many of the artists she esteemed, Paul Klee, for example, Clarice admired and even envied the spontaneous felicity and unforced ease of childhood expression. As her experience in creating *Água viva* had proven, that kind of writing was terribly difficult, even, or especially, for a mature artist who had spent years perfecting her language. "Make no mistake," she later wrote, "I only achieve simplicity through hard work."[12]

That simplicity came naturally to a child, who had none of the self-conscious refinement of the adult artist. For Clarice, caught in "the shipwreck of introspection," Andréa's lack of linguistic self-consciousness suggested an innocence now lost to her, a final chance to relive the happy and innocent years when she too still had a father and a mother. In 1975, enchanted by her "spiritual daughter," Clarice published a small edition of Andréa's stories, such as the following:

> On a moonlit night something happened by the sea that is hard to describe. I was sitting on a bench, near the beach. It wasn't very cold, but the waves like fans were calling the wind to dance an unknown dance. The sea was gray like the sky.
>
> It turned blue-green and didn't stop changing colors. Then the tide came in, came in . . . And then went back out, back out . . .
>
> And everything stopped. The moon started to turn off and went dark.
>
> I went to sleep and dreamed about everything that happened by the sea.[13]

In her letters, Clarice sent the little girl ready-made phrases to use in her stories. She also confided many of her fears, telling her, for example, of a nightmare: that she had left Brazil and returned to find her name had been stolen. From their correspondence, it seems that Clarice imagined Andréa's future literary career as completely as she imagined the buzz of the insects of the Italian summer afternoons of all those trips she never managed to take, offering a presumably baffled Andréa all sorts of practical advice about her career. The nine-year-old girl was "not to abuse commas," "to always keep a simple humility in life as in literature," and to "try to write in prose, even poetic prose, because from a commercial point of view nobody publishes books of poetry."[14]

Andréa, who eventually became a lawyer, grew very attached to Clarice and was hurt when her older friend, apparently going through a difficult time, temporarily vanished. "Why don't you write?" the girl asked. "Why do you disguise your voice when you call to speak to Daddy?"[15] Clarice was still dependent on Andréa's father, but her relationship with Andréa became one of the closest in her life. The two often shared meals together, and on one occasion Clarice took her to buy a puppy.[16]

A puppy was a particularly appropriate gift for Andréa. Clarice was as drawn to animals as she was to children, and in similar ways; in her writings they are often inextricable. Where she writes about a child, or for children, she always writes about an animal, too. Her own childhood memories were inseparable from her memories of the animals—dogs, cats, hens—that surrounded her in Recife. The connection was so automatic that the first chapter of her first book, *Near to the Wild Heart*, is a memory of Joana as a girl, playing with the hens in the yard. Every one of the children's books she later wrote concerns animals. As she grew older and increasingly nostalgic for childhood, her connection to animals grew stronger, and they take an ever more important role in her writing.

One animal in particular now became as close to Clarice as she was to Andréa Azulay: her dog Ulisses. This mutt's eccentricity gave him a wide reputation for being as extraordinary as his owner, who wrote about him in several books and even composed an entire book in his voice, a children's story called *Almost True*.[17] In that book, Ulisses introduces himself by saying, "I'm a little impolite, I don't always obey, I like to do whatever I want, I pee in Clarice's living room."

In the late 1960s, the director Luiz Carlos Lacerda, whose first love, like Clarice's, had been Lúcio Cardoso, worked on a screenplay with Clarice based on "The Egg and the Hen." Arriving at her apartment to discuss this project, which never materialized, he sat on a sofa beneath a whole wall of portraits of the mistress of the house, an intimidating constellation of almond-shaped eyes staring down at him.

Clarice went into the kitchen, and he lit a cigarette, placing it in an ashtray when she came back in. When he reached back down for his cigarette, it had vanished. Baffled, he thought, It's true what they say: the woman really is a witch. At a loss, he lit another, but after only a couple of minutes, it, too, disappeared. By now completely spooked, he looked over to see Ulisses the dog spitting out the butt.

In 1974, a woman who came to interview Clarice (for the same magazine, *O Pasquim*, in which Henfil had attacked her) was struck by the dog, "who madly swallowed all the cigarette butts, sometimes still partly lit, that the interviewers put out in the ashtray.... She calmly let him do whatever he wanted."[18] Ulisses was a part of her return to childhood, and to motherhood. She told an interviewer that "I bought Ulisses when my sons grew up and went their own way. I needed to love a living creature who would keep me company. Ulisses is mixed-race, which guarantees him a longer life and a greater intelligence. He's a very special dog. He smokes cigarettes, drinks whisky and Coca-Cola. He's a bit neurotic."[19]

Ulisses was a friend to Clarice, of course, and her love of animals and children was a love of their innocence and warmth. They eagerly absorbed the love that had brought her so many disappointments when directed at adults. Unlike Clarice, increasingly sinking in the "shipwreck of introspection," animals were enviably simple. "How I envy you, Ulisses, since all you do is be."[20]

In all of Clarice's writings, the animal, especially the horse, was a metaphysical ideal, a union of "impression and expression." The hens who laid eggs were intimately connected to the mystery of birth. And like children such as Andréa Azulay, animals had a special relationship to language. Animals and children, particularly babies, spoke a language that was not made of words with meanings, which Clarice always mistrusted, but of pure sound.

Clarice had many names for her dog Ulisses: "Vicissitude," "Pitulcha," "Pornósio." Her son's name, Pedro, may have been ordinary enough, but when he was only a few months old his mother had already embroidered it spectacularly, as she wrote Elisa and Tania: "Euríalo (that's Juquinha's new name) is already receiving affection in your names. I'll tell you straightaway what his names are: Juquinha, Euríalo, Júbilo, Pinacoteca, Vivaldi, Evandro, etc. He answers to any of these names. He also answers to any other name, he's so dim-witted."[21]

This naming recalled an old habit of Clarice's: when she was a little girl in Recife, she had even given names to all the tiles in her shower, and when Joana is first encountered as a child, she has already established an unconscious link between an occult language and the world of animals, as in the dialogue from *Near to the Wild Heart.*

> "Daddy, I made up a poem."
> "What's it called?"
> "Me and the sun." Without waiting long she recited: "The hens who are in the yard already ate two earthworms but I didn't see it."

It is not a coincidence that "The Egg and the Hen" has an animal theme and is written in a language that is almost, but not quite, nonsensical. Another great story, "Dry Study of Horses," is also abstract, and similarly is about animals. In her last book, the incomplete *A Breath of Life: Pulsations*, she writes:

> If I could describe the inner life of a dog I would have reached a summit. Angela [the book's protagonist] also wants to enter the living-being of her Ulisses. I was the one who transmitted to her this love for animals. . . .
>
> Oh God, and I who compete with myself. I detest myself. Happily other people like me, that's a relief. I and my dog Ulisses are mutts. . . .
>
> I know how to speak a language that only my dog, the honorable Ulisses, my dear lord, understands. It's like this: dacoleba, titban, ziticoba, letuban. Joju leba, leba jan? Tutiban leba, lebajan. Atotoquina, zefiram. Jetobabe? Jetoban. That means something that not even the emperor of China would understand.[22]

For her entire life as a writer, Clarice had pushed against the limits of language; here, abandoning intelligibility, she breaks through them entirely, attaining the ideal to which *Água viva* had alluded, when she aimed not at the mind but at the senses. In another fragment, not published in *A Breath of Life*, she explicitly makes the link between nonsensical language and precisely those realms of life that are impossible to define and describe: "Angela—Batuba jantiram lecoli? adapiu quereba sulutria kalusia. I enjoy speaking this way: it is a language that resembles an orgasm. Since I don't understand, I hand myself over: tilibica samvico esfolerico mazuba! I am the water of a lovely cistern."[23]

The "language that resembles an orgasm" is, like an orgasm itself, as far beyond intellect as the words "tilibica samvico esfolerico mazuba." In this language, "impression and expression" are united. Without moral or human meaning, these words are the linguistic equivalents of the insides of the cockroach or the bark of a dog; like music, they are nothing but sound.

How could language, which by definition carries meaning, achieve a meaningless purity? The question had always intrigued Clarice Lispector. In *Água viva,* she had wanted to compose a kind of music of words, or a book that, like an abstract sculpture, could be seen (and not read) from an airplane. In *A Breath of Life*, she says that she wants to write a book that would be like a dance, "pure movement."[24]

Delight in meaninglessness and sonorous words rings throughout Clarice Lispector's work. Perseu, in *The Besieged City*, shares it:

> "They feed on basic microvegetation, infusorials, etc."
> "Etc.!" he repeated brilliant, unconquerable.[25]

The state-without-language is what Ulisses the dog had in common with Martin: "he, too, pure, harmonious, and he too without meaning."[26]

Still, Clarice's writing, even at its most abstract, always has a comprehensible meaning, a human grammar. Nothing in her work resembles "tilibica samvico esfolerico mazuba." These words call to mind the meaningless words the cabalists created as a stimulus to meditation. For the Jewish mystic, creating and contemplating random combinations of letters was a path to hidden knowledge, and even a means of discovering the Holy Name itself: that word which, by definition, can belong to no human tongue.

But as the mystics also knew, a meaningless language is a mortal danger. Clarice was aware of this, too. She often mentioned, in *The Foreign Legion*, for example, her fear of "going too far" in her writing: "I restrain myself, as if holding the reins of a horse that could gallop off and take me God knows where."[27]

God knows where: it is no coincidence that the manuscript containing this nonsense is incomplete and would not be published in her lifetime. Even more than the cockroach of *G. H.*, "tilibica samvico esfolerico mazuba" is the end of the search, artistic and spiritual, that Clarice Lispector had begun decades before, in *Near to the Wild Heart*, when she had sought "the symbol of the thing in the thing itself."

Sounds, shapes, and movements can be independent of meaning. But language, by definition, cannot. The Name that is beyond human meaning cannot be pronounced. "I write through words that hide others—the true words. Since the true ones cannot be named," she wrote.[28] And so if Clarice Lispector had pursued a divine meaninglessness throughout her life, she knew, as she neared the end of that life, that senseless babble was as close as she was going to get to the "true words."

Perhaps the best solution would have been to stop writing entirely. She increasingly despaired of her "damned profession that gives no rest."[29] But because she had to write, she could not say "Atotoquina, zefiram." Her own definition of madness, after all, was "losing the common language." She was not kidding when, in *A Breath of Life*, she wrote, "And I—all that's left for me is to bark at God."[30]

39

HEN IN BLACK SAUCE

"If I could describe the inner life of a dog I would have reached a summit," Clarice wrote, and though she did not try to describe the nonsensical language of animals she nonetheless wrote more and more for children, about animals. Her dog Ulisses was the protagonist of *Almost True*, written in the mid-1970s and published after her death, a book that is a kind of satire of the social fiction then being produced by artists chafing at Brazil's censorship and dictatorship.

Ulisses, the narrator, ventures to a neighbor's yard and finds chickens being oppressed by a crooked fig tree, who has entered into an alliance with a witch who has tricked the chickens into believing that the sun never sets. This atmospheric inversion makes the cocks crow themselves hoarse and wears out the hens, who lay eggs without rest. The fig tree plans to sell the eggs and become a millionaire—until the poultry revolt. Victorious, the chickens win back their right to sleep, crow, and lay eggs whenever they like.

The book has a magical, happy ending, as do all her books for children. But the best children's literature is scary, and in a book published in 1974, *Laura's Intimate Life*—dedicated to, among others, Andréa Azulay—Clarice does not spare the gore. "I understand a hen, perfectly. I mean, the intimate life of a hen, I know how it is," she once said.[1] She had grown up with hens, of course, and the hen and the egg form one of her central themes.

The short book's heroine is a hen named Laura, the same name Clarice gave to the doll she bashfully confessed to buying in *Loud Object*. Laura's intimate life ("I'll explain right away what 'intimate life' means. It's this: intimate life means that we don't have to tell everyone what happens in our house") is not especially complex.[2] She is married to a vain cock named Luís who has an exaggerated idea of his influence over the sun. And she is terrified of being killed.

As a prolific egg producer, she is not in immediate danger, or so she has been led to believe. Clarice tells some cute stories about Laura before abruptly informing her young readership, "There's a way of eating hens called 'hen in black sauce.' Have you ever eaten it? The sauce is made with the hen's blood. But you can't buy a dead hen: she has to be alive and killed at home to be able to use the blood. And I don't do that. I don't kill hens. But it's good food. You eat it with well-cooked white rice."[3]

This grisly recipe fascinated Clarice. She refers to it in *Loud Object*, and it is the subject of a conversation in *An Apprenticeship*:

> I don't remember what restaurant in Tijuca Forest has hen in black sauce, nice and dark because of the thick blood that they know how to make there. When I think of the voracious delight with which we eat the blood of others, I realize how brutal we are, Ulisses said.
>
> I like it too, said Lori softly. Me of all people, who could never kill a hen, I like them so much alive, moving around their ugly necks and looking for worms. Wouldn't it be better, when we go there, to eat something else? she asked a bit fearfully.
>
> Of course we should eat it, we have to remember and respect the violence we have. Small violences save us from greater. Who knows, if we didn't eat animals, we would eat people in their blood. Our life is brutal, Loreley: we are born in blood and with blood the possibility of perfect union is forever cut: the umbilical cord. And many are they who die with blood spilled inside or out. We have to believe in blood as an important part of life. Brutality is love as well.[4]

Laura, the hen, is a proud mother, and the references to the cruelty of the world and the umbilical cord in the passage from *An Apprenticeship* suggest that Clarice, here as so often, was thinking of her mother's fate and, increasingly, her own. Previous assurances to the contrary, the same gloomy destiny hangs over an aging and less productive Laura.

> The cook said to Miss Luísa, pointing at Laura:
>
> "That hen isn't laying many eggs and is getting old. Before she gets sick or dies of old age we could cook her in black sauce."
>
> "I won't ever kill that one," Miss Luísa said.

> Laura heard it all and was afraid. If she could have thought, she would have thought this: it's much better to die being useful and tasty for people who always treated me well, these people for example who never once killed me. (The hen is so dumb that she doesn't know you only die once, she thinks we die once a day.)

The choice falls on her fourth cousin, Zeferina, who that evening is served on a silver platter, "all cut into pieces, some nicely browned," in a sauce of her own blood. As death seems to be inevitably nearing, Clarice rescues the hen with a dramatic deus ex machina, a one-eyed, chicken-size inhabitant of the planet Jupiter named Xext, "pronounced Equzequte." He invites her to make a wish. " 'Ah,' said Laura, 'if it's my destiny to be eaten, I want to be eaten by Pelé!' " Xext assures her that she will never be eaten, and that is that. "Laura is alive and well," the story ends.

It is hard to read this story and not think of Clarice's own childhood stories, the reason she became a writer in the first place: to save another female threatened with an incomprehensible death. But the story's gallows humor, and its ironic extraterrestrial denouement, belong to an adult, and Clarice, as much as she liked Laura, was not a sentimental child. She had not saved her mother, and though she saved Laura in the pages of the book, a real Laura would be sacrificed in honor of the one she invented.

"On the day *Laura's Intimate Life* came out," Olga Borelli remembered, "to celebrate we went out to eat just that: a hen in black sauce. She then gave me a copy of the book with a dedication: 'To Olga, to the little Laura whom we ate.' "[5]

Laura's Intimate Life was one of three books Clarice published in 1974. Her newfound prolificacy may have had something to do with a financial situation that had sharply deteriorated since she lost her job at the *Jornal do Brasil*. Money had always been a worry for her. As she explained to a journalist in 1971, "I need money. The position of a myth is not very comfortable."[6] Her great dream, according to her son Paulo, was to get rich and to dedicate herself entirely to literature.[7]

Since 1967, the newspaper had been her main source of income, and though she still had her alimony from Maury, she could not easily replace the money. After thirty years of publishing her highly regarded and sometimes best-selling books, which had been translated in countries from Czechoslovakia to Venezuela, she earned almost nothing from them. This was not an exceptional situation. Even Brazil's most important writers struggled. In the twentieth century, only three writers managed to live from their books: Erico Verissimo, Jorge Amado, and Fernando Sabino.

In a group interview with Clarice at the end of 1976, her friend Affonso Romano de Sant'Anna remarked, "In a better organized, more developed country, a writer like you would have ... a comfortable standard of living. I think Clarice's position reflects the problem of the Brazilian writer." Clarice expressed her wonderment that it could be otherwise: "A book that's well received by the critics in the United States makes the author rich! A book!"[8]

At this time, she approached several wealthier friends, including Marina Colasanti and Maria Bonomi, offering to sell them some of her paintings. Clarice had been portrayed by many of Brazil's leading artists, and she still had the valuable De Chirico portrait. Maria Bonomi did not want to take advantage of her friend's need and at the time could not afford what she thought would be a fair price. Marina Colasanti said that the subject came up every once in a while: "I remember going back to her house and the pictures were still there. I don't think she ever really had to sell them."[9]

To try to make ends meet, she began to translate English and French works, often for Álvaro Pacheco's Artenova. For another publisher, she adapted classics for children, including the stories of Edgar Allan Poe and Oscar Wilde's *The Picture of Dorian Gray*. She also translated *Burning Lights*, the Yiddish memoir of Bella Chagall, Marc Chagall's first wife. She presumably translated this from the English or French, but the story of Mrs. Chagall's childhood in Vitebsk, today in Belarus, would have kindled memories of the stories her family told her about their own past.

Clarice may not have chosen all the titles she translated, but she did have a choice with at least one publisher that employed her,[10] and it is nonetheless remarkable how many of them deal with the same themes of crime, sin, and violence that so often appear in her own work. There were the Poe stories and *Dorian Gray*, there were two novels by Agatha Christie, and there was Anne Rice's *Interview with the Vampire*.[11] (She had once said that her "ideal would be to write something that at least in the title recalled Agatha Christie.")[12]

Perhaps the choice of books is a coincidence, but Clarice's interest in crime was not simply metaphysical. "Though incapable of an act of violence," Olga Borelli wrote, "she only watched powerful films. Crime movies exercised a great attraction over her.... She enjoyed detective novels. Principally those of Georges Simenon."[13] As early as 1946, in Rome, she had written to Elisa that she longed to be back in Brazil, where they could watch detective movies together.[14] In a story published in 1974, she quoted Goethe: "There is no crime we have not committed in our thoughts."[15]

Her work as a translator was not distinguished, and she seems to have thrown her translations together in off hours. "I work quickly, intuitively," she said. "Sometimes I check the dictionary, sometimes not."[16] This lassitude was partly inspired by the pittance she was paid. Álvaro Pacheco, who paid translators by the page, remembered the pathetic spectacle of Brazil's greatest writer coming to his office with a few pages at a time.

This did not encourage her to do her best. In 1976, one of Pacheco's assistants chastised her translation of a French book. Among its faults were "entire sentences omitted," "words translated by deduction, or by the closest sound to a Brazilian word," "modification of the meaning of words and even reversal of the sentence's meaning." She concluded haughtily, "I think that you have been assisted in this translation by someone who did not take the work very seriously."[17]

Clarice's nostalgia for childhood may have been growing more intense at this time because she herself was growing older. The fire cost her the queenly beauty for which she had been famous and made her physically fragile. Her addictions to cigarettes and prescription drugs had weakened her. She was only fifty-four when she published *Where Were You at Night*, the collection of stories she published in 1974. But sadness about growing old casts a shadow across the book, in which, for the first time, she wrote about the melancholy and helplessness of aging.

In these short works, the fervently searching Clarice Lispector, the woman whose stunning ambition had not shied from direct conflict with God and the universe, is no longer desperate, as she had been as recently as five years earlier, in *An Apprenticeship*, to "humanize herself." Life itself has humbled and domesticated her, and *Where Were You at Night* has none of the rebellion of *Near to the Wild Heart*, the rococo of *The Besieged City*, the heroic allegories of *The Apple in the Dark*, or the mystic glory of *G. H.*

The author of *Where Were You at Night* has retreated from her previously Himalayan heights, and her language reflects a new modesty. The book is short, about a hundred pages, divided into seventeen stories. Its powerful and direct emotional appeal is typical of her last books. Through her characters—avatars of herself, as tenuously fictionalized as always—she is asking another question, so basic that it is unanswerable: What is a person to do with herself?

The housewives of *Family Ties*, struggling to balance the demands of family and marriage, have given way to women who are struggling to find a place for themselves now that their husbands and children have departed. The title of the first story, "In Search of a Dignity," refers to this attempt to find a new life for themselves once they have outlived their usefulness as wives and mothers.

In this story, Mrs. Jorge B. Xavier—she does not even have her own name—is on her way to a conference: "The conference might even have already started. She was going to miss it, she who made an effort not to miss anything *cultural* because that was how she kept herself young inside, since even on the outside nobody imagined that she was almost 70, everyone guessed she was around 57."[18] En route, she gets trapped in the cavernous entrails of Rio's immense Maracanã Stadium. It is an unexpectedly hot day, as hot as summer, though it is midwinter.

"There has to be an exit," she repeatedly thinks, her panic increasing. At length a man turns up to help her, and she realizes that the meeting was not *in* the stadium but nearby. She does not want to appear crazy to the man who helps her find her way out, but when she gets onto the street and into a taxi, she can remember only a part of the name of the street she is looking for. By the time she and the patient driver finally track down the address, she is exhausted, feeling foolish and old, and has to sit down.

As the man in the stadium and the taxi driver had done, an acquaintance at the conference takes charge of her, finding another taxi to take her home. She is an old woman, unable to fend for herself, being handed off from one caretaker to another. But the new taxi driver does not know the way to her neighborhood, and she cannot explain it. The streets, like the hallways of the stadium, feel like an exitless labyrinth. The driver hails down another taxi who knows the way, and hands her over to him.

Arriving at home, she throws herself onto her bed, her body "as anonymous as a hen's," awaking to a sexual fantasy about the matinee idol Roberto Carlos. "So the lady thought this: in my life there was never a climax as in the stories you read. The climax was Roberto Carlos.... There she was, trapped in an out-of-season desire just like the summer day in the middle of winter. Trapped in the tangle of the halls of Maracanã. Trapped in the moral secret of old women. She wasn't used to being almost seventy years old, she lacked practice, she didn't have any experience at all." But she sees her weak old body: "Were her lightly rouged lips still kissable? Or was it by chance disgusting to kiss an old woman's mouth?" "It was then that Mrs. Jorge B. Xavier bent brusquely over the sink as if she was going to vomit out her insides and interrupted her life with a shattering muteness: there! has! to! be! an! exiiiiit!"[19]

"The Departure of the Train," the next story, also shows an old woman trying in vain to revolt against the irrelevance that age has forced upon her. As her long string of names suggests, Mrs. Maria Rita Alvarenga Chagas Souza Melo is a wealthy lady, "but you reach a certain point—and it doesn't matter what you were." Like Mrs. Jorge B. Xavier, Maria Rita is in search of dignity: " 'I'm old but I'm rich, richer than everyone else in this compartment. I'm rich, I'm rich.' She glanced at her watch, more to see its thick gold than to see what time it was. 'I'm very rich, I'm not just any old lady.' But she knew, oh she knew very well that she was just any old lady, a little old lady spooked by the slightest things."[20]

She sits across from a younger woman, Angela Pralini, who has just left her lover. Angela watches Maria Rita as she thinks about the man she has left, Eduardo, and "seeing the old Maria Rita was afraid to grow old and die."[21]

Clarice was never far from the surface of her fictions—Angela Pralini, for example, lost her mother when she was nine and has a dog named Ulisses—and in this story the irrepressible author suddenly bursts to the forefront.

> The old woman was as anonymous as a hen, as a certain Clarice had said on the subject of a shameless old woman who was in love with Roberto Carlos. That Clarice made people uncomfortable. She made the old woman shout: there! has! to! be! an! exiiiiit! And there was. For example, that old woman's exit was the husband who would be back the next day, it was the people she knew, it was her maid, it was an intense and fruitful prayer when faced with despair. Angela said to herself as if biting herself in rage: there has to be an exit. For me as for Maria Rita.[22]

In a copy of the book Clarice gave to Autran and Lucia Dourado she scrawled, in the almost illegible handwriting that was a legacy of her injury in the fire, "This book is no good. I'll only make allowance for 'In Search of a Dignity,' 'Dry Study of Horses,' and 'The Departure of the Train.' " "Dry Study of Horses" is a hallucinatory, abstract collection of short prose poems about horses that also includes a quick stylized summary of *The Besieged City*.

Many of the other stories had been published elsewhere, but to the three stories she approved of Clarice might also have added the title story, "Where Were You at Night." As in "The Departure of the Train," in which the voices of Angela and Maria Rita alternate and comment on each other, "Where Were You at Night" is a series of voices captured at random throughout a single night. In this kaleidoscope of characters, the author herself is close by: " 'My life is truly a novel!' cried the failed woman writer." The only Jewish character named as such anywhere in Clarice's work also appears, perhaps a fictionalized memory of her father: " 'I am Jesus! I am a Jew!' screamed in silence the poor Jew." Praying to God, he says, "Deliver me from the pride of being a Jew!" But if the story mourns this poor man and speaks of "the person living unanaesthetized the terror of life," it also betrays the light touch and subtle wit that readers rarely expect, but frequently meet, in Clarice's writing: "As a child Max Ernst was taken for Baby Jesus during a religious procession. Later he provoked artistic scandals."[23]

Clarice combines this playfulness with the abstraction of "The Egg and the Hen" in the sparkling "Report on a Thing," the thing being an alarm clock called Sveglia:

> I went five years without getting a cold: that is Sveglia. And when I got a cold it lasted three days. Then I had a dry cough. But the doctor prescribed me antibiotics and I got better. Antibiotics are Sveglia.
>
> This is a report. Sveglia doesn't allow stories or novels or anything else. It only allows transmission. It can hardly stand my calling this a report. I call it a report on the mystery. And I do what I can to make it a dry report like extra-dry champagne. But sometimes—I beg your pardon—it gets wet. A dry thing is made of sterling silver. Gold is already wet. Could I speak of diamonds in relation to Sveglia?
>
> No, it just is. And in truth Sveglia has no intimate name: it remains anonymous. In any case God has no name: he remains perfectly anonymous: no tongue can pronounce his real name.[24]

40

PORNOGRAPHY

Like Mrs. Jorge B. Xavier and Mrs. Maria Rita Alvarenga Chagas Souza Melo, Clarice Lispector feared that she, "the failed woman writer," had become outmoded, superfluous. As Olga Borelli remembered, she quite literally did not know what to do with herself. "She always said: 'Now what?' Can you imagine being friends with someone who is constantly saying: 'Now what?' Now... let's have something to eat, have tea in such and such a restaurant—we would go to the Méridien. We'd finish the tea, pay the bill, and she'd be asking: 'Now what?' Now we're going home to watch TV. 'Now what? Now what? Then what? Then what?' Clarice was like that."[1]

By the middle of the 1970s, Clarice's reputation as an eccentric genius, more or less unfit for society, had grown to legendary proportions. Autran and Lucia Dourado invited her to lunch almost every Sunday. In the late afternoon, sitting in their apartment, she would take a sleeping pill and begin removing her jewelry so that she would not fall asleep wearing her bracelets and earrings. They would put her in a cab and dispatch her to her house, where she sometimes arrived sound asleep.

When, in this "mystic phase," she received them at her house, the lights were usually out, the curtains shut, a single candle flickering on the coffee table, half-illuminating the gallery of portraits that commemorated the vanished beauty of her youth. "Those who pray, pray to themselves, calling themselves by another name. The flame of the candle. Fire makes me pray. I have a secret pagan adoration for the red and yellow flame." She was increasingly incapable of small talk. "God, death, matter, spirit" were the subjects of her everyday conversation.[2] Every once in a while, though, she resolved to reengage, and did so with characteristic élan. Olga Borelli remembered:

> There were periods in which she made up her mind to break out of her solitude and communicate with the outside world. She would repaint the walls in white, decorate the living room with foliage, have the maid polish her few pieces of silver, the chandelier, rearrange the paintings. She would make a guest list. She would take from the sideboard the crystal and china that she reserved for special occasions, spread out her best linen tablecloth, and order Rio's most famous *vatapá* (she never had a good cook). She would light her long jasmine incense-burner, fill the ice bucket, bring out a bottle of whisky and lemon-juice cocktails, and torture herself waiting for the guests.[3]

These excursions into society were not always successful, as Olga's friend Gilda Murray remembers. Once, Clarice and Olga had planned a birthday party for Clarice two months in advance. At the appointed hour, the guests, including Chico Buarque and Maria Bethânia, the famous singers, began to arrive. Clarice opened the door, very welcoming and polite, leading one guest after another into the living room. As more and more people appeared, Clarice turned, astonished, to Olga, and whispered, "What do you think got into them? It's almost like they planned it!"[4] She had no idea she had invited them.

On another occasion, Clarice's old friend Walther Moreira Salles, who had been ambassador in Washington in the 1950s, invited her to what he described as an "intimate dinner." When she arrived at his mansion in Gávea, one of the most beautiful houses in Rio de Janeiro, she found him waiting with two couples she had never met. By the time the salad was being served, she had already decided to leave. Rising from her chair and pointing a finger at the ambassador, she shouted, "Walther, you betrayed me!" before storming out.[5]

What was Moreira Salles's crime? When Clarice told Luiz Carlos Lacerda the story, he realized that she had no idea that her outrage might suggest that she and Walther were sexually involved. "Do you think I did something stupid?" she asked, utterly astonished. He thought she had. What would the other guests think? "But I didn't know those people! There was absolutely no *intimacy* there!"[6]

Moreira Salles had betrayed her by misusing a word.

Despite her social difficulties, Clarice was often invited to literary conferences. Affonso Romano de Sant'Anna and Marina Colasanti recall her at a seminar on literary theory, where two scholars were discussing epistemology. Clarice vanished. When Affonso called her to see if she was all right, she answered, "That whole discussion made me so hungry. I came home and ate an entire chicken."[7]

Alberto Dines remembers hearing her work discussed in terms of structuralism. She leaned over and grumbled, "I don't even have any idea what that is, structuralism." For Dines, it was a very Jewish contrarianism, a way of mocking the pomposity of the grandees.[8]

Her irreverence hid a genuine frustration that she was not understood through the haze of terminology and theory. Nélida Piñon recalled her at yet another conference, where she "rose indignantly from her chair, ordering me to follow her." She said, "Tell them that if I had understood a single word of all that, I wouldn't have written a line of any of my books."[9]

As a young writer, she had keenly followed critical appraisals and accepted even the harshest judgments. "Everything he says is true," Clarice wrote Lúcio Cardoso about a devastating review of *The Chandelier*—though she added that the critic was acting "like the man who beats his wife every day because she must have done *something*."

Now, with a lifetime of work behind her, she was no longer interested in the opinion of the critics. She proved this with the bravura of *The Via Crucis of the Body*, the last of the three books she published in 1974. The woman who had spent years revising her books now dashed one off in the course of a single weekend.

In *Loud Object*, she had written, "I wouldn't write a story here because then it would be prostitution. I don't write to please anybody. But it's great when I do please. I have to follow the pure line and keep my 'it' uncontaminated."[10] In *Via Crucis*, she explicitly links storytelling and prostitution.

The book is defiantly, spectacularly sexual in a way Clarice had never been before and would never be again. In its eighty-odd pages, we meet a drag queen, a stripper, a horny nun, a sixty-year-old lady with a teenage lover, a couple of murderous lesbians, an old woman masturbating, and an English secretary who has ecstatic intercourse with a being from the planet Saturn.

As a provocation to her critics, it is not subtle. ("She was subject to judgment," the first line of the first story reads. "That is why she never told anybody anything.")[11] In a foreword that she calls an "explanation," Clarice explains the book's genesis. Her publisher at Artenova, Álvaro Pacheco, had commissioned three stories based on true events. At first she hesitated, but, feeling a nascent inspiration, she decided to accept the challenge.

Just as she had when she started writing for the *Jornal do Brasil*, however, she distances herself from the whiff of whorishness she associated with writing for money. "I simply want to say that I write on impulse and not for money," she emphasizes on the first page. Imagining the reactions, she uses a metaphor alluding to the punishment meted out to a biblical prostitute: "They will throw stones. Which hardly matters. I don't joke around, I'm a serious woman."[12]

She had her doubts about publishing the stories and asked Pacheco if she could use a pseudonym. He said she ought to be free to write whatever she wanted, and Clarice agreed. "One person"—this may have been Olga Borelli—"read my stories and said this isn't literature, this is trash. I agree. But there is a time for everything. There is also a time for trash."[13]

It was less that she savored the provocation as that she increasingly did not care what people thought of her work. In the story "Day after Day," she writes, "Who knows if this book is going to add something to my oeuvre. My oeuvre be damned. I don't know why people think literature is so important. And as for my good name? it can be damned too, I have other things to worry about."[14]

The Via Crucis of the Body added to Clarice's reputation for being weird and unpredictable—and even, for the first time, "pornographic." Her interest in deviant sexuality did not, at least as far as is known, derive from personal experience. As she writes in her preface, "If there are indecencies in these stories it's not my fault. Needless to say they didn't happen to me, my family, or my friends. How do I know? Knowing. Artists know things."[15]

Some friends found her touchingly naïve on the subject of sex. Maria Bonomi, who left her husband to begin a relationship with a woman around this time, was peppered with "technical questions" by an intrigued Clarice. This interest is further substantiated by a tantalizingly brief and possibly apocryphal reference to Clarice's having "swapped imported pornographic magazines" with the celebrated poet Carlos Drummond de Andrade.[16]

"I was even frightened... by how much I knew about the subject," she told an interviewer when the book came out. "Álvaro gave me three ideas, three facts that really happened: an Englishwoman who said she had slept with an alien; a woman in Minas who thought she had been impregnated by the Holy Ghost; and the Argentine man who lived with two women. The rest was my imagination."[17]

Despite the exoticism of some of its settings and characters, only a person of the most rigid and archaic moral principles could find the book scandalous. Clarice's tone ranges from the serious to the farcical, as in "The Body," in which two women who share a male lover kill him and bury him in the garden, where he provides excellent mulch for their roses. The stories are written with a freedom and spontaneity that Clarice must have found exhilarating.

The Via Crucis of the Body is remarkable as a portrait of Clarice's creative life captured in real time, her fiction intruding into her everyday life, and her existence as a mother and a housewife constantly penetrating and undermining her fiction. The imaginative, "fictional" stories alternate with diary-like notes of her daily activities: the phone rings; she runs into a man she used to know; her son Paulo arrives for lunch. These alternating tableaux add up to a picture of May 11 to 13, 1974, the days Clarice spent writing the book. That weekend, on Sunday, May 12, significantly included Mother's Day. And the theme that unites the collection is not, in fact, sex. It is motherhood. A transsexual has an adopted daughter, to whom he is a "true mother." The woman who bears an immaculately conceived child knows that he will walk the via crucis: "They all do."[18]

In the parts of the book that include her day-to-day jottings, Clarice writes, "My dog is scratching his ear and with so much delight that he's even moaning. I am his mother." Meeting a wreck of a man, once a promising poet she had known in college, she writes, "Today is Sunday, May 12, Mother's Day. How can I be a mother to this man?"[19] On that same day, Clarice's son Paulo remembered, they went out to lunch to celebrate. When she was paying, "in place of dating the check the 10th of May (*maio*) she wrote the 10th of mother (*mãe*), 1974."[20]

The most shocking aspect of the book has to do precisely with the connection between motherhood and illicit sex, though there is nothing teasing or pornographic about the fact that on Monday, May 13, 1974, the day after Mother's Day, Clarice Lispector wrote her only explicit description of rape.[21]

"Pig Latin" is a story about Cidinha, a prim English teacher from Minas Gerais, who is on a train to Rio de Janeiro. Two men enter her compartment, "one tall, thin, with a small moustache and a cold look in his eyes, the other short, potbellied, and bald." "There was an uneasiness in the wagon. As if it were too hot. The girl worried. The men on alert. My God, the girl thought, what do they want from me? There was no answer. And to top it all off she was a virgin. Why, but why had she thought about her own virginity?"[22]

The men begin speaking an incomprehensible tongue, which Cidinha soon recognizes as pig Latin. But she has to pretend not to understand, because they are saying that as soon as the train enters a tunnel they will rape her. "Save me, Virgin Mary! save me! save me!" she inwardly begs, as the men prattle in the childish language. They can always kill her, they say, if she puts up a fight. Lighting a cigarette to buy some time, inspiration strikes her: "If I pretend to be a prostitute, they'll lay off, they don't like sluts."

> So she hitched up her skirt, grimaced sensually—she didn't even know she knew how, so little did she know about herself—opened some buttons to leave her breasts halfway exposed. The men suddenly startled.
>
> "Eshay isway azycray."
>
> She's crazy, they meant.
>
> And there she was boogying like a samba dancer from the slums.[23]

The men laugh at her, and her antics are spotted by the conductor, who decides that he'll turn her in to the cops at the next station. When she is escorted onto the platform, a young woman with a suitcase gets in, casting the whorish Cidinha a disparaging gaze. Cursed and despised, Cidinha spends three days in jail. "There was a fat cockroach crawling across the floor."[24]

When she is finally released, she takes the next train to Rio. "So little did she know about herself": to her terror, she realizes that "when the two had talked of raping her, she had wanted to be raped. She was brazen. Iway amway away ookerhay. That was what she discovered. Eyes downcast." Walking through the streets of Rio, she sees a newspaper headline. A girl has been raped and murdered in a train. "So it had happened. And to the girl who had looked down on her."[25]

Without Cidinha's unexpected realization that she had desired the men, "Pig Latin" would lose much of its impact. For Clarice, who found God inside a roach, the conventional, moral solution was never attractive. Still, perversely, this is a happy ending. The way she deflects her protagonist's rape recalls the stories she told as a child, her vain attempts to cure her mother. The horror is transferred from a woman with a name and a history to someone anonymous—as if by magic.

41

THE WITCH

"Trash indeed," huffed the leading newsmagazine *Veja*, reacting with foreseeable thickness to the bait in *The Via Crucis of the Body*.[1] "One critic said it was trash, dirty, unworthy of me," said an unsurprised Clarice.[2] Even the *Jornal do Brasil*, where she had worked for so many years, piled on. Its critic opined that "it would have been better not to have published the book, rather than being forced to defend herself with this phony contempt for herself as a writer."[3]

"My kids liked it and that's the judgment that interests me the most," Clarice said. "Usually, after reading reviews of my work, positive or negative, I stop writing for two or three days in order to forget that I'm a writer."[4] The subject of good and bad literature, of "being a writer," in any case no longer interested her. "Any cat, any dog is worth more than literature," she wrote in *Via Crucis*.[5]

The literature of Clarice Lispector, however, was increasingly interesting to others, both at home and abroad. The pornographic tingle that attached itself to her name with the publication of *Via Crucis* added to her notoriety in Brazil, and by the time the book appeared in mid-1974 she already enjoyed a wide reputation throughout Latin America.

In August 1974, she was with her friend and fellow writer Lygia Fagundes Telles in Cali, Colombia, for another conference. They had traveled together in the same plane, which suddenly started to bounce around wildly in the air. Seeing Lygia's alarm, Clarice took her arm and laughed. "Don't worry," she said, "because my card-reader already told me, I'm not going to die in a disaster!"[6]

Once they had arrived intact, Clarice, as usual, avoided the bigwigs, preferring to walk around the city. In August of the next year, she returned to Colombia. This appearance, though brief and by most accounts unremarkable, has become a central part of the legend of Clarice Lispector. Perhaps impressed by her appearance in Cali the year before, a Colombian aristocrat named Simón González invited her to participate in his First World Congress of Sorcery:

> We feel that this will be for you an important experience, eminently revealing, fraught with new insights, whether your field of research be witchcraft or parapsychology, astrology or alchemy, ancient magic or modern sorcery, extrasensory perception or any other of the countless means whereby men and women become aware not only of capacities ordinarily untapped within themselves but also of a pulsing reality beyond their senses, and mystic realms of love, joy, and power never attained by unbelievers.[7]

"Everyone is having a convention these days. So why not Satan?" the *Evangelical Missions Quarterly* wondered.[8] And Satan, sure enough, did it in style, luring notables such as the spoon-bending Uri Geller to Bogotá, where two thousand people paid $275 to participate in the gathering's forty seminars, and where an estimated 150,000 individuals, presumably less committed, visited the various occultists offering their services and wares in a hall open to the public. The spectacular opening, the *New York Times* reported, on a stage dominated by "a huge white plaster reproduction of a pre-Columbian idol," featured "150 young women in black and colored robes swirling to a voodoo dance on a moonlit outdoor stage."[9]

Perhaps not surprisingly, the press took a somewhat patronizing interest in Clarice's participation in the convention, even before she left Rio. She herself took it seriously. "At the conference I plan to listen more than speak," she told *Veja*. "I will only talk if I can't avoid it, but I will speak about the magic of the natural phenomenon, since I think it is entirely magic that a dark and dry seed contains within it a brilliant green plant." Creating another one of the paradoxes that were a trademark, she said, "Magic as well is the fact that we invented God and that, miraculously, He exists."[10]

She prepared several versions of a speech but did not read any of them.[11] Instead, she limited herself to a brief introduction that summed up her entire approach to writing and its relationship with the world it reflects and creates:

> I have little to say about magic. In truth I think that our contact with the supernatural must be made in silence and in a profound solitary meditation. Inspiration, in all forms of art, has a touch of magic because creation is a thing that is absolutely inexplicable. No one knows anything about

> it. I do not think that inspiration comes from outside, from supernatural powers. I suppose that it emerges from the deepest *I* of a person, from the deepest individual, collective, and cosmic unconscious. But it is also true that everything that has life and is called by us "natural" is in truth as inexplicable as if it were supernatural. It happens that all I have to give you is just my literature. Now someone is going to read in Spanish a text I wrote, a kind of story called "The Egg and the Hen" which is really mysterious for me and has a secret symbology. I ask you not to listen only with your reason because, if you just try to reason, everything that will be said will escape your understanding. If a dozen listeners feel my text I will consider myself satisfied.[12]

Clarice was very fat, the Mexican journalist Horácio Oliveira recalled, and her lipstick a loud shade of red. She sat silently while, to the amusement of the audience, someone reading her story rambled on for two hours about an egg. "Nobody understood a word," Oliveira said. After it was translated and printed, Oliveira wrote, everyone understood it was the most brilliant thing at the conference.[13] But Clarice had no illusions about the impression she made. "My presentation, in English, was not a resounding success," she reported. "'The Egg and the Hen' is mysterious and does indeed have a bit of occultism. It is a difficult and profound story. That is why I think the audience, very mixed, would have been happier if I had pulled a rabbit out of my hat. Or fallen into a trance. Listen, I never did anything like that in my life. My inspiration does not come from the supernatural, but from unconscious elaboration, which comes to the surface as a kind of revelation. Moreover, I don't write in order to gratify anybody else."[14]

When she returned home, she was besieged by the press, until, "worn down by persistence or perhaps fatigue," she conceded an interview to the same journalist who had met her before the trip. She emphasized that the reports of her walking around Bogotá dressed in black were mistaken. "For her, the reporter who saw her strangely dressed and covered with amulets was the victim of poor vision, excessive imagination, or bad faith."[15]

As usual, though, the mythology was resistant to facts. The few days she spent in Colombia were enough to earn her a lasting moniker: "the great witch of Brazilian literature," in Affonso Romano de Sant'Anna's phrase.[16] "Be careful with Clarice," her old friend Otto Lara Resende told the Canadian writer Claire Varin when she came to Brazil to do research on Clarice. "It's not literature. It's witchcraft."[17]

Ironically, or psychically, enough, Clarice seems to have anticipated this latest wrinkle in her legend, even before she heard of the Bogotá conference. The year before, in *Where Were You at Night*, she had imagined a ditzy journalist calling up a friend: "Claudia, sorry for calling so early on a Sunday! But I got up with a fabulous inspiration: I'm going to write a book about Black Magic! No, I didn't read that book about the Exorcist, people said it was no good and I don't want everybody saying I copied it. Think about it. Human beings have always tried to communicate with the supernatural, from ancient Egypt with the secret of the Pyramids, to Greece with its gods, to Shakespeare in *Hamlet*. Well, I'm going to do it too."[18]

Back in Rio, Clarice announced, as she did periodically, that she was tired of, "indeed nauseated by," literature. This was not a pose: writing increasingly exhausted her and she feared it had become an obsessive tic. "I am writing because I don't know what to do with myself," she wrote in one of the fragments that would become *A Breath of Life*. "I mean: I don't know what to do with my spirit."[19]

She was tired of writing, but she was equally unable to halt the restless creative urge that throughout her life had pushed her from one experiment to the next. Just as Lúcio Cardoso turned to painting after his stroke made it impossible for him to use language, Clarice, too, began to paint. She had been dabbling in painting since the time of *Água viva*. In the first versions of the manuscript, the narrator is a writer; in the published version she has been transformed into a painter.

That book began with Michel Seuphor's evocation of a "painting totally free of dependence on the figure—or object—which, like music, illustrates nothing, tells no story, and launches no myth." *Água viva* was full of allusions to painting and its connection to creation: "And now just as in painting all I say is: egg and that is enough."[20] In *Vision of Splendor*, an anthology of mainly older works she published in 1975, she wrote, "If I knew how to paint, I would struggle to manage to paint the complete shape of an egg."[21]

By the middle of 1975, she was painting in earnest. Olga Borelli published a note in which Clarice described the process by which she began producing these weird works. "What relaxes me, incredible as it may seem, is painting," she said. "Without being in any way a painter, and without learning any technique. I paint so badly it's not even funny and I don't show my quote-unquote 'paintings' to anyone. It's relaxing and at the same time exciting to play with colors and forms for no reason at all. It's the purest thing I do."[22]

Many of her pictures have the same fascination as certain of her abstract writings. Like *Água viva*, they give the impression of having been composed without any modification or elaboration, of being "brainstorms." But unlike the painstakingly refined *Água viva*, their colors and forms *were*, in fact, applied directly, without subsequent editing, to their wooden supports. Clarice could not polish her paintings as she could her words, and this immediacy gives them a primitive, visceral impact.

"I painted a picture that a friend advised me not to look at because it would hurt," Clarice said. "I agreed. Because in this painting which is called fear I managed to express, maybe even magically, all the fear-panic of a being in the world."[23] Dated May 16, 1975, *Fear* shows a bright blob dabbed with eyes and a mouth, hurtling through black space. Looking at it, one might recall what a man said in Washington after reading "The Buffalo," included in *Family Ties*: "He said the whole story seemed to be made of entrails."[24]

She did not, in fact, have any training in painting, but it is not true that she had no technique. "I am so upset that I never perfected what I invented in painting," she wrote in *A Breath of Life*. "Or at least I've never heard of this way of painting: it consists of taking a wooden canvas—Scotch pine is the best—and paying attention to its veins. Suddenly then a wave of creativity comes out of the subconscious and you go along with the veins following them a bit—but maintaining your liberty."[25]

Using this method, she created Rorschach-like images that do indeed seem to be direct flashes of her subconscious life. They have none of the beauty of the language that made her famous. But it may have been easier for her to use color and form to reach the state "beyond thought" that she had sought in mystical writings such as *The Passion According to G. H.* or *Água viva*. After a lifetime of writing, her mastery of her language was so complete that she now had to deliberately seek its roughness and novelty.

In language, she feared that she could not attain "the symbol of the thing in the thing itself" without being reduced to gibberish and "barking at God." Perhaps in painting, without the imperfection of words, she could reach that goal more directly. The goal, though, was unchanged. "My ideal," she wrote, "would be to paint a picture of a picture."[26]

42

THE THING ITSELF

"A picture of a picture," a representation of a representation, the symbol of the thing in the thing itself: the ideals Clarice sought in her painting inevitably came from, and led her back to, her writing. The phrase above, like so many of her thoughts on painting, appears in *A Breath of Life (Pulsations)*, the book she began sketching out around 1974.[1]

She would not live to see it published. At her death, a mountain of fragments remained to be "structured" by Olga Borelli. But if an unfinished, posthumously published work necessarily feels incomplete, and if readers will naturally wonder if what we are reading is what the author would have wanted us to read, *A Breath of Life*, like so many of Clarice Lispector's works, achieves "the precious and precise harmony between expression and substance" to an almost spooky degree.

Not only published but also, to some extent, *written* after Clarice's death, *A Breath of Life* is completed and perfected precisely by its incompletion and imperfection. This is the kind of uncanny paradox in which she had always delighted, and it was exactly what she anticipated and intended when writing it: "This I suppose will be a book made apparently out of shards of a book. But in fact it is about portraying quick flashes of me and quick flashes of my character Angela. I could grab onto every flash and go on about it page after page. But it so happens that the essence of the thing is sometimes in the flash.... My life is made of fragments and that's how it is for Angela."[2]

These fragments form a dialogue between an author and a character, Angela Pralini, the same name Clarice used for the woman in the train in *Where Were You at Night*. A discarded subtitle of *Água viva* was "Monologue with Life," and *A Breath of Life* could be called a dialogue with life, between a godlike artist who infuses the breath of life into his creation, and that speaking, breathing, dying creation herself: Angela Pralini.

The miracle of creation through words was the same wonder that had always fascinated Clarice, but in her other meditations on the subject, *The Apple in the Dark*, for instance, the fictional edifice is less visible, the author hidden in the tangles of her dense and allusive allegory. The author and her creation were often identical: "I am Martin," Clarice said in an interview, referring to the protagonist of *The Apple in the Dark*.[3] This was exactly what Álvaro Lins had criticized in *Near to the Wild Heart*, speaking of its "feminine" incapacity to disguise the author in her work: "There is, however, in masculine temperaments, a greater tendency to hide the author behind his creations, to disconnect from the finished and completed work. That means that a writer can put all of his personality into a work, but diluting himself inside it so that the spectator sees only the object and not the man."

This was not a criticism that Clarice Lispector had taken to heart, to say the least. In her last books, the identity of the divine author with her creations reaches a poetic climax. In *A Breath of Life*, both Angela and the male author character Clarice interposes between herself and Angela *are* Clarice Lispector, far more than any of her previous creations had been. Even in a body of work as richly autobiographical as Clarice's, no character, not Martin or Joana or G. H., had ever been as boldly and transparently Clarice. Angela says:

> The object—the thing—always fascinated me and in a certain sense destroyed me. In my book *The Besieged City* I speak indirectly of the mystery of the thing. A thing is a specialized and immobilized animal. Years ago I also described a wardrobe. Then came the description of an immemorable clock called Sveglia: an electric clock that terrified me and that would terrify any living person in the world. Then it was the telephone's turn. In "The Egg and the Hen" I talk about the crane. It is my timid approach to the subversion of the living world and of the threatening world of the dead.[4]

The male author, Angela's purported creator, also bears certain similarities to Clarice Lispector, though she distances him with irony. "I never had a vocation for writing," he says, "the number fascinated me since I was a boy. The only reason I awkwardly and daily write down notes is because I can't have a conversation with my wife."[5]

There is more to this distancing than irony, though. Clarice emphasizes over and over again the fictional qualities of this and all writing. Angela and "the author" are her creations; so, too, is the "I". "The I who appears in this book is not I. It is not autobiographical, you all know nothing of me. I never have told you and I never shall tell you who I am. I am all of yourselves."[6]

Painting had prepared Clarice for her new experience in writing. After returning from Bogotá, she described her two previous books, *Where Were You at Night* and *The Via Crucis of the Body*, as "light" and "direct," and announced that she would not be continuing in that direction: "I am afraid of acquiring a detestable facility. I don't want to write out of habit but out of necessity, as has been the case until now. A while ago I thought about stopping, but a desire came to me that was so strong that I started again. Today, I am thinking once again about abandoning literature. If I continue, it will be the old Clarice Lispector, since my vein of 'light' literature has run out. But the experience was important. After all, profundity is not the only thing that exists. The surface is a real aspect."[7]

Just how much she understood of the surface as "a real aspect" is most immediately visible in her paintings. Her technique is the opposite of the trompe l'œil. By allowing herself to follow the grain of the wood she painted over, she covers the surface at the same time that she calls attention to its reality, and thus to the artificiality of her own creation. She is not trying to make a piece of canvas look like wood or marble. She is not creating a fake surface but, by following the contours suggested by a natural surface, making that natural surface reveal its depths. The tension between the "natural" and the "invented," between the "real aspect" of the surface and the profundity of human artifice, is the source of the paintings' disquieting power.

In *A Breath of Life*, Angela Pralini is a painter. More significantly, Angela Pralini is a painting, the "picture of a picture" that Clarice sought, and *A Breath of Life* is a picture of Clarice creating her. In creating the character, she does not strive to paint over the raw material, in this case the author herself; the canvas is never occulted by the creation overlaying it. Few characters in fiction are as self-consciously fictional, as obviously avatars of their creator, as Angela Pralini.

"I call the grotto by its name and it begins its murky life," Clarice had written in *Água viva* of one of her paintings. The process of infusing a "breath of life" into inanimate objects was one of her oldest mystical themes; the link between language and creation was the same link that she had pondered so poetically in her many books, in *The Apple in the Dark*, for instance, or in Virginia's rumination on the anise liquor. "The thought... was the taste of anise," she wrote three decades earlier in *The Chandelier*. Now Clarice's thought about Angela Pralini *is* Angela Pralini. "Does Angela feel that she is a character?" the author wonders. "Because as for me I sometimes feel that I am someone's character. It is uncomfortable being two: I for me and I for others."[8]

At the same time, Clarice longs to be two. She desperately longs to be someone other than herself. With Angela, and with her male "author," Clarice is literally trying to escape her own self. "Angela is my attempt to be two." And: "I and Angela are my interior dialogue—I in conversation with myself. I am tired of thinking the same things."[9]

Plagued by these doubts about the fragility and the reality of her creation, the divine author nonetheless revels in the creation: "As I was saying: it was God who invented me. And so do I—as in the Greek Olympiads the athletes who ran passed forward the burning torch—so too do I use my breath and invent Angela Pralini and make her a woman."[10]

The two characters enter into an incantatory dialogue that lasts throughout the book, shedding names, changing roles, and engaging in mystical speculations that burn with a fierce intensity as the author, in this case the "real" author, Clarice Lispector, feels her death approaching.

AUTHOR: I am in love with a character I invented: Angela Pralini. Here she is speaking:
ANGELA: Ah how I would love to have a languid life.
I am one of the interpreters of God.
AUTHOR: When Angela thinks about God, is she thinking about God or me?
ANGELA: Who makes my life? I feel that someone orders me about and destines me. As if someone created me. But I am also free and do not obey orders.[11]

Angela has been planning a "novel of things,"[12] but the author knows she will not finish it. Like the young Clarice, who only finished law school because of a friend's taunt that she never finished anything, the author notes that "Angela never finishes what she starts. Second because the random notes for her book are all fragmentary and Angela doesn't know how to unify and construct. She will never be a writer."[13]

But as in law school, it is Clarice herself who cannot finish what she started. Page after page, the author wonders what to do with Angela. By this, it becomes clear, she means whether to allow Angela, and thus herself, to die. The author has given her life, and the author now must decide whether, and how, to unmake it. "And suddenly—suddenly! a revolted and demoniacal avalanche bursts up inside me: I'm wondering whether it's worth it for Angela to die. Do I kill her? does she kill herself?" the "author" writes. "I want to justify death."[14]

Yet Clarice still cannot justify Angela's. She tries throughout to find a way to let her character go. "At the hour of my death—what do I do? Teach me how to die. I don't know," Angela implores.[15] But Clarice Lispector, at the end of her own life, is still addicted to the spells she cast as a child, still searching for the words that might mean salvation. At the very end of the book, an eerie and astonishing paragraph recalls Clarice's very first magical stories:

> Last night I had a dream within a dream. I dreamed that I was calmly watching actors working on a stage. And through a door that was not locked men came in with machine guns and killed all the actors. I began to cry: I didn't want them to be dead. So the actors got up off the ground and said: we aren't dead in real life, just as actors, the massacre was part of the show. Then I dreamed such a good dream: in life we are actors in an absurd play written by an absurd God. We are all participants in this theater: in truth we never shall die when death happens. We only die as actors. Could that be eternity?[16]

She could not save her mother, but she still hoped to save someone, even a character as unabashedly artificial as Angela Pralini, and Clarice's desire—"I am looking for someone whose life I can save. The only one who allows me to do this is Angela. And as I save her life, I save my own"[17]—gives the book its tragic magnificence. This is no longer a fictional author talking. This is Clarice Lispector.

Clarice knew all too well that if she let Angela die, she herself would have to follow. On the very last page she spares her creation, allowing her to drift off, a figure vanishing from a stage: "I pull back my gaze my camera and Angela starts getting small, small, smaller—until I can see her no longer."[18] Angela may have been the painting of a painting—"The I who appears in this book is not I"—but she was also quite literally Clarice. Olga Borelli understood that the connection was not theoretical: "She asks to die. . . . I left out one sentence. I left it out to spare the family's feelings. I mean, the book was fragments, and one fragment touched me deeply, in which she says 'I asked God to give Angela a cancer that she can't get rid of.' Because Angela doesn't have the courage to kill herself. She needs to, because she says 'God doesn't kill anyone, it's the person that dies.' Clarice also said that everyone chooses the way they die."[19]

43

LISPECTORIAN SILENCE

On November 28, 1975, after a Thanksgiving dinner with his daughter, Clarissa, and her American family, Erico Verissimo died in Porto Alegre. Clarice was stunned. "It was such a shock that my blood pressure dropped to almost zero and I had to lie in bed, without the strength to move so much as my hands," she wrote Mafalda. "Excuse me for letting you down at a time like this. I too wanted to see you in order to—as incredibly illogical as it seems—, for you to console me."[1]

For Clarice it was a sad end to a tough year, one that included publishing headaches, as so often before. Early in the year, Álvaro Pacheco's Artenova had brought out a compilation of the interviews she had done through the years with notable Brazilians, under the title *The Whole Body*. This brought to five the number of books she had published with him: *Água viva*, *The Via Crucis of the Body*, *Where Were You at Night*, and the anthology *The Imitation of the Rose*.

"Artenova wasn't a publisher, it was a printing press," said Alberto Dines, who was also published there for a time.[2] Clarice liked Pacheco at first, when he took a chance on *Água viva*. But she, a perfectionist in her writing, loathed the slovenliness with which her books were published. Especially compared with the stylish editions Autor and Sabiá had produced for her, the Artenova productions do indeed stand out as astonishingly ugly. The first edition of *The Via Crucis of the Body*, for example, is decorated with an inexplicably grotesque brownish-yellowish African mask.

But she let this slide until she began to feel that he was cheating her out of her royalties. "He didn't enjoy paying authors for their work," Dines said of Pacheco.

"He thought he was doing authors a favor by publishing them." Despite her legal training, Clarice had never been able take care of her own contracts; this incompetence when it came to business was part of the childlike helplessness Dr. Azulay had noticed. But now, when her paychecks became too insultingly pitiful, even she smelled a rat. "Even published in Portugal and translated in France, the United States, and other countries, and even with my work published in countless school anthologies of Brazilian authors, I never could live exclusively from literature. The reason, however, is not that the public isn't interested in my work, but an unjust exploitation that only benefits publishers."[3]

She rang Artenova to discuss the matter. After several attempts, she managed to schedule a meeting with Pacheco and immediately got into a taxi. Arriving thirty minutes later, she was told to wait: the boss had gone out to lunch with a group of foreigners. When he finally returned, a leisurely two hours later, he gave her a grand total of 140 cruzeiros: her royalties for half a year, for all five books. Olga said that she never saw Clarice so enraged. She stormed out and gave the money to a beggar.[4]

Her friend Nélida Piñon, a novelist of Spanish parentage who was well-connected in her ancestral country, put her in touch with Carmen Balcells, the Barcelona literary agent who represented so many first-rate Latin American authors, from Gabriel García Márquez to Júlio Cortázar and Mario Vargas Llosa. ("When Cervantes appeared," the Mexican writer Carlos Fuentes said, "Carmen Balcells was right there.")[5] At long last, but still years after it would have made a difference in her career, Clarice had professional representation.

❧

With these unpleasant chapters behind her, 1976 was shaping up to be a better year. Early on, Clarice consulted the *I Ching.* "What attitude should I take in 1976?" she asked the ancient Chinese text. "What awaits me this year?"

> Answer: 42. "I win."
> How should I do my book?
> Answer: 8 of "Unity, Coordination."
> Will I have sublimity, daring, perseverance?
> Response: 55. "Abundance."[6]

The book was right, after a fashion. She would have "abundance" of a widespread and sustained recognition that throughout most of her life had arrived only in reluctant bits and pieces. A bit amazed by all the attention, she made note of everything that had been happening, as if she couldn't believe her good fortune.

This year there is so much happening around me, God knows why, since I don't know. 1) The *Colóquio Letras* [a Portuguese literary magazine] asked me for a story; 2) the Argentine literary magazine *Crisis*, considered perhaps the best in Latin America, asked me for an interview; 3) *Manchete* interviewed me; 4) a paper from São Paulo interviewed me; 5) Bogotá invited me; 6) students from the Communications Department in São Paulo are making a non-profit film based on a novel of mine, *An Apprenticeship*; 7) TV Globo scheduled a "special" adapted from one of my stories for next January; a magazine invited me to do a book review section (I turned them down because I'm not a critic, and because I wanted to avoid the fuss of having my name in the spotlight); 8) I was invited to the city of Marília, in São Paulo, for a debate with students; 9) lots of unknown people call me, even more than before, to talk and sometimes to confess; 10) I'm going to be invited by the professor and critic Affonso Romano de Sant'Anna to speak with the students at the Catholic University about my experience of creation; 11) I was the Brazilian representative in a story collection with different writers from Latin America; I think they should interview all the young writers, some are very good and they have a lot to say; 12) Julio Cortázar sent me a message saying he'd like to meet me; 13) several translations came out of my books (but I earn little from them); 14) Marília Pera, in her one-woman show, uses phrases of mine from *Água viva*; 15) two Brazilian magazines published my stories, not to mention that last year Benedito Nunes wrote a book interpreting me.

This all leaves me a bit perplexed. Could it be that I'm fashionable? And why did people complain they didn't understand me and now seem to understand me?

One of the things that makes me unhappy is this story about the sacred monster: other people fear me for no reason, and I end up fearing myself. The truth is that some people created a myth around me, which gets in my way: it drives people off and I end up alone. But you know that I'm very easy to get along with, even if my soul is complex. Success almost pains me: I looked at success as an invasion. Even a little bit of success, such as I sometimes have, disturbs my inner ear.[7]

An interviewer asked her to describe what a friend is.

"Someone who sees me as I am. Who doesn't mystify me. Who treats me as an equal. Who allows me to be humble."

"It makes you uncomfortable to be treated as a famous person, doesn't it?"

"Too much praise is like too much water for a flower. It rots it."

"It gets frightened?"

"It dies."[8]

At the same time, her sister Tania said, toward the end of her life Clarice knew how peerless her achievement had been, and this knowledge was a private comfort for the difficulties she had suffered in her life. By 1976, her success was at last being widely recognized and celebrated. Though ambiguous, it was a kind of consolation.

On April 7, 1976, her son Paulo, who was twenty-three, married. He had already been living on his own for over a year. Rosa Cass recalled that "Clarice almost keeled over on the spot" when he first broached the subject, asking for his share of Maury's child support in order to set up on his own. But Rosa advised her to let him go: "You'll have more of him that way than if you try to cling on," she said.[9]

And she did cling. Paulo lived close by in Leme and ate lunch with her almost every day. He soon became engaged to a woman named Ilana Kaufman. "Clarice was overjoyed that Ilana was Jewish," said Rosa, who told Clarice that if she had been a pushy *yiddishe mama* Paulo never would have married a Jewish girl. Clarice wholeheartedly agreed, and reportedly told Elisa that Paulo's marriage was a way of making up for her own.[10]

Clarice was also nervous about the wedding. Perhaps part of this was because she knew Maury and Isabel would be coming up from Montevideo, the first and only time Clarice would meet her ex-husband's second wife. By then, however, Clarice was very grateful to Isabel for taking charge of Pedro, and the early frostiness of their relationship had warmed.

She begged Maria Bonomi to come from São Paulo, saying that she feared being left alone. Faced with Clarice's insistence, Maria came, though she did not understand how the mother of the groom could lack for company. But she was surprised to see that Clarice's premonitions were right: the other guests gave the "sacred monster," with all her social inhibitions, wide berth, and Maria was glad she was there to keep her company.

Clarice was not entirely ignored, of course. An aunt came up to her and mentioned, to Clarice's tremendous astonishment, that Mania Lispector had been a writer, too, keeping a diary and writing poems. Clarice had no idea. Perhaps her mother had stopped writing after all the disasters that overcame her and her family in their homeland, or perhaps she continued the habit in Brazil until, in the face of her advancing illness, she could no longer summon the energy. In any case, Clarice had never known that they had writing in common. Clarice's own writing had always been so intimately connected with her mother that the news came as a shock. "It was a present to learn that," she said.[11]

Later in the month of April, she was invited to a book fair in Buenos Aires, whence she traveled with Olga Borelli and where she was surprised to see her books in unauthorized, and thus unpaid-for, Spanish translations. She was also surprised at the level of interest her work provoked in Argentina. "I was amazed when I got there, I didn't know they knew me," she said upon her return. "They gave me a reception, thirty journalists. I spoke on the radio. All a bit on automatic pilot because (laughing) it was all so strange, it was so unexpected that I was just going through the motions. I didn't even notice that I was on the radio. Who knows (Pause) A woman there kissed my hand."[12]

A month later, she had another occasion to remember her mother. On May 30, 1976, Clarice and Olga arrived in Recife. On the plane she ran into Alberto Dines and told him that she was going to "stuff herself with the Jewish food" that her aunt, Mina Lispector, had promised to prepare for her. Mina's son Samuel had made the trip possible. He had prospered in the low-end jewelry business; he later built an apartment building on the Avenida Boa Viagem, Recife's most exclusive street, and named it in honor of his beloved cousin.

She stayed in the Hotel São Domingos, on the same Praça Maciel Pinheiro, the *pletzele*, where she had spent her childhood. The old house from whose balcony the paralyzed Mania had sat staring away her final days, and which the family had had to leave because they were afraid it was going to fall over, was still defying gravity. "The only thing different is the color," Clarice said.[13] She sat on the benches in the square listening, enraptured, to the distinctive Pernambuco dialect of the fruit sellers.

Clarice was not a good speaker, Samuel's wife, Rosa Lispector, remembered, after the presentation at a cultural center. She was anxious about being photographed. After her event, the press rushed forward, and Clarice cried, "No pictures, no pictures!" Rosa noted that Olga spoke to her as if she were a child: "Don't you want to go to the bathroom?" she asked gently, and Clarice allowed herself to be led to the bathroom.[14] She inspired in Rosa the same protective feeling. When she found out Clarice's shoes were hurting and that they wore the same size, Rosa simply removed hers and gave them to Clarice, ending up barefoot herself. When a reporter asked her what had had the greatest impact on her life, "I think it was my birth," she answered, "and its mystery."[15]

She would never again see the city of her childhood, but after years without traveling, Clarice was in demand. In July 1976 came word of a great honor. Her lifetime achievement was to be honored by the Federal District Cultural Foundation in Brasília. The prize came with a whopping 70,000 cruzeiro cash award.

Before she left for Brasília, she gave an interview to a journalist named Edilberto Coutinho. Unlike the many journalists who had to make do with a few grudgingly proffered phrases, Coutinho found her in such a chatty mood that if he hadn't taken the initiative to leave he feared she would have talked all night.[16]

"I was extremely happy," she said. "I didn't expect it. A complete surprise. But then came a terrible depression. I, winning all that money and so many children out there who need it."

"Why don't you make a donation to those children?" Coutinho asked.

"Because the adults would keep the money. Listen here, I already tried to change the world. That's why I went to law school. I was interested in the problem of prisons. But ever since I got the news of the prize, all I can think is: children starving to death, children dead of starvation. But who am I, my God, to change things?"

In a confessional mood, she spoke a bit about the Jews as a chosen people—"That's ridiculous. The Germans ought to be because they did what they did. How did being chosen ever help the Jews?"—and about her vanity, which had nothing to do with her writing: "I like for people to think I'm pretty," she confessed. "That, yes. It does me an enormous amount of good. I've had many admirers. Some men couldn't forget me in ten years. There was the American poet who threatened to commit suicide because I didn't feel the same way. I think about those things a lot."[17]

In Brasília, relieved and delighted, she said, "I really needed this money. I feel humbled, since I don't deserve it," she said. "Someone told me that when they give us a prize it's because they think we're retired. But I shall never retire. I hope to die writing."[18]

On October 20 she gave a long interview for the Museum of Image and Sound in Rio de Janeiro, which collected recordings of notable individuals. The interview was conducted by close friends, including Marina Colasanti and Affonso

Romano de Sant'Anna. The familial atmosphere allowed Clarice to let down her guard and talk comfortably. But despite her friendly disposition, it was becoming increasingly clear that she was unwell.

In that same month, she visited Porto Alegre, home of Mafalda Verissimo, for a writers' conference. "When I saw her again," the writer Luiz Carlos Lisboa said, "I was shocked: she was already very sick, with large bags around her eyes, and hardly recognized me. For the first time I noticed that she was hiding her arm. Even so, you could still glimpse the stunning woman she had been in her youth."[19]

Caio Fernando Abreu, a young writer from Porto Alegre who was literally obsessed with her—"I eventually had to forbid myself to read Clarice Lispector. Her books gave me the feeling that everything had already been written, that there was nothing left to say"—remembered this trip: "She—who almost didn't speak, smoked a lot, and could hardly stand to be around people—invited me to a café on the Rua da Praia. We went. Dense, Lispectorian silence. At the bar, through the cigarette smoke and with that extremely strange accent, she suddenly asked: 'What's the name of this city again?' And she had been in Porto Alegre for three days."[20]

Back in Rio, she was briefly hospitalized. She wrote Mafalda to promise to wean herself from sleeping pills and tranquilizers.[21] But after so many years, this was easier said than done. One macabre anecdote from around this time suggests just how tormented she was by her inability to sleep, and how lost she was to the dreadful addiction that resulted from it. Clarice, who liked being attractive more than she liked being a great writer, hired a makeup artist named Gilles to come to her house once a month and apply "permanent" makeup.

Month after month, surrounded by magazines and papers, and with her typewriter close at hand, Clarice sat for Gilles's sessions. He touched up the blonde in her eyebrows and applied false eyelashes and flesh-colored lipstick. She talked a bit about herself, telling him, for example, that she had left her husband because she wanted to be a writer, and mentioning that she didn't see the point in living any more. But these confessions had not prepared Gilles to be awakened by the famous writer at one in the morning, or to have her schedule her makeup sessions for the middle of the night.

Like so many others who felt her vulnerability and made exceptions for her they would not have made for anyone else, Gilles agreed to come. Occasionally, when he arrived at her apartment, she would be sound asleep: she had taken her pills. Clarice had warned Siléa, her live-in assistant, and Gilles of the possibility and instructed them to make her up anyway. The patient esthetician did what he could. The false eyelashes, he remembered, were the biggest challenge.[22]

44

SPEAKING FROM THE TOMB

The most enduring image of Clarice Lispector at the end of her life, perhaps the most enduring image of Clarice Lispector at any time of her life, comes from an interview she gave in February 1977.[1] This was the only time Clarice ever spoke in front of a camera, and because these images are unique the interview has had a much greater impact on her popular image than the interviews she gave when she was younger, healthier, or more energetic.

The footage is difficult to watch. With her famously penetrating gaze, Clarice stares straight at the interviewer, her face an almost immobile mask. She sits in a drab leather chair, clutching a big white purse in her left hand and a Hollywood cigarette in her right, burned, hand. Smoking incessantly in the middle of a giant gray studio, punctuating the interview with long, pregnant silences, she answers the questions in her strange and unmistakable voice.

Everyone in the room felt a sense of portent, said the interviewer, a Jewish journalist named Julio Lerner. He was aware of the tremendous weight of the moment and felt a responsibility to history: "Neither Kafka, nor Dostoevsky, nor Fernando Pessoa, nor Peretz" would ever be captured on film. It was up to him to capture Clarice Lispector. He had thirty minutes.[2]

She had arrived at the studios of TV Cultura in São Paulo with Olga Borelli to participate in a program about film. The director of the station took the chance to ask her for a personal interview, which invitation, to general astonishment, she accepted. Lerner was hauled out of his office and given no time to prepare for the interview. "In only five minutes I get a studio and a team outside the normal hours to interview her. It is 4:15 in the afternoon and I only have half an hour.... At five the children's program begins and I'll have to be out of studio B fifteen minutes before."

Meeting her, he was "pierced by the most unprotected gaze a human being can cast on another." In an extremely hot studio—February is the height of the southern summer—under heavy lighting, he began to ask the first questions that occurred to him.

"Is it harder for you to communicate with adults or with children?"

"When I communicate with a child, it's easy, because I'm very maternal. When I communicate with an adult, I'm actually communicating with the most secret part of myself. And that's when it gets difficult."

"Are adults always solitary?"

"Adults are sad and solitary."

"And children?"

"Children . . . have their imagination. They're free."

"At what point do you think a human being starts becoming sad and solitary?"

"That's a secret." [She pauses.] "Sorry, I'm not going to answer." [Another pause.] "At any point in life, a slightly unexpected shock is all it takes. And that happens. But I'm not solitary. I've got lots of friends. And I'm only sad today because I'm tired. Usually I'm happy."

She discusses her ambiguous fame:

"Do you consider yourself a popular writer?"

"No."

"Why not?"

"Well, they even call me hermetic. How can I be popular and hermetic at the same time?"

"And what do you think of that description—'hermetic'?"

"I don't understand it. Because I'm not hermetic for myself. Well, there's one story of mine that I don't understand very well."

"Which one?"

" 'The Egg and the Hen.' "

"Among all your writings, there's always, naturally enough, a prodigal son. Which one do you have the tenderest feelings for?"

" 'The Egg and the Hen,' which is a mystery for me. A thing I wrote about a gangster, a criminal named Mineirinho, who was shot thirteen times, when one shot was enough. And who was devoted to St. George and had a girlfriend. And which completely revolted me. . . ."

"What, in your opinion, is the role of the Brazilian writer today?"

"To speak as little as possible. [...]"

"Do you have contact with young university students?"

"Sometimes they seek me out, but they are really scared of getting in my way, they're scared that I won't... meet them."

"Why not?"

"I don't know. I don't know why."

"But the ones who manage..."

"Then they're perfectly welcome to visit me, to have coffee with me, to come to my house. I greet them as friends."

"What do the young students who seek you out normally want to talk about?"

"It's surprising. They get me."

"What does that mean, they get you?"

"It's that I thought, that I sometimes think that I'm isolated, and then I see university students, very young people, who are completely by my side. I'm surprised and it's gratifying, isn't it?..."

"Of all your writings, which one do you think most speaks to young people?"

"It depends. It entirely depends. For example, my book *The Passion According to G. H.*, a Portuguese teacher from Pedro II [an elite Rio high school] came to my house, said he'd read it four times, and he didn't know what it was all about. The next day a young girl, seventeen years old, came over and said that that book was her very favorite. I mean, you can't understand it."

"Has this happened with your other books as well?"

"It has. It either touches people, or it doesn't. I mean, I guess the question of understanding isn't about intelligence, it's about feeling, about entering into contact. So the Portuguese and literature teacher, who ought to be the one most prepared to understand me, didn't, and the seventeen-year-old girl read and reread the book. It seems I gain by rereading, which is a relief."

"Do you think that this difficulty belongs only to certain people today and that the younger generations will understand you immediately?..."

"I don't have the slightest idea. I don't have the slightest idea. I know that nobody used to understand me and now they understand me."

"How do you explain that?"

"I think everything changed because I didn't change, no. I didn't... as far as I know, I made no concessions."

This is the last remnant of the young Joana's defiant pride in her uniqueness, now uttered in the resigned voice of a woman who knows she is at the end of her life. It is followed by the most uncanny moment in the interview, Clarice's apparent announcement of her impending death.

> "Do you ever write something only to tear it up again?"
>
> "I put it aside or te...No, I tear things up," she says, abruptly annoyed.
>
> "Is that reaction purely rational or more of a sudden emotion?"
>
> "Anger, a little bit of anger." [Her tone hardens; her eyes are downcast and her hands are fiddling with a pack of cigarettes.]
>
> "With whom?"
>
> "With myself."
>
> "Why, Clarice?"
>
> "Who knows. I'm a little tired."
>
> "Of what?"
>
> "Of myself."
>
> "But aren't you born again and refreshed with every new work?"
>
> "Well." [She takes a deep breath before finally looking up.] "For now I'm dead. We'll see if I can be born again. For now I'm dead... I'm speaking from my tomb."

The camera pans out to reveal a room as bare, hot, and silent as the room in which G. H. encountered the cockroach. The cameraman and Olga Borelli said nothing as an intern stood softly crying. Clarice whispered a request to Lerner that the footage be broadcast only after her death. The wish would be respected.

45

OUR LADY OF THE GOOD DEATH

This was not the first time that Clarice had proclaimed that she was about to die. She imagined her death in many of her writings. "Ah how she wanted to die," she wrote in *An Apprenticeship*. "She had never tried dying before—what an opening she had before her."[1] "I almost know what it will be like after my death," she told a Portuguese journalist in 1975. "The living room empty, the dog dying of loneliness. The windows of my house. Everything empty and calm."[2]

There was the line Olga cut from *A Breath of Life*—"I asked God to give Angela a cancer that she can't get rid of"—and there was her unexpected declaration to Olga, two years before: "I'm going to die of a nasty cancer." There was the phone call she placed to Jacob David Azulay: "She had heard about my mother's death and wanted to offer some comforting words. My mother had died a few days before, of an intestinal complication. When I told Clarice this, she said: 'Look, Dr. Azulay, I'm going to die exactly like your mother.' And this was in 1972! I remember that she frequently said to me: 'Doctor, I won't live to see the end of this year.' Living for her was torture. She no longer wanted to live."[3]

She had, Olga said, "an unbearable genius, for herself and for others."[4] By June 1977, she was already feeling the first signs of illness. Perhaps a foreboding of the end inspired her to depart, almost without warning, for Paris, where she planned to spend a month with Olga. She got there on June 19 but wanted to go home as soon as she arrived. The city was full of painful memories—of her lost friends Bluma Wainer and San Tiago Dantas, of her years with Maury, of her departed beauty and youth—and five days later she was back in Rio de Janeiro.

After her return, the journalist Norma Couri, Alberto Dines's wife, spoke to her. During the conversation, Clarice mentioned that when she was walking down the street, she always went against the oncoming tide of people.[5] "She was a brutal example of the singularity of the human person," a friend wrote when she died.[6] Her inflexible individuality would find its last and greatest expression in the book she published in October: *The Hour of the Star*.

Much of Clarice Lispector's subsequent fame, her enduring popularity among a broad public, rests on this thin book, in which she managed to bring together all the strands of her writing and of her life. Explicitly Jewish and explicitly Brazilian, joining the northeast of her childhood with the Rio de Janeiro of her adulthood, "social" and abstract, tragic and comic, uniting her religious and linguistic questions with the narrative drive of her finest stories, *The Hour of the Star* is a fitting monument to its author's "unbearable genius."

In her legendary interview with Julio Lerner, Clarice mentioned a book she had just completed. "Thirteen names," Clarice smiled, when asked what it was called. "Thirteen titles." "It's the story of a girl who was so poor that all she ate was hot dogs. That's not the story, though. The story is about a crushed innocence, about an anonymous misery." But she refused to tell Lerner the protagonist's name: "It's a secret."[7]

This is Macabéa, who, far more than the elderly women in *Where Were You at Night*, is superfluous and useless, more so, even, than Laura the hen: "Anyway I never saw anyone clumsier than that hen. Everything she does is pretty much wrong. Except eating. And, of course, she knows how to make an egg."[8] Macabéa is so poor that she hardly eats, and, Clarice says, her ovaries are dried up.

She is a poor girl from Alagoas, the state where the Lispectors first landed in Brazil, who has migrated, like the Lispectors and so many millions of others, to the metropolis of Rio de Janeiro. Her strange name, Macabéa, comes from a promise her mother made to a saint widely venerated in northeastern Brazil, Our Lady of the Good Death.[9] It alludes to the biblical story of the Maccabees, the band led by Judas Maccabaeus, one of the greatest heroes of Jewish history.

The Maccabees are the stars of the Chanukah celebration, and Clarice would have known their story from childhood. Judas Maccabaeus and his brothers defied the orders of a foreign king who desecrated the Temple in Jerusalem, ordered the Jews to worship false gods, and tried to destroy those who resisted. Resistance was not the easiest path, as an officer told Judas's father, Mattathias: "Mattathias answered and spake with a loud voice, Though all the nations that are under the king's dominion obey him, and fall away every one from the religion of their fathers, and give consent to his commandments: Yet will I and my sons and my brethren walk in the covenant of our fathers. God forbid that we should forsake the law and the ordinances."[10]

Judas Maccabaeus's story of sacrifice and doomed struggle against impossible odds would have appealed, like the climax of his glorious "good death," to Clarice Lispector, who had spent her life fighting through a crowd headed in the opposite direction.

The "failed woman writer," of course, was the last person to think of herself as a heroine. But the suggestion of the Maccabees' manly and warlike valor is even more ironic when applied to their namesake, Macabéa, a smelly, dirty, starving typist living with four other girls in a cheap boardinghouse in a scummy part of downtown Rio, the Rua do Acre.

As she had on her last visit to Recife, when she sat in the Praça Maciel Pinheiro listening, captivated, to the dialect of the fruit sellers, Clarice in her final years often went with Olga to a market, the Northeastern Fair, held in São Cristóvão. This was near the area, north of downtown, where she, her father, and sisters had lived when they first moved from Recife to Rio. It represented a double return: to the northeast of her childhood and to the Rio de Janeiro of her early adolescence, before her father's death.

At the fair, poor northeastern migrants gathered, and Macabéa's dodgy boyfriend, Olímpico, appeared there one day, Olga Borelli remembered.

> Take the Olímpico of Macabéa, he was born in a trip to the São Cristóvão fair, which is the northeastern market. We had walked around quite a bit on that visit, and she was eating *beiju* and eating *rapadura* and listening to the Northeastern songs. Suddenly she said: "Let's sit on that bench." She sat down and wrote, I think, about four or five pages about Olímpico, described Olímpico completely and she herself says in the book: "I caught the eye of a man from the Northeast." She got his entire story. Distractedly, she picked up on everything around her at that market. And she was wolfing down her *beiju* and talking about one thing and another and laughing at the singer. You'd never have guessed that Clarice was already working on that character.[11]

Macabéa's genesis was similar, Clarice writes at the beginning of the book: "On a street in Rio de Janeiro I suddenly got a glimpse of the feeling of perdition in the face of a northeastern girl. Not to mention that I as a boy grew up in the Northeast."[12]

As in *A Breath of Life*, the narrator of this "true though invented" story is a man, Rodrigo S. M.,[13] but behind him Clarice Lispector is even more visible than usual. The book opens with a "Dedication by the Author (Actually Clarice Lispector)," who a couple of pages later says,

> I know there are girls who sell their bodies, their only real possession, in exchange for a nice dinner instead of a mortadella sandwich. But the person I am going to talk about hardly has a body to sell, nobody wants her, she's a virgin and innocuous, nobody would mind if she dropped off the face of the earth. Moreover—I discover now—nobody would mind if I vanished either, and even my writing somebody else could do just as well. Another writer, yes, but it'd have to be a man because a woman writer could get all weepy and maudlin.[14]

The symphonic dedication—"So I dedicate this thing here to old Schumann and his sweet Clara who today alas are bones"—in which Clarice recalls all the musicians and spirits who have "inhabited her life" and remembers "her former poverty, when everything was more sober and dignified and I had never eaten lobster," is one of the most beautiful pages in her oeuvre; it is followed by the thirteen titles she mentioned in her interview with Julio Lerner.

The Hour of the Star
It's My Fault
Or
The Hour of the Star
Or
Let Her Deal with It
Or
The Right to the Scream

CLARICE LISPECTOR

.As For the Future.
Or
Singing the Blues
Or
She Doesn't Know How to Scream

Or
A Feeling of Loss
Or
Whistling in the Dark Wind
Or
There's Nothing I Can Do
Or
Register of the Preceding Facts
Or
Cheap Tearjerker
Or
Discreet Exit through the Back Door

Between the fourth and fifth titles, Clarice Lispector signed her name, not in the shaky handwriting that was a legacy of the fire a decade before, but clearly, boldly, a final assertion of the creator's identity.

The number thirteen was not casually chosen. Speaking of the composition of *Água viva*, Olga Borelli said, "When she had me type for her, she would say: 'Count to seven, put seven spaces in the paragraph, seven. Then, try not to go past page 13.' So superstitious! When it was a story, she would say: 'Tighten it up. Don't leave so much space so that it doesn't go past page 13.' She really liked the numbers nine, seven, and five. It's sort of a strange thing about Clarice, but she would ask the publisher not to go past page number x, to end the book there. It's a bit cabbalistic, isn't it? She had a lot of that."[15]

The book begins with Rodrigo S. M.'s lengthy search for the story he is going to tell. "So that's why I don't know if my story is going to be—be what? I don't know anything about it, I still haven't worked up the nerve to write it. Will things happen? They will. But what? I don't know that either."[16]

At last the story of Macabéa begins, a girl who was "incompetent for life," a girl who earns less than the minimum wage. "Some people have it. Some people don't. It's very simple: the girl didn't have it. Didn't have what? That's it: she didn't have it."[17] At work, she makes too many mistakes—she has a third-grade education—and invariably dirties the paper.

Macabéa stinks, but her roommates, afraid of offending her, cannot bring themselves to tell her so: "She didn't have that delicate thing called charm. Only I find her charming. Only I, her author, love her." She is an orphan who "no longer knew what it was to have a father and mother, she had forgotten the taste." But she is not unhappy, because her self-consciousness is as rudimentary as her education. "She thought that people should be happy. So she was."[18]

Clarice's identification with the girl who "didn't have it" is so complete, she writes, that she hopes she never has to describe a lazar, because she would break out in leprosy. "When I think that I could have been born her—and why not?—I tremble. And it seems a cowardly escape not being her, I feel guilty as I said in one of the titles."[19]

Macabéa has her pleasures, though. "I am a typist and a virgin and I like Coca-Cola," she thinks with satisfaction. Like Clarice Lispector, she likes listening to Clock Radio, which offered " 'the correct time and culture,' and no music, just dripping in the sound of falling drops—each one the drop of a minute passing by. And especially the radio station used the intervals between those drops of minutes to run commercials—she loved commercials. It was the perfect station because also between the drops of time it gave little lessons about things she might need to know some day. That was how she learned that the Emperor Charlemagne was known as Carolus in his own country."[20]

She fantasizes about buying a tub of cream she saw advertised in an old newspaper "for the skin of women who simply were not her," a product so luscious that she dreamed of eating it.[21] And once, for the only time in her life, she lies to her boss in order to spend the day sitting by herself in her lousy boardinghouse.

And she has her boyfriend, who enters her life on a rainy street.

> "And if you'll allow me, what's your name, little lady?"
>
> "Macabéa."
>
> "Maca what?"
>
> "Bea," she had to finish.
>
> "Sorry but that sounds like a disease, a skin disease."[22]

Olímpico de Jesus never grows much more charming, but Macabéa, who has nobody else, is, of course, charmed by him. His surname is "the surname of those who have no father," and his first name is another reference to the story of the Maccabees, to the false god the Jews refused to worship when the Temple was polluted and called "the temple of Jupiter Olympius" (in Portuguese, Zeus Olímpico). Like the pagan idols, which were covered with precious metals, Olímpico has saved up for months in order to have a perfectly good tooth removed and replaced with one of gold.[23]

> They didn't know how to take a walk. They walked through the heavy rain and stopped in front of a hardware store where the window display featured piping, tin cans, large bolts, and nails. And Macabéa, afraid that the silence might already mean separation, said to her new boyfriend:
>
> "I just love bolts and nails, what about you, sir?"[24]

This comical scene recalls another, more ghoulish, which the writer José Castello described, dating from the time Clarice was writing *The Hour of the Star*:

> Clarice has halted before a shop window on the Avenida Copacabana and seems to be looking at a dress. Embarrassed, I come up to her. "How are you?" I say. It takes her a while to turn around. She doesn't move at first, but then, before I dare repeat the greeting, she turns slowly, as if to see where something frightening had come from, and says: "So it's you." At that moment, horrified, I notice that there is nothing in the shop window but undressed mannequins. But then my silly horror becomes a conclusion: Clarice has a passion for the void.[25]

Macabéa shares this passion: "Most of the time she had without realizing it the void that fills the souls of the saints. Was she a saint? So it seems. She didn't know that she was meditating because she didn't know what the word meant. But it seems to me that her life was a long meditation on the nothing."[26]

Macabéa's relationship with the loathsome Olímpico, whose ambitions include working as a butcher and becoming a congressman, ends when Olímpico discovers a more promising prospect in her colleague Gloria, whose father works in a butcher shop and who eats three square meals a day—and who, unlike Macabéa, with her withered ovaries, has hair bleached "egg-yellow."[27]

Gloria is a know-it-all who constantly dishes out advice to Macabéa, including sending her to a cheap doctor who gives the girl more advice, telling her she has a touch of tuberculosis and then suggesting she eat more "nice Italian spaghetti," a dish the half-starved Macabéa has never heard of.

When Gloria suggests that Macabéa visit her psychic, Clarice suddenly, violently butts in.

> I am absolutely tired of literature: only muteness keeps me company. If I still write it's because I have nothing better to do in the world while I wait for death. The search for the word in the dark. My small success invades me and exposes me to glances on the street. I wanted to stagger through the mud, my need for abjection I can hardly control, the need for the orgy and the worst absolute delight. Sin attracts me, prohibited things fascinate me. I want to be a pig and a hen and then kill them and drink their blood. I think of Macabéa's sex, mute but unexpectedly covered with thick and abundant black hairs—her sex was the only vehement sign of her existence.[28]

When Clarice resumes the story, Macabéa borrows money from Gloria and goes to the psychic, Madame Carlota, a former hooker who lives in a luxury Macabéa had never imagined—"Yellow plastic covering the couches and chairs. And even plastic flowers. Plastic was the greatest"—and who overwhelms Macabéa with her affectionate words. She is a "fan of Jesus": "I'm just wild about him," she tells her bedazzled visitor, launching into her inspirational life story: sought after by visitors to the red light district, she "only got syphilis once but penicillin cured [her]."[29] When her charms had faded, Jesus wasted no time in setting up her and a colleague with a brothel of their own.

Madame Carlota finally tires of talking about herself, spreads Macabéa's cards, and sees her horrible destiny before her. But "(explosion) suddenly it happened: Madame's face lit up all illuminated." She tells Macabéa that as soon as she walks out of her house her life will change entirely. "Madame was right: Jesus was finally paying attention to her." She learns that she is about to meet a rich foreigner named Hans, "blond with blue or green or brown or black eyes," who will fall in love with her and buy her a fur coat. Macabéa stammers:

> "But you don't need a fur coat in the heat of Rio . . ."
>
> "You'll have it just to dress up. It's been a while since I've had such good cards. And I'm always honest: for example, I was open enough to tell that girl who just left that she was going to be run over by a car, she even cried a lot, didn't you see her bleary eyes?"[30]

Dazzled, amazed, already burning with passion for Hans, Macabéa's life has been changed: "And changed by words—we have known since Moses that the word is divine." As she walks out of Madame Carlota's house, "pregnant with the future," she is struck by a giant yellow Mercedes.[31]

At the suggestion of Marina Colasanti and Affonso Romano de Sant'Anna, Clarice, in her last years, had frequented a fortune-teller in the working-class neighborhood of Méier. This woman, with the Dickensian name of Miss Nadir, often gave Clarice rosy prognoses: "Health tending to improve, nothing seriously wrong. Ex-husband to leave posting with son, who is well and making a lot of progress. Happiness will chase away problems! Romance confirmed and in your house. Not family love," Miss Nadir wrote on October 7, 1976, for example.[32]

"I went to a fortune-teller who told me about all kinds of good things that were about to happen to me," she told Julio Lerner in the interview with TV Cultura, "and on the way home in the taxi I thought it'd be really funny if a taxi hit me and ran me over and I died after hearing all those good things."[33] The combination was typical of Clarice: of wanting to believe, of seeking out fortune-tellers and astrologers, only to dismiss their pronouncements with a dark and ironic joke.

Yet in the same dark and ironic fashion, Madame Carlota's predictions do come true. Macabéa does "meet" the foreigner she has been promised. And by now, after a fashion, Clarice did believe. In the book's dedication to the musicians, she wrote, "And—and do not forget that the structure of the atom is invisible but nonetheless known. I know of many things I have never seen. And so do you. There is no proof of the existence of the truest thing of all; all we can do is believe."[34]

"God is the world," she wrote on the first page of *The Hour of the Star*, a final distant echo of the Spinoza she had read as a student. "The truth is always an interior and inexplicable contact. My truest life is unrecognizable, extremely interior and not a single word can describe it."[35]

Macabéa, who like Clarice meditates on the nothing and "bathes in the no," is a kind of saint: "In the poverty of body and spirit I reach saintliness, I who want to feel the breath of my beyond. To be more than I, who am so little." Macabéa has "reduced herself to herself. And so have I," writes Clarice, "from failure to failure, reduced myself to myself but at least I want to meet the world and its God." "Like the northeasterner, there are thousands of girls spread though the slums, vacancies in boardinghouse beds, working behind counters till they drop. They don't even notice that they are easily substitutable and that they could just as soon not exist at all. Few complain and as far as I know none of them protest because they don't know to whom. Could this whom exist?"[36]

The tormenting question persists. "She prayed but without God, she didn't know who He was and therefore He did not exist," Clarice wrote of Macabéa.[37] But at last she herself did know who He was. When the book came out in October 1977, she sent Alceu Amoroso Lima a copy. This was the same Catholic writer who had contributed an introductory essay to the first edition of *The Chandelier*. In that book, he had written thirty-one years before, "there is the most complete **absence of God**." Now he received a copy of *The Hour of the Star* with an inscription in Clarice's shaking hand: "I know that God exists."[38]

"Before I could read and write I already made up stories," Clarice once said, remembering her earliest childhood. "I even invented, with a somewhat passive friend of mine, a never-ending story.... I started, everything got very difficult, they both died.... Then she came in and said they weren't actually as dead as all that. And then it all started over again."[39]

In *The Chandelier*, Virginia is killed by an oncoming car, but in *Near to the Wild Heart* the child Joana pulls off the same magic trick Clarice had performed as a child: "Joana had already dressed the doll, had already undressed her, she had imagined her going to a party where she would shine among all the other girls. A blue car crossed the girl's body, killed her. Then along came the fairy and the girl came back to life."[40]

Clarice could not let Angela die; now, at the end of *The Hour of the Star*, she still wants to rescue poor Macabéa. As soon as the Mercedes strikes, she rushes back to save her, only to pull herself back: "I could happily start again at the point that Macabéa was standing on the sidewalk—but it's not up to me to say that the blond and foreign man looked at her. Because I've gone too far and cannot turn back now."[41]

"I'm going to do everything I can to keep her from dying," Clarice writes on the next page. "But what an urge to put her to sleep and to go to bed myself." The rest of the book is Clarice's desperate effort to save her. "Is Macabéa by chance going to die? How do I know?" she writes. "And not even the people there knew. Though just in case a neighbor had lit a candle next to the body. The luxury of the rich flame seemed to sing glory."[42]

For pages and pages Clarice holds the girl's fate in her hands. "For now Macabéa is nothing more than a vague feeling on the dirty cobblestones. I could leave her on the street and simply not finish the story," she writes, exactly as she had done with Angela. Yet doubt has crept in. "But couldn't she be needing to die? Since there are times when a person needs a little bitty death and doesn't even know it."[43]

Macabéa crimps into the fetal position.

> Then—lying there—she had a moist and supreme happiness, since she had been born for the embrace of death. Death which is my favorite character in this story. Was she going to say farewell to herself? I don't think she is going to die because she wants to live so much. And there was a certain sensuality in the way she had huddled up. Or is it because pre-death resembles intense sensual throes? Because her face looked like a grimace of desire. Things are always days before and if she doesn't die now she is like us on the day before her death, forgive me for reminding you because as for me I can't forgive my clairvoyance.[44]

This time, the character will not stand up again. Clarice lets her beloved Macabéa die.

"But do not mourn the dead," she insists. "They know what they are doing."[45]

In October, only a couple of days after the publication of *The Hour of the Star*, Clarice Lispector was suddenly hospitalized. In the taxi on the way to the hospital, she said, "Let's pretend that we're not going to the hospital, that I'm not sick, and that we're going to Paris," Olga Borelli remembered.

> So we started making plans and talking about everything we would do in Paris. The taxi driver, poor thing, already tired from working all night long, timidly asked: "Can I go on the trip too?" And Clarice said: "Of course you can, and you can even bring your girlfriend." He said: "My girlfriend is an old lady, seventy years old, and I don't have any money." Clarice answered: "She's coming too. Let's pretend you won the lottery." When we got to the hospital, Clarice asked how much it was. Only twenty cruzeiros, and she gave him two hundred.[46]

Clarice had said that "everyone chooses the way they die," and the way she chose was spookily appropriate. After a lifetime writing about eggs and the mystery of birth—in *The Hour of the Star* she insistently referred to Macabéa's withered ovaries—she herself was now suffering from an untreatable ovarian cancer.

After an exploratory operation on October 28, she was transferred to a public hospital, the Hospital da Lagoa, and from her room she had a view of Rio's tremendous mountains and the Botanic Garden she so loved. She received few visitors: Tania and Elisa; Paulo and his wife, Ilana; Rosa Cass; Olga Borelli; Nélida Piñon; Autran Dourado; Siléa Marchi.

The diagnosis was terminal, but she was not told the news. "Clarice talked a lot," Siléa said. "She was very alert.... Moreover, she knew nothing about her illness and indicated, to everyone she talked to, how optimistic she was and how much she wanted to go home as soon as possible."[47]

The woman who had so often announced her own death gave no sign of knowing what was happening to her. She continued creating her magical fictions. In her nearly illegible handwriting, she drew up guest lists for the gatherings she would host back home. "She got very excited thinking about these lunches and about the relatives and friends she would invite. It would be a party. Which never happened," Olga said.[48]

But it is more likely, as many who accompanied her final weeks felt, that she knew perfectly well what was happening. For their sake, she put on a bold face. "A person knows when they're dying," said Rosa Cass, who at Clarice's request smuggled a black Caracu beer into the hospital. (She had also requested an *igurke*, a kosher pickle.) She laughed at the situation: "What nonsense," she told Rosa, when asked about its gravity. But Rosa remembered that Clarice often camouflaged her real feelings. "Clarice never let on what she was thinking."[49]

She was less tactful with one of her doctors, who was pained by the worried patient's persistent questions about what they were going to do with her.[50] And the words she wrote or dictated to Olga show that Clarice meant it when she said that she hoped to die writing: "Inside the most interior of my house I die at the end of this year exhausted." On her deathbed, she returned to the myth she had made about her name, the lily on the breast (*lis no peito*).

> I am an object loved by God. And that makes flowers blossom upon my breast. He created me in the same way I created the sentence I just wrote: "I am an object loved by God" and he enjoyed creating me as much as I enjoyed creating the phrase. And the more spirit the human object has, the greater God's satisfaction.
>
> White lilies pressing against the nudity of my breast. The lilies I offer to whatever hurts inside you. Since we are beings and needy. Even because certain things—if not given away—wither. For example—beside the warmth of my body the petals of the lilies would wilt. I call out to the light breeze for my future death. I will have to die because otherwise my

> petals will wilt. And that is why I give myself to death every day. I die and am reborn.
>
> I have also already died the death of others. But now I am dying intoxicated with life. And I bless the warmth of the living body that withers the white lilies.
>
> Desire, no longer moved by hope, calms and longs for nothing....
>
> I will be the impalpable substance that has no memory of the year before.[51]

Heavily sedated, she was still dictating words to Olga on the morning of December 9, 1977.

> Sudden lack of air. Long before the metamorphosis and my indisposition, I had already noticed in a painting in my house a beginning.
>
> I, I, if memory serves, shall die.
>
> And you do not know how much a person weighs who has no strength. Give me your hand, because I have to hold it so that nothing hurts this much.[52]

The day before her death, Olga Borelli reported, Clarice Lispector suffered a powerful hemorrhage.

> She turned very pale and lost a great deal of blood. Desperate, she got up from her bed and walked toward the door, wanting to leave the room. The nurse stopped her there. Clarice looked at her angrily and said, distressed:
>
> "You killed my character!"[53]

After their first meeting seven years before, Clarice wrote Olga Borelli that she hoped to have her near at the hour of her death. Now, at ten-thirty in the morning of December 9, 1977, she died holding Olga's hand.

"She became her own fiction," wrote Paulo Francis. "It is the best possible epitaph for Clarice."[54]

EPILOGUE

Clarice Lispector could not be buried the following day, her fifty-seventh birthday, because it fell on the Sabbath. On December 11, 1977, in the Israelite Cemetery of Cajú, not far from the port where Macabéa spent her rare off-hours, Clarice Lispector was laid to rest in the Orthodox ritual. Four women from the burial society, the Chevra Kadisha, washed her body inside and out, wrapped it in a white linen sheet, placed her head on a pillow filled with earth, and nailed her inside a simple wooden coffin. The Ninety-first Psalm, the funeral prayer El malei rachamim, and the burial Kaddish were read. There were no speeches from among the mourners. Three spadefuls of dirt were tossed upon the coffin as the words from Genesis rang out: "Dust you are and unto dust you shall return."

On the tombstone, engraved in Hebrew, the hidden name: Chaya bat Pinkhas. Chaya, daughter of Pinkhas.

Do not read what I write as a reader would do. Unless this reader works, he too, in the soliloquies of the irrational dark.

If this book ever comes out, may the profane recoil from it. Since writing is a sacred thing which no infidel can enter. I am making a really bad book on purpose in order to drive off the profane who want to "like." But a small group will see that this "liking" is superficial and will enter inside what I am truly writing, which is neither "bad" nor "good."

Inspiration is like a mysterious scent of amber. I have a small piece of amber with me. The scent makes me the sister of the sacred orgies of King Solomon and the Queen of Sheba. Blessed be your loves. Could it be that I am afraid to take the step of dying at this very instant? Careful not to die. Yet I am already in the future. This future of mine that shall be for you the past of someone dead. When you have finished this book cry a halleluiah for me. When you close the last page of this frustrated and dauntless and silly book of life then forget me. May God bless you then and this book ends well. That I might at last find respite. May peace be upon us, upon you, and upon me. Am I falling into discourse? may the temple's faithful forgive me: I write and that way rid myself of me and then at last I can rest.

—CLARICE LISPECTOR
(1920–1977)

ACKNOWLEDGMENTS

This book would have been much the poorer without the help of people all around the world who gave of their time, their archives, their memories, their knowledge, and their friendship.

I owe a special debt to Clarice Lispector's relatives. Over the years, Paulo Gurgel Valente has done so much—from creating the archives of her papers to ensuring the continued publication of materials relating to her life—to preserve and perpetuate his mother's great legacy. He was helpful and encouraging from the start, offering many valuable suggestions in the manuscript and generously providing many of the illustrations. And to my irrepressible honorary *vovó,* Ambassadress Eliane Weil Gurgel Valente. Getting to know the warm, entertaining, and unstintingly supportive Eliane was in itself reward enough for writing this book. I have spent many happy hours with Clarice's cousin, the prima ballerina Cecília Wainstok Lipka, who offered me hard-to-find documents, as well as her kindness and friendship. Clarice's grandniece, the filmmaker Nicole Algranti, has been extremely liberal with her private archive and with her memories of her aunt Elisa Lispector. I am grateful to Bertha Lispector Cohen in Rio, her brother, Samuel Lispector, and her sister, Vera Lispector Choze, in Recife, for sharing their memories of Clarice's early years. Thanks also to Ambassadress Marilu de Seixas Corrêa, Minister Mitzi Gurgel Valente da Costa, and Isaac Chut.

To Alberto Dines, great biographer and journalist, scholar of Jewish Brazil, and friend of Clarice Lispector, who despite his many commitments always found time to reply to even my most trivial questions; and to Humberto Werneck, a one-man encyclopedia of Brazilian life, whose inexhaustible erudition and unfailing flair for anecdote allowed me to create a much richer picture of the literary culture around Clarice Lispector.

To the journalist Rosa Cass, who spent hours recalling her long friendship with Clarice Lispector in her apartment in Flamengo; and to the distinguished writer Renard Perez, as gracious to me as he had been to Clarice and Elisa Lispector.

To the librarians and archivists who smoothed my path: Eliane Vasconcellos, Deborah Roditi, and Leonardo Pereira da Cunha at the Arquivo-Museu de Literatura Brasileira at the Fundação Casa de Rui Barbosa, Rio de Janeiro; Cristina Zappa and Manoela Purcell Daudt d'Oliveira at the Instituto Moreira Salles, Rio; Cristina Antunes and José Mindlin, who allowed me to examine the manuscript of *Near to the Wild Heart* preserved in Mr. Mindlin's legendary library in São Paulo; Maria Manuela Vasconcelos, who helped me locate Clarice Lispector materials in the Biblioteca Nacional in Lisbon and shared her own memories of the writer; and Dr. Tânia Neumann Kaufman of the Arquivo Histórico Judaico de Pernambuco, whose own writings on Jewish Recife were such a rich historical source. In Kahal zur Israel, the oldest synagogue in the New World, Dr. Kaufman introduced me to Beatriz Schnaider Schvartz, whose tour of Boa Vista, where she and Clarice Lispector grew up, was one of the most memorable days in the research and writing of this book.

To my fellow *claricianos*, whose enthusiasm for our common subject made the solitary work of writing a biography much more collegial: Claire Varin, the pioneer Canadian researcher whose books and conversation were such a bountiful source of inspiration; Nádia Battella Gotlib, Brazil's greatest authority on Clarice Lispector, whose biographical research uncovered so many essential facts about Clarice's life, and whose help with the photographs saved me many headaches; Teresa Cristina Montero Ferreira, whose own biography is packed with the fruits of her exhaustive research; Sonia Roncador, who shared her rare copy of the second draft of *Água viva*; and Earl E. Fitz, who helped put me in touch with Sonia Roncador and shared his own thoughts and writings on Clarice Lispector. A special word is due Nelson Vieira, brilliant teacher and scholar, who first fired my enthusiasm for Clarice when I was an undergraduate and who was among the first to understand Clarice as a Jewish writer.

To Juan Sager of the University of Manchester, who provided my research with an unexpected boost by giving me the Clarice materials collected by his late partner, Giovanni Pontiero, her English translator, who was working on his own biography at the time of his death; and to Ann Mackenzie of the University of Glasgow, who led me to Professor Sager.

To Minister Carlos Alberto Asfora of the Brazilian embassy in The Hague, who familiarized me with the ways of Itamaraty. His tireless dedication to promoting Brazilian culture abroad has been an inspiration to me and so many others, and his introduction to Ambassador Gilberto Saboia put me in touch with Clarice's diplomatic circle.

To Nachman and Shulamit Falbel, who have been my home away from home in São Paulo ever since they unexpectedly entered my life during my first semester in college.

To Denise Milfont, whose beautiful house overlooking the Bay of Guanabara, like Denise herself, is an isle of repose during my often hectic stays in Rio de Janeiro.

To "The Group" from Paraty—Paul Finlay, Ravi Mirchandani, Amy Tabor, Jocasta Hamilton, João Crespo, Fiona Smith, Raffaella de Angelis, Fiona McMorrough, and Diane Gray-Smith—who have so consistently provided comic relief on my research trips to Brazil. Among them, I owe a special debt to Alison Entrekin, who has so cheerfully placed her vast knowledge of the Portuguese language at my disposal; to Matthew Hamilton, agent, editor, and co-conspirator; and of course to the unremittingly glamorous Sheila O'Shea, who, Group or no Group, has been, for more than a decade, one of the best things in my life.

To the biographers who offered a novice guidance and encouragement: Judith Thurman's biography of Colette helped inspire this one, and her early insistence that organization is the key to biography spared me many headaches. Frederick Brown's *Flaubert* and *Zola* offered models of integrating literary criticism with life narrative, and his admonition to rely primarily on my own readings of Clarice's work helped focus this book. Edmund White warned me of what I was in for, in person and in the chapter of *My Lives* about his own adventures writing *Genet*.

My visit to Ukraine would have been much less rewarding without Santiago Eder's suggestion that I get in touch with Kate Brown, whose *Biography of No Place* did so much to illuminate the mysterious world Clarice Lispector came from. Kate, in turn, put me in touch with Mary Mycio. Some of my favorite memories of writing this book involve eating pizza in Kiev, Mary's Geiger counter at the ready, and staying up into the wee hours watching dressage videos in her apartment. Mary led me to Victoria Butenko, who helped with Ukrainian translation. Daniel Mendelsohn recommended Alexander Dunai as a guide through the wilds of Podolia. Alex's vast knowledge of Jewish and Ukrainian culture immeasurably enriched, and indeed made possible my fascinating expedition to Clarice Lispector's birthplace. I am also grateful to Ambassador Renato L. R. Marques and his auxiliaries at the Brazilian embassy in Kiev.

To all those who helped this project with kindnesses great and small: Jeferson Masson, who shared with me his extensive research into the life and work of Elisa Lispector; Ana Luisa Chafir, who spent an unforgettable evening telling me about her great-aunt Bluma Chafir Wainer; Muniz Sodré Cabral, who remembered Clarice's psychoanalyst Inês Besouchet; Joel Silveira, the journalist who knew Clarice Lispector in wartime Italy; Ambassadress Isabel Gurgel Valente, who offered valuable information about her late husband, Ambassador Maury Gurgel Valente; Sábato Magaldi and Edla van Steen, who spent an evening in São Paulo telling me about Lúcio Cardoso and the Brazilian theater; Ambassadress Sara Escorel de Moraes, who shared her memories of Clarice in Rio and Washington; Major Elza Cansanção Medeiros, veteran of the Brazilian Expeditionary Force, for her memories of Brazil's involvement in World War II, and her fellow field-nurse, Virgínia Portocarrero; the director Luiz Carlos Lacerda, who recalled the dazzling impression Lúcio Cardoso and Clarice Lispector made on him as a young man; the outstanding novelist Autran Dourado and his wife, Lucia, who remembered Clarice inside and outside the literary milieu of Rio de Janeiro; Marina Colasanti, who told me about her experience reading Clarice's *crônicas* in the palace where she lived as a refugee from Italian Africa; Gilda Murray, who remembered her experiences as a young woman with Clarice and her great friend Olga Borelli; Antonio Olinto, who welcomed me in a Copacabana apartment filled with an astonishing collection of African art; Álvaro Pacheco, who described publishing some of Clarice's last works; Ilka Soares, who spoke to me about her collaboration in Clarice's journalism; Helena Valladares, Fernando Sabino's first wife, who remembered the impression Clarice made as a young woman in Rio; Lygia Marina de Moraes, Fernando Sabino's third wife, who told me about the memorable day she met Tom Jobim and Clarice Lispector; Maria Alice Barroso, the novelist who so fondly remembered her friend Elisa Lispector; Moacir Werneck de Castro, who helped me understand Bluma Wainer and the Brazilian journalists of the 1940s; Marlos Nobre, one of the musicians to whom *The Hour of the Star* is dedicated; Ivan Lessa, whose vivid and hilarious memories of *Senhor* magazine and of Rio de Janeiro in the early 1960s made one want to be there; the dazzling Maria Bonomi, who (with Lena Peres) spent a morning in Amsterdam telling me about going to the White House "dressed as Clarice"; the essayist José Castello, who sent me his own writings about Clarice; Clarissa Verissimo Jaffe, who talked about Clarice during her Washington years; Caetano Veloso, who encouraged this project; Ana Paula Hisayama, who provided me with the Brazilian books I could not find closer to home; Magdalena Edwards, who pointed me to Elizabeth Bishop's letters about Clarice in the Harvard and

Princeton libraries; the great translator Gregory Rabassa, who recalled meeting Clarice in Austin; Richard Zenith, the leading authority on Fernando Pessoa, who helped me navigate the archives of Portugal; Danuza Leão, who talked to me about her late husband, Samuel Wainer; George Andreou, who provided a welcome impulse at a moment when this project most needed it; Dorothea Severino, who offered me her rare typescript of *Água viva*; Paulo Rocco, who told me about publishing Clarice; Eva Lieblich Fernandes, who recounted her own fraught experience of wartime immigration to Brazil; Joëlle Rouchou, who provided me with her remarkable book about Samuel Wainer and the Jewish world around him; the actress Marilena Ansaldi, who shared her warm memories of Olga Borelli; Klara Główczewska, who helped me with the finer points of Polish spelling; the outstanding novelist Bernardo Carvalho, who dug a rare item out of the archives of the *Folha de S. Paulo*; Jonathan Milder of the Food Network, who was intrigued as I was by recipes involving blood sauces; my old friend Jeremy Wright, who found Clarice materials in Austin; the gorgeous Norma Couri, who shared her memories of Clarice and her own impressive archive; Paulo de Medeiros, whose early reading offered many valuable suggestions; Želimir Galjanić, who read the manuscript in an early phase; Amber Qureshi, a friend I can always count on; Yuko Miki, my *cúmplice* in Brazilian studies for so many years; Jerome Charyn, a Clarice enthusiast who put me in touch with Michel Martens, who met her in Rio; and Luciane Moritz Sommer, Portuguese teacher turned friend.

To my literary agent, Jim Rutman, distant compatriot of Clarice Lispector, who took on a complex project and saw it through many nail-biting moments with his dry wit and inimitable tact.

To my editor, Cybele Tom of Oxford University Press, whose willingness to grapple with difficult intellectual issues helped me think them through and clarify them. Also at Oxford, I am grateful to Christine Dahlin, who shepherded a complex manuscript through production; to Sarah Russo, a publicist who gets up early; and to Samara Stob, who directed the marketing effort.

To the team at Haus Publishing in London: Harry Hall, Claire Palmer, Robert Pritchard, and most especially the delectable Barabara Schwepcke, who has built from scratch one of Britain's most welcoming homes for international literature.

To my dear friend Carol Devine Carson, who designed the beautiful jacket; and to Reginald Piggott, who designed the family tree and maps.

To my parents, Jane and Bertrand C. Moser, who always encouraged even my most recondite enthusiasms.

Finally, to those friends and collaborators who did not live to see the publication of this book: Gibson Barbosa, former minister of foreign relations; Marly de Oliveira, distinguished Brazilian poet; and Rosa Lispector, wife of Clarice's cousin Samuel.

When I met him, Marco Antonio de Carvalho was completing his biography of Rubem Braga, a labor of love of many years. His untimely death on June 25, 2007, deprived him of the pleasure of seeing the publication of his admirable book.

And to the last of the brilliant Lispector girls, Tania Lispector Kaufmann, who passed away on November 15, 2007. From the moment she first opened the door to her Copacabana apartment, I fell for Tania: ninety years old, hardly able to walk but always dressed to the nines, her hair and makeup flawless, her mind perfectly sharp, and her spirit as warm and generous as the day, all those years before, when she "adopted" the little sister grieving for her mother.

Marie-Claude de Brunhoff, *in memoriam.*

Aan Arthur Japin en Lex Jansen is dit boek, met liefde en vriendschap, opgedragen.

NOTES

Introduction

1. Fernando Sabino and Clarice Lispector, *Cartas perto do coração* (Rio de Janeiro: Record, 2001), 67, 59–62.

2. Clarice Lispector, "Já andei de camelo, a esfinge, a dança do ventre (Conclusão)," in *A descoberta do mundo* (1984; Rio de Janeiro: Livraria Francisco Alves Editora S.A., 1994), 379.

3. Instituto Moreira Salles, *Cadernos de literatura brasileira: Clarice Lispector,* vols. 17 and 18 (São Paulo: Instituto Moreira Salles, 2004), 53.

4. Ibid., 92; Edilberto Coutinho, *Criaturas de papel: Temas de literatura & sexo & folclore & carnaval & futebol & televisão & outros temas da vida* (Rio de Janeiro: Civilização Brasileira, 1980), 168.

5. Gregory Rabassa, *If This Be Treason: Translation and Its Dyscontents: A Memoir* (New York: New Directions, 2005), 70.

6. Laura Freixas, *Clarice Lispector: Vidas literarias* (Barcelona: Ediciones Omega, 2001), 16.

7. Hélène Cixous and Deborah Jenson, *"Coming to Writing" and Other Essays* (Cambridge, Mass.: Harvard University Press, 1991).

8. Nádia Battella Gotlib, *Clarice: Uma vida que se conta* (São Paulo: Ática, 1995), 485.

9. Ibid., 52.

10. "Meus livros têm 'recadinhos': Quais? Os críticos é que dizem . . . ," *O Globo,* May 15, 1961.

11. "Clarice Lispector diz que Escreve sem ter Esquemas," *[Curitiba],* July 25, 1970.

12. María Esther Gilio, "Tristes trópicos: Con Clarice Lispector en Río," *Triunfo,* June 5, 1976.

13. Quoted in Federico Mengozzi, "Mistérios de Clarice," *Época.* Edition no. 342, December 12, 2004, n.p.

14. Clarice Lispector, *De corpo inteiro* (São Paulo: Editora Siciliano, 1992), 199.

15. Antônio Hohlfeldt, "Uma tarde com Clarice Lispector," *Correio do povo,* January 3, 1971.

16. Isa Cambará, "Clarice Lispector: Não escrevo para agradar a ninguém," *Folha de S. Paulo,* September 10, 1975.

17. Teresa Cristina Montero Ferreira, *Eu sou uma pergunta: Uma biografia de Clarice Lispector* (Rio de Janeiro: Rocco, 1999), 258.

18. Clarice Lispector, "Amor," in *Laços de família* (São Paulo: Francisco Alves, 1960).

19. Lispector, "Perfil de um ser eleito," in *Descoberta,* 416.

20. Sérgio Fonta, "O papo: Clarice Lispector," *Jornal de Letras* 259 (1972).

21. Lispector, "Brain Storm," in *Descoberta,* 262.

22. Ibid., 75.

23. *Le Monde,* September 19, 1970.

24. Clarice Lispector, *Um sopro de vida: Pulsações* (Rio de Janeiro: Editora Nova Fronteira, 1978), 25.

25. Clarice Lispector, *Água viva* (1973; Rio de Janeiro: Editora Artenova, 1993), 40.

26. Lispector, "Minha próxima e excitante viagem pelo mundo," April 1, 1972, in *Descoberta.*

Chapter 1

1. Amylton de Almeida, *Gazeta,* 1986, quoted in Nelson Vieira, *Jewish Voices in Brazilian Literature: A Prophetic Discourse of Alterity* (Gainesville: University Press of Florida, 1995), 120.

2. Olga Borelli, *Clarice Lispector, esboço para um possível retrato* (Rio de Janeiro: Editora Nova Fronteira, 1981), 43.

3. Gotlib, *Clarice,* 66.

4. Lispector, "Esclarecimentos—Explicação de uma vez por todas" in *Descoberta,* 345, italics in original.

5. Clarice Lispector, Teresa Montero, and Lícia Manzo, *Outros escritos* (Rio de Janeiro: Rocco, 2005), 95. Tongue-tie is a relatively common birth defect, but it rarely lingers into adulthood. Dr. Pedro Bloch assured her that it was easy to fix, she wrote, but she declined the operation for fear of the pain.

6. Alberto Dines quoted in Vieira, *Jewish Voices,* 120.

7. Instituto Moreira Salles and Carlos Mendes de Sousa, "A revelação do nome," in *Cadernos de literatura brasileira: Clarice Lispector* (São Paulo: Instituto Moreira Salles, 2004), 144.

8. Interview, Renard Perez; Renard Perez, *Escritores brasileiros contemporâneos,* 2nd ed. (Rio de Janeiro: Civilização Brasileira, 1970), 69.

9. Quoted in Claire Varin, *Langues de feu: Essai sur Clarice Lispector* (Laval, Québec: Trois, 1990), 54–55.

10. Clarice Lispector, *O lustre* (Rio de Janeiro: Livraria Agir Editora, 1946), 185.

11. Carlos Mendes de Sousa, *Clarice Lispector, figuras da escrita* (Minho: Universidade de Minho Centro de Estudos Humanísticos, 2000), 164.

12. Sérgio Milliet, quoted in ibid., 21.

13. Lêdo Ivo, quoted in Instituto Moreira Salles, *Cadernos,* 50.

14. Sousa, *Figuras,* 22.

15. Lispector, "Crônica social" in *Descoberta,* 199, quoted in Varin, *Langues,* 97.

16. Emanuel Brasil, *Nossos clássicos: Clarice Lispector (No. 120)* (Rio de Janeiro: Agir, 1994), 138–39.

17. Ferreira, *Eu sou.*

18. Sousa, *Figuras,* 22.

19. Lêdo Ivo, quoted in Instituto Moreira Salles, *Cadernos,* 48.

20. "Clarice, um mistério sem muito mistério," *Correio da Manhã,* November 2, 1971; Instituto Moreira Salles, *Cadernos,* 59.

21. Julio Lerner, "A última entrevista de Clarice Lispector," *Shalom,* June–August 1992.

22. "She tried at all costs to hide her Jewish background," one critic typically asserted. Edgar Cézar Nolasco, "Restos de Ficção: A criação biográfico-literária de Clarice Lispector," Universidade Federal de Minas Gerais, 2003, 9. For other examples of this misconception, see Sousa, *Figuras,* 27.

23. Lispector, "Pertencer," in *Descoberta,* 110, emphasis added.

24. Anna Reid, *Borderland: A Journey through the History of Ukraine* (Boulder, Colo.: Westview Press, 1999), 132.

25. Ibid., 147.

26. Marcus Eli Ravage, *The Jew Pays: A Narrative of the Consequences of the War to the Jews of Eastern Europe* (New York: Knopf, 1919), 27.

Chapter 2

1. Nathan [a.k.a. Norman] Hofferman, *The 20th Century and I*, records of the Chechelnicker Benevolent Association of New York, YIVO Institute for Jewish Research, New York.

2. A Jewish cemetery proves that Jewish life persisted in Chechelnik long after the Holocaust, though the remaining Jews have either gone to the cities or emigrated.

3. C. T. Vovk, S. V. Taranets', and V. A. Kosakivsky, *Narisi z istoryi Chechel'nika: Z naidavnishikh chasiv do nashikh dniv* (Vinnitsa, Ukraine: "Komp'iuterna verstka ta khudozhne oformlennia redaktsii gazeti 'Chechel'nits'kii visnik'," 2000), 41. Neighboring Savran, where Elisa was born, and the related Savranka also bear Turkic names.

4. Ibid., 42.

5. Clarice Lispector, *Onde estivestes de noite* (Rio de Janeiro: Editora Artenova, 1974), 45.

6. Quoted in Vovk et al., *Narisi*, 62–63.

7. Gershom Gerhard Scholem, *Major Trends in Jewish Mysticism* (New York: Schocken Books, 1995), 337–38.

8. Kate Brown, *A Biography of No Place: From Ethnic Borderland to Soviet Heartland* (Cambridge, Mass.: Harvard University Press, 2004), 67, 59–62.

9. Borelli, *Esboço*, 11.

10. Coutinho, *Criaturas*, 170.

11. Scholem, *Major Trends*, 349.

12. Tania Lispector Kaufmann, Elisa and Clarice's sister, affirmed that the book is "about eighty percent true." Its chronology and the places it describes the family passing through are all traceable in other sources, not least in the "nonfictional" *Retratos antigos*, and the general outline of the story is common to many other memoirs and histories of the period. It is usually easy to see where Elisa is inserting novelistic flourishes. In any case, her main concern seems to be to provide a record of the suffering of her family.

13. Elisa Lispector, *Retratos antigos*, 8. Collection of Nicole Algranti, Teresópolis, Rio de Janeiro.

14. He may also have worked, at least for a time, as a *shochet*, a kosher butcher. According to *In Exile*, he abandoned his profession, set up a tea house for his wife to run, and dedicated himself to Talmudic studies. (These descriptions may be fictional; in *Retratos* Elisa says he was a shopkeeper.)

15. E. Lispector, *Retratos*. Other sources mention eight children: Ferreira, *Eu sou*, 20; "eight children" is also the number given in Elisa Lispector, *No exílio; Romance* (1948; Rio de Janeiro: Editora Pongetti, 1971), 51.

16. E. Lispector, *Retratos*, 9.

17. Ferreira, *Eu sou*, 19; author's visit to Jewish Cemetery of Barro, Recife.

18. Ferreira, *Eu sou*, 17.

19. E. Lispector, *Retratos*, 10.

20. E. Lispector, *Exílio*, 21, 24.

21. E. Lispector, *Retratos*, 14.

22. E. Lispector, *Exílio*, 21.

23. E. Lispector, *Retratos*, 16–17.

24. Ibid.

25. Ibid., 20.

26. E. Lispector, *Exílio*, 51, 29.

27. E. Lispector, *Retratos*, 21.

28. Ibid.

29. Lerner, "Última entrevista."

30. E. Lispector, *Retratos*, 21.

31. Ibid., 23.

32. Ferreira, *Eu sou*, 21.

33. Isidore Singer and Cyrus Adler, eds., "Agricultural Colonies in the Argentine Republic," in *The Jewish Encyclopedia: A Descriptive Record of the History to the Present Day*, 12 vols. (New York: Funk & Wagnalls, 1906).

34. He, too, later came to Recife.

35. Ferreira, *Eu sou*, 21–22.

36. Israel Wainstok, *Zichrones fun a fater* (Rio de Janeiro: Impresso nos Estabelecimentos Gráficos "Monte Scopus," 1955).

37. S. An-Ski, *The Enemy at His Pleasure: A Journey through the Jewish Pale of Settlement during World War I*, trans. Joachim Neugroschel (New York: Metropolitan Books, 2002), 3–4.

38. Ibid., 15.

39. David Engel, "World War I," in Gershon David Hundert, ed., *The YIVO Encyclopedia of Jews in Eastern Europe*, 2 vols. (New Haven: Yale University Press, 2008), 2:2034.

40. Ibid., 2:2033.

41. Joachim Neugroschel, introduction to An-Ski, *Enemy*, ix–x.

42. From the beginning, the Ukrainian nationalist movement was unusually hospitable to Jews. There were several reasons for this. Mykhailo Hrushevski, the president of the Ukrainian revolutionary government, the Central Rada, was an outspoken advocate of the rights of national minorities. As Hrushevski realized, the Ukrainians and the Jews needed each other. The ethnic Ukrainians were principally agrarian, whereas the cities were heavily Russian, Jewish, and Polish. The Ukrainian national movement needed a bourgeoisie, and an alliance with the Jews was natural. But the very concept of "Ukrainian Jewry" did not exist. The Jews of the Russian Empire thought of themselves as Russian Jews, and they feared that if the supernational state fractured, they would be vulnerable to the new nationalisms. If the Jews were to adhere to the new government, they would have to identify with the Ukraine rather than Russia. The Rada, long before it declared independence, therefore emphasized its friendliness to minorities. The parliament set aside large blocks of seats for Russians, Poles, and Jews. In the lower house, the Jews were even disproportionately overrepresented. The government created the world's first Ministry of Jewish Affairs. These moves were designed to establish the principle of self-determination for minorities, including the Ukrainians, within a larger Russian state. "By granting extraterritorial autonomy to their minorities," Henry Abramson has written, "the Ukrainians took the high moral ground in their negotiations with the [All-Russian] Provisional Government over greater territorial autonomy for Ukraine as a whole." Henry Abramson, *A Prayer for the Government: Ukrainians and Jews in Revolutionary Times, 1917–1920* (Cambridge, Mass.: Harvard University Press for the Harvard Ukrainian Research Institute and Center for Jewish Studies, 1999).

43. Ibid., 61.

44. Ibid., 80.

45. This proposal, like so much else during this critical time, was rendered toothless by the endless infighting of the Zionists and the Socialists. The Zionists, who insisted on using Hebrew, which almost nobody spoke, faced off against the equally intransigent Socialist parties, who used Yiddish, the language of the vast majority of the Jews. The Ministry of Jewish Affairs, caught between the two extremes, dithered throughout the end of 1917 and the beginning of 1918.

46. The Jewish parties, along with the Russians, universally opposed the declaration. The Ukrainians thought that the least the Jews could do in return for the Rada's unusual liberality was to support Ukrainian national aspirations, and were angered when they did not.

47. Abramson, *Prayer*, 88.

48. Ibid., 100–101.

49. E. Lispector, *Retratos*, 17.

50. Ferreira, *Eu sou*, 23–24.

51. E. Lispector, *Exílio*, 59. In *Retratos antigos* she writes, "In one of the first pogroms that followed the Red Revolution, when the Bolsheviks were still hardly established, Grandfather died pierced by several bullets, as he ran up the stairs of what had until then been his own house, later used to quarter troops."

Chapter 3

1. American Jewish Congress, Israel Goldberg, and Committee on Protest against the Massacres of Jews in Ukrainia and Other Lands, *The Massacres and Other Atrocities Committed against the Jews in Southern Russia* (New York, 1920), 5, 13–14.

2. Ibid., 12.

3. This is the town Elisa names in her book.

4. E. Lispector, *Retratos*, 23.

5. E. Lispector, *Exílio*, 32–33, emphasis added.

6. E. Lispector, *Retratos*, 15.

7. Interview with Claire Varin, Laval, Québec, January 7, 2006.

8. Clarice Lispector, *Objecto gritante (II)*, 1971, 155, Dorothea Severino Collection, Nashville, Tennessee.

9. Orlando Figes, *A People's Tragedy: The Russian Revolution, 1891–1924* (New York: Viking, 1996), 678.

10. American Jewish Congress et al., *Massacres*, 15–16.

11. For a description of this pogrom, see Bernard Lecache, *Quand Israël meurt* (Paris: Editions du "Progrès civique," 1927), 181. On 182–89 there is a description of the pogrom in Pinkhas Lispector's native Teplyk, where Tania was born four years earlier. The family may have been in Teplyk, though Elisa names Haysyn.

12. American Jewish Congress et al., *Massacres*, 8–15.

13. Lispector, *Descoberta*, 110–11; "Pertencer," in *Descoberta*, June 15, 1968.

14. http://www.schoolscience.co.uk/content/4/biology/abpi/diseases/disease10.html; Brown, *Biography*, 255, n. 61.

15. Brown, *Biography*, 72–73.

16. In Ukraine, Israel, and the United States, the author consulted several experts on Jewish and Ukrainian folk medicine. None knew what Clarice was referring to when she mentioned "a common superstition" linking pregnancy with curing illness. When women in Chechelnik were asked about this superstition, they exclaimed in immediate recognition.

17. Lispector, "Esclarecimentos—Explicação de uma vez por todas," in *Descoberta*, 345.

18. E. Lispector, *Exílio*, 37.

19. Ibid., 40.

20. Lispector, "As crianças chatas," August 19, 1967, in *Descoberta*, 15.

21. E. Lispector, *Exílio*, 53.

22. I. Wainstok, *Zichrones*, 12.

23. E. Lispector, *Exílio*, 63.

24. One of Mania's Rabin cousins, Abraham, had married a woman named Rebecca Chichilnitsky in Buenos Aires. Her name indicates an origin in the town.

25. E. Lispector, *Exílio*, 70.

26. Vovk et al., *Narisi*, 80.

Chapter 4

1. Sousa, *Figuras*, 177.

2. Instituto Moreira Salles and Sousa, "A revelação do nome," 165.

3. Lispector, *Sopro*, 127. Quoted in Sousa, *Figuras*, 178.

4. Clarice Lispector, *Visão do esplendor: Impressões leves* (Rio de Janeiro: Livraria Francisco Alves Editora S.A., 1975), 21.

5. Lispector, *Sopro*, 32–33.

6. Ibid., 15.

7. Clarice Lispector and Teresa Montero, *Correspondências* (Rio de Janeiro: Rocco, 2002), 291, [June] 28, [1974?].

8. Sousa, *Figuras*, 181; Borelli, *Esboço*, 61. In a late story, "As manigançãs de dona Frozina," a character says, "Listen, Miss Fronzina, there are worse names than yours. There's one named Fleur de Lis—and since they thought it was a bad name they gave her an even worse nickname: Minhora." ("Minhora" sounds like *minhoca*, worm.) In Lispector, *Onde*, 88.

9. Clarice Lispector, *A paixão segundo G. H.* (1964; Rio de Janeiro: Editôra do Autor, 1991), 24; Sousa, *Figuras*, 186.

10. E. Lispector, *Exílio*, 73.

11. David W. Tschanz, "Typhus Fever on the Eastern Front in World War I," http://entomology.montana.edu/historybug/WWI/TEF.htm.

12. Vidkun Quisling and Fund for the Relief of the Jewish Victims of the War in Eastern Europe, *The Truth about the Ukrainian Horror: Official Report* (London: Fund for the Relief of the Jewish Victims of the War in Eastern Europe, 1922), 18.

13. Ibid.

14. E. Lispector, *Exílio*, 75.

15. Ibid., 80.

16. Lispector, "Falando em viagens," in *Descoberta*, 380.

Chapter 5

1. Clarice was born in December 1920, and they were certainly in Bucharest in January 1922. They left Chechelnik at some time after a birth certificate was issued to her in Chechelnik on November 14, 1921. For this birth certificate, see Nádia Battella Gotlib, *Clarice Fotobiografia* (São Paulo: Edusp / Imprensa Oficial, 2007), 37. Elisa mentions that they went from Soroca and paused, for some reason, in the tiny village of Vertiujeni, near Soroca on the Dniester. This suggests that they were traveling by boat, for there is no other reason they would have lingered in such an insignificant town on their way to Kishinev.

2. Martin Gilbert, *Atlas of Russian History* (New York: Dorset Press, 1972), 107.

3. I. Wainstok, *Zichrones*, 10.

4. E. Lispector, *Retratos*, 24–25.

5. E. Lispector, *Exílio*, 82.

6. E. Lispector, *Retratos*, 25.

7. Ferreira, *Eu sou*, 32.

8. E. Lispector, *Retratos*, 24.

9. Ferreira, *Eu sou*, 29.

10. Howe, *World of Our Fathers*, 42.

11. E. Lispector, *Exílio*, 89–90.

12. Jeff Lesser, *Welcoming the Undesirables: Brazil and the Jewish Question* (Berkeley: University of California Press, 1995), 7.

13. Moreno Brandão, "Alagoas em 1925," in *Livro do Nordeste (comemorativo do 1. centenário do Diário de Pernambuco)*, 1925, Recife Secretaria da Justiça, Arquivo Público Estadual, reprint, 1979, 162–63.

14. Francisco Ignacio Marcondes Homem de Mello and Francisco Homem de Mello, *Geographia-atlas do Brazil e das cinco partes do mundo* (Rio de Janeiro: F. Briguiet, 1912). This excludes the Federal District, the city-state of Rio de Janeiro.

15. Brandão, "Alagoas em 1925."

16. E. Lispector, *Retratos*, 24.

17. I. Wainstok, *Zichrones*, 17.

18. Julio Lerner, *Clarice Lispector, essa desconhecida* (São Paulo: Via Lettera, 2007), 44–45; "*Compaaaa rôpáaaaaa*," interview with Olga Borelli.

19. E. Lispector, *Exílio*, 96.
20. Ibid., 97.
21. Ibid., 100.
22. Ibid., 102.
23. Ibid., 104.

Chapter 6

1. Undated letter from Tania Lispector Kaufmann, via Zélia Oliveira, to Giovanni Pontiero, in author's collection.

2. *Folha*, December 10, 1977: "Pernambuco marca tanto a gente que basta dizer que nada, mas nada mesmo das viagens que fiz por este mundo contribuiu para o que escrevo. Mas Recife continua firme."

3. Lispector, "Esclarecimentos–Explicação de uma vez por todas," in *Descoberta*, 345.

4. C. R. Boxer, *The Dutch in Brazil, 1624–1654* (Oxford: Clarendon Press, 1957); Eleazar Córdova-Bello, *Compañías holandesas de navegación, agentes de la colonización neerlandesa* (Seville: Escuela de estudios hispano-americanos, 1964).

5. Manoel Calado, *O valeroso Lucideno. E triumpho da liberdade: Primeira parte* (Lisboa: Por Paulo Craesbeeck impressor & liureiro das Ordões Militares, 1648).

6. Erico Verissimo, *Brazilian Literature: An Outline* (New York: Macmillan, 1945), 17; Arquivo Histórico Judaico de Pernambuco, Kahal zur Israel.

7. Arquivo Histórico Judaico de Pernambuco, Kahal zur Israel.

8. The Jesuit António Vieira wrote, "The principal motives for the rebellion were that they had taken a lot of money from the Hollanders and could not or did not want to repay them." Quoted in Pedro Calmon, *História do Brasil*, vol. 2 (Rio de Janeiro: José Olympio, 1971).

9. In E. van den Boogaart, Hendrik Richard Hoetink, and Peter James Palmer Whitehead, *Johan Maurits van Nassau-Siegen 1604–1679: A Humanist Prince in Europe and Brazil: Essays on the Occasion of the Tercentenary of His Death* (The Hague: Johan Maurits van Nassau Stichting, 1979).

10. José Honório Rodrigues, *Historiografia e bibliografia do domínio holandês no Brasil* (Rio de Janeiro: Departamento de Imprensa Nacional, 1949).

11. Interview with Tânia Neumann Kaufman, Recife, August 15, 2006.

12. Angela Maria de Castro Gomes, *Em família: A correspondência de Oliveira Lima e Gilberto Freyre, Coleção Letras em série* (Campinas: CECULT Mercado de Letras, 2005), 123–26.

13. Malamud, born in 1908 at Mogilev-Podilsky (Podolia), was an old friend. When they moved to Rio, the Lispector family stayed at his parents' boardinghouse in Flamengo, and later, as a lawyer, he assisted Clarice in her attempt to attain Brazilian citizenship. Samuel Malamud, *Escalas no tempo* (Rio de Janeiro: Editora Record, 1986), 112.

14. Avrum Ishie, quoted in Tânia Neumann Kaufman, *Passos perdidos, história recuperada: A presença judaica em Pernambuco* (Recife: Editora Bagaço, 2000), 197.

15. For the descriptions of the economy, social structure, and geography of Jewish Recife, the author is indebted to Tânia Neumann Kaufman, director of the Arquivo Histórico Judaico de Pernambuco, as well as to Beatriz Schnaider Schvartz, of the same institution.

16. Interview with Nachman Falbel, São Paulo, July 21, 2006.

17. Tania Lispector Kaufmann, quoted in Gotlib, *Clarice*, 67–68.

18. "Não houve muitas amizades com os pernambucanos." Undated letter from Tania Lispector Kaufmann to Giovanni Pontiero, in author's collection.

19. Tânia Kaufman et al., *Passos Perdidos, História Desenhada: A Presença Judaica em Pernambuco no Século XX* (Recife: Arquivo Histórico Judaico de Pernambuco, 2005), 1: 47–48.

20. "Tentativa de explicação," interview with Leo Gilson Ribeiro, *Correio da manhã*, March 21, 1965.

21. Quoted in Gotlib, *Clarice*, 22.

22. Ibid., 480–81.

23. Lispector et al., *Outros escritos*, 137–38.

24. Letter from Tania Lispector Kaufmann to Giovanni Pontiero, August 20, 1992, in author's collection.

25. Letter from Tania to Giovanni Pontiero, August 20, 1992, in author's collection.

26. Lispector et al., *Outros escritos*, 138, 139.

27. Lerner, "Última entrevista."

28. Lispector et al., *Outros escritos*, 139. Also see Instituto Moreira Salles, *Cadernos*, 58.

29. Quoted in Gilio, "Tristes trópicos: Con Clarice Lispector en Río."

30. Letter from Tania Lispector Kaufmann to Giovanni Pontiero, August 20, 1992, in author's collection.

31. Lispector, "As grandes punições," in *Descoberta*, 36.

32. He was also, however, a thief and a liar. Around 1927 he traveled to the United States, where he married the present author's grandmother, Elizabeth Lurie, then a graduate student in philosophy at the University of Chicago. They traveled to Mexico together for research into the Jewish communities of that country. In Mexico, he was caught stealing rare manuscripts from the National Archive and was expelled from the country. The Yiddish press in Mexico published a note on the subject that was picked up by a Jewish newspaper in New York, which was then picked up by a Jewish newspaper in Buenos Aires, which made its way to Recife, where the first Mrs. Nachbin learned that her husband had illegally married another woman. The second marriage was annulled and Jacob Nachbin expelled from the United States; he was in Spain by 1935 and in Paris by 1938, where he disappeared without a trace. See Nachman Falbel, *Jacob Nachbin* (São Paulo: Nobel, 1985); Nachman Falbel, *Estudos sobre a comunidade judaica no Brasil* (São Paulo: Federação Israelita do Estado de São Paulo, 1984).

33. Lispector, "As grandes punições," in *Descoberta*, 36.

34. Ibid., 320.

35. Claire Varin and Clarice Lispector, *Clarice Lispector: Rencontres brésiliennes* (Laval, Québec: Trois, 1987), 69. This quote was originally in the interview with Edgar Proença, "Um minuto de palestra . . . ," *Estado do Pará*, February 20, 1944. Clarice repeated the affirmation many years later in an interview with *O Pasquim*, Rio de Janeiro, June 9, 1974: "Clarice, to what point do you identify with your characters? To what degree are you the Joana of *Near to the Wild Heart*, a lucid person that one doesn't meet in reality?" "Well, Flaubert once said: I am Madame Bovary." Quoted in Lícia Manzo, *Era uma vez–eu: A não-ficção na obra de Clarice Lispector: Ensaio* (Curitiba: Governo do Estado do Paraná, Secretaria de Estado da Cultura; The Document Company, Xerox do Brasil, 1998), 3.

36. Lispector, "Bichos (Conclusão)," in *Descoberta*, 363.

37. Quoted in Coutinho, *Criaturas*, 167.

38. Interview with Luiz Carlos Lacerda, Rio de Janeiro, August 1, 2006.

39. In Instituto Moreira Salles, *Cadernos*.

40. Varin and Lispector, *Rencontres*, 138–41. This interview is also published in Lispector et al., *Outros escritos*.

41. Clarice Lispector, *Perto do coração selvagem* (Rio de Janeiro: A Noite, 1943), 86.

42. Clarice Lispector, *A mulher que matou os peixes* (Rio de Janeiro: Sabiá, 1968).

43. Quoted in Gotlib, *Clarice*, 73.

44. Lispector, "Um encontro perfeito," in *Descoberta*, 42.

45. Lispector and Montero, letter to Lúcio Cardoso, July 13, 1941, *Correspondências*, 15.

46. Interview with Olga Borelli.

47. Lispector, *Perto*, 54, 155 (1943 ed.).

48. Fernando Pessoa, *Heróstrato e a busca da imortalidade*, trans. Manuela Rocha, ed. Richard Zenith, vol. 14 of *Obras de Fernando Pessoa* (Lisbon: Assírio & Alvim, 2000), 174.

49. Lispector, *Perto*, 97 (1943 ed.).

50. Lispector, "O vestido branco," in *Descoberta*, 80.

51. Lispector, *Perto*, 181 (1943 ed.).

52. Fragment found among Clarice Lispector's last notes. See also Varin, *Langues*, 162.

53. Lispector, *Perto*, 12 (1943 ed.).

54. Ibid., 181.

55. Clarice Lispector, "A Report on a Thing" in *Soulstorm: Stories*, trans. Alexis Levitin (New York: New Directions, 1989), 136.

56. "Até que, finalmente envoltas, elas aspiravam o seu brilhante e sufocante ar." Lispector, *Perto*, 155 (1943 ed.).

Chapter 7

1. Quoted in Ferreira, *Eu sou*, 37.

2. E. Lispector, *Exílio*, 109.

3. Lispector et al., *Outros escritos*, 137–38.

4. Lispector, "Restos de Carnaval," in *Descoberta*, 82.

5. E. Lispector, *Exílio*, 123.

6. Ibid., 110–11.

7. Ibid., 115–16.

8. Quoted in Ferreira, *Eu sou*, 37.

9. E. Lispector, *Exílio*, 132.

10. E. Lispector, *Retratos*, 19.

11. E. Lispector, *Exílio*, 133.

12. "Sepultamento de Clarice será simples e discreto," *O Globo*, December 11, 1977. See also Olga Borelli, interviewed in *Manchete*, 1981, quoted in Gotlib, *Clarice*, 481.

13. Lispector, "San Tiago," in *Descoberta*, 62.

14. Lispector, *Visão*, 19.

15. Varin and Lispector, *Rencontres*, 191; interview with Marisa Raja Gabaglia, 1973.

16. Quoted in Gotlib, *Clarice*, 94.

17. Lispector, "O que eu queria ter sido," in *Descoberta*, 153.

18. Rachel Donadio, "The Irascible Prophet: V. S. Naipaul at Home," *New York Times*, August 7, 2005.

19. Interview with Julio Lerner, quoted in Varin and Lispector, *Rencontres*, 213.

20. Lispector, *Sopro*, 11.

21. Clarice Lispector, *A maçã no escuro* (1961; Rio de Janeiro: Livraria Francisco Alves, 1992), 300.

22. Lispector, "As grandes punições," November 4, 1967, in *Descoberta*, 36.

23. Undated letter from Tania Lispector Kaufmann to Giovanni Pontiero, in author's collection.

24. Lispector, "Lição de Piano," in *Descoberta*, 48.

25. Undated letter from Tania Lispector Kaufmann to Giovanni Pontiero, in author's collection.

26. Fragment quoted in Varin, *Langues*, 65.

27. Lispector, "Medo da eternidade," in *Descoberta*, 309.

28. Quoted in Gotlib, *Clarice*, 71.

29. Bertha presented the speech in Yiddish. However much Hebrew Clarice learned as a child, she almost certainly forgot much or most of it by the time she was an adult. When Bertha moved to Israel years later, thinking she, too, had forgotten everything, she discovered that with the same amount of Hebrew education as Clarice she was well prepared for a new country. Interview with Bertha Lispector Cohen, Rio de Janeiro, August 3, 2006. There are only two explicit references to Yiddish in Clarice Lispector's writings. In a late work she wrote, "Capitou? Understood? Farstein? D'accord?"; in a newspaper column she referred to her father's saying "He is a person," which, though she does not say so, is a translation of the Yiddish "Er is a mensch," he is a good man, or a real man. Lispector, *Visão*, 49. Elisa remembered this same expression in the previously cited *Retratos antigos*.

30. Quoted in Ferreira, *Eu sou*, 44.

31. Ibid., 43.

32. Clarice Lispector. *Objecto gritante*, 1971, 7, Clarice Lispector Archive, Arquivo-Museu de Literatura Brasileira, Fundação Casa de Rui Barbosa, Rio de Janeiro (hereafter cited in notes as CLA).

33. Quoted in Gotlib, *Clarice*, 94.

34. Quoted in Manzo, *Era uma vez*, 128; Interview with Lícia Manzo, Rio, October 23, 1996.

35. Clarice Lispector, *A legião estrangeira* (Rio de Janeiro: Editôra do Autor, 1964), 15.

36. Ibid., 21.

37. Ibid., 23–24.

Chapter 8

1. Ferreira, *Eu sou*, 48.

2. David Wainstok, *Caminhada: Reminiscências e reflexões* (Rio de Janeiro: Editora Lidador Ltda., 2000), 278.

3. Thomas E. Skidmore, *Politics in Brazil, 1930–1964: An Experiment in Democracy* (New York: Oxford University Press, 1967), 4.

4. See http://www.getulio50.org.br/textos/gv3.htm.

5. Boris Fausto, *Getúlio Vargas* (São Paulo: Companhia das Letras, 2006), 128.

6. Skidmore, *Politics*, 23.

7. Lesser, *Welcoming*, 59. There were rumors that Barroso's anti-Semitism came from his own Jewish origins: Barroso was reportedly a Brazilianization of "Baruch." There is no evidence that this is true.

8. Gustavo Barroso, *Os Protócolos dos sábios de Sião: O Imperialismo de Israel. O Plano dos Judeus para a Conquista do Mundo. O Código do Anti-Cristo. Provas de autenticidade, documentos, notas, e comentários. Texto completo e apostilado por Gustavo Barroso* (São Paulo: Agência Minerva Editora, 1936).

9. Alzira Alves de Abreu et al., eds., "Gustavo Barroso," in *Dicionário histórico-biográfico brasileiro* (Rio de Janeiro: FGV Editora/FGV CPDOC, 2001).

10. Lesser, *Welcoming*, 61.

11. Interview with Bertha Lispector Cohen, Rio de Janeiro, August 3, 2006.

12. Interview with Samuel Lispector, Recife, August 15, 2006.

13. D. Wainstok, *Caminhada*, 280.

14. "I. S.," quoted in Kaufman, *Passos*, 134–35.

15. D. Wainstok, *Caminhada*, 280.

16. Ibid.

Chapter 9

1. Samuel Lispector quoted in Gotlib, *Clarice*, 71.

2. Interview with Tania Lispector Kaufmann, Rio de Janeiro, August 1, 2006; interview with Cecília Wainstok Lipka, Rio de Janeiro, July 29, 2006.

3. Interview with Tania Lispector Kaufmann, Rio de Janeiro, August 1, 2006.

4. Quoted in Gotlib, *Clarice*, 84.

5. Interview with Tania Lispector Kaufmann.

6. Ferreira, *Eu sou*, 54.

7. Undated letter from Tania Lispector Kaufmann to Giovanni Pontiero, in author's collection.

8. Interview with Tania Lispector Kaufmann.

9. Gotlib, *Clarice*, 83.

10. "Amo a matemática desde os dez anos de idade," interview with Leopoldo Nachbin, *Manchete* [ca. 1969].

11. Interview for Museu de Imagem e Som, in Lispector et al., *Outros escritos*, 160.
12. Interview with Cecília Wainstok Lipka.
13. Arnaldo Franco Júnior, "Clarice, segundo Olga Borelli," *Minas Gerais Suplemento Literário*, December 19, 1987.
14. This is pointed out by Varin, *Langues*, 126.
15. Lispector, *Onde*, 73, quoted in Varin, *Langues*, 126.
16. Unpublished note reproduced in Varin, *Langues*, 124.
17. Lispector, *Água viva*, 37.
18. Ibid., 13. "Continuo com capacidade de raciocínio—já estudei matemática que é a loucura do raciocínio—mas agora quero o plasma—quero me alimentar diretamente da placenta."
19. Lispector, "A Descoberta do mundo," in *Descoberta*, 114.
20. Gotlib, *Clarice*, 39.
21. Suzana Bernstein Horovitz, quoted in ibid., 99.
22. Clarice Lispector, "Felicidade clandestina," in *Felicidade clandestina* (Rio de Janeiro: Sabiá, 1971), 15–18.
23. Lispector, "Escrever," in *Descoberta*, 304.
24. Quoted in Lerner, "Última entrevista"; "Tentativa de explicação," interview with Leo Gilson Ribeiro.
25. Hermann Hesse, *Der Steppenwolf* (1927; Berlin: G. Fischer Verlag, 1961), 42.
26. "Traktat des Steppenwolfes," 4, in ibid.
27. "Traktat," 6, 7, in ibid.
28. Lispector, *Sopro*, 45.
29. Lispector, "Ainda impossível," in *Descoberta*, 437.

Chapter 10

1. Ruy Castro, *Carmen: Uma biografia* (São Paulo: Companhia das Letras, 2005), 13.
2. Renato Pinto Venâncio, "Presença portuguesa: De colonizadores a imigrantes," in *Brasil, 500 anos de povoamento* (Rio de Janeiro: IBGE, Centro de Documentação e Disseminação de Informações, 2000).
3. Lispector, "Viajando por mar, 1a parte," in *Descoberta*, 377.
4. *Folha,* December 10, 1977: "Pernambuco marca tanto a gente que basta dizer que nada, mas nada mesmo das viagens que fiz por este mundo contribuiu para o que escrevo. Mas Recife continua firme."
5. Lispector, "O manifesto da cidade," in *Visão*, 53.
6. Interview with Alberto Dines, São Paulo, July 22, 2006.
7. Interview with Tania Lispector Kaufmann, Rio de Janeiro, August 1, 2006.
8. Interview with Cecília Wainstok Lipka, Rio de Janeiro, July 29, 2006.
9. D. Wainstok, *Caminhada*, 78.
10. See Beatriz Kushnir, *Baile de máscaras: Mulheres judias e prostituição: As polacas e suas associações de ajuda mútua* (Rio de Janeiro: Imago Editora, 1996); Isabel Vincent, *Bodies and Souls: The Tragic Plight of Three Jewish Women Forced into Prostitution in the Americas* (New York: William Morrow, 2005).
11. Lesser, *Welcoming*, 83.
12. Ibid., 74.
13. Ibid., 8.
14. Quoted in Kaufman, *Passos*, 159.
15. I. Wainstok, *Zichrones*, 16.
16. Gotlib, *Clarice*, 101.
17. Interview with Tania Lispector Kaufmann, Rio de Janeiro, August 1, 2006.

18. Gotlib, *Clarice*, 136.
19. Lesser, *Welcoming*, 105.
20. Ibid., 108.
21. Lispector, "O que eu queria ter sido," in *Descoberta*, 153.
22. Interview for Museu de Imagem e Som, in Lispector et al., *Outros escritos*, 140.
23. Letter to Fernando Sabino, August 14, 1946, in Sabino and Lispector, *Cartas*.
24. Quoted in Gotlib, *Clarice*, 147.
25. Stefan Zweig, *Begegnungen mit Menschen, Büchern, Städten* (Vienna: H. Reichner, 1937).
26. Lispector, "A Descoberta do mundo," in *Descoberta*, 114.
27. Gotlib, *Clarice*, 143–44.
28. Lispector, "Persona," in *Descoberta*, 77.
29. Ferreira, *Eu sou*, 67.
30. Lispector, "Escândalo inútil," in *Descoberta*, 95.
31. Lesser, *Welcoming*, 58.
32. Ibid., 49, 54. "Mas se, em vez de se reproduzir entre si, a população brasileira estivesse em condições de subdividir ainda mais os elementos daninhos de sua atual constituição étnica, fortalecendo-se através de alianças de mais valor com as raças européias, o movimento de destruição observado em suas fileiras se encerraria, dando lugar a uma ação contrária."
33. *Pan* (Rio de Janeiro), vol. 1, 1935.
34. "Triunfo" in Lispector et al., *Outros escritos*, 12–13.
35. E. Lispector, *Retratos*, 26–27.
36. Ibid.
37. Ibid.
38. Interview with Tania Lispector Kaufmann, Rio de Janeiro, August 1, 2006.
39. Sabino and Lispector, *Cartas*, August 14, 1946, 54.
40. Varin, *Langues*, 214.
41. Paulo Gurgel Valente quoted in Sílvia Leal Fernández, "Um ano sem Clarice," *Desfile*, December 1978, 176–83; also quoted in Aparecida Maria Nunes, *Clarice Lispector Jornalista: Paginas femininas & outras paginas* (São Paulo: Editora Senac, 2006), 64.
42. The other two were the Chilean Lugoni and the Argentine Gálvez. Alberto Dines, *Morte no paraíso: A tragédia de Stefan Zweig*, 3rd ed. (Rio de Janeiro: Rocco, 2004), 327.
43. Marco Antonio de Carvalho, *Rubem Braga: Um cigano fazendeiro do ar* (Rio de Janeiro: Editora Globo, 2007), 282.
44. Dines, *Morte*, 328.
45. "Convite à leitura," *Vamos Lêr!* Rio de Janeiro, August 6, 1936, quoted in A. M. Nunes, *Jornalista*, 42.
46. Lerner, "Última entrevista."
47. "Eu e Jimmy," in Lispector et al., *Outros escritos*, 17, 18–19. Her subsequent publications in *Vamos Lêr!* were an interview with Tasso da Silveira (December 19, 1940); the story "Trecho," January 9, 1941; a translation of "The Missionary" by Claude Farrère, February 6, 1941; and her first piece of reportage, "Uma visita à casa dos expostos," July 8, 1941.
48. Interview with Tania Lispector Kaufmann, Rio de Janeiro, August 1, 2006.
49. Ferreira, *Eu sou*, 75.
50. Quoted in Gotlib, *Clarice*, 165.

Chapter 11

1. Mario Carelli, *Corcel de fogo: Vida e obra de Lúcio Cardoso (1912–1968)* (Rio de Janeiro: Editora Guanabara, 1988).

2. Interview with Humberto Werneck, São Paulo, July 23, 2006.

3. Maria Helena Cardoso, *Por onde andou meu coração: Memórias* (Rio de Janeiro: José Olympio, 1967), 272.

4. Ibid., 265–66.

5. Carelli, *Corcel*, 27.

6. Ibid., 34.

7. Ferdinand Denis, *Résumé de l'histoire littéraire du Portgual, suivi du résumé de l'histoire littéraire du Brésil* (Paris: Lecointe et Durey, 1826), 516.

8. Joaquim Maria Machado de Assis, "Instinto de nacionalidade," 1873, http://www.geocities.com/athens/olympus/3583/instinto.htm.

9. Quoted in Manuel Bandeira and Ralph Edward Ingalls Dimmick, *Brief History of Brazilian Literature, Pensamiento de América* (Washington, D.C.: Pan American Union, 1958), 144.

10. "Literatura da vanguarda no Brasil," in Lispector et al., *Outros escritos*, 105–7.

11. Perez, *Escritores brasileiros contemporâneos*, 86.

12. Schmidt also published other important writers more identified with regionalism and modernism, such as Jorge Amado, Graciliano Ramos, and Rachel de Queiroz.

13. Lispector, "As grandes punições," November 4, 1967, in *Descoberta*, 36.

14. Irving Howe, *World of Our Fathers* (New York: Harcourt Brace Jovanovich, 1976), 11.

15. Interview with Rosa Cass, Rio de Janeiro, July 29, 2006.

16. Interview with Edla van Steen, São Paulo, July 23, 2006.

17. Tristão de Athayde et al., *10 romancistas falam de seus personagens* (Rio de Janeiro: Edições Condé, 1946), 56.

18. João Etienne Filho, quoted in Carelli, *Corcel*, 32.

19. Interview with Luiz Carlos Lacerda, Rio de Janeiro, August 1, 2006.

20. Lispector, "Lúcio Cardoso," in *Descoberta*, 171.

21. Interview with Rosa Cass.

22. Quoted in Ferreira, *Eu sou*, 88.

23. Maria Helena Cardoso, *Vida-vida: Memória* (Rio de Janeiro: José Olympio, 1973), 194.

24. Interview with Rosa Cass.

25. Interview with Luiz Carlos Lacerda.

26. Carelli, *Corcel*, 59.

27. The story "Obsessão" was published only posthumously, in *A Bela e a Fera*. These are the stories Clarice sent to a contest held by the publisher José Olympio. After the results were announced, she requested the return of her originals, only to learn that they had never arrived. A. M. Nunes, *Jornalista*, 65–66.

28. Clarice Lispector, "Obsessão," in *A bela e a fera* (Rio de Janeiro: Nova Fronteira, 1979), 43.

29. Ibid., 44, 45.

30. Ibid., 47.

31. Ibid., 48, 52.

32. Ibid., 45, 52, 53.

33. Ibid., 58.

34. Ibid., 65.

35. Ibid., 69.

36. Ferreira, *Eu sou*, 77.

37. "Onde se ensinará a ser feliz," *Diário do Povo* (Campinas), January 19, 1941, in Lispector et al., *Outros escritos*, 34.

38. In Lispector et al., *Outros escritos*, 45. A similar, later treatment of her obsessive theme of crime and punishment would appear in a ghost-written piece about the California killer Caryl Chessman. A. M. Nunes, *Jornalista*, 78.

39. Clarice Lispector, *Objecto gritante*, ca. 1971, 143, collection of Dorothea Severino, Nashville, Tenn.

40. Gershom Gerhard Scholem, *On the Kabbalah and Its Symbolism* (New York: Schocken Books, 1996), 2, 34.

41. In Coutinho, *Criaturas*, 168.

42. In another age, following the Exodus from Spain, the great cabbalist Isaac Luria, in Safed, created a powerful symbol for the withdrawal of God from his people. This is the concept of the *tsimtsum*, which literally means "concentration" or "contraction" but in cabbalistic parlance is best translated as "withdrawal" or "retreat." It is the basic precondition for creation.

43. Scholem, *Major Trends*, 350.

44. Lispector and Montero, letter to Lúcio Cardoso, July 13, 1941, *Correspondências*, 15.

45. Stefan Zweig, *Die Welt von Gestern: Erinnerungen eines Europäers* (1942; Stockholm: Bermann-Fischer, 2003), 482.

Chapter 12

1. Benedictus de Spinoza and Arnold Zweig, *Les pages immortelles de Spinoza* (Paris: Éditions Corrêa, 1940). Her copy, with notes, dated February 14, 1941, is in the Instituto Moreira Salles, Rio de Janeiro. Her notes read, "Chamamos de acaso a combinação de causa e efeito que a razão não percebe nem explica. Mas tudo existe necessariamente." "Nossa infelicidade vem de que somos incompletos faíscas do fogo divino, como queriam os índios (or possibly "indus") e perdemos o sentimento do todo." "Tudo que é, é porque alguma coisa foi anteriormente. Os fatos se ligam ao passado e não ao futuro (controle íntimo)." (The last two words are difficult to read.) "Dentro do mundo não há lugar para outras criações. Há apenas a oportunidade de reintegração e de continuação. Tudo o que pode existir, já existe certamente."

2. Lispector, *Perto*, 130.

3. Ibid., 131.

4. Ibid.

5. Ibid., 132–33 (1943 ed.). The last quote is from *Ethics*, part 2, "Of the Nature and Origin of the Mind," proposition 13.

6. Lispector, *Lustre*, 50.

7. Clarice Lispector, *A cidade sitiada* (Rio de Janeiro: A Noite, 1948), 89.

8. Clarice Lispector, *Uma aprendizagem ou o livro dos prazeres* (1969; Rio de Janeiro: Sabiá, 1993), 25.

9. Spinoza and Zweig, *Les pages immortelles de Spinoza*, 48–49.

10. Ibid., 48.

11. This is an accidental echo of the earliest Jewish mystics. For them, the holiness of God was utterly transcendent of any moral meaning, representing nothing but its own glory. Scholem, *Major Trends*, 60.

12. Lispector and Montero, letter to Lúcio Cardoso, July 13, 1941, *Correspondências*, 15.

13. Clarice published the first part of *Cartas a Hermengardo* on July 26, 1941, in *Dom Casmurro*. This is the story of the same name that appears in Lispector et al., *Outros escritos*, 20–22. The second part, which was not included in that (or any other) collection, appeared on August 30, 1941, in the same publication. Clarice denied writing poetry, and her sister Tania was not aware of this activity, she said in an undated letter to Giovanni Pontiero (in author's collection): "Clarice não escrevia poesias. É possível que na adolescência tenha feito algumas, mas não as publicou." In fact, she published at least two: "Descobrí o meu país," which appeared on October 25, 1941, in *Dom Casmurro*, and "A mágoa," published on January 5, 1947, in the *Diário de São Paulo*. This poem is reproduced in Varin, *Langues*, 103–4. For Clarice's two known poems, see Benjamin Moser, "A Newly Discovered Poem by Clarice Lispector," *Brasil / Brazil: A Journal of Brazilian Literature*, no. 36, year 20 (2007). On November 23, 1945, Manuel Bandeira wrote her, "Você é poeta, Clarice querida. Até hoje tenho remorso do

que disse a respeito dos versos que você me mandou. Você interpretou mal minhas palavras. Você tem peixinhos nos olhos; você é bissexta: faça versos, Clarice, e se lembre de mim." Also see interview in *O Pasquim*, June 3–9, 1974: "Olga Savary: Did you ever write poetry, Clarice?—No.—You never even tried?—Never.—Not even when you were a teenager? Sérgio Augusto: —Because your texts are very poetic.—But I am not poetic." Sousa, *Figuras*, 68–69. For Lúcio Cardoso on her poetry, see Ferreira, *Eu sou*, 104.

14. Quoted in Gotlib, *Clarice*, 154.

15. Interview with Tania Lispector Kaufmann, Rio de Janeiro, August 1, 2006.

16. Lispector and Montero, letter from Maury Gurgel Valente, January 5, 1942, *Correspondências*, 18–19.

17. Lispector and Montero, letter from Maury Gurgel Valente, January 9, 1942, *Correspondências*, 24–26.

18. Ibid., 25.

19. Lispector and Montero, letter to Maury Gurgel Valente, January 2, 1942, *Correspondências*, 17.

20. Lispector and Montero, letter to Maury Gurgel Valente, January 6, 1942, *Correspondências*, 20.

21. Lispector and Montero, undated letter to Maury Gurgel Valente, *Correspondências*, 23.

22. Lispector and Montero, letter from Maury Gurgel Valente, January 9, 1942, *Correspondências*, 24.

23. Lispector and Montero, letter to Maury Gurgel Valente, January 11, 1942, *Correspondências*, 27.

24. Clarice Lispector, letter to Tania Lispector Kaufmann, January 1942, in *Minhas queridas* (Rio de Janeiro: Editora Rocco, 2007), 23.

25. Lispector and Montero, letter from Maury Gurgel Valente, January 12, 1942, *Correspondências*, 28.

26. Lispector and Montero, letter to Getúlio Vargas, October 23, 1942, *Correspondências*, 35.

27. Lispector and Montero, letter to Getúlio Vargas, June 3, 1942, *Correspondências*, 33.

28. Ferreira, *Eu sou*, 92–93.

29. Lispector and Montero, letter to Getúlio Vargas, June 3, 1942, *Correspondências*, 33.

30. André Carrazzoni to Andrade Queiroz, Ministry of Justice, June 10, 1942, CLA.

31. "Conversas com P.," in Lispector et al., *Outros escritos*, 87.

32. Interview with Tania Lispector Kaufmann, August 1, 2006; interview with Bertha Lispector Cohen, Rio de Janeiro, August 3, 2006.

33. Lispector, *A bela e a fera*, 44; "Eu e Jimmy," in Lispector et al., *Outros escritos*, 17.

34. "A fuga" ("Rio 1940"), in Lispector, *A bela e a fera*, 101–2.

35. "Gertrudes pede um conselho," September 1941, in Lispector, *A bela e a fera*, 31.

Chapter 13

1. Lispector, *Perto*, 113–14 (1943 ed.).

2. Ibid., 119.

3. Ibid., 102, 97, 100.

4. Ibid., 159–60.

5. Ibid., 161.

6. Ibid., 198.

7. Ibid., 56.

8. Benedictus de Spinoza. *Korte verhandeling van God, de mensch en deszelvs welstand*, ca. 1660, 1/10, 4, Koninklijke Bibliotheek, The Hague. "Nu goet en kwaad en zijn noch zaaken nog werkingen. ERGO en zijn goet en kwaad niet in de Natuur. Want indien goet [of] en kwaad zaaken of werkingen zijn, zo moeten zij dan hare beschrijvinge hebben."

9. Benedictus de Spinoza, *The Collected Works*, ed. Edwin Curley (Princeton: Princeton University Press, 1985), 1:441.

10. Lispector, *Perto*, 90 (1943 ed.).

11. Ibid., 216–17.

12. Lispector and Montero, letter to Getúlio Vargas, June 3, 1942, *Correspondências*, 33.

13. Untitled clipping, April 24, 1944, Album CL/j 23–26, p. 9, CLA.

14. Gotlib, *Clarice*, 172.

15. Ferreira, *Eu sou*, 93.

16. Untitled clipping, April 24, 1944, Album CL/j 23–26, p. 9, CLA.

17. Quoted in Gotlib, *Clarice*, 167.

18. Quoted in ibid., 173.

19. Interview with Joel Silveira, Rio de Janeiro, August 25, 2006.

20. Jurema Finamour, "Clarice Lispector," *Jornal de Letras*, September 1960.

21. Dinah Silveira de Queiroz in *O Jornal*, January 1944. This citation and the following are borrowed from the most extensive survey of the early criticism of Clarice Lispector, and *Perto do coração selvagem* in particular: "Ovação," in Sousa, *Figuras*, 59–71; Oscar Mendes, "Um romance diferente," *O Diário* (Belo Horizonte), August 6, 1944; Guilherme Figueiredo, "O sentimento das palavras," *Diario de Notícias* (Rio de Janeiro), January 23, 1944; Lêdo Ivo, *Jornal de Alagoas*, February 25, 1944; Otávio de Freitas Júnior, in *A Manhã* (Rio de Janeiro), May 13, 1944.

22. *A Manhã*, October 13, 1944, in Sousa, *Figuras*, 61.

23. Lêdo Ivo in *Jornal de Alagoas / A Manhã*, February 25, 1944, in Instituto Moreira Salles, *Cadernos*, 49.

24. Lêdo Ivo, "Viva Clarice Viva," in *Melhores crônicas de Lêdo Ivo*, ed. Gilberto Mendonça Teles, *Coleção Melhores Crônicas* (São Paulo: Global Editora, 2004), 161.

25. Jorge de Lima, "Romances de Mulher," *Gazeta de Notícias*, November 1, 1944.

26. Lêdo Ivo, "Viva Clarice Viva," in *Melhores crônicas de Lêdo Ivo*, ed. Gilberto Mendonça Teles (São Paulo: Global Editora, 2004).

27. Antonio Candido, "Perto do coração selvagem," *Folha da manhã*, July 16, 1944. See also Antonio Candido, "No raiar de Clarice Lispector," in *Vários escritos* (São Paulo: Livraria Duas Cidades, 1977), 124–31.

28. Sérgio Milliet, *Diário crítico de Sérgio Milliet* (1944; São Paulo: Editora Brasiliense, 1981), January 15, 1944, 3:27–32.

29. Lispector, *Perto*, 47, 150 (1943 ed.).

30. In União Brasileira de Escritores, *Boletim Bibliográfico Brasileiro*, vol. 9 (Rio de Janeiro: Estante Publicações, 1961), 210, quoted in Varin, *Langues*, 97–98.

31. Milliet, *Diário crítico de Sérgio Milliet*, January 15, 1944, 3:27–32. The article was reprinted on March 10, 1944, in *A Manhã*, Rio, and on March 31 in the *Diário da Bahia*.

32. "Eu tinha me preparado, não sei porque especialmente, para um começo acido e um fim solitário. Suas palavras me desarmaram. De repente me senti até mal em ser tão bem recebida. Eu que não esperava ser recebida at all. Além do mais, a repulsa dos outros—eu pensava—haverá de me tornar mais dura, mais presa no caminho do trabalho que eu escolhera. PS. O nome é meu mesmo.

Remetente: Clarice Gurgel Valente

Central Hotel

Belém—Pará"

Typed and signed aerogram sent from Belém do Pará, concerning a review of *Perto do coração selvagem* published in the *Estado de São Paulo* on January 26, 1944. Private collection, provided by Livraria Dantes, Rio de Janeiro.

Chapter 14

1. Samuel Wainer, *Minha razão de viver: Memórias de um repórter*, ed. Augusto Nunes (São Paulo: Planeta, 2005), 69.

2. Elio Gaspari, *O sacerdote e o feiticeiro: A ditadura derrotada* (São Paulo: Companhia das Letras, 2003), 41.

3. Frank D. McCann, "Brazil and World War II: The Forgotten Ally. What did you do in the war, Zé Carioca?" *Estudios Interdisciplinarios de América Latina y el Caribe* 6, no. 2 (1995).

4. Ibid.

5. For the story of the persecution of the Japanese Brazilians during the war, see Fernando Morais, *Corações sujos: A história da Shindo Renmei* (São Paulo: Companhia das Letras, 2000).

6. Kaufman, *Passos*, 203.

7. Ibid.

8. Letter to Manuel Pimenta da Cunha from Manaus, December 30, 1904, in Francisco Venâncio Filho, *Euclydes da Cunha e seus amigos* (São Paulo: Cia. Editora Nacional, 1938).

9. Letter to Tania Lispector Kaufmann and Elisa Lispector, March 18, 1944, in Borelli, *Esboço*, 106.

10. Lispector, letter to Tania Lispector Kaufmann, February 23, 1944, in *Minhas queridas*, 27.

11. Lispector and Montero, letter to Lúcio Cardoso, February 6, 1944, *Correspondências*, 36–37.

12. Interview with Eliane Gurgel Valente. Paris, December 3, 2007.

13. Sara Escorel Rodrigues de Moraes, born in São Paulo, whose husband Lauro Escorel wrote about *Perto do coração selvagem* twice in October 1944: Lauro Escorel, "Crítica Literária," *A Manhã*, October 20, 1944, and Lauro Escorel, "Prêmio da Fundação Graça Aranha de 1943," *A Manhã*, October 29, 1944.

14. Lesser, *Welcoming*, 58.

15. Fábio Koifman, *Quixote nas trevas: O embaixador Souza Dantas e os refugiados do nazismo* (Rio de Janeiro: Editora Record, 2002).

16. Interview with Eva Lieblich Fernandes, Mainz, September 2, 2007.

17. René Decol, "Uma certa Aracy, um chamado João," *Folha de S. Paulo*, December 18, 2006. Other Brazilian diplomats who risked their careers to help Jews were Almeida Rodrigues and his wife, as well as Nogueira Porto.

18. Lispector and Montero, letter to Tania Lispector Kaufmann, February 16, 1944, *Correspondências*, 38–40.

19. Álvaro Lins, "A Experiência Incompleta: Clarice Lispector," in *Os mortos de sobrecasaca: Obras, autores e problemas da literatura brasileira: Ensaios e estudos, 1940–1960* (Rio de Janeiro: Editôra Civilização Brasileira, 1963), 187, quoted in Manzo, *Era uma vez*, 22–23. The term "magic realism" was first used in the 1920s by the German art critic Franz Roh to refer to a style of painting also known as the Neue Sachlichkeit. It was not commonly used in Latin America until the 1960s, when the Venezuelan writer Arturo Uslar Pietri popularized it in reference to (mainly Spanish American) fiction.

20. Lispector and Montero, letter to Tania Lispector Kaufmann, February 16, 1944, *Correspondências*, 38.

21. Lispector, "Ao correr da máquina," in *Descoberta*, 367.

22. Affonso Romano de Sant'Anna, *Jornal do Brasil*, October 25, 1986, untitled clipping, CLA. Cf. *Água viva*.

23. Lispector and Montero, undated letter to Lúcio Cardoso (end of March, beginning of April 1944), *Correspondências*, 42.

24. Ibid., 58.

25. Ibid., 60.

26. Lispector and Montero, undated letter to Tania Lispector Kaufmann, February 16, 1944, *Correspondências*, 38.

27. Ibid.

28. Proença, "Um minuto de palestra..."

29. Lispector and Montero, undated letter to Lúcio Cardoso (end of March, beginning of April 1944), *Correspondências*, 42.

Chapter 15

1. While there, Clarice got in touch with Lauro Escorel, a diplomat who had published a warm review of *Near to the Wild Heart* and whose wife, Sara, was the only other Jewish spouse in Itamaraty. They went to lunch, where she met a young man who had recently entered the foreign service and who would become the great Pernambuco poet João Cabral de Melo Neto. Ferreira, *Eu sou*, 107.

2. Ibid., 109–10.

3. Lispector and Montero, letter to Lúcio Cardoso, July 25, 1944, letter to Lúcio Cardoso, mid-September 1944, *Correspondências*, 48, 54.

4. Interview with Eliane Gurgel Valente, Paris, December 3, 2007.

5. Lispector and Montero, letter to Lúcio Cardoso, mid-September 1944, *Correspondências*, 54.

6. Lispector, "Estive em Bolama, África," in *Descoberta*, 381. There is another reference to this experience in "Objecto Gritante," CLA.

7. Lispector and Montero, undated letter to Lúcio Cardoso, *Correspondências*, 54.

8. Interview with Tania Lispector Kaufmann, Rio de Janeiro, August 1, 2006.

9. Kaufman, *Passos*, 159.

10. Lispector and Montero, *Correspondências*, 55.

11. Lispector and Montero, letter to Tania Lispector Kaufmann and Elisa Lispector, Algiers, August 19, 1944, *Correspondências*, 51.

12. Letter to Natércia Freire, Naples, February 29, 1945, Biblioteca Nacional, Lisbon.

13. Letter to Natércia Freire, Rio de Janeiro, March 13, 1972, Biblioteca Nacional, Lisbon.

14. Lispector and Montero, letter to Lúcio Cardoso, mid-September 1944, *Correspondências*, 55.

15. Lispector, letter to Tania Lispector Kaufmann, August 7, 1944, in *Minhas queridas*, 40.

16. Issued at Lisbon, August 7, 1944, CLA.

17. Lispector and Montero, *Correspondências*, 49.

18. Ibid., undated letter to Lúcio Cardoso, *Correspondências*, 55.

19. Lispector and Montero, letter to Tania Lispector Kaufmann and Elisa Lispector, Algiers, August 19, 1944, *Correspondências*, 51.

20. Ibid., 49–52.

21. See http://www.anvfeb.com.br/majorelza.htm.

22. Lispector and Montero, *Correspondências*, 50, 55.

23. Interview with Cecília Wainstok Lipka, Rio de Janeiro, July 29, 2006.

24. According to the Italian Embassy in Brasília. See http://www.ambbrasilia.esteri.it/Ambasciata_Brasilia/Menu/I_rapporti_bilaterali/Cooperazione_politica/Storia/.

25. Ferreira, *Eu sou*, 112–13.

26. Norman Lewis, *Naples '44* (1978; New York: Pantheon Books, 2002), 29.

27. Ibid., 79.

28. Ibid., 99.

29. Sabino and Lispector, *Cartas*, 7.

30. Rubem Braga, *Com a F.E.B. na Itália: Crônicas* (Rio de Janeiro: Livraria Editora Zelio Valverde, 1945).

31. Lispector and Montero, *Correspondências*, 56.

32. Lispector, letter to Elisa Lispector, December 18, 1944, in *Minhas queridas*, 65.

33. Lispector, letter to Elisa Lispector, January 12, 1945, in *Minhas queridas*, 69.

34. Lispector and Montero, *Lettere* (Mondadori) "Quaderni della Medusa," in *Correspondências*.

35. Lispector and Montero, undated letter to Lúcio Cardoso [~1944], *Correspondências*. 54.

36. Braga, *Com a F.E.B.*, 74.

37. Elza Cansanção Medeiros, *E foi assim que a cobra fumou* (Rio de Janeiro: Marques-Saraiva, 1987), 56.

38. Braga, *Com a F.E.B.*, 75.
39. Ibid., 80.
40. Medeiros, *E foi assim*, 86.
41. Interview with Nádia Batella Gotlib, Ribeirão Preto, July 23, 2006.
42. *Pan.* Vol. 1, Rio de Janeiro, 1935.
43. Medeiros, *E foi assim*, 71.
44. Elza Cansanção Medeiros, "Saldando uma dívida de gratidão," written "seven years later," that is, approximately 1952. CLA.
45. Interview with Major Elza Cansanção Medeiros, Rio de Janeiro, September 12, 2006.
46. Braga, *Com a F.E.B.*, 32.
47. Lispector and Montero, letter to Lúcio Cardoso, March 26, 1945, *Correspondências*, 70.
48. Elza Cansanção Medeiros, "Saldando uma dívida de gratidão."
49. Interview with Joel Silveira, Rio de Janeiro, August 25, 2006.
50. Lispector, "O maior elogio que recebi," in *Descoberta*, 79.

Chapter 16

1. Interview with Eliane Gurgel Valente, Paris, December 3, 2007.
2. Lispector, letter to Elisa Lispector, November 13, 1944, in *Minhas queridas*, 58.
3. Lispector and Montero, undated letter to Lúcio Cardoso, September, *Correspondências*, 56.
4. Lispector, letter to Elisa Lispector, April 20, 1945, in *Minhas queridas*, 85.
5. Lispector, letter to Elisa Lispector, September 1, 1945, in *Minhas queridas*, 94.
6. Lispector and Montero, letter to Lúcio Cardoso, March 26, 1945, *Correspondências*, 70.
7. Lispector and Montero, letter from Lúcio Cardoso, undated (December 1944), *Correspondências*, 60.
8. Lispector and Montero, letter to Lúcio Cardoso, March 26, 1945, *Correspondências*, 70.
9. Borelli, *Esboço*, 11.
10. Lispector, *Perto*, 13 (1943 ed.).
11. Lispector, *Lustre*, 130.
12. Ibid., 53–54.
13. Ibid., 67–68, 87, 273.
14. Ibid., 84, 80.
15. Ibid., 103.
16. Ibid., 125–27.
17. Ibid., 60.
18. Lispector, "Carta atrasada," in *Descoberta*, 288–89. The book she refers to is *The Besieged City*.
19. Cândido, "Perto do coração selvagem." See also Cândido, "No raiar de Clarice Lispector," in *Vários escritos*, 124–31.
20. Lispector, *Lustre*, 137.
21. Ibid., 64.

Chapter 17

1. Gotlib, *Clarice*, 194.
2. Interview with Eliane Gurgel Valente, Paris, April 16, 2006.
3. Quoted in ibid., 32. The friend, according to Eliane Gurgel Valente, was most likely Borges da Fonseca.

4. Lispector and Montero, letter to Tania Lispector Kaufmann and Elisa Lispector, May 9, 1945, *Correspondências*, 72.

5. José Augusto Guerra, "Talvez da Europa venha a renovação," 1949; no other information, CLA.

6. Lispector and Montero, letter to Tania Lispector Kaufmann and Elisa Lispector, May 9, 1945, *Correspondências*, 72–74.

7. Quoted in Gotlib, *Clarice*, 201.

8. Claire Varin reports that Ungaretti told this to Rubem Braga, interview, Laval, Québec, January 7, 2006.

9. The chapter "La zia" ("The Aunt"), published in the magazine *Prosa* (Rome), CLA.

10. Lispector, *A mulher que matou os peixes*, 21–23.

11. Lispector and Montero, letter to Tania Lispector Kaufmann, September 1, 1945, *Correspondências*, 76.

12. Lispector, "Bichos—I," in *Descoberta*, 359.

13. Lispector and Montero, *Correspondências*, 59; letter to Lúcio Cardoso [Naples, 1944].

14. Lispector and Montero, letter to Tania Lispector Kaufmann and Elisa Lispector, May 9, 1945, *Correspondências*, 72–74.

15. Letter to Natércia Freire, August 27, 1945, Biblioteca Nacional, Lisbon.

16. Lispector, letter to Elisa Lispector, September 1, 1945, in *Minhas queridas*, 94.

17. Lispector and Montero, letter to Tania Lispector Kaufmann, September 1, 1945, *Correspondências*, 75.

18. Lispector and Montero, undated letter to Lúcio Cardoso from Naples, *Correspondências*, 63.

19. Interview with Eliane Gurgel Valente, Paris, December 3, 2007.

20. Lispector and Montero, letter from Rubem Braga, March 4, 1957, *Correspondências*, 219.

21. Lispector, "Ao correr da máquina," in *Descoberta*, 367.

22. Gilda de Mello e Souza, "O lustre," *Estado de S. Paulo*, July 14, 1946.

23. Letter to Tania Lispector Kaufmann and Elisa Lispector, November 26, 1945, quoted in Borelli, *Esboço*, 109. Full letter in Lispector, *Minhas queridas*, 97.

24. Reproduced in Varin and Lispector, *Rencontres*, 142–43.

25. Lispector, "Trechos," in *Descoberta*, 405.

26. Lispector, letter to Tania, William, and Márcia Kaufmann, February 2, 1941, in *Minhas queridas*, 22.

27. Quoted in Ribeiro, "Tentativa de explicação."

28. Lispector and Montero, letter to Tania Lispector Kaufmann, September 1, 1945, *Correspondências*, 75.

29. Lispector, letter to Tania Lispector Kaufmann and Elisa Lispector, December 3, 1945, in *Minhas queridas*, 51.

30. Skidmore, *Politics*, 48.

31. Interview with Joel Silveira, Rio de Janeiro, August 25, 2006.

32. Interview with Ana Luisa Chafir, Rio de Janeiro, August 1, 2006.

33. According to Moacir Werneck de Castro. Fernando Sabino was also surprised by this, coming to the capital from provincial Minas Gerais. "And the women—theirs or someone else's, or everyone's, or nobody's—who sat at the table with the men, discussed politics and literature with them, heard and used dirty words. In Minas there was nothing like that; it was news to me." Fernando Sabino, *O tabuleiro de damas* (Rio de Janeiro: Record, 1988), 107.

34. Carvalho, *Braga*, 328.

35. Interview with Alberto Dines, São Paulo, July 22, 2006.

36. Interview with Humberto Werneck, São Paulo, July 23, 2006; Sabino, *Tabuleiro*.

37. Sabino and Lispector, *Cartas*, 7.

38. Ibid.

39. Humberto Werneck, *O desatino da rapaziada: Jornalistas e escritores em Minas Gerais* (São Paulo: Companhia das Letras, 1992), 99.

40. According to Nelson Rodrigues, in Ruy Castro, *Ela é carioca: Uma enciclopédia de Ipanema*, 2nd ed. (São Paulo: Companhia das Letras, 1999), 289.

41. Sabino and Lispector, letter to Fernando and Helena Sabino, Otto Lara Resende, and Paulo Mendes Campos, April 21, 1946, *Cartas*, 9.

42. Letter from Bern, May 5, 1946, quoted in Borelli, *Esboço*, 112–13.

43. "Letras e artes: O crime, Conto de Clarisse [*sic*] Lispector," CLA. The quotes are from this version, not the subsequent "Crime do professor de matemática" published in 1961.

Chapter 18

1. Letter to Tania Lispector Kaufmann, May 8, 1946, in Borelli, *Esboço*, 114.

2. Joëlle Rouchou, *Samuel, duas vozes de Wainer*, 2nd ed. (Rio de Janeiro: UniverCidade, 2004), 191.

3. Letter to Elisa Lispector and Tania Lispector Kaufmann, April 29, 1946, in Borelli, *Esboço*, 110–11.

4. Sabino and Lispector, letter to Helena Valladares Sabino, Fernando Sabino, Paulo Mendes Campos, Otto Lara Resende, April 21, 1946, *Cartas*, 9–10.

5. Letter to Elisa Lispector and Tania Lispector Kaufmann. April 29, 1946, in Borelli, *Esboço*, 110–11.

6. Lispector, "O medo de errar," in *Descoberta*, 245.

7. Lispector and Montero, letter to Elisa Lispector and Tania Lispector Kaufmann, May 5, 1946, *Correspondências*, 80.

8. Lispector, letter to Elisa Lispector and Tania Lispector Kaufmann, December 11, 1946, in *Minhas queridas*, 141.

9. Lispector and Montero, letter to Lúcio Cardoso, August 13, 1947, *Correspondências*, 146.

10. Ribeiro, "Tentativa de explicação."

11. Sabino and Lispector, letter from Fernando Sabino, May 6, 1946, *Cartas*, 15.

12. Oswald de Andrade, "[O Lustre]," *Correio da Manhã*, February 26, 1946; Souza, "O lustre." Souza's is probably the best essay on the book.

13. In Ferreira, *Eu sou*, 133.

14. Another reason for their silence was the appearance of a sensational debut that consumed the attention of literary Brazil. João Guimarães Rosa, a diplomat of humble provincial background, who, with his wife Aracy, had distinguished himself in wartime service in Hamburg, published *Sagarana*. The title was characteristic of his greatly learned and densely allusive work, the Germanic *saga* combined with the native Brazilian *rana*, a Tupí-Guarani word meaning "in the fashion of, a kind of." The result, "A Kind of Saga," was the most important work of fiction to appear in the country since *Near to the Wild Heart*.

15. Lispector and Montero, letter from Lúcio Cardoso, May 1947, *Correspondências*, 133.

16. Letter to [Lúcio Cardoso], [May 8, 1946?], quoted in Olga Borelli, *Clarice Lispector: Esboço para um possível retrato* (Rio de Janeiro: Editora Nova Fronteira, 1981), 115.

17. Sabino and Lispector, letter to Fernando Sabino, June 19, 1946, *Cartas*, 21.

18. Letter to Tania Lispector Kaufmann, May 8, 1946, in Borelli, *Esboço*, 114.

19. Lispector, *Perto*, 32 (1943 ed.), quoted in Manzo, *Era uma vez*, 15.

20. Letter from Maury Gurgel Valente, July 8, 1959, in Manzo, *Era uma vez*, 20.

21. Sabino and Lispector, letter from Fernando Sabino, July 6, 1946, *Cartas*, 28.

22. Letter to Tania Lispector Kaufmann and Elisa Lispector, May 12, 1946, in Borelli, *Esboço*, 119.

23. This letter appears in Borelli, *Esboço*, 122. The order is not clear in the other editions, and it does not appear in her book of collected correspondence. It is also quoted, in a different order, in Manzo, *Era uma vez*, 29–30.

24. Letter to Tania Lispector Kaufmann, May 8, 1946, in Borelli, *Esboço*, 114.

25. Gotlib, *Clarice*, 226.

26. Sabino and Lispector, letter to Fernando Sabino, July 27, 1946, *Cartas*, 35.

27. Lispector, *Perto*, 32 (1943 ed.).

28. Lispector, *Sopro*, 52.

29. Lispector, "Lembrança de uma fonte, de uma cidade," in *Descoberta*, 286.

30. Joseph A. Page, *Perón, a Biography* (New York: Random House, 1983), 196.

31. Quoted in Ferreira, *Eu sou*, 147.

32. Ibid.

33. Letter to Tania Lispector Kaufmann, May 8, 1946, in Borelli, *Esboço*, 114.

34. Sabino and Lispector, letter to Fernando Sabino, June 19, 1946, *Cartas*, 20–23.

35. Sabino and Lispector, letter to Fernando Sabino, July 27, 1946, *Cartas*, 35.

36. Lispector and Montero, letter from Bluma Wainer, July 22, 1946, *Correspondências*, 92.

37. The spelling of the last name cannot be confirmed. The document is number CL/dp 17–300 in the CLA. See Eliane Vasconcellos, *Inventário do arquivo Clarice Lispector* (Rio de Janeiro: Ministério da Cultura, Fundação Casa de Rui Barbosa, Centro de Memória e Difusão Cultural, Arquivo-Museu de Literatura Brasileira, 1994), 87.

38. Franco Júnior, "Clarice, segundo Olga Borelli."

39. Lispector, letter to Tania Lispector Kaufmann, October 22, 1947, in *Minhas queridas*, 176.

40. Ulysses Girsoler, "Psychodiagnostique de Rorschach" [1947–48], CLA.

41. Letter from Ulysses Girsoler, July 9, 1947, CLA.

42. Quoted in Borelli, *Esboço*, 44.

43. Sabino and Lispector, letter to Fernando Sabino, July 27, 1946, *Cartas*, 35.

44. Letter to Tania Lispector Kaufmann, May 8, 1946, in Borelli, *Esboço*, 114.

45. This same letter, in a slightly different form, appears in Lispector and Montero, *Correspondências*, 165–67, dated January 6, 1948. It also appears in Borelli, *Esboço*, 126.

Chapter 19

1. Lispector, "Lembrança de uma fonte, de uma cidade," in *Descoberta*, 286.

2. Lispector, *Cidade sitiada*, 18, 86.

3. Benedito Nunes, "Clarice Lispector ou o naufrágio da introspecção," *Colóquio / Letras*, no. 70 (1982).

4. Letter from Bluma Wainer, March 19, 1947, CLA.

5. Lispector, *Cidade sitiada*, 69, 130.

6. Ibid., 96, 106.

7. Letter possibly addressed to Elisa Lispector and Tania Lispector Kaufmann, 1947, in Borelli, *Esboço*, 130; Lispector, *Cidade sitiada*, 106.

8. Lispector, *Cidade sitiada*, 110.

9. Ibid., 111.

10. Ibid., 112, 123.

11. Lispector and Montero, letter to Elisa Lispector and Tania Lispector Kaufmann, from Paris, January, 1947, *Correspondências*, 116.

12. Lispector, *Cidade sitiada*, 174.

13. Ibid., 16.

14. Ibid., 23–26.

15. Ibid., 129, 168.

16. Ibid., 121.

17. Ibid., 18, 62, 76, 18.

18. Ibid., 172, 22.

19. Lispector, *Objecto gritante (II)*, 143.

20. Lispector, *Cidade sitiada*, 32.

21. Answering her sister, who thought chapter 11, "The First Deserters," superfluous, it shows "the connection of Perseu with the rest, is that he didn't need, like Lucrécia, to go out in search of reality, he was part of the truth. . . . Perseu was what Lucrécia couldn't manage to be." Letter to Tania Lispector Kaufmann, November 5, 1948, Lispector and Montero, *Correspondências*, 177.

22. Lispector, *Cidade sitiada*, 20.

23. Ibid., 91.

24. Ibid., 18.

25. Lispector, "Perfil de um ser eleito," in *Descoberta*, 416, quoted in Regina Lucia Pontieri, *Clarice Lispector: Uma poética do olhar* (São Paulo: Ateliê Editorial, 1999), 17.

Chapter 20

1. Lispector et al., "Conversas com P.," in *Outros escritos*, 87.

2. Lispector, "Lembrança de uma fonte, de uma cidade," in *Descoberta*, 286.

3. Lispector, "A entrevista alegre," in *Descoberta*, 56.

4. Lispector, "As três experiências," in *Descoberta*.

5. Ibid.

6. Lispector, letter to Elisa Lispector and Tania Lispector Kaufmann, September 11, 1948, in *Minhas queridas*, 198.

7. Lispector, letter to Elisa Lispector and Tania Lispector Kaufmann, September 21, 1948, in *Minhas queridas*, 201.

8. Letter to Zuza and Mozart Gurgel Valente Sr., September 25, 1948, in Gotlib, *Clarice*, 260.

9. Quoted in Ferreira, *Eu sou*, 154.

10. Lispector and Montero, letter to Tania Lispector Kaufmann, November 5, 1948, *Correspondências*, 177.

11. Lispector, "Virgem em todas as mulheres," in *Descoberta*, 163.

12. Lispector, "Hoje nasce um menino," in *Descoberta*, 424.

13. Lesser, *Welcoming*, 2.

14. Wainer, *Minha razão*, 133–34.

15. E. Lispector, *Exílio*, 7–8.

16. The birth of the State of Israel was not the immediate impulse for writing the book, however, which was complete by the middle of 1947 and published the next year, when Elisa added the preface.

17. Renard Perez, "Lembrança de Elisa Lispector," (1996), 2. Unpublished typescript, author's collection.

18. "Os novos: Elisa Lispector," *Revista Panorama*, August 1947.

19. According to the errata attached to the first edition.

20. Elisa Lispector, *Além da fronteira* (1945; Rio de Janeiro: Leitura, 1988), 4.

21. Ibid., 7.

22. Antonio Carlos Villaça, on flap copy of 1988 edition.

23. E. Lispector, *Além da fronteira*, 42.

24. Via Ivan Lessa. Maria Alice Barroso recalled another lover with whom Elisa occasionally traveled (interview, Rio de Janeiro, May 10, 2007).

25. Perez, "Lembrança de Elisa Lispector," 4.

26. Clarice Lispector, *A hora da estrela* (Rio de Janeiro: Livraria J. Olympio Editora, 1977), 51.

27. Elisa Lispector, *Corpo a corpo* (Rio de Janeiro: Edições Antares, 1983), 43.

28. E. Lispector, *Além da fronteira*, 20, 13, 43.

29. Quoted in Ferreira, *Eu sou*, 150.

30. Letter to Tania Lispector Kaufmann, July 7, 1948, in Gotlib, *Clarice*, 258.

31. Lispector and Montero, letter to Tania Lispector Kaufmann, November 5, 1948, *Correspondências*, 177.

32. Lispector, letter to Tania Lispector Kaufmann and Elisa Lispector, February 19, 1949, in *Minhas queridas*, 214–15.

33. Gotlib, *Clarice*, 262.

34. Lispector and Montero, letter to Tania Lispector Kaufmann, November 5, 1948, *Correspondências*, 177.

35. Interviews with Cecília Lipka and Eliane Gurgel Valente, Rio de Janeiro, July 29, 2006, and Paris, December 3, 2007.

36. Quoted in Gotlib, *Clarice*, 257–58.

37. Letter to Elisa Lispector and Tania Lispector Kaufmann, March 25, 1949, in ibid., 262.

38. Lispector, "Viajando por mar (1ª parte)," *Descoberta*, 377.

39. Quoted in Gotlib, *Clarice*, 480.

40. Ribeiro, "Tentativa de explicação"; Ferreira, *Eu sou*, 159.

41. Lispector and Montero, letter from Bluma Wainer, April 3, 1947, *Correspondências*, 123.

42. Letter from Bluma Wainer, March 24, 1948, CLA.

43. Lispector and Montero, letter from Bluma Wainer, October 2, 1947, *Correspondências*, 155.

44. Lispector and Montero, letter from Bluma Wainer, July 15, 1947, *Correspondências*, 137.

45. Lispector and Montero, letter from Bluma Wainer, March 3, 1948, *Correspondências*, 168.

Chapter 21

1. Lispector and Montero, letter from Lúcio Cardoso, July 26, 1947, *Correspondências*, 144.

2. Octávio de Faria, quoted in Carelli, *Corcel*, 54.

3. See Thomas E. Skidmore, *Black into White: Race and Nationality in Brazilian Thought* (1974; New York: Oxford University Press, 1993).

4. M. H. Cardoso, *Vida-vida*, 231.

5. Lispector and Montero, letter to Lúcio Cardoso, August 13, 1947, *Correspondências*, 147.

6. Letter, October 20, 1947, in Carelli, *Corcel*, 55.

7. Ferreira, *Eu sou*, 42.

8. Octávio de Faria, quoted in Carelli, *Corcel*, 55.

9. M. H. Cardoso, *Vida-vida*, 42.

10. Lispector and Montero, letter from João Cabral de Melo Neto, February 15, 1949, *Correspondências*, 186.

11. Lispector, "A pecadora queimada e os anjos harmoniosos," in *Legião*, 179–92.

12. The first review was on September 1. On September 4, 1949, the book was written about in *O Jornal*.

13. Marly de Oliveira quoted in Pontieri, *Poética*, 37.

14. Sérgio Milliet, *Diário crítico de Sérgio Milliet* (1953; São Paulo: Martins, 1982), 7:33–34, quoted in Pontieri, *Poética*, 38–39.

15. Varin and Lispector, *Rencontres*, 99.

16. João Gaspar Simões, "Clarice Lispector 'Existencialista' ou 'Supra-realista,'" *Diário Carioca*, May 28, 1950, in Vilma Arêas and Berta Waldman, eds., *Clarice Lispector: Remate de Males*, vol. 9, *Revista do Departamento de Teoria Literária* (Campinas: Universidade Estadual de Campinas, 1989), 178, quoted in Pontieri, *Poética*, 41–46. Simões was one of the Portuguese cultural figures whom Clarice had met and impressed in Lisbon in 1944.

17. For this interview (1976) for the Fundação Museu de Imagem e do Som, see Lispector et al., *Outros escritos*, 135–71. See also Lispector, "Carta atrasada," in *Descoberta*, 288–89; *Jornal de Letras*, interview, September 1960, quoted in Sousa, *Figuras*, 72.

18. Interview, Fundação Museu de Imagem e do Som, 1976, in Lispector et al., *Outros escritos*. See also Lispector, "Carta atrasada," in *Descoberta*, 288–89.

19. Quoted in Gotlib, *Clarice*, 269.
20. Lispector, "O caso da caneta de ouro," in *Descoberta*, 53.
21. Lispector and Montero, letter to Tania Lispector Kaufmann, October 23, 1950, *Correspondências*, 191.
22. Letter to Tania Lispector Kaufmann and Elisa Lispector, November 1950, quoted in Gotlib, *Clarice*, 276.
23. Lispector and Montero, letter to Tania Lispector Kaufmann, October 23, 1950, *Correspondências*, 191.
24. Letter to Tania Lispector Kaufmann and Elisa Lispector, November 1950, quoted in Gotlib, *Clarice*, 276.
25. Ibid., 192.
26. Lispector and Montero, letter to Tania Lispector Kaufmann and Elisa Lispector, November 28, 1950, *Correspondências*, 233–34.
27. Lispector, "As pontes de Londres," in *Descoberta*, 418.
28. Coutinho, *Criaturas*, 170. It seems, from this interview and from other hints, that she was planning to name this child João.
29. Lispector, *G. H.*, 150.
30. Interview with Marco Antonio de Carvalho and Ana Luisa Chafir, Rio de Janeiro, August 1, 2006.
31. Carvalho, *Braga*, 286.
32. Rubem Braga, "O gêsso," in *A cidade e a roça* (Rio de Janeiro: Livraria José Olympio Editôra, 1957), 178.
33. Skidmore, *Politics*, 79–81.
34. Quoted in ibid., 79.
35. Wainer, *Minha razão*, 190.
36. A. M. Nunes, *Jornalista*, 132–33.
37. Ibid., 133.
38. Columns of July 17, 1952, and September 19, 1952, quoted in ibid., 169, 172.
39. Columns of May 15, 1952, and May 22, 1952, quoted in Clarice Lispector and Aparecida Maria Nunes, *Correio feminino* (Rio de Janeiro: Rocco, 2006), 56, 59.
40. From *Jornal do Brasil* but not included in *Descoberta*, quoted in A. M. Nunes, *Jornalista*, 137.
41. Column of September 5, 1952, quoted in Lispector and Nunes, *Correio*, 120–21.
42. Column of May 22, 1952, quoted in Lispector and Nunes, *Correio*, 125.

Chapter 22

1. Clarice Lispector, "Amor," in *Alguns contos*, Os Cadernos de Cultura ed. (Rio de Janeiro: Ministério da Educação e Saúde, Serviço de Documentação 1952), 34.
2. Ibid., 32–33.
3. "Amor," in *Laços de família*, 26.
4. Lispector, "Brain Storm," in *Descoberta*, 261.
5. "Amor," in *Laços de família*, 27, 30, 31.
6. For this reading I am indebted to Manzo, *Era uma vez*, 46.
7. "Amor," in *Laços de família*, 29.
8. Sabino and Lispector, *Cartas*, 124n.
9. Manzo, *Era uma vez*, 44. When *Family Ties* appeared in 1960, one newspaper wrote that Clarice had finally returned to Brazilian letters, after having published no books for more than ten years (i.e., since *The Besieged City* of 1949).
10. This piece was published in *A Manhã* in October 1946.
11. Lispector, *Alguns contos*, 42.
12. "Amor," in *Laços de família*, 34, 35, 36.
13. "Amor," in *Laços de família*, 36.

14. Lispector, "Viajando por mar (1ª parte)," in *Descoberta*, 377. The name of this woman was Avani Cardoso Ferreira dos Santos, according to Ferreira, *Eu sou*, 185.

15. Sabino and Lispector, letter to Helena Valladares Sabino and Fernando Sabino, February 2, 1953, *Cartas*, 91.

16. Wainer, *Minha razão*, 221–22.

17. Quoted in Gotlib, *Clarice*, 285.

18. Lispector, letter to Elisa Lispector, February 21, 1953, in *Minhas queridas*, 241.

19. Perez, *Escritores brasileiros contemporâneos*, 152.

20. Verissimo, *Brazilian Literature*, 1.

21. *Manchete*, interview, January 4, 1969, in Instituto Moreira Salles, *Cadernos de literatura brasileira: Erico Verissimo* (São Paulo: Instituto Moreira Salles, 2003), 16:28–29.

22. Lispector, *Onde*, 115. This comment appears only in the first edition of the book, which carries the incorrect title *Onde estivestes de noite?*

23. Erico Verissimo, *Solo de clarineta; Memórias* (1973; Porto Alegre: Editora Globo, 2005), 1:290.

24. Ibid., 1:299.

25. Interview with Clarissa Verissimo Jaffe, Washington, June 12, 2007.

26. Luis Fernando Verissimo, "Clarice," *O Globo*, undated clipping from author's collection.

27. Ferreira, *Eu sou*, 187.

28. Mafalda Verissimo, interviewed by Vera Regina Morganti, in Vera Regina Morganti et al., *Confissões do amor e da arte* (Porto Alegre: Mercado Aberto, 1994), 142–43, quoted in Manzo, *Era uma vez*, 62–63.

29. Ibid. For the apposite quote from *The Apple in the Dark* I am also indebted to Manzo, *Era uma vez*, 63.

30. Lispector and Montero, letter from Rubem Braga, May 23, 1953, *Correspondências*, 196.

31. E. Lispector, *Exílio*.

32. See http://www.fortunecity.com/lavender/tomatoes/792/bloch4.htm.

33. Sabino and Lispector, letter to Fernando Sabino, July 28, 1953, *Cartas*, 99.

34. Sabino and Lispector, letters to Fernando Sabino, July 28, 1953, and from Fernando Sabino, August 30, 1953, September 10, 1953, October 5, October 21, October 27, 1953, *Cartas*.

35. Lispector, letter to Tania Lispector Kaufmann and Elisa Lispector, May 10, 1954, *Minhas queridas*, 253.

36. Letter to Pierre de Lescure, May 6, 1954, CLA.

37. Ibid.

38. Varin, *Langues*, 32.

39. Letter to Pierre de Lescure, June 20, 1954, CLA. She regretted her unkind words about the translation (by Denise-Teresa Moutonnier), which eventually did incorporate her improvements. The book came out with a bright cover designed by Henri Matisse and a preface by Paulo Mendes Campos. Three years later (May 14, 1957) she was still apologizing for her behavior: "Je ne saurai m'excuser de mon mauvais temperament," she wrote Lescure.

Chapter 23

1. Wainer, *Minha razão*, 231.

2. Ibid., 254.

3. Ibid., 261.

4. Skidmore, *Politics*, 142.

5. Lispector and Montero, letter to Mafalda Verissimo, August 14, 1954, *Correspondências*, 204.

6. The address was Rua Marquês de Abrantes, 126/1004, Flamengo.

7. Sabino and Lispector, letter to Fernando Sabino, September 25, 1954, *Cartas*, 118.

8. Sabino and Lispector, letter to Fernando Sabino, August 30, 1953, *Cartas*, 104.

9. Paulo Gurgel Valente, "Entrevista comigo mesmo: Clarice," in Clarice Lispector, *Dez contos selecionados de Clarice Lispector* (Brasília: Confraria dos Bibliófilos do Brasil, 2004), i.

10. Quoted in Gotlib, *Clarice*, 312.

11. Interview in Lispector et al., *Outros escritos*, 161.

12. Lispector, "Crônica social," in *Descoberta*, 199.

13. Interview with Eliane Gurgel Valente, Paris, December 3, 2007.

14. Lispector, "Trechos," in *Descoberta*, 405.

15. In 1937, as Rio's federal *interventor*, Amaral Peixoto visited a Jewish agricultural colony, and "what he seemed to find 'very agreeable' was that there were few Jews actually living there." Lesser, *Welcoming*, 87. With what degree of conviction he held these views is unclear; at the very least, like so many other highly placed people, he did not resist the anti-Semitic views then prevailing. The result was to block the escape paths of the Jews of Europe. As neither Alzira Vargas nor Hélène Moreira Salles were widowed at the time Clarice wrote this piece, the person in question was likely Yvonne Muniz, whose husband, the Esperantist and atomic energy advocate João Carlos Muniz, was in Washington from 1953 to 1956.

16. Ferreira, *Eu sou*, 188.

17. Undated letter from Alzira Vargas do Amaral Peixoto to Clarice Lispector, CLA. The book was published in 1960.

18. Ferreira, *Eu sou*, 197.

19. Valmiki Villela Guimarães, "Clarice Lispector em duas histórias," *Minas Gerais Suplemento Literário*, December 19, 1987.

20. Ferreira, *Eu sou*, 198.

21. Ibid., 198–99; interview with Maria Bonomi, Amsterdam, October 18, 2006.

22. João Cabral de Melo Neto, *Agrestes: Poesia (1981–1985)* (Rio de Janeiro: Editora Nova Fronteira, 1985). According to Teresa Cristina Montero Ferreira, this poem describes a true event in Washington.

23. Quoted in Coutinho, *Criaturas*, 170.

24. Lispector et al., "Conversas com P.," in *Outros escritos*, 83.

25. Quoted in Gotlib, *Clarice*, 287.

26. Quoted in Ferreira, *Eu sou*, 183, 86.

27. Interview with Sara Escorel de Moraes, Rio de Janeiro, October 5, 2007.

28. Lispector et al., *Outros escritos*, 84.

29. Lispector and Montero, letter to Elisa Lispector and Tania Lispector Kaufmann, April 23, 1957, *Correspondências*, 230.

30. Lispector, letter to Elisa Lispector and Tania Lispector Kaufmann, November 27, 1953, in *Minhas queridas*, 248.

Chapter 24

1. Lispector, "Estado de graça–Trecho," in *Descoberta*, 91. This phrase is also used in the long passage *An Apprenticeship* when Lori enters the state of grace (156).

2. Lispector, *Maçã*, 32.

3. Lispector, "As grandes punições," November 4, 1967, in *Descoberta*, 36.

4. Lispector, *Maçã*, 264.

5. Spinoza, *Collected Works*, 1:543.

6. Lispector, *Maçã*, 200.

7. Spinoza, *Collected Works,* preface to part IV, *Ethica.*

8. Lispector, *Lustre*, p. 103.

9. Lispector, *Maçã*, 11.

10. Ibid., 20, 21.

11. Ibid., 24.
12. Ibid., 28–29, 30–31.
13. Ibid., 29.
14. Ibid., 39, 44.
15. Ibid., 52, 61.
16. Ibid., 62, 76.
17. Ibid., 89, 83.
18. Ibid., 88, 89, 100–101.
19. Ibid., 102, 104.
20. Ibid., 121. "Originally, everything was conceived as one great whole, and the life of the Creator pulsated without hindrance or disguise in that of his creatures. Everything stood in direct mystical rapport with everything else, and its unity could have been apprehended directly and without the help of symbols. Only the Fall has caused God to become 'transcendent.'" Scholem, *Major Trends*, 224.
21. Lispector, *Maçã*, 143, 163–64.
22. Ibid., 168–69.
23. Ibid., 129.
24. Lispector, "O maior elogio que recebi," in *Descoberta*, 79.
25. Lispector, *Sopro*, 11.
26. Lispector, *Maçã*, 305.
27. Ibid., 163–64.
28. Ibid., 213.
29. Ibid., 164.
30. Ibid., 211.
31. Scholem, *Major Trends*, 132.
32. Lispector et al., *Outros escritos*, 45.
33. Scholem, *Major Trends*, 25, 217.
34. The book contains other concepts that resemble earlier Jewish mystical writings. There is the attitude that sexuality is close to the original life of God; there is the mystical equation of God and Nothing; there is the idea, so prominent in the *Zohar*, that the development of language is related to the process of life in God. Most of these ideas have precedents in Clarice's earlier work and seem to have developed from her own insights, not from any prolonged study of other writers.
35. Ribeiro, "Tentativa de explicação."
36. Elizabeth Bishop and Robert Lowell, letter from Elizabeth Bishop to Robert Lowell, July 2, 1963, in *Words in Air: The Complete Correspondence between Elizabeth Bishop and Robert Lowell*, ed. Thomas Travisano with Saskia Hamilton (New York: Farrar, Straus and Giroux, 2008), 479.
37. Letter to Natércia Freire, August 27, 1945, Biblioteca Nacional, Lisbon.
38. Scholem, *Major Trends*, 24.
39. Lispector, *Maçã*, 214.
40. Ibid.
41. Ibid.
42. Quoted in Chayim Bloch, *The Golem: Legends of the Ghetto of Prague* (Vienna: The Golem, 1925), 26–27.

Chapter 25

1. Sabino and Lispector, letter to Fernando Sabino, September 21, 1956, *Cartas*, 140.
2. Sabino and Lispector, letter to Fernando Sabino, May 7, 1956, *Cartas*, 128.

3. Sabino and Lispector, letter from Fernando Sabino, June 8, 1956, *Cartas*, 130–32.

4. Sabino and Lispector, letter from Fernando Sabino, January 1957, *Cartas*, 189–91.

5. Sabino and Lispector, letter from Fernando Sabino, September 26, 1956, *Cartas*, 144.

6. Fernando Paixão and Maria Celeste Mira, *Momentos do livro no Brasil* (São Paulo: Editora Atica, 1995), 108–9.

7. Sabino and Lispector, letter from Fernando Sabino, December 19, 1956, *Cartas*, 183.

8. Lispector and Montero, letter from Rubem Braga, December 7, 1956, *Correspondências*, 210.

9. Sabino and Lispector, letter to Fernando Sabino, December 14, 1956, *Cartas*, 180.

10. Sabino and Lispector, letter from Fernando Sabino, March 30, 1955, *Cartas*, 124.

11. Letter from Erico Verissimo, September 3, 1961, CLA.

12. Sabino and Lispector, letter from Fernando Sabino, June 8, 1956, *Cartas*, 130–32.

13. Sabino and Lispector, letter to Fernando Sabino, July 12, 1956, *Cartas*, 133.

14. Lispector and Montero, letter from Rubem Braga, March 4, 1957, *Correspondências*, 219. The story was "O Gêsso," published in *A cidade e a roça*.

15. Lispector and Montero, letter from Erico Verissimo, December 9, 1958, *Correspondências*, 239.

16. Elio Gaspari, *As ilusões armadas: A ditadura envergonhada* (São Paulo: Companhia das Letras, 2002), 382.

17. Lispector and Montero, letter to Mafalda and Erico Verissimo, January 17, 1957, *Correspondências*, 212.

18. Ferreira, *Eu sou*, 193.

19. Lispector and Montero, letters from João Cabral de Melo Neto, February 6, 1957, and undated (around 1958), *Correspondências*, 216, 248.

20. Sabino and Lispector, letter to Fernando Sabino, July 12, 1956, *Cartas*, 134.

21. Letter from Nahum Sirotzky, November 12, 1958, CLA.

22. Paulo Francis, "Clarice: Impressões de uma mulher que lutou sozinha," *Folha de S. Paulo*, December 15, 1977.

23. Interview with Nahum Sirotzky, Tel Aviv, August 30, 2007.

24. Francis, "Clarice: Impressões de uma mulher que lutou sozinha."

25. Caetano Veloso, *Tropical Truth: A Story of Music and Revolution in Brazil* (New York: Knopf, 2002), 12.

26. Caetano Veloso, "Clarice segundo suas paixões," *Jornal do Brasil*, November 24, 1992.

27. Lispector and Montero, letter to Fernando Sabino, October 5, 1953, *Correspondências*, 202.

28. Lispector, *Laços*, 39.

29. Ibid., 40.

30. "Imitação da rosa," in *Laços*, 50.

31. Ibid., 54.

32. Ibid., 59.

33. Ibid., 39, 42.

34. Ibid., 44.

35. Mafalda Verissimo interviewed by Vera Regina Morganti, in Morganti et al., *Confissões do amor e da arte*, 142–43, quoted in Manzo, *Era uma vez*, 63.

36. Ribeiro, "Tentativa de explicação."

37. Quoted in Gotlib, *Clarice*, 305.

38. E. Lispector, *Corpo a corpo*, 60–61.

39. Maury Gurgel Valente to Clarice Lispector, July 28, 1959, quoted in Gotlib, *Clarice*, 317–21.

40. Interview with Isabel Gurgel Valente.

41. Ibid.

Chapter 26

1. Quoted in Paulo Prado, *Retrato do Brasil: Ensaio sobre a tristeza brasileira* (1928; São Paulo: Duprat-Mayença, 1997), 50.

2. Joaquim Ferreira dos Santos, *Feliz 1958: O ano que não devia terminar* (Rio de Janeiro: Editora Record, 1997), 15.

3. Ibid., 14. In 1960 this was around US$352 million (US$1=85 cruzeiros).

4. Paulo Gurgel Valente, "Entrevista comigo mesmo: Clarice," in Lispector, *Dez contos*, ii.

5. Sabino and Lispector, letter from Fernando Sabino, February 16, 1959, *Cartas*, 198–99.

6. Mauritônio Meira, "Clarice Lispector volta às editoras: 'Laços de Família,'" *O Globo*, March 27, 1960.

7. Mauritônio Meira, "Clarice Lispector não quer se enfeitar com penas que não sejam suas," *O Globo*, January 10, 1960.

8. Mauritônio Meira, "Clarice Lispector volta às editoras: 'Laços de Família,'" *O Globo*, March 27, 1960.

9. Letter from Civilização Brasileira, April 24, 1959, CLA.

10. Francis, "Clarice: Impressões de uma mulher que lutou sozinha."

11. Lispector, "Em busca do outro," in *Descoberta*, 119.

12. August 21, 1959, quoted in A. M. Nunes, *Jornalista*, 197.

13. Ibid., 219. *Correio da Manhã*, Rio de Janeiro, August 21, 1959, 5.

14. *Correio da Manhã*, December 19, 1960, quoted in ibid., 220.

15. Interview with Eliane Gurgel Valente, Paris, December 3, 2007.

16. Borelli, *Esboço*, 13.

17. Quoted in Manzo, *Era uma vez*, 68.

18. Santos, *Feliz 1958*, 41.

19. Quoted in A. M. Nunes, *Jornalista*, 254.

20. *Diário da noite*, September 19, 1960, quoted in ibid., 266–67.

21. *Diário de S. Paulo*, July 31, 1960.

22. União Brasileira de Escritores, *Boletim Bibliográfico Brasileiro*, 9:210; Varin, *Langues*, 97–98.

23. "Meus livros têm 'recadinhos.'"

24. Assis Brasil, "Laços de família," *Jornal do Brasil*, September 2, 1960.

25. *Jornal do Comércio*, August 13, 1960, CLA.

26. Gotlib, *Clarice*, 335.

27. Temístocles Linhares, "Romances femininos," *Estado de São Paulo Suplemento Literário*, November 18, 1961, quoted in Diane Marting, *Clarice Lispector: A Bio-bibliography* (Westport, Conn.: Greenwood Press, 1993), 100.

28. Luis Fernando Verissimo, "Clarice," *O Globo*, undated clipping, author's collection.

29. "Na Berlinda," publication unknown, March 17, 1963, CLA.

30. "Clarice e *A Maçã no Escuro*," *Diário de Notícias*, July 30, 1961, quoted in Manzo, *Era uma vez*, 70.

31. CLA.

32. Lispector, "Anonimato," in *Descoberta*, 72.

33. Ibid., 49.

34. Skidmore, *Politics*, 197.

35. Lispector et al., *Outros escritos*, 166.

36. Interview with Nahum Sirotzky, Tel Aviv, August 30, 2007.

37. Francis, "Clarice: Impressões de uma mulher que lutou sozinha."

38. Lispector, "Falando em viagens," in *Descoberta*, 380.

Chapter 27

1. Interview with Sara Escorel de Moraes, Rio de Janeiro, October 5, 2007.
2. Interview with Isabel Gurgel Valente, Rio de Janeiro, August 3, 2006.
3. Ibid.
4. Interview with Isabel Gurgel Valente, Rio de Janeiro, August 3, 2006.
5. *Jornal do Brasil*, June 29, 1968, quoted in Varin, *Langues*, 166.
6. Quoted in Gotlib, *Clarice*, 312.
7. Letter to Mafalda Verissimo, November 17, 1957, Lispector and Montero, *Correspondências*, 235.
8. *Correio da manhã*, May 4, 1960, quoted in A. M. Nunes, *Jornalista*, 229.
9. Though some of her children's books had multiple dedicatees.
10. Olga Borelli interview with Lícia Manzo, in Manzo, *Era uma vez*, 96.
11. Francis, "Clarice: Impressões de uma mulher que lutou sozinha."
12. Lerner, "Última entrevista."
13. Quoted in Manzo, *Era uma vez*, 90.
14. Otto Lara Resende, "Mãe, filha, amiga," *O Globo*, December 10, 1977.
15. Reynaldo Jardim Silveira, in undated newspaper clipping, CLA.
16. Castro, "Paulo (Paulinho) Mendes Campos," in *Ela é carioca*, 286–90.
17. Ibid., 289.
18. Interview with Marina Colasanti, Rio de Janeiro, August 2, 2006 (Marina Colasanti to Millôr Fernandes).
19. Interview with Ivan Lessa, London, December 15, 2006.
20. Interview with Isabel Gurgel Valente, Rio de Janeiro, August 3, 2006.
21. Clarice Lispector, *A via crucis do corpo* (Rio de Janeiro: Editora Artenova, 1974), 25. Lispector, "A perigosa aventura de escrever," in *Descoberta*, 191.
22. Elizabeth Bishop to Ilse and Kit Barker, October 29, 1962, original letter in the Kit and Ilse Barker Collection of Elizabeth Bishop, Manuscripts Division, Department of Rare Books and Special Collections, Princeton University Library. Used with permission.
23. Bishop and Lowell, letter from Elizabeth Bishop to Robert Lowell, January 8, 1963, *Words in Air*, 438–39.
24. M. H. Cardoso, *Vida-vida*, 67–68.
25. Lúcio Cardoso and Mario Carelli, *Crônica da casa assassinada*, critical ed. (Nanterre, France: ALLCA XX, Université Paris X, Centre de recherches latino-américaines, 1991), 641.
26. Ibid., 642.
27. M. H. Cardoso, *Vida-vida*, 81.
28. Ibid., 159.
29. Bishop and Lowell, letter from Elizabeth Bishop to Robert Lowell, January 18, 1963, *Words in Air*, 439.
30. Elizabeth Bishop and Clarice Lispector, "Three Stories by Clarice Lispector," *Kenyon Review*, no. 26 (1964), reprinted in Elizabeth Bishop, *Poems, Prose, and Letters*, ed. Robert Giroux and Lloyd Schwartz (New York: Library of America, 2008).
31. Bishop and Lowell, letter from Elizabeth Bishop to Robert Lowell, May 26, 1963, *Words in Air*, 457.
32. Bishop and Lowell, letter from Elizabeth Bishop to Robert Lowell, July 12, 1963, *Words in Air*, 479.
33. Letter from Gregory Rabassa to Giovanni Pontiero, November 13, 1992, in author's collection.

34. Quoted in Lispector et al., *Outros escritos*, 94.
35. Lispector, "Falando em viagens," in *Descoberta*, 379.
36. Letter from Gregory Rabassa to Giovanni Pontiero, November 13, 1992, in author's collection.
37. Lispector et al., *Outros escritos*, 107, 109.
38. Ibid., 110.

Chapter 28

1. Clarice Lispector, "Nota da editora: Clarice em edição popular," in *Perto do coração selvagem*, 2nd ed. (São Paulo: Francisco Alves Editora, 1963).
2. Julio Lerner, "A última entrevista de Clarice Lispector," *Shalom*, June–August 1992.
3. Quoted in Gotlib, *Clarice*, 357.
4. Lispector et al., *Outros escritos*, 96.
5. Lispector, "O verdadeiro romance," in *Descoberta*, 328.
6. Lispector, *G. H.*, 27, 28.
7. Ibid., 29–30, 37.
8. Ibid., 41, 46.
9. Ibid., 48, 47.
10. Ibid., 49.
11. Lispector, *Cidade sitiada*, 41.
12. August 8, 1952, quoted in A. M. Nunes, *Jornalista*, 173.
13. Lispector, *G. H.*, 51.
14. Lispector, *Legião*, 21.
15. Lispector, *G. H.*, 64.
16. Ibid., 46.
17. Ibid., 73, 67.
18. Ibid., 78.
19. Lispector, *Cidade sitiada*, 18.
20. Ibid., 67.
21. Ibid., 75.
22. Ibid., 121.
23. Lispector, *G. H.*, 80.
24. Ibid., 81, 89.
25. Ibid., 87.
26. Ibid., 98, 97, 98.
27. Varin, *Langues*, 74.
28. Lispector, *G. H.*, 96.
29. Varin, *Langues*, 44.
30. Lispector, *G. H.*, 75; quoted in Varin, *Langues*, 58.
31. Lispector, *Legião*, 221.
32. Lispector, *G. H.*, 104.
33. Ibid., 25, 85.
34. Ibid., 106.
35. Scholem, *Major Trends*, 25.
36. Joseph Dan, *The Early Kabbalah*, trans. Ronald C. Kiener (New York: Paulist Press, 1986), 94.
37. Lispector, *G. H.*, 179.
38. Ibid., 139.
39. Clarice Lispector, *A paixão segundo G. H.: Edição crítica*, ed. Benedito Nunes, *Coleção Arquivos* (Paris: ALLCA XX, 1988), 107.

40. Or also, later: "God is what exists, and all contradictions are inside the God, and for that reason do not contradict Him." Lispector, *G. H.*, 179; Spinoza, *Collected Works. Ethics*, part I, proposition 33.
41. Lispector, *G. H.*, 106, 87.
42. Ibid., 167, 163.
43. Interview for Museu de Imagem e Som, October 20, 1976, in Lispector et al., *Outros escritos*.
44. Lispector, *Maçã*, 259.
45. Lispector, *G. H.*, 146.
46. Ibid.

Chapter 29

1. Quoted in Gotlib, *Clarice*, 480.
2. Walmir Ayala, " 'A Paixão segundo G. H.' Um romance de doação," *Jornal do Comércio*, December 1, 1964.
3. Rubem Braga, "Trata-se de uma revolução," in Jean-Paul Sartre, *Furacão sôbre Cuba* (Rio de Janeiro: Editôra do Autor, 1961), 202.
4. Ibid., 5.
5. John W. F. Dulles, *Carlos Lacerda, Brazilian Crusader*, 2 vols. (Austin: University of Texas Press, 1991), 1:314.
6. Gaspari, *Ditadura envergonhada*, 177, 80.
7. Wainer, *Minha razão*, 326.
8. Lispector, "San Tiago," January 6, 1968, in *Descoberta*, 62.

Chapter 30

1. Lispector, "Como se chama," in *Legião*, 139.
2. Ibid., 198.
3. Lispector, "A legião estrangeira," in *Legião*, 108.
4. Sabino and Lispector, letter to Fernando Sabino, February 8, 1947, *Cartas*, 84. In the letter she mentions that she has been sending things, including poems, to *A Manhã* and *O Jornal:* "Tudo ligado pelo título geral de 'Children's Corner.' "
5. Reynaldo Jardim Silveira, obituary, CLA.
6. Lispector, *Perto*, 49 (1980 ed.).
7. Lispector, "Desenhando um menino," in *Legião*, 206.
8. Ibid., 209.
9. Ibid., 200.
10. Lispector, "Literatura e justiça," in *Legião*, 149.
11. Lerner, "Última entrevista."
12. Lispector, "Mineirinho," in *Legião*, 253.
13. Lispector, "A experiência maior," in *Legião*, 142.
14. Lispector, *G. H.*, 146.
15. Lispector, "Romance," in *Legião*, 139.
16. Lispector, "A pesca milagrosa," in *Legião*, 143.
17. Lispector, "Abstrato e figurativo," in *Legião*, 151.
18. Lerner, "Última entrevista."
19. Lispector, "O ovo e a galinha," in *Legião*, 57–58.
20. Lispector, "Brasília: Cinco dias," in *Legião*, 163.
21. Lispector, "Não soltar os cavalos," in *Legião*, 197.

Chapter 31

1. Interview with Rosa Cass, Rio de Janeiro, July 29, 2006.
2. Ibid.
3. Instituto Moreira Salles and Sousa, "A revelação do nome," 144.
4. Carelli, *Corcel*, 64.
5. Sabino and Lispector, letter to Fernando Sabino, December 11, 1956, *Cartas*, 179.
6. Lispector, "Conversas," in *Descoberta*, 137.
7. Here and following: Ferreira, *Eu sou*, 223–26.
8. Lispector, "Morte de uma baléia," in *Descoberta*.
9. Lispector, "A revolta," in *Descoberta*, 203.
10. Borelli, *Esboço*, 12.
11. Lispector, "Meu Natal," in *Descoberta*, 164.
12. Ibid., 65.
13. Lispector, *Dez contos*.
14. Lispector, "A não-aceitação," in *Descoberta*, 204.

Chapter 32

1. Lerner, "Última entrevista."
2. Lispector, "Hermética?" in *Descoberta*, 76.
3. Lispector, *A mulher que matou os peixes*, 7.
4. Interview with Leo Gilson Ribeiro, quoted in Gotlib, *Clarice*, 383.
5. Lispector, "Amor imorredouro," in *Descoberta*, 22.
6. Dinah Silveira de Queiroz, Elsie Lessa, and Rachel de Queiroz, for example.
7. Lispector, "Fernando Pessoa me ajudando," in *Descoberta*, 139.
8. Lispector, "Trechos," in *Descoberta*, 406.
9. Lispector, "Ana Luisa, Luciana e um polvo," in *Descoberta*, 84–85.
10. Lispector, "Adeus, vou-me embora!" in *Descoberta*, 93.
11. Lispector, "Sentir-se útil," in *Descoberta*, 75.
12. Manzo, *Era uma vez*, 97 and following. The quotes from Clarice Lispector are taken from an undated clipping titled "Minha Secretária."
13. Interview with Hélio Pelegrino [*sic*], *Manchete* [undated clipping], CLA.
14. Isa Cambará, "Escritora mágica," *Veja*, July 30, 1975, in A. M. Nunes, *Jornalista*, 85.
15. A. M. Nunes, *Jornalista*, 88. She later asked other friends to do the same, though not all were as immediately understanding as Pellegrino. Manzo, *Era uma vez*, 191. She mentions Affonso Romano de Sant'Anna and his wife, Marina Colasanti; there were others as well.
16. Instituto Moreira Salles, *Cadernos*, 52.
17. Ibid., 50.
18. Resende, "Mãe, filha, amiga."

Chapter 33

1. Lispector and Montero, letter to Paulo Gurgel Valente, April 22, 1969, *Correspondências*, 267.
2. Interview with Yolanda Costa e Silva, "Já viajei por todo o mundo, mas não vi nada como a Amazônia." In *Manchete*, "Diálogos possíveis coem Clarice Lispector" [undated clipping], CLA.
3. Gaspari, *Ditadura envergonhada*, 231.
4. Ibid., 274.
5. "Frases que ficaram," *O Jornal*, February 25, 1968.

6. Lispector, "Estado de graça—Trecho," in *Descoberta*, 91.
7. Zuenir Ventura and Carlos Scliar, quoted in Gotlib, *Clarice*, 380–81.
8. "Marcha da liberdade toma conta da cidade," *Última Hora*, Rio de Janeiro, June 26, 1968, CLA.
9. Ventura and Scliar, quoted in Gotlib, *Clarice*, 380–81.
10. Interview with Julio Lerner, quoted in Varin and Lispector, *Rencontres*, 213.
11. Gaspari, *Ditadura envergonhada*, 299.
12. Ibid., 316–18.
13. Elio Gaspari, *As ilusões armadas: A ditadura escancarada* (São Paulo: Companhia das Letras, 2002), 362.
14. Ferreira, *Eu sou*, 247.
15. Alberto Dines, *100 páginas que fizeram história: Grandes momentos do jornalismo brasileiro nos últimos 80 anos* (São Paulo: LF&N, 1997).
16. Lispector, "Pertencer," in *Descoberta*, 110.
17. E. Lispector, *Corpo a corpo*, 44.
18. In obituary. Same story recounted in Manzo, *Era uma vez*, 144–45.
19. Eudinyr Fraga, "Clarice," undated typescript, in author's collection.
20. Interview with Rosa Cass, Rio de Janeiro, July 29, 2006.
21. Quoted in Varin, *Langues*, 32.
22. Marly de Oliveira, *A suave pantera* (Rio de Janeiro: Orfeu, 1968).
23. Letter to Marly de Oliveira, July 11, 1968, private collection, courtesy of Livraria Dantes, Rio de Janeiro.

> Marly queridinha, realmente não recebi carta sua antes desta que voce enviou por intermédio de Rosa. Meu endereço é.... Estou sentindo falta de você muito maior do que eu sabia que ia sentir. Parece que se criou um pequeno vácuo na minha vida, e ninguém consegue preencher nem de longe a sua vaga. Estou sentindo muita dificuldade com minha novela: é a primeira de que eu falei para os outros, e é a primeira cujo final eu já sei como é. Há ainda o espectro de "A Paixão Segundo G. H.": depois desse livro tenho a impressão desagradável de que esperam de mim coisa melhor. Mas estou lutando contra esse limiar de depressão procurando um jeito melhor de trabalhar e também me valendo de d. Catarina (nunca conte a ninguém da minha análise: escrevi todos os meus livros antes de d. Catarina, exceto o "Mistério do Coelho Pensante," que estava aliás escrito desde o tempo em que tinha seis anos; de modo que é uma pista fácil de me explicar dizendo que escrevo assim por causa da análise. Eliane Zagury foi uma que me perguntou se eu faço ou fiz análise, eu neguei, e ela disse que era porque meus livros tinham a profundeza que só se atinge na análise).... Quanto a mim mesma, estou apaixonada e a pessoa em questão simplesmente me disse, com outras palavras é claro, que ele não me quer. Mas a dor não está sendo grande."

24. M. H. Cardoso, *Vida-vida*, x.
25. Ibid., 232, 335, 340–41.
26. Quoted in ibid., x.

Chapter 34

1. Lispector and Montero, letter to Paulo Gurgel Valente, January 26, 1969, *Correspondências*, 261.
2. For example, Leo Gilson Ribeiro, Claire Varin, and Vilma Arêas.
3. Lispector, "Menino a bico-de-pena," October 18, 1969, in *Descoberta*, 256.
4. Norma Pereira Rêgo, "Lispector: Sempre em tom maior," 1969, undated clipping, CLA.
5. Lispector, *Aprendizagem*, 39.
6. Pessoa, *Heróstrato*, 174.

7. Rêgo, "Lispector: Sempre em tom maior."
8. Lispector, *Aprendizagem*, 22.
9. Lispector, "As dores da sobrevivência: Sérgio Porto." September 28, 1968, in *Descoberta*, 142.
10. Ibid., 79.
11. Lispector, *Aprendizagem*, 138–39.
12. There are many examples of this process in Manzo, *Era uma vez*, 105.
13. Lispector, *Aprendizagem*, 20–21.
14. Ibid., 105, 98.
15. Quoted in Sant'Anna, untitled clipping, *Jornal do Brasil*, October 25, 1986, author's collection.
16. Sabino and Lispector, letter from Fernando Sabino, January 29, 1969, *Cartas*, 203.
17. Lispector, *Aprendizagem*, 70.
18. Ibid., 35.
19. Ibid., 61–62.
20. Ibid., 63–64.
21. Ibid., 161, 125.
22. Lispector, "Humildade e técnica," in *Descoberta*, 251.
23. Lispector, *Aprendizagem*, 118–19.
24. Ibid., 114–15, 154–55, 158.
25. Ibid., 133.
26. Ibid., 95.
27. Ibid., 78, 128.
28. Ibid., 174, 181–82.

Chapter 35

1. Quoted in Manzo, *Era uma vez*, 102–3.
2. Ibid., 103.
3. Quoted in Ferreira, *Eu sou*, 249.
4. Lispector and Montero, *Correspondências*, 276.
5. Lispector, *Objecto gritante (II)*, 46.
6. Here and following, including Lícia Manzo's fascinating interview with Azulay: Manzo, *Era uma vez*, 93–94.
7. Elisa Lispector, *O muro de pedras* (Rio de Janeiro: Livraria José Olympio Editora, 1963).
8. Elisa Lispector, *O dia mais longo de Thereza* (Rio de Janeiro: Gráfica Record Editora S.A., 1965).
9. E. Lispector, *Corpo a corpo*, 13.
10. Lispector, letter to Elisa Lispector, May 1, 1945, in *Minhas queridas*, 48.
11. Lispector, letter to Tania Lispector Kaufmann, February 22, 1947, in *Minhas queridas*, 48.
12. Lispector, letter to Tania Lispector Kaufmann, August 13, 1947, in *Minhas queridas*, 171.
13. Lispector, letter to Tania Lispector Kaufmann and Elisa Lispector, July 25, 1956, in *Minhas queridas*, 273.
14. Lispector, "A vidente," in *Descoberta*, 43.
15. Ibid., 93.
16. "Uma visita à casa dos expostos," *Vamos Lêr!* July 8, 1941, in Lispector et al., *Outros escritos*, 35–42.
17. Olga Borelli, "Liminar: A difícil definição," in Lispector, *A paixão segundo G. H.: edição crítica*, xx–xxiii.
18. Franco Júnior, "Clarice, segundo Olga Borelli," 8.

19. Remy Gorga Filho, "Clarice Lispector: Eu não sou um monstro sagrado," *Revista do livro*, May-June 1970.

20. Ribeiro, "Tentativa de explicação."

21. Borelli, *Esboço*, 26.

Chapter 36

1. Quoted in Gotlib, *Clarice*, 399–400.
2. Ibid., 398.
3. Leo Gilson Ribeiro, "Auto-inspeção," *Veja*, September 19, 1973.
4. José Castello, *Inventário das sombras* (1999; Rio de Janeiro: Editora Record, 2006), 30.
5. Alexandrino Severino, "As duas versões de Água viva," *Remate de Males*, no. 9 (1989).
6. Letter to Alexandrino Severino, June 23, 1972, CLA.
7. Lispector, *Objecto gritante*, 32. In *Água viva* the Ukrainian reference is deleted.
8. Ibid., 29–30, 72, 74.
9. Quoted in Severino, "As duas versões de Água viva."
10. "Objecto Gritante," quoted in Manzo, *Era uma vez*, 142.
11. Lispector, *Objecto gritante*, 44, 63. The remark about her mother reappears in the essay on Brasília published in *Visão do esplendor*, and it also recurs, in slightly modified form, in the story "Soulstorm," published in *Where Were You at Night*: "The sacred monster died: in its place a girl was born who was alone."
12. Ibid., 66–67.
13. Too much concision, she later complained. About half of the book was cut, either by the publisher or by Clarice's heirs. See Franco Júnior, "Clarice, segundo Olga Borelli."
14. Franco Júnior, "Clarice, segundo Olga Borelli."
15. Ibid.
16. Letter to Marly de Oliveira, undated, private collection. Courtesy of Livraria Dantes, Rio de Janeiro. "Você sabe como sou quanto a cartas. Mas hoje a saudade apertou mais e eis-me aqui escrevendo para você.... Não sei porque você gostou do meu livro "Objeto Gritante." Pois, passado o primeiro ímpeto, fui reler e fiquei horrorizada. É tão ruim, tão ruim, que não vou publica-lo, já o retirei da editora."
17. Franco Júnior, "Clarice, segundo Olga Borelli."
18. Quoted in Gotlib, *Clarice*, 410.
19. Franco Júnior, "Clarice, segundo Olga Borelli."
20. Interview quoted in Lispector et al., *Outros escritos*.
21. Lispector, *Água viva*, 16.
22. Ibid., 37.
23. Ibid., 22.
24. Ibid., 31.
25. Ibid., 78.
26. Ibid., 59, 51, 27, 88, 71.
27. Ibid., 16.
28. Franco Júnior, "Clarice, segundo Olga Borelli."
29. Lispector, *Água viva*, 13.
30. Lispector, "Abstrato e figurativo," in *Legião*, 151.
31. Lispector, *Água viva*, 15.
32. Ibid., 34.
33. Ibid., 35.

34. Lispector. *Objecto gritante*, 7.

35. Lispector, *Água viva*, 60–61.

36. Ibid., 43.

Chapter 37

1. Borelli, *Esboço*, 42.

2. The tensions in the country claimed a victim close to Clarice. On September 4, 1969, the leftist guerrillas pulled off their most spectacular feat, kidnapping an American ambassador, Charles Elbrick. Though he was released unharmed after seventy-eight hours in exchange for captured guerrillas, the incident took a heavy toll on Clarice's brother-in-law Mozart Gurgel Valente, who was chief of staff of Itamaraty as well as a friend of Elbrick's. Soon thereafter he achieved one of the highest positions in the ministry, being named ambassador to Washington. But he had been exhausted by his previous, difficult position, and died in Washington on December 21, 1970, leaving Eliane a widow.

3. Gaspari, *Ditadura derrotada*, 504.

4. See http://jbonline.terra.com.br/destaques/110anosjb/110anosjb_impr_C2_13.html.

5. Gaspari, *Ditadura derrotada*, 49–50.

6. Ibid., 293.

7. Another matter complicating Brazil's relationship with the Arabs was its long-standing support for Portugal's brutal colonial wars in Africa, which, along with Portugal's own geriatric tyranny, were then approaching their end.

8. Interview with Alberto Dines, São Paulo, July 22, 2006.

9. Ibid.

10. Interview in *Pasquim*, June 3, 1974, quoted in A. M. Nunes, *Jornalista*, 94.

11. Dênis de Moraes, "Humor de combate: Henfil e os 30 anos do Pasquim," *Ciberlegenda* 1999. The attack appeared in *O Pasquim*, no. 138, February 22–28, 1972.

12. Fonta, "O papo: Clarice Lispector."

13. Ferreira, *Eu sou*, 263.

14. Interview with Alberto Dines. Gershom Scholem has demonstrated Kafka's deep roots in the Jewish mystical tradition.

Chapter 38

1. Quoted in Manzo, *Era uma vez*, 163.

2. Ferreira, *Eu sou*, 264.

3. Quoted in Manzo, *Era uma vez*, 163–64.

4. Ibid.

5. Ibid.

6. Lispector, "A entrevista alegre," in *Descoberta*, 56.

7. Lispector. *Objecto gritante*, 47–48.

8. Ibid., 109–10.

9. Lispector, *Água viva*, 71. The comment also appears in Lispector, *Objecto gritante*, 45.

10. Lori, a primary school teacher, was also most at ease around children: "What always saved me were my pupils, the children," she tells Ulisses, the children "she now loved with a mother's love." Lispector, *Aprendizagem*, 160–62.

11. Lispector and Montero, letter to Andréa Azulay, June 27, 1974, *Correspondências*, 290.

12. Lispector, *Hora*.

13. Andréa Azulay, *Meus primeiros contos* (Rio de Janeiro: Edição limitada confeccionada por encomenda de Clarice Lispector e prefaciada por ela, 1975), quoted in Manzo, *Era uma vez*, 168.

14. Lispector and Montero, letters to Andréa Azulay, July 7, 1974, and undated ("Uma história de tanto amor"), *Correspondências*, 292–93, 307.

15. Letter to Andréa Azulay, January 4, 1974, CLA.

16. Manzo, *Era uma vez*, 169.

17. Clarice Lispector, *Quase de verdade* (Rio de Janeiro: Rocco, 1978).

18. Varin and Lispector, *Rencontres*, 31.

19. Elizabeth Lowe, "The Passion According to C. L.," *Review*, no. 24 (1979), quoted in Varin and Lispector, *Rencontres*, 62. Luiz Carlos Lacerda thought that Ulisses started swallowing cigarettes after the fire that almost killed Clarice in an attempt to protect her, though she seems to have bought him afterward.

20. Olga Borelli quoted in Manzo, *Era uma vez*, 171.

21. Lispector, letter to Elisa Lispector and Tania Lispector Kaufmann, March 25, 1949, *Minhas queridas*, 219.

22. Lispector, *Sopro*, 64.

23. In Varin, *Langues*, 70.

24. Lispector, *Sopro*, 15.

25. Lispector, *Legião*, 23, 26.

26. Lispector, *Maçã*, 45.

27. Lispector, "Não soltar os cavalos," in *Legião*, 197.

28. Lispector, *Sopro*, 78.

29. Ibid., 79.

30. Ibid., 48.

Chapter 39

1. Quoted in Gotlib, *Clarice*, 73.

2. Clarice Lispector, *A vida íntima de Laura* (Rio de Janeiro: J. Olympio, 1974), 1.

3. Ibid.

4. Lispector. *Objecto gritante*, 56–57; Lispector, *Aprendizagem*, 115.

5. Quoted in Gotlib, *Clarice*, 415.

6. Hohlfeldt, "Uma tarde com Clarice Lispector."

7. Jorge de Aquino Filho, "Minha Mãe Clarice Lispector," *Manchete*, February 13, 1982.

8. In Lispector et al., *Outros escritos*, 167.

9. Quoted in Manzo, *Era uma vez*, 191–92.

10. See Pedro Paulo de Sena Madureira (from the publisher Nova Fronteira) in Ferreira, *Eu sou*, 270.

11. For a partial list of Clarice Lispector's translations, see Marting, *Clarice Lispector: A Bio-bibliography*, 176.

12. Lispector, *Descoberta*, 53.

13. Borelli, *Esboço*, 31.

14. Lispector, letter to Elisa Lispector, January 2, 1946, in *Minhas queridas*, 53.

15. Lispector, *Onde*, 57.

16. Lispector et al., *Outros escritos*, 167.

17. Letter from Anna Maria da Silva Telles Watson, Editora Artenova, April 26, 1976, CLA. Watson may have been on to something. Rumor has it that in order to help her friend, Olga Borelli's sister Helena did many of her translations for her.

18. Lispector, *Onde*, 8.

19. Ibid., 19–20.

20. Ibid., 25.

21. Ibid., 32.
22. Ibid., 38–39.
23. Ibid., 63, 68, 61, 65.
24. Ibid., 78.

Chapter 40

1. Franco Júnior, "Clarice, segundo Olga Borelli."
2. Borelli, *Esboço*, 34–35.
3. Ibid., 40.
4. Interview with Gilda Murray, São Paulo, September 19, 2006.
5. Interview with Luiz Carlos Lacerda, Rio de Janeiro, August 1, 2006.
6. Ibid.
7. Interview with Marina Colasanti, Rio de Janeiro, August 2, 2006.
8. Interview with Alberto Dines, São Paulo, July 22, 2006.
9. Manzo, *Era uma vez*, 162.
10. Lispector, *Objecto gritante*, 55.
11. Lispector, *Via crucis*, 15.
12. Ibid., 9–10.
13. Ibid., 10.
14. Ibid., 65.
15. Ibid., 9.
16. José Maria Cançado, "O 'vício impune' da leitura," *Folha de S. Paulo*, October 25, 1992.
17. Celso Arnaldo Araújo, "Uma escritora no escuro—Clarice Lispector," *Manchete*, May 3, 1975, in A. M. Nunes, *Jornalista*, 96.
18. Lispector, *Via crucis*, 81–82, 44.
19. Ibid., 68, 57.
20. Aquino Filho, "Minha Mãe Clarice Lispector," quoted in Claire Williams, *The Encounter between Opposites in the Works of Clarice Lispector* (Bristol, England: Hispanic, Portuguese, and Latin American Monographs, 2006), 177–78. The date is slightly misremembered.
21. Marta Peixoto points to two other stories that refer symbolically to rape, both from *Family Ties*: "Preciousness" and "Mystery in São Cristóvão." Neither is as explicit nor so clearly tied up with the memory of Clarice's mother. See Marta Peixoto, "Rape and Textual Violence," in *Passionate Fictions: Gender, Narrative, and Violence in Clarice Lispector* (Minneapolis: University of Minnesota Press, 1994).
22. Lispector, *Via crucis*, 86.
23. Ibid., 87.
24. Ibid., 89.
25. Ibid.

Chapter 41

1. Bruna Becherucci, "Lixo, sim: Lançamento inútil," *Veja*, July 31, 1974.
2. Araújo, "Uma escritora no escuro—Clarice Lispector," in A. M. Nunes, *Jornalista*, 96.
3. Emmanuel de Moraes, "A via-crucis de Clarice," *Jornal do Brasil*, August 17, 1974.
4. Araújo, "Uma escritora no escuro—Clarice Lispector," in A. M. Nunes, *Jornalista*, 96.
5. Lispector, *Via crucis*, 53.
6. Carlos Graieb, "A ciranda de Lygia," *Veja São Paulo*, August 6, 2008.
7. Letter from Simón González, 1975, CLA.
8. Robert L. Nicklaus, "Occult Conventioneers," *Evangelical Missions Quarterly*, January 1, 1976.
9. "Moonlight Dance Opens a Congress of Sorcery," *New York Times*, August 26, 1975.

10. Lispector et al., Montero, and Manzo, *Outros escritos*, 120, 122.

11. One version began, "I do not seek the magic of the supernatural. But I tremble all over when, such as recently happened, I was worried and solitary and without a future—when suddenly without any warning, at dusk, a rainfall came to relieve all of my electric energy and calm me down allowing me to sleep profoundly relieved. The rain and I had a magical relationship. The next day I read in the paper, to my great surprise, that the rain that for me was like white magic, had been black magic for other people: the paper said that the rain was hail, that it knocked over houses, that it prevented the flight of airplanes." Borelli, *Esboço*, 56–57.

12. Quoted in Marilene Felinto, "Lispector foi a congresso de bruxaria," *Folha de S. Paulo*, August 2, 1992.

13. Horácio Oliveira, untitled newspaper clipping, December 23, 1977, CLA.

14. Isa Cambará, "Clarice Lispector: Não escrevo para agradar a ninguém," *Folha de S. Paulo*, September 10, 1975.

15. Ibid.

16. Sant'Anna, untitled clipping, *Jornal do Brasil*, October 25, 1986, CLA.

17. Castello, *Inventário das sombras*, 28.

18. Lispector, *Onde*, 68.

19. Lispector, *Sopro*, 22.

20. Quoted in Varin, *Langues*, 184.

21. Lispector, *Visão*, 64.

22. Borelli, *Esboço*, 70.

23. "Esboço de uma possível pintora," *Jornal do Brasil*, November 4, 1992.

24. Lispector, letter to Elisa Lispector and Tania Lispector Kaufmann, May 8, 1956, *Minhas queridas*, 269.

25. Lispector, *Sopro*, 55.

26. Ibid.

Chapter 42

1. Claire Williams points out that Lucrécia, too, is a "picture of a picture": "Any picture of her was more real than she herself was," for example. Williams, *Encounter*, 59; Lispector, *Cidade sitiada*, 71.

2. Lispector, *Sopro*.

3. Lispector et al., *Outros escritos*.

4. Lispector, *Sopro*, 108.

5. Ibid., 82.

6. Ibid., 25.

7. Cambará, "Clarice Lispector: Não escrevo para agradar a ninguém."

8. Lispector, *Sopro*, 32.

9. Ibid., 38, 65.

10. Ibid., 77.

11. Ibid., 131.

12. Ibid., 105.

13. Ibid.

14. Ibid., 152.

15. Ibid., 165.

16. Ibid., 162–63.

17. Ibid., 166.

18. Ibid., 167.

19. Olga Borelli, "Não dá para analisar Clarice," *Brasil / Brazil: Revista de Literatura Brasileira* (2001): 96, quoted in Manzo, *Era uma vez*, 207.

Chapter 43

1. Lispector and Montero, letter to Mafalda Verissimo, November 28, 1975, *Correspondências*, 310.

2. Interview with Alberto Dines, São Paulo, July 22, 2006.

3. Quoted in Gotlib, *Clarice*, 436–37.

4. Borelli, *Esboço*, 47–48; Manzo, *Era uma vez*, 190.

5. Juan Cruz, "Carmen Balcells: Autorretrato de una dama," *El País*, March 11, 2007.

6. Borelli, *Esboço*, 58.

7. Ibid., 25, 26.

8. Gotlib, *Clarice*, 443–44.

9. Interview with Rosa Cass, Rio de Janeiro, July 29, 2006.

10. This account is a bit suspect: Elisa, after all, had never liked the idea of Clarice's marrying a Gentile.

11. Coutinho, *Criaturas*, 170.

12. Gotlib, *Clarice*, 438–39.

13. Ibid., 479–80.

14. Interview, Rosa Lispector, Recife, August 18, 2005.

15. Gotlib, *Clarice*, 480.

16. Ferreira, *Eu sou*, 283.

17. Coutinho, *Criaturas*, 155–56.

18. Untitled clipping [Brasília?], CLA.

19. Untitled clipping [Porto Alegre?], CLA.

20. "Entrevista com Caio Fernando Abreu," *Estado de São Paulo*, December 9, 1995.

21. Gotlib, *Clarice*, 293.

22. Ferreira, *Eu sou*, 275. Gilles probably inspired the story of a makeup artist in *A via crucis do corpo*, "Ele me bebeu."

Chapter 44

1. This interview is widely available on the Internet.

2. Lerner, "Última entrevista."

Chapter 45

1. Lispector, *Aprendizagem*, 136.

2. Jacinto Rego de Almeida, "Um encontro com Clarice Lispector," *Jornal de Letras (Lisbon)*, April 14, 1992.

3. Quoted in Manzo, *Era uma vez*, 206–7.

4. Quoted in ibid., 209.

5. Interview with Norma Couri, São Paulo, July 22, 2006. There is another reference to this habit in Varin, *Langues*, 95.

6. Resende, "Mãe, filha, amiga."

7. Lerner, "Última entrevista."

8. Lispector, *A vida íntima de Laura*.

9. Lispector, *Hora*, 59–60.

10. 1 Maccabees 1:18–21.

11. Franco Júnior, "Clarice, segundo Olga Borelli."

12. Lispector, *Hora*, 26.

13. Ibid.
14. Ibid., 27–28.
15. Franco Júnior, "Clarice, segundo Olga Borelli."
16. Lispector, *Hora*, 36.
17. Ibid., 39, 40.
18. Ibid., 42, 44, 43.
19. Ibid., 55, 54.
20. Ibid., 52, 53.
21. Ibid., 54.
22. Ibid., 59.
23. 2 Maccabees 6:2. For this reference, see Nelson Vieira, "A expressão judaica na obra de Clarice Lispector," in *Clarice Lispector: Remate de Males: Revista do Departamento de Teoria Literária*, ed. Vilma Arêas and Berta Waldman (Campinas: Universidade Estadual de Campinas, 1989), 209.
24. Lispector, *Hora*, 60.
25. Castello, *Inventário das sombras*, 26.
26. Lispector, *Hora*, 54.
27. Ibid., 76.
28. Ibid., 88.
29. Ibid., 90, 92.
30. Ibid., 95–96.
31. Ibid., 98.
32. Quoted in Ferreira, *Eu sou*, 286.
33. Lerner, "Última entrevista."
34. Lispector, *Hora*, 22.
35. Ibid., 25.
36. Ibid., 34, 35, 32, 28.
37. Ibid., 50.
38. Published under his pseudonym: Tristão de Athayde, "Requiem para Clarice," *Jornal do Brasil*, January 12, 1978.
39. Lispector et al., *Outros escritos*, 139.
40. Lispector, *Perto*, 13 (1980 ed.).
41. Lispector, *Hora*, 99.
42. Ibid., 100, 101.
43. Ibid., 102.
44. Ibid., 103.
45. Ibid., 104.
46. "Sepultamento de Clarice será simples e discreto." See also Olga Borelli, interviewed in *Manchete*, 1981, quoted in Gotlib, *Clarice*, 481.
47. "Sepultamento de Clarice será simples e discreto."
48. Quoted in Gotlib, *Clarice*, 481–82.
49. Interview with Rosa Cass, Rio de Janeiro, July 29, 2006.
50. Ferreira, *Eu sou*, 291.
51. Quoted in Gotlib, *Clarice*, 483.
52. Borelli, *Esboço*, 60–62.
53. Quoted in Gotlib, *Clarice*, 484.
54. Francis, "Clarice: Impressões de uma mulher que lutou sozinha."

WORKS CITED

Abramson, Henry. *A Prayer for the Government: Ukrainians and Jews in Revolutionary Times, 1917–1920.* Cambridge, Mass.: Harvard University Press for the Harvard Ukrainian Research Institute and Center for Jewish Studies, 1999.

American Jewish Congress, Israel Goldberg, and Committee on Protest against the Massacres of Jews in Ukrainia and Other Lands. *The Massacres and Other Atrocities Committed against the Jews in Southern Russia.* New York, 1920.

An-Ski, S. *The Enemy at His Pleasure: A Journey through the Jewish Pale of Settlement during World War I.* Translated by Joachim Neugroschel. New York: Metropolitan Books, 2002.

Andrade, Oswald de. "[O Lustre]." *Correio da Manhã,* February 26, 1946.

Aquino Filho, Jorge de. "Minha Mãe Clarice Lispector." *Manchete,* February 13, 1982.

Araújo, Celso Arnaldo. "Uma escritora no escuro—Clarice Lispector." *Manchete,* May 3, 1975.

Arêas, Vilma, and Berta Waldman, eds. *Clarice Lispector: Remate de Males.* Vol. 9, *Revista do Departamento de Teoria Literária.* Campinas: Universidade Estadual de Campinas, 1989.

Assis Brasil. "Laços de família." *Jornal do Brasil,* September 2, 1960.

Athayde, Tristão de. "Requiem para Clarice." *Jornal do Brasil,* January 12, 1978.

Athayde, Tristão de, Amado Fontes, Cornelio Penna, Erico Verissimo, Graciliano Ramos, Jorge Amado, José Geraldo Vieira, José Lins do Rego, Lúcio Cardoso, Octavio de Faria, and Rachel de Queiroz. *10 romancistas falam de seus personagens.* Rio de Janeiro: Edições Condé, 1946.

Ayala, Walmir. " 'A Paixão segundo G. H.': Um romance de doação." *Jornal do Comércio,* December 1, 1964.

Azulay, Andréa. *Meus primeiros contos.* Rio de Janeiro: Edição limitada confeccionada por encomenda de Clarice Lispector e prefaciada por ela, 1975.

Bandeira, Manuel, and Ralph Edward Ingalls Dimmick. *Brief History of Brazilian Literature, Pensamiento de América.* Washington, D.C.: Pan American Union, 1958.

Barroso, Gustavo. *Os Protócolos dos sábios de Sião: O Imperialismo de Israel. O Plano dos Judeus para a Conquista do Mundo. O Código do Anti-Cristo. Provas de autenticidade, documentos, notas, e comentários. Texto completo e apostilado por Gustavo Barroso.* São Paulo: Agência Minerva Editora, 1936.

Becherucci, Bruna. "Lixo, sim: Lançamento inútil." *Veja,* July 31, 1974.

Bishop, Elizabeth. *Poems, Prose, and Letters.* Edited by Robert Giroux and Lloyd Schwartz. New York: Library of America, 2008.

Bishop, Elizabeth, and Clarice Lispector. "Three Stories by Clarice Lispector." *Kenyon Review*, no. 26 (1964): 501–11.

Bishop, Elizabeth, and Robert Lowell. *Words in Air: The Complete Correspondence between Elizabeth Bishop and Robert Lowell.* Edited by Thomas Travisano with Saskia Hamilton. New York: Farrar, Straus and Giroux, 2008.

Bloch, Chayim. *The Golem: Legends of the Ghetto of Prague.* Vienna: The Golem, 1925.

Boogaart, Ernst van den, Hendrik Richard Hoetink, and Peter James Palmer Whitehead. *Johan Maurits van Nassau-Siegen 1604–1679: A Humanist Prince in Europe and Brazil: Essays on the Occasion of the Tercentenary of His Death.* The Hague: Johan Maurits van Nassau Stichting, 1979.

Borelli, Olga. *Clarice Lispector, esboço para um possível retrato.* Rio de Janeiro: Nova Fronteira, 1981.

———. "Não dá para analisar Clarice." *Brasil/Brazil: Revista de Literatura Brasileira* (2001).

Boxer, C. R. *The Dutch in Brazil, 1624–1654.* Oxford: Clarendon Press, 1957.

Braga, Rubem. *A cidade e a roça.* Rio de Janeiro: José Olympio, 1957.

———. *Com a F.E.B. na Itália: Crônicas.* Rio de Janeiro: Livraria Editora Zelio Valverde, 1945.

Brandão, Moreno. "Alagoas em 1925." In *Livro do Nordeste (comemorativo do 1. centenário do Diário de Pernambuco).* 1925; Recife Secretaria da Justiça, Arquivo Público Estadual, 1979.

Brasil, Emanuel. *Nossos clássicos: Clarice Lispector (No. 120).* Rio de Janeiro: Agir, 1994.

Brown, Kate. *A Biography of No Place: From Ethnic Borderland to Soviet Heartland.* Cambridge, Mass.: London: Harvard University Press, 2004.

Cabral de Melo Neto, João. *Agrestes: Poesia (1981–1985).* Rio de Janeiro: Editora Nova Fronteira, 1985.

Calado, Manoel. *O valeroso Lucideno. E triumpho da liberdade.: Primeira parte.* Lisboa: Por Paulo Craesbeeck impressor & liureiro das Ordões Militares, 1648.

Calmon, Pedro. *História do Brasil.* Vol. 2. Rio de Janeiro: José Olympio, 1971.

Cambará, Isa. "Clarice Lispector: Não escrevo para agradar a ninguém." *Folha de S. Paulo*, September 10, 1975.

———. "Escritora mágica." *Veja*, July 30, 1975.

Cançado, José Maria. "O 'vício impune' da leitura." *Folha de S. Paulo*, October 25, 1992.

Cândido, Antônio. "Perto do coração selvagem." *Folha da manhã*, July 16, 1944.

———. *Vários escritos.* São Paulo: Livraria Duas Cidades, 1977.

Cardoso, Lúcio, and Mario Carelli. *Crônica da casa assassinada.* Critical ed. Nanterre, France: ALLCA XX, Université Paris X, Centre de recherches latino-américaines, 1991.

Cardoso, Maria Helena. *Por onde andou meu coração: Memórias.* Rio de Janeiro: José Olympio, 1967.

———. *Vida-vida: Memória.* Rio de Janeiro: José Olympio, 1973.

Carelli, Mario. *Corcel de fogo: Vida e obra de Lúcio Cardoso (1912–1968).* Rio de Janeiro: Editora Guanabara, 1988.

Carvalho, Marco Antonio de. *Rubem Braga: Um cigano fazendeiro do ar.* Rio de Janeiro: Editora Globo, 2007.

Castello, José. *Inventário das sombras.* 1999; Rio de Janeiro: Editora Record, 2006.

Castro, Ruy. *Carmen: Uma biografia.* São Paulo: Companhia das Letras, 2005.

———. *Ela é carioca: Uma enciclopédia de Ipanema.* 2nd ed. São Paulo: Companhia das Letras, 1999.

Cixous, Hélène, and Deborah Jenson. *"Coming to Writing" and Other Essays.* Cambridge, Mass.: Harvard University Press, 1991.

"Clarice e *A Maçã no Escuro.*" *Diário de Notícias*, July 30, 1961.

"Clarice Lispector diz que Escreve sem ter Esquemas." [Curitiba], July 25, 1970.

"Clarice, um mistério sem muito mistério." *Correio da Manhã*, November 2, 1971.

Córdova-Bello, Eleazar. *Compañías holandesas de navegación, agentes de la colonización neerlandesa.* Seville: Escuela de estudios hispano-americanos, 1964.

Coutinho, Edilberto. *Criaturas de papel: Temas de literatura & sexo & folclore & carnaval & futebol & televisão & outros temas da vida.* Rio de Janeiro: Civilização Brasileira, 1980.

Cruz, Juan. "Carmen Balcells: Autorretrato de una dama." *El País,* March 11, 2007.

Dan, Joseph. *The Early Kabbalah.* Translated by Ronald C. Kiener. New York: Paulist Press, 1986.

Decol, René. "Uma certa Aracy, um chamado João." *Folha de S. Paulo,* December 18, 2006.

Denis, Ferdinand. *Résumé de l'histoire littéraire du Portgual, suivi du résumé de l'histoire littéraire du Brésil.* Paris: Lecointe et Durey, 1826.

Dines, Alberto. *100 páginas que fizeram história: Grandes momentos do jornalismo brasileiro nos últimos 80 anos.* São Paulo: LF &N, 1997.

———. *Morte no paraíso: A tragédia de Stefan Zweig.* 3rd ed. Rio de Janeiro: Rocco, 2004.

Dulles, John W. F. *Carlos Lacerda, Brazilian Crusader.* 2 vols. Austin: University of Texas Press, 1991.

"Entrevista com Caio Fernando Abreu." *Estado de São Paulo,* December 9, 1995.

"Esboço de uma possível pintora." *Jornal do Brasil,* November 4, 1992.

Escorel, Lauro. "Crítica Literária." *A Manhã,* October 20, 1944.

———. "Prêmio da Fundação Graça Aranha de 1943." *A Manhã,* October 29, 1944.

Falbel, Nachman. *Estudos sobre a comunidade judaica no Brasil.* São Paulo: Federação Israelita do Estado de São Paulo, 1984.

———. *Jacob Nachbin.* São Paulo: Nobel, 1985.

Fausto, Boris. *Getúlio Vargas.* São Paulo: Companhia das Letras, 2006.

Felinto, Marilene. "Lispector foi a congresso de bruxaria." *Folha de S. Paulo,* August 2, 1992.

Fernández, Sílvia Leal. "Um ano sem Clarice." *Desfile,* December 1978.

Ferreira, Teresa Cristina Montero. *Eu sou uma pergunta: Uma biografia de Clarice Lispector.* Rio de Janeiro: Rocco, 1999.

Figes, Orlando. *A People's Tragedy: The Russian Revolution, 1891–1924.* New York: Viking, 1996.

Finamour, Jurema. "Clarice Lispector." *Jornal de Letras,* September 1960.

Fonta, Sérgio. "O papo: Clarice Lispector." *Jornal de Letras* 259 (1972): 5.

Fraga, Eudinyr. "Clarice." Unpublished typescript, Author's collection.

Francis, Paulo. "Clarice: Impressões de uma mulher que lutou sozinha." *Folha de S. Paulo,* December 15, 1977.

Franco Júnior, Arnaldo. "Clarice, segundo Olga Borelli." *Minas Gerais Suplemento Literário,* December 19, 1987.

"Frases que ficaram." *O Jornal,* February 25, 1968.

Freixas, Laura. *Clarice Lispector: Vidas literarias.* Barcelona: Ediciones Omega, 2001.

Gaspari, Elio. *As ilusões armadas: A ditadura envergonhada.* São Paulo: Companhia das Letras, 2002.

———. *As ilusões armadas: A ditadura escancarada.* São Paulo: Companhia das Letras, 2002.

———. *O sacerdote e o feiticeiro: A ditadura derrotada.* São Paulo: Companhia das Letras, 2003.

Gilbert, Martin. *Atlas of Russian History.* New York: Dorset Press, 1972.

Gilio, María Esther. "Tristes trópicos: Con Clarice Lispector en Río." *Triunfo,* June 5, 1976.

Girsoler, Ulysses. "Psychodiagnostique de Rorschach," [1947–48]. Clarice Lispector Archive, Arquivo-Museu de Literatura Brasileira, Fundação Casa de Rui Barbosa, Rio de Janeiro.

Gomes, Angela Maria de Castro. *Em família: A correspondência de Oliveira Lima e Gilberto Freyre, Coleção Letras em série.* Campinas: CECULT Mercado de Letras, 2005.

Gorga Filho, Remy. "Clarice Lispector: Eu não sou um monstro sagrado." *Revista do livro,* May–June 1970, 112–15.

Gotlib, Nádia Battella. *Clarice: Uma vida que se conta.* São Paulo: Editora Atica, 1995.

———. *Clarice Fotobiografia.* São Paulo: Edusp / Imprensa Oficial, 2007.

Graieb, Carlos. "A ciranda de Lygia." *Veja São Paulo,* August 6, 2008.

Guimarães, Valmiki Villela. "Clarice Lispector em duas histórias." *Minas Gerais Suplemento Literário,* December 19, 1987.

Hesse, Hermann. *Der Steppenwolf.* 1927; Berlin: G. Fischer Verlag, 1961.

Hofferman, Nathan. *The 20th Century and I.* Records of the Chechelnicker Benevolent Association of New York.

Hohlfeldt, Antônio. "Uma tarde com Clarice Lispector." *Correio do povo,* January 3, 1971.

Howe, Irving. *World of Our Fathers.* New York: Harcourt Brace Jovanovich, 1976.

Hundert, Gershon David, ed. *The YIVO Encyclopedia of Jews in Eastern Europe.* 2 vols. New Haven: Yale University Press, 2008.

Instituto Moreira Salles. *Cadernos de literatura brasileira: Clarice Lispector.* Vols. 17 and 18. São Paulo: Instituto Moreira Salles, 2004.

———. *Cadernos de literatura brasileira: Erico Verissimo.* Vol. 16. São Paulo: Instituto Moreira Salles, 2003.

Instituto Moreira Salles and Carlos Mendes de Sousa. "A revelação do nome." In *Cadernos de literatura brasileira: Clarice Lispector.* São Paulo: Instituto Moreira Salles, 2004.

Ivo, Lêdo. *Melhores crônicas de Lêdo Ivo.* Edited by Gilberto Mendonça Teles. São Paulo: Global Editora, 2004.

Kaufman, Tânia Neumann. *Passos perdidos, história recuperada: A presença judaica em Pernambuco.* Recife: Editora Bagaço, 2000.

Kaufman, Tânia, Amaro Braga, Danielle Jaimes, and Roberto Cirne. *Passos Perdidos, História Desenhada: A Presença Judaica em Pernambuco no Século XX.* Vol. 1. Recife: Arquivo Histórico Judaico de Pernambuco, 2005.

Kaufman, Tânia Neumann. *Passos perdidos, história recuperada: a presença judaica em Pernambuco.* Recife, Pernambuco, Brasil: Editora Bagaço, 2000.

Koifman, Fábio. *Quixote nas trevas: O embaixador Souza Dantas e os refugiados do nazismo.* Rio de Janeiro: Editora Record, 2002.

Kushnir, Beatriz. *Baile de máscaras: Mulheres judias e prostituição: As polacas e suas associações de ajuda mútua.* Rio de Janeiro: Imago Editora, 1996.

Lara Resende, Otto. "Mãe, filha, amiga." *O Globo,* December 10, 1977.

Lecache, Bernard. *Quand Israël meurt.* Paris: Editions du "Progrès civique," 1927.

Lerner, Julio. *Clarice Lispector, essa desconhecida.* São Paulo: Via Lettera, 2007.

———. "A última entrevista de Clarice Lispector." *Shalom,* June–August 1992, 62–69.

Lesser, Jeff. *Welcoming the Undesirables: Brazil and the Jewish Question.* Berkeley: University of California Press, 1995.

Lewis, Norman. *Naples '44.* 1978; New York: Pantheon Books, 2002.

Linhares, Temístocles. "Romances femininos." *Estado de São Paulo Suplemento Literário,* November 18, 1961.

Lins, Álvaro. *Os mortos de sobrecasaca: Obras, autores e problemas da literatura brasileira: Ensaios e estudos, 1940–1960.* Rio de Janeiro: Editôra Civilização Brasileira, 1963.

Lispector, Clarice. *Água viva.* 1973; Rio de Janeiro: Editora Artenova, 1993.

———. *Alguns contos.* Os Cadernos de Cultura ed. Rio de Janeiro: Ministério da Educação e Saúde, Serviço de Documentação, 1952.

———. *A bela e a fera.* Rio de Janeiro: Nova Fronteira, 1979.

———. *A cidade sitiada.* Rio de Janeiro: A Noite, 1948.

———. *De corpo inteiro.* São Paulo: Editora Siciliano, 1992.

———. *A descoberta do mundo.* 1984; Rio de Janeiro: Livraria Francisco Alves Editora S.A., 1994.

———. *Dez contos selecionados de Clarice Lispector.* Brasília: Confraria dos Bibliófilos do Brasil, 2004.

———. *Felicidade clandestina.* Rio de Janeiro: Sabiá, 1971.

———. *A hora da estrela.* Rio de Janeiro: Livraria J. Olympio Editora, 1977.

———. *Laços de família.* São Paulo: Francisco Alves, 1960.

———. *A legião estrangeira.* Rio de Janeiro: Editôra do Autor, 1964.

———. *A maçã no escuro.* 1961; Rio de Janeiro: Livraria Francisco Alves, 1992.

———. *Minhas queridas*. Rio de Janeiro: Editora Rocco, 2007.

———. *A mulher que matou os peixes*. Rio de Janeiro: Sabiá, 1968.

———. *O lustre*. Rio de Janeiro: Livraria Agir Editora, 1946.

———. *Objecto gritante*, 1971, Clarice Lispector Archive, Arquivo-Museu de Literatura Brasileira, Fundação Casa de Rui Barbosa, Rio de Janeiro.

———. *Objecto gritante (II)*, 1971, Dorothea Severino Collection, Nashville, Tenn.

———. *Onde estivestes de noite*. Rio de Janeiro: Editora Artenova, 1974.

———. *A paixão segundo G. H.* 1964; Rio de Janeiro: Editôra do Autor, 1991.

———. *A paixão segundo G. H.: Edição crítica*. Edited by Benedito Nunes, *Coleção Arquivos*. Paris: ALLCA XX, 1988.

———. *Perto do coração selvagem*. 2nd ed. São Paulo: Francisco Alves Editora, 1963.

———. *Perto do coração selvagem*. Rio de Janeiro: A Noite, 1943.

———. *Quase de verdade*. Rio de Janeiro: Rocco, 1978.

———. *Soulstorm: Stories*. Translated by Alexis Levitin. New York: New Directions, 1989.

———. *Um sopro de vida: Pulsações*. Rio de Janeiro: Editora Nova Fronteira, 1978.

———. *Uma aprendizagem ou O livro dos prazeres*. 1969; Rio de Janeiro: Sabiá, 1993.

———. *A via crucis do corpo*. Rio de Janeiro: Editora Artenova, 1974.

———. *A vida íntima de Laura*. Rio de Janeiro: J. Olympio, 1974.

———. *Visão do esplendor: Impressões leves*. Rio de Janeiro: Livraria Francisco Alves Editora S.A., 1975.

Lispector, Clarice, and Teresa Montero. *Correspondências*. Rio de Janeiro: Rocco, 2002.

Lispector, Clarice, Teresa Montero, and Lícia Manzo. *Outros escritos*. Rio de Janeiro: Rocco, 2005.

Lispector, Clarice, and Aparecida Maria Nunes. *Correio feminino*. Rio de Janeiro: Rocco, 2006.

Lispector, Elisa. *Além da fronteira*. 1945; Rio de Janeiro: Leitura, 1988.

———. *Corpo a corpo*. Rio de Janeiro: Edições Antares, 1983.

———. *No exílio: Romance*. 1948; Rio de Janeiro: Editora Pongetti, 1971.

———. *O dia mais longo de Thereza*. Rio de Janeiro: Gráfica Record Editora S.A., 1965.

———. *O muro de pedras*. Rio de Janeiro: Livraria José Olympio Editora, 1963.

———. *Retratos antigos*. Unpublished typescript, collection of Nicole Algranti, Teresópolis, Rio de Janeiro.

Lowe, Elizabeth. "The Passion According to C. L." *Review*, no. 24 (1979): 34–37.

Machado de Assis, Joaquim Maria. "Instinto de nacionalidade." 1873. http://www.geocities.com/athens/olympus/3583/instinto.htm.

Malamud, Samuel. *Escalas no tempo*. Rio de Janeiro: Editora Record, 1986.

Manzo, Lícia. *Era uma vez–eu: A não-ficção na obra de Clarice Lispector: Ensaio*. Curitiba: Governo do Estado do Paraná Secretaria de Estado da Cultura: The Document Company, Xerox do Brasil, 1998.

Marcondes Homem de Mello, Francisco Ignacio, and Francisco Homem de Mello. *Geographia-atlas do Brazil e das cinco partes do mundo*. Rio de Janeiro: F. Briguiet, 1912.

Marting, Diane. *Clarice Lispector: A Bio-bibliography*. Westport, Conn.: Greenwood Press, 1993.

McCann, Frank D. "Brazil and World War II: The Forgotten Ally. What did you do in the war, Zé Carioca?" *Estudios Interdisciplinarios de América Latina y el Caribe* 6, no. 2 (1995). http://www.tau.ac.il/eial/VI_2/mccann.htm

Medeiros, Elza Cansanção. *E foi assim que a cobra fumou*. Rio de Janeiro: Marques-Saraiva, 1987.

Meira, Mauritônio. "Clarice Lispector não quer se enfeitar com penas que não sejam suas." *O Globo*, January 10, 1960.

———. "Clarice Lispector volta às editoras: 'Laços de Família.'" *O Globo*, March 27, 1960.

Mengozzi, Federico. "Mistérios de Clarice." *Época*. December 3, 2004.

"Meus livros têm 'recadinhos': Quais? Os críticos é que dizem…" *O Globo*, May 15, 1961.

Milliet, Sérgio. *Diário crítico de Sérgio Milliet*. Vol. 7. 1953; São Paulo: Martins, 1982.

———. *Diário crítico de Sérgio Milliet*. Vol. 3. 1944; São Paulo: Editora Brasiliense Ltda., 1981.

"Moonlight Dance Opens a Congress of Sorcery." *New York Times*, August 26, 1975.

Moraes, Dênis de. "Humor de combate: Henfil e os 30 anos do Pasquim." *Ciberlegenda* no. 2, 1999. http://www.uff.br/mestcii/denis3.htm

Moraes, Emmanuel de. "A via-crucis de Clarice." *Jornal do Brasil*, August 17, 1974.

Morais, Fernando. *Corações sujos: A história da Shindo Renmei*. São Paulo: Companhia das Letras, 2000.

Morganti, Vera Regina, Regina Zilberman, Maria da Glória Bordini, and Nydia Guimarães. *Confissões do amor e da arte*. Porto Alegre: Mercado Aberto, 1994.

Moser, Benjamin. "A Newly Discovered Poem by Clarice Lispector." *Brasil / Brazil: A Journal of Brazilian Literature*, no. 36, year 20 (2007): 36–45.

Nicklaus, Robert L. "Occult Conventioneers." *Evangelical Missions Quarterly*, January 1, 1976, 5–12.

Nolasco, Edgar Cézar. "Restos de Ficção: A criação biográfico-literária de Clarice Lispector." Universidade Federal de Minas Gerais, 2003.

Nunes, Aparecida Maria. *Clarice Lispector Jornalista: Paginas femininas & outras paginas*. São Paulo: Editora Senac, 2006.

Nunes, Benedito. "Clarice Lispector ou o naufrágio da introspecção." *Colóquio / Letras*, no. 70 (1982): 13–22.

Oliveira, Marly de. *A suave pantera*. Rio de Janeiro: Orfeu, 1968.

"Os novos: Elisa Lispector." *Revista Panorama*, August 1947.

Page, Joseph A. *Perón, a Biography*. New York: Random House, 1983.

Paixão, Fernando, and Maria Celeste Mira. *Momentos do livro no Brasil*. São Paulo: Editora Atica, 1995.

Peixoto, Marta. *Passionate Fictions: Gender, Narrative, and Violence in Clarice Lispector*. Minneapolis: University of Minnesota Press, 1994.

Perez, Renard. *Escritores brasileiros contemporâneos*. 2nd ed. Rio de Janeiro: Civilização Brasileira, 1970.

———. "Lembrança de Elisa Lispector." 1996. Unpublished typescript, author's collection.

Pessoa, Fernando. *Heróstrato e a busca da imortalidade*. Translated by Manuela Rocha. Edited by Richard Zenith. Vol. 14 of *Obras de Fernando Pessoa*. Lisbon: Assírio & Alvim, 2000.

Pontieri, Regina Lucia. *Clarice Lispector: Uma poética do olhar*. São Paulo: Ateliê Editorial, 1999.

Prado, Paulo. *Retrato do Brasil: Ensaio sobre a tristeza brasileira*. 1928; São Paulo: Duprat-Mayença, 1997.

Proença, Edgar. "Um minuto de palestra..." *Estado do Pará*, February 20, 1944.

Quisling, Vidkun, and Fund for the Relief of the Jewish Victims of the War in Eastern Europe. *The Truth about the Ukrainian Horror: Official Report*. London: Fund for the Relief of the Jewish Victims of the War in Eastern Europe, 1922.

Rabassa, Gregory. *If This Be Treason: Translation and Its Dyscontents: A Memoir*. New York: New Directions, 2005.

Ravage, Marcus Eli. *The Jew Pays: A Narrative of the Consequences of the War to the Jews of Eastern Europe*. New York: Knopf, 1919.

Rêgo, Norma Pereira. "Lispector: Sempre em tom maior." 1969. Clipping, Clarice Lispector Archive, Arquivo-Museu de Literatura Brasileira, Fundação Casa de Rui Barbosa, Rio de Janeiro.

Reid, Anna. *Borderland: A Journey through the History of Ukraine*. Boulder, Colo.: Westview Press, 1999.

Ribeiro, Leo Gilson. "Auto-inspeção." *Veja*, September 19, 1973.

———. "Tentativa de explicação." *Correio da manhã*, March 21, 1965.

Rodrigues, José Honório. *Historiografia e bibliografia do domínio holandês no Brasil*. Rio de Janeiro: Departamento de Imprensa Nacional, 1949.

Rouchou, Joëlle. *Samuel, duas vozes de Wainer.* 2nd ed. Rio de Janeiro: UniverCidade, 2004.

Sabino, Fernando. *O tabuleiro de damas.* Rio de Janeiro: Record, 1988.

Sabino, Fernando, and Clarice Lispector. *Cartas perto do coração.* Rio de Janeiro: Record, 2001.

Santos, Joaquim Ferreira dos. *Feliz 1958: O ano que não devia terminar.* Rio de Janeiro: Editora Record, 1997.

Sartre, Jean-Paul. *Furacão sôbre Cuba.* Rio de Janeiro: Editôra do Autor, 1961.

Scholem, Gershom Gerhard. *Major Trends in Jewish Mysticism.* New York: Schocken Books, 1995.

———. *On the Kabbalah and Its Symbolism.* New York: Schocken Books, 1996.

"Sepultamento de Clarice será simples e discreto." *O Globo*, December 11, 1977.

Severino, Alexandrino. "As duas versões de Água viva." *Remate de Males*, no. 9 (1989): 115–18.

Simões, João Gaspar. "Clarice Lispector 'Existencialista' ou 'Supra-realista.'" *Diário Carioca*, May 28, 1950.

Singer, Isidore, and Cyrus Adler, eds. *The Jewish Encyclopedia: A Descriptive Record of the History to the Present Day.* 12 vols. New York: Funk & Wagnalls, 1906.

Skidmore, Thomas E. *Black into White: Race and Nationality in Brazilian Thought.* 1974; New York: Oxford University Press, 1993.

———. *Politics in Brazil, 1930–1964: An Experiment in Democracy.* New York: Oxford University Press, 1967.

Sousa, Carlos Mendes de. *Clarice Lispector, figuras da escrita.* Minho: Universidade de Minho Centro de Estudos Humanísticos, 2000.

Souza, Gilda de Mello e. "O lustre." *Estado de S. Paulo*, July 14, 1946.

Spinoza, Benedictus de. *The Collected Works.* Edited by Edwin Curley. Vol. 1. Princeton: Princeton University Press, 1985.

———. *Korte verhandeling van God, de mensch en deszelvs welstand.* ca. 1660. Koninklijke Bibliotheek, The Hague.

Spinoza, Benedictus de, and Arnold Zweig. *Les pages immortelles de Spinoza.* Paris: Éditions Corrêa, 1940.

Tschanz, David W. "Typhus Fever on the Eastern Front in World War I." http://entomology.montana.edu/historybug/WWI/TEF.htm.

União Brasileira de Escritores. *Boletim Bibliográfico Brasileiro.* Vol. 9. Rio de Janeiro: Estante Publicações, 1961.

Varin, Claire. *Langues de feu: Essai sur Clarice Lispector.* Laval, Québec: Trois, 1990.

Varin, Claire, and Clarice Lispector. *Clarice Lispector: Rencontres brésiliennes.* Laval, Québec: Trois, 1987.

Vasconcellos, Eliane. *Inventário do arquivo Clarice Lispector.* Rio de Janeiro: Ministério da Cultura, Fundação Casa de Rui Barbosa, Centro de Memória e Difusão Cultural, Arquivo-Museu de Literatura Brasileira, 1994.

Veloso, Caetano. "Clarice segundo suas paixões." *Jornal do Brasil*, November 24, 1992.

———. *Tropical Truth: A Story of Music and Revolution in Brazil.* New York: Knopf, 2002.

Venâncio, Renato Pinto. "Presença portuguesa: De colonizadores a imigrantes." In *Brasil, 500 anos de povoamento.* Rio de Janeiro: IBGE, Centro de Documentação e Disseminação de Informação 2000.

Venâncio Filho, Francisco. *Euclydes da Cunha e seus Amigos.* São Paulo: Cia. Editora Nacional, 1938.

Verissimo, Erico. *Brazilian Literature: An Outline.* New York: Macmillan, 1945.

———. *Solo de clarineta: Memórias.* 1973; Porto Alegre: Editora Globo, 2005.

Vieira, Nelson. "A expressão judaica na obra de Clarice Lispector." In *Clarice Lispector: Remate de Males: Revista do Departamento de Teoria Literária.* Edited by Vilma Arêas and Berta Waldman. Campinas: Universidade Estadual de Campinas, 1989.

———. *Jewish Voices in Brazilian Literature: A Prophetic Discourse of Alterity.* Gainesville: University Press of Florida, 1995.

Vincent, Isabel. *Bodies and Souls: The Tragic Plight of Three Jewish Women Forced into Prostitution in the Americas.* New York: William Morrow, 2005.

Vovk, C. T., S. V. Taranets', and V. A. Kosakivsky. *Narisi z istoryi Chechel'nika: Z naidavnishikh chasiv do nashikh dniv.* Vinnitsa, Ukraine: "Komp'iuterna verstka ta khudozhne oformlennia redaktsii gazeti 'Chechel'nits'kii visnik'," 2000.

Wainer, Samuel. *Minha razão de viver: Memórias de um repórter.* Edited by Augusto Nunes. São Paulo: Planeta, 2005.

Wainstok, David. *Caminhada: Reminiscências e reflexões.* Rio de Janeiro: Editora Lidador, 2000.

Wainstok, Israel. *Zichrones fun a fater.* Rio de Janeiro: Impresso nos Estabelecimentos Gráficos "Monte Scopus," 1955.

Werneck, Humberto. *O desatino da rapaziada: Jornalistas e escritores em Minas Gerais.* São Paulo: Companhia das Letras, 1992.

Williams, Claire. *The Encounter between Opposites in the Works of Clarice Lispector.* Bristol, England: Hispanic, Portuguese, and Latin American Monographs, 2006.

Zweig, Stefan. *Begegnungen mit Menschen, Büchern, Städten.* Vienna: H. Reichner, 1937.

———. *Die Welt von Gestern: Erinnerungen eines Europäers.* 1942; Stockholm: Bermann-Fischer, 2003.

ILLUSTRATION CREDITS

p. 1: Courtesy of Cecília Wainstok Lipka

p. 2 (top two images): Courtesy of Nicole Algranti, Elisa Lispector Archive

p. 2 (bottom image): Arquivo Nacional, Rio de Janeiro

p. 3 (top image): Courtesy of Instituto Moreira Salles, Rio de Janeiro, and Paulo Gurgel Valente

p. 3 (bottom image): Courtesy of Instituto Moreira Salles, Rio de Janeiro, and Paulo Gurgel Valente

p. 4 (top image): Courtesy of Acervo Fundação Joaquim Nabuco, Recife. Coleção Benício Dias

p. 4 (bottom image): Museu-Arquivo de Literatura Brasileira, Fundação Casa de Rui Barbosa, Rio de Janeiro. Courtesy of Paulo Gurgel Valente

p. 5: Courtesy of Instituto Moreira Salles, Rio de Janeiro, and Paulo Gurgel Valente

p. 6 (top, left): Courtesy of Rafael Cardoso, Cardoso Family Archive

p. 6 (top, right): Museu-Arquivo de Literatura Brasileira, Fundação Casa de Rui Barbosa, Rio de Janeiro. Courtesy of Paulo Gurgel Valente

p. 6 (bottom): Courtesy of Cecília Wainstok Lipka

p. 7 (top): Author's collection

p. 7 (bottom): Museu-Arquivo de Literatura Brasileira, Fundação Casa de Rui Barbosa, Rio de Janeiro. Courtesy of Paulo Gurgel Valente

pp. 8 and 9 (all images): Museu-Arquivo de Literatura Brasileira, Fundação Casa de Rui Barbosa, Rio de Janeiro. Courtesy of Paulo Gurgel Valente

p. 10 (top): Museu-Arquivo de Literatura Brasileira, Fundação Casa de Rui Barbosa, Rio de Janeiro. Courtesy of Paulo Gurgel Valente

p. 10 (bottom): Courtesy of Nicole Algranti, Elisa Lispector Archive

p. 11 (top): Museu-Arquivo de Literatura Brasileira, Fundação Casa de Rui Barbosa, Rio de Janeiro. Courtesy of Paulo Gurgel Valente

p. 11 (bottom): Museu-Arquivo de Literatura Brasileira, Fundação Casa de Rui Barbosa, Rio de Janeiro. Courtesy of Paulo Gurgel Valente

p. 12 (top): Museu-Arquivo de Literatura Brasileira, Fundação Casa de Rui Barbosa, Rio de Janeiro. Courtesy of Paulo Gurgel Valente

p. 12 (bottom): Personal archive of Mafalda Volpe Verissimo. Courtesy of Acervo Literário de Erico Verissimo, Porto Alegre

p. 13: Museu-Arquivo de Literatura Brasileira, Fundação Casa de Rui Barbosa, Rio de Janeiro. Courtesy of Paulo Gurgel Valente

p. 14 (top and bottom, left): Museu-Arquivo de Literatura Brasileira, Fundação Casa de Rui Barbosa, Rio de Janeiro. Courtesy of Paulo Gurgel Valente

p. 14 (bottom, right): Courtesy of Nádia Battella Gotlib

p. 15 (top and bottom images): Museu-Arquivo de Literatura Brasileira, Fundação Casa de Rui Barbosa, Rio de Janeiro. Courtesy of Paulo Gurgel Valente

p. 15 (middle image): Courtesy of José Mario Rodrigues, Recife

p. 16 (top two images): (Left) Reproduction from the original video by Ibraim Leão, Ribeirão Preto. Courtesy of Nádia Battella Gotlib. Original image, Fundação Padre Anchieta—TV Cultura. (Right) Museu-Arquivo de Literatura Brasileira, Fundação Casa de Rui Barbosa, Rio de Janeiro. Courtesy of Paulo Gurgel Valente

p. 16 (bottom image): Courtesy of Paulo Gurgel Valente

INDEX